An Encyclopaedic Dictionary of Heraldry

An Encyclopaedic
Dictionary of Heraldry

BY

JULIAN FRANKLYN AND JOHN TANNER

ILLUSTRATED BY

VIOLETTA KEEBLE

THE QUEEN'S AWARD
TO INDUSTRY 1966

PERGAMON PRESS

OXFORD · LONDON · EDINBURGH · NEW YORK
TORONTO · SYDNEY · PARIS · BRAUNSCHWEIG

Pergamon Press Ltd., Headington Hill Hall, Oxford
4 & 5 Fitzroy Square, London W.1
Pergamon Press (Scotland) Ltd., 2 & 3 Teviot Place, Edinburgh 1
Pergamon Press Inc., Maxwell House, Fairview Park, Elmsford, New York 10523
Pergamon of Canada Ltd., 207 Queen's Quay West, Toronto 1
Pergamon Press (Aust.) Pty. Ltd., 19a Boundary Street,
Rushcutters Bay, N.S.W. 2011, Australia
Pergamon Press S.A.R.L., 24 rue des Écoles, Paris 5ᵉ
Vieweg & Sohn GmbH, Burgplatz 1, Braunschweig

First edition 1970

Library of Congress Catalog Card No. 69–19596

*Printed in Great Britain by Hazell Watson & Viney Limited
Aylesbury, Bucks*

08 013297 9

Contents

Preface

THERE are numerous books described as 'dictionaries of heraldry' that are dictionaries only in the loose sense of their main contents being arranged in alphabetical order; the majority of them are 'armorials', some are 'ordinaries'. The familiar *Papworth*, given its full title, is not only almost unrecognizable, but it covers the entire field: *An Alphabetical Dictionary of Coats of Arms Belonging to Families in Great Britain and Ireland Forming an Extensive Ordinary of British Armorials*... [followed by a brief description of the system].

On the other extreme some books never referred to, or thought of, as dictionaries, or glossaries, or as encyclopaedias of the subject, actually are: conspicuous among these stands *The Art of Heraldry* by A. C. Fox-Davies.

Should one be asked (either inquiringly or aggressively) 'What, then, is a dictionary?', the answer would not be easy to give, neither could it be narrowed down to some simple descriptive phrase such as 'a word-book'.

A dictionary is a book wherein the words of a language, or of a subject, following each other in alphabetical order, have their signification expounded by means of an explanatory phrase. There are many dictionaries doing simply that. Others succeed in doing less: the definitions being not even a phrase but one word more or less synonymous with the keyword, and possibly less familiar to the general user. A better dictionary is one in which an indication of pronunciation is given. Better still are those that give parts of speech and a key to usage. The best dictionaries deal with a word's etymology and semantics, give examples from literature of the word at work, and call the reader's attention to similar words whether homophonous or not.

The best dictionary, which does all these things and more in a most exhaustive, learned, and reliable manner, is *The Oxford English Dictionary*, to which monumental opus we give acknowledgement in general here, but have done so specifically in the text of our glossary.

Again the inquiring voice: 'What is a glossary?' And without hesitation we answer: 'A collection arranged in alphabetical order of obscure, obsolete, technical, or otherwise specialized terms with their meanings', and, in anticipation of further interrogation, add, gratuitously, that an encyclopaedia is a dictionary of subjects, giving a more or less extensive essay instead of a brief definition.

From the foregoing it is manifest that we are aware of the signification of the words constituting our title, and in offering this work as 'an encyclopaedic dictionary of heraldry' we are deceiving neither ourselves nor our audience. Were it simply a dictionary of heraldry it would be confined to an interpretation of the words used in the highly specialized language of

vii

heraldry: were it an encyclopaedia of the subject it would contain longer and more detailed articles on such subjects as the Court of the Lord Lyon, the College of Arms, the history and function of heralds, marshalling, heraldic art, and other major topics.

Heraldry is an organic subject: meanings change, and the emphasis falls on different aspects at varying periods. As recently as the end of the XIX century, brisures and helmets of rank were regarded as of paramount importance, and compartments were not given a moment's consideration: today, helmets of rank are quietly retiring in favour of tilting-helmets, and no recently devised supporters are in want of support.

Aware of this mutability we have endeavoured to defeat time, the great destroyer, by being—not prophetic—but objective. The matter that A declares to be of primal importance is given no more limelight than is the other matter which he thinks might well have been omitted, because the latter subject, according to B, is fundamental.

There are no norms. Each heraldist is a law unto himself; each knows all: everyone else is in error, and the very misprints of one who bears a reputation for scholarship become sacrosanct. We are ourselves not immaculate, but our transgressions, whatever they be, are not those of partizanship.

The critic who complains that our etymologies are both erratic and inadequate is paying us a compliment, for though we claim to be lexicographers in a small way we do not claim to be etymologists at all. The derivation cyphers in square brackets, for example [dial.], [O.E.], [M.E.], that follow a number of catchwords are there to serve a specific purpose.[1] At some time in the not too distant past a self-appointed pundit declared the language of heraldry to be Old French, and this has been repeated so often, and printed in so many books, that a simple denial has no effect.

The language of heraldry is not Old French. It is not even Anglo-Norman-French. It is a polyglot aggregate largely Middle English laced with dialect, but not without a seasoning of Arabic, Slavonic, Old High German, modern French, and here and there a few words of Old French.

Words that were current in Middle English, but were similar in form to their equivalents in Old French, are Middle English—not Old French. The cyphers in square brackets will enable the user of this book to make a rough count, and so convince himself that the language of heraldry is most accurately described as 'the language of heraldry'.

The other critic who complains, somewhat peevishly, that he fails to understand why the authors have devoted a column and a half to X and have totally omitted Y, is not making an oblique confession of obtuse understanding: he has our sympathy, for we cannot understand it either. However, he also has our gratitude: for though we cannot guarantee to reduce our wordage on X, we do promise to include something on Y in the addenda to our second edition.

It may be hazardous for authors to mention their second edition in the preface of their first—'The man who once did sell the lion's skin while the beast lived was killed with hunting him',[2] but we experience no trepidation: our lion is placidly dormant and, as a good heraldic lion should be, without competition on his territory.

We do not imply that there are no other dictionaries on the subject. There are several, first among them being *A Glossary of British Heraldry*, which is anonymous, but known to the

---

[1] When such cyphers appear without the square brackets they indicate translation—not derivation.
[2] Shakespeare, *Hen. V*, IV. 3.

general user as *Parker's Glossary* from the imprint of the Oxford publisher who issued it in 1847. (It is, in fact, the work of H. Gough.) There is also William Berry's *Encyclopaedia Heraldica*, published by Sherwood Gilbert & Piper in 1828, in four ponderous volumes two of which are an armorial.

A Dictionary of Heraldry by Charles Norton Elvin, published in 1889 by Kent & Company, compresses much into one slender volume.

These works are illustrated: the first with neat, precise, uninspired line drawings of appropriate coats of arms and, when wanting, with 'figures'; the second with dull copper-plate engraving, the examples appearing on ugly-shaped shields, the whole page divided into boxes; the last, also dividing its pages into boxes, dispenses with shields and is, from the artistic point of view, somewhat superior to Berry's work. They are not competitive because they very rarely appear on the market, and when they do they are so highly priced that only a millionaire or an endowed library can consider purchasing them.

In addition to these dictionaries there is hardly a book on heraldry that does not boast among its appendices a glossary. All are inadequate, most are inferior, many are misleading; but a few, in spite of the brevity of the definitions, are reliable in their interpretation of the words employed in the text of the volume.

This book, in so far as it is a dictionary, gives, in addition to definitions of the terms employed in heraldry, some indication of their usage: further, it includes the major terms used in foreign heraldry with reference to their country and their translation. These foreign terms include Dutch, French, German, Italian, Latin, Spanish, Swedish, and, last but by no means least, Afrikaans.

The heraldic importance of this Dutch–South African language cannot be too heavily stressed. The Government of the Republic of South Africa formed, almost immediately upon gaining autonomy, its own Bureau of Heraldry; hence Afrikaans is a language that will take a greater and greater percentage of space in the catalogue of the world's armorial bearings as time advances, and it must be borne in mind that Afrikaans, notwithstanding its origin, is not modern Dutch: the ability to struggle with a blazon in the latter tongue will not suffice to translate the former.

We, like all lexicographers, depend upon others for information on matters to which we have no access, and our grateful thanks are due to: Dr C. Pama for the list of Afrikaans terms; to Dr J. von Cuyp for Dutch and German; to Dr C. Schaffer for Swedish; and to Baron Stabile for Italian and Spanish terms.

The encyclopaedic coverage extends beyond the realms of the devising, granting, and usage of armorial bearings, banners, crests, supporters, and quarters. We include a brief account of all the authentic orders of chivalry together with descriptions of the world's major State orders of merit and decorations, both civil and military. This field is vast and perhaps deserves a major work to itself, but we have tried to include and make identifiable every order and decoration which the heraldist is likely to come across in the course of his studies.

We owe a debt of gratitude to Sir Thomas Innes of Learney, Her Majesty's Lord Lyon King of Arms, for calling our attention to the work of Sir Francis James Grant, K.C.V.O., on the historic Scottish Officers of Arms, published by the Scottish Record Society in 1945, and thus enabling us to complement the references to English historical heralds and pursuivants, biographical notes on whom, by the late H. Stanford London, Norfolk Herald Extraordinary, were published in 1963 by the London Survey Committee, in a magnificent volume entitled *The College of Arms*. It is a modern augmentation of the Rev. Mark Nobel's work published in 1804 under the more expansive title of *A History of the College of Arms and the Lives of all the Kings, Heralds and Pursuivants from the Reign of Richard III.*

The literary productions of Her Majesty's Garter King of Arms, Sir Anthony Richard Wagner, K.C.V.O., D.Litt., F.S.A., have been a deep and prolific well of information particularly on the subject of rolls of arms, in which special aspect of the subject he is the unchallenged authority as is evidenced by his *Aspilogia: A Catalogue of English Mediaeval Rolls of Arms*, published in 1950 by the Society of Antiquaries.

To all of these, and to the hundreds of scholars who have, through the generations, published informative books, we owe a debt of gratitude, and we trust that the shades of those no longer with us will, in the comfort and security of the heraldic heaven, accept this book of arms as a token of our thanks for, and appreciation of, the pleasure and enlightenment their works have afforded us.

Our heaviest debt is due to Violetta Keeble, the Herald-painter who has executed the unique, kinetic illustrations in this volume. Her work possesses the accuracy of form that is essential for the instant recognition of heraldic charges as well as the freedom of execution that gives life to what is all too often stereotyped to the point of ossification. Notwithstanding that we, the authors, have, under the appropriate headings, informed our readers that bagwins and yales, griffins, dragons, wyverns, cockatrices, and opinici, are composite fictitious monsters, we find ourselves, when looking at these vital drawings, wondering if after all there are some of them about, even if not to be found in zoological gardens and game reserves.

If the blazon asks for 'three trout, naiant', Violetta Keeble gives us three trout that from the poise of their fins are clearly naiant; not three fish (which might be herrings) arranged in the order two above and one below in a horizontal position on the fishmonger's marble slab.

When she draws a bluebottle it cannot appear as a heliotrope: her hop-bines on their poles are the pride of Kent, and they will fetch their price in Borough High Street; no one will mistake them for bind-weed wrapped around a park-paling. In short, Violetta Keeble brings to heraldry, in addition to the essential craftsmanship and knowledge of the subject, the high artistic ability that arises from true vision.

These illustrations constitute in themselves a graphic reference book, and to enable the reader to have full benefit of them we add two appendices. Each drawing has a number corresponding to that of the blazon which appears at the foot of the facing page, and they are placed in numerical order, from 1 to 474, and arranged, as far as is practicable, in the form of an ordinary: nevertheless, the first appendix is an index to the page number where each appears. The sixteen colour plates which are extra to the black-and-white drawings are included, but they, being distinguished by roman numeration, are grouped at the end of the list.

In selecting the achievements of arms wherewith to illustrate this book, many different aspects had to be taken into consideration, the chief one being to find a coat of arms in which the subject of the article was the main characteristic of the composition. This could, in some cases, be done: a garb, a maunch, a bend, but, space being limited, the majority of the drawings exemplify two, three, or even more of the subjects dealt with in the text.

The second appendix is an analysis of the blazon so that the user may find all examples of the figure under inquiry. For example, at 'fleur-de-lys' will appear about twenty numbers;

each is that of an achievement in which the fleur-de-lys, in various settings, makes its appearance. At 'lion' there is a reference number to every lion performing in these pages, whatever attitude he may assume. To specialize on one position only, then the position itself must be consulted too. All numbers under 'lion' that are also under 'passant', segregate lions passant. When numerals in parentheses follow an entry in the dictionary, the reference is to the drawing in which the subject matter is strongly and unmistakably illustrated.

We have aimed at producing a book to enlighten the novice, assist the learned, and, perhaps, prove of some use to the professional, and we trust that we have achieved our objective. One matter remains to be mentioned in this preface. When a work is published under a joint authorship, the reader, being human, has his curiosity aroused. The question 'which did what?' presents itself irritatingly. To appease this natural inquisitiveness we voluntarily append the information. If the question is put to either of the partners in this book he will answer that he did all of it with the exception of such passages as ultimately prove to be erroneous, and they are the work of the other fellow.

JULIAN FRANKLYN
JOHN TANNER

List of Abbreviations

abvn	abbreviation	illus.	illustration
Afk.	Afrikaans	It.	Italian
alt.	alternative	K.	King
c.	circa (about that time)	L.	Latin
ca.	cant, or canting	lit.	literally
Ch.	Charles	M.E.	Middle English
D.	Dutch	N.B.	*nota bene* (mark well; take special notice)
dial.	dialect		
Ed.	Edward	*ob.*	*obiter* (died)
Eliz.	Elizabeth	obs.	obsolete, or obsolescent
e.g.	*exempli gratiâ* (for example)	O.E.	Old English (Anglo-Saxon)
equiv.	equivalent	O.F.	Old French
er.	erroneous (or erroneously)	Q.	Queen
f.	founded	qtr	quarter
f.d.l.	fleur-de-lys	q.v.	*quod vide* (which see)
fm	from	r.	rare
frmd	formed	Ric.	Richard
Fr.	French	Sp.	Spanish
Gael.	Gaelic	SS	Saints
Geo.	George	Swd.	Swedish
Ger.	German	Teut.	Teutonic
Gk	Greek	u.o.s.	unless otherwise stated
Hen.	Henry	via	through, by way of
i.e.	*id est* (that is; namely)	Wm	William

Glossary

Note: The ~ mark indicates repetition of the keyword

A

A.: abvn for 'argent' (q.v.) for which 'arg.' is also used.

à bouché: [Fr.] of a shield having cut, in dexter-chief, a slot which turns downward to act as a lance-rest. A steel hook of the same shape, but turning upward, was sometimes attached to the breastplate. Notwithstanding that an armorial shield may carry a charge in dexter-chief, to render the shield ~ does not, as a rule, spoil the design.

à couché: [Fr.] reclining, resting, hence descriptive of an art-form that depicts the shield tilted over to the dexter. There are many heraldists who admire this system of display and they seem oblivious to its many serious defects. Chief among the objections is that it may be deceptive; a cross appearing to be a saltire, and a saltire a cross. Simple ordinaries suffer a similar distortion, a bend sinister appearing to be a pale, a pale a bend, a fess a bend sinister, and a bend a fess. The system was imported into British heraldry from the Continent at an early period, and its antiquity is made an excuse for bad taste; further, we are told that some of the Garter stall-plates are in this form. It might be mentioned, in passing, that some of the Garter stall-plates were made on the Continent.

In foreign heraldry shields ~ are less offensive to the eye than they are in British heraldry chiefly because the ordinaries are rare in continental arms. Shields ~ are supposed to be hanging up from the guige, but in a full achievement the helmet of rank complete with the crest pirouettes perilously on the sinister-chief corner of the shield, and the mantling is draped in the usual way at each side, whereas, to be logical, we should be presented with a plan of the helmet and crest, and the mantling ought to hang, lank and limp like a wet overcoat, and so conceal the majority of the shield's area.

The ~ form, having survived so long, will probably remain with us, but it ought to be employed with caution and restraint. (I, XVI)

aan albei kante rond uitgesny: Afk., flaunches.

aansiende: Afk., caboshed.

Aaron's rod: see **Aesculapius, rod of.**

abacot: er. for 'bycocket', a cap peaked back and front. See also **maintenance, cap of.**

abaissé: [Fr.] of a charge or an ordinary that appears on the field in a position lower than normal, but in Fr. blazon merely 'in base'; also spelt 'abased'. (398)

abased: see previous entry.

abatement of honour: er.; assumed to be a general term for marks of distinction for

I

bastardy; actually an alt. term for 'rebatements' (q.v.).

abatido: Sp., in base.

abbassato: It., in base.

abbreviation: standard ~s are often employed for the metals (q.v.) and tinctures (q.v.), i.e. A. or arg. = argent; O. = Or; B. = azure; G. or gu. = gules; S. or sa. = sable; V. or ver. = vert; P. or pur. = purpure; ppr = proper. Furs (q.v.) are indicated by tricking (q.v.) the elements, but in spite of attempts to standardize ~ for ordinaries (q.v.), beasts, common charges (q.v.), and attitudes, no system has been universally accepted. Engravers' 'signatures' are not ~s.

Aberdene, John de: Herald-painter to the Lyon Court, 1364.

abeyance: [L.] dormant; suspended; arms go into ~ when a family becomes extinct.

abgerissen: Ger., erased.

abgewendet: Ger., addorsed.

abimé: Fr., fess point.

abismé: of a charge (q.v.) depicted disproportionately small, as, e.g., a brisure (q.v.).

abouté: [Fr.] to abut; to touch; placed end to end or conjoined (q.v.); also spelt 'abouti(e)'.

abouti(e): see previous entry.

abraised: [either fm O.E. 'abraid', to twist back, or fm O.E. 'abreid', apart] of wings inverted.

abrojo: Sp., caltrap.

absconded: hidden; gone away secretly; hence, of a charge (q.v.) rendered invisible by its being covered with another which is a later addition, often an augmentation (q.v.). Sometimes 'occulted by' is used in its stead. (55)

abyss: obs.; the area surrounding the actual fess point (q.v.).

academic arms: see **community, arms of.**

acanalado: Sp., invected.

acanthus: the conventionalized leaf of

Acanthaceae spinosus; employed with oakleaves in heightening the crowns of kings of arms (q.v.).

accessories: a term sometimes substituted for 'exterior decoration' (q.v.).

accidental forms: changes of a minor, or of a secondary character, as, e.g., rendering beasts' heads originally couped (q.v.) as erased (q.v.); or the straight sides of an ordinary (q.v.) as of one of the lines of partition (q.v.) with a view to creating a difference (q.v.).

accolée: [M.E.] lit. 'embracing'; hence, of two shields displayed side by side, generally tilted inward, the corners overlapping; r. alt. for 'collared' (q.v.).

accompagnée: [Fr.] obs. alt. for 'between'.

accorné: [Fr.] obs. alt. for 'attired' (q.v.) or 'horned' (q.v.) in English blazon, but current in Fr. blazon.

accosted: [fm L. via Fr.] obs. for 'beside'; hence, between.

accoutred: [L.] obs. alt. for 'equipped with'.

accroché: [Fr.] obs.; of two charges (q.v.) conjoined (q.v.) by hooking together.

accroupi: r. alt. for 'couchant' (q.v.); applicable only to the coney (q.v.) in British heraldry, but in current Fr. blazon 'lion ~ ' refers to a lion sejant.

accrued: [L.] r. obs. term for a tree in full growth.

achievement of arms: the total armorial display including the exterior decoration (q.v.). (I, III, V, VI, X, XIV, XVI)

acolarado: Sp., collared.

acorn: [O.E.] always in its cup, and provided with a short length of stalk; when blazoned 'slipped' (q.v.) and 'leaved' (q.v.) the stalk is long enough to carry two leaves, one each side, but a greater number may appear if specified. (427)

acornado: Sp. horned.

acorned: of an oak-tree (q.v.) fructed (q.v.).

ad oram positus: L., in orle

2

Adam and Eve: used as charges in the achievement of the Worshipful Company of Fruiterers.

adder: [O.E.] generic term for a snake or a serpent (q.v.).

adder's tongue: a type of fern; *Ophioglossum*; also lily of the valley. Sometimes depicted like oats with ears drooping.

addice: [O.E.] alt. for 'adze' (q.v.).

addorsed: [M.E.] back to back; two creatures erect may be ∼ (see also **barbel**), but most examples of its use refer to wings; a bird with wings ∼ has them raised to the maximum and resting one against the other; obs. spelling 'adossé'. (115; XVI)

addossati: It., addorsed.

adelaartje: D., eaglet.

adler: Ger., eagle.

adoption, indication of: see **bastardy, indication of.**

adosados: Sp., addorsed.

adossé: see **addorsed.**

adossés: Fr., addorsed.

adumbrated: see **entrailed.**

adumbratio: L., adumbrated.

advancers: the terminal tynes (q.v.) of a stag's attires (q.v.).

adventail: [O.F.] lit. air-hole; hence, the visor (q.v.) of a close-helmet. Variously spelt 'adventayle' and 'aventail', the last being preferable. Wrongly defined as 'shield'.

adze: (frmd on 'addice' (q.v.)) a carpenter's surfacing axe, having the bit at right-angles to the haft (q.v.). (339)

aeroplane: introduced into heraldry to take its place among the prosaic objects, and blazoned volant: this is an incongruous mixture. If the object had to be imported, its own term 'airborne' might well have accompanied it.

Aesculapius, rod of: a staff entwined with a serpent; also called rod of Aaron, Hermes, Mercury. The symbol of healing. (78).

affixed: see **staple.**

affrontée: [M.E.] of a beast presenting full-face and breast to the observer; the whole body turned and facing outward (see also **gardant**); obs. alt. spellings 'affrontant' and 'affronted'.

afgekanteeld: D., raguly.

afgerukt: D., erased.

afgewend: Afk., addorsed.

Africa, Order of the Star of: f. 1920 in five classes. Insignia—*Badge:* a white enamel star of nine points with gold rays between the arms, each ray surmounted by a small silver star of five points; a central medallion in gold depicts a symbolic female figure reaching for the light, and is surrounded by a red band bearing the legend in gold *Light and Darkness*; the badge is ensigned with a laurel wreath in green. *Star:* the unensigned badge in larger size. *Riband:* blue with a central red stripe.

African Star, Order of the: (Belgium) f. 1888 in five classes with three medals. Insignia—*Badge:* white enamelled star of five points, edged blue, with a central medallion of blue enamel bearing a silver star and the inscription *Travail et Progres*, the whole encircled by a green and gold wreath ensigned with a gold crown. *Star:* the badge superimposed on a ten-point silver star with the cypher of Leopold I below the crown. *Riband:* pale blue moire with a light gold central stripe.

agacella: a gazelle.

Agatha, Order of St: (San Marino) f. 1923 in five classes. Insignia—*Badge:* gold-edged white enamelled cross surmounting a laurel wreath, with a central medallion depicting St Agatha. *Star:* the badge surmounting an eight-point silver star. *Riband:* crimson, with narrow stripes of gold and white at each edge.

Agincourt King of Arms: a name of office created by K. Hen. V but apparently complimentary only.

aggruppato: It., sejant.

Agnus Dei: see **lamb, Paschal.**

agrafe: [Fr.] a hook and eye, the former S-shape, the latter U-shape; a dress-fastener; a military-belt clasp.

águila: Sp., eagle.

aguilated: see **aquilated.**

águileta: Sp., eaglet.

aguise: [Teut.] lit. to dress; array in garments; hence, 'aguised', but frequently confused with 'aiguise' (q.v.).

aguzado: Sp., pointed at each end.

aguzzato: It., pointed at each end.

aigle: Fr., eagle.

aiglette: Fr., eaglet.

aiguise: [Fr.] a shape of 'aiguille', a mountain peak; hence, of objects pointed; alt. spelling 'eguisee'.

aigulated: see **aquilated.**

Aikman, James: Dingwall Pursuivant, 1460.

ailes: (possibly frmd on 'aiglet', 'aiglette', an eaglet; or on aigrette, the white heron, crested; hence, a tuft of feathers) obs. alt. for 'wings'.

ailette: see **emerass.**

ainent: obs. of a beast running.

Air Force Cross: f. 1918 for acts of valour or devotion to duty whilst flying, though not in operation against the enemy. Decoration is of silver, being a 'thunderbolt in the form of a cross, the arms conjoined by wings, base-bar terminating with a bomb, surmounted by another cross composed of aeroplane propellors, the four ends inscribed with the royal cypher. In the centre a roundel, thereon a representation of Hermes mounted on a hawk in flight bestowing a wreath . . . the whole ensigned by an Imperial Crown.' Reverse bears the royal cypher and '1918'. *Riband:* 1¼ inches in width; alternate stripes of crimson and white ⅛ inch in width, diagonally at 45° to the wearer's left.

Air Force Medal: f. 1918 for award to non-commissioned ranks of the Royal Air Force on the same conditions as pertain for the Air Force Cross. Insignia: a silver oval bearing an effigy of the sovereign; the reverse, within a wreath of laurel the date 1918 and Hermes on a hawk bestowing a wreath. *Riband:* 1¼ inches in width, alternate red and white stripes $\frac{1}{16}$ in. wide running at 45° diagonally to the wearer's left.

aire: the nest of a pelican in her piety (q.v.).

Airedale terrier: popular among dogs (q.v.), appearing notably as supporters (q.v.) for the Duke of Westminster.

aisle: [L.] a wing, applied in heraldry (although now obs.) to a bird's wings, but strictly applicable only to the wing of a building.

---

1. A white hart lodged, ducally gorged and chained gold.
   K. Ric. II. Armorial badge.

2. The stump of a tree eradicated proper.
   K. Hen. IV (Woodstock). Armorial badge.

3. A falcon on a fetterlock Or.
   Edmund Langley, Duke of York. Armorial badge.

4. A sunburst.
   K. Hen. VII. Armorial badge.

5. A wine-flask argent, corded azure.
   John de Vere, Earl of Oxford. Armorial badge.

6. A swan argent ducally gorged and chained Or.
   Humphrey de Bohun, Earl of Hereford. Armorial badge.

1

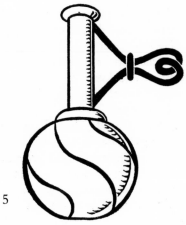

2

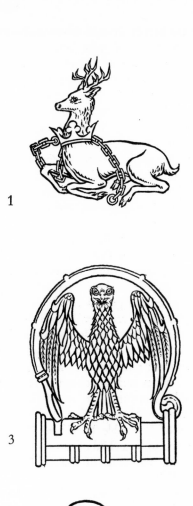

3

4

5

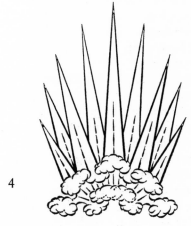

6

aisur: [dial.] r. alt. for 'azure' (q.v.).

Aitchison, Andrew: Unicorn Pursuivant, 1646.

Aiyl Fauste Faire Pursuivant: see **Il Faut Faire Pursuivant.**

ajoure: obs. alt. for 'voided' (q.v.).

Al-Hussein, Order of: (Jordan) f. 1949 by K. Abdullah; has one class only; primarily for heads of states. Insignia: a collar of two gold chains linking sixteen diamond-set red enamelled plaques and sixteen platinum stars, from which is suspended the badge, a gold oval with twenty diamonds set in platinum roses surrounding a red enamel centre inscribed *Abdullah ben Hussein.*

aland: see **dog.**

alant: see **dog.**

alatus: L., winged.

alaunt: see **dog.**

Albany Herald: see **Lyon Office.**

albatross: a sea-bird of the Pacific Ocean, *Diomedea exulans*; the great ~ exceeds all other sea-birds in size; uncommon but not unknown in arms.

alberia: r. alt. for a field argent.

Albert Medal: f. 1866 for gallantry in saving life at sea or on land, in two classes. Insignia—First class: an oval gold badge, enamelled blue for sea, red for land, with a monogram of V & A in gold (with an anchor for sea awards) surrounded by a bronze garter with, raised in gold, the words *For Gallantry in Saving Life at Sea* (or *Land* as applicable). Second class: the design is worked throughout in bronze. *Ribands:* first class—alternate stripes of blue and white (sea); alternate stripes of red and white (land). Second class—white, edged with blue with a central blue stripe (sea), white edged with red with a central red stripe (land).

alce: see **griffin.**

alchemist's symbols: astrologers believe that planets have influence, or control, over inanimate objects as well as over the fate of human beings. To each sphere is allocated a specific group of gases, liquids, and solids including, *inter alia*, metals; hence, the alchemists worked on similar suppositions and employed the cyphers of the planets to denote various metals. These are: Jupiter, ♃, tin; Mars, ♂, iron; Moon, ☽, silver; Mercury, ☿, quicksilver; Saturn, ♄, lead; Sun, ☉, gold; Venus, ♀, copper. These symbols are employed in the arms of mining companies, of other bodies corporate connected with metals, and also those of private persons.

ale-warmer: a hollow, cone-shaped vessel usually drawn with a pommel at the apex (which is necessarily baseward) and always with a handle on the sinister: this may be a simple, bulged grip; a Greek 'ear' (as employed on an urn (q.v.)); or a pattern of interlaced stout wire. In the XV and XVI cents. it was a common domestic utensil, and so not remarkable as a charge (q.v.); now, when such an object is rarely seen outside museums, it is of infrequent occurrence in arms. That in the achievement of Dunstable Municipal Council is believed to be a child of error, due to misdrawing the arms of Dunstable Priory. (306, 327)

aleanje: Sp., scimitar.

alembic: [Arabic] a pear-shape glass vessel, the narrow end drawn off into a long, tapering tube set at a declining angle; used by the alchemists for distilling; a retort. (199)

alerion: see **allerion.**

aleron: r. form of 'ailette' (q.v.).

alésé: Fr., couped.

Alexander, David: Snowdoun Herald, 1828. Dingwall Pursuivant, 1823.

aleyon: a fictitious water-bird resembling, in its appearance, the swan. It does not swim, but reclines luxuriantly upon its floating nest which is dirigible by the bird's magical powers.

alferes: [Arabic via Fr.] a cavalryman, particularly a Standard- or Ensign-bearer; hence, alt. for 'ensign', an officer, but not for 'ensign', a flag.

Alford, Laurence: Bluemantle Pursuivant, 1484. Former Rose Blanche.

alisée cross: see **globical.**

Alishay Pursuivant Extraordinary: a name of office formerly employed in Scotland.

Alisone, James: Bute Pursuivant, 1661.

Alisza Herald: a Scottish Officer of Arms, c. 1426.

Allan, Thomas: Carrick Pursuivant, 1643.

Allan, Wm: Ormonde Pursuivant, 1807.

allerion: [Fr.] an eagle without beak and claws. Three on a bend (q.v.) appear in the old arms of the Duchy of Lorraine, the word ~ being an anagram of the name.

allettato: It., finned.

alliance, arms of: an impaled (q.v.) marital achievement (q.v.). (43)

alligator: [Sp.] a large saurian that has been introduced into heraldry in comparatively recent times.

allocamelus: a composite fictitious beast having an ass's head and a camel's body; thought to be the hybrid offspring of an ass and a camel.

allume: [Fr.] obs. for a beast's eyes when gules.

allusive arms: an achievement in which a charge, or combination of charges, make indirect reference to a name or to an incident of family history: in the latter category e.g. the arms of Binning of Easter Binning have introduced a covered wagon which alludes to an ancestor's feat of concealing in a load of hay a party of select fighting men who overpowered the English garrison of Linlithgow Castle.

alpaca: a Peruvian llama having a coat of long, fine wool; makes a few appearances in arms for ca. reasons.

alpe: a name applied, generally for ca. reasons, to the bullfinch.

Alphabet, the Great: a book-form roll of arms by Thomas Wall (q.v.) containing painted shields and blazons. 1530.

alphyn: a r. monster similar to the tygre (q.v.) but having cloven hooves on the fore- and eagle's claws on the hind-legs.

altar: a pagan ~ is always intended; generally depicted as a round (very r. square) plinth or a truncated column. An ~ flammant has flames of fire proper rising from the centre of the top flat surface.

altar-tomb: the rectangular table-tomb; may be in elevation or arrasways, but r. in British heraldry.

alzado: Sp., in chief.

alzato: It., in chief.

ambulent: [L.] mis-spelling of 'ambulant'; lit. 'walking'; hence, r. alt. for 'passant' (q.v.).

amethyst: [L.] a gem-stone, manganese-quartz, sometimes containing iron and sodium; purple or violet in colour; hence, ~ in heraldry refers to the tincture purpure, and is not connected with segregative blazon (q.v.).

ammanche: see **emmanche.**

ammonites, fossil: see **shell.**

amorini: see **supporters.**

amphiptere: see following entry.

amphisbaena: a composite fictitious creature being a snake with a head at each end, four short legs terminating in claws, and a pair of membraneous wings in the middle; also named the 'amphiptere'.

amphisian cockatrice: see **cockatrice.**

anade: Sp., duck.

ananas: fruit of the pine-apple plant, *Ananassa sativa.* (146)

anchor: [O.E.] a hook by means of which a ship, or boat, may hold to the ground (i.e. the sea- or river-bed). It consists of a rod in the upper end of which an eye is forged and through which a ring is attached for the purpose of securing the ~ to the chain or cable: at the lower end it is welded into the centre of the segment of a circle with, at each end, an arrow-head shape fluke. Crossing, just below the forged eye in the shank (heraldic term 'beam' (q.v.)), is the stock (heraldic term 'timber' (q.v.)), set at 90° to the arms.

An ~ blazoned as 'cabled' has a length of line secured to the ring, entwining the beam and falling smartly away at the point. An ~ chained has chain instead of cordage, but, again, it must fall away from the arms. An ~ 'fouled' is one in which the cable, or the chain, does not clear the flukes, but is wound about the arm, normally the sinister. The 'fouled' ~, particularly that of the Admiralty, may have been created not by bad seamanship, but by artistic exuberance.

The ~ is employed in arms as an allusive charge, in, e.g., the achievement of a family with a seafaring tradition, or in the civic heraldry of seaports and ship-building areas where it is to be expected, but it also appears without reference to the sea, or to ships, being the emblem of Hope,

and it even good-naturedly joins in the fun of being a simple ca. on the surname Hope. (335)

anchoratus: L., anchored.

anchored: of a cross with ornamental terminals when it is to reach the edges of the shield; an alt. term is 'fixed', and also 'throughout' is employed. Alt. forms are 'anchory', 'ancre', 'ancred', but it always refers to a cross throughout, in contact with the edge of the shield, not to a cross with the limbs terminating in anchors, nor even in flukes of anchors as is sometimes er. stated.

ancient: see **colour party.**

ancred: r. alt. spelling of 'anchored' (q.v.).

Anderson, Alexander M'Culloch: Marchmont Herald, 1830. Dingwall Pursuivant, 1828.

Anderson, David: Unicorn Pursuivant, 1796.

Anderson, James: Carrick Pursuivant, 1526.

Anderson, Wm: Lyon Clerk Depute, 1828. Marchmont Herald, 1836. Carrick Pursuivant, 1833.

andreaskors: Swd., saltire.

andreaskors sammanflätat med en gen-ombruten ruta: Swd., fret.

---

7. Sable, a bars-gemel Or between in chief two fleurs-de-lys and, in base, a chalice surmounting a spear in bend, argent, headed gules.
    Col. H. A. Lewis, M.B.E., O.StJ., C.L.J.

8. Barry wavy of four azure and argent: on a chief of the second a cross gules charged with a lion of England.
    Former London County Council.

9. Barry nebuly Or and sable.
    Blount.

10. Barry argent and azure, a bendlet compony of the first and gules.
    Avensley.

11. Barry wavy of four argent and azure, on a chief gules a Saxon crown gold.
    Greater London Council.

12. Or, a mural crown gules between two barrulets azure and three wolf's heads sable.
    Seale.

7

8

9

10

11

12

Andrew (?——?): Clarenceux King of Arms, 1334. Norroy King of Arms 1338. Former Windsor Herald, but 'Windsor' may have been his surname.

Andrew, cross of St: see **saltire**.

Andrew, Imperial Order of St: (Russia) f. 1698 as a one-class order that carried with it automatic admission to four other orders. Insignia—*Collar:* linked gold and enamel medallions depicting, alternately, a black double-headed Imperial eagle surmounted by a medallion of St George and the dragon, a blue St Andrew's cross, and the letters *S.A.P.R.* (*Sanctus Andreas Patronus Russiae*), a white trophy of arms surmounted by the monogram of Peter the Great ensigned with a crown. *Badge:* the double-headed Imperial eagle surmounted by St. Andrew crucified on his cross, the arms of which bear the initials *S.A.P.R.*, ensigned with the Imperial crown, beneath which crossed swords could be placed to denote a military award. *Star:* of silver with eight points; a central medallion of gold depicts the Imperial eagle surmounted by St Andrew's cross and surrounded by a blue band bearing the inscription, in Russian, *Faith and Loyalty. Riband:* sky blue.

Andrew, St: is depicted in a number of Scottish coats of arms.

anellato: It., ringed.

angels: [O.E.] a group of invisible beings in human form, but winged, of a higher order than mankind, who are the servitors and the messengers of the Deity. In British heraldry appear chiefly in the capacity of supporters (q.v.). They are represented as female, crined (q.v.) of long golden tresses, habited in a long robe, frequently close-girt (q.v.). Whether ~ are acting as supporters or not they are depicted, u.o.s., affrontée, the long wings addorsed (q.v.) and inverted.

It is a regrettable fact, but one that ought not to be omitted, that ~ are often very badly drawn; they appear lacking in dignity, and 'sugary'. However, there exists in relation to them an emotional content, and attempts to depict them as strong, worthy messengers and representatives of the Lord are resisted. Included among ~ are the arch~, particularly Michael and Gabriel, the former sometimes confused with St Michael.

A well-known example of ~ supporters that do not conform to the conventions are those in the achievement of the Royal House of France; these are masculine, clad in plate-armour, and wearing the tabard (q.v.) of France ancient (q.v.).

angemmes: see **trefoil**.

angle¹: [O.E.] a barbed fish-hook by which latter description it is sometimes blazoned. Four, in cruciform juxtaposition, butt to butt, make cross hamecon.

angle²: Fr., angled.

angled: an obs. line of partition: 'per fess ~' consists of a straight line from dexter flank to the centre of the shield where it drops at 90° to the depth of one-third of the shield's width, breaks at right angles to the sinister, and continues to the flank; the entire line with its two square breaks, rotated clockwise, gives 'per bend ~', 'per pale ~', 'per bend sinister ~'.

angles, pair of: an article consisting of two chevron-shaped elements interlaced, all four horns finishing with an annulet. Supposed to represent a belt fastener, but likely to have originated in a monogram.

anglesado: Sp., engrailed.

Anglevert: a French mistake for 'Eagle Vert' (q.v.).

angolata: It., angled.

angora: an Asiatic goat (q.v.) specified in

PLATE I The Most Noble Order of the Garter Stall-plate in St. George's Chapel, Windsor.
Quarterly I and IV: sable, a cross engrailed Or, for *Ufford*. II and III: gules, a cross moline
argent, for *Beke*.
CREST: a blackamoor couped at the shoulders, crined and ducally crowned Or.
Sir Wm Willoughby, fifth Lord Willoughby de Eresby, K.G. (Installed under K. Hen. IV)

a number of achievements. It is noted for its silky coat.

angulado: Sp., angled.

Angus Herald Extraordinary: a name of office formerly employed in Scotland.

anilée, croix: Fr., cross moline.

anillada, cruz: Sp., cross annuletty.

anillado: Sp., ringed.

anille: r. alt. for 'millrind' (q.v.).

animé: [Fr.] animated; excited; spoiling for a fight; hence, of a beast depicted with eyes gules, not, as often er. stated, one breathing fire and exuding flames from the ears which is blazoned 'incensed' (q.v.).

anitrella: It., duck.

anjou: a spear with a f.d.l. (q.v.) shaped head.

Anjou King of Arms: an officer of arms maintained by the Duke of Bedford before 1436.

ankerkruis: Afk., cross moline.

Anne, Order of St: Anne, daughter of Peter the Great, married the Duke Charles Frederick of Schleswig-Holstein, who f. the Order in four classes, in her memory in 1735. Their son succeeded to the throne of Russia in 1742 and the Order was henceforth in the gift of the czars. Insignia—*Badge:* a gold-rimmed red enamel cross paty with gold scroll decorations between the arms; a white central medallion depicts St Anne in a country setting; the first- and second-class badges were ensigned with an enamelled Imperial crown. *Star:* silver of eight points; a red enamel cross on a central medallion is surrounded by a red band inscribed, in gold, *Aman. Just. Piet. Fid* (i.e. *Amantibus, Justitiam, Pietatem, Fidem*). *Riband:* red with yellow edges.

annet: [dial.] name for the seagull or kittiwake.

annodated: double curved, as the letter S.

annodato: It., nowy.

annulet: [L.] a ring, considered to be as thick as it is wide; hence, of square section but not necessarily so depicted; the brisure (q.v.) of the fifth son. (423)

annulets, cross of: from a central annulet (q.v.) four lengths of chain consisting of annulets interlaced extend outward to the edge of the shield.

annuletty: semé (q.v.) of annulets.

annuletty, cross: a cross humetty (q.v.) having each limb terminating in an annulet (q.v.); alt. forms 'annuletted' and 'annuly'.

annulus: L., annulet.

Annunciation, Order of the Most Sacred: (Italy, Savoy) f. 1362 by Amadeus VI as the 'Order of the Collar'; revised by Charles III in 1518 and renamed the 'Annunziata'. A one-class order of fifteen members who were addressed as 'Cousins of the King'. Insignia—*Badge:* a representation of the Annunciation surrounded by entwined knots of Savoy in gold ribbon embellished with gold roses and the letters *F.E.R.T.* (a cypher referring to Amadeus's relief of Rhodes) suspended from a gold chain of alternate knots of roses and ribbons. *Star:* the badge on a gold and silver star of eight points each of seven rays. *Riband:* blue moire.

anserated: r. obs. alt. for 'lionced' (q.v.).

anshient: see **colour party**.

Anstis, John[1]**:** Garter King of Arms by nomination 1714 but, being a Jacobite, not created till 1719. Former Norfolk Herald, 1707.

Anstis, John (Junior)[2]**:** Garter King of Arms concurrently with his father; became sole, 1730. Former Blanch Coursier Herald, 1726.

ant: see **emmet**.

Antarctic and Arctic stars: a r. method of blazoning 'two estoiles', and not necessarily having reference to the Pole star which is so blazoned. (102)

antelope, heraldic: a composite fictitious

beast, being in appearance an heraldic tygre (q.v.) with cloven hooves, and on the head a pair of short, straight horns with serrated backs. (280)

Antelope Pursuivant: an obs. English name of office; from the badge (q.v.) of Bohun (c. 1419).

Anthony, cross of St: see **tau-cross.**

antic: mis-spelling of 'antique'; applied to various objects, including ornate escutcheons.

antilop: Swd., antelope, heraldic.

antilop naturling: Swd., antelope proper.

Antiquaries Roll: (c. 1360) in book form, eleven vellum leaves 10 by 14¼ in., painted, 352 shields with names over.

antique [L] lit. ancient, of the past, descriptive of shields (see **antic**), lamps, and other objects.

antique boot: see **Dutch boot.**

antique crown: a circlet heightened with ten triangular rays, five only of which appear in drawing, the outer ones being in profile; also described as a radiated crown and as an eastern crown. In Scotland, ~ may refer to a ducal coronet (q.v.). (231, 235, 378)

antique shield: a shield used as a charge, scroll-edged and highly ornate, appearing notably in the arms of Bermuda (Somer's Island), assigned by royal warrant, 1910,

viz.: 'argent, on a mount vert a lion sejant affrontee gules supporting between the forepaws an antique shield azure, thereon a representation of the wreck of the ship "The Sea Venture", all proper.' At the end of the first decade of XX cent. armorial taste, if still a little redolent of the florid Victorian days, was not so bad as this seems to indicate: it is clearly an attempt on the part of the devisor to capture the heraldic spirit, which was decidedly bad, of 1609—the date of the incident—in which he has succeeded admirably.

anvil: [O.E.] the armourer's ~ is intended, but it is generally so badly drawn as to appear to be that of a watchmaker. The shape is admittedly similar; nevertheless, in old prints the armourer's ~ does not have a flimsy, diminutive appearance. The blacksmith's ~, massive and shapely, is of pleasing appearance and it is a pity there are not more of them. (318)

Ap Howel, Fulk: Lancaster Herald, 1538. Former Rouge Dragon Pursuivant, 1536; former Guisnes Pursuivant, 1523.

apalmada: Sp., appaumé.

ape: [O.E.] a non-specifying term for any kind of monkey. What is generally depicted closely resembles the chimpanzee, *Anthropopithecus troglodytes*, and has a long, rope-like tail. His usual attitude is passant, on all

---

13.   Argent, three bears heads erased sable muzzled Or.
     Berwick.

14.   Per pale gules and vert an elephant, on his back a tower triple towered Or.
     Corporation of Coventry.

15.   Gules, a wolf statant argent.
     Lowe.

16.   Argent, a bear sejant erect sable muzzled gules.
     Lynsey.

17.   Or, a camel passant between three cloves sable.
     Clove.

18.   Gules, a horse forcene argent.
     Corporation of the County of Kent.

13

14

15

16

17

18

fours, and he is either collared or gorged (q.v.) about the loins. When chained, it is not 'reflexed over the back' in a graceful manner, but allowed to trail along behind. The chain sometimes terminates in 'an ~'s cog', a capstan-shaped weight. There is at least one example of both a night-~ (q.v.) and a winged-~. (190)

Apollo: appears in the arms of the Worshipful Society of Apothecaries of the City of London.

appalmata: It., appaumé.

appalmed: r. alt. spelling of 'appaumé' (q.v.).

appaumé: [Fr.] open; of the human hand when presenting the palmer surface. (228; IV)

appensus: L., stringed.

apple: [O.E.] fruit of the tree *Pyrus malus*, cultivated in many varieties, and employed in heraldry often for ca. reasons. Always depicted pendant u.o.s., and with a short stalk.

apple of Granada: see **pomegranate.**

Appollonia, St: see **fanged tooth.**

apre: a fictitious beast described by various writers as 'a bull with a bear's tail', 'an emasculated bull with a short tail', etc., that seems to make but one appearance on the heraldic scene, i.e. as the sinister supporter of the Muscovy Company.

apricot: a plum-like fruit, *Prunus armeniaca*; employed in heraldry for ca. reasons.

Aquarius: in the act of pouring libations; is the sinister supporter of the Metropolitan Water Board.

aquila: It., eagle.

aquilated: [L.] of a cross the limbs of which terminate in eagle's heads; of an ordinary (q.v.) exteriorly decorated with eagles' heads; of a field semé (q.v.) of eagles' heads; alt. spellings 'aguilated' and 'agulated'.

Aquilon: the It. name for both the north and the north-east winds, poetically enlikening them to a mighty bird swooping down out of the mountains. Depicted in heraldry as a cherub's head (q.v.) with pursed lips and distended cheeks, in the act of blowing, and sometimes described as borée. The ~ is also blazoned as Boreas, the Greek god of the north wind.

aquilotto: It., eaglet.

Aquitaine King of Arms: a XIV cent. office for service in the English territory of France. See also **Guyenne King of Arms.**

Arabic alphabet: see **script.**

Arabic numerals, blazon by: see **segregative blazon.**

arbalest: [Fr.] a cross-bow, depicted with the crank-handle engaged and the bow (or lath) bent; alt. spelling 'arbalète'.

arbalète: see previous entry.

arch: [M.E.] the heraldic ~ is the semi-circular keystoned Roman type erected on a pillar at each end. A double ~ is on three and a triple ~ on four. The pillars consist of three parts each of which may be coloured differently from the other parts, and from the ~ itself: the base, which may be of one, two, or three degrees (q.v.); the round pillar itself and the caps, capitals, or imposts, being the square, flat stones at the top of each pillar, upon which the ~ rises. The ~, like the bridge (q.v.) and the castle (q.v.), may vary greatly in appearance; special ~ are sometimes devised. (413)

archangels: see **angels.**

Archduke: [L.] pertaining, originally, to the Royal House of Austria, the Emperor Frederick III having conferred, in 1453, the title Archduke of Austria on his son Maximilian and his heirs. See also **Duke.**

arched: see **enarched.**

archer's bow: see **bow[1].**

archy: see **enarched.**

Arctic star: see **Antarctic and Arctic stars.**

arg.: see **A.**

argent: [L. via Fr.] silver; one of the

heraldic metals, represented in art by white (q.v.). Cross-hatching (q.v.) blank.

argenteus: L., argent.

argento: It., argent.

arm (human): generally embowed erect, and couped at the shoulder. A dexter ~ has the elbow to the dexter, and clenched hand to the sinister. 'An ~ embowed, the upper part in fess' is orientated from shoulder to elbow in fess, the forearm raised and inclined towards the shoulder. 'An ~ embowed fesswise' has the elbow downward, the fist and shoulder end raised. Two ~s counter-embowed have the clenched fists resting together and chiefward. Two ~s counter-embowed and interlaced are also erect, the dexter forearm surmounting (q.v.) the sinister, and the sinister upper ~ surmounting the dexter. ~s are depicted bare u.o.s., and the whole arm, from shoulder to fist, is intended unless 'couped at the elbow' (when it cannot be embowed) or 'a cubit ~' (q.v.). (290, 294)

arma inquirenda: see **false heraldry.**

armatus: L., armed.

armed: of the teeth and claws of carnivora; the horns of ungulates, and of the beak and claws of predatory birds. A lion (q.v.) will be ~ gules u.o.s. except when either the field or the lion himself is gules, when azure is substituted.

armed cap-à-pie: see **cap-à-pie.**

armellino: It., ermine.

armes à enquerré: see **false heraldry.**

armes parlantes: see **canting arms.**

armig: see next entry.

armiger: [L.] orig. an attendant upon a knight, an esquire; hence, one possessed of armorial bearings (q.v.). XV cent. usage— a minor title following a surname similar to the modern 'Esq.'; 'John Bull, Armig.'

armigerous: having, being possessed of, being entitled to display, armorial bearings.

armillary sphere: a celestial sphere in outline only, consisting of hoops representing the equator, tropics, polar circles, etc.; specialized and uncommon.

arming buckles: see **arming points.**

arming doublet: a r. alt. for 'tabard' or 'surcoat'.

arming points: the straps and buckles attached at intervals to pieces of plate-armour for the purpose of securing each part to the next, the buckles being lozenge-shape.

arminos: Sp., ermine.

armorial: [Fr.] pertaining to coats of arms or to heraldry in general; a directory in which the arms of the entrants are recorded in a, b, c, order, or extended to cover ordinaries (q.v.) of arms, textbooks, and other books dealing with heraldry.

armorial bearings: the achievement (q.v.) of any person or body-corporate having the right to bear arms.

Armorial de Gelre: see **Gelre, Armorial de.**

armorist: [Fr.] one who possesses a knowledge of heraldry.

armory: [Fr.] heraldry; the whole subject of coats of arms.

armoury: a collection of weapons, a place in which a collection of weapons is housed; a mis-spelling of 'armory' (q.v.).

armoyé: a r. term applied to fabrics, i.e. mantling (q.v.), comparisons (q.v.), housings (q.v.), etc., when diapered with armorial charges.

Arms, Wall's Book of: see **Book of Arms, Thomas Wall's.**

Armstrong, Edmond Clarence Richard: Bluemantle Pursuivant, 1923.

Armstrong, Harry: Carrick Pursuivant, 1699.

armys: archaic spelling of 'arms'.

arrache: [M.E.] to tear; to pull away; to pull up by the roots; hence, in English blazon, a r. obs. alt. for 'erased' (q.v.), but current in Fr. blazon.

arrancado: Sp., erased.

arraswise: [frmd on Gk 'arris'] an obtruding or external corner; applied to any object on the field (or forming the crest) that is to present a corner affrontée, often a book (q.v.); similar to but not identical with 'in perspective' (q.v.); ~ is generally used in blazoning a small object.

arrestato, leone: It., a lion statant. See also **fermo, leone**.

arrière, volant en: [Fr.] of a winged insect flying away from the spectator; seen from behind.

arrondi: rounded; strictly implying that an object is to be depicted 'in the round' by means of shading, but er. extended to describe an object that is curved, e.g. 'a cultivated rose stalked ~' is to be depicted as pendant from a curved stem.

arrow: [O.E.] u.o.s. is erect, the head baseward, but most frequently appearing as a sheaf of ~, i.e. three, one erect surmounted by two in saltire, the heads baseward. ~ is barbed of its head, flighted of its feathers, and notched when the short length of shaft protruding beyond the flights is to be of another colour. ~ proper has the shaft brown, barbed, and

flighted argent, but 'proper' often refers only to the shaft. (94, 459, 105; IV)

art, symbolic figure of: a female figure wreathed about the temples with laurel, vested argent and close-girt, holding in the dexter hand a book and in the sinister an oval palette and brush.

artichoke, Jerusalem: a kind of sunflower with edible roots, *Helianthus tuberosus*; sometimes used for ca. reasons. Jerusalem is a distortion of the Ita. name Girasole.

Arundel Herald: formerly the name of office of the herald maintained by the Earl of Arundel; now used for a herald extraordinary. See also **Extraordinary Officers of Arms**.

ascendant: progressing upward, but not an alt. for 'rizant' (q.v.): applicable to vegetable charges; hence, growing.

ascents: alt. for 'degrees' (q.v.).

ashen keys: the fruit (or seed) of the ash-tree, *Fraxinus excelsior*, which grow in clusters and are so depicted.

Ashmole, Elias: Windsor Herald, 1660.

Ashmolean Roll: (c. 1334) vellum true roll (q.v.) 7½ in. by 16 ft. 3in., containing 489 names and blazons. On the dorse is written a collection of heraldic notes of a later date.

---

19. Sable, three nags trotting argent within a bordure Or.
    Trotter.

20. On a mount of three peaks vert a lamb sable the dexter fore-leg flexed and supporting in bend sinister a staff; flotant therefrom a banner ermine charged with a cross entrailed.
    Gross, Francis (Richmond Herald, c. 1750).

21. Sable, three goats clymant argent.
    Thorold.

22. Sable, a horse upright argent bridled Or.
    Cabell.

23. Argent, a ram statant sable armed Or.
    Layton.

24. Argent, a Paschal lamb, passant, Or.
    Duntze of Tiverton.

19

20

21

22

23

24

Ashwell, John: Lancaster King of Arms, 1426. May have been former Leopard Herald, Exeter Herald, and Cadran Pursuivant. It is also stated that he was a former Bluemantle Pursuivant.

Ashwell, Robert: Windsor Herald during the reign of K. Hen. VI. Former Rouge Croix Pursuivant; former Antelope Pursuivant.

asker: see **newt.**

asp: see **serpent.**

aspectant: r. obs. alt. for 'respecting each other' (q.v.); also written 'aspecting'.

aspen: see **poplar.**

aspersed: [L.] sprinkled with; alt. for 'semé' (q.v.).

aspis: a circular Gk shield.

ass: a now unpopular (due to its association with stupidity) but formerly dignified (because of its religious significance), charge: asses' heads are more common than the beast itself. (256)

Assessors of the Lyon Court, Lords: see **Court of the Lord Lyon.**

assis: r. alt. for 'sejant' (q.v.).

assultant: r. alt. for 'salient' (q.v.).

assumption, arms of: all armorial devices that were taken into use before control was established: such arms generally passed from father to son, and also became associated with the feudal estate; in fact, it is sometimes by no means clear to which family an armorial device should be attributed when an estate has changed hands. Since all heraldic incunabulae were chosen by the users, and composition did not far exceed the application of the various lines of partition to ordinaries, multiples of ordinaries, sub-ordinaries, and diminutives, it followed that duplication of devices was likely to occur, particularly when the armigers concerned came from distant parts of the country and the spread of the use of armorial bearings increased the likelihood. It was largely to prevent such duplication, and the repetition of disputes such as that between Scrope and Grosvenor (q.v.), that armorial control was established. ~ already in existence were by no means unrecorded: they had appeared again and again in Parliament rolls, tournament rolls, and other occasional rolls, as well as in seals and on monuments: they were, perhaps, more firmly established than arms granted by patent at a later period. There is no comparison between ~ and arms in use today by what the users please to describe as 'prescriptive right', notwithstanding that some go so far as to cite ~ as their precedent.

assurgeant: [L.] lit. rising from; hence, of any heraldic beast represented as emerging from water, either water proper, or a plain point barry-wavy, which generally represents water. See also **fountain.**

astral crown: devised to serve in the arms of persons connected with aviation, consists of a circlet heightened with four pairs of wings displayed and conjoined at the tips. In drawing, one complete pair of wings appears in the centre, and a single wing at each side.

astroid: [Gk.] having the conventionalized form of a star; hence r. alt. for 'mullet' (q.v.).

asureus: L., azure.

ater: L., sable.

Athene, the Goddess: represented in the civic arms of Athens.

Athill, Charles Harold: Clarenceux King of Arms, 1919. Former Norroy K. of A., 1919; former Richmond Herald, 1889; former Bluemantle Pursuivant, 1882.

Athlone Herald: an officer of arms, created in 1690 by K. James II in exile at St Germain-en-Laye.

Athlone Pursuivant: see **Ulster Office.**

Atkinson, Edmund: Somerset Herald, 1550. Former Bluemantle Pursuivant, 1545; former Hampnes Pursuivant, 1544.

Atkinson, John: Somerset Herald, 1794. Former Rouge Croix, 1784.

Atkinson's Roll: (temp. K. Hen. VI) eighty-eight shields blazoned in a manuscript book containing also other matter.

attired: [M.E.] lit. adorned; hence, of a stag's (q.v.) antlers.

attires: [M.E.] headdress; hence, a stag's antlers. (38)

attoney: a shape of the word 'tournament' as employed in the blazon of arms of the Worshipful Company of Armourers.

attribution, arms of: coats of arms attributed to historic characters who flourished centuries before the rise of armory, to saints, and to fictitious characters. Some ~ have acquired a factual status, e.g. those attributed to K. Ed. Confessor; and the armorial motifs attributed to various other Saxon kings, and to their kingdoms, are to be traced in the modern civic heraldry of some county councils.

au pied fiché, croix: Fr., a cross fitchy at the foot.

Auchmouty of Drummeldrie, David: Dingwall Pursuivant, 1712.

auger: [O.E.] a boring tool consisting of a strip of steel twisted throughout, ground at one end to a central projecting point with cutting edges at each side facing in opposite directions, and, at the other, turned over to form a socket through which a lever may be threaded so that the tool can be rotated, the workman using both hands. It may be blazoned by its alt. name 'a wimble' and employed for ca. reasons in the arms of the family of Whimble; has, at different periods, been differently drawn. In one it is represented as a carpenter's crankbrace, fitted with a spoon-bit; in another as a gimlet (which

last is employed sometimes under its own name). It should be noted that the archaic names of tools are deceptive: 'wimble' is also a generic term for any wood-boring tool.

augmentation of honour: an addition, bestowed by the sovereign, to an achievement of arms in recognition of special services. Origin unknown, but attributed to K. Ed. III who bestowed, in ~ 'two round buckles on their straps', to be worn quarterly (q.v.) with 'azure, three pelicans vulning themselves argent', the arms of Sir John Pelham who captured the French king at the battle of Poictiers.

In the event of one who is non-armigerous qualifying for such recognition of service, the sovereign may bestow, by royal warrant and sign manual, an achievement of arms which itself has the status of an ~, that is being the personal gift of the sovereign it is above normal administration. Thus it was that the arms of ~ bestowed upon Col. Carlos by K. Chas. II were allowed to be perpetuated by his nephew on his death without issue. At the same turbulent period the family of Lane received in ~ a canton of England in recognition of Jane Lane's service in conducting the fugitive king to the coast: a crest in ~ was added, e.g. 'a strawberry roan horse, couped at the flanks holding between the hooves the crown royal'.

In the XVIII and during the XIX cents., ~ of the 'landscape' type became popular; e.g. on a chief, an entire battle scene. This had the effect of spoiling the artistic merit of more than one old coat of arms; nevertheless, the ugliness is tolerable since it is the result of so high an honour.

Supporters in ~ were granted (posthumously), by extended limitations (q.v.)) to Speke, the explorer. As recently as 1963 an ~ was bestowed on the Rt Hon. C. V.

Massey, ex-Governor-General of Canada; namely, a canton (azure) of the royal crest for Canada. (168)

Aulet Pursuivant: a privately maintained officer of arms of whom no more than the name is known. Possibly identical with Aurtt Herald (q.v.).

aulned: r. obs. alt. for 'bearded'; in reference to vegetation—barley, etc.

aure: r. obs. alt. for 'gutty d'Or' (q.v.).

Auriol, Robert, Earl of Kinnoull: Lord Lyon King of Arms, 1796.

Aurtt Herald: a privately maintained officer of arms (c. 1450) of whom but little is known.

aurum: L., Or.

ausgebogt: Ger., engrailed.

ausgebrochen: Ger., voided.

A.V.: see **Mary, the Blessed Virgin.**

avant-mur: with a wall, or section of wall, attached. Various heraldic structures, bridges, castles, towers, etc., may be ∼.

avelane, cross: from a central roundel (q.v.) four tulip-like elements, the petals parted at the extremities, extend outward: the five parts of ∼ are conjoined (q.v.). It is

said to be formed on, and is certainly named from, the filbert nut, i.e. hazel, *Corylus avellana.*

avellanus: Sp., hazel nuts.

aventail: see **adventail.**

averdant: r. alt. for 'vert' (q.v.) but only applied to a mount (q.v.) or other piece of ground, since it implies grass covered.

aversant: [L. via O.F.] reversed; backward; of a human hand when the dorsal surface is depicted.

avhugget: Swd., couped.

Avis, Military Order of: (Portugal) f. in Spain and introduced into Portugal in 1162 as a religious–military order. Revised in 1789 in three classes: Grand Cross (sash over right shoulder, and star); Commander (neckbadge and star); Knight (breast badge). Insignia—*Badge:* green enamelled cross fleury edged gold. *Star:* eight-point silver-gilt, bearing the badge on a centre medallion of white enamel. *Riband:* green.

avmotsatt tinktur: Swd., counterchanged.

avslitet: Swd., erased.

awl: the leather-workers sewing awl is intended u.o.s. Symbolic of the character-

---

25. Argent, two foxes salient counter-salient in saltire, the sinister surmounting the dexter, gules.
     Williams.

26. Ermine, a calf passant gules.
     Cavell.

27. Argent a bull passant gules armed and unguled Or.
     Bevill.

28. Argent, a squirrel sejant gules, cracking a nut Or.
     Nutshall.

29. Argent, three cows passant sable, eyed gules, collared Or.
     Benedictine Alien Priory of Cowick, Devon.

30. Argent, on a point wavy barry-wavy of azure and argent, an ox passant gules, armed and unguled Or.
     Corporation of the City of Oxford.
     [*Note:* This is also expressed: Argent, an ox gules armed and unguled Or, passing a ford of water in base proper.]

25

26

27

28

29

30

istic of penetration—shrewdness—but also of ca. value. (313)

awned: r. alt. spelling of 'aulned' (q.v.).

axe: [M.E.] a wedge-shaped cutting-tool, generally convex on the edge, hafted (q.v.) or helved, of a long, slightly curved handle: sometimes blazoned as either a 'felling ~' or a 'woodsman's ~'. The pole-~ (q.v.) is both a weapon of war and a butcher's tool, which latter aspect is emphasized when it is blazoned as a 'slaughter ~ '.

aylet: [dial.] the tern; a sea-bird of the genus *Sterna*, having long, slender wings and a forked tail; known also as the sea-swallow. Erroneously applied to the Cornish chough (q.v.).

ayrant: [L. via Fr.] of a bird of prey on a nest.

Aztec Eagle, Order of: (Mexico.) f. 1933 in six classes. Insignia—*Badge:* an Aztec eagle in gold, holding a red enamel snake, on a blue medallion surrounded by a gold border and an open five-point star, each point separated by an eagle's head on a rectangle. *Star:* the badge on a round gold plaque. *Riband:* gold moire.

azur: Fr. and It., azure.

azure: [Arabic] dark blue, represented in engraver's cross-hatching by parallel horizontal lines.

azzur: D., azure.

azzuro: It., azure.

B.: abvn for 'azure' (blue) to differentiate sharply from abvn A. for 'argent' (q.v.).

bacillus: L., baton (of office).

badelaire: (alt. spelling 'badelar') see **sabre.**

badge, heraldic: [M.E.] a ~, cognisance, or cullison is a device, not part of, but extra to a coat of arms, and the subject of a grant by the kings of arms. It is exclusive to the use of the grantee, may be used to brand property and to be a mark of identity for a man's servants and others (under the feudal system—his foot soldiers). A ~, unlike a crest (q.v.), does not appear upon a wreath of the colours (q.v.) or other crest bearing item, but in Scotland a crest appearing within the circlet of a strap-and-buckle becomes a badge, and thus enables an heraldic heiress (q.v.) to transmit to male issue the time-honoured historic crest of, e.g., a Clan. Without a ~ an armiger's normal display of flags is confined to the household banner (irrespective of sailing flags, if any), but the possession of a ~ necessitates the wearing of a standard (q.v.) (1–6)

Badge of Ulster: see **Ulster Office.**

badger: so called from the blaze (q.v.) on its forehead; nocturnal, hibernating, related to both the weasel (q.v.) and the bear (q.v.), *Meles vulgaris.* Noted for its fierceness and courage in fighting to defend its home, hence of symbolic significance. Also named 'brock', 'bauson', and 'gray'; hence of wide ca. value.

Badges, Barnard's Roll of: (1475) 8½ by 12 in., being a muster-roll connected with the invasion of France led by K. Ed. IV, giving names and armorial badges, most of which are illustrated by rough marginal pen-drawing, of the dukes, earls, bannerets, knights, and others contributing their quota of 'spears and lances' to the host. The heralds and the craftsmen accompanying the expedition are also mentioned, and due respect is extended to the accountancy clerks, described as 'tellers of the Kynges mony in his Receyt at Canterbury'.

Badges, Sir John Fenn's Book of: (c. 1470) bold drawing in ink on paper of fifty-seven armorial badges; the book is marked 'Wyllm Forthe', who may have been the first owner. The name is accompanied by his cypher, a figure 4 reversed between Roman text letters W and F. See also **merchants' marks.**

bag: a sack, or a bale, bunched into lugs at the corners, generally stated to contain some form of merchandise, as the '~ of madder' crest of the Worshipful Company of Dyers, and often wrapped about with cordage of a colour differing from that of the ~ itself.

bagpipes: see **hare.**

bagril: a minnow (ca.).

bagwin: a composite fictitious beast having the body of a horse and the head of an heraldic antelope provided with a pair of long, curving horns.

bail: [M.E.] lit. a stake or palisade; hence, a bar or strip of metal forming the face-protecting grid of a non-visored helmet.

Baillie, Michael: Marchmont Herald, 1698.

bâillone: [Fr.] of a lion rampant holding in its mouth a baton.

Bailly, Wm: Albany Herald, 1452.

Bainbridge, Andrew Ferguson: Herald-painter to the Lyon Court, 1884.

Baird of Newbyth, Sir John: Lord Lyon Depute, 1663.

balaai: Afk., charged.

balance: see **hand-balance.**

bale: see **bag.**

bale-fire: [O.E.] a fire kindled in the open air; a beltane or need-fire; a funeral pyre; a bonfire; hence, a r., chiefly Scottish, term for a beacon fired (q.v.).

Balfour, John: Albany Herald, 1568. Unicorn Pursuivant, 1528.

Balfour, Robert: Procurator Fiscal to the Lyon Court, 1631.

Balfour, Sir David: Lord Lyon Depute, 1650.

Balfour of Denmilne, Sir James: Lord Lyon King of Arms, 1630.

Balfour Paul, Sir James, K.C.V.O.: Lord Lyon King of Arms, 1890.

Balfour Paul of Cakemuir, Lt.-Col. John Wm: Marchmont Herald, 1939. Falkland Pursuivant, 1927.

balk: Swd., bend.

balken: Ger., fess.

Ball, Henry: Windsor Herald, 1686. Former Rouge Croix Pursuivant, 1677; former Rose Rouge Pursuivant, 1675.

Ballard, John: Windsor Herald during the reign of K. Ed. IV. Former Rouge Croix Pursuivant (K. Hen. VI); former Wallingford Pursuivant (K. Hen. VI).

Ballard's Book: (c. 1465–90) vellum, about 95 pages, some of which are blank, 10½ by 14½ in. A collection, being in the main a series of local rolls (q.v.) including Cheshire, South Wales and adjacent territory, Warwickshire, Staffordshire, and Leicestershire: shields, crests, and armorial badges relating to Cheshire and Lancashire, the same for Yorkshire. Shields of families in Devon and Cornwall, Berkshire, Oxfordshire, Hampshire, Surrey, Sussex, and Buckinghamshire. There is also an ordinary (q.v.) of roundels.

Balliol Roll: (c. 1432) a list of Scottish lords and knights; shields painted with names over; written on the dorse of Cooke's Ordinary (q.v.). The ~ is considered to be the oldest roll of Scottish arms.

ballista: see **mangonel.**

ballock knife: see **kidney dagger.**

balm: a fragrant herb, ~-mint, *Melissa officinalis,* drawn without conventionalization, and of r. occurrence in arms.

Balsillie, John: Islay Herald, 1667.

band, a: sometimes applied to the binder-twine that holds a garb (q.v.) together.

banda: It. and Sp., bend.

bande: Fr., bend.

bandeau: [Fr.] r. alt. for 'wreath of the colours' (q.v.).

bande batonnée: [Fr.] baston.

banded: of the binder-twine round a garb when of a colour differing from that of the straws. Of any ring, or ferrule, that may, in a similar manner, surround any object.

bandera: Sp., banner.

banderole: a trumpet-banner, being a small gonfanon (q.v.) on which is emblazoned the full achievement, i.e. shield, crest, mantling, supporters, and compartment, if any, attached to a trumpet and carried outward, over the flexed arm of the trumpeter. An alt. spelling of 'bannerol' (q.v.). The term is also applied to a streamer: formerly to helmet-streamers, now sometimes to the vexillium (q.v.) of a crosier (q.v.).

bandiera: It., banner.

bandrol: see **bannerol.**

bandula: L., bendlet.

Banelee: Rothesay Herald, 1507. Former Bluemantle Pursuivant, 1503; former Risebank Pursuivant, 1501.

banier: D., banner.

Bannatyne, Patrick: Islay Herald, 1588.

banner: [M.E.] a rectangular flag, fringed of the colours, originally measuring in the dip (q.v.) about twice the length of the fly (q.v.); now roughly square and emblazoned with the armorial devices that distinguish the shield of an armiger: exterior decorations are not included.

Every armiger, irrespective of social rank, ought to possess and, on appropriate occasions, fly a ∼ of his arms, but in England a mis-applied modesty has made a museum piece of the ∼. In Scotland, however, one's neighbours would take greater offence at a breach of flag etiquette than it is supposed they would take in England by its observance.

The sovereign's Household Banner, miscalled 'the Royal Standard', and the National Banner of Great Britain and Northern Ireland, known as the Union Jack (q.v.) are about twice as long in the fly as they are high in the dip, and this proportion governs the shape of most flags. The extension in length was developed at sea, where the shape was found to be more easily visible in a high wind; a short, square mast-head ensign being inclined to develop a rapid vibration throughout.

The ensigns carried upon a vertical frame by trade unionists on May Day, although often having high artistic merit, are not ∼s. Any flag, including a ∼, may function as a charge (q.v.) (243)

banner-roll: see previous entry.

---

31. A bull's head erazed sable: on a chief of the last three pheons Or.
     Tipping.

32. Argent, on a mount vert a stag lodged between two oak trees all within a ring of park-pales and a gate proper.
     Corporation of the City of Derby.

33. Argent, a hart trippant azure.
     Hertington.

34. Argent, a bull's head caboshed azure, armed Or.
     Turnbull.

35. Azure, on a mount vert a stag pascuant proper.
     Lennon.

36. Azure, a reindeer trippant, ermine.
     Walstone.

31

32

33

34

35

36

Bannerett's Roll: see **Parliamentary.**

bannerol: a gonfanon (q.v.) fringed of the colours and carried in a funeral procession; alt. spellings 'banderole', 'bandrol', and 'banner-roll'.

bannière: [Fr.] banner.

Baptist, St John the: see **lamb, Paschal.**

Baptist, head of St John the: described as 'decollated' and 'on a charger'; is one of the crests of the Worshipful Company of Tallow Chandlers.

bar¹: [M.E.] a horizontal ordinary, one-fifth of the width of the shield, two of which appear together being their own width apart: a single ~ may appear accompanying some other ordinary, generally a chief (q.v.). (253, 465, II)

bar²: continental name of the barbel. See also **tench.**

bar-shot: a missile consisting of two cannon-balls joined by a length of iron rod, used largely in naval warfare as a means of increasing the chances of cutting the enemy's rigging and shattering masts.

bar-sinister: a crass, vulgar phrase believed to have signification in relationship to bastardy and to heraldic differencing. The explanation that it is an altered form of the French heraldic term 'barre' meaning a bend sinister, formerly employed as a mark of distinction, is constantly being given notwithstanding that it is arrant nonsense. It is an example of the egocentric theorizing in which experts in any subject are also expert: they take a hammer to make a stitch, and a needle and thread to drive a nail. The phenomena of linguistics are not to be resolved by application of the grammar of heraldry.

The term ~ is a specimen of euphemistic slang having its origin in the servants' quarters. 'Bastard', as frequently pronounced 'bar-sterd' as 'bass-tard', was too robust a word to fall from the lips of the footman and the scullery-maid: truncated to 'bar-' and suggestively followed by the sibilant 'sinister', it was, in addition to being euphemistic, a fine piece of 'below-stairs' wit: the production of a bastard in the family was bad, quite sinister in fact, and the combination sounded highly heraldic.

The servants were not learned in heraldry: if they had knowledge of a few terms it is doubtful whether they could have attached them to the figures they described; hence, to imply that they were conversant with Fr. terms, could compare them with English, and had knowledge of archaic marks of distinction, is to attribute the song of the nightingale to the crow.

barbed: [M.E.] of a rose, provided with visible caylix; of an archer's arrow, provided with a head differing in colour to the shaft; of a barbel fish, provided with aggressive spines beside the mouth.

barbel: see **tench.**

barber's pole: see **wreath of the colours.**

barbetado: Sp., finned.

barbican: [M.E.] a fortified gate-house, represented as a narrow Gothic archway, closed, in a crenellated wall with, at each end, a tower terminating in a cone-shaped roof.

Barbour, Alexander: Kintyre Pursuivant, 1684.

barbula: L., barbed.

bard: Swd., bordure.

bardado: Sp., comparisoned.

bardato: It., comparisoned.

barded: [Arabic] of a horse comparisoned, furnished, or saddled.

Bardolf Herald: active in 1399; an officer of arms maintained by Lord Bardolf.

barea: Sp., bend sinister.

barensteel: Afk. and D., label.

Barker, Justinian: Rouge Croix Pursuivant, 1541. Former Risebank Pursuivant.

Barker, Sir Christopher: Garter King of

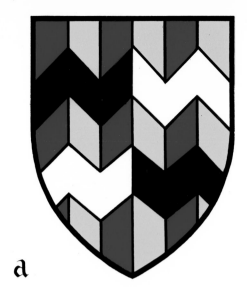

a

b

c

PLATE II (a) Paly gules and Or, two bars dancetty, both per pale, the upper sable and argent, the lower argent and sable.

Central Electricity Generating Board

(Paly gules and Or suggests heat and light. The bars dancetty represent the jagged electrical flash and the colours, sable and argent, symbolize both coal and water, the two main sources of energy employed to drive the turbines that rotate the generators.)

(b) Quarterly gules and azure: in the first and fourth a leopard's face; in the second and third a covered cup between, in chief, two buckles tongues to the dexter, all gold.

Worshipful Company of Goldsmiths (London)

(First and fourth is the hallmark: second and third, products of the craft.)

(c) Vert, issuant from sinister-base three piles wavy conjoined in point in dexter-chief.

Milk Marketing Board

(Symbolizing rivers of milk flowing far and wide from our lush, green pastures.)

Arms, 1536. Former Norroy K. of A. (also 1536); former Richmond Herald, 1522; former Suffolk Herald, 1517; former Lisle Pursuivant, 1513.

Barkham, George: Lancaster Herald under Cromwell, 1658.

Barnabas, St: represented by his hand in the municipal arms of Bornavino, Russia.

barnacle[1]: [L.] the wild, Arctic goose, *Anas leucopsis*, which visits the British Isles in winter. Thought to have grown upon the tree where it was seen resting following its arrival. Alt. spellings 'barnicle' or 'bernicle'.

barnacle[2]: an instrument made from flexible branches to grip the nose of a restive horse: applied to an instrument of torture used upon the human nose. In spite of the oft-repeated statement that the heraldic ∼ is a representation of the former, it is far more reasonable to believe, because of the shape depicted, that it is of the latter. (144)

Barnes Pursuivant: maintained by Lord Berners, 1520–33.

baron: [L.] In England, from the Conquest to about the time of Ed. I, a ∼ was one who paid homage to the king, or to one of the great lords, and undertook certain commitments in return for the lease of a substantial holding of land. All ∼s of the time were so by virtue of tenure, and at an early date they were recognized as being in two categories, the 'greate' ∼s, who held directly of the king by military service, and 'lesser' ∼s; the former received direct summonses to the King's Council, whereas Magna Carta decreed that the latter would be called only through the sheriffs.

No title was inherent in a barony at this stage, and recognition of the rank as that of the lowest in the peerage grew only when summonses to the Council, which was to evolve into the House of Lords, were made at the will of the king and not by right of tenure. From the time of Ed. I ∼s were made by writ or letters patent and, over a lengthy period of time, their right to the title 'lord' and to a seat in the House of Lords became established.

In Scotland a feudal barony retains some of its original character, for it does not carry the title 'lord' and does not entitle the holder to a seat in the House; it is still, theoretically, a rank achieved by tenure or possession, for the holder must own the 'caput' of an original barony, although this may nowadays consist of a mere token which can be bought, together with the right to the barony.

On the Continent of Europe 'barones' evolved, *mutatis mutandis*, in much the same way as in England, and came to be recognized as the lowest rank of hereditary titled nobility (see **noble**). Baronies in the Scottish sense, by the form of tenure which links the title to possession of a certain property, are found in other countries, e.g. Malta and Sicily.

baronet: a degree of nobility created by letters patent. Possesses the title 'Sir', although ∼s are not knighted by virtue of their baronetcy; and their title is hereditary, although they are not peers; hence the early definition that they were 'neither peers nor gentlemen'. The honour was f. in 1611 by K. James VI and I, and confirmed by K. Ch. I, who later, in 1629, decreed that ∼s of Scotland and Nova Scotia should wear round their necks 'an orange tawny riband whereon shall be pendent an inescutcheon argent, a saltire azure, thereon an inescutcheon of the Arms of Scotland, with an Imperial Crown above the scutcheon, and encircled on an oval band the motto *Pax Mentis Honestae Gloria*'. In 1929 K. Geo. V instituted a neck-badge for ∼s of the United Kingdom, namely:

'A shield of the Arms of Ulster, viz. on a silver field a left-hand gules, surmounted by an Imperial crown enamelled in its proper colours, the whole enclosed by an oval border embossed with gilt scrollwork having a design of shamrocks and of roses and thistles combined, and for those ~s who were created ~s of England, of Ireland, and of Great Britain respectively, and for all other ~s other than baronets of Scotland, a design of roses, thistles and shamrocks combined, such a badge to be suspended from an orange riband with a narrow edge of blue on both sides, the total breadth of the riband to be one inch and three quarters, and the breadth of each edge to be one quarter of an inch.' The badge is not worn in miniature.

baronet, badge of: a mark of distinction (q.v.), being either an escutcheon or a canton, whichever is the more suitable to the shield's contents; also called 'The Badge of Ulster', being 'argent, a sinister hand appaumé, couped at the wrist, gules'. This armorial embellishment, described by K. James VI and I as 'the arms of Ulster', is a version of the inescutcheon therefrom. (IV)

baron-et-femme: lit. man and woman; hence, alt. description of an impaled (q.v.) marital achievement (q.v.).

baron's coronet: a silver-gilt circlet heightened with six pearls (q.v.) each 2 in. in diameter, four only of which are depicted; used to ensign a baron's shield.

barque: see **ship.**

Barr, James: Albany Herald, 1694.

barre: Fr., bend sinister.

barrel: see **tun.**

barrulet: second diminutive of the bar (q.v.), being one-quarter the width of the parent (or half a closet (q.v.)); employed as a satellite, one running on each side of a bar, and exterior to it. (12, 77, 420; IV)

barrulety: a term used in old heraldry for 'barry' (q.v.) of many pieces: as many as twenty is not uncommon.

barrully: see following entry.

barry: of a field (q.v.) an ordinary (q.v.) or a charge (q.v.) carrying an equal number of barrulets (q.v.) of alternate metal and tincture: six is the standard and no number need be given, but it must be for eight: ten has a special term, i.e. 'barrully'. ~, which is one of the major variations of the field (q.v.), may consist of alternate fur (q.v.) and tincture. The word 'pieces' is sometimes added after the number. (8, 9, 10, 11; X, XII, XIV)

barry-bendy: a compound variation of the field created by lines drawn fesswise (as though for barry (q.v.)) crossed by lines in

---

37. Gules, a stag at gaze attired Or.
    Jones.

38. Argent, a buck's head caboshed gules attired Or.
    Trye.

39. Vert, three hounds courant bendwise at random argent: on a chief of the last a stag at speed proper.
    Wildish.

40. Argent fretty vert, a stag springing sable.
    Warnett.

41. Azure, a thistle vert flowered gules between three urcheons sable.
    Harris.

42. Azure, a talbot trippant Or.
    Burgoigne.

37

38

39

40

41

42

bend (as though for bendy (q.v.)) producing a series of lozenges that incline to the dexter. ~ may be of either metal or fur and tincture, the metal commencing in the first whole shape in dexter-chief. ~ sinister creates similar shapes that incline in the contrary direction. (444)

Barrye, Thos: Unicorn Pursuivant, 1570.

bars-gemel: see **closet**.

bartizan: a turret, corbelled out at each corner of the top storey of a Scottish castle, often machicolated. The ~ appears as a charge in some Scottish achievements.

barwise: of a number of small charges crossing the field from flank to flank, in two or more rows: the canton (q.v.) in the flag of U.S.A. is 'azure, fifty mullets in nine barwise rows of alternately, six and five'.

bascinet: see **basinet**.

bascule: [Fr.] a bridge, pivoted and counterpoised, that may be raised and so put out of action, and lowered to afford transit; a drawbridge.

base: [M.E.] all of the field (q.v.) below fess point (q.v.); the lower part of a charge (q.v.); on the Continent 'a ~' is an ordinary (q.v.), but in British heraldry the plain point (q.v.) serves the same purpose, although some old writers describe 'a ~'. Charges below fess point are 'in base'.

based-esquirre: see **esquirre**.

basilisk: see **cockatrice**.

basinet: a basin-shaped skull cap, generally worn as an extra protection within the pot helm; alt. spelling 'bascinet'.

basket: many different kinds of ~ appear in arms, always blazoned by name as 'bread-~', 'fish-~'.

basket-makers' tools: the arms of the Worshipful Company of Basket Makers constitute an almost unique group of prosaic objects, i.e. 'a prime, an iron, a cutting knife and an outsticker', each of which is no doubt fundamental to the trade, but not one of which has either character or form.

bastardy, indication of: the bearing of coat-armour is, notwithstanding that the point is no longer stressed, an honour, albeit a minor honour; hence it follows, in spite of deeply ingrained popular fallacy, that illegitimate offspring of an armiger, either sons or daughters, are not stigmatized by a punitive addition to the achievement. When an armiger has acknowledged his paternity, and has made the necessary arrangements with the heraldic authority, his illegitimate offspring will receive a grant of the pronominal (q.v.) quarter of his arms 'suitably differenced'. The mark of difference employed is not for the purpose of declaring the irregularity of the new armiger's birth, but simply to indicate that he is not the heir to any titles or estates that may be associated with the achievement of arms to the use of which he has been admitted.

There is not a mark of difference that is specifically the mark of the bastard, but there are prevailing fashions: an early form was the bend sinister, later reduced to the baston, and ultimately curtailed to the baton, and metal was reserved for illegitimate offspring in the Royal Family. Borders have also been employed as differences, and the prevailing fashion is a bordure wavy; hence, it follows that 'a mark of bastardy' does not, and never did, exist.

An adopted child is in precisely the same position armorially as an illegitimate. If he is to perpetuate his foster father's arms he must receive a grant of the pronominal quarter 'suitably differenced'. The prevailing mark is a plain canton on the shield, and on the crest a cross-crosslet.

The idea that such marks of distinction may be abandoned after being in use for three generations is absurd.

baston: [M.E. fm O.F.] lit. baton, a rod; the second diminutive of the bend sinister, being one-quarter the width of the parent (or half a scarpe (q.v.)).

bastone: It., baston.

bastonnades: r. alt. for 'bretesse' (q.v.).

Basynge's Book: (c. 1395) vellum, 8 in. by 11½ ft, painted, 407 shields with names over.

bat: [M.E.] a flying-mouse of nocturnal habits, having membranous wings; *Chiroptera vesperti lionidae*. Also called 'reremouse' and 'flittermouse'. (143)

Bath, Most Honourable Order of the: f., first, at a date uncertain; revived by K. Geo. I, 1725. Originally a one-class order it now has three classes in Military and Civil divisions. Insignia—Grand Crosses—a mantle of crimson satin lined with white taffeta with the star on the left breast; a gold collar of nine crowns and eight sceptres with roses, thistles, and shamrocks issuant, linked by seventeen knots enamelled argent; a badge (Mil. Div.) of a gold Maltese cross pommetty, gold lions in the angles, bearing centrally the sceptre, rose, thistle, and shamrock device between three gold crowns, encircled with the motto *Tria juncta in uno* in gold on red, encompassed by two laurel branches issuant from an escroll inscribed *Ich Dien*. Civ. Div.: *Badge:* an oval gold filigree representation of the military badge's central device, encircled by the motto in gold; badges worn from the collar or from crimson riband over right shoulder. The Mil. Div. star is of silver rays charged with simplified mil. badge. Civ. Div. star is of silver rays bearing centrally three crowns encircled by the motto in gold on red. Knight Companions wear similar but smaller badges from a crimson riband round the neck; their stars are of four rays, with smaller rays between, with a central device as for G.C.B. (Civ.), the Mil. Div. being distinguished by laurel leaves and *Ich Dien*.

Companions wear badges as for K.C.B.s, but smaller.

Bath King of Arms: a title created in XI *anno regnum* K. Geo. I in connection with the Order of the Bath (q.v.); not an officer of arms in ordinary.

baton¹: [Fr.] a staff of a special size, shape, and pattern, being the symbol of authority, (as the Earl Marshal's ∼ borne in saltire (q.v.) behind his arms).

baton²: [M.E. fm O.F.] the third diminutive of bend sinister, being a baston (q.v.) couped (q.v.) at each end to half its length. The ∼'s primary function is to act as a special mark of difference (q.v.); sometimes called 'ribbon sinister'.

battering-ram: a tree-trunk provided with an iron armament at one end and having two iron bands, with rings at the top, at intervals along its length. The ∼ has the armament in the form of a ram's head. It may be all of one colour but is likely to be 'armed' of its head, i.e. the head of a colour differing from the cylinder. It may have several colours, being 'banded' or 'garnished' of one, 'ringed' of another, 'headed' of the ram's head which in turn may be 'armed' of its horns. (460)

battle-axe: consists of two parts; the head—called the blade—and the shaft, which is often curved forward towards the end—called the stave. The blade conforms to the proportions of an equilateral triangle; the cutting edge, which faces dexter, is convex; the other two sides, concave. The truncated apex merges into a socket out of which issue two spikes; one, being a continuation of the blade, faces the sinister, the other, in line with the stave, points chiefward. (455)

battled-embattled: see **grady**.

battlements of a castle (or of a tower): crests are sometimes issuant of the ∼ (or a tower) instead of upon a wreath of the colours (q.v.). What is intended is the upper part of a round-tower (q.v.) which should always be drawn as corbelled out, thus made distinct from a mural crown (q.v.) which, too, on occasions, has issuant from it a crest. (136)

batune: r. obs. alt. for 'potent' (q.v.).

baudrick: a swordbelt.

bauson: see **badger.**

bauteroll: r. alt. spelling of 'boteroll' (q.v.).

bay: see **laurel.**

bay, at: an uncommon term for a beast with its head lowered, awaiting attack.

Bayley, Wm Goodall: Islay Herald, 1851. Bute Pursuivant, 1838.

beacon: [O.E.] an alarm signal consisting of an iron cage erected on three legs, one of which was provided with branches to facilitate climbing, which was kept filled with inflammable materials. These ~s, placed on high hills or on church towers or city gates, were in charge of a watchman whose duty was to fire it when he saw that the next nearest had been fired; thus was the warning of an enemy's approach conveyed from the coast inland with great rapidity. The ~ in heraldry varies little, if at all, from the real thing, and is generally blazoned as 'in full flare', 'fired', or 'inflamed'. Sometimes described as a cresset.

beaked: [M.E.] referring to the colour of the beak of a non-predacious bird.

beaker: see **jug.**

beam: an heraldic term for the shaft, shank, or stem of an anchor (q.v.) often, but not invariably, employed; shank is, perhaps, second in frequency.

bean: [O.E.] the fruit, or seed, of the climbing plant, *Faba vulgaris*, which develop in pods and are so blazoned and depicted; 'beancod' and 'beanpod' are frequently employed in blazon.

bear: [O.E.] genus *Ursus:* has no special characteristic and is sometimes employed for ca. reasons. The usual attitude is sejant erect, and he is often muzzled. The head, when appearing alone, can easily be mistaken for that of the boar (q.v.) and similarly may be either couped close or couped at the neck. The paw, either couped or erased, is more slender than that of a lion,

---

43. Or, a greyhound courant between three garbs azure [for Moreton of Chilworth Manor], *impaling*, azure, issuant of a crescent in base Or, two ostrich feathers argent: in chief, a mullet of six points of the second [for Schintz].

44. Per fess argent and sable a lion rampant counterchanged.
     Basket, Dorset [II & III qtr].

45. Or, a lion rampant regardant, gules, holding in the dexter paw a cross-crosslet fitchy azure.
     Guthry.

46. Argent, a greyhound skipping in bend, sable.
     Atwood.

47. Or, a lion rampant trononné gules within a bordure wavy and quarterly azure and of the second charged with a mullet in centre-chief and, in centre-base, a crescent of the first.
     Maitland.

48. Argent, a lion rampant queue-fourché and double knowed purpure.
     Storey.

43

44

45

46

47

48

has longer and less-curved claws, and sleek fur. (13, 16)

bearded: see **comet** and **ear**.

Beauchamp, John: Portcullis Pursuivant, 1633.

beauvoir: r. alt. spelling of 'beaver' (see **beaver²**).

beaver¹: an amphibious rodent employed chiefly for ca. reasons.

beaver²: the visor of a close-helmet (q.v.).

beckée: see **becqué**.

Becket's Murderer's Roll: see **Calveley's Book**.

beckit: archaic name for the Cornish chough (q.v.).

Beckit, St Thomas: commemorated in the allusive arms of the Muncipal Corporation of Canterbury, i.e. 'three Cornish choughs, formerly called beckits' (q.v.).

becqué: [Fr.] beaked; of the beak of a non-predacious bird; also spelt 'beckée'.

Bede, The Venerable: commemorated in the civic arms of Jarrow, Durham.

bedekt: D., charged.

Bedford Herald: maintained in the service of the Duke of Bedford, 1428.

bee: [Teut.] a hymenopterous insect living in herds having a queen (female), a few drones (male), and numerous neuters (workers). They gather honey and excrete wax: symbolic of industriousness. Sometimes, particularly when acting as a crest, the ~ is depicted 'statant' (q.v.) in profile with wings, of which there are four, elevated; but generally 'volant in arrière', i.e. flying from the spectator. A ~-hive is of the basket, domed variety, and is generally surrounded by ~s blazoned as 'promiscuously volant' or as 'diversely volant'; sometimes simply 'sans nombre'. (79)

beetle¹: any coleopterous insect having shell-like wing-covers; r. and blazoned by descriptive name, e.g. stagbeetle.

beetle²: see **hammer**.

beetroot: [O.E.] a vegetable charge, Cheno podiaceae, employed in continental arms.

beffroy: obs. term for 'vair' (q.v.).

Begbie, Patrick: Ormonde Pursuivant, 1769.

behalsbandet: Ger., collared.

beiderseits gespitzt: Ger., pointed at each end.

bekleidet: Ger., vested.

belegt: Ger., charged.

belfry: see **church**.

Belgian Croix de Guerre: see **Croix de Guerre** (Belgium).

belic: r. obs. alt. for 'gules'.

bell, church: a musical instrument cast in a special quality bronze; cylindrical, closed at the head by a dome with an external central ring, termed the canon, and curved outward at the open end, the curvature being termed the skirt: suspended within is a rod terminating in a ball, termed the tongue or clapper, which is visible below the skirt. ~ may have the canon, the skirt, and the clapper of differing colours. (356)

Bell, George: Angus Herald Extraordinary, 1500.

bell, hawk's: a small, hollow, spherical brass or silver container, provided with a ring for its suspension, and having in the lower half a slit to enhance vibration which is caused by the tumbling of a piece of flint, or a nodule of metal housed within. A hawk is always belled on one leg whether mentioned in the blazon or not; it may also be double-belled, i.e. one on each leg. (359)

Bellasis, Edward: Lancaster Herald, 1882. Former Bluemantle Pursuivant, 1873.

belled: see **bell, hawk's**.

Bellesme Pursuivant: maintained by the Earl of Salisbury, 1421.

Bellew, Hon. Sir George Rothe: Garter King of Arms, 1950. Former Somerset

Herald, 1926; former Portcullis Pursuivant, 1922.

bellfroy: obs. alt. for 'vair' (q.v.).

bellota: Sp., acorn.

bellows: [O.E.] a domestic utensil employed for creating a current of air in order to stimulate a sluggish fire. No change in pattern occurred from the late XIV cent. when they make their appearance in arms to the end of the XIX cent. when they went out of general use. (319)

Beltz, George Frederick: Lancaster Herald, 1822. Former Portcullis Pursuivant, 1817; former Brunswick Herald, 1814.

bend: [O.E.] lit. a band, tape, tie, or connecting piece; hence, an ordinary (q.v.) commencing in dexter-chief, passing over the fess point, and terminating baseward of the sinister flank. It should not be less than a fifth of the shield's width or, if charged, more than a third. The complementary ordinary is ~ sinister, which slopes in the opposite direction. (87, 88, 108; III, XI)

bend, in: of an object, or a number of objects crossing the field in the direction of and position of a bend (q.v.).

bendlet: first diminutive of the bend (q.v.) being half the width of the parent; obs. alts. 'garter' or 'gartier'. (86)

bendulatus: L., bendy.

bendy: of a field (q.v.), an ordinary (q.v.), or a charge carrying an equal number of bendlets (q.v.) of alternate metal and tincture: there seems to be no standard number as there is for barry (q.v.) and for paly (q.v.), but eight serves the purpose best when ~ is acting as one of the major variations of the field. ~-sinister is composed of alternate metal and tincture bendlets descending from sinister to dexter. ~ or its complement may be of a fur and a tincture.

Bengal tiger: a tiger proper; *Panthera tigris*, a comparative newcomer into heraldry, depicted without conventionalization. The heraldic tygre (q.v.), an old inhabitant of the field, is a fictitious creature.

beneficent rain-dragon: see **dragon**.

Bennet of Whiteside, Patrick: Ross Herald, 1816.

Benolt, Thomas: Clarenceux King of Arms, 1511. Former Norroy K. of A. 1510; former Windsor Herald, 1404; former Rouge Croix Pursuivant; former Berwick Pursuivant.

Bensilver Pursuivant: active in 1443. Possibly identical with Biencele, Biencole, Biendelle, or Bientele and Bien Colier. Biendelle was maintained by Sir Richard Woodville, Lord Rivers; Bien Colier carried dispatches in 1444; but who maintained ~ is unknown.

beque, alt. spelling of 'becqué' (q.v.).

bereift: Ger., banded.

berly: obs. alt. for 'barry' (q.v.).

bernak: r. obs. alt. for a barnacle (see **barnacle**[1]).

Berry, George: Rouge Croix Pursuivant, 1487.

Berwick Pursuivant: an officer of arms formerly attached to the Governor of Berwick. A Garrison Pursuivant for the Scottish border.

besamt: Ger., seeded.

besant: Swd., bezant.

besät: Ger., semé.

besca: r. term sometimes applied to a spade (q.v.); probably originally for ca. reasons.

besom: [Teut.] a bunch of thin, flexible twigs lashed round the end of a short, rigid handle, used as a sweeping brush; formerly the domestic household broom and associated with witchcraft, being the vehicle upon which the journey to the Sabbat was made. The ~ is still employed by gardeners who use them in the autumn for clearing the fallen leaves; hence, there are numerous reasons for the employment of the ~ in heraldry.

beson: see **boson.**

Besource Pursuivant: active in 1380 when he received largesse (q.v.) from John O'Gaunt, but his master is not known.

beströdd: Swd., semé.

Beul Pursuivant: maintained by the captain of Bayeux Castle. Active in 1446.

beurtelings gekanteel: Afk., embattled-counter-embattled.

bevally: an obs. term which seems to have been applied by writers rather than by officers of arms.

bevapnad: Swd., armed.

bevilled: an obs. line of partition: 'per fess ~' consists of a straight line from dexter flank to a little beyond the centre of the shield where it breaks and descends in bend sinister for a third of the shield's width then, returning to the horizontal, reaches the sinister flank: this line with its two (roughly) 45° breaks, rotated clockwise gives 'per bend ~', 'per pale ~', 'per bend sinister ~'.

bevrugte: Afk., fructed.

bewehrt: Ger., attired or horned.

bewinkelt: Ger., angled.

Beyren Herald: see **Gelre, Armorial de.**

bezaaid: D., semé.

bezant: [O.F.] a roundel (q.v.) Or, representing the coin minted at Byzantium and used during the Middle Ages as currency over a wide area; the ~ is not shaded.

bezanty: semé (q.v.) of bazants (q.v.).

Bible: see **book.**

bicapitated: of a beast having two heads.

bicorporate: lit. two-bodied of twin beasts (generally lions or fish) having but one head between them. A lion ~ may be sejant affrontée (q.v.) or else rampant and counter-rampant, the common head, in centre-chief (q.v.) being 'gardant' (q.v.). A development of the same freak-evolution is a beast tricorporate: one head (gardant) shared by three bodies. 'A tricorporate lion rampant disposed in triangle' is a sufficient blazon: the head gardant is in fess point, and a body in the rampant attitude extends into each corner of the shield, but this is not the only method of filling the space: 'a tricorporate lion, one passant, one rampant and one salient' will place the common head gardant

---

49. Argent, a lion rampant double-queued purpure ducally crowned Or.
    Folliott.

50. Argent, a lion salient gardant gules.
    Jermy.

51. Argent, a lion passant gardant gules.
    Clare.

52. Or, a lion rampant sable holding erect in the dexter fore-paw a sabre proper within a double tressure flory-counter-fleury of the second.
    MacCausland.
    (This is the much-quoted achievement wherein the sabre was blazoned as 'a crooked saw'.)

53. Argent, a lion passant coward, sable.
    Herwell.

54. Gules, three lions passant gardant in pale Or dimidiated with azure, three hulks of ships in pale argent.
    Cinque Ports.

49

50

51

52

53

54

in dexter-chief. Both of these compound freaks belong to the late Middle Ages, are normally no longer employed, but survive in old arms and in recent arms based on old. (273)

Bien Alaunt Pursuivant: probably maintained by the Earl of Warwick.

Bien Colier Pursuivant: see **Bensilver Pursuivant.**

Biencele Pursuivant: see **Bensilver Pursuivant.**

Biencole Pursuivant: see **Bensilver Pursuivant.**

Biendelle Pursuivant: see **Bensilver Pursuivant.**

Bientele Pursuivant: see **Bensilver Pursuivant.**

Bigland, Ralph[1]**:** Garter King of Arms, 1780. Former Clarenceux K. of A., 1774; former Norroy K. of A., 1773; former Somerset Herald, 1759; former Bluemantle Pursuivant, 1756.

Bigland, Sir Ralph[2]**:** Garter King of Arms, 1831. Former Clarenceux K. of A., 1822; former Norroy K. of A., 1803; former Richmond Herald, 1780; former Rouge Dragon Pursuivant, 1774.

biljett: Swd., billet.

billed: [O.E.] r. alt. for 'beaked' (q.v.).

billet: a plain rectangle which, in its major axis, ought not to be less than twice, or more than three times, the minor axis. A ~ always stands on its narrow side but obviously 'three ~s in bend' will recline bendwise. It is frequently defined as representative of a block of wood; this is, however, er. The ~ represents a letter which was something of importance in the XIII cent.: a block of wood was not. A sheet of paper (or even vellum) was not thick enough to cast a shadow; hence, ~s, being letters, are not shaded. (103, 418, 471)

Billett, James: was severally Antelope Pursuivant, Rouge Croix Pursuivant, and Chester Herald during the reign of K. Hen. VI.

billetty: semé (q.v.) of billets (q.v.).

binnenzoom: D., orle.

binnesoom: Afk., orle.

bird bolt: a short, blunt arrow, similar to (if not identical with) the quarrel (q.v.). A ~ may be double or triple headed. (463)

biremed: [frmd on Gr. 'bireme', a fishing-boat] a r. term employed in Scotland to express 'oars in action' or 'oars over the side', in connection with a lymphad (q.v.). (VI)

birt: [dial.] a turbot (ca.).

birth-brieves: see **Lyon Office.**

bis: [? L. (evil-smelling)] alt. spelling 'bisse'; an obs. term for a serpent.

bisante: It., besant.

bisante di argento: It., plate.

bisca: a fictitious beast, being a gigantic serpent (q.v.) with a pug-dog-like head and long donkey-like ears. It has an engrailed (q.v.) dorsal-fin, and seems to have been evolved from the Germanic 'lindwurm'. As the armorial badge of the dukes of Milan it is 'swallowing a child'.

bischofsmütze: Ger., mitre.

bishop, a: [L.] identifiable by vestments, mitre, and crosier (q.v.) or pastoral staff (q.v.).

bisse: see **bis.**

bit[1]**:** [Teut.] the metal rod attached to the bridle (q.v.) that enters the horse's mouth and by means of the reins enables the rider, or the driver, to maintain control of the animal. Two types appear—the snaffle-~ and the manage-~. The former consists of an iron bar jointed loosely in the middle the ends passing through vertical side-irons and terminating in rings; the latter is, in principle, the same with S-shaped side-irons on the outside of which there is fitted at each end of the ~-bar, and before the rings, discs, or washers, having an invected (q.v.) circumference and known as bosses, or ~-

bosses, which may stand alone as charges. The manage-∼ has also a lower bar, or a length of chain that passes under the horse's lower jaw. The snaffle-∼ was used to guide draught horses, the manage-∼, which gave greater control, was used when riding.

bit²: the cutting element in any tool that consists of two parts (see also **brace and bit**). The brace is the crank; the ∼ is the auger attached.

bizantius nummus: L., bezant.

bjälke: Swd., fess.

Black, Wm: Messenger-at-Arms to the Lyon Court, 1762.

Black Eagle, Noble Order of the: (Prussia) f. 1601 as a one-class order for princes and up to thirty noblemen, each of whom was required to prove eight noble ancestors. In 1848 hereditary nobility was abolished as a requirement, and it was decreed that recipients should also wear the Order of the Red Eagle (q.v.) at the neck. Insignia—*Badge:* a gold-edged dark blue cross paty notched with, between the arms, four black eagles displayed; a gold central medallion bears the initial *F. Star:* silver, of eight points; a central medallion of orange enamel, surrounded by a gold riband, depicts the displayed eagle holding in his dexter claw a green laurel wreath, and in his sinister golden thunderbolts. *Collar:* blue medallions alternating with gold shields bearing the eagle, linked in gold, interspersed with eight sets of the initials *F.R.* in light green edged with gold. *Riband:* of orange worn as a sash from the left shoulder to right hip. Knights who also held the Garter could have a star on which the garter was entwined.

Black Star of Benin, Order of the: f. 1889 and became a French Colonial Order in 1896 with five classes. Insignia—*Badge:* a five-point black star on a blue and white enamel cross, gold rays between the arms,

ensigned with a green and gold wreath. *Star:* the badge surmounting an eight-point star. *Riband:* light blue moire.

blackamoor: [M.E.] of strongly negroid racial characteristics, 'peppercorn' hair, receding brow, retroussé nose, thick lips, and prognathous jaw; he is wreathed about the temples with a torse (q.v.) instead of foliage. The ∼ is always depicted facing either dexter or sinister, but not affrontée (q.v.). A ∼ head is very often enwrapped about the neck by a serpent, and when some heraldic monster is to be depicted devouring a man, it is the unfortunate ∼ who is chosen for the offering. (145, I)

blade: see **battle-axe**.

bladed: of any plant, but particularly ears of grain (q.v.) having leaves differing in colour to the other parts.

Blair, John: Lyon Clerk Depute, 1799.

Blaise, St: patron of Dubrovnik, Yugoslavia; appears in the municipal arms.

Blanc Sanglier: a pursuivant maintained by K. Ric. III.

Blanch Coursier Herald: an *ex-officio* name of office formerly attached to the Genealogist of the Order of the Bath (q.v.).

Blanch Lyon Pursuivant: name of office of an officer of arms formerly maintained by the Earl of Arundel.

Blanchlyverer Pursuivant: a name of office which appears to have been employed for one officer of arms only, 1418–19.

Blanquefort Pursuivant: served as a Gascon adherent of K. Hen. VI.

blasted: see **branch**.

blatt: Swd., azure.

blau: Ger., azure.

blauw: D., azure.

blaze: [M.E.] lit. a white mark on an animal's brow making it conspicuous; hence, to attract attention; hence, to blaze arms, i.e. to blazon (q.v.).

blazing star: see **comet**.

blazon: [M.E.] a concise and complete verbal description of a coat of arms according to a set of rules laid down by Gerard Legh in XVI cent. and which have not been improved upon. First, the field is fully described: this may be done in one word, e.g. 'gules', 'vair', 'argent', or it may demand a sentence, e.g. 'per fess, in chief barry wavy of Or and vert and, in base, gyronny of argent and azure'. Secondly, everything on the field that is in contact with it, must be described: paramount among these will be the ordinary which, after being named, e.g. 'a bend', 'a fess', must have its contours revealed, e.g. 'engrailed', 'embattled', and, finally, the colour has to be mentioned.

An ordinary is likely to repose between a number of charges all of which must be described next, their number, disposition, and colour (or colours), following: e.g. 'gules, a fess engrailed Or between eighteen mullets, twelve in chief, five, four, and three and, in base, six: three, two, and one'. When charges are of more than one kind, the ~ assumes a slightly different form,

e.g. 'Or, a fess gules cotised wavy azure between, in chief, two fleurs-de-lys vert and in base a mascle, sable'.

Disposition of charges need not be, but often is, mentioned when there are three only and no special instruction: 'argent, three torteaux *two and one*', is overstated: 'two and one' is the general and normal arrangement of three charges but 'argent, three torteaux *in bend* (or *in fess*; or *in pale*; or *one and two*) is essential information.

The colours of the charges are stated last, and must be delayed when various pieces are all of the same colour: e.g. 'a fess, plain cottised, between three lozenges azure'. This, which looks to the uninitiated as though the writer has forgotten to mention the colours of the fess and its cottices, is correct as it is written: the fess, the cottices, and the lozenges are all azure: in fact, the word 'all' is often interpolated, and, if the group is a large one, is helpful.

When an armorial device is without an ordinary and there are two kinds of charges, those disposed in the direction of an ordin-

---

55. Sable a lion passant Or between, in chief, three bezants and, in base, a point wavy barry-wavy argent and azure: *in augmentation*, a canton of the second charged with an escallop between two palmer's staves sable. *Sir John Hawkins.*

56. Argent, a lion sejant sable. *Meggison.*

57. Argent, a lion's gamb erect, couped, within a bordure engrailed sable. *Bedford.*

58. Azure, a lion statant Or. *Edmund Bromfeld* (Bishop of Llandaff, 1389–93).

59. Or, a lion dormant azure: on a chief of the last two equilateral triangles interlaced between, on the dexter a harp and, on the sinister, a lily leaved and slipped, all of the field. *David*, Bombay.

60. Per pale argent and sable, a leopard's face Or jessant-de-lys, counterchanged. *Withew.*

55

56

57

58

59

60

41

ary are mentioned first and stated to be between the others, e.g. 'sable, three billets in bend between two fusils, argent'. When the composition does not permit of this expedient, dominance gives precedence and dominance is controlled by position, that on (or nearest to) fess point being first, e.g. 'ermine, an ogress between four torteaux, two in pale and two in fess', or 'gules, a cross humetty argent between three fleurs-de-lys Or'.

In some achievements there is no dominant charge; hence, the number of and the position of the charges is enough: e.g. 'Or, ten heurtes, four, three, two, and one'; or '. . . four, four, and two'; or '. . . two barwise rows of five each', etc.

All the foregoing (imaginary) examples constitute achievements in two layers only; one is the shield itself, two is the combination of the shapes upon it, but three layers to an achievement is common. The most usual way in which this comes about is by the ordinary carrying charges, an addition indicated by the interpolation of the word 'on' before the ordinary, e.g. 'vair, on a bend Or between two bezants, three mullets gules'. As well as, or instead of, the ordinary carrying charges to provide the third layer, the charges on the field may do so, e.g. 'sable, three plates each charged with a mullet gules'.

After the contents of the shield have all been fully described the bordure, if present, is given, e.g. '. . . all within a bordure Or'; or '. . . a bordure engrailed sable'; or '. . . a bordure gules bezanty'; or '. . . charged with eight . . .'.

A chief or a canton, either of which surmounts a bordure, follows and, last, the brisure (distinguished by the suffixed words 'for difference') is mentioned often without reference to its colour, which, since the mark of difference is ephemeral, is of no importance, and which is subject to rule.

The repetition of both colours and numbers is, as far as is reasonable, avoided; the former by numerical reference, the latter by the phrase 'as many'; e.g. 'argent, on a cross gules between four mullets, vert, as many billets of the field' (or 'of the first') or 'argent, billetty sable, on a fess gules a sword, fesswise, proper, pommelled and hilted Or, the point to the dexter; on a chief of the third, on a pale of the second, a mullet pierced round of the fifth'. It should be observed that 'proper' is counted. Such avoidance of repetition ought not to be carried to excess. If the coat of arms is crowded it may be better to write 'also (say) purpure', than to write 'also of (say) the seventh'.

On completion of the description of the shield the ~ concerns the exterior additions; '. . . ensigned with a helmet befitting his degree, mantled of his liveries, whereon is set for his CREST, upon a wreath of the colours . . .'. The crest is not necessarily one simple object; it may consist of a group assembled laterally, vertically, or in depth; the last arrangement is indicated by the words 'in front of', e.g. 'in front of an oak-tree issuant proper a fylfot set saltire-wise, argent'.

In the event of an achievement having a compartment and supporters they are detailed last.

It will be observed from the foregoing that ~ is as near a perfect system of expression as may be attained in a world of imperfections, but its use demands the application of skill. To make a drawing from ~ is comparatively simple; to write ~ from a drawing is more difficult; and both to devise an armorial achievement and describe it is most difficult; hence the ~ in many a patent of arms is obscure and sometimes even misleading. It is the inherent difficulty of verbal expression, and the average reader's obtuse understanding that have influenced the inclusion of a drawing in the patent, and the words '. . . as in the margin may be more plainly seen'.

Blinsell, John: Islay Herald, 1596. Bute Pursuivant, 1590.

block-brush: [M.E.] heath, similar to broom (q.v.) anciently used by butchers to scrub their chopping-blocks.

blodius: used by old writers as an alt. for 'gules' (q.v.), but probably never adopted by the heralds.

bloedkleur: Afk., sanguine.

blokkies: Afk., billets or delves.

blomkruis: Afk., cross patonce.

blou: Afk., azure.

Blount, Walter Aston: Clarenceuɴ King of Arms, 1822. Former Norroy K. of A., 1859; former Chester Herald, 1834; former Blanch Coursier, 1831; former Arundel Herald, 1830.

Blount v. Blunt: see **Chivalry, Court of.**

Blue Ensign: the flag of the Royal Naval Reserve, Royal Naval ships other than vessels of war, and of ships of the Merchant Navy when under the command of an ex-naval officer; a blue flag with the Union in the canton (q.v.).

bluebottle: an heraldic name for the corn-flower (q.v.) (161)

Bluemantle Pursuivant: see **College of Arms.**

blut fahne: see **regalienfeld.**

Blyth, David: Dingwall Pursuivant, 1538.

boar: [O.E.] the male of the swine, *Sus scrofa*, the domestic (uncastrated) pig; the wild ~ is blazoned as a 'sanglier'. ~s are armed of their tusks (or tushes), and may be 'bristled', which state is indicated by short, stiff, upstanding hair on the back only. This, due to over-conventionalization, is sometimes drawn as though it were a

dorsal fin. ~-tail is curled, and has a tufted end. The head, a frequent charge, particularly in Scottish achievements, may be erased (q.v.) but is generally couped (q.v.) which severance may be made in two ways: either 'couped at the neck' or 'couped close'. The former elongates the figure, the latter, cutting immediately behind the ears, gives a rather triangular appearance. ~ head erect is couped close and set with the snout chiefward. (200)

boat: almost anything afloat between a racing-skiff and a catamaran may appear in answer to this vague and sloven form of blazon. It might even include a Thames lighter (q.v.), a wherry, a dinghy, Noah's Ark, or a coracle, although this last, built of frame and skin and used by Celtic fisher-folk, is likely to be individualized.

bock: alt. for or mis-spelling of 'buck' (q.v.).

bogenflanken: Afk. flaunches.

bogus arms: see **prescriptive right.**

Bolivar, Order of the Bust of: (Vene-zuela) f. 1854 in five classes. Insignia—*Badge:* twenty-eight rays with a central gold medallion portraying Bolivar, the medallion surmounted by a circlet of blue enamel inscribed *Simon Bolivar. Star:* for grand crosses, of eight points with the badge's circlet and medallion superimposed; for grand officers the medallion is replaced by the Venezuelan arms. *Riband:* red, light blue, orange, in equal stripes.

bolt: see **quarrel.**

bolt, bird: see **bird bolt.**

bolt, door: the common fastener consis-ting of a rod or bar free to slide in sockets and engage with a staple. Employed only for ca. reasons. (330)

bolt-container: see **distillatory.**

boltant: a r. term sometimes applied to a coney (q.v.) when courant (q.v.).

boltheyd: obs. term for a bull's head.

bombshell: a hollow cannonball having a

round hole (depicted in chief), through which the shell was stuffed with tallow-impregnated tow and ignited. Fired at the enemy's baggage-train, or stores, it acted as an incendiary missile. A ~ is always ignited and blazoned either as 'flammant' or as 'issuant of flames of fire proper'; sometimes simply as 'fired'. Alt. term 'fire-ball'. (166)

Bon Espoir Pursuivant: active in 1419. Probably maintained by the Earl of Huntingdon.

Bon Rapport Pursuivant: a privately maintained officer of arms; active c. 1450.

bonacon: an ox-like monster having crumpled horns, its mode of defence being flight, and the voiding of excrement that burns pursuers.

bonasus: alt. for 'bonacon' (q.v.).

bones, broken: the two parts are set in line (fess-, pale-, or bendwise), the jagged, broken ends inward. A device employed in the arms of exalted members of hitherto persecuted minorities. (297)

Bontemps Pursuivant: probably privately maintained, but employed on the king's business in 1434.

bontvair: Afk., verry.

bontwerke: Afk., fur.

book: appears very frequently in both academic and ecclesiastical achievements. A ~ may be either open or closed, and is provided with clasps known as 'seals' which are generally visible and the number stated in the blazon. The orientation of a ~ when closed must be given; e.g. 'a closed book, palewise, sealed of three seals to the dexter', etc. Arraswise (q.v.) a ~ may present either its head and spine, or its head and fore-edge, which is indicated by, in the latter case, the seals being blazoned.

An open ~, generally so blazoned, is necessarily palewise, and, well drawn, is represented leaning back—into the shield—a little. The seals appear on the dexter side. An open ~ is 'leathered' of the turn-over of the hide, and 'garnished' of the visible edges—usually dexter, sinister, and baseward—of the pages which, even when not coloured, are 'garnished argent'.

The two pages presented to the view are seldom left blank. When no text-matter is blazoned a good herald-painter gives the visual impression of the 'scrip-block' of a medieval manuscript ~, but advantage is often, quite rightly, taken of the 'double spread' to say something. Obviously, if the words are to be read, only very few can

---

61.   Sable three ounces statant in pale Or spotted of the field.
Sir James Bourchier.

62.   Azure, three loggerheads Or.
Corporation of Shrewsbury (Salop).

63.   Gules, three leopards' faces inverted jessant-de-lys Or.
See of Hereford (from the arms of *Thomas de Cantelupe*, Bishop 1275–82).

64.   Barry-wavy of six argent and gules, three crevices Or.
Atwater.

65.   Argent, a dolphin embowed azure, finned gules.
Monypenny, Kent.

66.   Argent, two lobster-claws in saltire, the dexter surmounting the sinister gules.
Tregarthick.

61

62

63

64

65

66

45

appear, and these few should, in a natural manner, proceed from the verso to the recto; however, far too often the script crosses the 'gutter' of the ~, and even when it does not, inexpert lettering together with wrong punctuation and hyphenation make it appear to do so.

A special ~ may be blazoned as 'a music ~', 'a song ~', in which cases it is enough for the pages to be ruled with repetitions of the five musical lines with mere indications of clef and stave; however, the Worshipful Company of Parish Clerks have, for crest (q.v.), '. . . a prick-song-book, open' which is inscribed with staff-notation.

A ~, either open or closed, may be blazoned by its title, particularly the Holy Bible. (127, 132, 473)

Book of Arms, Thomas Wall's: a book-form roll in blazon. 1530.

Book of Crests, Thomas Wall's: the second part of 'Wall's Book of Arms' (q.v.) contains blazon of about 650 crests. 1538.

book-form rolls: see **rolls of arms.**

boordsel: D., bordure.

boot: see **Dutch boot.**

bordato: It., fimbriated.

borde: Fr., fimbriated.

Bordeaux Herald: an English officer of arms, serving as garrison and general duties herald in Bordeaux under K. Ric. II and K. Hen. VI.

bordura: It. and Sp., bordure.

bordure [M.E.] a border, being a band, one-fifth of the width of the shield, which it surrounds. In old heraldry used frequently as a mark of difference (q.v.) and still largely so employed in Scotland. A ~ may be of one colour, or may, irrespective of any parting of the field, be themselves party in the direction of any of the ordinaries. When carrying charges the number is eight in modern heraldry; in the past there was neither rule nor custom in this matter;

hence, there is a tendency to overcrowding. A chief (q.v.) or a canton (q.v.) surmounts a ~.

Upon impalement (q.v.) a ~ is deprived of the section that would march with the palar line, and this applies also to the orle (q.v.) and to the tressure (q.v.), both of which are sometimes described as diminutives of the ~.

Variations of the ~ are 'gyronny' (q.v.), compony and counter-compony' (q.v.) (also called 'gobony' and 'counter-gobony'), and 'chequey' (q.v.). Only three rows of chequers go to the width of the ~ and the corners remain square. In the other variations, which are reductions of gyronny, the corners are diagonal, thus forming triangles. In colouring the metal should begin in the first whole square. (170, VIII)

Boreas: see **Aquilon.**

borée: see **Aquilon.**

boreyne: a monster having a bull's head and trunk, dragon's claws in place of hooves, a dorsal fin, and a tongue terminating in a spear-head.

Borough, Sir John: Garter King of Arms, 1634. Former Norroy K. of A., 1623; former Mowbray Herald, 1623.

Boroughbridge Roll: (1322) an occasional roll recording the names and arms of the king's supporters at the battle of Boroughbridge. A vellum true roll 7 in. by 9 ft. 7 in. There are 214 entries written on the dorse of a roll of royal writs relating to Thomas, Earl of Lancaster's rebellion.

Borthwick, James: Lyon Clerk and Keeper of the Records, 1597. Rothesay Herald, 1597.

Borthwick, John: Unicorn Pursuivant, 1619.

boson: frmd on Teut. 'bolzen', a blunt arrow, or bird bolt (q.v.); alt. spelling 'beson'.

Boswell, Alexander: Lyon Clerk Depute, 1881.

Boswell, Wm: Lyon Clerk Depute, 1794.

Boswell of St Boswells, Robert: Lord Lyon King of Arms, 1795. Lyon Clerk and Keeper of the Records, 1770. Lord Lyon Depute, 1770.

boteroll: see **chape.**

botonado: Sp., seeded.

botonée: Fr., seeded.

bottonato: It., seeded.

bottony, cross: a cross humetty (q.v.) having each limb terminating in a rounded trefoil (q.v.); also termed 'cross trefly'. (205, 214)

Bouchard, Peter: Richmond Herald in the service of John, Duke of Bedford, c. 1430.

boucle: Fr., ringed.

bouget, water: see **water-bouget.**

Bough, Samuel: Dingwall Pursuivant, 1864.

Boulogne Pursuivant: a name of office of an English officer of arms created by K. Hen. VIII in 1544; abandoned in 1550.

Bound, John: Rouge Croix Pursuivant, 1704.

bourchier knot: a half-hitch followed by a second half-hitch tied in the same direction; a 'granny'; orientated fesswise.

bourdon: a term applied to a palmer's or pilgrim's staff (q.v.) for ca. reasons, the word having reference to the ball-terminal.

bourrelet: Fr., torse.

boutonné: Fr., seeded.

bow[1]: a springy length of wood, the two ends of which were connected by a cord which, when drawn, bent the ~ and, when released, discharged the arrow. An English archer's ~ was of yew, and was 6 ft in length. The blazon must state how a ~ is orientated, i.e. fesswise, palewise, bend-wise, and which way the string is to face, e.g. 'a ~ palewise, string to the dexter'. A ~ may be drawn as a plain arc, or given some shape, as a double ogee. Alt. terms:

'string-~', 'archer's ~', 'hand-~', and 'long-~'. (462).

bow[2]: see **key.**

bowen knot: a grummet laid out square and turned over at the corners forming external loops.

bowl [O.E.] a vessel, almost hemispherical in shape but with a flat bottom: sometimes blazoned as a 'standing-~' or as a 'wassail ~': may differ in colour inside and outside.

Bowyer's Book: (c. 1440) paper $8\frac{1}{4}$ by $11\frac{1}{2}$ in. Each page ruled in three columns: 1, blazon; 2, painted shield; 3, name: total of 153, including arms attributed to Saxon monarchs.

Boyd, Wm: Unicorn Pursuivant, 1741.

Boys, Wm: Lancaster King of Arms, 1436. Former Anjou K. of A., 1427; former Exeter Herald, 1417; former Dorset Herald, 1413.

braccio destro: It., arm, dexter.

braccio sinistro: It., arm, sinister.

brace and bit: a woodworking tool for the purpose of drilling holes. It consists of a crank having, at the upper extremity, a disc-shaped handle on which the operator applies pressure; in the centre, a grip by which it is rotated and, at the lower end, an expanding chuck into which a bit (cutting tool) of the appropriate diameter is secured. (160)

braced: r. term sometimes applied to sub-ordinaries interlaced (q.v.), particularly chevronels.

Brackley's Book, Friar: (c. 1440–60) in book form, painted with seventy-three shields, one to a page, exemplifying alliances between the Pastons, the Barreys, and the Mawtebeys. Contains also obituary notes.

Bradfer-Lawrence's Roll: (temp. K. Hen. VI) a book $5\frac{3}{4}$ by 8 in. of seventy-four leaves and two vellum arranged in seven sections:

1, twenty-two pages each carrying one shield (à bouché (q.v.)) with helmets, crests, and names over, those on versos depicted contourné; hence, over the double spread, charges are respecting (q.v.); 2, sixty-four shields four to a page, some painted, some partly painted, some in line only; 3, a treatise on heraldry condensed from the work of Bado Aureo, with one illustrative line drawing; 4, named and painted shields of earls, lords, and knights totalling 108. The next section, 5, begins with a headnote of the metals and tinctures, followed by twenty-two names and blazons written in two columns; 6, contains 152 painted shields with names at the side; and 7, a list of family arms with surnames only over. In this section there are 138 shields the majority of which are painted.

Bradshaw, John: Windsor Herald, 1626. Former Rouge Croix Pursuivant, 1624; former Rose Rouge Pursuivant, 1624.

branch: [M.E.] the limb of any tree which may be couped (q.v.), slipped (q.v.), or truncated. A ~ should carry five sprigs (q.v.), but a greater or a lesser number may be depicted. When blasted, or starved, or withered the ~ is without foliage; lopped, the sprigs are cut off square. A ragged staff (q.v.) is a ~ lopped.

brasses, monumental: also called 'sepulchral brasses' and 'funerary brasses', are effigies of the dead taking the form of an engraved brass plate instead of sculpture in the round in stone. Their employment, particularly in the southern part of England, extends from the XII to XVIII cents., and, down to the XV cent., they represent a very high form of artistic expression.

The raw material, known as Cullenplate, from Cologne having been a centre of manufacture, and also as Latten, had an intrinsic value with the result that many thousands of ~ were stolen from the churches, a depression in the stone that had housed them being all that is left.

The military figures, in addition to being depicted with their shields armorially emblazoned, are very frequently clad in a surcoat of their arms, and are accompanied by their wives. The ladies generally wear a mantle on which the arms of their fathers are impaled with those of their husbands, and the couple, standing under a gothic canopy are often surrounded by shields of arms. Many ~ were originally enamelled in brilliant colours, minute traces of which are, here and there, to be seen in an undercut groove. In addition to the military figures there are brasses commemorating Church

---

67. Azure, crusilly, and two barbels addorsed Or within a bordure engrailed gules.
    John de Bar.

68. Azure, three bream naiant Or.
    Breame, Essex.

69. Vert, three flying-fish naiant in pale argent.
    Garmston, Lincoln.

70. Gules, three lucys haurient, Or.
    Lucy.

71. Gules, an inescutcheon between three lucy's heads couped haurient, argent.
    Geddes of Tweeddale.

72. Azure, a flying-fish haurient in bend argent on a chief of the second a rose gules between two torteaux.
    Henry Robinson (Bishop of Carlisle, 1598).

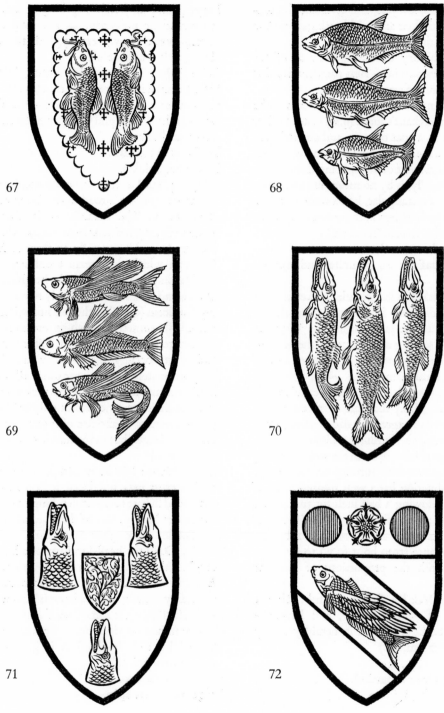

67

68

69

70

71

72

dignitaries, lawyers, and civilians, all complete with their armorial bearings as well as those of their wives.

The history of the appearance of the merchant-class in ~ runs parallel with that of their use of armorial bearings.

In many of the civilian brasses is to be seen a merchant's mark (q.v.) instead of, or as well as, a coat of arms, and a merchant's mark on the dexter impaling, on the sinister, an achievement of arms, being those of the wife's family, is by no means uncommon.

brazier: a rectangular, latticework iron box raised on short legs at the corners, used as a grate; also termed 'firechest'.

breached: see **castle.**

bread, loaf of: see **manchet** and **wastel-cake.**

bread-basket: a flat, circular basket of open weave, differing in no way from the ~ brought to the table during the Victorian era, and serving as a charge in the arms of charitable institutions, and sometimes in ecclesiastical arms. The ~ is generally blazoned as 'filled with wastel cake' (q.v.).

breadth: [M.E.] the unit of measurement employed to express the size of a flag (q.v.): 9 in., being the finishing width of narrow-bunting which is $9\frac{1}{2}$ in. in the weft, allowing for a quarter-inch turning on each edge. Broad-bunting has a weft measurement of 19 in., allowing a half inch for turning on each side; hence, finishing two ~ (18 in.). A flag of sixteen ~ measures 12 ft in the dip. The distance from hoist (q.v.) to fly (q.v.) varies with the proportions of different flags.

bream: [M.E.] a freshwater fish, *Abramis brama*, of yellow colour, and having a hump-back; employed in heraldry chiefly for ca. reasons. (68)

bretesado: Sp., bretessy.

bretessy: see **embattled.**

breuke: Afk., brissure.

brey: [M.E.] the heraldic spelling of 'bray', to pound or pulverize; an alt. term for 'hemp-break' (q.v.) er. applied to the barnacle (see **barnacle[2]**).

Brice, John: Bluemantle Pursuivant, 1484.

brick: drawn in perspective; ca. only.

brick-axe: a tool appearing notably in the arms of the Worshipful Company of Brick-layers and Tilers.

brick-kiln: see **kiln.**

bride: Fr., bridled.

bridge: [Teut.] a stone structure consisting of arches carrying a road over a river or a deep valley. The heraldic ~ is always masoned (q.v.), has a flat road surface with a balustrade, and is generally on three arches 'through which the stream transfluent' as the blazon puts it. A ~ may be heightened at each end by a tower (probably representing barbicans (q.v.) but the toll-house is not excluded); sometimes such an erection in the centre represents a chapel. When birds and beasts occupy the ~ they are disproportionately large. ~ are often allusive in civic arms and also ca. They vary somewhat in their appearance, not only because of the presence or absence of towers, or of birds and beasts, but in the number of their arches. (410)

Bridge House Mark: an annulet ensigned with a cross paty interlaced with a saltire conjoined in base to a barrulet. Employed in the dexter base quarter of the civic arms of the London Borough of Southwark.

bridle: [O.E.] the head-furniture of a horse to which the bit (q.v.) and reins are attached. As well as making an appearance in a secondary capacity when a horse is blazoned as 'bridled' (q.v.), it sometimes features as a charge in its own right but (a weakness enhanced by bad drawing) it is generally quite unrecognizable.

bridled: see **horse.**

brigantine[1]: see **ship.**

brigantine²: r. obs. alt. for a suit of mail.

brill: a flat-fish, *Rhombus vulgaris*; also named 'brett'; employed in heraldry for ca. reasons.

Brilliant Star, Order of the: (Zanzibar) f. 1875 in two classes. Insignia—*Badge:* a five-armed cross of ten points in red enamel, surmounting a gold laurel wreath, with a centre medallion depicting Sultan Bargash-Ben-Said for the first class, and his name in Arabic for the second class, the whole pendent from a small gold wreath. *Star:* of eight points, in silver, bearing the badge medallion. *Riband:* red moire with white stripes at the edges for the first class, and green stripes for the second class.

brimsey: [dial.] an heraldic name for the 'gad-bee' or 'gad-fly' by which titles it is also blazoned, as well as 'horse-fly'. Any fly of genus *Oestrus*, or of the genus *Tabanus*; depicted with four wings set back at a sharp angle from the thorax, two legs visible before and two behind. (81)

briquet: Fr., ferris.

bristled: see **boar**.

brisure: [Fr.] an addition to a coat of arms (q.v.) to distinguish between the senior house and cadet branches; also employed as marks of cadency to distinguish between younger sons, or cadets, in chronological order. Eldest son (or heir-apparent), a label (q.v.) of three points: his son, being heir-presumptive, uses, during the lifetime of his grandfather, a label of five points; second son, a crescent (q.v.); third son, a mullet (q.v.); fourth son, a martlet (q.v.); fifth son, an annulet (q.v.); sixth son, a f.d.l. (q.v.); seventh son, a rose (q.v.); eighth son, a cross moline (q.v.); ninth son, a double quatrefoil (q.v.); daughters do not use ~s. This system is (theoretically) in use in England. Scotland has an efficient system of its own named the Stodart System (q.v.).

The ~ must be depicted smaller than they would be if appearing as charges, and of any heraldic colour not otherwise used in the achievement (or the one used least if all are in use); and they may be of metal (q.v.) on metal, or of tincture (q.v.) on tincture without producing false heraldry (q.v.). The bordure (q.v.), the bend (q.v.), the bend sinister (q.v.), and their diminutives have been employed as marks of difference and to some extent are still so employed. Accidental forms (q.v.) and fields semé (q.v.) acted as differences in the early days of heraldry. Much emphasis was placed on the correct employment of ~s down to the late XIX cent. when slackness in the matter began to be countenanced. Today, ~s are totally ignored in English heraldry, although, of course, their use is still official. In these days of outspoken criticism so weak and ungainly a system of differencing would, if enforced, bring ridicule upon the authority.

British Empire, Most Excellent Order of the: f. June 1917 in five classes with Civil and Military Divisions. Insignia—*Knights Grand Cross:* a mantle of rose-pink satin lined with pearl grey silk, the star embroidered on the left; a silver-gilt collar with six medallions of the Royal Arms and six royal cyphers of K. Geo. V linked by cables, bearing centrally the Imperial crown between two sea-lions; a chipped silver eight-point star bearing centrally a gold medallion with effigies of K. Geo. V and Q. Mary surrounded by a circle gules with the motto *For God and the Empire* in gold; a badge of a cross patonce enamelled pearl fimbriated Or, surmounted by a gold medallion as in the star, ensigned with the Imperial crown Or; reverse bears the royal cypher of K. Geo. V; the badge is worn from the collar or from a broad riband over the right shoulder. *Knight Commanders:* a badge as for Grand Crosses but smaller in size, worn from the riband round the neck; a chipped silver star of four greater and four lesser points bearing a medallion as before. *Commanders:* a neck riband and badge as for Knight Commanders. *Officers:* a silver-gilt version of the badge worn from the left breast. *Members:* a silver version of the badge worn from the left breast. Ladies may be admitted to the Order; their insignia is identical save that for all ranks but Dame Grand Cross the badge is worn from a bow on the left breast. There is a silver medal attached to the Order—the British Empire Medal—awarded for services not qualifying for admission to the Order; *obverse:* Britannia, with the order's motto and, in the exergue, the words *For Meritorious Service.* *Reverse:* Royal Cypher and the words *Instituted by King George V.* The riband for all grades of the Order and the medal is of rose-pink edged with pearl-grey, the Military Division being distinguished by an additional central stripe of pearl-grey. A silver emblem of two oak-leaves on the riband denotes an award for gallantry.

British Empire King of Arms: a title of a complimentary character bestowed upon a member of the Most Excellent Order of the British Empire.

British Royal Arms: see **Royal Arms, the British**

broach: a technical charge, used by embroiderers, drawn in heraldry like a wooden fork, round in section, having several shapes of beading along its length, and terminating in two long, slender prongs. It is a combined bobbin and spindle.

broad-arrow: depicted without a shaft; two blades, with parallel back and front edges, are set at an angle to a shank; the blades may be at any angle so the ∼ can fit into the restricted space afforded by an ordinary without appearing distorted. It must be noted that the backs of the blades of a ∼ are straight.

broad-axe: used for shaping barrel-staves; appears notably in the arms of the Worshipful Company of Coopers and in those of some families. (316)

brock: see **badger.**

brocket: [M.E.] used as an alt. for 'stag' (q.v.) for ca. reasons. Lit. either a young stag—second year—with its first antlers, or a Brazilian stag having short, pointed horns instead of antlers.

brod: a Scottish armorial flag of the gonfanon (q.v.) type.

Brodie, George: Rothesay Herald, 1753. Carrick Pursuivant, 1747.

---

73. Argent, a tortoise turgiant in fess vert. *Gawdy.*

74. Argent, a python regardant and, in chief, three teals, proper. *Teal.*

75. Argent, a serpent knotted between three sinister gauntlets argent. *Milman.*

76. Azure, a lizard extended in pale argent between three mullets and, in chief, a ducal coronet Or. *Champagne* (Ireland).

77. Argent, eight barrulets sable, overall, a caduceus, Or. *Times Publishing Co. Ltd.*

78. Or, on a pale between two lions rampant azure, a rod of Aesculapius of the field. *Payne,* Tasmania.

73

74

75

76

77

78

Brodie of that Ilk, Alexander: Lord Lyon King of Arms, 1727.

Brodie, James: Marchmont Herald, 1729.

Brodie, John: Rothesay Herald, 1746.

Brodie, Thomas: Lord Lyon Depute, 1754. Lyon Clerk and Keeper of the Records, 1769.

brogue: see **shoe**.

Broke Pursuivant: in the service of Lord Broke; active 1489.

broken spear: see **lance**.

broken sword: see **sword**.

Bromley, Roger: Chester Herald to K. Ric. III. Bluemantle and Falcon Pursuivant to K. Ed. IV.

Brooke, John Charles: Somerset Herald, 1777. Former Rouge Croix, 1773.

Brooke, Ralph: York Herald, 1592. Former Rouge Croix Pursuivant, 1580.

broom: [O.E.] *planta-genista*, formative in the name Plantagenet. The shrub *Cytisus scoparius*.

Brown of Balmangan, Wm: Albany Herald, 1516. March Pursuivant, 1515.

Brown, John[1]**:** Dingwall Pursuivant Extraordinary, 1565.

Brown, John[2]**:** Ormonde Pursuivant, 1855.

Brown, Robert: Carrick Pursuivant, 1706.

Brown, Thomas: Herald-painter to the Lyon Court, 1866.

Brown, Thomas Austin: Herald-painter to the Lyon Court, 1880.

Brown, Wm: Albany Herald, 1546.

Browne, George: Bluemantle Pursuivant, 1764.

Browne, Robert[1]**:** Richmond Herald to K. Hen. VII. Former Rouge Croix Pursuivant (K. Ed. IV); former Guisnes Pursuivant (K. Ed. IV).

Browne, Robert[2]**:** Rouge Croix Pursuivant, 1634.

Browne, Robert[3]**:** Bluemantle Pursuivant, 1641. Former Blanch Lyon, 1640.

Browne, Thomas: Garter King of Arms, 1774. Former Clarenceux K. of A., 1773; former Norroy K. of A., 1761; former Lancaster Herald, 1744; former Bluemantle Pursuivant, 1737; former Blanch Lyon Pursuivant, 1727.

Bruce roll: (c. 1370) vellum book, $9\frac{1}{4}$ by $14\frac{1}{2}$ in., containing Scottish arms painted on banners, and also arms of France and the Netherlands. Names have been inserted later.

Bruges, Richard: King of Arms of the Northern Province, 1399, but styled 'Lancaster K. of A.' instead of Norroy K. of A. Former Lancaster Herald, 1380. His name is also rendered 'Del Brugge'.

Bruges, Wm: Garter King of Arms, 1415. Former Guyenne K. of A. (q.v.), 1413; former Chester Herald, 1398.

Bruges' Garter Book: (c. 1430) paper book, $11\frac{1}{4}$ in. by 1 ft 3 in. Each page contains a portrait (full-length figures). There is one of K. Ed. III, another of St George before whom kneels Garter King of Arms. The rest are the Founder Knights of the Order of the Garter (q.v.). Each knight holds a frame in which is painted small shields of arms of those who succeeded him in his stall at St George's Chapel, Windsor. Hollar (1607–77), the engraver, used the book as reference for the plates in Elias Ashmole's (q.v.) *Institution of the Order of the Garter*, 1672.

brunatre: [Fr.] the colour brown as employed in continental arms; not tenné (q.v.).

Brunswick Herald: one of the offices attached to the Order of the Bath (q.v.).

brush, a fox's: see **fox**.

brush, block: so called when appearing in the arms of the Worshipful Company of Butchers; otherwise identical with 'broom' (q.v.).

brush, treble flat: a prosaic object used only by the Worshipful Company of Plasterers.

brusk: r. obs. alt. for 'tenné' (q.v.).

bubble: the ordinary soap- or water-~; employed for ca. reasons only; very r.

buck: a male fallow-deer; should be distinguished in drawing by having palmated tynes (q.v.), but is frequently represented as a stag (q.v.).

bucket: see **well-bucket**.

Buckingham Herald: maintained by the dukes of Buckingham (down to 1514) and also described as Buckingham Pursuivant.

buckle: [M.E.] a metal frame carrying a tongue, or pin, that engages in a hole punched in a strap-end, and so acts as a fastener. Heraldic ~ may be square (lozengewise), oblong, round, or oval; they may be provided with a central cross-bar to which the tongue is attached, but if this is absent the tongue depends from the chiefmost part of the frame u.o.s. A ~ with the tongue blazoned as 'pendent' is reversed, so that the tongue hangs outside the frame. Any ~ may be described as a 'belt ~', but when the term 'gar-~' is used it refers to an oblong ~ with the long sides curved inward, probably a 'garter-~', An alt. term for any ~ is a 'fermail'. When a ~ is secondary to a strap one side only of the frame, and the point of the tongue appears. (178, 245; II, IV)

Bucky Pursuivant: a not very well authenticated name of office; c. 1490–1.

budget: alt. spelling of 'bouget' (water) (q.v.).

bugle: [M.E.] a bull, hence ~-horn or hunting-horn; a primitive musical instrument cut from a bull's horn, provided with two bands, or ferrules, to which a sling, or a strap, or cord is attached, finishing in a bowknot. (134)

bull: the male of the Bovidae. A frequently employed heraldic beast, being symbolic of strength and virility, the usual attitudes are rampant (q.v.) and passant. The ~ is armed of its horns, unguled of its hooves, and may be 'ringed' when a nasal ring is indicated. When the ~ is to appear in its natural colours, the term 'proper' is inappropriate; 'pied' of a metal and a tincture serves the same end: 'a ~ argent, pied sable' or 'a ~ argent, pied gules'. It is particularly important for a ~ to be depicted entire. If it is not, the beast will appear to be an ox (q.v.) or even a cow (q.v.). (27)

bunting¹: a small bird, similar to a lark, of the sub-family Emberizinae. An insessor; hence to be depicted with three toes forward and one backward. Sometimes spelt 'bunton'.

bunting²: a stout woollen fabric, 9½ in. wide, used in the construction of flags. The finishing width, when sewn, is 9 in. which equals '1 breadth' of flag measurement.

bunton: see **bunting¹**.

burbot: [Fr.] a freshwater fish, *Lota vulgaris*; also called 'ling' and 'coney-fish' because it is inclined to lurk in holes in the river's banks.

burdock: [M.E.] chiefly Scottish for a dock-leaf; sometimes reduced to 'bur'. Actually *Arctium lappa* or *Xanthium strumarium*.

burelete: Sp., torse.

burgee: a small pennant emblazoned with a yacht club's device; flown by owners of small craft.

burgeony: a decadent form of f.d.l. having its petals closed.

burgher arms: achievements of arms granted to merchants and other citizens in the Teutonic area by burgomeisters or other civic authorities. ~ were considered inferior to nobiliary arms which were granted by heralds on behalf of grand dukes, landgraves, and other hereditary rulers; hence, ~ were generally subject to restrictions, e.g. no helmet-crest or mantling was permitted, and the shield was generally heart-shape. Time straightened the chief, and added a crest.

Burghill, Francis: Somerset Herald, 1700. Former Mowbray Herald, 1677.

burgonet: a steel skull-cap, similar to a basinet (q.v.).

Burke, Sir Henry Farnham: Garter King of Arms, 1918. Former Norroy K. of A. 1911; former Somerset Herald, 1887; former Rouge Croix Pursuivant, 1880.

burletto: It., torse.

burling-iron: a technical charge, being a kind of tweezers with one broad and one narrow blade; used in the homespun textile industry for removing false threads.

Burma, Order of: f. by K. Geo. VI as a one-class order with twenty-eight members, sixteen from the Burma Army and the remaining twelve from severally the Burma Frontier Force and the Military Police. Insignia—*Badge* (worn about the neck): a gold medallion, issuant rays of gold, charged with a peacock in his pride azure, all within an azure border inscribed *Order of Burma* ensigned with the Imperial crown. *Riband:* light blue.

Burnet, Alexander: Procurator Fiscal to the Lyon Court, 1650.

Burnett, George: Lord Lyon King of Arms, 1866. Former Lyon Depute, 1863.

bustard: a large strong-flying bird, *Otis tarda*, also called the seapie. Not of very common occurrence. (121)

Bute Pursuivant: see **Lyon Office.**

Butler, Alfred Trego: Windsor Herald, 1931. Former Portcullis Pursuivant, 1926.

butt: [M.E.] a generic term for flat-fish; employed in heraldry for ca. reasons.

butterfly: see **papillon.**

buttoned[1]: of a strap fastened with an ornamental buckle (q.v.).

buttoned[2]: sometimes used in place of 'garnished' (q.v.) when the decoration consists of studs or rivets.

buttrice: a farrier's knife.

Bysley, Thomas: York Herald, 1528. Former Bluemantle Pursuivant, 1522; former Risebank Pursuivant (K. Hen. VII).

Bysshe, Henry: Somerset Herald under Cromwell; dismissed at the Restoration.

Bysshe, Sir Edward: Garter King of Arms by usurpation under Cromwell, 1646; at the Restoration was permitted to fill the office of Clarenceux K. of A., 1661.

---

79. Azure, semé of bees volant, Or: a basket-hive of the last.
    Burgh, Kenningspark.

80. Sable, three papillon Or.
    Sabyn.

81. Vert, three gad-flies argent.
    Bodringan.

82. Or, a liver-bird sable holding in the beak a sprig of laver, vert: on a chief of the last a grasshopper of the field.
    Martin's Bank Ltd.

83. Or, three spiders azure.
    Chettle.

84. Argent, six emmets gules, three, two, and one.
    Tregent.

79

80

81

82

83

84

cabbage: r. in British heraldry, but not uncommon on the Continent. (395)

cabellado: Sp., crined.

cabley: twisted; given the appearance of laid rope; 'wreathed' is an alt. term. (259)

cabley, cross: the representation of a length of laid rope throughout (q.v.) in fess (q.v.) surmounted (q.v.) of another in pale.

caboshed: [M.E.] of the head of a horned beast when severed close behind the ears and set affrontée (q.v.). (34)

cabré: [Fr.], alt. for 'forcené' (q.v.).

cabria: Sp., chevron.

cabria curva: Sp., embowed.

cadency, marks of: see **brisure.**

cadet: any male offspring other than the firstborn; hence, a younger son or brother: a line or 'house' descended from such a one: under the feudal system, not liable for military service because he would never hold the family estates in feudal fee; hence, not necessarily armigerous.

Cadran Herald: maintained by the Earl of Dorset, 1415.

caducée: Fr., caduceus.

caduceo: It. and Sp., caduceus.

caduceus: [Gk] a wand; a baton (q.v.) of office; a rod, winged at the upper end and entwined (q.v.) with two serpents (q.v.) wound in opposite directions; the symbol of healing. (77)

Caerlaverock, Roll of: an occasional roll written in Norman-French rhyming couplets, contains 906 lines, is illustrated with both banners and shields and tells, at an intensely exciting tempo, the story of the siege, in A.D. 1300, under K. Ed. I, of Caerlaverock Castle, Dumfries. The authorship of this masterpiece of literature, like that of many rolls, remains unknown. There have been numerous theories propounded in the past, all of which have now been rejected, it being manifest that the poem, with its illustrations, was the work of one

of the heralds accompanying K. Ed. I on his Scottish campaign.

Caernarvon Pursuivant: a recent (1911) name of office for an extraordinary who functioned at the investiture of Edward Prince of Wales (now Duke of Windsor).

Calais Pursuivant: an office created by K. Ed. IV which expired in 1558.

Calais Roll, the Second: see **Styward's Roll.**

Calais Roll, the Third: (c. 1348) vellum true roll (q.v.), $7\frac{1}{2}$ in. by 8 ft. 2 in., containing twenty-four painted shields of those killed in the siege of Calais, 1345–8. It begins with the genealogy of English kings.

Calatrava, cross of: alt. term for a cross floretty (q.v.).

Calder, John: Bute Pursuivant, 1561.

Caledonius, St: in association with St Hemeterius, the patrons of Santander, Spain, appear in that town's municipal arms.

calf: the young of the Bovidae; generally employed for ca. reasons. (26)

calopus: a composite fictitious beast having the body of a wolf and the head of a cat to which a pair of short, curving horns are sometimes added; alt. title 'challoup'.

caltrap: a device consisting of four spikes extending from a common centre so that when dropped on the ground three spikes formed a pyramid supporting the fourth which was upstanding. These objects, scattered on open ground, constituted an effective means of inhibiting a cavalry charge. Alt. terms 'galtraps' and 'chevaltraps'. (457)

Calvary, Cross: see **Latin cross.**

Calveley Herald: a privately maintained officer of arms, active in 1383, and probably in the service of Sir Hugh Calveley.

Calveley's Book, Sir George: (c. 1350–1450) vellum book, painted with about 876 shields and arranged in five sections: 1, Becket's Murderers' Roll, 320 painted shields

PLATE III Gules, at the chiefward end of a bend nebuly between three leopard's faces jessant-de-lys
Or, a chaplet of laurel vert: ensigned with a baron's coronet and issuant therefrom a peer's
helmet mantled of his liveries, whereon is set for CREST, upon a wreath of the colours a
dexter arm embowed, vambraced, and gauntleted Or grasping in bend sinister a broken
tilting-spear enfiled with a chaplet of laurel as in the arms.

SUPPORTERS: On each side a leopard gardant gules semé-de-lys and ducally crowned Or.

Lord Alfred Tennyson (Poet Laureate)

with names over; 2, Lancashire roll, 116 shields of county families; 3, Cheshire roll, 220 shields of county families and religious houses; 4, Kent roll, 100 county families; 5, College of Arms MS., twenty shields tricked (q.v.) by Robert Glover (q.v.).

calygreyehound: a cat-like monster having antlers similar to a stag's.

calyptratus: L., hooded.

Cambodia, Order of: f. 1864 in five classes, to be conferred by Cambodia and France. Insignia—*Badge:* an oval eight-point star of forty-eight rays with a red-rimmed central medallion of blue enamel bearing the arms of Cambodia; it is ensigned by a crown in gold (silver for the fifth class). *Star:* the central medallion on a silver star of eight points. *Riband:* red, edged green (Cambodia); white edged orange (France).

Cambridge Herald: maintained by the Earl of Cambridge, 1380.

Camden, Wm: Clarenceux King of Arms, 1597. Former Richmond Herald, 1597.

Camden Roll: (c. 1280) vellum true roll, 6¼ in. by 5 ft 3 in., painted, 270 shields on face, 185 French blazons on dorse.

camel: [L.] a large, long-necked, hump-backed quadruped, having broad cushioned feet suited to walking upon sand, used as a beast of burden in Asia and Northern Africa; functions in heraldry chiefly as a supporter. (17)

cameleon: a mis-spelling of 'chameleon' (q.v.).

camelopard: an heraldic name for the giraffe, whose long neck and spotted hide suggested that it was a hybrid, the offspring of the camel and the leopard. Given a pair of long, curved horns it is called 'camelo-pardel'.

campaned: r. alt. for 'belled' (q.v.); employed in Scottish heraldry.

Campbell, Archibald: Marchmont Herald, 1796. Bute Pursuivant, 1776.

Campbell, Robert: Carrick Pursuivant, 1582.

Campbell, Sir Duncan Alexander Dundas: Carrick Pursuivant, 1907.

Campbell of Lawers, Sir James: Lord Lyon King of Arms, 1658.

Campbell, Wm: Darnaway Pursuivant Extraordinary, 1498.

cancellato: It., fretty.

Candalle Herald: in the service of the Earl of Kendal (1430); also modernized to 'Kendal Herald'.

cannell: Fr., invected.

cannet: [Fr.] a duckling; alt. for a duck; used in continental heraldry for a duck without feet or beak.

cannon: see **chambers.**

canter: r. alt. for the unicorn (q.v.).

cantherius: L., chevron.

canting arms: [L.] an achievement in which the description of the figures is homophonous with the name; a rebus, or pictorial pun, also described as 'armes parlantes', and, er., as 'allusive arms' (q.v.).

canton: a sub-ordinary, being a square, one-third of the width of the shield which, u.o.s., occupies the dexter-chief corner. 'A sinister ∼' indicates that it shall appear on the other side. The term includes the dexter-chief quarter, whether it is ruled off or not, and the dexter-chief 'box' created by a plain cross (q.v.). A ∼ on a chief (q.v.) ought to be slightly smaller than the chief's width in order not to appear like a chief party per 'side' (q.v.). 'Canton' is Sp. and 'cantone' Fr. (165)

cantoned: of a cross between four charges; used more commonly in Scottish than in English blazon.

cap of estate: see **maintenance, cap of.**

cap of dignity: see **maintenance, cap of.**

cap of maintenance: see **maintenance, cap of.**

cap-à-pie: [Fr.] from head to foot; descriptive of a man clad in armour, from a chevalier (q.v.) to a knight genuant (q.v.); alt. term 'armed at all points'.

caparaçonne: Fr., comparisoned.

capelot: r. alt. for a cap of maintenance (q.v.).

capital cross: supposed to refer to a cross humetty the limbs of which terminate in Greek column capitals; a term adopted by writers but not by heralds.

capitalization: it is correct to write a blazon (or any other sentence) entirely in capital letters; it is equally correct to use all small letters for the same purpose. It is more correct to write blazon and anything else in mixed upper and lower case, and it is most correct to conform to modern usage in the matter. The employment of the majuscule for the ordinaries, the charges, and the colours in blazoning recent coats of arms is wrong, not because of the capitals, but in respect of the custom of educated people, and the general appearance of a page of print. There is today no need to follow the fashion of the early XVIII cent. There is, however, one exception: the word 'Or', when meaning 'gold', should always be capitalized. Either 'Or' or 'or' must be written, and the less confusing of the two is 'Or'.

capitals: see **arch.**

capo: It., chief.

capo d'Angio: see **Guelphic and Ghibelline chiefs.**

capo dell'imperio: see **Guelphic and Ghibelline chiefs.**

cappelain: [Fr.], r. alt. for 'mantling' (q.v.).

caps: see **arch.**

capuchin: a monk's hood.

caravel: a shapely small craft, having one mast rigged with two square sails; similar to a lymphad (q.v.) but without fore- and stern-castles. The hull is of necessity 'carvel built', e.g. having the planks abutted edge to edge, giving a smooth surface. That in the crest of the Worshipful Company of Vintners has the mainsail charged with a cartwheel, the emblem of St Martin de Tours, their patron saint. (189)

carbonchlo: It., escarbuncle.

carbuncle: also spelt 'carboncle'; a truncated form of escarbuncle (q.v.).

carbunculus: L., escarbuncle.

card¹: [M.E.] a kind of sharp-toothed comb used in preparing fibres for spinning; hence, variously blazoned as a 'flax ~', or as a 'wool ~'; or alt. as a flax-, stock-, wool-, or jersey-comb. Drawn like a curry-comb (q.v.).

card²: playing ~s appear very r. The Worshipful Company of Playing Card Makers have them.

Cardinal's hat: see **hat, ecclesiastical.**

---

85. Per bend embattled à plomb argent and gules.
    Von Scheldorfer, Bavaria.

86. Gules, two bendlets, vair.
    Fagg, Wiston.

87. Azure, a bend Or.
    Scrope.

88. Per bend embattled argent and gules.
    Earl of Cork and Orrery.

89. Gules a bend vert, fimbriated Or.
    O'Dulin.

90. Or, three piles conjoined in point gules, surmounted of a bend azure.
    Riddell of Sunart.

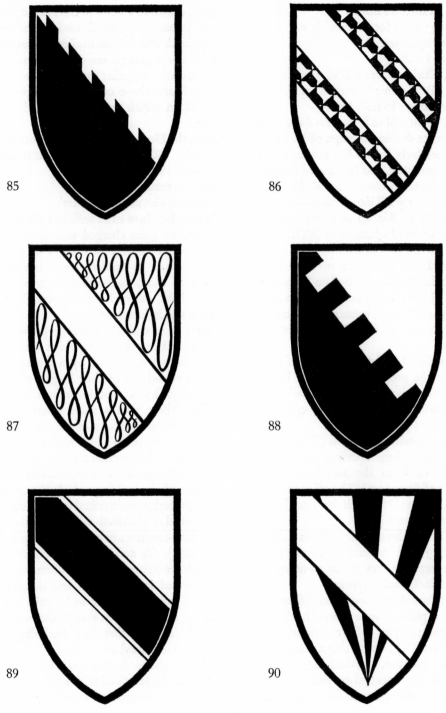

85

86

87

88

89

90

career, in full: see **horse.**

careering: r. alt. for 'forcené' (q.v.).

cargado: Sp., charged.

caricato: It., charged.

Carlill, Christopher: Clarenceux King of Arms, 1510. Former Norroy K. of A. 1494; former Carlisle Herald, 1486.

Carlill, Wm: said to have served the Duke of Clarence during the reign of K. Ed. IV as consecutively Falcon Pursuivant, Rouge Croix Pursuivant, and Richmond Herald.

Carlisle Herald: created by K. Ed. III in 1327. The name fell into desuetude and was revived by K. Ric. III and employed till c. 1550. Revived again, early XVIII cent., as title for an extraordinary (q.v.).

Carlisle Roll: (1334) an occasional roll (q.v.) in book-form, painted on 128 vellum leaves $7\frac{3}{8}$ by $10\frac{1}{8}$ in., containing armorial bearings of 277 earls, bannerets, and knights in the vanguard of K. Ed. III's army at Carlisle.

carnation[1]**:** [M.E. fm L.] a shade of pink; obs. for the proper (q.v.) tint of human flesh; written both 'carnat' and 'car'.

carnation[2]**:** the name of the cultivated gillyflower (q.v.). (382)

Carolina Herald: appointed (1705) by the Government of the Province of Carolina, and chosen from the members of the College of Arms (q.v.). The office seems to have died in 1715 with its first holder (Laurence Cromp (q.v.)).

carp: [L.] a freshwater fish, *Cyprinus carpio*, inhabiting still waters; uncommon in British heraldry, but of frequent occurrence in Indian achievements.

Carrick Pursuivant: see **Lyon Office.**

carrot: a plant, *Daucus carota*, having an edible root; employed for ca. reasons.

cartouche: [Fr.] an oval shape, having the long axis palewise, on which arms may be depicted; the appropriate shape for the arms of a priest, also used for the arms of a lady; drawn to a point in chief and in base, i.e. 'a pointed $\sim$', much used for the arms of schools and ecclesiastical establishments; of frequent general use on the Continent, particularly in Spain; extended in usage to include any shape other than a legitimate shield on which arms are depicted. (404, 407)

Cary, the Hon. Philip Plantagenet: York Herald, 1923. Former Bluemantle Pursuivant, 1919.

cask: see **tun.**

casque: r. obs. alt. for 'helmet'.

Castile, bordure of: a sufficient blazon for a bordure gules charged with castles Or; the correct number of charges on a bordure, u.o.s., in modern times is eight—three in chief, one each side at honour-point level, one each side at nombril-point level, one in base point.

castle: a crenellated building presenting, u.o.s., its front elevation, which consists of two towers connected by a frontage of about two-thirds of their height, pierced, centrally, by a Gothic archway above which there rises a third tower which according to the shape of the space to be filled, may be either a little higher or a little lower than the external towers; hence, the blazon often states 'a $\sim$ triple-towered'.

The whole building which is masoned (q.v.) whether so described in the blazon or not, is also provided with a number of window-apertures or cruciform loop-holes (or both), the number and disposition of which are left to the artist's discretion, are mentioned in the blazon and designated 'lights' only if they are to be voided of a colour differing from that of the $\sim$ itself, which indicates that they (including the entrance archway) are open.

When the $\sim$ is closed the Gothic arch ought to be provided with a pair of doors hung upon ornamental strap-hinges unless the portcullis is down, which may be described as coulissé, i.e. closed, from the grooves in which it rises and falls.

The nature of the ~ is such that a great deal of latitude exists regarding its appearance. Some towns and cities that have developed round a ~, and whose arms are based on a seal depicting the structure, have shapes that are peculiar to themselves.

To be surrounded by a moat is blazoned as 'rising out of water proper' or as 'on a point barry-wavy argent and azure'.

A ~ may be behind a wall, or a palisade, and blazoned as 'within' either; or surrounded by broken ground representing earthworks, and blazoned as 'fortified'. The building may also be blazoned as 'breached' when it will be depicted with a large, jagged gap in the wall, and, perhaps one of the towers shattered. Alt. terms applied to a ~ of any kind, or in any state, are 'fort', 'fortress', 'citadel', and 'chateau'. In the heraldry of the Rhineland a ~ is often a view of the local 'schloss', slightly conventionalized. (432)

castle, elephant and: see **elephant**.

Castle of Good Hope Decoration: (S. Africa) f. 1952 for valour in action. Insignia —*Badge:* five-point star, in gold, representing the outline shape of the castle, surmounted by a medallion depicting van Riebeck arriving at Table Bay in 1652; the medallion is surrounded by a wreath and the name of the decoration in both Afrikaans and English. *Riband:* green with a miniature of the badge worn centrally.

castrensis, r. obs. alt. for 'palisado' (q.v.).

catamount: condensation of 'cat o' the mountains', a wild-cat. His usual attitude is sejant, with the sinister fore-paw raised. He occasionally assumes other heraldic attitudes but in all of them he is gardant (q.v.) u.o.s. A ~ proper is tabby, and in old blazon he is sometimes called 'a tabby'.

Among other obs. terms will be found 'musion' (the mouser; hence, domestic cat), probably abandoned on account of its being easily confused with musimon (q.v.) and leyzard which survives in the arms of the Worshipful Company of Skinners.

Alt. terms current are numerous: 'cat-o'-mountain', 'mountain-cat', 'civet-cat', 'spotted-cat', and 'wild-cat'. The ~ has two terms exclusive: when rampant (q.v.) he may be termed 'éffarouché', and when statant with back raised and tail expanded he is 'hérissone'. A ~ is of very common occurrence in Scottish heraldry because the wild-cat still inhabits the highlands. (187)

cathedral church: see **church**.

Catherine wheel: representing the medium of St Catherine of Alexandria's martyrdom: depicted as a massive, broad wooden cartwheel, the spokes extending through and beyond the rim where they are drawn to points, and curved in a clockwise direction. The ~ often appears with six spokes only: from the point of view of the wheelwright, there should be eight. (345)

Cathrow, James: Somerset Herald, 1813. Former Rouge Dragon Pursuivant, 1797.

cauda: L., tail.

cauldron: a cooking-vessel having bulging sides, an arched handle over the top which engages in rings attached to the rim, and three short legs to prevent its rolling when stood down; alt. terms 'flesh-pot', 'porridge pot', 'cooking-pot', and 'pot'. (147)

cedar: [O.E.] an evergreen tree famous as ~ of Lebanon; *Pinus cedrus*.

Cedar, National Order of the: (Lebanon) f. 1958 in five classes. Insignia—*Badge:* a star of five points, gold-rimmed and tipped, in red enamel, bearing an Arabic inscription and a depiction of a cedar tree surmounted by a laurel wreath, all surmounting a silver plaque surrounded by a laurel wreath. *Star:* a star as in the badge having gold cedar branches and cones in each arm, with an Arabic inscription, a laurel wreath set centrally, surmounting a silver plaque of ten points. *Riband:* white, edged orange.

celery: a plant having edible stems; employed for ca. reasons.

celestial, crown: an antique crown (q.v.) having each ray terminating in a mullet (q.v.).

celestial sphere: see **globe, celestial.**

celestials: see following entry.

celestiaulx: [Fr.] a r. alt. term for 'sunburst' (q.v.); an alt. spelling is 'celestials'.

celosia: Sp., fret.

celosiado: Sp., fretty.

Celtic cross: the representation of a stone cross set upon a plinth, the head being a circle pierced with four quadrants.

cenidor: Sp., bar.

censer: an incense burner: the thurible; a perforated metal vessel in which the burning gums and spices are contained, suspended on chains and carried, swinging, from the hand, often in procession, during a religious service. Due to Protestantism, very r. in British heraldry.

centaur: [Fr.] differs in no way from the ~

of classical mythology: the head, trunk, and arms of a man merging into the body, four limbs and tail of a stallion. Symbolic of virility.

centrato: It., banded.

centre-base: the central area in the lower portion of the shield, below fess point.

centre-chief: the central position at the top of the shield; roughly a square of about one-third the shield's width.

cercele: a truncated form of recercele (q.v.).

cerise: obs. for a torteau (q.v.); also spelt 'serise'.

chabot: see **perch.**

Chad. St: clad in vestments, is the dexter supporter of the achievement of the City Council of Lichfield.

chafant: of a boar (q.v.) charging.

chaffinch: a common British bird, *Fringilla coelebs.* See also **spink.**

chain: of frequent appearance both as a primary and a secondary item. A ~ ought always to be of square (i.e. rectangular) links; round links are blazoned as so many annulets interlaced. Lengths of ~ may cross the field in the direction of an ordinary (q.v.), or be formed into annulets (q.v.),

---

91. Argent, three crapawdys sejant sable.
    Botreaux.

92. Argent, on a bend between two Cornish choughs sable, beaked and legged gules, three escallops of the field.
    Rowley.

93. Sable, on a bend between two nag's heads erased argent, three fleurs-de-lys azure.
    Pepys.

94. Barry-wavy of eight argent and gules gutty d'eau, on a bend between six arrows barbed and flighted gules, three fountains.
    Mansergh.

95. Argent, a bend gules between six tiler's nails sable.
    John Tyler (Bishop of Llandaff, 1706–24).

96. Sable, three mullets pierced round in bend between two bendlets and as many annulets Or.
    Hippisley, Berkshire.

91

92

93

94

95

96

crosses (q.v.), and other shapes. When appearing as a secondary item, attached to the collar of a beast, ~ is, as a rule, 'reflexed over the back'. (167, 326, 328)

chain, cross of: from a central annulet (q.v.) four lengths of square-linked chain extend outward to the edge of the shield.

chain, a fret of: see **chains of Navarre.**

chain-shot: a cannon-ball having four short lengths of chain attached, in chief, in base, and at each side.

chained: of a beast having a length of chain attached to a collar, coronet, or other circlet about the neck. Chain in heraldic art should be 'square', i.e. of rectangular, not of oval links, and terminate in an annulet (q.v.). ~ supporters (q.v.) generally have the appendage 'passing between the fore-limbs and reflexed (i.e. looped) over the back'. Inanimate charges may also be ~.

chains of Navarre: a device assumed by the Royal House of Navarre after the battle of Talosa (1212) was brought into British heraldry by Isobel, daughter of Philip IV of France, consort of K. Ed. II, who bore the arms in right of her mother, Joan, heiress of Hen. I of Navarre. It is often misleadingly blazoned as 'a fret of chain'. (325)

Chakri, Most Illustrious Order of the Royal House of: (Thailand) f. 1884 in one class limited to forty-three members. Insignia—*Badge:* an eight-pointed star of curved gold-rimmed white enamel spokes, with a central medallion of blue enamel bearing a design in diamond chippings; the medallion is surrounded by a gold-rimmed band of red enamel and a gold laurel wreath; the whole ensigned with a royal umbrella of seven tiers supporting a sunburst. *Star:* the badge surmounting a multi-rayed star of ten points. *Riband:* yellow, with the badge worn centrally.

chalice: [O.E.] a shallow cup; specifically, the vessel used in the celebration of the Eucharist, being a broad, curved cup on a central stem that curves outward forming a foot of about the same diameter as the cup itself. In the centre of the stem there is generally a knopf. The ~, symbolic of a layman's interest in Church government, and in ecumenacy, may be of any heraldic colour but is likely to be gold unless the field is of metal. (7)

challoup: see **calopus.**

Chalmers, Roderick: Ross Herald, 1724. Herald-painter, 1724.

Chaloner, Robert: Lancaster Herald, 1667. Former Bluemantle Pursuivant, 1660.

chambers: big guns, generally of the type employed in naval warfare. They are orientated fesswise with muzzle to the dexter, and may be 'discharging'. 'Chamber-pieces on their carriages' remain naval guns with the appropriate carriages, graded at the rear, and running on small, solid cast-iron wheels. 'Field-pieces' indicates the earliest pattern guns of the Horse Artillery, with large wheels and carriages curving downward to ground-level behind. Allusive, and ca. on the name 'Chambers'. (149, 458)

chameleon: [M.E.] a lizard-like reptile of the saurian order, genus *Chamaeleo*, having a prehensile tail and eyes that focus separately. Known chiefly for its apparent changes of skin colour in varying circumstances, notwithstanding which it is generally vert in heraldry. Formerly believed to live on air because the extending and retraction of its long, coiled tongue is too rapid to permit of unskilled observation.

chamfrain: [O.F.] plate-armour for a horse's head; alt. spelling 'chamfron', but not, as sometimes printed, 'chanfrein', which is a different word.

Chandos Herald: originally maintained by Sir John Chandos, but annexed to the Crown c. 1370.

change of name: see **surname.**

chape: an ornamental U-shape fitting with which the end of a scabbard is closed, and which appears as a charge without the scabbard. One horn of the U is generally longer than the other, and the curvature is chiefward. Also blazoned as a 'crampette' and as a 'boteroll'. (434, 451)

chapé: in Fr. blazon described as a parting of the field consisting of two straight lines issuant in centre-chief (q.v.) and extending to severally the dexter and the sinister-base. In British blazon it would be a pile (q.v.) throughout (q.v.) issuant in base.

chapeau: [Fr.] see **maintenance, cap of.**

chapel: see **church.**

chaperon: [M.E.] a small shield carried on the forehead of the hearse-horse at an armorial funeral.

chaperonado: Sp., jessed.

chaplet: a wreath (q.v.) without stems or ribbon, carrying flowers, generally roses; one in chief, one in base, and one at each side. A ~ of rue (q.v.) is not, strictly a ~; and there is reason to doubt the existence of a ~ graminy (of grass). The term ~ is often er. used instead of 'garland' (q.v.) or 'wreath' (q.v.). (237)

charge: [M.E.] the representation of any object, animate or inanimate, or of any geometrical shape or combination of shapes appearing upon the shield and constituting the armorial device (q.v.). Prefixed by the word 'common' the reference is generally to one of the numerous, time-honoured inanimate objects, often having a symbolic, or an allusive value, that constitute the figures of heraldry.

chargé: [Fr.] charged.

Charles, Nicholas: Lancaster Herald, 1608. Former Blanch Lyon Pursuivant, 1603.

Charles, Order of St: (Monaco) f. 1858 in five classes. Insignia—*Badge:* a red-edged white enamel Maltese cross, the points pommetty, surmounting a gold and green laurel wreath; a red central medallion bears the crowned cypher of K. Ch. III, and is surrounded by a gold-rimmed white band inscribed *Princeps et Patria* in gold; the whole is ensigned with a gold crown. *Star:* the unensigned badge on a silver eight-point star. *Riband:* red, white, red, edged with white.

Charles XIII, Order of: f. 1811 as a one-class order to be awarded solely to distinguished Swedish Freemasons. Insignia—*Badge:* a gold-rimmed red enamel cross ensigned with a crown, with a central medallion of white enamel bearing in gold the cypher of Ch. XIII. *Star:* a cross paty notched of red enamel. *Riband:* red.

Charles' Roll: (c. 1285) vellum true roll, 11 in. by 8 ft 6 in. painted, 486 shields; names over.

chart: [L.] lit. a map of the sea rather than the land, in which coastlines, submerged rocks, shallows, and sandbanks are indicated. A few appear in the armorial bearings of famous navigators, and pioneers of marine discovery and expansion, but details cannot appear and they are poor heraldry.

chase, in full: of a dog when depicted in pursuit of its quarry; the small animal running ahead is not mentioned in the blazon; alt. 'in full course' and 'in full cry'.

chateau: see **castle.**

chatterer: a name for the crested lark; employed for ca. reasons.

chaussée: Fr., caltrap.

chausses: [O.F.] shoes, or half-boots; allied also to leg-guards of mail.

Cheale, John: Norroy King of Arms, 1741. Former Arundel Herald Extraordinary, 1741.

checky: see **chequy.**

cheese-slip: a name applied to the wood-louse (q.v.).

chef: Fr., chief.

chequy: [M.E.] a variation of the field consisting of squares of alternate metal (or fur) and tincture; there ought to be five squares fesswise and eight palewise unless the field ~ is charged with a fess when there should be two rows of five in chief, and the same in base but cut by the contour of the shield. ~ represents either the chessboard or the chequered cloth used as an abacus before the adoption of Arabic numerals. Metal should start in dexter-chief. (261, 446)

cherry: [M.E.] a small stone-fruit which grows in clusters and is so depicted; *Prunus cerasus*.

cherub: [Hebrew] represented in sacred and legendary (hence in heraldic) art as a winged child's head. More likely to appear as a crest (q.v.) than as a charge (q.v.), and most likely to be seen as a form of non-heraldic external decoration, particularly ensigning a lozenge. In addition to the ~, heraldry finds employment for the seraph, also depicted as a child's head, but surrounded by six wings. Both are pluralized by the suffix 'im'. (159)

Cheshire Roll: see **Calveley's Book, Sir George.**

chess rook: see **rook, chess.**

Chester Herald: see **College of Arms.**

chevalier: [M.E.] a sufficient description of the figure of a man in armour, mounted on a barded (q.v.) horse, proceeding to the dexter; also a title of honour.

cheval-trap: see **caltrap.**

chevelé: Fr., crined.

chevin, see **chub**[1].

chevron: [L.] an ordinary (q.v.), one-third of the width of the shield, taking the form of an inverted V. In the XVI cent., when esoteric meanings were attached to the figures of heraldry, the ~ was enlikened to the gable end of a house and it was declared the appropriate ordinary for a civilian; hence it will be seen in the arms of many livery companies. When a ~ carries charges (say three) one on each side will slope with the ordinary, that in the centre will be orientated palar of the field; furs also remain palar. (174, XV)

chevron, in: of a number of objects placed upon the field in the position of a ~.

chevronel: first diminutive of the chevron, being half the width of the parent.

chevronny: of a field (q.v.), an ordinary (q.v.), or a charge (q.v.) carrying an equal number of chevronels (q.v.) of alternate metal and tincture. A field ~ of less than eight pieces is inclined to be deceptive in appearance at the upper corners; hence, though one of the major variations of the field ~ is not of frequent occurrence in

---

97. Azure, on a bend engrailed argent three daws argent.
Dawson.

98. Argent, on a bend sable three chess-rooks of the field.
Bunbury.

99. Argent, on a bend vert three spades Or.
Sweetington.

100. Azure, on a bend argent, a cutlass proper, hilted and pomelled Or.
Tatnall (1).

101. Or, on a bend engrailed sable, three horseshoes argent.
Ferrara.

102. Ermine, on a bend azure a magnetic needle pointing to the pole star.
Petty.

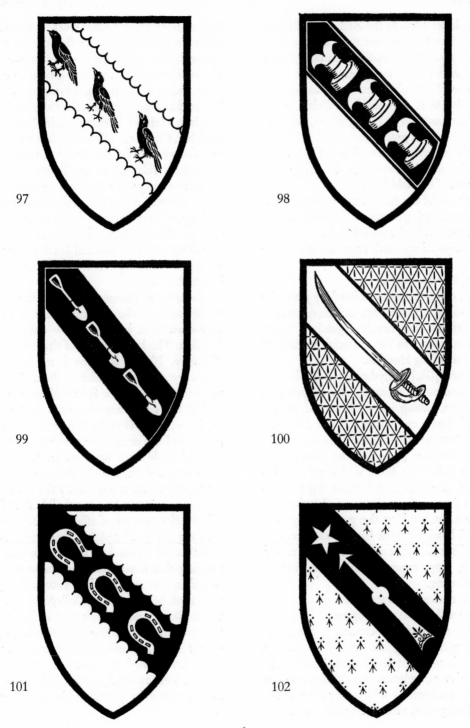

British heraldry. In the XIII cent., diminutives (q.v.) were narrow, as many as twenty pieces was not uncommon; hence, ~ was then of better appearance.

cheyne: [Fr.] r. obs. term for an acorn.

chibol: [M.E. and dial.] a Welsh onion, *Allium fistulosum*; a spring onion, depicted complete with green head.

chief[1]: an ordinary one-third of the width of the shield, occupying the uppermost section of the field (q.v.).

chief[2]: all of the field above fess point; the line constituting the top of the shield; hence, charges (q.v.) blazoned (q.v.) as 'in chief' are disposed upward, near the top of the shield.

chief, in: see **chief[2]**.

child: children appear in heraldry generally in a secondary capacity, and are often then illustrative of a family legend: a naked infant appears in the armorial bearings of the Foundling Hospital.

chimera: [Gk.] in mythology, a fire-breathing composite monster, the offspring of Typhon, having a lion's head and neck, a goat's body, and whose tail was a serpent. The ~ was slain by Bellerophon who rode upon Pegasus (q.v.) for the occasion. In some prints the form is that of a snake-tailed, fire-breathing lion having a demi-goat issuant from between the shoulder blades. In heraldry the goat's body with lion's head and neck has the addition of a maiden's face. The snake-tail has its mouth open, fangs exposed, and barbed tongue protruding.

china-cocker tree: see **trees**.

Chinese dragon: see **dragon**.

chisel: a cutting tool consisting of a bar of steel with the edge on one end. ~ vary in their shape and in their application: masons, bricklayers, sculptors, and other workers in stone use a cold ~ which they drive with a mallet (q.v.) or a hammer (q.v.); carpenters,

turners, horners, and other workers in such softer mediums have a handle attached to one end, and apply their ~ by pressure. The ~ does not lend itself to artistic treatment and is without symbolism; hence it is r. used and usually in an allusive setting.

Chitting, Henry: Chester Herald, 1618.

Chivalry, Court of: a Court of Canon Law, presided over by the Earl Marshal, wherein all matters relating to the honour of a gentleman may be tried, and judgement given. The major function of the Court was to legalize and enforce decisions of the College of Arms (q.v.); hence, complaints of infringement of armorial bearings were among the most important matters brought before the ~.

The cause of Blount *v*. Blount is famous in the annals of the ~ because, during the long-drawn-out hearing the ~ ceased to function. The last mention of the cause of Blount *v*. Blount is to be found in the Chancery Records under 9 June 1737, wherein is reported the failure of an appeal against the admission of certain evidence by the ~. By 1741 no judgement had been given, and the arms, 'barry nebuly of six Or and sable', are recorded in *Wotton's Baronetage* with the note 'In suspense'.

No judgement was given by the ~, and subsequently canon law was abolished. This led to a chaotic state of affairs. There arose a strong body of opinion that with the abolition of canon law the ~, notwithstanding that it was not specifically mentioned in the reforms, had automatically been abolished; hence the College of Arms was no longer an authoritarian body, and arms supplied by the Heraldic Stationer, or simply taken into use at the whim of anyone who wished to make an armorial display, were as 'legal' and as 'authentic' as those granted by patent in the approved way.

The matter was not put to the test until 1954 when the Corporation of the City of Manchester petitioned the Earl Marshal for a ~ to be held to resolve their complaint against the Manchester Palace of Varieties Ltd., who were making display of the arms of the Corporation.

The difficulty of conducting a trial under canon law with barristers instead of proctors was overcome and the Lord Chief Justice, wearing the crimson robe of a Doctor of Civil Law, acting as surrogate for the Earl Marshal, who was present, occupied the judgement seat in his own Court. Judgement was given in favour of the plaintiff, and the authenticity of the College of Arms was thereby heavily stressed. This revival of the ~ made indisputably clear that 220 years of abeyance did not destroy or render invalid the ~, and that ponderous though the machinery may now be, the ~ can function to protect armigers against infringement. The holding of this first ~ in the reign of Her Majesty Q. Eliz. II was epoch-making, and a high-water mark in the history of English law. Known alternatively as the Earl Marshal's Court, which is the name given to what is now virtually the entrance hall of the C. of A. building in Q. Vic. St, E.C.4. This chamber, though still fitted with the barrier and the judgement seat (known as the Earl Marshal's Throne), was not considered suitable to be used in the 1954 revival.

chough, Cornish: [M.E.] a small, black bird having red beak and legs; a member of the crow family, *Fregillus Graculus*; the ~ is always sable beaked and membered gules: if he is blazoned of any other colours he is not a ~. Blazoned in old heraldry as a 'beckit'. (176)

Christ, Order of: can claim to be, in some respects, a continuation of the Knights

Templar, but its foundation as the Order of Christ dates from 1318, when K. Denis of Portugal established it primarily to defend Algarvia. The foundation was ratified by Pope John XXII in 1319, who gave the knights the properties of the defunct templars and ordained that they follow the Cistercian rule; the right to create knights of the Order was at the same time assumed by the Holy See, and the Order thereafter developed two separate identities, *viz*:

ORDER OF CHRIST: (Portugal) pre-1910 insignia—*Badge:* a gold-rimmed oval medallion of white enamel bearing a red cross surmounted by a white cross; above the cross a Sacred Heart surmounting a white enamel star of eight points. *Star:* a silver star of twenty-two rays, the top ray ensigned with a Sacred Heart, with a central medallion of white bearing the cross as on the badge. *Riband:* scarlet. Post-1918 insignia (the Order was dormant in Portugal from 1910 to December 1918)— *Badge:* a gold-rimmed red enamel cross surmounted by a white enamel cross. *Star:* as above, without the Sacred Heart. *Riband:* scarlet.

ORDER OF CHRIST: (Vatican) one class only. Insignia—*Badge:* a red enamel cross surmounted by a white cross; usually, but not always, ensigned with a crown; the badge is worn either from a scarlet neck-riband or from the gold collar, consisting of enlinked gold knots and medallions depicting the Papal tiara and the crossed keys of St Peter, with a knight's trophy of arms in the centre from which the badge depends. *Star:* a silver star of twenty-two points, with a central laurel wreath surrounding a white enamel medallion bearing the badge in miniature.

Christ and St Benedict of Avis, Order of: (Portugal) f. c. 1320, in one class, for those who had received both the Order of Christ

(q.v.) and the Order of Aviz (q.v.). Insignia—*Badge:* a gold oval medallion surmounted by two smaller oval medallions,
side by side, bearing the badges in miniature
of the Orders of Christ and of Aviz; the
whole ensigned with a crown. *Star:* the
unensigned badge, in circular shape, surmounting a silver star of twenty-one points
which is ensigned between the uppermost
points with a red enamel Sacred Heart.
Riband: red, green, in equal widths.

Chrysanthemum: see **sephium.**

Chrysanthemum, Order of the: (Japan)
f. 1877 in one class. Insignia—*Badge:* a star
of thirty-two white enamelled gold-edged
rays; between the four longest rays are four
chrysanthemums in silver, between green
leaves; centrally a gold-edged cabochon
garnet, the whole ensigned by an enamelled

chrysanthemum on gold. *Star:* a larger
version of the badge. *Riband:* crimson,
edged violet.

Chrysogonus, St: appears in the municipal
arms of Zadar, Yugoslavia.

chub: [M.E.] a freshwater fish, *Leuciscus
cephalus,* also called 'chevin' by which
name it may be blazoned; employed in
heraldry chiefly for ca. reasons.

church: generally drawn as the typical
church building with its row of gothic
windows and, normally at the dexter end,
the tower out of which rises the spire. The
blazon is less standardized than is the
graphic representation: 'a ~ with a spire',
'perspective view of a ~', 'a cathedral ~',
'a chapel' will all be found as well as
specific references such as 'the ~ of
Falkirk'. Reductions, too, occur: 'a ~

---

103. Azure, on a bend cottised argent three
      billets sable.
      Haggerston, Northumberland.

104. Paly argent and sable, on a bend gules
      three martlets Or.
      Burdett of Burthwaite.

105. Gules, on a bend between in chief a serpent
      knowed and, in base, a stag trippant Or,
      an arrow pointing upward to a bee volant
      proper: upon a chief argent, on waves of
      the sea, a paddle-wheel ship under both
      steam and canvas, also proper.
      Municipal Corporation of Barrow-in-Furness.

106. Sable, three walnut-leaves between two
      bendlets, argent.
      Waller.

107. Or, an Imperial eagle sable beaked and
      membered gules, dimidiated with bendy
      of the last and argent.
      Municipal Corporation of Nuremberg.
      [*Note:* This is the 'superior' of two coats of
      arms worn by the municipality. The
      secondary achievement is depicted at
      No. 284.]

108. Per bend sinister gules and argent; on a
      bend sinister embattled azure between in
      chief, a demi-lion issuant Or holding in
      his paws a battle-axe of the third the haft
      curved of the fourth and, in base, issuant of
      a point wavy barry-wavy vert and Or, a
      tower sable, masoned argent, ports and
      lights also Or; an open crown gold
      jewelled of the first between two fleurs-
      de-lys argent.
      Viscount Dunrossie.

103   104

105   106

107   108

porch', 'a ~ tower', 'a belfry', 'a steeple'. There are no church interiors. (409)

church bell: see **bell, church.**

church flags: the Church of St Martin in the Fields, Trafalgar Square, London, being the Parish Church of the Admiralty, has the status of a Naval Shore Establishment, is H.M.S. 'St M. in the F.', and has the right to fly the White Ensign (q.v.). It is the only church building from which a secular flag ought to be flown; nevertheless, churches all over the country fly, from time to time, the Union Jack, and prices for various sizes will be seen in the catalogues of ecclesiastical outfitters.

On occasions when flags are flown from a church tower, a simple cross of St George would be in order, and more appropriate than a Union Jack. More appropriate still would be a St George with, in the canton, the arms of the diocese, and most appropriate a banner charged with the emblem of the saint of the parish's dedication.

Archbishops and bishops fly a banner of the arms of the see (being arms of office (q.v.)) impaling their family arms; hence, are aware of correct usage, but no objection seems to be raised to the misuse of the Union Jack.

cicada: see **grasshopper.**

ciclamoro: It., annulet.

cimera: Sp., crest.

cimier: Fr., crest.

cimiero: It., crest.

cimiterre: Fr., scimitar.

cinople: alt. spelling of 'sinople' (q.v.).

cinquefoglie: It., cinquefoil.

cinquefoil: see **trefoil.**

cinta: It., orle.

cintre: Fr., banded.

circular bordure: a circle described with its centre on fess point; hence, a ~ gules on a field argent has the appearance of gules, a plate (q.v.). It is r. even on the Continent

where many forms strange to the British eye are comparatively popular.

cirkelomgeven: D., banded.

citadel: see **castle.**

civet-cat: see **catamount.**

civic arms: see **community, arms of.**

civic crown: see **garland.**

civic mace: the staff of office, carried by the official mace-bearer before the mayor of a municipal corporation, and which rests upon a stand during the deliberations of such a body corporate. The symbol of civic authority. The maces in the possession of various local government bodies throughout the country differ but little in form, and in spirit and significance not at all, from the mace of the House of Commons. The ~ is employed not only in public arms, but in the achievements of persons who are, or have been prominent in either national or local government. It is also the symbol of magisterial authority. Notwithstanding that its application might be fairly wide, the ~ is granted with reserve. (188)

civic wreath: see **garland.**

clairevoies: r. alt. for 'interstices' (q.v.).

Clare Roll: (c. 1456) vellum true roll (q.v.), 10 in. by 2 ft. 8 in. Two columns; left—an English poem of eighteen stanzas, seven lines each; right—a Latin translation. It takes the form of a dialogue between a layman and a friar, the former asking, the latter answering, questions on the genealogy and history of the Lords of the Honour of Clare. Illuminated (below) with eleven shields of the lords of the honour, each impaling (q.v.) the achievement of his wife's family with names over, gilded and painted.

Clarence Herald: also named Clarenceux Herald, was maintained by dukes of Clarence. In 1420 both Clarenceux King of Arms (q.v.) and ~ met other English officers of arms on the Continent; hence,

d

b

c

PLATE IV (a) Azure, a lion rampant and, in chief, a terrestrial globe between two estoiles Or.

John Dryden (Poet Laureate)

(b) Gules, two arrows in saltire argent, barbed and flighted of the same, debruised of as many barrulets compony Or and azure between two oval buckles in pale of the third, all within a bordure engrailed, also of the third.

Lord Macaulay

(c) Quarterly I and IV: Or, two mullets in chief and a crescent in base azure within an orle of the second, for *Scott*. II and III: Or, on a bend azure three mascles of the first: in sinister-chief, a buckle of the second, for *Haliburton*. Over all, on an inescutcheon, the badge of the baronet, *videlicit*; argent, a sinister hand erect, appaumé, couped at the wrist gules.

Sir Walter Scott, Bt

there can be no doubt of the existence of both.

Clarence Roll: (temp. K. Hen. VI) 102 painted shields of noblemen and ecclesiastics.

Clarenceux King of Arms: see **College of Arms.**

clarendon: see **clarion.**

claricimbal: see **clarion.**

claricord: Sp., clarion.

claricorde: Fr., clarion.

claricordium: D., clarion.

clarine: [Fr.] a r. alt. term for a beast collared and belled.

clarion: [M.E.] a primitive musical instrument, being a shepherd's pipe; in heraldic art, highly conventionalized. A number (strictly, eight) of short cylinders, each a little higher than the previous one from dexter to sinister, are issuant from a square block having, on the underside, a downward extension, erupting on the sinister and curving over to the dexter, thus forming a handle. In the course of its history it has been mistaken for, and blazoned as, a lance-rest (see **à bouché**), and as a ship's rudder, and has numerous alt. terms: 'clarendon', 'claricimbal', 'claricord', 'clavecimbal', 'lance-rest', 'organ-rest', 'rest', 'rudder', and 'shepherd's pipes'; all except ∼ and organ-rest are now obs. (357)

Clarkson, James: Kintyre Pursuivant, 1724.

clausum: L., close.

clavado: Sp., cloue.

clavecimbal: see **clarion.**

claw, a bird's: the leg severed below the thigh. See also **quise, erased à la.**

clayed: see **cleed.**

claymore: [Gael.] a sword (q.v.) having a basket hand-guard.

cleché, cross: a cross composed of four narrow triangles conjoined (q.v.) apex to apex, the base of each outward, and brought to a point of 90°. The word, from L.

through Fr., has reference to a key or to a key-hole. A ∼ in modern heraldry has limbs roughly the shape of an angular key-hole; in old heraldry ∼ might apply to any cross voided (q.v.). When voided and pommetty ∼ is the cross of Toulouse.

cleed: pertaining to a bird's pounce (q.v.) or to a boar's hoof; alt. spellings 'clayed', 'cleyed', 'clewed', and 'clowed'.

Clerk, Adam: Ormonde Pursuivant, 1636.

Clerk Cragie of Dunburney, George: Lord Lyon Depute, 1823.

clewed: see **cleed.**

cley: see **klee.**

cleyed: see **cleed.**

clock: a timepiece appearing only in the achievement of the Worshipful Company of Clockmakers.

Clopton, Hugh: Rouge Dragon Pursuivant, 1691. Former Blanch Lyon Pursuivant 1690.

close: [M.E.] closed; shut; of a helmet with the visor down; of a bird with wings folded. (254)

close-girt: of a long robe, or other form of clothing, drawn in by means of a cord about the waist: the colour of the cord is usually given, and the statement is made that it is tasselled, whether or not of another colour.

closet: [M.E.] first diminutive of the bar (q.v.) being half the width of the parent and always appearing in association with another, the two being their own width apart and constituting an inseparable item blazoned as 'bars-gemel' (or 'gemelle'). (153)

closing nails: see **nails.**

cloud: as well as its being symbolized by nebuly (q.v.). A ∼ proper is frequently employed. (292)

Cloud and Banner, Order of: (China) f. 1935 in nine classes. Insignia—*Badge:* an eight-point white-enamelled star bearing a faceted design surmounting (for the first, second, and third rank) an eight-point faceted star of either gold or silver. A central medallion of blue enamel depicts a banner and white clouds. The three ranks are distinguished one from another by small red stars in the upper arm of the white star. The star of the order is the same as the badge, but on a larger scale. *Ribands:* for the first class—red edged white; for the second class—white edged red; for the third class—yellow with two blue stripes; for the fourth class—blue with red and white stripes and white and red stripes at alternate edges; for the fifth class—blue red and yellow stripes with yellow and red stripes at alternate edges; this, in reverse, is used by the sixth class. The seventh class has white with red and yellow stripes and yellow and red stripes at alternate edges; for the eighth class—white with yellow and blue and blue and yellow stripes at alternate edges. The ninth class has the colours of the eighth reversed.

cloué [Fr.] nailed; of an object on which a number of dots represent nail-heads (see **trellis**). The same word is current in Fr. blazon.

clove: [M.E.] the flower-butt of *Caryophyl-lus aromaticus*, dried, and used as spice; the symbolic device of the Worshipful Company of Grocers. (17)

clowed: see **cleed**.

cloyshacke: [Gael.] alt. for a harp (q.v.).

cloyshackle: frequent mis-spelling of cloy-shacke (q.v.).

club: [M.E.] a crude weapon consisting of a length of rough log, whittled down at one end to reduce the diameter sufficiently to make it convenient to be gripped in the hand. A 'spiked ~' is depicted with a number of iron studs protruding at varying angles and irregular intervals from the butt end. The ~ makes its appearance in heraldry in conjunction with the savage (q.v.), it being held in his outer hand when he does duty as a supporter (q.v.).

clymant: see **goat**.

Clyne, David: Lyon Clerk Depute, 1807. Lyon Clerk and Keeper of the Records, 1819.

coal-pick: see **pick**.

coat-armor: a generic term relative to armorial bearings.

cob¹: see **herring**.

cob²: a male swan.

cobweb: see **spider**.

---

109. Argent, a chevron engrailed between three martlets azure.
Bramston.

110. Gules a tournament barrier argent: on a chief Or an eagle displayed sable.
Giovio.

111. Or, two ravens in pale proper within a bordure gules.
Corbet.

112. Azure, on a chevron ermine between three bird-bolts a rose gules slipped and leaved proper between two daws incontrait sable.
Dawson (2).

113. Sable, a hawk's leure argent.
Longueville.

114. Argent, an eagle displayed sable charged on the breast and on each wing with an open crown of the field.
Barclays Bank.

109

110

111

112

113

114

Cochrane, Sir Arthur Wm Stewart: Clarenceux King of Arms, 1927. Former Norroy K. of A. 1926; former Chester Herald, 1915; former Rouge Croix Pursuivant, 1904.

cock: [O.E.] a male bird, particularly the male of the domestic fowl, *Gallus domesticus*; often employed in arms for ca. reasons. When blazoned as a game-~ the reference is to the fighting bird and it ought to be more vigorously depicted than is the barnyard fowl. The ~ is armed of beak, claws, and spurs, crested of his comb, and jelloped of his wattles. Sometimes blazoned 'dunghill-~'. (124)

cockatrice: a composite fictitious beast, hatched from an egg laid by a cock, having a cock's head and legs, a pair of wings either feathered or membraneous, the body bird-shape tapering to a long, curling snake-like tail, terminating in a barb. The ~ has scales except on the thighs which are feathered. If, having attained the age of nine years the ~ lays an egg on a laystall, and this is guarded by a toad, the resultant offspring will differ from the parent by having at the nether extremity, a second head, being that of a dragon. This creature named the basilisk, has a death-dealing eye, one glance from which turns the victim into a block of stone. It is also known as the amphisian ~, and may in fact be identical. (282).

cocke: r. alt. for 'zule' (q.v.).

Cocke, John: Lancaster Herald, 1559. Former Portcullis Pursuivant, 1553.

cockle-shell: debased term for 'escallop' (q.v.).

coconut-tree: a tree of the order Palmae, depicted with a tall trunk having at the top a bunch of foliage inclined upward. Not intended for the 'cocoa', *Theobroma cacao*.

cocquel: a spelling of 'cockle'; a debased alt. term for 'escallop' (q.v.).

cod: [M.E.] a large sea-fish, *Gadus morrhua*; also known in heraldry as 'sea-lucy', or 'sea-gad'. The ~, as well as sea ling (q.v.), was used in the production of 'stock-fish' (q.v.) and therefore assumed economic importance. ~-head appears both as a charge and as a crest, and when 'a fish's head' is blazoned a ~-head is to be understood.

coffee: the shrub, *Coffea arabica*, from the roasted seeds of which the beverage so named is made. Blazoned, generally, as a ~-tree.

cog, ape's: see **ape.**

cog, mill: an iron rod bent in a semicircle of small diameter at one end, and into a crank at the other. Near the crank end the rod is enfiled (q.v.) with an iron ring. The semicircular end was placed under the hopper in a windmill, the collar acted as a bearing, and the crank was rotated from the general machinery; the purpose was to keep the hopper agitated and the grist flowing. Sometimes blazoned as a 'spinning cog', which is an implement so very close in its appearance as to be practically the same thing. The application was different: the latter being the hook to which the yarn was secured in a rope walk. Alt. term 'mill-clack'.

cognisance: [O.F.] a badge, or any device peculiar to a feudal chief and used as the distinctive mark of all his followers and men-at-arms.

coheiresses: see **heraldic heiress.**

coif-de-mailles: head-covering of mail; a sort of protective hood.

coiled-snakes: see **shell.**

cointise: [M.E.] quaint dress ornament; hence, the lady's scarf or sleeve attached crestwise to a knight's helmet as a mark of favour during a tournament.

Cokayne, George Edward: Clarenceux King of Arms, 1894. Former Norroy K. of

A., 1882; former Lancaster Herald, 1869; former Rouge Dragon Pursuivant, 1859. (G.E.C., author of *The Complete Peerage*.)

Colbarne, Wm: York Herald, 1565. Former Rouge Dragon Pursuivant, 1554. Also called 'Wm Cowarne'.

Coldharbour: a Thames-side property in Dowgate Ward, a little westward of Old Swan stairs, granted by K. Ric. III to the heralds for their residence and office. K. Hen. VII dispossessed the heralds and bestowed the property on his mother, Margaret Beaufort, for life.

Collar Pursuivant: a name of office derived from the collar of SS's, and employed down to 1488.

collar of SS's: a neck-ornament consisting of pairs of SS's connected by short lengths of chain at top and bottom. A Lancastrian device, still employed by the Lord Chief Justice, the Lord Mayor of London, and the heralds of arms. This (and the Yorkist collar) were insignia of allegiance before Tudor times when they came into use by civilians (merchants and others) solely for their decorative value. Eventually the wearing of collars was restricted to knights.

collared: of a beast having about the neck a strap and buckle (q.v.).

collarinato: It., collared.

Collars of orders of chivalry: may be an integral part of the insignia of a grand cross of an order—as with all British orders that have a grand cross rank—or be awarded as an extra mark of distinction. In both cases the badge of the order is, on stipulated days and under certain conditions, worn pendant from the collar and not from the riband. Some awards of honour are restricted to collars only, such as the Royal Victorian Chain and the Order of Al-Hussein (q.v.), and are worn on all appropriate occasions. Collars may be displayed surrounding their holder's arms.

College of Arms: a body of officers of arms, being functionaries of the Royal Household, incorporated in the second regnal year of K. Ric. III (i.e. 1484). In these specialists is vested the duty of devising, and granting by royal letters patent, coats of arms and other armorial devices to Her Majesty's English, Welsh, and Commonwealth subjects. Scottish subjects are provided for by the Lyon Office (q.v.). Their further public duty is that of making proclamations, and of organizing and marshalling royal processions. The ~ consists in thirteen persons: three kings of arms, six heralds of arms, and four pursuivants of arms who are subject to the jurisdiction of the Earl Marshal (q.v.). The senior member of the College is Her Majesty's Garter Principal King of Arms of Englishmen, whose title is whittled down to Garter Principal King of Arms, further to Garter King of Arms, and, ultimately, to Garter. The office was created by K. Hen. V in 1415. Before that date the senior officer of arms in the service of the crown was styled 'Roy d'armes d'Angleterre'.

The country is divided into two provinces by the River Trent: Clarenceux King of Arms, whose title is derived from the town of Clare, has jurisdiction south of the Trent; Norroy King of Arms, north of the Trent: the latter's territory was increased, and his title enhanced, by the addition of Ulster after the southern part of Ireland became independent and set up its own heraldic and genealogical authority.

The six heralds derive their titles from those of royal dukedoms, i.e. Windsor, Richmond, Somerset, Lancaster, York, and Chester; and the four pursuivants are named after royal badges: Rouge Croix, Rouge Dragon, Bluemantle, Portcullis. They are domiciled in a building in Q. Vic. St, City of London, E.C. 4, where each occupies a suite of chambers, employs his own office staff, and conducts his heraldic and genealogical practice independently, but they function in concert in other duties, and meet to confer in matters of general interest to the College, at a monthly Chapter. Persons making inquiries are received by Her Majesty's Officer of Arms in Waiting, which Office lasts for one week, and is taken in turns: all applicants for a grant of arms become, and remain, the client of the 'duty officer' by whom they are first received.

~ is an extension of the Court, not a department of State: the officers of arms are created by royal warrant, they are not government officials. On State occasions when the officers of arms are engaged on public business, they wear their traditional costume, the tabard, or Her Majesty's coat; a sleeveless, tunic-like jacket emblazoned back and front with the Royal Arms as marshalled for England, and on each shoulder a half-cape similarly decorated: with this court-levee knee-breeches, stockings and shoes are worn, and the headdress is the pointed, laced hat except at functions of the Order of the Garter when the Garter bonnet takes its place. The ~ possesses a wealth of records and collections including some most beautiful illuminated manuscripts. The constitution of the ~ is such that these documents, even when of historical importance, are private property to which there is no public right of access.

College of Arms Trust: a fund set up for the purpose of building, furnishing, and supplying a Museum of Heraldry to which the general public shall have access. At present, exhibition cases only are envisaged: it is hoped that a reading room, which would be highly appreciated by heraldists and other antiquaries, may be added later.

College of Heralds: a colloquial misnomer of the 'College of Arms' (q.v.).

college-pot: see **pewter-pot.**

---

115. Argent, a falcon with wings addorsed and inverted azure, armed and membered gules, belled and jessed Or, between three spearheads sable.
Ernast.

116. Azure, three eagles' heads erased each holding in the beak a patriarchal cross Or.
Corporation of Lyme Regis Dorset [or *King's Lynn*, Norfolk].
[*Note:* The eagles' heads in this achievement are sometimes described as dragons' heads, the patriarchal crosses as crosses-crosslet fitchy.]

117. Vert, a swan naiant in water proper beaked Or.
Van Juchen.

118. Sable, a goshawk perched on a stock issuant in base argent, armed jessed and belled Or.
Hawker.

119. Quarterly of six pieces azure and argent three doves of the last membered gules each holding in the beak an olive-branch Or.
Worshipful Company of Tallow Chandlers.

120. Azure, an eagle with wings displayed Or, holding in the beak a penner and ink-horn sable stringed gules, standing on a closed book of the last garnished of the second.
Worshipful Company of Scriveners.

115 116

117 118

119 120

Collen, George Wm: Portcullis Pursuivant 1841.

colleté: Fr., collared.

Collingborne's Book: (XV cent.) a paper book, 8½ by 11¾ in. It contains 179 painted shields, some having brisures (q.v.); twenty blazons in French of arms not illustrated, forty-eight painted shields with names over being an ordinary of crosses, several miscellaneous shields, and sixteen painted crests with helmets and mantling; finally, twenty shields of French noblemen, nineteen painted, one tricked (q.v.).

Collins's Roll: (c. 1295) vellum true roll, 3¾ by 32 ft 7½ in., painted, 598 shields with names.

Collona: It., column.

collone: Fr., column.

Collyer, James: Lancaster Herald during the reign of K. Ed. IV. Former Bluemantle and Cadran Pursuivant during the reign of K. Hen. VI.

Colombus Pursuivant: see **Ulster Office.**

color naturalis: L., proper.

colour party: six persons—two junior lieutenants, two sergeants, and two privates; the commissioned ranks carry the colours on parade, the other four act as guards; hence, a military junior lieutenant came to be known as an ensign which word, by a familiar process of phonetics, turned into 'ancient', alt. spelling 'anshient'. It is correct to refer to the colour and to other flags as ensigns but er. to apply the word 'ancient'.

colt: see **horse.**

columbine: [M.E.] the flower *Aquilegia vulgaris*, which, in addition to the general use that might be made of any flower in heraldry, has attracted special interest by its use in the achievement of the Worshipful Company of Cooks where it does not seem to be appropriate. It may be representing preserving-ginger which came from Colombo, and was called 'colambyne'. An-

other reasonable theory is that *Aquilegia* had medicinal qualities, but it is most likely to be nothing more complex than a crude pun: 'columbinus', L., a pigeon or dove; hence, the contents of a pie. This idea is strengthened by the fact that the crest a cock-pheasant, and both the supporters of the Cooks' arms dexter, a buck; and sinister a doe, both proper, are edible. (169, 381)

column: see **pillar.**

columna: Sp., column.

comb¹: the toilet comb that is used as a charge is square in form and has teeth cut into each of two sides, generally chiefward and baseward. The roots of the teeth at the spine generally form a curve, the longest teeth central, the shortest at each end. When the ~ appears in a secondary capacity, as, e.g., in the hand of a mermaid (q.v.), it has only a single row of teeth. Sometimes blazoned 'square ~'. (320)

comb²: see **card¹.**

combatant: of two lions when one, contourné (q.v.), occupies the dexter half of a shield and the other, rampant, fills the sinister half. The inference is that the king of the beasts will not share his territory: three lions, each being king in his own corner of the shield do not molest each other, but more than three are assumed to be separated by an ordinary. Since, from very early times, six lions without an ordinary have been employed, the term 'lioncels', meaning 'cubs', was invented to account for it.

combed: sometimes used as an alt. for 'crested' with reference to a cock's (q.v.) comb.

comble: a diminutive, being half the width of a chief (q.v.); employed only on the Continent.

comet: [L.] also described as 'a blazing star', consists of two parts, the head and the tail which often vary in colours. The head may be represented as either a mullet (q.v.) or as an estoile (q.v.) conjoined to the apex of either a straightedged or a wavy ray (q.v.). A ~ is described as 'bearded' of its tail. (135)

cometa: It. and Sp., comet.

comète: Fr., comet.

Comfort Pursuivant: created by K. Ed. IV for service in France, but the origin of the name of office does not appear.

commercial arms: see **community, arms of.**

common charge: see **charge.**

community, arms of: the armorial bearings of a body corporate, as, e.g., a university, a school, a municipal council, or a limited company; hence, ~ is a collective term, diffuse in meaning. The incisive subtitles are better: for universities and schools 'academic arms'; for municipal councils, public utility organizations and the like, 'public arms' with specializing 'civic arms'; for limited companies, 'commercial arms'.

comparisoned: a debased form of 'caparisoned' [L.] applied to the horse (q.v.) when provided with a saddle-cloth.

compartment: [frmd on L. 'comport', to carry] see **supporters.**

compass¹: [M.E.] a drawing instrument consisting of two legs pivoted together, one extremity being a steel point, the other a socket to hold a pencil, used for describing circles. Carpenter's ~ has both legs pointed, the circumference being scratched on the wood. Normally orientated palewise, pivot chiefward, points a little apart, but may be 'expanded' (er. blazoned 'extended') when they are flat across the shield; hence, fesswise. (157)

compass²: an instrument consisting of a magnetic needle, poised above a card which is inscribed in degrees, employed at sea to direct the steering of a ship. Also blazoned

'mariners ~'. The ~-card and the needle appear separately.

complexions, blazon by: see **segregative blazon.**

complicated: r. obs. term meaning 'semirisant'.

componado: Sp., compony.

componné: Fr., compony.

compony: [L.] of an ordinary (q.v.) or a bordure (q.v.) divided into squares of alternative metal and tincture: also called 'gobony' (or 'gobinated'). A bordure consisting of two tracks, each ~ metal alternating with tincture both round the shield and across the bordure, is blazoned 'counter-compony'. (10, 173, IV)

composed, arms: a primitive form of announcing armorially a marriage by the expedient of adding to the husband's achievement a charge from the paternal arms of the wife. Such additions, after two or three generations, made the marital achievement both overcrowded and unrecognizable. Also termed 'arms compounded'.

compositis: L., compony (q.v.).

composto: It., compony (q.v.).

compounded arms: see **composed, arms.**

Comrie, James: Messenger-at-Arms to the Lyon Court, 1675.

conchiglia: It., escallop.

conchilium: L., escallop.

concession, in: an obs. term of blazon applicable to charges in augmentation (q.v.) when they are items of regal heraldry.

Conde: Sp., Count.

Condé Pursuivant: serving in France in 1428; name of office probably derived from Condé sur Noireau.

condor: a giant vulture found in the Andes, *Sarcorhamphus gryphus.*

Condor of the Andes, Order of: (Bolivia) f. 1921 in five classes. Insignia—*Badge:* gold-edged blue cross paty notched, the eight points tipped with gold balls; gold trumpet flowers between the arms; a central medallion depicts Mount Potosi and the sun in gold, surrounded by the inscription *La Union Es La Fuerze MCMXXI* in gold on white; the badge is ensigned by a gold condor. *Star:* the badge with the medallion showing a condor flying in front of Potosi. *Riband:* green.

coney: [L. via M.E.] a rabbit. (255)

coney-fish: see **burbot.**

confronty: r. alt. for 'respecting' (q.v.).

conger: see **eel.**

conjoined: [M.E.] fastened together; linked; touching. (264)

conjunct: obs. alt. for 'conjoined' (q.v.).

Conke Pursuivant: a name of office current in the reign of K. Hen. VII; taken from the town of Concarneau, Brittany.

Conspicuous Gallantry Medal: f. 1874 as an award to petty officers and seamen of the Royal Navy, and non-commissioned officers and men of the Royal Marines. In 1942 men of the Empire's flying services became eligible for the award and, in 1943, it was extended to include Merchant Navy personnel. *Medal: obverse:* the crowned head of the conferring monarch (the king's bust in naval uniform for Ed. VII and Geo V), surrounded by appropriate legend, e.g.

Edwardus VII Rex Imperator; reverse: the words *For Conspicuous Gallantry* within a laurel wreath broken by a crown. *Riband:* (naval) originally blue, white, blue in equal thirds, changed in 1921 to white with $\frac{1}{8}$ in. navy-blue edges; the flying services riband is of sky-blue with navy-blue edges.

Conspicuous Service Cross: see **Distinguished Service Cross.**

Constable [L.] originally denoting an office-holder in royal courts, the word developed widely different connotations at various times and from country to country. In France, from medieval times to 1814, the Constable of France was appointed by the king to command the army, to be the arbiter in affairs of chivalry, and to adjudicate on military offences.

After the Norman invasion the office of Lord High Constable was instituted in England for similar duties. The earls of Hereford were the first hereditary holders of the office, followed by the earls of Essex and the dukes of Buckingham. The office lapsed after Buckingham's attainder, and the duties are now exercised as necessary, e.g. at coronations, by the Earl Marshal (q.v.).

From the time of K. Hen. VII, high constables were elected at the court-leets of

---

121. Azure, three bustards rizant Or.
  Nevill.

122. Per saltire vert and argent, two popinjays of the first.
  Stoker.

123. Argent, a chevron between three coots sable.
  Southcott.

124. Argent, three cocks gules, armed, crested and jelloped sable.
  Cockayne, Rushton.

125. Argent, an ostrich sable, holding in the beak a horseshoe Or.
  Marnham.

126. Argent, a chevron between three herons sable.
  Henshaw.

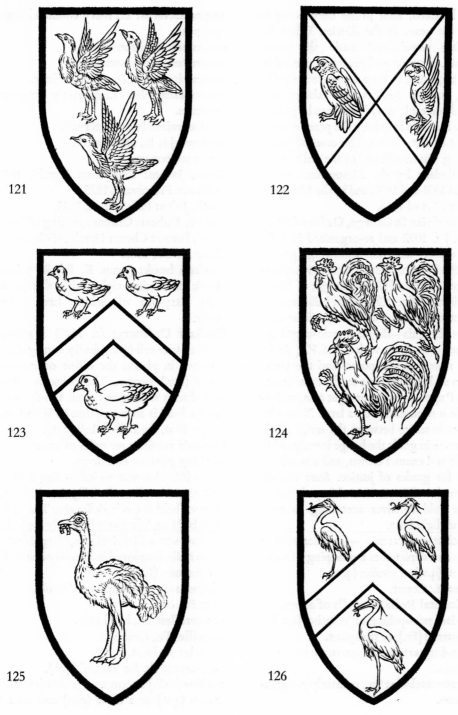

121

122

123

124

125

126

each hundred, their prime duty being to keep the peace in the district. When increasing populations made this more difficult, petty or parliamentary constables were appointed to keep the peace in smaller areas, such as manors and tithings, and special constables could be sworn by justices of the bench to help keep the peace at times of riot or disturbance. The onus of peace-keeping was transferred to the police force constabulary by the Metopolitan Police Acts of 1831 and 1840, and by the Municipal Reform Act of 1835.

Constantinian St George, Order of: (Two Sicilies) f. 1092 and re-organized in 1695, this Order has the following grades: Bailiff of Justice; Grand Cross; Knight of Justice; Knight of Grace; Knight of Merit; Knight of Office; Chaplains; ladies may be admitted as Dames of the first four categories. Insignia—*Badge:* a gold-edged red enamel cross flory with *I.H.S.V.* (*In hoc signo vinces*) on the points and the Greek letters alpha and omega on the cross arm; a large *P* appears on the upright arm, and the whole is surmounted by a large *X* forming a cross in saltire between the arms; all the letters are in gold; the badge is ensigned by a gold and enamel crown, and a trophy of arms for grades of justice. *Star:* the un-ensigned badge on a multirayed star of either gold or silver according to rank. *Riband:* light blue.

constellation: various ∼ are blazoned by name and depicted as a grouping of either mullets (q.v.) or estoiles (q.v.).

Conte: It., Count.

Continental Rolls: see **rolls of arms.**

contoise: mis-spelling of 'cointise' (q.v.).

contourné: [Fr.] see **rampant.**

contra-inquartato: It., quarterly per grand quarters.

contracuartelado: Sp., quarterly per grand quarters.

contrafasciatus: L., barry counterchanged per pale.

contrapal: Sp., trononné.

contraveros: Sp., countervair.

contravittatus: L., per bend sinister.

contre-escartelé: Fr., quarterly per grand quarters.

contre-vaire: Fr., countervair.

controvajo: It., countervair.

cony: see **coney.**

Cook, James: Snowdoun Herald, 1845. Unicorn Pursuivant, 1825.

Cook, John: Islay Herald, 1811.

Cooke, Robert: Clarenceux King of Arms, 1567. Former Chester Herald, 1562; former Rose Herald, 1562.

Cooke's book: (temp. K. Ed. II) painted book containing eighty-nine shields the first sixty-one of which have names over.

Cooke's Ordinary: (c. 1340) a painted vellum true roll (q.v.), badly damaged and defaced in places: the oldest ordinary of arms (q.v.) known. The contents—about 650 shields with names over. On the dorse at the head is an inscription in Welsh, and at the foot, the Balliol Roll (q.v.).

Cooke's version: see **rolls of arms.**

cooking pot: see **cauldron.**

coot: [M.E.] a water-bird having a broad white patch where the bill joins the brow; hence, 'bald as a ∼'; *Fulica atra.* The ∼ has webbed feet. The name formerly applied to various water-birds including the guillemot, *Uria troile.* Employed in heraldry chiefly for ca. reasons. (123)

coppers: see **wyre-drawers' tools.**

coq: Fr., cock.

coquerelles: Fr., hazel nuts.

coquille: Fr., escallop.

coracle: see **boat.**

corbeau: r. alt. for 'corbie' (q.v.).

corbie: [O.F.] a term used in Scotland for a raven (q.v.) or a crow (q.v.) and used to describe such birds in heraldry for ca. reasons; also spelt 'corbyn'.

Corbin Pursuivant: name of office used in 1431 by a servant of the Duke of Bedford. Possibly from 'corbyn', a crow (q.v.), in the arms of Richard Gethin whom ~ served under the Duke of Bedford.

Corbyn: see **corbie.**

cordado: Sp., stringed.

cordal: cords of mixed silk and gold thread attached to a mantle, or with which a figure may be close-girt (q.v.).

cordato: It., stringed.

cordé: Fr., stringed.

corded: of a package, bale, or bag when tied about with cord of a different colour.

corded, cross: a cross humetty (q.v.) having each limb wound about with cords that cross salterwise in the centre.

Cork Pursuivant: see **Ulster Office.**

cormorant: see **liver-bird.**

cornato: It., attired, horned.

cornet [L.] a r. alt. term for the hunting- or bugle-horn (q.v.).

corneta: Sp., lit. cornet; hence, a bugle-horn.

cornette: Fr., cornet; hence, a bugle-horn.

cornflower: lit. any wild flower that grows among corn; in heraldry the 'bluebottle', *Centaurea cyanus*, is indicated. Drawn with but little conventionalization it is similar in appearance to the thistle; when 'proper' it is azure, cupped vert. The ~, or bluebottle, is also called 'heydoddes' for ca. reasons.

corno da caccia: It., bugle-horn.

cornucopia: [L.] the horn of plenty, a goat's horn inverted and disgorging fruit and flowers; also a conch-shell so disposed: a ~ may be employed for a specific purpose, and represented as disgorging a special product or symbol, as, e.g, bezants.

Cornwall Herald: created by K. Ric. II, probably to serve the Duke of Cornwall.

coronas: Sp., crown or coronet.

coronatus: L., crowned.

corone: It., crown or coronet.

coronets, peer's: see under the various coronets—**baron's coronet: earl's coronet,** etc.

coronetted mitre: a mitre (q.v.) issuant of a ducal coronet, proper to the use of only the Lord Bishop of Durham, on account of Co. Durham having been, till the XIX cent., a Palatinate. Dunelm also has a sword in saltire with a crozier (q.v.) behind his shield: other bishops use two croziers in saltire.

cortado: Sp., per fess.

cortinado: Sp., chape.

Cosoun, John: Clarenceux King of Arms 1425. Former Mowbray Herald, 1416; former Arundel Herald, 1413.

cost: [O.E.] an alt. for 'cottice' (q.v.).

Cotgrave, Hugh: Richmond Herald, 1566. Former Rouge Croix Pursuivant, 1553.

Cotgrave's Ordinary: (c. 1340) contains 556 blazoned arms with 219 painted in the margin.

cotice: Fr., bendlet.

cotissa: It., bendlet.

cotiza: Sp., bendlet.

cottice: [O.F.] second diminutive of the bend (q.v.) being a quarter the width of the parent; half a bendlet (q.v.).

cotticed: [Fr.] of any ordinary (q.v.) that runs between a pair of its second diminutives (q.v.); alt. spellings, 'cottised' and 'cotised'.

cotton: [M.E.] appears in heraldry in several forms: as ~-tree, *Gossypium*; as a hank of cotton thread; as a quill or spool of thread. (372)

Cottonian Roll: (XV cent.) contains 461 shields, a few in trick (q.v.), the majority painted, with names over. The MS. has been damaged by fire.

couchant: of a beast resting on its ventral surface, the fore-limbs extended forward, the head held up.

couché: see **à couché**.

coulissé: see **castle**.

coulter: [O.E.] lit. a vertically poised blade that procedes the plough-share; in heraldry an alt. term for a plough-share.

count [L.] the title 'count' derives from the early days of the Roman Empire when senators who were chosen to travel as companions and aides to the emperor became a permanent council, and thus their description as *comites principis* evolved into a title of honour. Comites continued to be royal servants of high rank, drawn on merit from any strata of society, until the feudal era when the title became hereditary, although throughout the middle ages the original connotation was never wholly lost. In France the title attained great status (since debased by liberal new creations) and comtes have ranked with dukes; even today the head of the Royal House of France is known as the Comte de Paris.

In Germany the equivalent title, 'graf', was also originally official in nature, but the access of power and wealth it brought to its holder ensured that it evolved into a hereditary distinction, and by *c.* 1150 grafs were territorial noblemen, some of whom became virtually territorial sovereigns. These latter ranked first in the hierarchy of grafs, and can be distinguished by the prefix 'erlaucht' (illustrious) and by use of a crown instead of a coronet to ensign their arms.

In Italy and Spain the titles of 'conte' and 'conde', respectively, have evolved in the same manner, from official nomenclature to hereditary distinction. The title proliferated freely in Italy, but has been more sparingly conferred in Spain; it has also been conferred in other countries, e.g. Russia, Japan, and Malta. See also **Margrave**.

counter ——: for compound terms preceded 'counter', e.g. counter-naiant, counter-passant, etc., see under **naiant, passant,** etc.

---

127. Azure upon a book open proper, having seven seals gold, leathered gules garnished Or the words *Dominus illuminatio mea*, in text-letters sable, all between three open crowns, also gold.
University of Oxford.

128. Argent, the Hebrew text-letter 'tawe' sable: on a chief gules a lion passant gardant Or, charged with the Roman capital text-letter H, also sable.
Regius Professor of Hebrew: Cambridge University (Arms of Office).

129. Per pale sable and argent three Gothic capital text-letters B counterchanged: on a chief of the second a bars-gemel wavy azure.
Municipal Corporation of Bridlington.

130. Azure, two rolls of paper in saltire Or banded gules between four bees volant of the second.
Harold Harmsworth (first Lord Rothermere).

131. Sable, a trefoil argent charged with a Gothic text-letter 'r' of the field.
Linne.

132. Azure, three garbs and, in dexter-chief, an estoile Or: on a chief of the last an open book argent garnished gold and leathered gules between two tulips, slipped and leaved proper.
Municipal Corporation of Spalding.

127

128

129

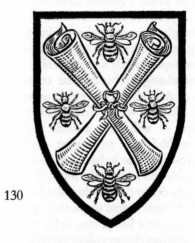

130

131

132

counter-ermine: an obs. term based on Fr. for 'ermines' (q.v.). The people who will not (or who cannot) conform to the rules and terms of modern blazon are inclined to make use of it. They also advocate such descriptions as 'argent, ermined sable', 'sable, ermined argent', 'Or, ermined sable', and 'sable, ermined Or' on the grounds that such a verbose jumble is easier.

counter-indented: appears in British heraldry only in the arms of Marie of Este, consort of K. James VI and I. Her second and third quarter (for Ferrara), i.e. France modern within a bordure counter-indented gules, appears to have a bordure compony of triangles azure and gules, the indentation being on the outer edge of the bordure.

counter-quartered: see **quarterly.**

counterchanged: having the colours reversed. A field party per pale argent and sable charged with a fess between three mullets ~ will have a sable mullet in dexter-chief and an argent mullet in sinister-chief: that in base will itself be per pale sable and argent; the fess will be sable from the dexter flank to the palar line where it will become argent to the sinister flank.

A paly, or a barry, etc., field, when ~, has the pieces change colour on each side of a line of partition. e.g. 'barry of argent and sable ~ per pale' will have the chiefmost piece beginning (on the dexter) argent, and becoming sable at the palar line; the second piece, beginning sable changes to argent, and so on to the basemost piece. When a variegated field carries charges ~ the charges are themselves variegated as the field, but with metal pieces on tincture, and tincture on metal.

In Scottish heraldry the term is used with greater freedom: e.g. what would be blazoned in England as 'per pale Or and gules, a mullet, also per pale vert and argent', in Scotland might be 'per pale Or and gules a mullet ~ of vert and argent'.

Total ~, that is, the complete reversal of the colour scheme, is used in Scotland for differencing: 'argent, three boar's heads couped close sable' for one branch of a family, and 'sable, three boar's heads, couped close argent' for another branch of the same family. English ~ may be described in Scotland as countercoloured. The word 'countercharged' sometimes seen in print, is an error. (154; Pl. I)

countercharged: see **counterchanged.**

countercoloured: see **counterchanged.**

county crown: a gold circlet heightened with four garbs (q.v.) Or between five points vert, used in Scotland to ensign (q.v.) and thus to distinguish the arms of a county council.

County Roll: (temp. K. Ric. II) book, $5\frac{1}{2}$ by $7\frac{3}{4}$ in., containing 700 shield outlines, of which number 504 were painted, twenty tricked (q.v.), and 176 blank. A local roll (q.v.) for Cheshire, Derbyshire, Essex, Kent, Lancashire, Norfolk, Shropshire, Staffordshire, Suffolk, and Sussex.

coupé: Fr., per fess.

couped: [Fr.] cut; of the head, trunk or limbs of a beast when finished at the place of severence by a straight line; of a cross (q.v.) with the elements shortened and finished square; of an ordinary (q.v.) or any appropriate charge (q.v.) that is represented as cut short. (399)

couple-close: second diminutive of the chevron, being a quarter the width of the parent (or half a chevronel (q.v.)): two are always associated (see **closet**) and are generally employed as external satellites to the chevron which may be blazoned as between ~, but is more likely to be described as 'cotticed' (q.v.).

courant: [L. via Fr.] a general term for running, applicable to any beast notwithstanding that there may be a specific term e.g. 'trippant' (q.v.). A beast ~ proceeds towards the dexter (q.v.); to the sinister (q.v.) it is counter-courant.

couronnes: Fr., crown or coronet.

course, in full: see **chase.**

Court of the Lord Lyon: a Court of Civil Law, being the Court of Chivalry over which the Lord Lyon King of Arms, being a judge of the Realm of Scotland, presides. All arms in use in Scotland are held by authority of the ~ which maintains its own Procurator Fiscal whose duty it is to proceed against all persons offending against the Law of Arms. It is an offence to use or display armorial bearings without the authority of the Lord Lyon, and persons so doing are mulcted of a fine which, like the fines imposed in any other court, are paid into the Treasury. As Judge of the ~ (also styled the Head Court), the Lord Lyon has power not merely to enforce the Laws of Arms as at present enacted but, if the law proves deficient in any particular circumstance, to 'prescryve' new ones. The ~ can, under the royal warrant, devise and grant augmentations of honour, and handle matters in relation to change of name. The Lord Lyon K. of A, although supreme in matters of law in his own Court, may take advice on matters of fact from the Hereditary Lords Assessors of the ~, e.g. the Lord High Constable of Scotland (at present the Countess of Errol) who, with the baton of office, sits on the right hand of the judgement seat; and the Earl of Angus (the Duke of Hamilton) who sits on the left.

The ~ normally sits twice a year but it may be convened at any time if the Lord Lyon thinks fit. The proceedings open with a procession announced by the court's trumpeters blowing a fanfare. First comes the Lyon Macer, followed by the heralds and pursuivants in their tabards. Then comes the Lord Lyon himself wearing the crimson robe and ermine cloak of a Great Officer of Scotland. He is attended by a page who wears a white blouse, red breeches, and a red velvet cap complete with an ostrich feather: his duty is to carry the long train of the Lord Lyon's crimson robe. Having traversed the Court the Lord Lyon takes his seat and places the baton of gold and blue enamel on the desk before him whereupon the Lyon Clerk 'fences' the Court by declaring: 'Forasmuch as this Honourable Court is called, by and under the ancient custom of Scotland, and as is required by the Act of Parliament 1587, Chapter 46: I therefore, in the name of Our Sovereign Lady Q. Eliz. II and in the name and on behalf of the Right Honourable the Lord Lyon K. of A. of Scotland, here present, do fence and fix this Court to sit, hold and continue, during his Lordship's pleasure, and I command all and sundry to reverence, acknowledge and obey the same, and I defend and forbid all manner of persons to trouble this Court, or take speech upon hand without leave asked and given as they will answer at their peril.'

Courtais, Jean: see **Sicily Herald.**

Courthope, Wm: Somerset Herald, 1854. Former Rouge Croix, 1839.

cousu: additional, generally applied to a chief (q.v.) and continental in usage.

coutel: [O.F.], r. alt. for 'dagger' (q.v.).

cow: [M.E.] the female of the *Bovidae*; employed in arms for ca. reasons. (29)

coward: [L.] descriptive of any beast to be depicted with the tail depressed and carried between the legs. (53)

Cowarne, Wm: see **Colbarne, Wm.**

crab: [O.E.] a crustaceous sea-creature; a sea-spider having ten legs and two claws. This decapod is generally depicted with its head to the dexter; hence, advancing in a chief-ward direction. Employed in heraldry chiefly for ca. reasons, but also as a symbol of gripping and holding power.

craftsman's marks: see **merchants' marks.**

Craig, Wm: Rothesay Herald, 1607.

cramp: [M.E.] an object of uncertain utility: it is represented as a bar of iron having a short length at each end bent over to within 45° of the bar and brought to a point; in chief it is bent to the sinister; in base, to the dexter. Two are sometimes set in saltire (q.v.) and may be so blazoned, but 'cross crampony', which strictly refers to the swastika (q.v.), is also applied. It has been defined as 'a carpenter's tool for holding two pieces of wood'. There is such a tool that has such a name, but it is emphatically not represented by this object. Another definition makes it a wall-anchor which is possible, but not very likely. When 'a kettle-hook' is blazoned precisely the same thing is depicted but they are accepted as two totally different objects. It is variously named 'cramp-iron', 'crampon', and 'crampoon', and its use is not confined to British heraldry, but on the Continent its purpose is clear and is revealed in its description, i.e.

'wolf-hook'. The shape is of respectable antiquity, it being the runic cypher for the yew-tree and for death.

crampette: see **chape.**

crampon: see **cramp.**

crampony, cross: see **swastika** and **cramp.**

crampoon: see **cramp.**

crancelin: r. alt. for 'crown of rue' (q.v.).

crane [O.E.] a long-legged, long-necked, long-billed big bird inhabiting marshy places, *Grus cinerea*. Depicted with a tufted head and standing (often in water) on the sinister leg, the dexter being flexed and raised with a piece of rock grasped in the claw. Thus the ~ is blazoned as 'in his vigilance', the assumption being that in the event of his attention wandering, the rock would fall and the splash so created have a stimulating effect. The rock may appear alone, when it will be blazoned as 'a vigilance' or as a '~'s vigilance'.

Cranston, John: Angus Herald Extraordinary, 1505.

crapawdy: [M.E.] a toad, *Buffo vulgaris*. Generally sejant (q.v.) and facing dexter (q.v.); sometimes sejant-affrontée (q.v.);

---

133. Sable, a demi-sun in his splendour, issuant in base Or: a chief dancetty of the last.
     A. C. Fox-Davies.

134. Per fess invected vert and gules, in chief two hunting-horns Or garnished of the second and stringed of the third; in base, the sun in his splendour also of the third.
     Forester.

135. Or, an estoile flaming in bend sable.
     Waldeck.

136. Argent, upon a rock issuant in base a leopard statant proper: on a chief wavy sable the upper half of a demi-sun in his splendour Or.
     Government of Nyasaland.

137. Azure, Jupiter's thunderbolt Or, shafted and winged argent.
     Tomyris.

138. Sable, three astronomical signs of Taurus, Or.
     Rt. Hon. Sir Wm Bull, Bt, P.C., F.S.A. (former Maltravers Herald Extraordinary).

133

134

135

136

137

138

'displayed', the back-view is presented, head in chief, limbs expanded as when leaping. (91)

Crawford, George: Procurator fiscal to the Lyon Court, 1636.

creciente: Sp., crescent.

crénelé: Fr., embattled.

crenelly: see **embattled.**

crescent: [L.] a convexo-concave figure of frequent occurrence, and er. supposed to represent the moon (q.v.). The heraldic ∼ is a decorative shape only, not a representative charge although it may, on some occasions, be of symbolic value since it is accepted as the badge of Islam.

The ∼ (which is the brisure (q.v.) of the second son), is broad in the middle, and has, running through the centre of its curvature, from tip to tip, a third line indicating that it is not flat, but rises to a ridge being thus triangular in section, and it ought to be shaded to enhance this effect, which is termed faceted (q.v.). Its normal orientation is with the horns chiefward, and sometimes another object, e.g. a cross, is issuant; the secondary object may also be unattached, and blazoned simply as 'within a ∼'. With the horns baseward it is 'a ∼ inverted'; with horns to the dexter, 'an increscent', and to the sinister 'a decrescent', both of which terms are applied er. to the crescent moon (q.v.). (401)

crescente: It., crescent.

cresset: see **beacon.**

crest: [L. via M.E.] lit. the summit; hence, a figure or a group of figures appearing above the helmet of rank (q.v.) and always 'resting on' or 'issuant from', generally a wreath of the colours (q.v.), sometimes a chapeau (q.v.) or a ducal coronet, peer's coronet, or heraldic crown. ∼, of unknown origin, developed later than coats of arms, and are not exclusive; numerous armigers (q.v.) having totally different

achievements, share a crest. The exaggerated use of the ∼ instead of the arms during the XVIII and XIX cents. resulted in families forgetting their shield of arms and claiming a crest only (which is absurd); the habit also had the effect of establishing the er. reference to a coat of arms as a 'family ∼'. (187–204)

crest-wreath: see **wreath of the colours.**

crested: see **cock.**

Crests, Wall's Book of: see **Book of Crests, Thomas Wall's.**

crevice: [M.E.] a name for the freshwater crayfish, *Astacus fluviatilis,* much like a lobster in form; alt. spellings 'crevise', 'crevish', 'crevisse', and 'crevys'; employed in heraldry largely for ca. reasons. (64)

crevise: see **crevice.**

crevish: see **crevice.**

crevisse: see **crevice.**

crevys: see **crevice.**

creyke: [dial.] see **rook.**

cri-de-guerre: [Fr.] see **escroll** and **motto.**

cricket: [M.E.] an orthopterous insect. *Acheta domestica;* similar in appearance to the grasshopper (q.v.).

crimping-iron: see **glazier's nippers.**

crined: [L.] descriptive of hair, either human or animal; a horse is ∼ of its mane.

crinita: It., crined.

crista: L., crested.

croce: It., cross.

crocketted mitre: a mitre (q.v.), having hook-like ornaments on the edges, like a Gothic pinnacle; now considered a decadent art-form.

crocodile: [L.] a large amphibious saurian, *Crocodilus niloticus;* r. but of significance in the armorial achievements of explorers and others whose work has been in connection with Egypt and the River Nile.

crocus: see **saffron.**

croissant: Fr., crescent.

croix: Fr., cross.

Croix de Guerre: (Belgium) f. 1915. Insignia—*Badge:* bronze cross paty notched, crossed swords between the arms, with a central medallion depicting a lion rampant, the whole ensigned by a crown. *Riband:* red with five narrow green stripes; in 1941 the Belgian Government in England authorized the continuing award of the croix, the riband having six green stripes—three at each edge.

Croix de Guerre (France) f. 1915. Insignia—*Badge:* a bronze cross paty with swords in saltire between the arms; a central medallion depicting a head symbolizing the Republic, crowned with a laurel wreath, is surrounded by the inscription *Republique Française. Riband:* green, edged red, with five equally spaced red stripes; in 1921 a Croix de Guerre for French and colonial troops serving abroad was authorized, of identical design but having *Theatre d'Operations Exterieurs* on the reverse, with a riband of blue having wide red edges; in 1939 the croix was confirmed for continuing award, the design being unchanged save for the date 1939 inserted on the reverse; the riband—red with four green stripes placed centrally.

Cromp, Laurence: first and only holder of the office of Carolina Herald (q.v.). York Herald, 1700. Former Portcullis Pursuivant, 1689.

cronel: a crown, or cover, or guard for a lance-point, as used in tournaments, giving the lance head the appearance of a f.d.l.

crosier: [L.] strictly, the insigne of an archbishop, but used indiscriminately also for a bishop: a cross paty (q.v.) within an annulet (q.v.) gold, raised upon a staff and carried in procession; alt. spelling 'crozier'. (226)

crosier-case: appears only in the arms of the bishopric of Basle; the same as the crosier-head in the civic arms, and probably repre-senting a leather, or an embroidered fabric, cover.

crosier-head: actually the crooked head of a pastoral staff (q.v.). It is employed, notably in the arms of the Swiss town of Basle, where it takes two forms. *Urban:* a simple, clean curve, facing dexter. *Rural:* a crocketed curve facing sinister; the field of both is argent, the former sable, the latter, gules. Both terminate in base with three points as 'erased' (q.v.).

cross: [O.E.] the fusion of a fess (q.v.) and a pale (q.v.); also known as a Greek cross and as a plain cross. All four limbs of the ~ extend to, and are in contact with the edges of the shield. When a ~ gules appears on an argent field it may be briefly described as a ~ of St George, which is the national ~ of England, surmounting, in the Union Jack (q.v.) the combined saltires (q.v.) of SS Andrew and Patrick. The palar element of the ~ is longer than the fesswise element solely because of the proportions of the shield: when a ~ appears upon a chief (q.v.) —as in the arms of the former London County Council—the opposite effect is obtained. (8, 218)

cross, conjoined in: of a number of small shapes set together in cruciform juxta-position; the lozenge (q.v.), the rustre (q.v.), the mascle (q.v.), and the fusil (q.v.) are the shapes most usually employed for this purpose.

cross couped: see **humetty.**

cross fourché: see **fourché.**

Cross of Honour: (South Africa) f. 1952 for gallantry in action. Insignia—*Badge:* a green enamel cross of eight points with gold eagles between the arms, and a central medallion bearing the South African flag, surrounded by the legend *Honoris Crux* in gold on red enamel. *Riband:* green with a red and white stripe at each edge.

cross sinople: see **sinople.**

cross-bow: see **arbalest.**

cross-crossed: see following entry.

cross-crosslet: a cross humetty (q.v.) with a short traverse (q.v.) on each limb; a r. alt. is 'cross-crossed'; ~, when extended to the limits of the field (which is very r.), is not 'anchored' (q.v.) nor 'fixed' (q.v.) but is ~ 'entire'. (212)

cross-hatching: see **hatching.**

cross-paty indented: see **eight points, cross of.**

cross-paty notched: see **eight points, cross of.**

crosses: see under the various crosses—**Latin cross, plain cross,** etc.

crow: see **rook.**

Crown, Most Exalted Order of the: (Malaysia) f. 1958 in one class. Insignia—*Collar:* twenty-two links of gold stars on a yellow enamel background alternating with a gold star and crescent above crossed kris. *Badge:* a five-point gold star with a medallion of yellow enamel bearing in gold a crescent, a crown, and the motto of the Order. *Star:* the badge surmounting a nine-point gold star. *Riband:* yellow with a central red stripe, and edged blue, white, blue.

Crown, Order of the: (Belgium) f. 1897 by K. Leopold II as K. of the Congo and absorbed by Belgium in 1908. The Order has five classes. Insignia—*Badge:* white enamelled star in ten points with gold rays between the arms; a central medallion of blue enamel depicts, in gold, the Belgian crown; the badge is ensigned with a gold and green laurel wreath. *Star:* the unensigned badge on a ten-point star with alternate rays in gold and silver.

Crown of India, Imperial Order of: f. by Q. Vict. in 1878 for ladies. Insignia—*Badge:* Imperial monogram in diamonds, pearls and turquoises with an oval pearl border, ensigned with a jewelled Imperial crown. *Riband:* light blue, edged white, worn as a bow on left shoulder.

Crown of Italy, Order of the: f. 1868 in five classes to commemorate the unification of Italy. Insignia—*Badge:* white enamelled cross with gold knots of Savoy between the arms; a central medallion depicts the crown of Savoy in gold on blue enamel. *Star:* silver, of eight points, surmounted by the badge's medallion surrounded by the inscription, in gold on white, *Victorius Emmanuel II Rex Italise MDCCCLXVIII,* and ensigned by a crowned Imperial eagle bearing the arms of Savoy on its breast.

---

139. Argent, a chevron between three hazel leaves vert.
Hazelrigg, Leicestershire.

140. Argent, a chevron between three pheons sable.
John Smert (Garter King of Arms).

141. Argent, a chevron sable between three sykes.
Sykes, Yorkshire.

142. Argent, a chevron between three estoiles sable.
Morduant.

143. Gules, a chevron between three bats sable.
George J. Bascom.

144. Argent, a fess azure between, in chief, two pairs of barnacles and, in base, a rose, all gules.
Thurning of Harroden Parva.

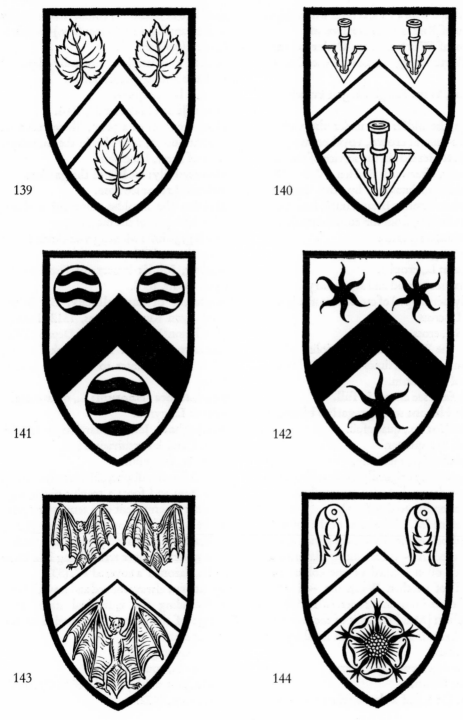

139

140

141

142

143

144

Riband: red with a wide central white stripe.

Crown of Rue: see **rue, crown of.**

Crown of Würtemberg, Order of the: see **Würtemberg, Order of the Crown of.**

Crowne, Wm: Rouge Dragon Pursuivant, 1638.

crowns, heraldic: see under the various crowns—**naval crown, royal crown,** etc.

Croyslett Herald: in the service of the Earl of Derby, afterwards K. Hen. IV, in 1390; probably maintained by the Earl of Warwick (Thomas Beauchamp); hence, the name of office, from the crosses-crosslets in the Beauchamp arms.

croze: see **grose.**

crucicula: L., crosslet.

crucifix: see **sacred** and **legendary.**

crusilly: semé (q.v.) of crosses-crosslet (q.v.).

crux: L., cross.

cruz: Sp., cross.

crwth: the Welsh word for 'violin' which instrument is sometimes so blazoned in the arms of Welshmen.

cry, in full: see **chase, in full.**

cryptic blazon: see **segregative blazon.**

cuadrifolio: Sp., quatrefoil.

cuartel: Sp., quarter.

cuartelado: Sp., quarterly.

cube: probably originally a dice without the spots, so drawn, but now apparently having no relationship to dice (q.v.).

cubit-arm: [M.E.] a section of the forearm couped below the elbow: the hand, u.o.s., is clenched. A ~ is bare unless blazoned as habited; often habited of one colour and 'cuffed' of another. When the ~ is thus clad the hand remains proper. (201, 293)

cucumber: [M.E.] the fruit of the creeping plant *Cucumis sativus*; used in heraldry for ca. reasons.

cuernas de ciervo: Sp., attires.

cuff: see **fanon.**

cuffed: [M.E.] of a sleeve when the wrist-band is to be of another colour: it is generally accompanying a cubit-arm (q.v.) which is habited (q.v.) and ~.

cuirass: a breastplate, normally depicted with the arming-points flotant.

cuisse, à la: see **quise.**

Cullen, John: Islay Herald, 1661.

culm: the stem of a plant, 'three culms of papyrus' occur, *inter alia*, in the municipal arms of Bury, Lancashire.

cultivated lily: see **lily of the garden.**

cultivated rose: see **rose.**

culverin: the heraldic name for a short, wide-bore gun of the mortar type.

Cuming, John[1]: Messenger-at-Arms to the Lyon Court, 1775.

Cuming, John[2]: Procurator Fiscal to the Lyon Court, 1808.

Cumming of Inverallochy, Sir Wm: Lord Lyon King of Arms, 1512. Former Marchmont Herald and Lyon Depute, 1508.

Cummyng, James: Lyon Clerk Depute, 1770. Herald-painter to the Lyon Court, 1770.

cumulationes armorum: L., quartering.

cuneus: L., gyron.

Cunningham, James: Marchmont Herald, 1625. Carrick Pursuivant, 1617.

cuore: It., fess point.

cup: [O.E.], a hemispheroidal vessel mounted on a stem and foot: a trophy given, e.g., as either a permanent or a temporary prize to the winner of an athletic contest. The ~ in heraldry is generally provided with a hemispherical cover terminating in a knob and is blazoned 'a covered ~'. (337)

cup, acorn: always slipped and leaved. Notwithstanding the individual status as a charge of the acorn, the kernel does not appear alone.

cuppy: see **engrailed.**

currens: L., courant.

Currie, James: Islay Herald, 1636. Ormonde Pursuivant, 1622.

curry-comb: a stiff brush used in grooming horses: depicted as rectangular in shape, the bristles downward. It is sometimes shown to have a side-handle, at others an arched strap over the back, but generally with no aid to gripping at all. It is r. in its occurrence.

curtalax: see **sabre.**

curtelace: see **sabre.**

curtilaxe: see **sabre.**

curvated: curved inward, generally having reference to the limbs of a cross.

curvo: It. and Sp., enarched.

cushion: [O.F.] lit. a bag constructed from fabric filled with feathers, flock, or some other resilient medium; in heraldry depicted, generally, square upon the field, but may be lozenge-wise. At each corner, whether blazoned or not, a tassel extends in line with the diagonal: the sides are sometimes fringed, but not unless so blazoned. The tassels may be different in colour to the ~ ; the fringes of yet a third. A ~ often appears secondarily as a rest for a beast (e.g. lamb) or an object (e.g. crown). Alt. terms 'pillow' and 'oreiller'. (224, 244).

Cuthbert, cross of St: a cross paty quadrate, often described and depicted as either the head of a Celtic cross or as a cross globical.

cutlass: see **sabre.**

cutting knife: see **basket-makers' tools.**

cyclamor: r. term for a circular orle (q.v.). In Fr. and Sp. blazon, an annulet.

cygnet: [M.E.] lit. a young swan; used as an alt. for swan without reference to the bird's age.

cymbal: a musical instrument similar to a gong; used for ca. reasons.

cymbalatus: L., gorged.

cypress: a tall, slender tree having dark green leaves, used as a symbol of mourning; *Cupressus sempervirens.*

Cyril and Methodius, Order of SS: (Kingdom of Bulgaria) f. 1909 as a one-class order. Insignia—*Badge:* a gold-edged cross paty of light-blue enamel, with red enamel flames surmounted by a silver f.d.l. between the arms; a central medallion depicts the saints, and is surrounded in blue on gold by the legend *Ex Oriente Lux. Star:* a gold Maltese cross with red flames surmounted by silver f.d.l. between the arms, bearing centrally the head of a seraphim surmounting six red enamel wings. *Riband:* light red.

Dacre knot: three loops, one in pale, one in bend, one in bend sinister the ends pendant, flotant and tasselled. The family embellish it with two other badges: the dexter end is looped round an escallop, the sinister round a ragged staff.

dagger: see **sword.**

Dagnell, Allen: York Herald, 1530. Former Guisnes Pursuivant, 1528.

Daill, John: see **Dale, John.**

daisy: generally the large ox-eye daisy or marguerite, *Chrysanthemum leucanthemum,* is intended, being a cant on the feminine personal name; but where no such interpretation exists the small, wild field-daisy, *Bellis perennis,* may be assumed. (379)

Dale, John: Snowdoun Herald, 1684. Kintyre Pursuivant, 1668. Also spelt 'Daill'.

Dale, Robert: Richmond Herald, 1721. Former Suffolk Herald, 1707; former Blanch Lyon Pursuivant, 1694.

Dallas, James: Lyon Clerk Depute, 1715.

Dalton, Laurence: Norroy King of Arms, 1558. Former Richmond Herald, 1547; former Rouge Croix Pursuivant, 1546.

Dalyell, Lt.-Col. Gordon: Unicorn Pursuivant, 1939.

dance: see following entry.

dancetty: a fesswise line of partition inclining sharply up, and equally sharply down again, forming three peaks across the shield: a fess ∼ may be blazoned as 'a dance'. (262)

Danish axe: a broad axe with a vertical tube in the flat, hammerlike butt through which the haft passes, slightly concave on the underside, more heavily concave on the upper-side, and distinguished by a deep engrailment in that surface similar to the seax (q.v.). It is the implement generally depicted as the headman's axe.

Dannebrog, cross of: a cross paty throughout gules fimbriated argent, in the arms of both Anne of Denmark, daughter of Frederick II, and consort of K. James VI and I, and Alexandra, daughter of K. Christian IX, and consort of K. Ed. VII.

Dannebrog, Order of: f., it is thought, in 1219 by K. Waldemar; the Order was revived in 1671 and given new statutes in 1693. In six classes and a cross of honour. Insignia—*Badge:* an oblong white enamel cross with gold-rimmed edges of red enamel; gold crosses between the arms, which bear the Order's motto *Gud og kon gen. Badge:* ensigned by the reigning monarch's cypher and crown; the sixth-class badge is worked in silver and enamel, and the Cross of Honour is unenamelled silver. *Star:* a seven-point silver star surmounted by the unensigned badge, with no cross between the arms, and bearing centrally a crowned letter W. *Riband:* white with crimson edges.

danse: r. alt. spelling of dance (q.v.).

Darge, James: Messenger-at-Arms to the Lyon Court, 1673.

Darnaway Pursuivant Extraordinary: a name of office formerly employed in Scotland.

dart: see **javelin.**

Davidson, Patrick: Ross Herald, 1567. Kintyre Pursuivant, 1557.

Davy-lamp: a miner's gauze-protected lamp, named after its inventor Sir Humphry Davy (1778–1829), employed in the arms of that family and, secondarily, in the arms of families, corporations, and commercial companies connected with coal-mining. Often 'in the outer hand of a miner proper' when acting as a supporter. Also blazoned as 'safety-lamp' and as 'miner's lamp'.

daw: [M.E.] the jackdaw *Corvus monedula*; generally employed for ca. reasons. (97, 112)

---

145. Argent, a chevron ermines between three blackamoors' heads.
Blaker, Sussex.

146. Gules, a chevron ermine between three ananas fruits Or.
Pyne.

147. Gules, a chevron between three flesh-pots Or.
Wethered.

148. Argent, a chevron between three lozenges ermines.
Shaw.

149. Argent, on a chevron sable another ermine between three chamber-pieces discharging.
De La Chambre, Sussex.

150. Sable, a chevron between three drums, argent.
Tabouris.

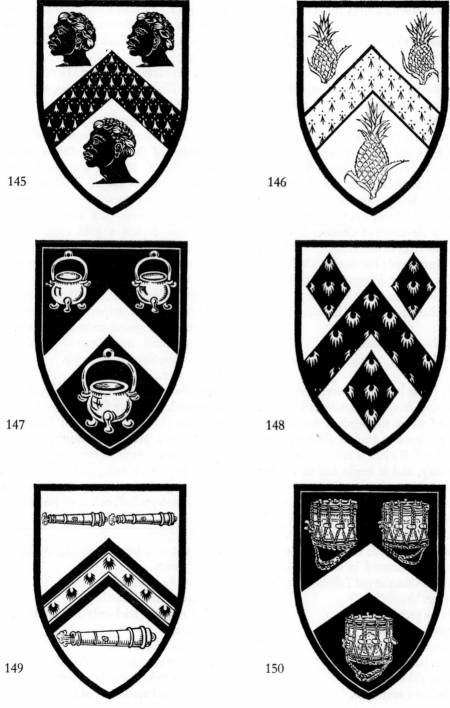

145

146

147

148

149

150

Dawes, Thomas: Rouge Croix Pursuivant, 1570.

days of the week, blazon by: see **segregative blazon.**

De Haviland, John: York Herald, 1872. Former Rouge Croix Pursuivant, 1866.

De la Gatta, Laurence: Rouge Croix Pursuivant, 1515.

De Laton's Roll, Sir Robert: (c. 1370) a roll of arms and names of kings, princes, dukes, earls, barons, knights, and esquires, written by Sir R. de L. at the dictation of his father, being part of the evidence adduced in the Scrope *v.* Grosvenor (q.v.) hearing in the Court of Chivalry (q.v.).

death's head: the human skull. Now seldom, if ever, employed; but in the XVIII cent. with the macabre interest and outlook of the period it was thought to be a sober, serious charge, and was in consequence admired.

debruised: see **surmounted.**

dechaussé: [Fr.], r. alt. for 'trononné' (q.v.).

decked: [Teut.] lit. to cover; specifically with fine, or decorative, attire. In heraldry, of a bird when the feathers are shaded, edged, or tipped of a colour differing from the bird itself. If a bird is to be ~ the patent will specify, and it ought not to be, but sometimes is, employed as artist's licence: e.g. Barclays Bank have an eagle sable; in some representations it is decked gold with, it must be confessed, a very fine effect.

decollated: beheaded; the head of St John Baptist is so blazoned in the arms of the Worshipful Company of Tallow Chandlers. Reduced to 'decollé'.

decollé: see previous entry.

decrement: see **moon.**

decrescent: see **crescent.**

decussius: [L.] saltire.

deeble: see **dibble.**

Deed Poll: see **surname.**

deer: [O.E.] the fallow deer which should be distinguished in drawing by flat, palmated tynes (q.v.), but which is very often drawn as a stag (q.v.).

Dees, Francis: Windsor Herald, 1510. Former Bluemantle Pursuivant, 1508. Also spelt 'Dyes'.

defamed: [L.] specifically of a lion, but applicable to any beast, deprived of his tail.

Defender of the Realm, Order of the: (Malaysian) f. 1959 in five classes and a medal. Insignia—*Badge:* a white enamel star of eleven points with a gold crescent and star between the arms; a central medallion depicts a gold cross and the Order's motto *Under God's Protection* in Jawi and Romanise. *Star:* the badge superimposed on a silver-gilt star of twelve points. *Riband:* blue, edged yellow, with white–red–white stripes centrally; a collar is granted to grand crosses, consisting of eleven linked medallions depicting the arms of the States of Malaysia.

degen: Ger., claymore.

degoullant: r. alt. for 'distilling' (q.v.).

degraded, cross: see following entry.

degrees: [L. via M.E.] steps; hence of a plinth or a platform consisting of three (u.o.s.) rises, each decreasing in area as ascending in altitude; normally a plinth sustaining a Latin cross (q.v.) and blazoned as 'a cross degraded', or '. . . on (so many) ~ (or grices)', or '. . . degraded of (so many) ascents'. (209)

dejected: of a beast or an object fallen or overthrown.

déjoint: Fr., trononné.

dekklede: Afk., mantling.

Del Brugge, Richard: see **Bruges, Richard.**

delad: Swd., per fess.

delf: see **rebatements of honour.** (155)

delph: see **rebatements of honour.** (155)

delve: see **rebatements of honour.** (155)

delyce: an archaic form of 'fleur-de-lys' (q.v.).

demarcation lines: alt. for 'lines of partition' (q.v.).

Demetrius, St: appears in the municipal arms of Bucharest.

demi: [L.] half; of a beast couped (q.v.) at the waist. Beasts so treated are generally in the rampant (q.v.) attitude and the tail couped at the same level accompanies the half-trunk. ~-beasts may also be erased. A ~ f.d.l. may be either per fess (q.v.) or per pale: the former is normal; the latter must be stated unless the circumstances of its appearance make any other severance absurd. (197, 288)

demi-vol: a single wing; tip baseward u.o.s.

Dendy, Edward Stephen: Chester Herald, 1859. Former Surrey Herald Extraordinary, 1856; former Rouge Dragon Pursuivant, 1848.

Denis, St: see **or(r)iflamme.**

dentato: It., indented.

dentelé: Fr., indented.

dentellado: Sp., indented.

Derby Herald: in the service of the Earl of Derby (c. 1390), subsequently K. Hen. IV.

Derby Place: more generally known as Derby House and, commonly, as the College of Arms or as the Herald's College. After their being deprived of Coldharbour (q.v.) the officers of arms were without a seat, and held their chapter meetings in each other's homes, or in any chambers where such hospitality was offered. ~ was presented to the College by Q. Mary I, when the address was given as on Benet's Hill, between the west-door of St Paul's and Paul's wharf. On obtaining vacant possession the officers of arms set up their chambers and library and enjoyed a measure of comfort until the edifice was lost in the Great Fire of 1666, whereupon they became tenants on sufferance in Whitehall Palace. ~ was re-

erected as a quadrangular building round a courtyard with access through an arch opening on Benet's Hill. In the mid XIX cent. one wing of this building was demolished with Doctor's Commons to make way for Q. Vict. St. (London, E.C.4), which remains the postal address.

Dering Roll: (c. 1275) vellum true roll (q.v.), 8¼ in. by 8 ft. 8 in. painted on a pale green background containing 324 shields in rows of six with names over. Sir Edward Dering (d. 1644) had a weakness for 'ancestors', which is manifested in shield No. 61 having been altered from 'Nic. de Crioll' to 'Ric. fiz Dering'.

Derval Herald: active in 1361, possibly in the service of Sir Robert Knollys; also known as Sire de Derval.

desbrancado: Sp., raguly.

descent, arms of: paternal, or family arms that descend from father to offspring; a normal armorial possession.

Desirous Pursuivant: an officer of arms in the service of the Crown, 1435.

Dethick, Henry: Richmond Herald, 1677. Former Rouge Croix, 1660.

Dethick, Nicholas: Windsor Herald, 1583. Former Bluemantle Pursuivant, 1565.

Dethick, Sir Gilbert: Garter King of Arms, 1550. Formerly Norroy King of Arms, 1547; former Richmond Herald, 1540; former Rouge Croix Pursuivant (same year); former Hampness Pursuivant, 1536.

Dethick, Sir Wm: Garter King of Arms, 1587. Former York Herald, 1570; former Rouge Croix, 1567.

detriment: see **moon.**

deurgesny: Afk., per fess.

developed: of a flag to be depicted as an emblazoned square, or rectangle, projecting from the staff; to be drawn without folds and draping.

Devenish, Robert: Norroy King of Arms, 1700. Former York Herald, 1675.

Devereux Roll: (XV cent.) a general roll (q.v.) in book form, painted paper $5\frac{1}{8}$ by $6\frac{1}{2}$ in., containing 180 shields with names and blazons. It begins with the achievement of Devereux, Earl of Essex, which is accompanied by a genealogical note.

device: [M.E.] an achievement (q.v.) of arms, or any single part; a charge; the armorial composition that the heralds or pursuivants devise (q.v.) for a petitioner.

devise[1]: [M.E.] to plan; invent; fashion; create; hence, the act of designing a coat of arms which, on approval, is granted by the kings of arms.

devise[2]: current Fr., blazon for 'motto' (q.v.).

devise, in: r. obs. alt. for the first diminutive (q.v.) of an ordinary (q.v.); 'a bend $\sim$' is a bendlet (q.v.).

Devoir Pursuivant: maintained by Walter Lord Hungerford; active in 1429.

Dewar of Balgonie, David: Snowdoun Herald, 1715.

d'Ewes Roll, Sir Symonds: see **Styward's Roll.**

dexter: [Gk via L.] pertaining to the right-hand; hence, the left-hand side of a shield when depicted. (The armed man carrying the shield is behind it.)

dexter-base: the area of the shield to the observer's left, in the lower portion of the shield.

dexter-chief: an area, roughly square, of about a third of the shield's width, situated at the top of the shield and to the observer's left.

dextra: It., dexter.

dextre: Fr., dexter.

dextrochère: Fr., dexter arm.

dez: r. alt. for 'dice' (q.v.).

d'Hozier: name of a family which, for several generations in the XVIII cent., held the monopoly of 'juge d'armes' of France.

diamond: see **segregative blazon.**

diapering: an artistic expedient to relieve the monotony of an extensive, uncharged area of field (q.v.) or ordinary (q.v.). $\sim$ was introduced early in XIII cent. into heraldic art when the arms of assumption (q.v.) then in use were basically of simple form, e.g. 'azure, a bend Or', for Scrope. The three plain sections acquired 'surface interest' by having a repeat pattern of a non-heraldic character executed upon them in a darker shade of the same colour. The illuminators of manuscripts and the makers of leaded lights used $\sim$ in a most effective manner. Today, competent heraldic artists introduce

---

151. Per pale Or and vert, a chevron between three whelk-shells all counterchanged.
Sir Neville Wilkinson (last Ulster King of Arms).

152. Sable on a chevron between three round-towers argent masoned of the field as many ogresses.
Towers.

153. Gules, on a chevron argent three bars-gemel sable.
Throckmorton, Coughton.

154. Per chevron embattled argent and gules three escallops counterchanged.
Hudson, Melton Mowbray.

155. Argent, a chevron gules fretty Or between three delves, sable.
Delves, Sussex.

156. Azure, a chevron Or between three limbecks argent.
Worshipful Company of Pewterers.

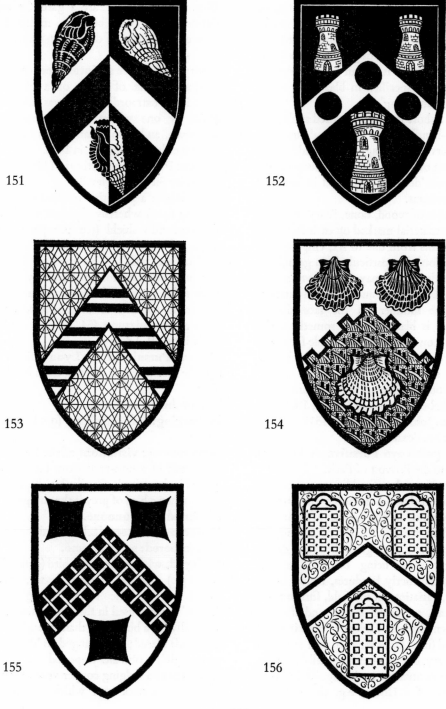

151   152

153   154

155   156

~ into their work whether in colour, or line-drawing, and an officer of arms might ask his artist to do so, but it must be emphasized that although ~ is an adjunct to heraldic art it is not an heraldic device, and is never specified in blazon. A r. alt. term is 'damasking'.

dibble: a short length of pointed stick with a cross-handle at the other end, used by gardeners for opening soft ground for the reception of seeds, roots, and young plants. Also spelt 'deeble'; employed in heraldry for ca. reasons.

dice: cubes of wood, bone, ivory, or other suitable material marked on each face with round spots from one to six, employed in 'casting lots', but particularly in gambling. In heraldry they may be drawn as flat squares, but most frequently are in perspective. The number on the face that is affrontée is blazoned, and sometimes the numbers on the two other visible faces will be stated; if not, the cube is heavily shaded. Very r. alt. term 'dez'.

Dick, George: Ormonde Pursuivant, 1725.

Dick, Robert: Rothesay Herald, 1804.

Dickson, John: Ross Herald, 1517.

diestea: Sp. dexter.

Dieu y pourvoye Pursuivant: 1430, attached to the Provost of Paris.

difference, marks of: additions to a coat of arms to distinguish between the various persons who, in the course of time, are entitled to wear it. Marks of cadency or brisures (q.v.) distinguish between cadets (younger sons, being brothers in one family). Formerly bordures, bends, bends sinister, variations of the field, furs in place of metals, accidental forms, and the like were employed. Cadency markings in England (in so far as they are used at all) are temporary, but ~ ,often originally brisures, become permanent to distinguish between branches of a House, e.g. the Duke of

Westminster bears 'azure a garb Or undifferenced'; Lord Ebury, 'a mullet for difference'. Marks of distinction (q.v.) are also ~.

dignity, cap of: see **maintenance, cap of.**

Diligens: name of office of a Scottish Pursuivant extraordinary: it was filled, in 1472, by one whose personal name is unknown, and who became Ross Herald, known only as 'Diligens', in 1476.

Diligent Pursuivant: active in 1431, maintained by Sir Ralph Neville.

dimidiation: a primitive method of marshalling (q.v.) whereby the dexter half of the husband's shield (cut per pale) was displayed on one shield with the sinister half of the wife's. This method led to deceptive combinations, particularly when both fields were of the same colour; and also to the apparent creation of some very incongruous mixtures. (54, 107)

dimidiatus: [L.] demy.

Dingwal Pursuivant: see **Lyon Office.**

dip: the measurement of a flag from head to foot.

dirk (or **durk**): see **sword.**

discharging: of chambers (q.v.) when firing.

disclaimer: see **visitations of the heralds.**

disclosed: of a non-predacious bird when poised in the attitude described as 'displayed' (q.v.) when a bird of prey is the charge.

disjointed: see **trononné.**

disjunctum, a latere: [L.], couped.

dismembered: see **trononné.**

displayed, with wings: of a bird (generally an eagle) perched, facing dexter, with wings raised. The terms 'rising' and 'rizant' are also used in this connection but generally for a bird other than an eagle.

disposed: placed; set; arranged, as 'disposed in triangle'; r. obs. alt. 'disponed'.

distillatory: a bulging copper vessel drawn inward to a neck over which is fitted a

DOMINUS·MIHI·ADIUTOR

PLATE V   Sable, on a cross engrailed argent a lion passant gules between four leopard's faces azure:
on a chief Or a rose of the third barbed and seeded proper between two Cornish choughs.
   Behind the shield a legantine and an archiepiscopal cross in saltire; the whole ensigned
with a cardinal's hat.
   SUPPORTERS: On each side a griffin per fess gules and argent, wings elevated, beaked, eared,
and tufted Or, each grasping, and displaying above the shield, a pillar gold: the whole
resting upon a plinth proper, inscribed in text-letters sable, *Dominus Mihi Adiutor*.
Thomas Wolsey (Cardinal)
[*Note:* This achievement has survived as the armorial bearings of Christ Church, Oxford.
This college, which was projected by Cardinal Wolsey, was to have borne the name
'Cardinal College'.]

spherical dome having a tube (or two tubes —one to each side) extending laterally, turned downward, and wound in a spiral forming a condensing coil (or coils) called 'worms'; below, and not joined to the coil, stands an open, cylindrical vessel termed the 'bolt-container'. (307)

distilling: exuding drops frequently of blood, and blazoned ' ~ guttae de sang', of a beast wounded, or a head or limb severed.

distinction, marks of: additions, of either a permanent or a temporary character, for the purpose of calling attention to some special status; e.g. the Badge of the Baronet (q.v.).

Distinguished Conduct Medal: f. 1854 to replace the Meritorious Service Medal, for N.C.O.s and men. The medal, of silver, originally bore a design of the Royal Arms surrounded by military trophies; since the reign of K. Ed. VII the obverse has borne the effigy of the conferring sovereign and the appropriate legend, e.g. *Edwardus VII Rex Imperator*; the reverse bears the legend, in four lines, *For Distinguished Conduct in the Field. Riband:* equal stripes of crimson, dark blue, crimson.

Distinguished Flying Cross: f. 1918 for acts of valour or devotion to duty 'performed whilst flying in active operations against the enemy'; decoration is of silver, being a 'cross flory terminated in the horizontal and base bars with bombs, the upper bar terminating with a rose, surmounted by another cross composed of aeroplane propellers charged in the centre with a roundel within a wreath of laurels a rose winged ensigned by an Imperial crown thereon the letters *RAF.*' Reverse bears the royal cypher and 1918. *Riband:* $1\frac{1}{4}$ in. in width, alternate white and violet stripes $\frac{1}{8}$ inch in width, diagonally at 45° from left to right.

Distinguished Flying Medal: f. 1918 for

award to non-commissioned ranks of the Royal Air Force on the same conditions as pertain for the Distinguished Flying Cross. Insignia: a silver oval bearing an effigy of the sovereign. *Reverse:* within a wreath of laurel the date 1918, and Athena Nike seated on an aeroplane, a hawk rising from her right arm above the words *for Courage. Riband:* $1\frac{1}{4}$ inches in width, alternate violet and white stripes $\frac{1}{16}$ in. wide running at 45° diagonally to the wearer's left.

Distinguished Service Cross: f. as Conspicuous Service Cross in 1901, the present designation was adopted in October 1914; amended for gallant and distinguished service at sea. A silver cross paty bearing centrally a roundel with the crowned royal cypher. *Reverse:* plain. *Riband:* equal stripes of blue, white, blue.

Distinguished Service Medal: f. 1914 for petty officers and men of the Royal Navy and N.C.O.s and men of the Royal Marines who show 'bravery and resource under fire'. The medal, of silver, bears the effigy of the conferring sovereign and the appropriate legend, e.g. *Georgius V. Britt. Omn. Rex et Ind: Imp. Reverse:* within a laurel wreath broken by a crown the words *For Distinguished Service. Riband:* equal stripes of blue, white, blue, the white having a narrow central stripe of blue.

Distinguished Service Medal: (India) f. 1907 for members of the Indian Regular Forces who distinguished themselves in peace or war. *Obverse:* effigy of K. Ed. VII and the legend *Edwardus VII Kaiser I Hind. Reverse:* a wreath of laurel surrounding the words *For Distinguished Service. Riband:* maroon with broad edges of blue.

Distinguished Service Order: f. 6 September 1886 under statute subsequently amended. From 5 February 1931 Companionship of the Order is conferred solely for gallantry, or for distinguished service in action. Insignia: a gold cross enamelled white, edged gold, bearing centrally in a wreath of laurel the Imperial crown in gold on red enamel; the reverse bears the royal cypher in gold, on red, with a laurel wreath. Worn from the left breast from a riband of red, edged blue.

Divine monogram: the sigil of the Christian Church before A.D. 400 when the cross was adopted; being in appearance a Roman capital X having a capital P struck through the intersection, but actually a combination of the greek cyphers *rho* (P) and *chi* (X). The ∼ appears chiefly in ecclesiastical heraldry.

divisa¹: It., bar.

divisa²: Sp., motto.

divise: Fr., bar.

divorce, effect of: the marriage, being made null and void by divorce, the marital achievement, either an impalement or the assumption of an escutcheon of pretence (q.v.), is no longer valid. Each party, irrespective of which was the plaintiff, must revert to the pre-marital achievement; hence, the ex-wife will be displaying her paternal arms on a lozenge, whereby she is armorially equal to her spinster sister. This might be a matter productive of some embarrassment; hence, a divorced woman, wishing to remain actively armigerous, may add to her lozenge a mark of distinction, e.g. a mascle the size and colour of which is subject to the same set of rules as those governing brisures (q.v.).

dock: see **burdock**.

docken: [dial.] a raven or a crow.

Dods of Muircleugh, Robert: Marchmont Herald, 1764. Herald-painter, 1764.

doe: [O.E.] female fallow deer, *Curvus dama*.

dog: makes its appearance early, the breed first represented being the greyhound, blazoned 'levrier' (frmd on O.F.–M.E. 'leveret', a hare). Also early is the hunting-hound, blazoned 'rache', alt. spelling 'ratch'. The keen scent and massive jaw, together with the soft, hanging ear characterize the hound which, bearing the name of 'talbot', survives as the heraldic dog to be depicted when no specific breed is mentioned. The 'alant' (mastiff or wolf-hound), is a ca. charge for all branches of the family of Allen, and is always represented with pricked ears. Sometimes spelt 'aland'.

---

157. Per chevron crenelly Or and sable, three pairs of compasses expanded counter-changed.
Cartwright.

158. Per chevron azure and Or: in chief, two fleurs-de-lys of the last and, in base, a joscelyn sable and of the first.
Joslin.

159. Per chevron azure and sable, three cherubim Or.
Chandler.

160. Argent, a chevron dovetailed between three braces and bits erect sable.
Worshipful Company of Furniture Makers.

161. Per chevron argent and vert, in chief, two bluebottles proper and, in base, a fountain.
Lord Chorley.

162. Per chevron sable and argent, in chief, two skillets, handles inward and saltirewise Or each over flames of fire proper and, in base, a cross paty fitchy of the first.
The National Society's Training College in Domestic Subjects.

157

158

159

160

161

162

In addition to these 'classic' heraldic dogs, most other breeds, blazoned by name, have appeared in arms, as a charge, as a crest, or as a supporter; and notwithstanding that they are to be depicted in recognizable form, they may, nevertheless, assume heraldic attitudes and be of heraldic colours; they may also be 'eared' of another colour. ~s are correctly blazoned as in any of the heraldic poses, but there are special terms for some of them. (42)

dog-fish: see **shark.**

dolphin: [M.E.] a marine mammal honoured in legend and folklore from pre-Christian times. Symbolic of love and kindness, diligence, and speed; the friend of mariners whom he would gladly rescue in the event of shipwreck. In 1349, the Province of Dauphiné was ceded to France, and the title Dauphin conferred upon the French king's eldest son who took the ~ as his ca. armorial device. In heraldic art the ~ is depicted naturalistically but with exaggerated fins and tail flukes. His normal orientation is naiant (q.v.), embowed (q.v.); when proceeding to the sinister, counter-embowed. If embowed is not specified it is taken for granted u.o.s.; the alt. is 'extended'—straight from head to tail. ~ may be 'finned' (q.v.) and 'scaled' (q.v.). (65)

domed: of a castle having a dome rising from within the battlements of the towers, which additions terminate in a flagstaff when the blazon states 'ensigns' or 'pennons flotant' to either dexter or sinister. The colour of and the charges upon such flags will be given.

Domville Roll: (c. 1470) vellum book, 11¼ in. by 1 ft. 3 in., painted with twenty shields to the page (four rows of five each), with names over, a total of 2840: the first 1760 are English family arms, so are the last 1039, but sandwiched between are forty-one saints, Saxons, and others.

Donaldson, Robert: Lyon Clerk Depute, 1755. Marchmont Herald, 1760.

door bolt: see **bolt, door.**

door staple: see **staple.**

doorsneden: D., per fess.

doppelgewolkt: Ger., nebuly.

doppelkreuz: Ger., patriarchal cross.

doppia: It., double; hence, of a cross with two traverse elements, as Patriarchal cross or cross of Lorraine.

doppio merlato: It., bretessy.

Dorc, Peter: Norroy King of Arms, 1780. Former Richmond Herald, 1764; former Bluemantle Pursuivant, 1763.

dormant [O.F.] lit. sleeping; hence, of a beast prone on its ventral surface, the fore-limbs extended and the head, with mouth shut and eyes closed, resting on them. (59)

dormiens: L., dormant.

dornen: Ger., engrailed.

Dorset Herald: in the service of Thomas Beaufort, Earl of Dorset, c. 1411; revived by K. Hen. VII in 1494 to serve Thomas Grey, Marquis of Dorset.

dory: [M.E.] a sea-fish, *Zeus faber*; also called 'St Peter's fish', spots on its skin being St Peter's fingermarks. Employed in ecclesiastical heraldry, and also for ca. reasons. The ~ is often associated with a key (q.v.) both being symbols of St Peter.

dosser: see **well-bucket.**

double arch: see **arch.**

double delta: two equilateral triangles interlaced: also named 'Solomon's seal' and 'Shield of David'. The symbol of Judaism, assumed as a 'national' badge by the Zionists.

double-attired: provided with four antlers.

double-belled: see **bell, hawk's.**

double-eared: see **jug.**

double-headed eagle: see **Imperial eagle.**

double quatrefoil: see **trefoil.**

double-queued: see **queued.**

doubled: [M.E.] of a cloak, other garment,

or mantling turned back to reveal some portion of the reverse side.

double tressure: see **tressure.**

Douglas, . . .: Lord Lyon King of Arms, 1410.

Douglas, Florens: Rothesay Herald, 1574.

Douglas, John: Albany Herald, 1768. Bute Pursuivant, 1765.

Douglas, Wm¹: Carrick Pursuivant, 1753.

Douglas, Wm²: Marchmont Herald, 1735.

Douglas, Wm³: Rothesay Herald, 1790. Unicorn Pursuivant, 1764.

Douglas of Earnslaw, James: Lord Lyon Depute, 1689.

Douglas of Torquhen, George: Marchmont Herald, 1775.

dove: [O.E.] a pigeon, Columbidae, depicted with a tuft extending backward from the crown of the head; a feature that remains when blazoned 'proper' which term indicates a pink beak and legs, although gules is frequently specified. The ~ is symbolic of gentleness and peace; it also represents the Holy Ghost, in which role it is blazoned as 'a holy ~' and is within a glory (q.v.). The ~ perched and close (q.v.) very often holds in his beak a sprig of foliage; frequently, but not necessarily, olive. A holy ~ is often affrontée with wings displayed (q.v.). (119)

dovetailed: shaped like a truncated equilateral triangle, as the tail feathers of a dove. A line of partition consisting of such shapes run on, each being open at the narrow end. An ordinary ~ has open facing open and closed, facing closed, i.e. inward and outward ~ equipoised. (219)

Downes, Dudley: Rouge Dragon Pursuivant, 1704.

drache: Ger., wyvern.

draco: [Gk] general term for a snake or a dragon; hence, applied to pennons (q.v.) and standards (q.v.), they being snake-like (i.e. long, narrow, and flexible) in character.

The term is sometimes written 'dracones' in the chronicles.

Dragance: name of office of a Scottish Pursuivant Extraordinary; filled in 1429 by one whose personal name is not on record.

dragon [M.E.] a composite fictitious beast, part serpent, part crocodile, having four short legs terminating in eagle-like claws, a long curled tail terminating in a barb and a pair of membranous wings. The ~ is generally depicted incensed (q.v.) and receiving its death blow from the lance of St George who, armour clad, is mounted on a charger. In Christian mythology the ~ is generally evil, which is contrary to the Oriental attitude, but in Scottish heraldry there is an example of a beneficent rain-dragon, being the sinister supporter of the arms of Harry Pirie-Gordon of Buthlaw, whose dexter supporter is a kelpie (q.v.). A Chinese ~ is wingless. In both Fr. and Sp. current blazon, ~ is extended to include 'wyvern', which, with a final 'e', applies to It. (278)

dragon's head and tail: see **stainand.**

Drake Pursuivant: see **Ulster Office.**

drawing-board: see **royne.**

drawing-iron: see **wyre-drawers' tools.**

dreiblatt: Ger., trefoil.

dreieckschild: Ger., shield.

dress, symbolic: when an article of attire is outstanding, and universally recognized as insignia of a specific calling, it is sometimes employed in the arms of persons who are, or who have been active in the particular office, i.e. a mitre for a bishop, a wig for a judge, etc. (242, 342)

drieblad: D., trefoil.

driehoekig vlaggetje: D., pennon.

drinking pot: see **pewter-pot.**

drops: see **label.**

drum: see **tabor.**

Drummond, Alexander: Marchmont Herald, 1704.

Drummond Hay, Edward Wm Auriol: Lyon Clerk and Keeper of the Records, 1823.

Drysdale, Thomas: Lyon Clerk and Keeper of the Records, 1632. Islay Herald, 1627.

dubbel getinneerd: D., bretessy.

dubbelde binnesoom: Afk., double tressure.

dubbelörn: Swd., double-headed eagle.

Dublin Herald: see **Ulster Office.**

Dublin Roll: (temp. K. Hen. VI) paper book 8¼ by 10¼ in. containing 324 shields the majority in line drawing but some painted. The text is a transcription of part of Nicholas Upton's work; the shields are marginal.

ducal coronet: an heraldic device, having no objective existence, consisting of a circlet, or headband, heightened with four conventionalized strawberry leaves, three of which appear in drawing—one central and one at each side depicted in profile only. Also termed 'an open crown' and, in Scotland, an 'antique crown'. The ~ is generally a secondary charge: objects are enfiled (q.v.) with beasts gorged (q.v.) with a ~. When it does duty as a crown the beast, on the object so decorated, is often blazoned as 'ducally crowned' (q.v.). As a primary charge it is by no means unimportant, and it rises to the eminence of regal heraldry in some continental achievements, e.g. the Arms of Sweden. A very frequent usage is for it to do duty as the base, or medium, from which a crest emerges, in which capacity it may be described as a 'crest coronet'. (194)

ducally crowned: crowned with a ducal coronet (q.v.).

ducally gorged: gorged with a ducal coronet (q.v.).

duciper: obs. term for a cap of maintenance (q.v.).

duck: see **shoveller.**

Dugdale, Sir John: Norroy King of Arms, 1686. Former Windsor Herald, 1675.

Dugdale, Sir Wm: Garter King of Arms, 1677. Former Norroy K. of A., 1660; former Chester Herald, 1645; former Rouge

---

163. Per chevron azure and gules three covered salts argent garnished Or, shedding on both sides the salt, also argent.
The Worshipful Company of Salters.

164. Per chevron indented grady argent and gules, in chief two yellow-horned poppies slipped and leaved proper and, in base, a seahorse, supporting between the legs an open book argent.
Eastbourne Training College.

165. Gules, a chevron Or between three crosses paty argent: on a canton ermine a buck's head erased and attired sable.
Strickland, Boynton.

166. Per chevron argent and Or, in chief two bombshells fired, and in base an eagle's head erased proper.
Hardy.

167. Azure, a chain couped in chevron between three mitres argent: at the dexter end of the chain a padlock of the last.
Benedictine Abbey, Evesham.

168. Per fess Or and azure, a chevron gules between three mullets counterchanged and, *in augmentation*, a canton of England.
Lane.

163

164

165

166

167

168

Croix Pursuivant, 1640; former Blanch Lyon Pursuivant, 1638.

duke: [L.] the senior rank in the peerage. The first dukes were appointed by Hadrian to command expeditions. When the Empire's military and civil administrations were separated, a duke commanded the troops in each of the frontier provinces. At this time his status was below that of the original counts (q.v.), who were still personal aides and companions to the emperor, but, under the Merovingian and Carolingian kings, dukes came to exercise authority over groups of counts, and the title became hereditary and slowly took precedence over others. Sovereign and semi-independent duchies evolved, and certain of their holders were elevated to, or adopted the style of archduke (q.v.) or grand duke (q.v.). The first English duke was the Black Prince, created Duke of Cornwall by his father, K. Ed. III, in 1337.

duke's coronet: a circlet decorated with engraving, heightened with eight strawberry leaves, five only of which appear in drawing, those at each side being in profile. The cap, which is of crimson velvet turned up ermine, is generally omitted in armorial achievements, the helmet of rank (q.v.) being issuant.

dun-fly: r. alt. for 'gad-fly' (see **brimsey**).

Dunbar, James: Snowdoun Herald, 1682. Dingwall Pursuivant, 1675.

Duncan, Archibald: Lyon Clerk Depute, 1825.

Dundas, Younger of Fingask, Thomas: Lord Lyon Depute, 1744.

dung-hill cock: see **cock.**

Dunnett, Wm: Carrick Pursuivant, 1836.

Dunstable Roll, the First: (1308) an occasional roll recording 235 names and arms of those competing in a tournament held at Dunstable.

Dunstable Roll, the Second: (1334) true roll containing 135 names and blazons.

Dunstan, St: represented by his insignia, i.e. fire-tongs, in the civic arms of the Corporation of the Borough of Stepney.

Duram of Largs, Sir Alexander: Lord Lyon King of Arms, 1660.

duriatus: L., diapered.

Durroit, Roger: Lancaster Herald, 'Roy de North d'Angleterre', c. 1386.

Dutch boot: also blazoned as 'antique boot'; is drawn as a high-legged riding boot turned over at the top of another colour. A ∼ is sometimes spurred. (251)

Duty Officer: see **College of Arms.**

dawl: [dial.] nightshade, *Solanum nigrum*, having white flowers and black poisonous berries; hence, deadly nightshade of the genus *Atropa*; also called 'belladonna'.

dwarsbalk: D., fess.

dwarsbalke: Afk., bar.

Dyes, Francis: see **Dees, Francis.**

Dynastic Orders: see **House Orders.**

e, redundant final: see **spelling.**

eagle: [O.F.] a large, predacious bird used as a military ensign by the Romans and as the armorial device of the Holy Roman Empire and by the Russian, Austrian, German, and French empires. As important in continental heraldry as the lion (q.v.) is in British, and popular in heraldry in places beyond the Continent of Europe. The ∼ is the national emblem of the U.S.A. where it represents the indigenous bald or white-headed ∼ *Haliaetus leucocephalus*. Its most frequent position is displayed (q.v.) when the wings may be either 'elevated' (i.e. having the tips in the dexter- and the sinister-chief corners of the field) or 'inverted' (i.e. having the tips directed downward). The former was considered typically British and the latter continental, but this distinction can no longer be made.

~s and other birds of prey are described as 'armed' of their beaks and talons but non-predacious birds are (or should be) blazoned as 'beaked and membered' (or 'beaked and legged'). The rules governing the coloration of ~ armament are the same as those applied to the lion (q.v.). When the ~ turns his head and faces sinister he may be blazoned as 'regardant' (q.v.). But, having an exclusive term to describe the position, it is more correctly employed, i.e. 'recursant'. In continental arms one ~ only may appear on a shield; British heraldry is more generous, allowing three. When these limits are exceeded the birds should be blazoned as 'eaglets' and, if argent, as 'ospreys'. An interesting newcomer into the company of ~s is the Rhodesian fish-~. (107, 110, 114, 253)

Eagle Pursuivant: in the service of the Crown in 1389.

Eagle Vert Pursuivant: maintained by the earls of Salisbury; named from the arms of Monthermer.

eaglet: see **eagle.**

ear: [O.E.] the head of any kind of grain, 'bladed' of its leaves. The particular plant intended will be specified, e.g. ~ of wheat, ~ of oats, etc., but there is no difference observable in the drawing, except in the case of barley, which is (and is blazoned as) 'bearded', and rye, the head of which droops as though the stem were broken.

eared[1]: of the head of a garb (q.v.) when of a different colour to the stalks (q.v.).

eared[2]: see **dog.**

earl: [O.E.] the oldest, and once the first, but now the third, rank in the British peerage. Earls originally were set over counties by the king to administer and to preside over the county court together with the local diocesan bishop. At the time of their appointment the king girded the new earl with the 'sword of the county' (hence 'belted earl'), and this custom persisted until the time of James VI and I. After the Norman invasion the rank was equated with that of count (q.v.), and became hereditary; an earl's wife is a countess.

Earl Marshal [O.E.] originally the king's farrier, the office of marshal has risen to be eighth in the list of great officers of State, and today the Earl Marshal is head of the College of Arms, attends the sovereign at opening and closing Parliament, presides over the Court of Chivalry, and arranges all important public royal functions, namely coronations, weddings, and state funerals. The marshals were at one time supreme military commanders, in which sense the name lingers as Field Marshal, Marshal of the Royal Air Force, etc., and had the duty of arranging all combats in the lists. The post was probably first held by the Marshal family, as marshals of the household only, and then devolved onto the Clares. Ed. II granted the title to his younger brother, Earl of Norfolk, and Rich. II conferred it on Thomas Mowbray, who was granted the style 'Earl Marshal' in 1386. The title suffered many vicissitudes as the royal and political scene changed, but in 1672 Ch. II entailed it on the male line of the Howards, who have held it proudly ever since. The Earl Marshal puts 'E.M.' after his signature, and places two batons in saltire behind his arms as an additament of office. The marshals of France similarly evolved, and are now the holders of the rarely awarded highest rank in the French army. There were also Marshals of Ireland, and until 1716 the Keiths were Great Marischals of Scotland.

Earl Marshal's Court: see **Chivalry, Court of.**

earl's coronet: a circlet heightened with alternate pearls (q.v.) set upon points (q.v.) and strawberry leaves. Five pearls and four strawberry leaves appear in drawing.

Eastern crown: see **antique crown.**

écartelé: Fr., quarterly.

ecclesiastical hat: see **hat, ecclesiastical.**

échancré: Fr., engrailed.

eclipsed: see **moon** and **sun.**

écoté: Fr., raguly.

écu: Fr., shield.

écu en losange: Fr., a lozenge when employed to carry the arms of a lady.

editions of rolls: see **rolls of arms.**

edoc: a term used chiefly in Scotland for a dock-leaf. See also **burdock.**

Edward, Medal: f. 1907 in two classes as an award for heroism in mines or quarries, and subsequently extended to other industries. Insignia: first class—silver medal with the royal effigy. *Reverse:* for mining and quarrying awards—a miner rescuing a comrade, and the words *For Courage*; for industrial awards—a classical female figure holding a wreath, with the words *For Courage*. Second class—as first class but in bronze.

'ée' word-terminal: see **spelling.**

eel: a snake-like fish, *Anguilla latirostris*; also called 'grig'; an old inhabitant of the heraldic field being of economic importance in the Middle Ages. The ∼ is generally secondary: as in the heron's beak (q.v.), a gauntleted hand, or a cooking-pot. The conger, or great sea-∼, is also employed, and an ∼-head is that of the latter.

eel-pot: see **weel.**

eendje: D., duck.

eenhoorn: D., unicorn.

éffarouché: see **catamount.**

effe: Afk., plain.

effe soom: Afk., plain bordure.

effet: [O.E.] a shape of the word 'eft' [O.E.]; a generic term covering any lizard or lizard-like creature often applied to the newt (q.v.) but also to any unspecified lizard.

effray: r. alt. for 'forcene' (q.v.).

egg: in British heraldry it is symbolic, and is a recent importation from the Continent where it is ca. and old established. An ∼ proper, badly drawn, appears as a tapering cartouche.

---

169. Argent, a chevron engrailed sable between three columbines azure.
Worshipful Company of Cooks.

170. Argent, a chevron vert within a bordure gules.
Boardman.

171. Argent, two chevronels round-embattled sable between two sprigs of oak slipped and fructed proper and, in base, a cog-wheel azure.
Lord Kirkwood.

172. Sable, two chevronels between as many owls in chief and, in base, a wolf's head erased argent.
Howatson.

173. Argent, a chevron between three garbs gules all within a bordure compony argent and azure.
Sheffield of Normanby.

174. Or, a chevron inverted gules.
Municipal Corporation of Newport, Mon.

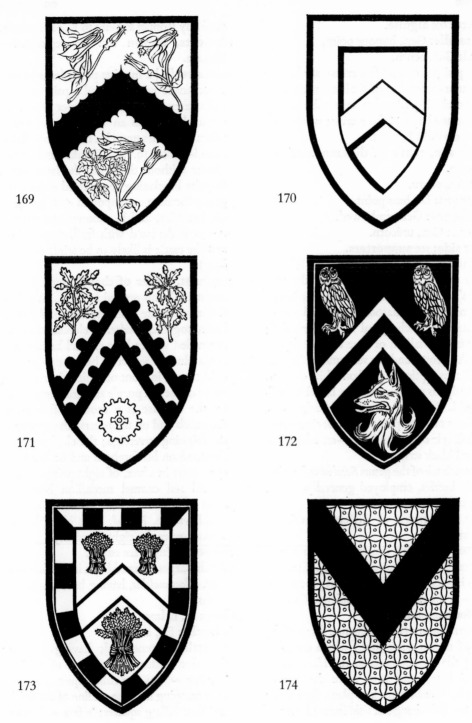

169

170

171

172

173

174

eguisce: see **aiguise.**

ehrenstelle: Ger., honour point.

eichel: Ger., acorn.

eight points, cross of: a cross paty having the outer extremities of the limbs narrowed, and notched (q.v.); when argent the ~ may be blazoned as a Maltese cross; when vert, as a cross of St Lazarus.

eighth son, mark of difference of: see **brisure.**

eikel: D., acorn.

eindepunt: D., base point.

eingebogen: Ger., embowed.

einhorn: Ger., unicorn.

either side: see **supporters.**

El-Rafidain, Order of: (Iraq) f. 1922 in three classes. El-Rafidain means 'the two rivers' and refers to the Tigris and Euphrates. Insignia: *Badge:* maroon enamelled star of seven points, each tipped with a silver ball; a central medallion of blue enamel depicts a gold cross, and is surrounded by an Arabic inscription in gold on white enamel; the badge is ensigned with a laurel wreath in gold. *Star:* the unensigned badge on a gold star of seven points. *Riband:* civil—red, with black edges; military—an additional central black stripe.

elder: a shrub of the genus *Sambucus,* bearing edible berries, employed generally for ca. reasons.

eldest son, mark of difference of: see **brisure.**

Eleanor cross: the ornate Gothic erections in stone, commemorative of Q. Eleanor, marking the route of her funeral procession. An ~ is the crest of the Municipal Council of Northampton.

electoral bonnet: a continental form of the cap of maintenance (q.v.) which ensigned (q.v.) the inescutcheon in the Hanovarian Royal Arms until 1816 when the Crown Royal of Hanover took its place, signalizing K. Geo. III's change of title from Elector of the Holy Roman Empire to K. of Hanover.

elements, blazon by: see **segregative blazon.**

elephant: [L.] a massive pachyderm having a prehensile proboscis and a pair of ivory tusks extending from the upper jaw. Very often blazoned as an 'elephant and castle' when he carries upon his back a crenellated round-tower (q.v.). Trunks and tusks appear without the beast, the latter often in pairs bracketing some third object, the group forming a compound crest (q.v.). In old heraldry, and in monumental brasses, the ~ is depicted with frail, slender legs, and the castle is likely to be triple-towered (q.v.).

Elephant, Order of the: (Denmark) f. in about 1457 and revised in 1693. Insignia— *Collar:* alternate gold elephants and towers linked together. *Badge:* an elephant in gold, enamelled white; blue enamel harnessings, and a blue carpet on its back, supporting a gold tower, in front of which sits a blacka-moor dressed in purple and holding a spear; on the obverse is a cross of five table-diamonds and on the reverse the cypher of the reigning sovereign; the elephant has a diamond on his forehead and brilliants for eyes. *Star:* in silver, of eight points, with a central red enamel medallion bearing a cross of six silver balls, surrounded by a laurel wreath. *Riband:* light blue (the sash is worn over the right shoulder).

elevated wings: see **eagle.**

elk: the largest horned beast in the family of deer, *Alces malchis,* having broad, spatulate horns.

elmo: It., helmet.

émanché: Fr., indented.

embattled: crenellated; having wall-top defensive battlements: as a line of partition 'per fess ~' has five rising squares, the end ones merging into the outline of the shield, and four falling squares: 'a fess ~' has five crenellations on the chiefmost edge, the lower edge remaining straight: if both edges are to be treated the blazon is 'a fess ~-counter-~' and the lower edge has its rising squares facing the falling squares of the upper edge: if falling are to face falling, and rising to face rising squares, the term used is 'bretesse', e.g. 'a fess (pale, bend, etc.) bretesse'. 'Crenelly' is an alt. term, but is obs.: a variation is 'round ~' in which the rising squares are semicircular at the top. (171). (The correct term for the falling squares is either 'embrasures' or 'crenells'; for the rising, 'merlons', but they are architectural and military, not heraldic terms.)

embelif: obs. for 'per bend sinister'.

embouché: [Fr.] of a fish's mouth when coloured differently from the body.

embowed: [M.E.] lit. bent as a bow; hence, of a fish, a marine-mammal, a serpent, or an inanimate object represented as conforming to a shallow S-shape: or of a human arm flexed at the elbow.

embrassé: a chevron (q.v.) or a field (q.v.) per chevron, from either the dexter or the sinister flank instead of from base.

embrasure: see **embattled.**

embrued: [M.E.] blood-stained; applied to an inanimate object, as a sword or a knife; alt. spelling 'imbrued'.

emerald: see **segregative blazon.**

emerass: a plate of steel attached frontally at the shoulder to cover the joint between the breastplate and the upper brassant. These varied in shape from roundels to escutcheons, and on them the arms might be painted: when they appear as charges they are indistinguishable from escutcheons. They are thought to be the origin of charges on the shoulders of supporters. Alt. term 'ailette'.

emmanché: [Fr.] a variation of the field (q.v.) which may also be described as 'barry-piley'. It was not employed in British heraldry until August 1957, when it was introduced into the arms granted by the Lord Lyon to Gordonstoun School, founded in 1934, by a German refugee. Because ~ (which has the alt. spelling 'enmanché') was unknown, a new method of expressing the pattern was attempted: i.e. 'per fess: in chief Or, a lymphad vert, the cutwater thereof a ram's head; the stern, a fish-tail raised and flexed inboard; under sail to the sinister, the square-sail proper, biremed with two banks of six oars each, in action, gules. In base, the sea barry-intradented argent and azure'. (Pl. VI.) A chief ~ would be termed, in today's heraldic idiom, 'per chevron throughout'—two straight lines of partition descending from centre-chief to the dexter- and the sinister-base corners of the chief.

emmet: [O.E.] an ant; a herd insect of the *Hymenopterous* order. Sometimes called a pismire, and likely to be depicted in numbers, 'a mount vert, semé of ants sable'. (84)

Empire Gallantry Medal: f. 1922 as the Medal of the Order of the British Empire for Gallantry. *Obverse:* the uncrowned effigy of the reigning sovereign. *Reverse:* the royal and Imperial cypher and the words *For Gallantry. Riband:* rose pink with pearl-grey edges (Civil); an additional central stripe of pearl-grey denotes an award in the Military Division. The medal was abolished when the George Cross (q.v.) was instituted in 1940, and holders of the medal were instructed to exchange it for the Cross.

enaluron: [Fr.] obs. for a bordure charged with birds.

enarched: of any ordinary given an upward curvature: a chief has only the baseward line curved, but the bend, the chevron, and the fess are curved (parallel) on both sides; alt. forms are 'arched' and 'archy', which latter is approaching obs.

encajado: Sp., indented.

encalved: mis-spelling of **enclaved** (q.v.).

enclaved: [O.F.] obs alt. for 'dovetailed' (q.v.); also spelt 'inclaved'.

encogido: Sp., sejant.

endorse: [M.E.] second diminutive of the pale (q.v.) being a quarter the width of the parent (or half the width of a pallet (q.v.)): a pale between two ~ may be blazoned 'endorsed', but is more likely to be described as 'cotticed' (q.v.).

endorsed: r. alt. for 'addorsed' (q.v.).

Endure: a Scottish Pursuivant Extraordinary, possibly maintained by the Earl of Crawford, since the holder of the office in 1455 was promoted to Lindsay Herald Extraordinary (q.v.) in 1463.

enfield: a composite fictitious beast having the slender body of a greyhound, the sleek head of a fox, the fore limbs of an eagle, with the hind-legs and tail of a wolf.

enfiled: [M.E.] encircled with; surrounded by. A sword (q.v.) passing through an open crown (q.v.) is ~ thereby.

englante: r. term relating to the oak-tree when fructed.

engolado: Sp., swallowing.

engoulé: Fr., swallowing.

engouled: [O.F.] of a beast into whose mouth is thrust a weapon, a cross, or even an ordinary. In continental arms an ordinary (particularly the bend), may issue at each end from the mouths of beasts (particularly lions), depicted in profile.

engrailed: [M.E.] a line of partition consisting of open semicircles conjoined in line at diameter level: 'per fess ~' the convexities are chiefward; per pale ~ they are to the dexter: when an ordinary is ~ the curvature on each side faces inward. ~ is complementary to 'invected' (q.v.). An obs. alt. term is 'cuppy'.

engrelé: Fr., engrailed.

engrossing-block: see **wyre-drawers' tools.**

enhanced: [M.E.] of an ordinary, or of a charge, raised on the field above its normal position. (398)

---

175. Argent, a mountain formal of ten peaks, one, two, three, and four vert: on a chief azure a dove of the field, beaked and membered gules, holding an olive-branch Or.
Baron Monti della Corte.

176. Argent, three Cornish choughs sable beaked and membered gules: on a chief of the last a lion passant gardant Or.
Corporation of the City of Canterbury, Kent.

177. Ermine, on a mount vert a hurst of oak-trees proper; on a chief engrailed gules the sun in his splendour between two hawks rizant, Or.
Ayerst, Kent.

178. Gules, a spur leathered and buckled Or: On a chief argent three cock's heads erased of the field, combed and wattled of the second.
Cockes.

179. Argent, on a mount vert a stork close ermine: on a chief gules three estoiles argent.
Lubbock of Lamas.

180. Ermine, a rose argent in solei Or, on a chief gules three roses of the second barbed and seeded proper.
Municipal Council of the West Riding.

175

176

177

178

179

180

enhendée, croix: Fr., cross patonce.

enhendida cruz: Sp., cross patonce.

enmanché: see **emmanché.**

enraged: r. alt. for 'forcené' (q.v.).

ensenzie: [Gael.] alt. spelling 'ensenye'; a slughorn (or slogan); a Scottish war-cry; a crest-motto.

ensign: an obs. title for a junior military lieutenant. Also a distinctive badge, mark or other device. See also **colour party.**

ensigned: [M.E.] an object is ~ with another when the relationship is one of altitude; e.g. the shield is '~ with a helmet ...', etc., not, as frequently written, surmounted (q.v.) with. A cross humetty ~ with an open crown (q.v.) means that the whole cross is visible, and an open crown rests on the chiefmost extremity of the upper limb; 'surmounted with', means that the centre of the cross is invisible.

entado: Sp., nebuly.

entchen: Ger., duck.

enté: Fr., nebuly.

entire: see **cross-crosslet.**

entoyre: (mis-spelling of Fr. 'entouré') lit. to surround; hence, of a bordure (q.v.) charged with inanimate objects; obs.

entrailed: [M.E.] lit. degutted, disembowelled; hence, of a charge drawn in outline only; also termed 'adumbrated', 'in umbra', 'in ombre', and by the generic term 'ghost charges'. 'A lion passant gardant in umbra' (*umbra leonis*) appears on the bend of Henry Scrope in the glass of York Minister, in which achievement it may be a unique form of augmentation (q.v.). No satisfactory explanation of the origin and significance of charges ~ has been given, and a large percentage of those (chiefly continental) to which reference is made in the literature appear to be merely unfinished drawings. Charges ~ are r. in British heraldry: Francis Gross, F.S.A.,

Richmond Herald in 1755, who wrote *A Classical Dictionary of the Vulgar Tongue*, had a ghost charge, but this may have been of continental origin. (20)

entwined: wrapped about; twisted round; alt. terms 'entwisted', 'enwrapped', and 'environed'.

entwisted: see **entwined.**

enty-in-point: precisely the same as 'point-in-point' (q.v.); alt. spelling 'entée'.

enury: [O.F.] of a bordure (q.v.) charged with beasts, particularly with lions, obs.

environed: see **entwined.**

enwrapped: see **entwined.**

equerre: see **esquirre.**

eradicated: [L.] of a tree, or other plant, pulled by force from the ground, and depicted complete with its roots: a plant proper (q.v.) ~ does not necessarily extend the natural shape to the exposed roots which are often drawn in decorative curves. (376)

erased: [L.] of a beast's head, limb, or paw when torn away from the body: the state is represented by three jagged peaks at the place of severance. (116)

erazed: alt. spelling of 'erased' (q.v.).

erect: [M.E.] lit. to direct upward; hence, of any object set palewise on the field or of a creature proceeding chiefward.

erectus: L., rampant.

ereplek: Afk., honour point.

erhon: Ger., in chief.

Eric, St: Patron of Sweden; represented in the municipal arms of Stockholm.

ermine: [M.E.] the arctic stoat, *Mustela Erminea*, when in its winter coat, i.e. white, with a black tip to the tail: represented in heraldry by the field argent powdered (q.v.) with ermine 'spots' sable. The ermine spot or point may be variously drawn, but its modern representation is as a blunt, narrow arrow-head with a triangle of dots at the point. If the colour-scheme is

PLATE VI Per fess, in chief Or, a lymphad vert, the cutwater a ram's head, the stern a fish-tail raised and flexed inboard, under sail to the sinister, the square-sail proper: biremed with oars in action gules. In base, the sea barry intradented argent and azure.

Gordonstoun School

reversed, argent spots on sable field, the fur is distinguished by the title 'ermines': a field Or powdered with sable spots is described as 'erminois', and this in reverse, a field sable with Or spots gives 'pean'. A decadent form, ermine with a gules line at each side of the spots, is termed 'erminites', but it is totally obs. (417)

ermine, counter: obs. term for 'ermines' (q.v.)

ermine, cross: four ermine spots set in cruciform juxtaposition, head to head, with a dot in each angle, but the four elements are not conjoined. (213)

ermined: an archaic method of blazoning the variations of ermine whereby ermines (q.v.) is rendered 'sable ermined argent'; erminois (q.v.) becomes 'Or, ermined sable'; and 'sable ermined Or' stands for pean (q.v.). There is a modern group attempting to revive the system.

ermines: see **ermine.**

erminites: see **ermine.**

erminois: see **ermine.**

ermites: an obs. term for 'ermine spots'.

erne: [O.E.] specifically the sea- or white-tailed eagle, *Haliaetus albicilla*, but extended to include all eagles.

erniedrigt: Ger., in base.

errant: r. obs. alt. for 'hauriant' (q.v.).

Erskine, David: Lyon Clerk and Keeper of the Records, 1724. Rothesay Herald, 1718. Lyon Clerk Depute, 1718.

Erskine, Sir John: Albany Herald, 1726.

Erskine, Sir Wm: Unicorn Pursuivant, 1707.

Erskine of Cambo, Sir Alexander: Lord Lyon King of Arms, 1672.

Erskine of Cambo, Sir Alexander (the Younger): Lord Lyon King of Arms, 1701 (joint).

Erskine of Cambo, Sir Charles[1]: Lord Lyon King of Arms, 1663.

Erskine of Cambo, Sir Charles[2]: Lyon

Clerk and Keeper of the Records, 1715. Bute Pursuivant, 1707.

escaillée: see **papelonné.**

escallop: a shellfish of the genus *Pecten*, represented in heraldry by its shell which was the insignia of St James of Compostella, the patron saint of pilgrims; hence, the badge worn by palmers who had visited the shrine, used in heraldry largely as a symbol of travel, but also for its sheer decorative value. It is always depicted with the outside (convexity) presented to the observer and, at the top, one on each side of the peak, are two square corners as though a rectangle were standing behind the shell. These, sometimes referred to as the ears, are the hinges of the shell: should they be omitted the ~ has the appearance of a vannet (q.v.). (92)

escallopée: semé of escallops.

escarbuncle: a charge having normally eight limbs (but six, ten, and twelve are also used), radiating as the spokes of a wheel from a central annulet (q.v.), each limb has a pommel in the centre and terminates in a f.d.l. The ~ is supposed to represent either a boss in the shield's centre or the ornamental heads of nails used to secure a sort of leather buffer to the shield. The word is sometimes truncated to 'carbuncle' which is also alternatively spelt 'carboncle'. (430)

escartellé: alt. for 'quadrate' (q.v.).

escheque: alt. for 'chequy' (q.v.).

eschiquete: alt. for 'chequy' (q.v.).

escocheon: r. alt. spelling of 'escutcheon' (q.v.).

escroll: see **ribbon[2].**

escudo: Sp., shield.

escudo femenino: Sp., a lozenge employed to carry the arms of a lady.

escutcheon[1]: [L] a shield; hence, descriptive of any shape within the bounds of which an armorial achievement is depicted; used loosely as alt. for 'coat of arms'.

escutcheon²: a charge consisting of a small shield, one-fifth of the width of the shield on which it appears, which may itself carry charges and occupy any position, however, when on the fess point it is an 'inescutcheon'. (421)

Esperance Herbert Pursuivant: in the service of Charles Somerset, Lord Herbert. 1523.

Esperance Pursuivant: maintained by Percy, Earl of Northumberland, but on more than one occasion was employed in the service of the Crown.

Esplin, James: Marchmont Herald, 1630.

Espoir Pursuivant: maintained by Sir John Lisle (1442).

esquire: an apprentice to a knight (q.v.); one aspiring to knighthood. Later, an English gentleman ranking below a knight; hence, 'squire'; a member of the landed gentry. In modern times debased to a mere substitute for 'Mr', used in addressing a male adult, without reference to class. An esquire in an order of chivalry still owes a duty of service, such as acting as banner-bearer, to his master.

esquire's helmet: see **helmet of rank.**

esquirre: [Fr.] the upper half of a canton (q.v.) party (q.v.) per bend; a gyron (q.v.). The lower half is a 'based-esquirre'.

essonier: of doubtful authenticity, defined by an early writer as a diminutive of the orle (q.v.) being of one-half the breadth. It is unknown in practical heraldry.

estaie: It., chevronel.

estandarte: Sp., standard.

estate, cap of: see **maintenance, cap of.**

estaye: Sp., chevronel.

estenzele: semé (q.v.) of sparks; r. in British heraldry; also spelt 'etincele'.

estoile: [O.F.] a shape consisting of six slender, wavy rays (q.v.) extending from a common centre, representing a star. The ~, with its six delicate limbs and constrained centre is very different in both appearance and function to the mullet (q.v.) with its five, stocky triangular limbs and extensive central area. The ~ alone represents the astronomical body. (142, 472)

Estoile Volant Pursuivant: also called 'Toell Volland'; was maintained by Sir Richard Wingfield, deputy of Calais,

---

181. Argent, on a mount vert a grape-vine fructed and leaved proper: on a chief azure, three mullets of the first.
Jaudon.

182. Sable, three lilies of the garden: a chief per pale azure and gules; dexter, a fleur-de-lys Or and, sinister, a lion passant gardant also Or.
Eton College.

183. Sable, five bezants in saltire: on a chief indented argent three tobacco plants vert.
Cardozo.

184. Azure, a fleece Or: on a chief sable three mullets argent.
Corporation of the City of Leeds, Yorkshire.

185. Vair, on a chevron gules three bezants: a chief gyronny Or and sable.
Lord Newlands.

186. Argent, on waves of the sea a representation of the ship 'Golden Hind' in full sail, all proper: on a chief enarched azure a terrestrial globe, also proper between two mullets of the field.
Honourable Company of Master Mariners.

181

182

183

184

185

186

1513–19. It is probable that the badge was a winged star, the wings from the ca. arms of Wingfield, the star from Lex Baux.

estoille: semé of estoiles.

estoily: of a cross, or other object, having wavy limbs, or rays, as an estoile (q.v.).

estrella: Sp., estoile.

etai: Fr., chevronel.

etendard: Fr., standard.

Ethiopia, Order of the Star of: f. 1874 in five classes. Insignia—*Badge:* first and second class—a gold filigree star of eleven large and ten small points alternately, bearing a central design of five Coptic crosses and scroll decoration; the whole ensigned with a Latin cross surmounting an ornate gold background. *Star:* the unensigned badge in larger size; third class—a five-point gold star, having centrally a green cabochon stone, each ray tipped with a crown, surmounting a circular gold plaque; fourth and fifth class—a gold or silver-gilt triangle ornately decorated, surmounted by an inverted triangle, two tips of which terminate in small crowns, the third tip being covered by a central medallion bearing a circular abstract leaf design. *Riband:* green, gold, red.

etincele: see **estenzele.**

étoile: Fr., estoile.

Ettrick Pursuivant Extraordinary: a former Scottish name of office, known only due to the holder being deprived, in 1571, for supporting rebels in Edinburgh Castle.

evacuatus: L., voided.

Eve: see **Adam and Eve.**

eviré: [L.] castrated, emasculated; of a lion to be drawn without indication of sex. (That numerous lions were so drawn in the XIX cent. was not due to the intention of the heralds but to the mock-modesty of the period. The Rev. C. Boutell, in his popular *Heraldry*, made a point of the respectability of the woodcuts of Mr Utting. Medieval artists suffered no such qualms, and beasts were sexed gules, or, when necessary, azure.)

ewer: see **jug.**

Ewing, James: Rothesay Herald, 1661.

Exeter Herald: maintained by Duke of Exeter, 1416.

exhaltation: of doubtful authenticity; defined by a XV cent. writer as a water-spout.

expanded: an object, usually a tool or an implement consisting of two parts attached one to another by a pivot and normally depicted closed, or folded, is described as ∼ when represented open, the two parts becoming continuous in line.

expansus: L., displayed.

extended: of an object that, normally depicted as curved, is to be represented as straight. Sometimes er. employed in place of 'expanded' (q.v.) which is the more correct, to describe objects consisting of two elements joined by a pivot, as compasses (q.v.) or barnacles (q.v.) when open.

extended limitations: a successful petitioner for a grant of arms receives a Royal Letters Patent in which instrument the device is detailed and the statement made that the achievement may be displayed by himself and his heirs and descendants for ever; thus the right to bear arms is lineal— not collateral. If, however, the petitioner in his generosity wishes to share the honour with his brothers and sisters, or if they are to share the expense, the grant can be made with ∼ to include all the offspring of the petitioner's father. When cousins are to be included the ∼ cover all descendants of the petitioner's grandfather. An extra-territorial Scot; one domiciled in (say) Canada might need ∼ for several generations to link up with a domiciled collateral.

extended, with tail: see **statant.**

exterior decoration: all the display in an achievement (q.v.) of arms that surrounds the shield, i.e. helmet of rank (q.v.), crest (q.v.), mantling (q.v.), and, when present, the supporters (q.v.), their compartment, (q.v.) and the motto scroll.

Exton, Everard: Rouge Dragon Pursuivant, 1659.

Extraordinary Officers of Arms: supernumeraries who may be attached to either the College of Arms (q.v.) or the Lyon Court (q.v.). In England these appointments are made by the Earl Marshal on the recommendation of the kings of arms and with royal assent. Persons recommended are those whose work has been accepted as a contribution to heraldic scholarship; they receive one of the Earl Marshal's titles, e.g. Norfolk Herald ∼, Fitzalan Pursuivant ∼, wear the tabard and enjoy all the privileges of the legitimate officers of arms, e.g. have access to the records and collections of the College of Arms, attend at Garter and at State functions. The appointment, once made, lasts for life. In Scotland, ∼ are appointed by the Lord Lyon (q.v.), generally for the purpose of their undertaking some special duties upon the completion of which their status as ∼ expires.

eye, human: always in the socket and complete with upper and lower lids, lashes, and brow. Rare in British heraldry where, in many of its appearances it is 'an ∼ in the sun', being a charge on the disc of the sun in his splendour (q.v.) and is often intended to symbolize the omnivoyance of the Deity. On the Continent, where it also sometimes symbolizes the eye of God, it is employed more extensively, and is sometimes represented as weeping. (295)

eyed: see **peacock.**

face, a leopard's: a leopard's head gardant (q.v.) without any portion of the neck: it is depicted with mane, and has on the brow a segment in which the typical leopard's spots appear. The leopards' faces in the arms of Shrewsbury are blazoned (q.v.) as 'loggerheads'. A ∼ having passing down behind it a f.d.l. the base of which protrudes from the open mouth thus concealing the lower jaw is a ∼ jessant-de-lys. A ∼ inverted j.d.l. is very often wrongly drawn: it is the ∼ only (not the f.d.l.) that is inverted. (62, 63, 194)

face, a lion's: a lion's head gardant (q.v.) without any portion of the neck. (194)

faceted: lit. having faces; hence, applicable to an ordinary or to an appropriate charge, e.g. a cross, when drawn so as to appear to be raised in the centre; sloping upward to a ridge, like a roof. In British heraldry this style of depiction is optional, except on a crescent when it is compulsory; hence, the term is seldom, if ever, used in blazon, but on the Continent it is common.

facettiert: Ger., faceted.

faggots: alt. for 'laths' (q.v.).

fahne: Ger., a flag.

Fairbairn, James: Snowdoun Herald, 1703.

faja: Sp., fess.

falchion: see **sabre.**

falcon: [L.] a generic term in heraldry for any member of the family Falconidae. Depicted with a short, hooked beak and powerful claws. The ∼ is generally perched and close (q.v.), always belled (q.v.), whether so blazoned or not, sometimes also jessed (q.v.) and vervelled (q.v.). A ∼ rizant (q.v.) is often so blazoned, but has a special term, i.e. 'surgerant'. When blazoned 'hooded' the bird is perched, close (q.v.), and has a blindfold over the head. When blazoned as '∼ trussing' it is depicted standing upon another bird, its victim, which is often prone upon its back. An alternative term is 'preying upon' and the nature of the victim is sometimes given, e.g. '. . . a mallard', '. . . a duck'. Alt. terms include 'hawk', 'goshawk', 'girfauk', 'hobby', and 'merlin', which last is often er. misspelt 'merlion', which term does not refer to a falcon.

falcon on a fetterlock: see **fetterlock** and **badges.**

Falcon (King of Arms): name of office derived from the falcon on a fetterlock (q.v.), 1359; employed also for a herald, a pursuivant, and, ultimately, a herald extraordinary (q.v.), this last as recently as 1813.

falconer's glove: see **glove.**

Falkirk Roll: (1298) vellum true roll 6¼ in. by 4 ft, contains 111 names and blazons of those who were engaged at the battle of Falkirk: it is the oldest known occasional roll (q.v.). On the dorse is inscribed the Nativity Roll (q.v.).

fallgatter: Ger., portcullis.

falot: r. in British heraldry; a lantern, similar to a globular lamp (q.v.) carried upon a pole; a continental development of the torch (q.v.).

false escutcheon: see **orle.**

false heraldry: arms in which tincture (q.v.) is charged upon tincture, or metal (q.v.) upon metal, except when the achievement (q.v.) is of sufficient importance to preclude error as, e.g., the arms of the Christian Kingdom of Jerusalem, viz. 'argent, a cross potent between four crosses humetty Or', when the term 'armes a enquerre' or 'arma inquirenda', is employed. ~ is often stated to refer to arms of assumption, which error arises from a misreading of 'Blason de Couleurs', by Jean de Courtais (*ob.* 1345), Sicily Herald, who applied the term to bogus arms not because they are unofficial, but because 'home-made' arms very often include ~ among their other errors. Notwithstanding that the arms of Jerusalem are frequently quoted it ought not to be assumed that they are the sole example of 'official ~'. In continental

---

187. On a wreath of the colours a catamount passant gardant proper, collared gemel, and charged on the body with a cross paty Or. *Macpherson.*

188. On a wreath of the colours, a griffin segreant gules holding in the dexter claw a representation of the mace of the Canadian House of Commons and in the sinister, a war-mace Or. *H. R. Jackman,* Toronto.

189. On a wreath of the colours a caravel Or laded with tuns proper; topsail and mainsail gules, the latter charged with a cartwheel of the first; from the masthead, flotant to the dexter, a pennon argent. *Worshipful Company of Vintners.*

190. On a wreath of the colours a winged monkey statant gules: about the loins a collar, chained Or. *Col. H. A. Lewis,* M.B.E., O. St J.

191. On a wreath of the colours an opinicus statant Or. *The Worshipful Company of Barbers.*

192. On a wreath of the colours a globical lamp Or ensigned with a crown royal. *The Worshipful Company of Tin-plate Workers.*

187   188

189   190

191   192

heraldry there is to be found a comparatively large number of coats embodying ~.

fält: Swd., field.

family orders: a description that should be
reserved for those royal orders conferred
by a sovereign solely on members of the
Royal Family. Occasionally the term is
extended to cover dynastic (q.v.) and house
(q.v.) orders. Family orders have taken
various forms; in Britain they have been
conferred on ladies only, and have consisted of a cameo or (more frequently) a
miniature of the sovereign, in a jewelled
oval band, worn from a bow on the left
breast.

fan¹: a semicircular piece of silk, or paper,
generally painted, or otherwise decorated,
attached to a number of thin, radial sticks
joined on a pivot, to enable it to be closed
into a small compass. Used in Europe down
to the end of the XIX cent. by ladies; in
Japan by both sexes for creating a cooling
breeze. Employed in the arms of the
Worshipful Company of Fanmakers. (323)

fan²: see **peacock.**

fan³: see **vannet.**

fanged tooth: a molar, the cusps chiefward
and the roots, described as the fangs, may
be of another colour. The ~ is very r. in
British heraldry, but appears in eastern
European achievements. It is the insigne
of St Apollonia, patron of toothache.

fanion: a small flag, generally rectangular,
and often notched in the fly, being the
ensign of the baggage train; also spelt
'fannion'.

fannion: see previous entry.

fanon: [M.E.] part of the Eucharistic vestments, being a strip of fabric 4 ft in length
carried doubled, and pendant from the left
wrist, in origin, a napkin. Commoner in
continental than in British heraldry, where
it is sometimes blazoned as 'a cuff'.

färger: Swd., colours.

farrier's knife: see **buttrice.**

fasce: Fr., fess.

fasces: [L.] the Roman symbol of authority,
carried in a consul's procession: it was a
bundle of rods bound round the haft (q.v.)
of an axe (q.v.), the blade of which pro-
truded. In heraldry employed to indicate
magisterial office. Palewise, the blade faces
dexter; fesswise, downward. (268)

fascia: It. and L., fess.

fasciatum: L., barry.

Father Time: see **hour-glass.**

Faucon: an archaic spelling of 'Falcon' (King
of Arms).

Fayery, Robert: Portcullis Pursuivant,
1516. Also known as 'Faythe', 'Venables',
and 'Spret'.

Faythe, Robert: see previous entry.

feather: [Gk] an ostrich ~ u.o.s.; are of
conventionalized form, somewhat wooden
in appearance, and with the tip canted over
to the sinister (q.v.): a ~ proper (q.v.)
appears fluffy, weak and decadent. If the ~
is to represent a pen, the quill will be of a
different colour, and the blazon will state
'penned' of that colour. A single ~ may
(but seldom does) do duty for a crest (q.v.),
but groups of them—always of an odd
number—are usual. Three ~, will have the
central one erect and those at each side
falling outward: more than three are
described as a plume of so many ~s, three
and two: the terms 'double plume', 'treble
plume', and so on are also used. A plume of
more than three rows may be blazoned as a
pyramid of ~s of so many heights. More
than five ~s in a plume might be described
as a panache. (470)

feh: Ger., vair.

felling axe: see **axe.**

Fellow, Wm: Norroy King of Arms, 1536.
Former Lancaster Herald, 1527; former
Marleon-de-Aye Pursuivant, 1522.

felon: [M.E.] generally depicted as a semi-clad, hairy, bearded human being with about the neck a rope blazoned as a 'halter'.

femblading: Swd., cinquefoil.

femme: see **baron.**

fencing the Lyon Court: see **Court of the Lord Lyon.**

fencock: alt. title for the 'heron' (q.v.).

fennel: [O.E.] a plant, *Faeniculum dulce*, used in cookery for preparing sauce and in heraldry for ca. reasons.

Fenwick's Roll: (temp. kings Hen. V. and VI) a general roll (q.v.) on vellum, which has been damaged and cut. It originally depicted 1035 shields including arms attributed to biblical characters and saints: also achievements of English nobility and armigerous commoners as well as ecclesiastical sees.

fer-de-fourchette: a r. term for a musket-rest (q.v.). There is also supposed to be a cross ~, but it seems to exist only in old textbooks.

fer-de-martel: see **martel.**

fer-de-moline: see **mill-rind.**

Ferdinand, Royal Military Order of St: f. 1815 and confirmed by Generalissimo Franco in 1940; in five classes. Insignia— *Badge:* a gold-rimmed white enamel Maltese cross; a green and gold wreath appears between the arms and the badge is similarly ensigned; a gold central medallion depicts a robed St Ferdinand holding a sword and an orb, and is surrounded by a red band inscribed in gold *Al Merito Militar. Star:* an unensigned larger version of the badge, on a red enamel cross fitchy, with very slender propeller-like arms, having centrally a gold cross paty encircled by eight linked gold balls. *Riband:* red with yellow stripes near the edges.

ferens: L., charged.

Ferguson, Walter: Bute Pursuivant, 1851.

fermaglio: It., buckle.

fermail: [reduced from Fr. 'fermaille'] see **buckle.**

fermo, leone: It., an alt. term with 'arrestato' for a lion statant.

fern-brake: [M.E.] a clump, or thicket of fern.

ferr: [dial.] a horseshoe.

ferrated: semé of horseshoes.

ferris: [frmed on 'fleerish'] a fire-iron; the conventionalized representation of the steel used in conjunction with flint to produce fire before the introduction of matches. A more or less square plate of steel had cut into one side a W-shaped slot thus providing a central point, with the sidepieces rising higher. These outer parts acted as guides, keeping the central point in contact with the flint. The heraldic drawing broadens the spaces between the striking point and the guides, and makes of the latter spirals similar to a ram's horns beneath which the plate often curves to a waist, and is sometimes set in a wooden holder. ~ has now gone out of use but a number remain in old established arms. Alt. term 'furison'. (322).

fess: [L.] an ordinary crossing the field from flank to flank at the level of the visual centre: the width is one-third of that of the shield. A final 'e' on the word is misleading— 'fesse' is a dialect word for pale blue.

fess, in: of a number of objects ranged across the field from flank to flank, at the visual centre: charges occupying the position of a fess (q.v.).

fess point: an imaginary dot occupying and indicating the visual centre of the shield: extended to include the area immediately surrounding it. See also **abyss.**

fesswise: horizontal; level; crossing the field, or orientated from flank to flank.

feswe: r. obs. alt. for 'fusil' (q.v.).

fetterlock: a manacle depicted as a semi-circle of iron hinged at one end to a bar and having at the other a disc that engages in a lock built into the bar. A falcon on a ~, i.e. perched on the bar and arched over by the semicircular part, was the heraldic badge of Edmund Langley (the fifth son of K. Ed. III) and, later, of K. Ed. IV, and may be seen in the ironwork in Westminster Abbey.

The ~, also blazoned as a 'manacle', 'shackbolt', and 'shacklebolt', generally takes the form mentioned above, but there are two other forms: the lockbar fitted with a short length of chain in place of the iron arch, and a rod of iron bent into a semicircle and having at each end an eye through which a straight rod may be pushed and then secured in position. The differences in terminology have no bearing on the pattern to be depicted. (3)

feverstahl: Ger., ferris.

fiammegiante: It., wavy.

fiancato: It., flaunches.

fiché, croix: Fr., cross fitchy. See also **au pied.**

fiddle: see **violin.**

field: the whole of the surface of the shield, lozenge (q.v.), cartouche (q.v.), or other shape upon, or within which, the armorial composition is depicted.

field-pieces: see **chambers.**

fife: see **hautboy.**

Fife Roll: (temp. K. Ed. I) vellum true roll 6 in. by 2 ft. 9 in., painted, thirty-one shields, named.

fifth son, mark of difference of: see **brisure.**

figibilis: L., fitchy.

fig-tree: the tree, *Ficus carica*; its fruit and its leaves, the last sometimes having reference to Gen. iii.7, all appear in heraldry and often for ca. reasons. (387)

figura: L., charge(d).

figured: having, as a secondary development, some part of the human form, generally the face, in, e.g., both sun (q.v.) and moon (q.v.); additional to what is specified in the blazon.

fijada: Sp., fitchy.

files: see **label.**

filet: [Fr.] lit. a thread, hence employed in current Fr. blazon for a narrow diminutive (q.v.). The same word, spelt 'filete' in Sp. and 'filetto' in It., has the same signification in those countries. See also **fillet.**

---

193. On a wreath of the colours, a pelican in her piety, argent, gutty-de-sang.
     Chandler.

194. Out of a ducal coronet gules a lion's face Or.
     Oxenden, Dene.

195. On a chapeau gules turned-up ermine a man's head and neck couped at the shoulders proper, bearded and crined Or.
     Hazelrigg, Leicester.

196. On a wreath of the colours, a hawk, close, Or, preying upon a mallard's wing, of the last, erased gules.
     Henshaw.

197. Out of a mural crown argent masoned sable a demi-lion issuant, of the last, gorged with a ducal coronet Or.
     Cooke, Yorkshire.

198. On a chapeau gules turned-up ermine an eagle with wings displayed Or, preying upon an infant in its cradle proper, swaddled of the first, the cradle laced gold.
     Stanley.

193

194

195

196

197

198

filiation, mark of: r. alt. for 'brisure' (q.v.).

filiera: It. and Sp., bordure.

filière: Fr., bordure.

fillet: [M.E.] diminutive of the chief (q.v.); a narrow band, one-quarter of the chief's depth, that is charged on the parent's basemost edge.

fillet cross: a plain cross (q.v.) composed of narrow elements. In the Middle Ages crosses, saltires, chevrons, pales, and the other figures of heraldry were narrower than those in current use, but the ~ is not a survival: it is modern and utilitarian, being on some occasions introduced in a quarterly shield to hold the design together, and thus strengthen the effect.

fimbria: L., bordure.

fimbriated: [L.] of any shape, but applied particularly to crosses having in their construction a narrow border which must not be shaded since it is not a cross charged with a bordure, but is a cross of (say) tincture having as part of its constitution an edging of metal (or vice versa). (89)

fimbriatus: L., fimbriated.

finch: [O.E.] the chaffinch, a common British song bird, *Fringilla calebs*; and for any bird of the sub-family *Fringillidae*; employed in heraldry chiefly for ca. reasons.

finger-ring: see **gem-ring.**

finned: [O.E.] of a fish, or of a composite fictitious beast that is in part piscine, when the fins are of a different colour to the body; generally referring to the dorsal fin.

fiocci: [It.] the tassels of an ecclesiastical hat (q.v.).

fiordalisata, croce: It., cross floretty.

fiordaliso: It., fleur-de-lys.

fiorenta, croce: It., cross flory.

fiorente: It., flory.

fir-tree: [M.E.] a generic name given to several different coniferous trees, always drawn with drooping branches.

fire-bucket: a tall, slender, leathern bucket with a metal ring at the top to which the bow-handle is attached, and a rigid circular foot. The ~ is not seen frequently, and there is a tendency for it to be taken as a joke; however, it should be noted that in London fire-prevention was a public concern, as revealed in 'The Mayor's Assize of Buildings', dated 1212, where in every citizen is enjoined to provide, inter alia, a fire-bucket.

fire-chest: see **brazier.**

fire-pan: r. alt. for 'beacon' (q.v.).

fireball: see **bombshell.**

firebrand: a billet of timber, conventionalized as a ragged staff and sometimes blazoned as 'a staff raguly' fired proper, or flammant. It represents the forerunner of the modern incendiary bomb, but when blazoned as a 'torch', although drawn in the same way, it is not of military significance, but is intended for an illuminant. Alt. term 'flambeau'. (336)

fired: see **lowe.**

firmé: lit. firm, rigid, r. alt. for 'throughout' or 'anchored'.

fish-basket: see **weel.**

fish-eagle: an innovation in corporate arms in Rhodesia; it is depicted volant (q.v.) and grasping a fish in its talons.

fish-hook: see **angle.**

fish's head: may be either couped (q.v.) or erased (q.v.) and orientated haurient (q.v.), naiant (q.v.), counter-naiant (q.v.), or urinant (q.v.). If the blazon says ~, a cod's head is understood, and if no orientation is given the head is to appear haurient. (71)

fish's skeleton: the spine and rib-bones, complete with head in the naiant (q.v.) position u.o.s.; r. in British, but common in continental heraldry.

fitch: see **foin.**

fitched: r. alt. for 'fitchy' (q.v.).

fitchet: see **polecat.**

fitchy: [Fr.] of a cross having the lower limb

drawn to a long, tapering point: in certain crosses the lower limb is removed, and the long spike is attached at the centre of the cross, notably in the cross paty (q.v.) and the cross-crosslet (q.v.). In such crosses, if the lower limb is to be retained, the blazon gives '~ at the foot' when the additional spike is not extended downward to more than half the length of the limb. '~ of all four' is a decadent and now obs. form. (221)

fitchy at the foot: see previous entry.

Fitzalan Pursuivant Extraordinary: named from one of the titles of the Duke of Norfolk, and first appointed to serve in connection with Q. Vic.'s coronation.

Fitzgerald, cross of: see **saltire.**

Fitzwalter Pursuivant: maintained by Lord Fitzwalter, 1485.

five wounds: see **sacred and legendary figures.**

fixed: see **anchored.**

fjallskura: Swd., invected.

flag: a piece of fabric of any size or shape whereon is emblazoned, either by painting or needlework, armorial bearings or other ensigns, attached by one side only to a cord and allowed to float on the wind from the top of a mast as a mark of identity, or as a signal, or for gala effect only. A colloquial term covering banner (q.v.), gonfannon (q.v.), guidon (q.v.), pennon (q.v.), standard (q.v.), and streamers of all kinds.

flagon: r. alt. for a ewer or jug (q.v.).

flambant: Fr., wavy.

flambeau: see **firebrand.**

flames of fire: often described as 'proper' (q.v.), may be either gules or Or, or gules shaded Or.

flaming sword: see **Michael, Archangel.**

flammant: [M.E.] see **lowe.**

flamulato: Sp., wavy.

flanch: [O.F.] a sub-ordinary, being the space enclosed by an arc commencing in

dexter-chief (q.v.) and having its horizontal diameter level with fess point (q.v.) where it is one-third the width of the shield. ~ are always borne in pairs, one on each side of the shield, and they often carry charges. Alt. spelling 'flaunch'. (427)

flanker: Swd., flanches.

flanks: [M.E.] the 'cheeks' of the shield; the areas on each side of the fess point; dexter flank and sinister flank.

flanque: Fr., flaunches.

flanquisado: Sp., flaunches.

flasque: [possibly frmd on 'flanque', O.F.] first diminutive of the flanch (q.v.) being of the same length from chief to base, but only two-thirds its width at fess-point level, and always borne in pairs, one on each side of the shield. (N.B.—it is argued that sub-ordinaries do not give rise to diminutives; hence, the ~ is a shape similar to, but not connected with, the flanch.)

flaunch: see **flanch.**

flax-breaker: see **hemp-break.**

flax-card: see **card[1].**

flea: [Teut.] a leaping insect, *Pulex irritans*, that feeds on blood; employed as a device in continental but not in British heraldry.

fleam: [O.F.] the barber-surgeon's blooding knife consisting of a blade with parallel edge and back, pivoted into a sheath which latter is extended in length by a curving finger-rest. Orientated upon the shield with the blade fesswise in chief, the sheath and its extension descending palewise; hence, in appearance a figure 2 inverted. Alt. spellings 'flegme' and 'phlegme'. The word is still current in the U.S.A. where it refers to a dental surgeon's gum-lancet. Employed in the arms of medical men and institutions. (324)

fleece: [O.E.] depicted as a lamb secured in a belt provided with a ring, its head and forequarters, its rump and hindquarters drooping, giving the appearance of being lifted for transport. It is also blazoned as 'toison d'Or'—the golden fleece—and is worn about the neck by members of that Order of Chivalry. (184)

flegme: see **fleam.**

flesh-hook: a domestic utensil for lifting boiled meat from the cauldron (q.v.) being a large, two-pronged fork, each prong having a barb on the outer edge; another form consists of a rod with three hooked prongs jutting at one side.

flesh-pots: see **cauldron.**

Fletcher, George: York Herald, 1752.

fleur-de-lys: a tripartite decorative shape having petal-like elements, the central one rising vertically, the other two curving outward, all three issuant from a band, or ring, beneath which the three elements terminate in shortened versions of what is above. ~ adopted by Louis VII; hence, representative of the French Royal Family, and of France as a Sovereign State. It is the brisure (q.v.) of the sixth son. Erroneously stated to be a conventionalized iris (Iridaceae) which was assumed to be a form of lily (Liliaceae), accepted as a symbol of the Holy Trinity, also

of the three Christian virtues, for both of which it may have been employed, but it is of pre-Christian origin, the earliest known example being on a cylinder-seal of Rameses III.

The ~ is of very frequent occurrence in the heraldry of all nations, both as an individual charge and as part of a compound of elements of design, and on most occasions it is used as a meaningless item of decoration. It may vary greatly in form: more than forty versions are known.

Fleur-de-lys Herald: created in 1435, and entrusted with a task in France.

Fleur-de-lys Pursuivant: named from the French quarter of the Royal Arms; promoted to f.d.l. Herald (q.v.) 1435.

fleurdelisée, croix: Fr., cross floretty.

fleuronné: Fr., flory.

flighted: see **arrow.**

flint: see **mineral.**

flittermouse: see **bat.**

float: a toothed cutting or scraping tool used in the production of archers' bows and preserved as a charge in the arms of the Worshipful Company of Bowyers.

---

199. On a wreath of the colours a furnace Or masoned sable, and thereon an alembic, also Or.
Municipal Council of Widnes.

200. On a wreath of the colours a boar statant ermine.
Bacon, Suffolk.

201. On a wreath of the colours a cubit-arm habited, per pale indented azure and Or, enfiled with an annulet of the last, the hand proper grasping a cross flory, erect, of the second.
Anson.

202. On a wreath of the colours, in front of a mount vert having thereon a portcullis sable, three water-bougets fesswise of the last.
Langman.

203. On a wreath of the colours a grenade sable fired proper and winged azure.
Lord Donovan.

204. On a wreath of the colours, on a charger argent irradiated Or the head of St John the Baptist, decollated proper.
Worshipful Company of Tallow Chandlers.

 199

 200

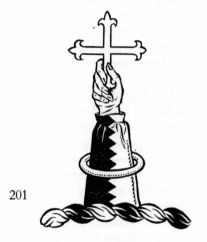 201

 202

 203

 204

flook: [Gael.] a name for the plaice (q.v.) occurring in Irish heraldry.

flor-de-lis: Sp., fleur-de-lys.

florado: Sp., flory.

flordelisada: Sp., floretty.

florence, croix: Fr., cross flory.

floretty cross: a cross humetty having the head of a f.d.l. extending beyond the flat extremity of each limb.

florenzada: Sp., flory.

floriated: decorated with a f.d.l.

flory, cross: a cross humetty having each limb terminating in a triple floral form as the head of a f.d.l. (q.v.). (208)

flounder: a small flat-fish, *Pleuronectes flesus*; employed in heraldry for ca. reasons. Also known as the fluke.

Flower, Wm: Norroy King of Arms, 1562. Former Chester Herald, 1547; former Rouge Croix Pursuivant, 1544; former Guisnes Pursuivant, 1536.

flower-pot: see **jug** and **lily-pot**.

flowers, blazon by: see **segregative blazon**.

fluke: see **flounder**.

flute: see **hautboy**.

fly¹: the free end of a flag; hence, equivalent to sinister (q.v.), but also the measurement from hoist (q.v.) to fly.

fly²: any winged insect other than a beetle, several different kinds of which function as charges. When the blazon states 'a fly' and does not specify (as, e.g., 'a gad-fly' (q.v.)), a common house-fly is intended.

flying-fish: in early heraldry depicted as fish with long, tapering feathered wings as those of a swallow. Accurately observed by Sir Francis Drake, and subsequently depicted with wings of the same size and shape but of fin, or membraneous material. (69, 72)

foi: [Fr.] consists of two human arms issuant from the flanks, the hands clasped at fess point; hence, the arms of Purefoy (Bishop of Hereford, 1554–7), e.g. 'gules, two arms issuant from the flanks, the hands conjoined argent between three hearts Or', are ca.

foin: [M.E.] the beech-marten, *Mustela foina*, also known as the 'fitch'; both forms for ca. reasons.

fontal: [L.] lit. fountain, or spring: depicted as a conch or other shell, or an urn (q.v.) whereout of water is transfluent. A ~ is generally supported by a nymph, and has reference to a river. The entire composition is rather ornate, and belongs to the period of 'landscape heraldry'.

förbättring: Swd., augmentation.

forcené: [Fr.] lit. insanely violent; hence, of a horse (q.v.) when rearing to attack: salient (q.v.) is sometimes used but ~ is preferable. Both hind hooves are on the ground though they are set wide apart. Very frequently a horse ~ is er. depicted rampant (q.v.). (18)

Fordyce, James: Snowdoun Herald, 1728.

forks, agricultural: may be specified in blazon by the particular purpose to which applied, a 'pitch-~', 'hay~', 'dung-~', but no difference is observable: a fork, irrespective of its use, may be drawn with either three or four tynes.

Forman, John: Rothesay Herald, 1578.

Forman, Sir Robert: Lord Lyon King of Arms, 1555. Former Ross Herald and Lyon Depute, 1554.

formy, cross: see **paty, cross**.

Forrester, Alexander: Carrick Pursuivant, 1557.

fort: see **castle**.

Forth, John Doddington: Portcullis Pursuivant, 1780.

fortified: see **castle**.

fortress: see **castle**.

foumart: [M.E.] a name for the polecat (q.v.); employed in heraldry generally for ca. reasons.

fountain: [L.] a roundel (q.v.) barry-wavy

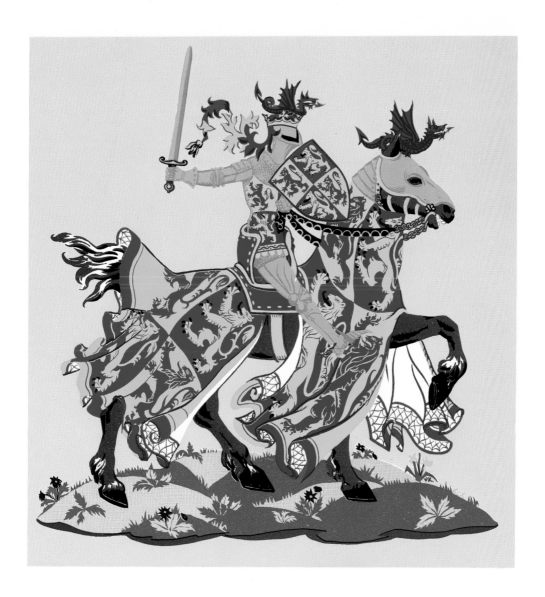

PLATE VII Quarterly Or and gules, four lions passant gardant counterchanged, and for his CREST
a wyvern, gules.

Owen Glendower

Arms emblazoned on shield, surcoat, and horsetrapper.
CREST (on both horse and rider) moulded in the round.

[*Note:* This achievement is now employed as an inescutcheon in the arms of H.R.H.
The Prince of Wales.]

(of six) argent and azure, representing a pool, or a spring, of pure water; hence, not to be shaded. See also **sykes.** (94)

fountain proper: an ornamental water-jet rising from the centre of a shallow basin back in to which it falls.

fourché: [Fr.] forked; bifurcated; of a cross having the extremity of each limb cleft, and turned outward: a lion queue-∼ has one tail emerging at the base of the spine, the second branching off from it. See also **double-queued.**

fourth son, mark of difference of: see **brisure.**

fox: [O.E.] a beast of the genus *Vulpes*; the head is rounded, the ears short, and the snout long and tapering: ∼ is a sleek animal having a long bushy tail which may itself appear as a charge, known as '∼-brush'. The head alone, affrontée, and with no portion of the neck, is ∼ mask. His second name, tod, by which he may be blazoned, puts him in many a ca. setting, and he may be, though rarely is, blazoned as 'reynard'. (25)

fracted: of a charge revealing a defect; fractured; broken.

fraises: see **trefoil.**

France, pretense to throne of: K. Ed. III, claimed, in 1340, the French throne in right of his mother, Isobel, daughter of Philip IV of France, consort of K. Ed. II. The claim was signified by the assumption of France Ancient quarterly with England. The royal heir-apparent's label, which had hitherto been azure, was changed to argent. K. Ch. V altered his arms to France Modern probably to difference from the French quarter of England's arms, but the English king also changed. (K. Hen. V's great seal is the first to display three f.d.l.)

France Ancient: arms worn by the King of France until 1405 when the change was made to difference from the French quarter

of the K. of England: azure semé-de-lys Or: but claimed to represent the Trinity.

France Modern: 'azure, three fleurs-de-lys Or': arms adopted by the King of France, K. Ch. V, in 1405 to difference from the King of England's assumed French quarter: 'azure, semé-de-lys Or', i.e. France Ancient.

francolin: see **pheasant.**

Franke, Henry: see **French, Henry.**

Franke, Thomas: see **French, Thomas.**

Franz Joseph, Order of: (Austria) f. 1849 in three classes for all classes of society according to merit. Insignia—*Badge:* a gold edged red cross globical, with narrow arms between which appears the encrowned double-headed black eagle bearing a gold chain from its beak; the lower portion of the chain forms the motto *Viribus Unitis;* a central white medallion bears *FJ* in gold; the whole ensigned with the Imperial crown. *Star:* silver of eight points, surmounted by the ensigned badge. *Riband:* dark red.

Fraser, Henry: Ross Herald, 1687. Herald-painter to the Lyon Court, 1687.

Fraser, John: Unicorn Pursuivant, 1426.

Fraser, Robert: Unicorn Pursuivant, 1585.

Fraser of Reilig, Major Charles Ian: Dingwal Pursuivant, 1939.

frectum simplex: L., fretty.

French, Henry: York Herald during the reign of K. Ed. IV. Former Bluemantle Pursuivant and Comfort Pursuivant. Also called 'Franke'.

French, Thomas: Bluemantle Pursuivant, 1484. Former Guisnes Pursuivant. Also spelt 'Franke'.

French Croix de Guerre: see **Croix de Guerre** (France).

Frere, James Arnold: Chester Herald, 1955. Former Bluemantle Pursuivant, 1948.

fret: [O.F.] a figure, sometimes given the status of a sub-ordinary, formed by a ribbon (q.v.) and a baton (q.v.) (hence, a saltire) interlaced with a mascle (q.v.). Also known as the Harrington knot, being a cognisance (q.v.) taken from the arms of that family. (415)

frette: Fr., fretty.

fretty: a variation of the field, or of an ordinary, or a charge. A field ~ carries eight costs (q.v.) interlaced with the same number of bastons (q.v.) (265)

Friar Brackley's Book: see **Brackley's Book, Friar.**

Frier, Robert: Herald-painter to the Lyon Court, 1857.

fructed: [L.] of a tree, or other plant, bearing its fruit: an oak is ~ of its acorns (q.v.), a pine of its cones, and a garb (q.v.) may be ~ of its head. (181)

fructen: Ger., fructed.

fruit: often employed for ca. reasons, always pendant u.o.s.

fruit trees: frequently have a ca. value and appear under their own names: apple-tree, pear-tree, walnut-tree, etc. Foreign fruits, such as fig, orange, lemon, also appear as trees. ~ in their conventionalization follow the general rules for trees (q.v.).

fruité: Fr., fructed.

frutado: Sp.

fruttifero: It.

fruttle: see **vannet.**

Fryth, Rowland: Lancaster Herald, 1712. Former Mowbray Herald Extraordinary, 1698.

fucile: It., ferris.

Fuirde, James: Unicorn Pursuivant, 1617.

Fuirde, Thomas: Unicorn Pursuivant, 1633.

fullstandigt vapen: Swd., achievement.

fummant: see **lowe.**

funerary brasses: see **brasses, monumental.**

funfblatt: Ger., cinquefoil.

fur: [M.E.] a garment lined with, or tailored from, the pelt of an animal, the wearing of which symbolized authority in the Middle Ages, and to a lesser extent still may do so. The furs employed in heraldry are represented by a conventionalized repeat pattern and standardized colour combinations. See **ermine, ermines, erminois, pean, vair, potent, white.**

furison: see **ferris.**

furled: of a sail when out of action and lashed to the boom or yard-arm.

Furness Coucher Book: (c. 1412) an illustrative roll of arms (q.v.) being the

---

205. Gules, on a cross bottony argent five ogresses.
   Humfrey.

206. Argent, a cross moline quarter-pierced, sable.
   Copley.

207. Argent, a cross sable pointed and voided of the field.
   Dukinfield, of Cheshire (the Civic Arms of the Borough are based on those of the family.)

208. Argent on a cross flory sable, four bezants.
   Whitgift (Bishop of Worcester).

209. Argent, a cross Calvary on three degrees gules.
   Legat of Edinburgh.

210. Argent, a Patriarchal cross gules voided of the field.
   Ashafen.

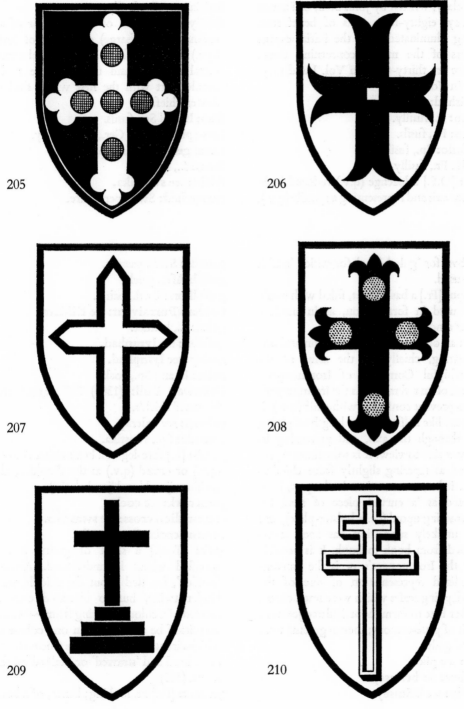

205

206

207

208

209

210

cartulary, written by John Stell, of Furness Abbey, eighty-four arms of benefactors being illuminated with the initial capital letters of the matter concerning them. There are thirty-three in Vol. I and fifty-one in Vol. II.

furnished: see **horse.**

fusato: It., fusilly.

fusées: Fr., fusils.

fuselado: Sp., fusilly.

fuselé: Fr., fusilly.

fusil: [O.F.] a lozenge (q.v.) reduced in its minor axis and representing a spindle (q.v.).

fusillatum: L., fusilly.

fusilly: a variation of the field (or of an ordinary or a charge) consisting of fusils (q.v.) set close in barwise rows of alternate metal (or fur) and tincture: the metal should start with the first whole fusil in dexter-chief.

fuso: It. and Sp., fusils.

fuss-spitz kreuz: Ger., cross fitchy.

fussangel: Ger., caltrap.

fusus: L., fusil.

fylfot: see **swastika.**

fyrstyckad: Swd., per saltire.

G: abvn for 'gules' (q.v.) for which 'gu.' is also used.

gabion: [Fr.] a basket that, filled with earth, was used in fortification, as in modern times sandbags were used.

gad[1]: an object of unknown origin and use, appearing, chiefly, in the arms of the Worshipful Company of Ironmongers; hence, often referred to as the Ironmonger's ∼ to prevent confusion with gad[2] (q.v.). It appears like half of a short length of piping cut through the axis, and presenting its convex side to view. It is sometimes represented as tapering slightly from chief to base. It has, at some time in the past, been defined as 'a curved piece of steel for hammering upon' (i.e. a bolster-plate), and this unlikely suggestion has been transcribed from book to book. It is possible that the Ironmonger's ∼ is the conventionalized representation of one of the overlapping scales which were sewn onto a leather base to form the articulated joints of a suit of plate-armour; these segments were called gads.

gad[2]: see **pike.**

gad-bee: see **brimsey.**

gad-fly: see **brimsey.**

gaende: Swd., passant.

gaffel: Afk., pairle.

gaffelkors: Swd., pairle.

Galdare Pursuivant: see **Kildare.**

galea: L., helmet.

galleon: see **lymphad.**

galley: see **lymphad.**

gallo: It. and Sp., cock.

Galloway Roll: (1300) 259 named and blazoned shields.

galtrap: see **caltrap.**

gamada: Sp., swastika.

gamb: [L.] fore-leg of a beast either couped (q.v.) or erased (q.v.) at the shoulder; alt. spellings 'jamb' and 'jambe'. (57)

gamecock: see **cock.**

gammadion cross: see **swastika.**

gamme croix: Fr., swastika.

garb: [Teut.] a sheaf of grain: if not specified wheat is understood. Always 'banded', i.e. tied about the middle with binder twine, but so blazoned only if banded of a colour differing from ∼ which may itself be of more than one colour in which circumstance it may be fructed (q.v.) of its head and 'strawed' or 'stalked' of the stems. (369)

gardant: [Fr.] lit. looking; hence, of a beast

with its head turned so that it appears full-face; the spelling 'guardant' may not be absolutely wrong, but it is most undesirable since it implies 'protecting'. (51)

garde-bras: [Fr.] part of a suit of plate armour, being a protective device for the elbow-joint. It consisted of overlapping segments, scales, or gads sewn onto a leather base, and sometimes provided with a central fan-like projection. The ~, sometimes spelt 'garde-de-bras', also 'garbraille' and 'gard brace', is in position, and closed, on an arm vambraced (q.v.), but when it appears as an individual charge it is generally expanded (q.v.) with arming points flotant, and is often so badly drawn that it is unrecognizable.

garden lily: see **lily of the garden.**

garden rose: see **rose.**

garden trowel: see **trowel.**

Gardner, David: Ormonde Pursuivant, 1607.

garland: a wreath (q.v.) without stems and ribbon. When of oak, carrying four bunches of acorns—one in chief, one in base, and one at each side; also called 'a civic-wreath', sometimes 'a civic crown'. (238)

garlic: [O.E.] a plant having a segmented, bulbous root of strong flavour, *Allium sativum*; used in continental cooking and heraldry; r. in British arms.

garnie: Fr., hilted.

garnished: embellished; ornamented, dressed; a book (q.v.) ~ has coloured edges to the pages; a bugle-horn (q.v.) ~ has coloured metal bands surrounding it; pieces of armour, including helmets, are ~ by rivet-heads, and ornamental edges overlaid on the steel.

Garrioch Pursuivant Extraordinary: see **Mar, John Earl of.**

garter: [M.E. fm O.F.] insignia of the highest order of English knighthood; arms of a K.G. are depicted 'within the Garter' (see **Royal Arms**); also the circle of a strap and buckle may be blazoned 'a demi-~' or a 'perclose'; it appears in the arms of office of ~ King of Arms; alt. for a bendlet (q.v.). (217)

Garter, Most Noble Order of the: Britain's premier order; f. by K. Ed. III in 1348. Insignia comprises: a garter of dark blue velvet adorned with gold, bearing the motto *Honi soit qui mal y pense*, worn by K.G.s below the left knee, and by ladies of the order above the left elbow; a mantle of blue velvet, taffeta lined, the star embroidered on the left breast, with a hood and surcoat of crimson velvet; a hat of black velvet plumed with ostrich and heron feathers attached by a band of diamonds; an eight-point silver star; bearing centrally the red cross of St George on a white ground, surrounded by the garter and motto; a gold collar of garters encircling red roses (by custom, although the statutes decree alternate red and white roses) alternating with white enamelled knots of cords; the George, being an enamelled figure of a mounted St George fighting the dragon, to be worn from the collar; the lesser George, being the former in gold or gilt badge form, surrounded by the garter, worn from a riband of 'kingfisher blue' over the left shoulder.

Garter King of Arms: see **College of Arms.**

gartier: see **bendlet.**

garvie: [Gael.] a sprat (see also **sparling**); employed mainly in Scots heraldry for ca. reasons.

gas-bracket: see **supporters.**

gastel: obs. term equivalent to 'roundel' (q.v.).

gate: [O.E.] generally of five horizontal bars, the hinge-strake, which is to the dexter, extending upward and sometimes curved over to the sinister: a diagonal, crossing all bars, descends from near the top of the extended hinge-strake, to the bottom corner of the latch-strake. Hanger-hinges and a tip-latch may be added at the artist's discretion. The ~ is employed for ca. purposes, particularly in civic arms when the borough has the suffix . . . gate'. (279)

Gatty, Sir Alfred Scott-: Garter King of Arms, 1904. Former York Herald, 1886; former Rouge Dragon Pursuivant, 1880.

gauntlet: A steel-clad leather glove used to protect the hand; an accessory to a suit of plate armour. Depicted as a 'mitten' without separate compartments for the fingers and thumb; erect u.o.s., the back invariably presented, the palmar surface not being armoured.

gaze, at: see **stag.**

geastet: Ger., raguly.

gebekt: D., beaked.

geblak[t]: Afk. and D., company.

gebleomd kruis: D., cross flory.

gebogen: Ger., arched.

gebonden: D., jessed.

geboord: D., fimbriated.

gebseek: Afk., differenced.

ged: see **pike.**

Geddes, James: Kintyre Pursuivant, 1785.

Gedding, Wm: see **Jenyns, Wm**[2].

gedeel: Afk. and D., pale.

gedek: Afk., surmounted.

Gedeminas, Order of: (Lithuania) f. 1928 in five classes. Insignia—*Badge:* an iron cross in saltire, with each arm bearing a white enamel insert and separated by three rays of gold; a diamond-shaped centre of red enamel, gold rimmed, bears Gedeminas's crest, the gates of Castle Trakai. *Star:* the badge on a silver star of nine-points. *Riband:* yellow with dark brown edges.

gedwarsbalk: Afk., barry.

geer: D., gyron.

gefesselt: Ger., jessed.

geflosst: Ger., finned.

gegeerd: D., gyronny.

gegenast: Ger., raguly.

gegenfeh: Ger., counter-vair.

gegenzinnen: Ger., bretessy.

gegolfd: D., wavy.

gegrifft: Ger., hilted.

gehaard: D., crined.

gehalsband: D., collared.

gehoornd: D., horned.

gehörnt: Ger., horned.

Geijer, Eric Neville: Rouge Dragon Pursuivant, 1926.

gekanteel(d): Afk. and D., embattled.

---

211. Sable, a Julian cross argent and, in chief, a crescent Or.
     Sir Edward Corne.

212. Or a cross-crosslet ermines between four ermine spots sable.
     Durrant of Scottowe.

213. Argent a cross ermine sable.
     Hudelton.

214. Per pale Or and gules, two crosses trefly dimidiated and issuant from the dexter and the sinister flanks, counterchanged.
     Cochrane (Sir Arthur) (Clarenceux King of Arms).

215. Argent, three crosses patonce, gules.
     Stainton.

216. Sable, three crosses pommetty Or.
     Feres.

211

212

213

214

215

216

gekapt: D., chape.

gekeper: Afk., chevronry.

gekleed: D., vested.

geknobbeld: D., nowy.

geknopt: D., seeded.

geledigd: D., voided.

gelelied kruis: D., cross floretty.

geleliedeen teengelelied: Afk., flory-counter-fleury.

gelockt: Ger., crined.

Gelre, Armorial de: an heraldic manuscript vellum book consisting of 124 folios measuring $8\frac{1}{2}$ by $5\frac{1}{2}$ in.; noteworthy for, in addition to its excellence of execution, its containing on folios 64r, 64v, and 65r the oldest extant roll of Scottish arms; forty-two in number. It is the work of Claes Heynen, Gelre Herault de Arms to the Duc de Gueldres (Duke of Guelderland) from 1334 to 1372. Some of the painting seems to be from the brush of Claes Heynen fils who succeeded his father in office, and was later named Beyren Herald, until 1411.

geluipaarde: D., passant.

gemalied: Afk., masculy.

gemanteld: D., mantled.

gem-ring: a finger-ring and sometimes so blazoned, particularly when the colour of the stone is specified, 'a finger-ring gemmed (jewelled or stoned . . .)'.

gem-stones, blazon by: see **segregative blazon**.

gemmed: see **gem-ring**.

genageld: D., cloue.

General Rolls: see **rolls of arms**.

genet: [L.] a weasel, formative in the name Plantagenet. *Genetta vulgaris*, indigenous to south of France.

genomborrad ruta: Swd., rustre.

genombruten ruta: Swd., mascle.

genombrutet: Swd., voided.

gentil, flowers: flowers of the genus *Amaranthus*; employed as a symbol of immortality.

Gentry Roll: (c. 1480) contents thirty-six shields; known only from tricked (q.v.) copies.

genuant: [L.] of a human figure, usually clad in armour, when kneeling.

geopende hand: D., a hand appaume.

George Cross: f. by K. Geo. VI on 24 September 1940, revised 8 May 1941; takes precedence after V.C. and before all other British orders and decorations. Cross of plain silver, the cypher *GVI* in the angles, with a centre medallion surrounded by the words *For Gallantry* depicting St George slaying the dragon; the reverse bears the recipient's name and date of award; the cross is worn at left breast from a dark blue riband terminating in a silver bar adorned with laurel leaves. When worn alone the riband bears centrally a silver miniature of the Cross.

George, Cross of St: see **cross**.

George, Order of St: (Bavaria) of legendary foundation, it was given practical f. in 1729 when it became an order with strong Church connections and endowments. Belief in the Immaculate Conception was a prerequisite of appointment. Insignia—*Badge:* red cross paty notched, white edged, gold-ball tipped; between the arms lozenge-shaped rays; a gold central medallion depicts the Virgin Mary, the reverse showing St George and the dragon; the arms of the cross bear the initials *V I B I* (*Virgini Immaculate Bavaria Immaculata*) and on the reverse the motto *Justus Ut Palma Florebit. Star:* a silver-edged blue Maltese cross with a central medallion bearing the red cross of St George. *Riband:* light blue with white and dark blue stripes near the edges.

George I, Order of: (Greece) f. 1916 in six classes. Insignia—*Badge:* a gold-edged white enamelled cross surmounting a laurel wreath with a central medallion depicting a royal crown and cypher in gold on maroon; the medallion is surrounded by a Greek inscription in gold on white enamel, and the badge is ensigned with a crown; for the fifth class the badge is on silver, for the sixth, bronze. *Star:* the ensigned badge on a silver star of eight points.

George Medal: f. by K. Geo. VI on 24 September 1940. A silver medallion portraying K. Geo. VI surrounded by the inscription *Georgius VI. D.G.Br. Omn. Rex et Indiae Imp*; reverse of St George slaying a dragon on the British coast, circumscribed by the words *The George Medal*.

geapal: Afk., pale.

gepeilt: Ger., per fess.

gerändert: Ger., fimbriated.

gerated: (possibly an anagram on 're-grated') a r. alt. for 'semé' (q.v.).

gerautet: Ger., lozengy.

geruit: Afk., lozengy.

gescheiden kruis: D., cross patonce.

gescherpt: D., pointed at each end.

geschlechtsteilen: Ger., membered.

geschuind: D., per bend.

geschulpt: D., invected.

geskaak: Afk., chequy.

geskaak in twee rye: Afk., counter-compony.

geskunisbalk: Afk., bendy.

geslachtsdeel: D., stringed.

gesp: D., buckle.

gespalten: Ger., per pale.

gespe: Afk., buckle.

geständert: Ger., gyronny.

gestuckt: Ger., compony.

getoomd: D., bridled.

getralied: D. and Afk., fretty.

gevierendeel: Afk. and D., quarterly.

geviert: Ger., quarterly.

gevind: D., finned.

gevleugelds draak: D., wyvern.

geweckt: Ger., fusily.

gewelfd: D., enarched.

gewolk: Afk., D., and Ger., nebuly.

gezähnelt: Ger., indented.

gezäumt: Ger., bridled.

gheronato: It., gyronny.

gherone: It., gyron.

ghianda: It., acorn.

ghost charge: see **entrailed.**

giavellotto: It., javelin.

Gibbon, Edward Howard: Norroy King of Arms, 1848. Former York Herald, 1842; former Mowbray Herald Extraordinary, 1842.

Gibbon, James: Carrick Pursuivant, 1827.

Gibbon, John: Bluemantle Pursuivant, 1671.

Gibbon, Matthew Charles Howard: Richmond Herald, 1846.

giglio: It., fleur-de-lys.

gillyflower: [M.E.] July flowers; the clove-scented pink, *Dianthus caryophyllus.* In dial. use, the wallflower, *Cheiranthus cheiri,* is called ~ ; hence, in blazon, when the wallflower is intended, the term 'wall-~' is employed. (388)

Gilman, Andrew: Ross Herald, 1860. Unicorn Pursuivant, 1859.

gimlet: see **auger.**

ginbalk: Swd., bend sinister.

ginstam: Swd., chief.

ginstyckad: Swd., bend sinister.

gipon: alt. spelling of 'jupon' (q.v.).

giraffe: see **camelopard.**

girfauk: see **falcon.**

giron: Fr., gyron.

gironné: Fr., gyronny.

gironnerad: Swd., gyronny.

girouettés: [Fr.] a method employed in French heraldry of blazoning vanes: the castle, tower, or other structure of such a colour is ~ of some other colour.

girt: see **close-girt.**

gitterraite: Ger., fret.

glaive: a javelin (q.v.), employed only for ca. reasons.

gland: Fr., acorn.

Glass, George: Rothesay Herald, 1724. Bute Pursuivant, 1715.

glazier's nippers: a long narrow thin plate of iron, rounded at each end, and having a narrow slot cut into each side and sloping at about 45° towards the centre. It was a device used to remove spiky corners and rough edges from sheets of glass; hence, it is applied symbolically beyond the confines of the glass-worker's craft. Alt. terms are 'grossing-iron' and 'crimping-iron'; 'graizier's nippers' must be included, but this last is obviously a perpetuated spelling mistake. (317)

Gledstanes of Quothquhan, John: Ormonde Pursuivant, 1577.

glevenkreux: Ger., cross flory.

gliding: [O.E.] alt. for 'glissant' (q.v.).

glissant: [O.E.] of a serpent extended in fess, the head raised, and supposed to be gliding (as it may be blazoned) to the dexter. Depicted with the length of the body raised in a series of humps, it is blazoned '~ wavy'.

globe celestial: seldom detailed, and generally depicted with a broad belt at the equator on which signs of the Zodiac appear. ~ may be blazoned as 'celestial sphere'.

globe terrestrial: a circular shape showing a few meridians and latitudes, with the land-masses very roughly indicated. When a '~ on its tripod' is blazoned a short length of rod extends northward and southward beyond the poles. These engage in sockets at each end of a semicircular carriage which is itself attached to three curving legs. A ~ may be 'demi-' or 'broken'. (227)

globical, cross: a cross having limbs that cover roughly the same area as those of cross paty (q.v.) but which has the two sides of each limb concave and the extremity convex; r. alt. term 'cross alisée', which may have been dropped on account of its frequent er. confusion with O.E. 'alise', a report, a rumour.

globical lamp: see **lamp.**

glory, a: [L.] a nimbus; a circular effulgence of mystical light surrounding a whole figure and represented by a circle of short radial lines. See also **halo.**

Gloucester King of Arms: served either Thomas of Woodstock, Duke of Glou-

---

217. Argent, a cross gules; on a chief azure a crown encircled with the garter between, on the dexter, a lion passant gardant, crowned; and, on the sinister, a fleur-de-lys, all Or.
Garter King of Arms (Arms of Office).

218. Argent, a cross potent between four crosses humetty Or.
Christian Kingdom of Jerusalem.

219. Per pale argent and sable a cross dovetailed: in the first and fourth quarters a fleur-de-lys, in the second and third a trefoil slipped, all counterchanged.
Fenton.

220. Argent, a tau-cross gules and, in chief, three wreathes vert.
Tawke, Sussex.

221. Gules, a heart between three crosses-crosslet fitchy, Or.
De Lisle-Adams.

222. Or, a cross engrailed interlaced with a gurge.
Syffard.

217

218

219

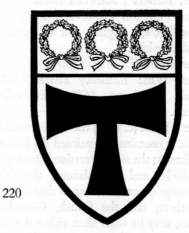

220

221

222

cester, or Thomas Despencer, Earl of Gloucester (c. 1400). K. Ric. III had a ~ but he seems to have been without a province. In the early XVIII cent. both K. of A. (q.v.) received ~ as an extra title and Wales for his province, but there was a strong protest from both Clarenceux and Norroy king of arms, and the name was withdrawn.

glove: Generally a 'falconer's' or a 'hawking' ~ will be specified. A ~ is orientated by the direction in which the fingers point: may be tasselled at the wrist (252).

gloved: see **hand.**

Glover, Robert[1]: Somerset Herald, 1570. Former Portcullis Pursuivant, 1568. The earliest known English roll of arms is named after him.

Glover, Robert[2]: see next entry.

Glover, Wm: Rothesay Herald, 1676. Carrick Pursuivant, 1676. Also called 'Robert'.

Glover's Roll: (c. 1255) the earliest version (Cooke's) contains 211 painted shields and 214 blazons; the second version (Harvey's), 215 shields and 218 blazons; the third (St George's) version is much shorter than the others; and the fourth, Grimaldi's version, may be older than either the first or the second. They are true rolls (q.v.) painted and blazoned on vellum.

glutinatus: L., masoned.

glutton: see **wolverene.**

goat: [O.E.] a quadruped of the genus *Capra*, distinguished in heraldic art by his long ogee horns and his beard. The agility of the ~ has secured for him the term 'clymant' as alt. to 'rampant' (q.v.). (21)

gobony: see **compony.**

God: represented in the arms of the Municipal Corporation of Bozi Dar, Bohemia. The town's name means 'gift of God'. See also **eye.**

gold: [Teut.] used as an alt. to the word 'Or'

(q.v.) in blazon (q.v.), but according to one school of thought it should be applied only to objects that are to be understood as constructed from gold, e.g. 'covered-cups, gold' but 'a lion Or'. (257)

golden: Ger., Or.

Golden Fleece, Order of the: f. 10 January 1429 at Bruges by Philip the Good, Duke of Burgundy. In time the Order, because of family interconnections, was claimed by both the House of Spain and the House of Austria, and the Grand Mastership remained in dispute until the Congress of Cambrai decreed in 1721 that each house should have an independent Order of the Golden Fleece. The Order has always been of the highest standing, and in the past its knights—it is a one-class order—have been granted great privileges, including exemption from all taxes and precedence before all peers save princes of the blood royal. The insignia consists of the badge, worn from neck by a crimson riband or from the collar, which latter has been issued in many designs. There is no star. The badge, for both Austria and Spain, is a golden sheep's fleece suspended at its middle, so that head and feet are in line, from a gold-mounted flintstone, issuant of gold-rimmed red enamel rays; the Spanish insignia surmounts the flames with an ornate gold device surrounding a red and gold rose, and at the base of the neck riband has an additional ornamentation in gold, containing a precious stone; the Austrian insignia surmounts the flames with a crown-like device in gold depicting Jason slaying the dragon; this is ensigned with gold-rimmed blue enamel scroll bearing in gold the motto *Pretium Laborum Non Vile*. Many variants of these badges exist, for numerous knights had their own insignia created, incorporating precious stones. Napoleon created in 1809 an 'Order of the Three Golden Fleeces' in

which the badge of three fleeces was ensigned by a crowned Imperial eagle; the
riband was red, edged white; there was no
star; the Napoleonic Order became defunct
in 1815.

Golden Lion, Order of: (Luxembourg) f.
1858 in five classes. Insignia—*Badge:* a
white Maltese cross, edged gold, with one
ornate N between the arms; a central
medallion of blue enamel depicts in gold a
lion rampant. *Star:* the badge's central
medallion, surrounded by a gold rimmed
white enamelled band bearing in gold the
motto *Je Maintiendrai,* surmounting a silver
eight-point star. *Riband:* orange with
blue stripes at the edges.

Golden Spur, Order of: (Vatican) re-
putedly f. by Pope St Sylvester in 332.
At one time the Order could be conferred
by numerous Papal and Roman dignitaries,
and carried with it the hereditary title of
count. The Order was reformed drastically
in 1841 and in 1905, and has subsequently
been granted sparingly. Insignia—*Badge:* a
gold cross paty notched with a central
medallion of white enamel bearing the gold-
crowned monogram of the Virgin Mary; a
gold spur is suspended between the two
points of the bottom arm of the cross; the
badge is ensigned by a military trophy of
arms. *Star:* the unensigned badge on a
silver star of eight points. *Riband:* red,
edged white.

Goldie, George: Ross Herald, 1839. Ormonde Pursuivant, 1835.

golfsgewysgeent: D., nebully.

golpe: A roundel (q.v.) purpure; employed
only in continental heraldry.

golwend: Afk., wavy.

gonfalon: see following entry.

gonfannon: [M.E.] formerly the name given
to a lance-pennon (q.v.); in modern usage a
flag constructed so as to be suspended by the
head from a spar which is itself supported

on a central staff. The foot of the ~ is
shaped in one of three ways; it may be
either triangular, or semicircular, or it may
have a number of short streamers pendant.
These pendants, of which there are usually
either three or six, may be rectangular with
flat ends, rectangular with rounded ends, or
triangular, points downward. ~s are
carried in solemn ecclesiastical procession,
with slight variations in funeral processions,
and they may function as charges on the
armorial field where they may themselves
carry charges. Alt. term 'gonfalon'. The
same word with slight deviation of spelling
occurs throughout Europe. (428)

Gordon, Charles: Unicorn Pursuivant,
1719.

Gordon, George: Kintyre Pursuivant,
1661.

Gordon, Herbert Lewis: Herald-painter
to the Lyon Court, 1943.

Gordon of Craig, Wm: Dingwal Pursuivant, 1761.

gore: see **rebatements of honours.**

gorge: r. alt. for a water-bouget (q.v.).

gorged: [M.E.] of a beast having the neck
encircled with some object other than a
collar (q.v.), generally with a coronet;
'gorged with a collar' is a frequent redund-
ancy.

goscelyn: see **joscelyn.**

goshawk: see **falcon.**

Gottand, St: appears in the public arms of
Gotha.

goud: Afk. and D., Or.

goutté: [M.E.] lit. drops, particularly of
viscous or semi-viscous liquid; hence pear-
shaped charges, orientated with the bulge
downward, but may, on occasion, be inverted. ~ in British heraldry only, have
individual names, but may, nevertheless, be
blazoned by their colours. 'goutté d'Or',
~ of gold; 'goutté d'eau', argent, ~ of
water; 'goutté de larmes', azure, ~ of tears;

'goutté de sang', gules, ~ of blood; 'goutté de poix', sable, ~ of pitch; 'goutté d'olive' or 'd'huile', vert, ~ of oil.

goutty: semé (q.v.) of gouttés; also spelt 'gutty' and 'guttae'. (267)

Govan, Wm: Islay Herald, 1676.

gradato: It., indented.

gradiens: L. passant.

grady: a fesswise line of partition in which a crenellation has, rising from it, a smaller crenellation, one-third of its own width; two double crenellations rise, one in the centre of the shield falls; ~, also termed 'battled–embattled'; may cross the shield chevronwise without having a descending section. (164)

Graf: Ger., see **count.**

Graham, Daniel: Dingwal Pursuivant, 1596.

Graham, Richard: Rouge Croix Pursuivant, 1722.

grain-tree: appears as the crest of the Worshipful Company of Dyers: represented as a straight stem bearing pairs of ovate leaves at intervals with, in the angle of junction, a red berry. The ~ is a child of error, it being thought that the 'berries'

were seeds: they were actually dead cochineal insects, adhering to imported cactus.

graminy chaplet: [Sp.] a circlet of woven grass, but apparently only theoretical.

grand duke: the first duke (q.v.) to be elevated to the status of grand duke was Cosimo I of Florence, by a patent of 1567 from Pius V. Napoleon conferred the title on his brother-in-law, Joachim Murat, in 1806, during which year the rulers of Baden, Hesse-Darmstadt, and Wurzburg assumed the title. The Congress of Vienna allowed the distinction to the sovereigns of Baden, Hesse-Darmstadt, Luxembourg, Mecklenburg-Schwerin, Mecklenburg-Strelitz, Oldenburg, and Saxe-Weimar. The Emperor of Austria (see also **archduke**), the King of Prussia, and the Grand Duke of Tuscany possessed the title, which was also borne by all descendants of the Russian Imperial House until 1886, when it was restricted to the sons, daughters, male grandchildren, brothers, and sisters of the emperor.

grand quarter: see **quarterly.**

grandee: [Sp.] lit. great; hence, a title borne by the highest Spanish nobility. It is not in itself a peerage rank, but in 1824

---

223. Ermine, a cross quarterly pierced, ermines. *Brugge, Richard del* (Lancaster Herald, 1380).

224. Gules, a cross argent, between four cushions, lozengewise, ermine, tasselled Or. *Redman, Wm* (Bishop of Norwich, 1595–1602).

225. Or, a cross raguly gules between four trefoils, slipped vert. *Clark.*

226. Or, on a cross between four fleur-de-lys azure, a crosier of the field. *Crozier.*

227. Per pale azure and gules, crusilly, and a cross moline voided Or: overall, on fess point a terrestrial globe proper. *Oceltine*

228. Or, on a cross gules between I, a dove holding in the beak a sprig of olive; II, an aloe; III, a staff erect entwined with a serpent and, IV, an alembic and receiver, all proper, a hand-balance of the first: on a chief azure, a stag lodged, also of the first. *Pharmaceutical Society of Great Britain.*

223

224

225

226

227

228

grandees were granted precedence in the Chamber of Peers. Their privileges have now been abolished but were at one time considerable, and included freedom from taxation and civil arrest. Grandees were of three classes: the first spoke and listened to the king with covered heads; the second spoke to him covered but uncovered for his reply; the third needed the king's permission to cover themselves; all were addressed by the king as 'my cousin'.

grannapye: [dial.] a duck; r. employed only for ca. reasons.

Grant, Francis James: Lyon Clerk and Keeper of the Records, 1898. Rothesay Herald, 1898. Carrick Pursuivant, 1886.

Grant, John: Marchmont Herald, 1884. Carrick Pursuivant, 1883.

Grant, Malcolm: Carrick Pursuivant, 1771.

Grant, Robert: Islay Herald, 1795. Unicorn Pursuivant, 1790.

grape: [M.E.] fruit of the vine, which grows in bunches and is so depicted; normally pendant, but may be erect. (394)

grapnel: a three-fluked, stockless anchor, used in old naval warfare for casting among the lines and spars of an enemy ship and so holding them for boarding and capture. The ∼ was also employed as an anchor (q.v.) for small boats, and, by dragging, as a means of securing drowned corpses, for which purpose it is still in use. Alt. term 'grappling-iron' may have four instead of three hooks, and a '∼ head' always has four since it forms a cross barely distinguishable from cross hamecon (q.v.).

grass: [O.E.] meadow-grass, generally blazoned as in tufts, each of so many blades, and sometimes the particular type is stated, e.g. 'cocksfoot ∼'. Tufts are occasionally miscalled 'spines', and blades may be referred to as 'piles', but such terms are seldom to be met with since ∼ is itself r.

grasshopper: [M.E.] an orthopterous insect,

winged, and noted for chiriping, i.e. the musical sound it produces by rubbing its legs against its wings. A ca. device for the House of Gresham. Sometimes blazoned as a 'cicada', notwithstanding that the latter is totally different, inhabiting trees and shrubs. The sole similarity is in the action of chirping. (82)

graverk: Swd., vane.

gray: see **badger.**

Gray, Wm: Dingwal Pursuivant, 1718.

grazier's nippers: see **glazier's nippers.**

Great Alphabet, the: see **Alphabet, the Great.**

Great Roll, the: see **Parliamentary Roll.**

Great Star of Jugoslavia, Order of the: f. 1954 in one class. Insignia—*Badge:* a plaque of gold scroll-work, surmounted by a central medallion of purple enamel depicting in gold the arms of socialist Jugoslavia; the arms being surmounted by a small red star of five points. *Star:* the badge on a silver star of ten points, the centre medallion surrounded by brilliants. *Riband:* purple.

Greek alphabet: see **script.**

Greek cross: see **cross.**

Greek Order of George I: see **George I, Order of.**

Green, Alexander: Kintyre Pursuivant, 1714.

Green, James: Bluemantle Pursuivant, 1719.

Greene, Charles: Lancaster Herald, 1729. Former Arundel Herald Extraordinary, 1727.

Greenwood, Richard: Rouge Croix Pursuivant, 1485.

gregor: see **partridge.**

grelot: [Fr.] r. alt. for a hawk's bell (q.v.).

grenade: a fireball or bombshell (q.v.) to which a short length of cylindrical neck is attached out of which the flames issue. The ∼, which was designed for throwing by hand, and the bombshell (q.v.) designed for

PLATE VIII England within a bordure of
France. (Gules, three lions passant
gardant in pale Or within a bordure
azure semé-de-lys of the second.)
John of Eltham, Earl of Cornwall
(John Plantagenet – second son of
K. Ed. II and Isobel of France)
Effigy in Westminster Abbey
Arms emblazoned on shield and
jupon.

firing from a gun differ only in the neck attached to the ~; hence, they are often confused and consequently misdrawn. (203)

Greve, Henry: Lord Lyon King of Arms, 1339.

Grey v. Hastings: the accidental death of John, sixth Lord Hastings and third Earl of Pembroke (*aet* 16 *anno*) in 1389, in a tournament caused the Hastings title and arms to be claimed by both Reginald (or Reynald) Lord Grey de Ruthyn, and Sir Ed. Hastings. The former's grandfather, Roger, Lord Grey had married Elizabeth, daughter of Lord Hastings by his first wife, Isobel de Valence. He now claimed the title and undifferenced arms, namely, 'Or a maunch gules', as heir-general of John, Lord Hastings and Earl of Pembroke, the last person seized of the Estates title and arms, he being descended from a sister of the whole-blood of John, third Lord Hastings.

Sir Ed. Hastings was descended from the eldest son of the second wife, Marjery Foliot, and he asserted his right to the title and arms as heir-male, he being great grandson of Sir Hugh Hastings, brother of the half-blood of the third Lord Hastings.

Judgement was pronounced (11 A.R. K. Hen. IV) against Sir Ed. Hastings who was condemned in costs. He entered an appeal and withheld payment of costs. This debt was 'bought' by Lord Grey de Ruthyn who thus became the creditor, and caused Sir Ed. to be arrested for debt and thrown into the Marshalsea Prison.

All Sir Ed. had to do to regain his freedom was, not settle the bill for £987 costs, but relinquish his claim to the arms and title. This he stubbornly refused to do, and suffered great privation and loss. Three and a half years after his arrest he wrote an admonitory letter to Lord Grey de Ruthyn and signed it 'Edward, Lord Hastings'. Ten years later the two men came to terms: Sir

Edward's son should marry Lord Grey's daughter and so resolve the problem; however, the iron wills of the fathers were inherited by their children and no marriage could be arranged.

Sir Edward died after having spent twenty-six years 'bounden in fetters of iron liker a thief or traitor, than like a gentleman of birth'. Before his passing he called upon his posterity to continue to make the claim, which was faithfully done by one or another of them whenever it seemed that an opportunity presented itself. During the Tudor period, male issue failed and Sir Edward's line was fragmented between co-heiresses. A descendant of one seized an opportunity to bring the matter to a hearing again in 1641, but the previous judgement was confirmed. Two hundred years later another opportunity occurred to bring the ancient dispute forward, and by a judgement of the House of Lords dated 18 May 1841, Sir Jacob Astley was summoned to Parliament by Writ as Baron Hastings, bearing Or a maunch gules; thus the judgement was reversed in favour of a descendant of the line of Sir Edward Hastings.

greyhound: see **dog**.

grice: [M.E.] lit. a sucking-pig; hence, a young boar.

grices: [M.E.] steps or stairs; hence, alt. for 'degrees' (q.v.). As spelt is correct, but 'greeces' (of which it is an earlier form) is permissible: all other expedients to distinguish it from the previous entry are barbarous.

gridiron: [M.E.] representing the medium of St Lawrence's martyrdom: an instrument consisting of parallel iron rods held together by cross-pieces, and provided with a handle, used for grilling meat over an open fire, and this culinary implement is used as an heraldic charge, it being the saint's emblem. However, a similarly arranged frame of rods was an instrument of torture by roasting to death, and was known as a ~.

Grierson, Andrew: Snowdoun Herald, 1665.

Grieve, John: Carrick Pursuivant, 1790.

griffin: [Gk.] a composite fictitious creature having the fore-quarters and wings of an eagle conjoined to the hind-quarters of an heraldic lion. Nevertheless, the assumption that the ~ was created by dimidiation (q.v.) is unjustified since the conception can be traced to the Archaic Civilization: the ~ head has the addition of a pair of asses' ears without which 'a ~ head' as a charge would be indistinguishable from that of an eagle. The wings are addorsed u.o.s., and it is blazoned either as 'armed' or as 'beaked and forelegged'. It may assume any of the heraldic postures but is most commonly seen in the rampant attitude which is described as 'segreant', a word of doubtful origin and meaning. A male ~, which is rare, is wingless, and has rays issuant at all its joints. It is also known as the alce. (188)

Griffin, Thomas: Richmond Herald in the service of George, Duke of Clarence, c. 1473.

Griffin Pursuivant: maintained by earls of Salisbury (1385); also spelt 'gryphon'.

griffon: alt. spelling of 'griffin' (q.v.).

grig: see **eel.**

grillage: a variation of the field (q.v.) in the category of fretty (q.v.) and trellis (q.v.) but consisting of interlaced fesswise and palewise pieces; r. in British heraldry.

grille: [Fr.] a grating; an arrangement of bars on strips of metal forming a mesh; hence, the face-guard of a non-visored helmet.

Grimaldi, Order of: (Monaco) f. 1954 in five clases. Insignia—*Badge:* a white enamel cross of eight points, each tipped with a gold ball; a gold central medallion depicts a mounted knight surrounded by the inscription *Rainier Grimaldi, Prince of Monaco*; the badge is ensigned by a gold crown (silver for the fifth class). *Star:* the badge's central medallion and inscription surmounting a silver star of sixteen straight edged points. *Riband:* white, with red stripes at the edges.

Grimaldi's Roll: (c. 1350) a vellum true roll 9½ in. by 9 ft. 11 in., painted with 167 shields, names and blazons over.

Grimsby, Wm: created a king of arms,

---

229. Gules, a crown royal Or.
M'Alpin.

230. Or, a crown vallary gules between three stags trippant proper.
Rogers.

231. Gules, three antique crowns Or within a bordure engrailed of the last.
Grant, Dalvey.

232. Azure, a mural crown within an orle of twelve anchors, Or.
Lendon.

233. Argent, a mural crown between three holly leaves vert.
Irwin.

234. Azure, three clouds argent irradiated Or, each ensigned with as many open crowns palewise, also Or.
Worshipful Company of Drapers.
[Note: Granted 1438, the patent being the oldest extant.]

229

230

231

232

233

234

1462, under the name either of Lancaster or Ireland.

gringoly: of a cross the limbs of which terminate in serpents' heads; of any object decorated with serpents; alt. term 'guivre'; use r. in British heraldry.

grip: Swd., griffin.

Groby Herald: maintained by Thomas Grey, Lord Ferrers of Groby, 1475.

groen: Afk. and D., vert.

grönt: Swd., vert.

groot uitgeschulpt: D., engrailed.

grose: probably a phonetical, hence, spelling error, 'croze' being intended: alt. term for 'royne' (q.v.).

Grose, Francis: Richmond Herald, 1755. Famous for his *Classical Dictionary of the Vulgar Tongue.* He was caricatured by Thomas Rowlandson, being the central figure in the foreground of the print depicting the Earl Marshal's Court in *The Microcosm of London.*

grosser reif: Ger. annulet.

grossing iron: see **glazier's nippers.**

grun: Ger., vert.

gryphon: alt. spelling of 'griffin' (q.v.).

Gryphon Pursuivant: see **Griffin, Pursuivant.**

gryphonmarine: a sea-griffin, being the fore part of an eagle dimidiated (q.v.) with the hind part of a fish; there is also a male ~ (see **griffin**); employed in Teutonic heraldry, but not in British.

gu.: see **G.**

guardant: see **gardant.**

guarded: a term equivalent to 'turned up' (q.v.) and sometimes employed to describe the visible fold of the ermine lining of the crimson cap filling a peer's coronet.

guarnecida: Sp., hilted.

guarnita: It., hilted.

gudgeon: [M.E.] a freshwater fish of small size, used for bait, *Gobio fluviatilis*; employed in heraldry chiefly for ca. reasons.

Guelphic and Ghibelline chiefs: peculiar to Italian heraldry, denoting a tribal allegiance. The Guelphic chief, *capo d'Angio*, is azure charged with a label of four points gules and, between the files, three f.d.l. Or. The Ghibelline chief, *capo dell'imperio*, is Or, charged with an eagle sable.

Guelphic Order, the Royal: f. 1815 by the Prince Regent in three classes, with Military and Civil divisions. Insignia: Knights Grand Cross—a silver eight-point star with crossed swords in gold for the Military Division; a red medallion superimposed bearing the so-called white horse of Hanover (q.v.) surrounded by a blue circle with the motto *Nec Aspera Terrent* and a laurel wreath; a badge of eight points terminating in gold balls with a lion between the arms, bearing centrally the star's device; the reverse bears the founder's initials with the date *MDCCCXV*; ensigned with the royal cypher and crossed swords for the Military Division, and worn from the riband over the right shoulder. Knight Commanders—a similar star and badge, the latter worn from the riband round the neck. Knights—the badge worn from the riband on the left breast. *Riband:* sky-blue moiré.

gueules: Fr., gules.

guidon: a tapering flag with a rounded fly, from hoist to fly about three times the measurement of the dip, fringed of the colours. The form of ensign carried by regiments of dragoons and by the Royal Horse Artillery.

guige: [O.F.] a strap attached to the back of the shield from which it might be supported.

guild marks: see **merchants' marks.**

Guillim, John: Rouge Croix Pursuivant, 1613. Former Portsmouth Pursuivant, 1604.

Guillim's Roll: (c. 1295) vellum true roll, painted, 148 shields, names over.

guion: Sp., guidon.

Guisnes Pursuivant: one of the garrison officers of arms in Picardy (1474). From Guines, near Calais.

guivre: alt. for 'gringoly' (q.v.).

guld: Swd., Or.

gules: [L.] red; crimson; from 'gule', the gullet. Notwithstanding the constant repetition of the fallacy that ~ derives from the Arabic 'gul', a (red) rose, the fact remains that it does not, nor is there the vaguest relationship. Engraver's cross-hatching, palewise parallel lines.

gull: see **perch.**

gun: [M.E.] generally, but not invariably, applied to ordnance, but also to the musket (q.v.) used notably in the arms of the Worshipful Company of Gunmakers. (46)

gunner: [dial.] a folk name for the sea-bream employed in ca. settings.

gunstone: see **ogress.**

gurge: [L.] a conventionalized representation of a whirlpool (as it is sometimes blazoned), being a spiral expanding from fess point; strictly argent and azure, but other colours are employed. A number of concentric annulets are not a ~ but are often thus blazoned. (222)

gurnard: [M.E.] a sea-fish having a large head, of the genus *Trigla*; employed in heraldry chiefly for ca. reasons. Also known as 'gurnet' and as 'tub-fish'; this last, alt. spelt 'tubbe', is a Cornish dial. word; hence, so blazoned in arms of Cornishmen.

gurnet: see previous entry.

gurze: a roundel (q.v.) sanguine (q.v.) employed only in continental heraldry.

gusset: see **rebatements of honour.**

Guthrie, Alexander[1]: Snowdoun Herald, 1571. Falklands Pursuivant, 1532.

Guthrie, Alexander[2]: Marchmont Herald, 1630.

Guthrie, Gilbert: Linlithgow Pursuivant Extraordinary, 1572. Marchmont Herald, 1588.

Guthrie, James: Dingwall Pursuivant, 1682.

guttae: see **goutty.**

Guyenne Herald: an obs. English name of office. There was also a ~ King of Arms.

Guyenne King of Arms: a XV cent. office for service in the English possessions in France. There was also a ~ Herald in the service of K. Hen. VI. During the reign of K. Hen. V this officer of arms was known as 'Guienne and Aquitaine K. of A.' (or vice versa). See also **Aquitaine King of Arms.**

gyron: [Fr.] an obs. sub-ordinary being the lower half of a quarter per bend; a 'based esquirre' (q.v.).

gyronny: [Fr.] of a field, or an ordinary (q.v.) party per pale, per fess, per bend, and per bend sinister, giving eight triangular pieces, alternately metal (or fur) and tincture; a gyron, as a sub-ordinary is the lower half of a quarter per bend (see **esquirre**); may be of six, ten, or twelve pieces; termed, strictly, mal-~. In Teutonic heraldry the lines forming ~ may be curved and, when translated into English blazon are described, e.g. 'Gyronny-curved, sable, and argent' for von Aldenburg. (185, 425)

haan: D., cock.

habick: an instrument formerly used by cloth workers: in its appearance it could easily be mistaken for a bow-handle that has been violently pulled from a back-door, the screws remaining in, and projecting beyond the terminals of the bow. It is notably employed in the arms of the Worshipful Company of Clothworkers.

habited: [M.E.] dressed, clad or clothed;

applicable to the human form in its various guises.

hackle: see **hemp-break.**

haddock: [M.E.] a small sea-fish *Gadus aeglefinus,* related to the cod (q.v.); employed in heraldry for ca. reasons.

haft: [Teut.] a handle, generally of a tool that has to be swung, or wielded, as, e.g., an adze (q.v.), an axe (q.v.), or a sledge-hammer (q.v.). The bit, or head, of such tools, although the smaller, is of superior importance, the blazon naming the tool, e.g. 'an axe argent, hafted azure'. Alt. 'helve'.

hahn: Ger., cock.

haie: see **weir.**

Haig, Sir Thomas Wolseley: Albany Herald, 1927. March Pursuivant, 1923.

Hailes Pursuivant Extraordinary: an officer of arms maintained and probably created by the Earl of Bothwell in 1488. Office filled by George Schoriswood in 1508.

hake: [M.E.] a large sea-fish, *Merlucius vulgaris,* similar to the cod (q.v.); employed chiefly for ca. reasons.

hakenkruis: D., swastika.

halberd: see **pike[1].**

halbmond: Ger., crescent.

Hales, Humphrey: York Herald, 1587. Former Bluemantle Pursuivant, 1584.

half-spade: see **spade.**

half-spear: see **lance.**

Halley, Thomas: see **Hawley, Thomas.**

Hallvard, St: appears in the municipal arms of Oslo.

halo: [L. via Fr.] a disc, generally Or, sometimes argent, surrounding the head of a saint, and other symbolic figures of sacred import. See also **glory.**

halsband: Swd., collar.

halter: see **felon.**

halvmåne, liggande: Swd., crescent.

hamade: a fess (q.v.) or a bar (q.v.), couped (q.v.); r. in British heraldry. (407)

hame: a primitive collar for a draught-horse; in appearance rather like a lyre (q.v.).

hamecon, cross: [Fr.] four fish-hooks set head to head in cruciform juxtaposition the hook curving in a clockwise direction.

Hamilton, Robert: Kintyre Pursuivant, 1821.

Hamilton, Wm[1]: Angus Herald Extraordinary, 1502.

Hamilton, Wm[2]: Procurator Fiscal to the Lyon Court, 1663.

hammer: [O.E.] a percussion tool, employed in one of its very numerous shapes

---

235. Gules, a tilting-spear fesswise proper between three antique crowns Or.
Grant.

236. Ermine, two wreaths in chief and a rose in base gules.
Peche.

237. Per pale sable and argent, a chaplet of roses counterchanged.
Nairn.

238. Argent, a garland of laurel vert between three pheons gules.
Conqueror.

239. Argent, a civic wreath acorned proper: on a chief azure a serpent knowed Or and a dove of the field, respecting.
Sutton.

240. Azure, a wreath argent and sable, belled in quadrangle Or.
Jocelyn, Earl of Royden.

235

236

237

238

239

240

and sizes by almost every workman: it is symbolic of force, dominance, aggression, irresistibility, and mastery; hence it has application far exceeding its allusive function in connection with crafts in which the ~ is notably employed, e.g. that of the blacksmith. It consists of two parts, the metal (generally steel) head, and the wooden handle, the former being the more important since the handle, styled the haft, may be of a secondary colour, e.g. 'a ~ Or, hafted gules'. A ~ may be crowned, or the haft may be enfiled (q.v.) of a coronet: on the field, the ~ is erect, head chiefward u.o.s. The head remains chiefward when two are in saltire (q.v.). It serves in the capacity of a crest and also as a secondary object grasped in the outer hand of a supporter (q.v.) either inclined over the shoulder or 'with head resting upon the ground'. Since the haft is long enough to enable the supporter to remain standing under these conditions, it is clear that a sledge-~ is involved, but the blazon does not say so.

In heraldry the term ~ includes mallets, itself an inclusive description of all wooden-headed percussion tools from the paviour's heavy maul, or beetle, a cylindrical head with flat faces—actually a section of tree-trunk—which may be blazoned 'mallet', 'maul', or 'square-~', via the carpenter's long-hafted square-headed mallet, the mason's (or sculptor's) short-handled basin-shaped tool, to the jeweller's minute box-wood ~. (315)

Hampnes(s) Pursuivant: one of the garrison officers of arms in Picardy (1360). The name of office, also spelt 'Hammes' and 'Hannes', is derived from the castle near Calais. Now called Hames Castle.

hand: generally couped at the wrist and presenting the palmar surface (appaumé (q.v.)), fingers extended. A dexter ~ has the thumb to the sinister; proper u.o.s., and

when of a heraldic colour may be blazoned as 'gloved' of that colour. 'Raised in benediction', the thumb, index finger and second finger are extended, the other two flexed on the palm. (291)

hand-balance: an instrument for weighing small quantities with accuracy: the beam is suspended in a frame which acts as a guide to the eye in judging whether the indicator-needle is vertical. The pans, which are often hemispherical, are suspended by three silken cords attached to hooks at each end of the beam. The apothecaries used the ~ to weigh drugs, and in the first quarter of the XX cent. they were employed by tobacconists. (285, 474)

hand-basket: see **wicker**.

hand-bow: see **bow**.

hanger: see **sabre**.

hank of thread: either cotton, or silk, may be specified. Always wound in a figure of eight and the end carried round the cross-over. Employed chiefly for ca. reasons.

Hannes Pursuivant: see **Hampnes(s) Pursuivant**.

Hanover, White Horse of: a misnomer for the horse in base of the inescutcheon on the Hanoverian Royal Arms, viz. 'gules, a horse courant argent', for Saxony.

Hanover Herald: one of the names of office which, in 1726, was added to that of Bath King of Arms (q.v.). See also **Gloucester King of Arms**.

Hanoverian Royal Arms: When K. Geo. I acceded to the British throne the Royal Arms were remarshalled by making IV for Hanover, i.e. 'per pale and per chevron, I, gules, two lions passant gardant in pale Or', for *Brunswick*. II, 'Or, semé of hearts proper a lion rampant azure', for *Lunenburg*. III, 'gules, a horse courant argent' for *Saxony*. 'Surtout, on an escutcheon of pretence gules, the Crown of Charlemagne, gold'. A re-marshalling took place in 1801 on the Act of Union with Ireland, during the reign of K. Geo. III, i.e. I and IV *England*; II *Scotland*; III *Ireland*; surtout, *Hanover*, 'ensigned with the Electoral Bonnet'. In 1816 Hanover became a kingdom: K. Geo. III abandoned his title of 'Elector of the Holy Roman Empire' and substituted 'King of Hanover'. Armorially signified by replacing the Electoral Bonnet with the crown royal of Hanover. Q. Vic., on her accession in 1837, relinquished the throne of Hanover and abandoned the inescutcheon.

harboured: r. alt. for 'lodged' (q.v.).

Hardy, Wm: Unicorn Pursuivant, 1554.

hare: [O.E.] a small fur-clad quadruped, *Lepus timidus*, having a cleft upper lip and disproportionately long hind-legs which enable it to run at high speed. The usual attitude is courant, since the creature is symbolic of speed, but it is also to be found rampant, salient, and sejant in which position it is likely to be 'playing the bagpipes'.

Hare, John: Richmond Herald, 1704. Former Rouge Dragon, 1700.

Harington Pursuivant: maintained by the Marquis of Dorset who became Lord of Harington in right of his wife. (1475)

Harleian Roll; (temp. K. Ed. II) a book written at the Abbey of St Augustine, Canterbury, containing miscellaneous material including a French poem by Guillaume de Wadington entitled 'Manuel des Pechez'. The shields, 191 in all, are painted, four to six on the head-margin of each (vellum) page. Names are over.

harnas en dek: D., comparisoned.

harness: armour for man or horse, or both.

häroldskåpa: Swd., tabard.

harp: a musical instrument consisting of a timber frame formed of one upright post with extending outward and upward from the foot another, and both joined by a top-strake between which and the upright the strings are stretched. Following the example

of the third quarter of the Royal Arms, the ~ often has the form of an angel, the top-strake being the wing, but this elaboration is not essential. In addition to its being the insignia of Ireland, it is symbolic of musicianship. Alt. term 'cloyshacke'. (360, 403 third quarter)

harpy: [Gk] in mythology the spirits of the wind, particularly the hurricane, and messengers of the gods: depicted as the head and breast of a woman, merging with the body and legs of a vulture.

Harrington knot: a mascle interlaced with a saltire; hence, a fret (q.v.) and differing from the other heraldic knots in never being depicted as constructed from cord: the nearest compromise is to represent the component parts as leather straps. There is a possibility that the ~ is the child of error: sloven speakers and half-attentive listeners are a perpetual partnership in the formative process of a living language. In the Middle Ages they were more potent than they now are, for then the spoken language did heavy duty, and even those who could read were at a big disadvantage due to the erratic, non-standardized spelling of the period. One sloven speaker, mentioning the Harrington net to one semi-attentive auditor, would be enough to create, and to perpetuate, the ~.

Harrison, George: Clarenceux King of Arms, 1803. Former Norroy K. of A., 1784; former Windsor Herald, 1774; former Bluemantle Pursuivant, 1767.

Harrison, George Harrison Rogers: Windsor Herald, 1849. Former Bluemantle Pursuivant, 1831; former Blanch Lyon, 1831.

Harrison, Humphrey: Albany Herald, 1754.

harrow: [M.E.] of two shapes, either triangular or square; consisting of heavy timbers securely fastened and provided with cross-bars on the underside of which are fixed hooks, teeth, or tynes, used for drawing over the land after the plough (q.v.). The square ~ has cross bars in two directions and may be mistaken for a badly drawn portcullis (q.v.); the triangular ~ has the bars parallel with the base only. In both kinds the point of the tynes should be visible.

hart¹: [M.E.] alt. name for the stag (q.v.), the male red deer.

hart²: Afk., fess point.

Hart, John: Chester Herald, 1567. Former Newhaven Pursuivant, 1562.

Hart, Robert¹: Ross Herald, 1546. Bute Pursuivant, 1528.

Hart, Robert²: Rothesay Herald, 1533.

hartskild: Afk., inescutcheon.

harvest-fly: an unidentifiable winged insect having two wings only which cover the area of the butterfly's (q.v.) four, depicted volant en arriere, with two legs extended forward and two behind.

Harvey's version: see **rolls of arms.**

haselneutkruis: Afk., cross avellane.

Hastings, Henry: Somerset Herald, 1773. Former Rouge Croix Pursuivant, 1752.

Hastings, Wm: see **Hasyng, Wm.**

Hastings Pursuivant: maintained by William Lord Hastings (1479).

Hasyng, Wm: Somerset Herald, 1528, maintained by the Duke of Richmond and Somerset. Former Nottingham Pursuivant, 1526; former Rouge Dragon Pursuivant, 1521; former Buckingham Herald, 1514. Also spelt 'Hastings'.

hat, ecclesiastical: a broad-brimmed, small-crowned hat having a pair of cords (which may be knowed (q.v.)), each terminating in one or more tassels, descending from the headband. The ~ is employed to ensign the arms of a priest in accordance with the injunction of Pope Innocent IV, delivered at the Council of Lyons, 1248, but the custom is not exclusive in the Catholic Church; it is a feature of Scottish ecclesias-

241. Sable, three spervers ermine garnished azure and gules; within the sperver in base a lamb couchant argent on a cushion Or; above the lamb a cross paty fitchy of the third.
Worshipful Company of Upholders (i.e. Upholsterers).

242. Azure, three mitres Or.
Episcopal See of Norwich.

243. Gules, a dexter arm vambraced issuant in dexter flank brandishing a sword erect, all proper: flotant to the dexter therefrom a a banner charged with a cross between sixteen escutcheons of the first. On the cross, a lion of England.
Sir Edward Lake (Arms of augmentation).

244. Gules, three oreillers ermine, tasselled and fringed sable, set lozengewise.
Redemaine.

245. Argent, three lozenge-buckles, tongues fesswise, points to the sinister gules.
Jernyngham.

246. Gules, three dexter arms in pale, embowed, vambraced argent; the hands clenched proper.
Armstrong.

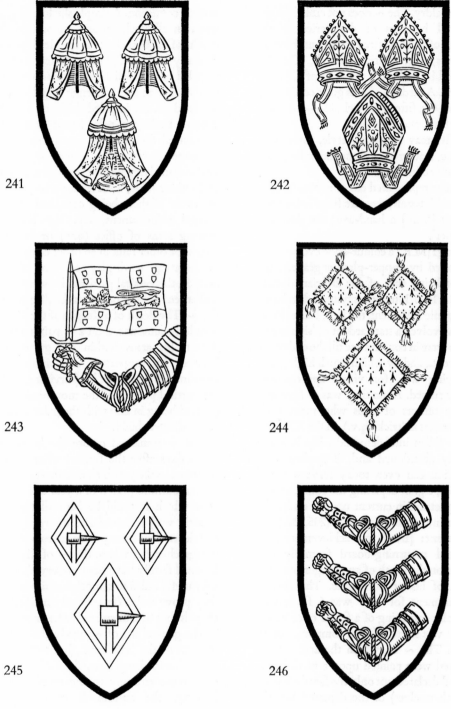

241

242

243

244

245

246

tical heraldry. The ~ does not embellish the armorial bearings of dignitaries of the Church of England (see **mitre**) but there are survivals; e.g. Christ Church, Oxford, founded by and using the arms of Cardinal Wolsey. A cardinal's hat is gules corded and tasselled Or, fifteen on each side—one, two, three, four, and five. (V)

hat, felt: may be of any style, turned-up, tricorne, feathered, and the like which will be specified in the blazon.

hatbands: represented either as braids, or as cords with tassels; separate from hats (q.v.).

hatchet: [M.E.] a hand-axe; the domestic 'chopper'.

hatching: [M.E.] a colour-code evolved and developed by copper-plate engravers, the earliest being that of the Belgian, Francquart, c.1623. Numerous systems developed and by mid XVII cent. the Rev. Father Petra Sancta evolved a standard set of 'signatures' which were in constant use till the end of the XIX cent., and by which much high-grade engraving was, for visual appreciation, utterly ruined. At no time was ~ favoured by the officers of arms who made their rough notes in 'trick' (q.v.). In the XX cent. ~ has fallen into desuetude, but it is not entirely abandoned and, if applied with discretion can even today serve a useful purpose, e.g. in depicting the roundels. For the signatures in current use, see under the various metals and tinctures. (205, 208)

hatchment: [frmd on 'achievement'] an armorial mourning-board formerly displayed on the death of an armiger over the porch of his or her home. The correct measurement for a ~ was 6 ft. square, generally consisting of a frame over which canvas was stretched, but sometimes of all wood. The ~ on which the arms of the deceased were painted upon a black background declared not only the family (by the arms themselves) of the departed but the marital condition. A simple shield and crest upon an all-black ground announced the death of a bachelor; a simple lozenge, similarly backed, that of a spinster; a shield impaled upon an all-black ground was that of a widower; and a lozenge impaled, that of a widow. An impaled shield on a background itself per pale argent and sable announced the death of one partner to a marriage; dexter sable, sinister argent revealed a surviving widow; but dexter argent and sinister sable, a surviving widower. In the event of there being complexities to a marital achievement, e.g. the husband bearing arms of office (q.v.) or being a knight or other rank in an order of chivalry necessitating a display of two shields accolée, the vertical partition between sable and argent did not occur on the diagonal of the ~. The death of a Knight of the Garter would be announced on a ~ painted with dexter, his arms within the garter and between his supporters, and sinister, his arms impaling those of his (surviving) wife, the vertical parting of the mourning background being in line with the palar parting of the sinister shield.

The ~ remained before the house for seven days after the funeral when it was removed to the parish church there to hang for a minimum period of a year and a day, after which it could be (and all too frequently was) removed and destroyed. Up and down the country there are to be found village churches where the ~ of the local baronial family have been preserved, and a very useful index to armorial family history they prove to be. (In privately maintained chapels they are, of course, to be expected.)

The general use of ~ survived down to the end of the XIX cent., but today, not solely due to changed social conditions, but even more strongly to the revolution in housing, the custom is comparatively extinct. A few of our leading families continue to use ~, and they are occasionally seen in cathedral and university cities where their continuance is more official than personal.

hauberk: alt. term for 'cuirass' (q.v.).

haurient: [L.] lit. drawing (air); inhaling hence, of a fish or a marine mammal when palewise with head in chief.

hause: r. alt. for 'enhanced' (q.v.). In Fr. blazon, with 'ss', 'in chief'.

hautboy: [Fr.] the archaic name for the oboe, a wood-wind musical instrument depicted in heraldry as a long, straight, tapering tube, having a mouthpiece in chief and opening to form the bell in base. In the upper end there is a row of holes to act as keys. The same form is taken by the fife, the flute, the horn (not to be confused with the hunting—or bugle—horn (q.v.)), and the trumpet; hence, it is likely that these are but alt. terms, not separate instruments made identical in heraldic art. A brass trumpet is depicted like the ~ bent in the form of a capital Roman S reversed, the mouthpiece chiefward, but without holes, keys, or other form of modulating mechanism.

havette: the original form of 'habick' (q.v.).

hawk: see **falcon**.

Hawker, John: Clarenceux King of Arms, 1839. Former Norroy K. of A., 1838; former Rouge Croix Pursuivant, 1794.

Hawkeslow, Wm: Clarenceux King of Arms, 1461. Former Guyenne K. of A.; former Leopard Herald; former Bluemantle Pursuivant; former Wallingford Pursuivant.

hawking-glove: see **glove**.

hawk's-bell: see **bell, hawk's**.

hawk's leg: distinguishable from that of the eagle (q.v.) only by its remaining belled (q.v.).

hawk's leure: see **leure**.

Hawley, Thomas: Clarenceux King of

Arms, 1536. Former Norroy K. of A., 1534; former Carlisle Herald, 1515; former Rouge Croix Pursuivant, 1509. The name is also spelt 'Halley'.

hawthorn: [O.E.] a thorn-bearing shrub having either white or pink blossom named 'may'; *Crataegus oxyacantha*. Blazoned as ~-tree.

Hay . . .: Islay Herald, 1506.

hay-fork: er. for 'shakefork' (q.v.).

hay-hook: see **horse-pricker**.

hazelnoten: D., hazelnut.

head: all animate charges are subject to dismemberment, the human form (q.v.) being no exception to severance of parts. The head is the most frequent in its occurrence. ~ may be couped, erased, or, in the case of horned cattle, caboshed (q.v.). (31, VI, XV)

Head Court: see **Court of the Lord Lyon**.

Heard, Sir Isaac: Garter King of Arms, 1786. Former Clarenceux K. of A., 1780; former Brunswick Herald, 1774; former Norroy K. of A., 1774; former Lancaster Herald, 1761; former Bluemantle Pursuivant, 1759.

hearse: an obs. charge constructed from three palets (q.v.) couped (q.v.) at each end interlaced (q.v.) with the same number of barrulets (q.v.), also couped at each end. Also applied indiscriminately to the harrow (q.v.), the portcullis (q.v.), and to a funeral candelabrum consisting of a metal trellis with a spike raised at every cross-over. Also spelt 'herse'.

heart: of the conventional art form, pointed below and depressed in the centre above. Always erect, often proper which is gules. Symbol of charity, but also employed for ca. reasons. Often crowned, and sometimes flammant. In the arms of Douglas the ~ is allusive (q.v.) to the attempt made to carry the heart of Bruce to the Holy land. (298)

heart-shape escutcheon: a heart-shape, instead of a normal shield is, on special occasions, introduced into British heraldry. Two hearts accolée (q.v.) were painted on the rudder of H.M.Y. 'Britannia' on the occasion of the wedding of H.R.H. Princess Margaret: a book-plate designed in the same manner was presented to K. Geo. V. and Q. Mary on the occasion of their wedding. Normally it is the shape on which Burgher arms must be displayed in Teutonic heraldry.

heartsease: [M.E.] a name for the pansy, *Viola tricolor*, and also for the wallflower, *Cheiranthus cheiri*.

heater-shape shield: a straight top, short shield; hence, sharply tapering and conforming roughly to an equilateral triangle. So called from its likeness to a laundresses smoothing iron or to a tailor's pressing iron of the period. The ∼ is not well-adapted to accommodate heraldic design, the base being pinched and constrictive to an heraldic beast. A bend (q.v.) on a ∼ leaves a far too extensive triangle of the field in sinister-chief (q.v.), and a corresponding small and narrow segment in dexter-base (q.v.).

heathcock: see **moorcock.**

heaume: [Fr.] a helmet; in Fr. heraldry any helmet is so called, in British (where it is r.)

it refers to the pot-helmet, and is, therefore an alt. spelling of 'helm' (q.v.).

hebilla: Sp., buckle.

Hebrew alphabet: see **script.**

hedgehog: see **urcheon.**

heights: see **feather.**

heiligenschein: Ger., halo.

heir apparent, mark of difference of: see **brisure.**

heir presumptive, mark of difference of: see **brisure.**

heiress, heraldic: see **heraldic heiress.**

helm¹: [O.E.] originally the great pot-helmet that rested on the shoulders, and with a representation of which medieval art ensigns the shield. Later, extended to include other head-protecting pieces of armour, and now loosely applied to the helmet of rank (q.v.).

helm²: Afk., general for helmet.

helmdecken: Ger., mantling.

helmet, close: a visored helmet with the visor down, drawn complete with the gorget. All pieces of plate armour that do duty as heraldic charges are badly drawn, and in this the ∼ is no exception: as a rule the neck is too narrow for the average man's fist to pass through, much less his head. Further, there is a convention of

247. Argent, three morions sable.
      De La Reur.

248. Or, three chapeaux vert, turned-up ermine.
      Sefton.

249. Gules, a maunch Or.
      Hastings.

250. Quarterly azure and Or, four pilia pastoralis counterchanged.
      Drokensford, John (Bishop of Bath and Wells, 1309–29).

251. Argent, a Dutch boot sable turned over Or, soled and heeled gules.
      Boot.

252. Sable, three dexter hawking-gloves, tassels pendant, in pale, argent.
      Vauneye.

247

248

249

250

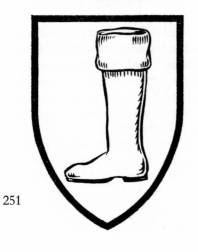

251

252

putting human, or else animal's faces, into helmets. (III, XIV, XVI)

helmet of rank: the representation of the head-protecting unit of a suit of armour, with which the shield is ensigned, indicates by its shape and its position the social status of the armiger. The royal helmet is of gold, is set affrontée (q.v.), is spherical in form, and the opening is protected by a grille (q.v.) of six bailes (q.v.). The helmet of a duke or of a marquis is of the same shape and is set affrontée but is of silver, garnished gold, with a grille of five gold bailes. The same shape ~ ensigns the shield of severally an earl, a viscount, and a baron, but for each it is set facing dexter and shows five of its ten bailes: it is steel, garnished gold. For baronets and knights the ~ is crested and visored, set affrontée, and open: the crimson lining is generally quilted: it is of silver. Esquires have the same, set facing dexter, and the visor closed. A shield may be ensigned with a tilting-helmet which does not indicate rank, and need not be set affrontée, hence, in recent times there is a strong and growing tendency for tilting-helmets to be depicted in preference to ~. A major objection to the latter is that many crests, being beasts either statant (q.v.) or passant, are not suited to a helmet set affrontée. ~ emerged in the post-Tudor period. In old heraldry the shield was ensigned with the 'pot-helm' of the period, and social status was not indicated by them.

helmkleed: D., mantling.

helmteken: Afk., crest.

helmtopsieraad: D., crest.

helmzier: Ger., crest.

helve: see **haft.**

Hembre Pursuivant: one of the officers of arms accompanying the English ambassador at Arras, 1475.

hemp-break: a technical charge, consisting of two long, slender iron plates hinged together at one end, the lower having four feet, the upper a handle extending from the free end, and both having teeth cut on the inner surfaces. Used in the process of loosening the fibres in the stems of the hemp plant and often employed in heraldry for ca. reasons. Alt. terms 'brey', 'hackle', and 'flax-breaker'. (341)

Henderson, Wm: Dingwall Pursuivant, 1566.

heneage knot: a series of interlaced loops of endless cord which finishes heart-shape.

Henlic Pursuivant: one of the officers of arms in attendance on the English ambassador at Arras in 1475.

Herald-painter: the description given in both the College of Arms (q.v.) and the Lyon Office (q.v.) to the artist (or to the senior artist) who is engaged on depicting, in the margin of a patent of arms, the achievement blazoned in the text, or otherwise depicting arms to embellish, or to illustrate, any other official heraldic document.

Notwithstanding that the artists specializing in this work may be equal in their ability whether they are Scottish or English, the professional status differs greatly. In England the Herald-painter to the College of Arms is merely an employee of the Chapter—probably a very highly valued and respected servant—to whom each individual officer of arms may or may not go when requiring the services of an artist. In Scotland, the Herald-painter to the Lyon Court is accorded the status of an officer of arms, and if he is not an officer of arms in ordinary he will have conferred upon him Extraordinary status.

An heraldic artist, whether officially employed, or free-lance, must possess an extensive knowledge of the subject and have a superior education in general history and in antiquarian studies. What is more, an abnormal skill in draughtsmanship and

PLATE IX *Left:* A Garter Principal King of Arms.
  Right: A Lord Lyon King of Arms.
    Note particularly the different marshalling of the Royal Arms for display in severally
England and Scotland: Garter: I and IV, *England*; II, *Scotland*; III, *Northern Ireland*; The
Lord Lyon: I and IV, *Scotland*; II, *England*; III, *Northern Ireland*.

in painting is required, with the ability to 'lay' gold-leaf, all combined with a special sense of design. The Herald-painter must be an admirer of both the artistic and the spiritual achievement of the Gothic age, and a devotee of chivalry. In the past, when the services of portrait-painters were in high demand, and a representation of the sitter's arms appeared on the canvas, it was not uncommon for the portraitist to employ a specialist to add the armorial bearings.

In modern times, armigers such as municipal corporations and commercial companies, wishing for a representation of their arms, place the order with a commercial studio or an advertising consultant in whose office a totally ignorant, and perhaps inferior, draughtsman will make a crude copy of the 'reference' supplied; hence, much armorial draughtsmanship is very bad indeed.

heraldic heiress: in Western culture the family is patrilineal and inheritance is by male primogeniture; hence, property descends from father to son. A patent of arms states that the grant is made to a man and his heirs and descendants forever; therefore a coat of arms is an incorporeal hereditament the possession of which, and the right and power of its transmission to offspring, is vested in heirs-male. All the offsprings of an armiger (female as well as male) have, as a birthright, freedom to wear their father's arms: the sons display on a shield (which in England is theoretically 'suitably differenced') and the daughters on a lozenge. In the mere use and display of the device there is equality between brother and sister: there is, however, a fundamental divergence in the powers carried by the rights inasmuch as each and all of the brothers in a family transmit the arms to their own offspring but the sisters do not. In the event of there being a daughter as sole offspring of the marriage

she becomes, on the death of her father, heiress of his property, and at the same time an ~ who can, if married to an armigerous husband, transmit her family arms to her own sons and daughters with consequent changes in the display of the arms. (See **marshalling**.) A number of sisters without a brother become co-heiresses, each enjoying the same armorial rights.

The circumstances of a woman's becoming an ~ may not be simple and straightforward as in the foregoing explanation: there may be complications as when, e.g., a woman becomes 'heiress in her issue' or is '~ of her mother but not of her father', and in like contingencies. A woman becomes 'heiress in her issue', when, during her lifetime there is a male representer of the house who, ultimately dying without issue (or without surviving issue) leaves his sister's son as the sole surviving claimant to the family arms. A woman is ~ of her mother but not of her father when, her mother being an heiress, and she the sole issue, has a brother of the half-blood, being issue of a second marriage by her father. The son of the second marriage is clearly the heir-apparent to his father's arms, but the daughter by the first marriage is heiress of her mother's arms which were worn in pretence (q.v.) by her father prior to the death of his first wife. On marriage, the husband of such an ~ cannot marshal his wife's paternal arms (these are to be transmitted through her brother of the half-blood) nor can he marshal his wife's maternal arms because his wife is of her father's family and bears his name. The solution to the problem is that this ~ bears her mother's family arms differenced by a dexter canton of her father's which is in perpetuity.

If the ~ is also a peeress in her own right, married to a commoner, the escutcheon of pretence, ensigned with her coronet of rank is displayed on her husband's shield which stands without supporters; and accolée (q.v.), on the sinister, a lozenge of her arms with her peerage supporters: if her husband is himself a peer his arms, complete with supporters, carries his wife's in pretence, and accolée, her lozenge and supporters.

heraldic tygre: see **tygre, heraldic.**

heraldry: [M.E.] the range of duties performed by certain officers of the royal household who, under the Earl Marshal's jurisdiction, organize processions, make proclamations, and devise and grant armorial bearings.

Heralds: see **College of Arms** and **Lyon Court.**

Herald's Roll: (c. 1270–80), the copy in the possession of the College of Arms (herald's version), consists of thirty-nine strips, each of five shields, cut from a vellum true roll (q.v.) and now mounted on paper. The Fitzwilliam version is a cut roll bound in book-form having thirty-nine leaves $9\frac{1}{10}$ by $10\frac{3}{4}$ in. containing 697 painted shields. Earl

of Bedford's version, a true roll painted with 705 shields. Everard Green's version, vellum true roll $11\frac{1}{8}$ in. by 33 ft, painted on the face with 665 shields. On the dorse there are 130 shields, painted c. 1525–30, marked 'Tilt Roll'.

Herbert Pursuivant: maintained by Lord Herbert of Gower, c. 1525.

Hereford Herald: maintained by Humphry de Bohun, Earl of Hereford till 1373 when, on the death of the Earl, ~ was taken into the royal service and held office under Kings Hen. IV and V, attending the latter's coronation in 1413.

heremelin: Ger. and Swd., ermine.

heremelijn: D., ermine.

herisson: [L.] a hedgehog also blazoned as urcheon (q.v.) Genus *Erinaceus*.

herissoné: a term applied only to the catamount (q.v.) meaning hedgehog-like, bristling.

herkruiste kruis: Afk., cross-crosslet.

Herman: Lancaster Herald in the service of the Duke of L., 1354.

---

253. Gules, on a fess wavy argent between, in chief, a Rhodesian fish-eagle displayed regardant, Or, grasping in the talons a fish of the second, in base, a night ape's face of the third, a bar wavy azure.
Corporation of Chingola.

254. Sable, on a fess between three close-helmets argent, a fox courant proper.
Kennedy.

255. Gules, on a fess Or between three coneys sejant argent, a crescent azure between two martlets sable.
Christmas.

256. Sable, a fess between three asses passant argent.
Sir Wm Aseu.

257. Azure, on a fess Or between three mounds gold banded gules, a horse courant of the last.
Moss of Middleton Hall.

258. Or, on a fess sable between three brocks passant proper, two cinquefoils pierced-round, argent, charged on each petal with an ermine spot of the second.
Broks, James (Bishop of Gloucester, 1554–8).

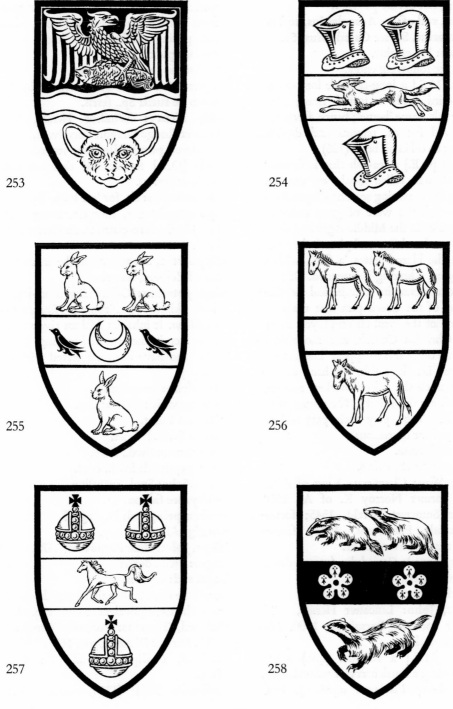

253

254

255

256

257

258

Hermes, hat of: see **petasus.**

Hermes, rod of: see **Aesculapius, rod of.**

Hermeterius, St: see **Caledonius, St.**

hermine: Fr., ermine.

herne: see following entry.

heron: [M.E.] a long-necked, long-legged water-bird with a tufted head; *Ardea cinerea*; alt. name 'herne'; hence, frequently employed for ca. reasons and depicted holding an eel in his beak. (126)

herring: [O.E.] a sea-fish that is found in large clusters, called shoals, off the coast during the spawning season; *Clupea harengus*. ~ fisheries were of great economic importance in the Middle Ages and the ~ soon found an honoured place in heraldry. When the blazon states 'a fish', without specifying, a herring is intended. Of common occurrence in ecclesiastical heraldry because of the Greek pun that made the fish one of the symbols employed by the early Christian Church, and more likely than any other fish to appear 'interlaced in triangle', i.e. three fish, the head of each resting upon the tail of another, and thus symbolizing the Trinity. The young of the ~, called 'cob', play their part and are employed for ca. reasons.

herse: see **hearse.**

hertengewei: D., attires.

Hervy, Wm: Clarenceux King of Arms, 1557. Former Norroy K. of A., 1550; former Somerset Herald, 1545; former Bluemantle Pursuivant, 1543; former Hampnes Pursuivant, 1541.

Herzog (gross): Ger., duke, (grand) duke.

herzstelle: Ger., fess point.

Hesketh, John: see following entry.

Heskett, John: Lancaster Herald, 1713. Former Portcullis Pursuivant, 1700. Also spelt 'Hesketh'.

heurte: [M.E.] a roundel (q.v.) azure, representing a hurtleberry or whortleberry (the bilberry *Vaccinium myrtillus*). Both roundel and berry may derive their names from 'hurt', a bruise; hence, blue in colour. Alt. spellings are 'hurte' and 'hurt'.

hew: see **pick.**

heydoddes: see **cornflower.**

Heynen, Claes: see **Gelre, Armorial de.**

hierro de fusil: Sp., ferris.

Hill, Henry: Windsor Herald, 1757. Former Rouge Dragon Pursuivant, 1755.

hilted and pommelled: see **sword.**

hind: [O.E.] female red deer; depicted without antlers.

hippocampus: alt. for 'sea horse' (q.v.).

hippogryph: a r. monster, being griffin (q.v.) in the fore-quarters, and horse in the hind.

Hippolytus, St: appears in the arms of the See of Zell-am, Austria.

hippopotamus: [Gk] a bulky, short-legged, thick skinned quadruped; *Hippopotamus amphibius*. It inhabits African rivers and is to be seen in the armorial bearings of persons who have been connected with that country.

hirondelle: see **martlet.**

hirschgeweih: Ger., attires.

hirst: see **hurst.**

hjalm: Swd., helmet.

hjälmkrans: Swd., torse.

hjalmprydnad: Swd., crest.

hjälmtäcke: Swd., mantling.

hobby: see **falcon.**

hoekenspringend: D., angled.

hoekig: Afk., dancetty.

Hoge, John: Bute Pursuivant, 1675.

hoger: Swd., dexter.

hogshead: see **tun.**

hoist: the side of a flag that is attached to the mast; hence, equivalent to dexter (q.v.).

Holford, Thomas: Portcullis Pursuivant, 1687. Former Blanch Lyon, 1686.

Holland, Philip: Portcullis Pursuivant, 1606.

Holland's Roll: (1310) contains forty-seven shields and is part of book of arms made for (or by) Joseph Holland, Antiquary.

Hollingsworth, John: Bluemantle Pursuivant, 1558. Former Risebank Pursuivant, 1554.

Hollingsworth, Thomas: York Herald during the reign of K. Ed. IV. Former Bluemantle Pursuivant and Rose Blanch Pursuivant.

holly, knee: see **knee-holm.**

holly leaves: see **sheaf.**

Holme, Sir Thomas: Clarenceux King of Arms, 1476 (resigned 1485; reappointed 1487). Former Norroy K. of A., 1464; former Windsor Herald, 1461; former Rouge Croix Pursuivant, 1457; former Falcon Pursuivant.

Holmes, Randall: Chester Herald, 1533. Former Montorgueil Herald, 1516, and former Montorgueil Pursuivant. He was also known as 'R. Jackson'.

Holme's Book, Randle: (temp. K. Hen. VI) paper book of seventy-one leaves $8\frac{1}{4}$ in. by 1 ft $1\frac{1}{2}$ in. A general roll, executed in bold pen drawing, being a most motley collection of real and fictitious arms including those attributed to Jesus Christ. An entry that is perhaps unique in a roll of arms is a Salerno prescription for the treatment of 'syetyka'. The whole was published in facsimile by Joseph Foster (who gave it the title of *A Tudor Book of Arms*), under the patronage of Lord Howard de Walden in 1904. See also **Le Neve's Book.**

Holme's Book, Sir Thomas: (c. 1446–90) paper book of 112 leaves $10\frac{1}{4}$ in. by 1 ft $2\frac{1}{4}$ in. The most important part of the contents, sub-titled 'The Military Roll', which is on permanent exhibition at the British Museum, depicts, on each page, two pairs of mounted warriors engaged in single combat alternately with sword and lance. Shields, surcoats (q.v.), and trappers (q.v.) are emblazoned; helmets provided with a bandeau (q.v.), but there are no crests. There are 248 figures with names over. The second part of the book is a general roll (q.v.) and also a local roll: the third part, a roll of the mayor and aldermen of London, an ordinary (q.v.) of arms with bends and a French roll.

Holy dove: see **dove.**

Holy Ghost, Order of the: (France) f. by K. Hen. III, in 1578, for a maximum of nine commanders and 100 knights. The Order was suppressed in 1791 and revived in 1814 by Louis XVIII; no conferments outside the Royal House of France have been made since 1830. Insignia—*Badge:* a gold-edged white-bordered green cross paty notched pometty, with silver f.d.l. between the arms; a central medallion bears a dove in either silver or white enamel; the reverse depicts St Michael slaying the dragon. *Collar:* of gold, formed of f.d.l. and flames, alternating with the crowned letters *HH.* *Star:* the badge on a silver plaque. *Riband:* light blue, worn over the right shoulder. *Motto: Duce et Auspice.*

Holy lamb: see **lamb, Paschal.**

Holy Sepulchre of Jerusalem, Equestrian Order of the: possibly f. by Godfrey de Bouillon in 1099. Revived under the protection of the Holy See on 24 January 1868 in three grades: Knights Grand Cross, Knights Commanders, and Knights. Insignia—*Badge:* a gold-rimmed red-enamel Jerusalem cross quartering similar smaller crosses, ensigned with a crown, or a trophy of arms, or left unadorned, according to type of membership. *Star:* eight-point, of silver, bearing centrally the badge on a medallion surrounded by two palm leaves tied by a gold band. *Riband:* black moiré edged with red.

Home of Linhouse, James: Lyon Clerk Depute, 1796, Lyon Clerk and Keeper of the Records, 1804.

hone-stone: a prosaic ca. device for the name of 'Hone' only.

Honour, Companions of: f. June 1917 to acknowledge outstanding services of national importance. Limited to sixty-five recipients. Insignia—*Badge:* a gold oval badge depicting a mounted knight in armour and an oak tree bearing the Royal Arms, surrounded by a blue enamel border with the motto *In Action Faithful and in Honour Clear* in gold; the whole ensigned with the Imperial crown. Worn round the neck from a riband of carmine bordered with gold thread.

honour point: an imaginary dot resting on the paler line, halfway between fess point (q.v.) and centre-chief (q.v.).

honourable: superior to; more important than; to be given precedence. ~ ordinaries (q.v.) distinct from sub-ordinaries (q.v.), and from diminutives (q.v.); metal (q.v.) more ~ than tincture; dexter more ~ than sinister; chief more ~ than base, etc.

hooded: see **falcon.**

hoofpunt: Afk., chief point.

hoofverdelings: Afk., lines of partition.

Hooke Campbell of Bangston, John: Lord Lyon King of Arms, 1754.

hooped: of the iron rings that hold a barrel or tun (q.v.) when differing in colour from the staves.

hop: fruit or cones of the climbing plant *Humulus lupulus*; used as flavouring matter in brewing; blazoned as '~-bines' or '~-vines', and the prop or pole, is mentioned, e.g. '~-bines fructed on their poles' and '~-poles sustaining their fruit'. The nature of the plant produces specimens of landscape heraldry (q.v.).

Horbury, Peter de: Norroy King of Arms, 1276.

horn: see **hautboy.**

Hornebrooke, Richard: Bluemantle Pursuivant, 1667.

horned: [O.E.] an obs. term of wide application; applied not only to ungulates, but to the antennae of insects, to the crest of certain birds (a plumicorn), to the 'feelers' of the snail, and even to the tusks of an elephant. The Fr. term 'accorné' has a similar coverage. See also **attired** and **armed.**

---

259. Argent, a stag salient gules attired Or. Surmounted of a fess wreathed of the second and third.
M'Corquodale.

260. Argent, on a mount vert an oak-tree proper debruised of a fess azure charged with a crescent between two mullets of the field.
Watts.

261. Azure, a fess chequy Or and gules between, in chief, three mullets and, in base, a crescent of the second.
Boyd, of Danson.

262. Azure, a fess dancetty the upper points flory.
Plowden.

263. Gules, a fess wavy and, in chief, three piles conjoined in point, also wavy, argent.
Isham, Lamport.

264. Per fess argent and sable, three fusils conjoined in fess and counterchanged.
The National Coal Board.

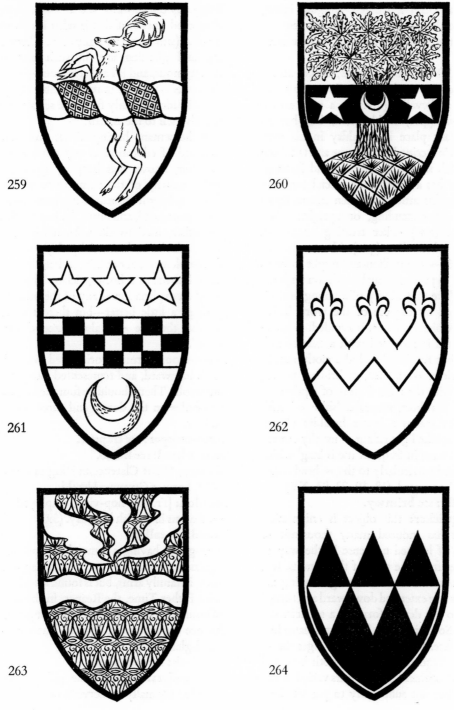

259

260

261

262

263

264

hornet: [O.E.] a winged, stinging insect, *Vespa crabro*; of infrequent occurrence.

horns: the points of a crescent, or a crescent-moon.

horse: [O.E.] *Equus caballus*; makes an inconspicuous and automatic appearance when a chevalier (q.v.) or a man armed *cap-à-pie* (q.v.) is blazoned, but has an important place in heraldry in his own right. He is crined of his mane and tail, both of which should be fulsome and flowing, and he has a number of special terms to describe his attitudes: when statant (q.v.) he is either standing, or upright; when courant (q.v.) either trotting or in full career; when salient (q.v.) either rearing, or forcené. ~ is a stallion and ought to be so drawn to prevent visual confusion with the mare. The masculinity of a young horse is indicated by the use of the word 'colt'; 'foal', which is neuter, is avoided. ~ comparisoned is provided with a saddle-cloth only, but furnished includes cloth, saddle, and bridle. ~ saddled, or bridled, is provided with the named piece of equipment alone. A robust, muscular 'shire ~' with fetlocks, makes a better heraldic charge than does the light riding ~ usually drawn. An alt. term in frequent use is 'nag' which is applied particularly to the ~ head either couped or erased. (18, 19, 22, 93, XV)

horse-fly: see **brimsey.**

horse-pricker: this object is enigmatical and it has induced many thousands of words of learned nonsense in the way of theories from the pens of the pundits. It is drawn as a horizontal rectangle having the sinister side extended downward and turned over to the dexter forming a semicircular hook. Sometimes the hook terminates in a lion's face. In the late Middle Ages the ~ was of frequent occurrence both here and on the Continent. Its contours varied somewhat, but not sufficiently to permit there

being any doubt—a ~ was a ~—but how it pricked horses, if that is what it did, remained (and remains) a mystery. Theorizing and guessing are, in such matters, synonymous, and it has been found—more than once—that the unrecognizable charge hides its identity only from the scholar but reveals itself to the artisan.

A horseman, having about the same standard of education as any other farm-labourer, knows that hanging up in any stable worthy of the name there will be found a length of stiff wire bent into a circle at one end, and into a shallow hook at the other, used to clear the horse's frog after a day's work on sticky clay soil, and this implement, about 8 in. in length overall is known as a horse-pricker. That is as good an explanation as any of the others—perhaps a little better—but there remains the fact that the ~ is also blazoned 'hay-hook'.

horse-shoe: normally orientated with the heels baseward, and represented like pendant scrolls. There should be four rectangular nail-holes on the dexter and three on the sinister.

horse-trapper: see **trapper.**

horse's head: see **horse.**

Horsley, Wm: Clarenceux King of Arms, 1419. Former Guyenne Herald.

houblon: [Fr.] the hop-vine; employed for ca. reasons in British heraldry. (393)

hound: see **talbot.**

hour-glass: having a somewhat depressing significance does not make many appearances in family arms, but is found associated with Father Time, the Reaper, in the arms of insurance companies and other long-term finance organizations. May be blazoned as 'sand-glass' (473)

houseleek: see **sengreen.**

house orders: those in the gift of, and awarded normally for services to, the head of a dynastic house who is a ruling sovereign or who is in *de jure* succession to a ruling sovereign.

housing: a horse-trapper (q.v.).

Howard, Sir Algar Henry Stafford: Garter King of Arms, 1944. Former Norroy and Ulster K. of A. 1943; former Norroy K. of A., 1931; former Windsor Herald, 1919; former Rouge Dragon Pursuivant, 1911; former Fitzalan Pursuivant Extraordinary, 1911.

Hubert, Order of St: (Bavaria) f. 1444 and could be bestowed on an unlimited number of princes and on twelve counts or barons. Insignia—*Badge:* a white Maltese cross pommetty with rays between the arms; a gold central medallion depicts St Hubert, surrounded by the motto, in gold on red, *Firm in Loyalty;* ensigned with a gold crown. *Collar:* of forty-two links, interlaced with golden ornaments; twenty-one links show St Hubert and twenty-one the motto, alternately in red and green enamel. *Star:* silver of eight points surmounted by the unensigned badge. *Riband:* dark red with light green borders.

Huchenson, Francis: Chester Herald, 1740, Former Arundel Herald, 1735. Also spelt 'Hutchenson'.

huitfoil: r. obs. alt. for an octofoil or double quatrefoil.

hulk: [O.E.] the hull of a dismasted ship no longer seaworthy; blazoned as 'the ~ of a ship' or as 'a demi ~'.

Hume, Wm: Unicorn Pursuivant, 1682.

humet: alt. term for 'hamade' (q.v.).

humetty, cross: [O.F.] a cross consisting of four limbs of equal length that are never in contact with the boundary of the shield; also termed 'cross couped'.

Hunter, Gilbert: Dingwal Pursuivant, 1617.

Hunter, Thomas[1]: Dingwal Pursuivant, 1656.

Hunter, Thomas[2]: Ross Herald, 1625.

Huntingdon Herald: maintained by the Earl of Huntingdon, c. 1450.

hunting-horn: see **bugle.**

hurst: a group of trees (q.v.).

Hutchenson, Francis: see **Huchenson, Francis.**

hutchett: [Fr.] r. alt. for a bugle-horn (q.v.).

Hutton, John: Bluemantle Pursuivant, 1528. Former Guisnes Pursuivant, 1527.

hydra: [Gk] a type of dragon (q.v.) having seven heads, each on a long snake-like neck. The ~ cannot be disposed of by decapitation: by the time a champion has struck off the seventh, the first is fully regrown and the rest are progressing favourably.

Hygiea: holding a serpent is the dexter supporter of the Metropolitan Water Board.

hyphenated name: see **surname.**

ibex: lit. a wild goat, *Capra ibex,* indigenous to the Apennines, having strong curved horns, deeply ridged; the heraldic ~ is indistinguishable from the heraldic antelope (q.v.) and may even be merely an alternative term.

Icelandic Falcon, Order of the: f. 1921 in five classes. Insignia—*Badge:* a gold-rimmed white enamel cross with a central blue medallion depicting a silver falcon. *Star:* the badge on a silver star of eight points. *Riband:* blue edged white divided by red.

Ich Dien Pursuivant: served the Prince of Wales, c. 1475.

icicle: a goutté d'eau (q.v.) inverted often does duty for an ~, but they may also be represented by piles (q.v.) wavy.

Il Faut Faire Pursuivant: maintained by Sir John Fastalf; named from his word (q.v.) or motto (q.v.).

illegitimate offspring, marks of distinction: see **bastardy, indication of.**

illeopardito, leone: It., a lion passant.

illuminated: see **moon.**

illustrative rolls: see **rolls of arms.**

imbeccato: It., beaked.

imbrigliato: It., bridled.

imbrued: see **embrued.**

impalement: the marshalling of two coats of arms upon one shield palewise: most commonly employed in a marital achievement (q.v.) when the arms of the husband are compressed into the dexter half and those of the wife into the sinister half of the combined display. If such lateral reduction will cause distortion the ∼ should be depicted on a shield that allows for broadening. The whole of each coat of arms appears in the appropriate half of the shield except when either achievement has a bordure of any kind, including the double tressure (q.v.) and the orle (q.v.) when the palar line is omitted (the sinister side if in the husband's arms, the dexter if in the wife's).

Arms of office (q.v.) are ∼ with the personal arms of the holder of the office for the time being, the official arms on the dexter. In the event of the office-holder wishing to display arms for his wife, two shields accolée (q.v.) will be employed: dexter, arms of office & personal arms; sinister, personal arms ∼ those of the wife's family. On the termination of office, or at the conclusion of marriage, such ∼ are broken. The arms on the dexter are 'impaling', those on the sinister, 'impaled by'. (43, 367, XV)

impartable: see **indivisible arms.**

Imperial crown: when Q. Vic. became Empress of India the depression in the arches of the crown royal was lifted, which style remained in use until India became independent; however, the Stationery Office did not revise its imprint until about fifteen years later and ∼ and crown royal have become interchangable terms on account of blazon sometimes remaining unaltered while the graphic representation has been modernized. The continental ∼ is like a mitre (q.v.) with an arch added. Before the Reformation, when numerous Catholic symbols appeared in arms, the ∼

---

265. Sable, a fess Or fretty of the field between three fleurs-de-lys, all within a bordure of the second.
Stule.

266. Per fess argent and sable, three pickaxes Or.
Piggott.

267. Azure, a fess engrailed Or gutty d'larmes between two daggers inverted in chief and, in base, a cross-crosslet fitchy of the second.
Pixley.

268. Azure, a fasces in pale Or, axe-head argent, debruised of a fess gules charged with three estoiles of the second.
Mazarin (Cardinal).

269. Per fess crenelly sable and argent, three five-barred gates counterchanged.
Yeats.

270. Barry wavy of eight argent and azure, a fess conjoined to a chevron enarched sable.
Lord Cole.

265

266

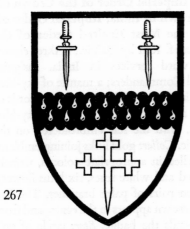

267

268

269

270

represented the Papal tiara, and was drawn in three tiers. (217, 229, 234)

Imperial eagle: a double-headed eagle displayed (q.v.) facing outward. Imperial status has been claimed for the single-headed eagle of the U.S.A.; hence, there is a tendency to describe the ∼ simply as 'a double-headed eagle'. In origin the ∼ is two single-headed eagles, the one absconded (q.v.) except for the head and neck, by the other. Said to have been first used by the Emperor Sigismund as a symbol of his sovereignty over both the Eastern and the Western Empire.

Imperial Service Order: f. August 1902 as a Companionship for Civil Servants working throughout the British Empire, to be awarded normally after at least twenty-five years' outstanding service. Insignia: (for men) a silver seven-point star bearing centrally a gold roundel containing the royal cypher, the whole ensigned with a crown; for ladies the star is replaced by a laurel wreath; worn on left breast from a riband of red, blue, red. There is a medal attached to the Order, of silver with the sovereign's head on the obverse and *For faithful Service* on the reverse, which may be awarded to government servants who do not qualify for the Companionship.

impost: see **arch.**

in die skildhoof: Afk., in chief.

incensed: see **animé.**

inchiavato: It., indented.

inchiodato: It., cloue.

inclaved: see **enclaved.**

incontrait: [Fr.], of two birds respecting (q.v.) each other. (112)

increment: see **moon.**

increscent: see **crescent.**

indelicate charges: some charges are, in modern times, considered a trifle indelicate, but in the Middle Ages such a display would

have shocked no one. With the progression of time slight changes have been made to spare the armiger's blushes: e.g. the counts of Colleoni of Milan now blazon their arms 'per pale argent and gules three hearts inverted counterchanged'. These charges were originally 'cullions' (i.e. testicles) making a ca. reference.

indented: a line of partition rising and falling in small, triangular peaks: low-grade draughtsmanship, making the triangles too small, produces a realistic portrait of a hack-saw blade: ∼ is a decadent form of dancetty (q.v.). (183)

India, Imperial Order of the Crown of: see **Crown of India, Imperial Order of.**

India, the Most Exalted Order of the Star of: f. 1861 by Q. Vic., in three classes, to reward services in India. Insignia: Grand Commanders; a mantle of sky-blue satin lined with white silk, tied by cords of white and silver terminating with sky-blue tassels, with the star embroidered on the left side. *Collar:* gold links joining emblems enamelled in appropriate colours, namely five red and white roses, six lotus flowers, and ten pairs of palm branches. The Imperial crown appears in the centre and from it depends the badge. *Star:* circle of golden rays, surmounted centrally by a five-point star of diamonds surrounded by a sky-blue enamelled band bearing in gold letters the motto *Heaven's Light Our Guide.* *Badge:* an onyx cameo depicting Q. Vic. in profile, surrounded by a sky-blue band and the motto, the band being decorated with four small lotus flowers equally spaced on its outer edge; the whole badge is ensigned with a five-point star of diamonds. *Riband:* sky-blue with white edges, worn by Grand Commanders over the right shoulder, the badge on the left hip: Knight Commanders have a silver star of the same pattern as Grand Commanders, and wear the badge round the neck; Commanders have the badge only, worn round the neck.

India, Order of British: f. 1837 in two classes: revised 1941. Insignia—*Badge:* a star of gold rays ensigned with a crown: a centre medallion of light blue depicting a lion statant in gold, surrounded by the inscription in gold *Order of British India*; the second-class badge has a medallion of dark blue and is smaller in size. *Riband* (worn round the neck): first class—dark red, 2 in. wide, with two central blue stripes; second class—dark red, 1½ in. wide, with one central blue stripe.

Indian Distinguished Service Medal: see **Distinguished Service Medal** (India).

Indian Empire, Most Eminent Order of the: f. 1878 in three classes, for services in India. Insignia—*Collar:* of gold, consisting of linked elephants, lotus flowers, Indian roses, peacocks in their pride, and a central Imperial crown. *Badge:* a crimson enamelled five-petalled rose, the petals bearing the letters *India*; a central medallion of gold depicts Q. Vic. and is surrounded by an indigo-enamelled band inscribed in gold *Victoria Imperatrix*; the whole being ensigned with the Imperial crown. *Star:* the badge's central medallion, ensigned by a crown, surmounting a ten-point star with alternate rays of gold and silver. *Mantle:* purple satin, lined white silk, with the star embroidered on the left breast. *Riband:* deep indigo.

indivisible arms: of a grand-quarter subquarterly (q.v.) when such a marshaling is the subject of a Royal Warrant supporting a 'name-and arms' clause. Also called 'impartable'.

inescutcheon: a small shield, one-fifth of the width of the shield whereon it occupies the fess point. The ~ is generally itself a coat of arms to which the armiger has, or will or may have a claim, or to which he is

the pretender; hence, the alt. term 'a shield of pretence'. Sometimes expressed as ' "A", bearing "B" in pretence'. (IV)

infamato: It., membered.

infamea: r. obs. alt. for 'defamed' (q.v.).

infant: see **child.**

infattning: Swd., orle.

inferriato: It., trellised.

inflamed: see **lowe.**

infulae vitae: see **mitre.**

ingehoekt: D., indented.

ingeskulp: Afk., invected.

ingollato: It., vorant.

ingot: see **minerals.**

ingulphant: of fish, when feeding.

ink-moline: generally defined as alt. for 'mill-rind' (q.v.), but unconvincing: perhaps 'ink-horn' was intended.

innenbord: Ger., **orle.**

Innes, Robert: Lyon Clerk Depute, 1675.

Innes of Blairton, Robert: Lord Lyon Depute, 1677.

inquartato: It., quarterly.

inquartato in croce di St Andrea: It., per saltire.

insigne: see following entry.

insignia: [L.] signs, or indicators of rank, honour, and other distinctions, as the stars, collars, and badges of an order of chivalry; the flags and emblems of a nation, or the armorial bearings of a gentleman. The word is plural and it is very commonly misused for 'insigne', the singular.

inter: [L.] alt. for 'between' and sometimes used to avoid several repetitions.

interlaced: woven; crossing alternately over and under. (426)

interlaced cross: see **parted** and **fretty.**

interstice: [L.] lit. an intervening gap; hence, any one of the lozenge (q.v.) shaped spaces through which the field (q.v.) is visible in either 'fretty' (q.v.) or 'trellis' (q.v.); e.g. 'gules fretty Or and in each ~ a fleur-de-lys argent'.

intortant: [L.] of a serpent wound tightly inward, forming a flat spiral.

intradented: a r. term: 'barry ~' was introduced into Scottish heraldry to express 'emmanché' (q.v.). (VI)

inumbratus: L., in umbra.

invected: [L.] complementary to 'engrailed' (q.v.); it is precisely the same line of semicircles conjoined, but is opposite in its application, i.e. 'per fess ~' the points are chiefward; 'per pale ~' they are to the dexter: when an ordinary is ~ the points on each side face inward. When either ~ or engrailed are employed in a parting of the field it is very common to see them drawn in reverse.

invectus: L., invected.

inverted, wings: see **eagle.**

inverted shields: see **Matthew Paris.**

involved: [M.E.] of a serpent formed into a ring and holding his tail in his mouth.

Ireland, Chief Herald of: see **Ulster Office.**

Ireland Herald Extraordinary: a Scottish officer of arms (c. 1500) now obsolete.

Ireland King of Arms: an English officer of arms, first mentioned in 1389; supposed to have jurisdiction in Ireland, but attached to the English authority. The name fell into desuetude in 1487.

Irish Genealogical Office, the: see **Ulster Office.**

iron, an: see **basket-makers' tools.**

iron-jack: see **knitting-frame.**

irradiated: see **ray.**

Isabella, the Catholic Order of: f. 1815; abolished 1931; revived 1938 in five classes. Insignia—*Badge:* a gold cross paty notched, the eight points tipped by gold balls, the arms enamelled red and separated by golden rays; a white central medallion depicts the Pillars of Hercules, a banner inscribed *Plus Ultra* and two crowned terrestrial globes; the medallion is surrounded by the inscription, in gold on white, *A Lealtad Acrisolada. Badge:* ensigned by a laurel wreath. *Star:* a large version of the badge, with the central medallion being ensigned with a crown and the cypher FY, the name of the Order added to the inscription, and the addition of a laurel wreath. *Riband:* orange, white edges.

Isidore, St: appears together with St Leander in the municipal arms of Seville.

---

271. Sable, a phoenix argent issuant of flames of fire proper.
Caine.

272. Argent, a unicorn clymant sable, armed and unguled Or.
Harling.

273. Azure, a lion bicorporate argent, ducally crowned Or.
Corporation of the Borough of Shoreditch (from the arms of Sir John de Shoreditch).

274. Azure, a salamander Or in flames of fire proper.
Cenino.

275. Azure, a Pegasus salient argent.
Honourable Society of the Inner Temple.

276. Azure, a winged lion statant-gardant, the head within a nimbus, all Or, resting the dexter fore-paw on an open book, argent.
Venice.
Note: This achievement can be shortly blazoned as *azure, the lion of St Mark.*

271

272

273

274

275

276

Islay Herald: see **Lyon Office.**

issuant: [M.E.] emerging from; arising at, or out of. A demi-beast ~ of a ducal coronet (q.v.) is a frequent crest theme; a pile (q.v.) ~ in base has its broad end in base point: a charge may be ~ of an ordinary (q.v.) or of another charge. (419, II, III)

Italian Solidarity, Order of the Star of: f. 1948 in three classes. Insignia: First-class badge—a five-point star, each ray tipped with a ball, having flames between the arms; a central medallion depicts the Good Samaritan; the badge is ensigned with a wreath. *Star:* the unensigned badge in larger size. Second class—a neck badge, as above. Third class—a breast badge without the flames; all the insignia is in gold. *Riband:* green, edged with a narrow red and white stripe.

Italy, Order of the Crown of: see **Crown of Italy, Order of the.**

ivy: the climbing plant, *Hedera helix* (symbol of Bacchus), employed by the Municipal Corporation of St Ives, Cornwall, as a ca. device.

jabalina: Sp., javelin.

jacens: L., see following entry.

jacent: r. obs. alt. for 'couchant' (q.v.).

jachthoren: D., bugle horn.

jacinth: obs. interchangeable with tenné (q.v.).

jack: see **pike**[1].

jackdaw: see **daw.**

Jackson, Randall: see **Holmes, Randall.**

Jacobean Union: see **Union Jack.**

Jacob's staff: alt. for 'palmer's staff' (q.v.).

jagdhorn: Ger., bugle horn.

jambe: see **gambe.**

James of Compostella, St: see **escallop.**

James of the Sword, Order of St: (Portugal) f. in 1390 as a semi-religious order it is now a State order in five classes. Insignia—*Badge:* a gold-rimmed red enamel cross cercelé fitchy at the foot, with green and gold palm branches between the arms; surmounting the two lower palms is the inscription, in gold, on a white band, *Sciencias, Letra, E Artes;* the whole is ensigned with a green and gold laurel wreath. *Star:* a silver star of twenty-two separate rays, with a central medallion of white enamel depicting the badge, surrounded by a red band bearing the inscription in gold, and by a gold wreath. *Riband* purple.

Januarius, Order of St: (Two Sicilies) f. 1738 in one class. Insignia—*Badge:* a gold-rimmed white-edged red cross paty notched, gold f.d.l. between the arms; centrally, an episcopally red-garbed depiction of St Januarius on a cloud, an open book in his left hand. *Star:* a silver version of the badge with St Januarius garbed in gold and holding a pastoral staff in his left hand, his right being raised in benediction; the cloud is replaced by an escroll bearing the motto *In Sanguine Foedus. Riband:* red worn from the right shoulder to left hip.

Japan, heraldry in: the Japanese system of heraldry is not based on the European system, is not influenced by it, and it emerges at a much earlier period than the XII cent. A.D. It can be traced to the early Heian Era, when the House of Fujiwara gained political ascendance—a date equivalent to 794 A.D. The device itself does not conform to a shield shape, and was not evolved upon the shield. The circle is the most usual shape, the semicircle, or fan-shape follows in frequency of usage, and after that comes the square and the rectangle.

PLATE X *Left:* Barry wavy azure and argent: on a chief of the last a cross gules charged with a lion passant gardant Or.

Former *London County Council*
accolée with

Right: Barry wavy argent and azure: on a chief gules a Saxon crown gold.

Greater London Council (successors to L.C.C.)

(The mural crown ensigned the achievement of the L.C.C. The G.L.C.'s shield has no exterior decoration.

Barry wavy azure and argent for the L.C.C. and barry wavy argent and azure for the G.L.C. is not an heraldic 'difference'; it is to give a sharper edge to the chief in each case.)

The device, called the 'mon', is a design exclusive to and a means of identification of a family, and there is a system of differencing to distinguish between one branch of a family and another. Although the design of the mon is subject to control, it may be of any colour. As it is worn on clothing the right to vary its colour is manifestly necessary. The use of mon was popularized at a period equivalent to 900–1000 A.D. when the court nobles invariably had their equipages decorated with a repeat pattern of their family mon. Devices were the subject of grant made either by the emperor himself or by a feudal superior, but there does not seem to have been at any period a body of officers of arms. Infringement of mon was a punishable offence. The higher the social status of the true owner the more severe the punishment which might go even as far as death. As we draw nearer to our own time, ~ follows the trend of heraldry throughout the world: less exalted persons are permitted the use of mon. The conventionalized chrysanthemum, known as the Royal mon, is familiar on account of its having become the State mon, making its appearance on postage stamps and the like. More exclusive in its use by the Royal House is the conventionalized paulownia (q.v.).

The theme of the early mon is invariably botanical: grasses, leaves, and flowers being used. As the use of the mon spread, other themes were introduced, and, finally, there came the prosaic object. The outstanding difference between the employment of such in Japan and in Europe is that on account of the Japanese sense of design, and delicacy of drawing, even umbrellas, or mouse-traps form a pleasing device.

javelin: [O.F.] a shaft about 3 ft in length, fitted with a barbed head like an arrow, used for throwing; also blazoned as 'dart'. In Fr. blazon the word has a final 'e'.

jaw-bone: infrequent, and generally employed in an allusive (q.v.) setting.

jefe: Sp., chief.

jelloped: see **jowlopped.**

Jenyns, Wm[1]: said to have served K. Hen. VII as Chester Herald and to have been, formerly, both Rouge Croix and Berwick Pursuivant, but not to be found in the records.

Jenyns, Wm[2]: Lancaster Herald, 1516. Former Guisnes Pursuivant, c. 1509. Also called 'Wm Gedding'.

Jenyn's Book, Thomas: (c. 1410) the most famous copy 'Queen Margaret's Book' (q.v.) on permanent exhibition in the British Museum; differs but little from Thomas Jenyn's version.

Jenyns' Ordinary, Wm: (c. 1380) in book form, fifty-one vellum leaves 8 in. by 11½ ft, containing 1611 painted arms, a few of which are on banners instead of shields.

jersey card: see **card[1].**

Jerusalem cross: alt. for 'cross potent'. See **potent, cross.**

Jerusalem Herald: George Ruxnen, published in 1522 *Thurnier Buch*, a study of tournaments.

jessant: [Fr.] shooting forth, or out of; extruding; an alt. continental spelling is 'issant', indicating a linguistic relationship to 'issuant', but ~ is not an alt. for 'issuant' (q.v.). (60)

jessant-de-lys: see **face, a leopard's.**

jessed: [L.] of a falcon (q.v.) having about the claw a strap to which the leash (q.v.) was attached by means of a ring described as a 'vervel' (or varval); hence, a falcon may be belled (q.v.), ~ and vervelled, each of a different colour.

jetton: a counter, token, or private coin; a disc of metal, engraved or embossed with a device; r. for ca. reasons only.

jewelled: see **gem-ring.**

Jew's-harp: a musical toy that is believed to have wandered into heraldry by accident; it makes one appearance only: 'argent, a Jew's harp in bend sable between six laurel leaves of the last' for Scopham. It is suggested that the object in bend was meant for a scoop—for ca. reasons—and bad drawing did the rest.

jiron: Sp., gyron.

jironado: Sp., gyronny.

Johanniterorden: [Ger.] see **Saint John, Order of.**

John [? . . . ?][1]: Lancaster Herald in the service of the Black Prince, 1358.

John [? . . . ?][2]: Chester Herald, 1393.

John Chad Decoration: (South Africa) f. 1952 as a reserve decoration. *Badge:* an oblong silver medallion depicting the Commissariat building at Rorke's Drift, the scene of a battle at which Lieutenant Chard won the Victoria Cross. *Riband:* red with a blue and white stripe at the edges, and the initials *J.C.D.* in the centre.

John Dory: a name applied to the dory fish (q.v.).

John (Tyndale): Chester Herald, 1447. The surname does not appear in the records. Hugh Stamford London assumes the sur-

name from a cognizance written in the signature of this John, and Wm Tyndale (q.v.) whose son he may have been.

John of Jerusalem, Order of St: see **Saint John of Jerusalem.**

Johnston, Graham: Herald-painter to the Lyon Court, 1898.

Joieulx Pursuivant: maintained by Lord Bonvill upon whom he was in attendance at the battle of St Albans, 1455.

Jones, Francis: Wales Herald Extraordinary, 1963.

Jones, Philip: York Herald, 1722.

joscelyn: a large annulet (q.v.) charged at top, bottom, and on each side with a small shape, such as a mullet; or carrying, on the outer edge, four hawk's-bells (q.v.) in those positions; ca. on the family name of Joscelyn, Goslin, etc.

jowlopped: [O.E.] a term employed to describe the wattles of a cock.

Joye Pursuivant: one of the officers of arms maintained by Lord Scales (c. 1450).

Joyner, John: Norroy King of Arms, 1522. Former Richmond Herald, 1511; former Calais Pursuivant, 1510.

jug: a domestic utensil, being a vessel deep in comparison with its diameter, used for handling such liquids as water, beer, milk,

---

277. Argent, a morse naiant azure.
      Silvester.

278. Argent, a dragon segreant wings elevated, azure.
      Almarade.

279. Argent, a wyvern with wings addorsed sable.
      Tilley.

280. Argent, an heraldic antelope gules; tusked, crined, horned and unguled Or.
      Antilupe.

281. Argent, an heraldic tygre statant gules within a bordure sable charged with eight fleurs-de-lys.
      Lone.

282. Argent, a cockatrice azure, combed, beaked, jelloped and membered gules.
      Dancye.

277

278

279

280

281

282

wine, etc. Standardized in heraldic drawing as of Grecian-vase shape, but varying in detail from the austere to the ornate by fluting and chasing. The lip is to the dexter and the handle to the sinister u.o.s. It may be styled 'a beaker', 'a ewer', 'a flagon', 'a pitcher', or 'a water-pot'. When depicted without a lip and with a handle at each side it is described as 'double eared' and it is most likely to be dignified by being a 'ewer' or a 'pitcher'; it may also be simply 'an urn', 'a vase', or 'a flower pot'.

Julian, Cross of St: a cross-crosslet (q.v.) set saltirewise (q.v.). (211)

jumel: r. alt. spelling of 'gemel' (q.v.).

Jupiter: see **segregative blazon.**

Jupiter's cross: a saltire of lightning-flashes surmounted by a cross of flame; alt. term 'thunder cross'.

Jupiter's thunderbolt: a composite charge consisting of a long, slender barrel-shape tubular element, termed the 'shaft', open at each end where it is issuant of flames of fire proper: the shaft, which may be decorated with chasing, is 'banded' about the middle and to this band a pair of wings (spread) is attached: the whole is in front of a saltire of lightning flashes, i.e. zigzag lines terminating baseward in arrow heads: sometimes blazoned without the classic reference. (137)

Jupon: [M.E.] a jacket, a development of the surcoat (q.v.), and a forerunner of the tabard (q.v.).

Justice, figure of: see **symbolic figures.**

Justice, sword of: see **sword.**

kaare: a name for the horse (q.v.).

Kaisar-I-Hind: f. 1900, the last order to be founded by Q. Vic., in three classes. *Obverse:* within an ornamental band the cypher of the reigning sovereign, the whole ensigned with the Imperial crown. *Reverse:* on a central scroll the words *Kaisar-I-Hind;* a design of foliage surrounded by a band inscribed *For Public Service in India;* ensigned with the Imperial crown; first class—gold; second class—silver; third class—bronze. *Riband:* lavender blue.

Kalvariekruis: Afk., cross Calvary.

kangaroo: a marsupial having highly developed hind-legs that enable it to progress by leaping forward. Of the family *Macropodidae,* and indigenous to Australia; hence, employed in the arms of Australians and those connected with that country.

kantenpfahl: Ger., trononné.

kanton: D. and Swd., canton.

karbonkel: D., escarbuncle.

karvskura: Swd., engrailed.

kedja: Swd., collar.

keel: D., gules.

keil: Ger., pile.

kelpie: [Gael.] a fictitious beast that finds its way out of Scottish folklore where it is a horse-like water-sprite, into heraldry where it serves as a supporter.

Kendal Herald: see **Candalle Herald.**

Kent Herald: see **Lyon Office.**

kenteken: Afk., badge.

keper: Afk. and D., chevron.

kepersgewyse geplaas: Afk., chevronwise.

kerkvaan: D., gonfannon.

Kerr, John: Herald-painter to the Lyon Court, 1804.

Kerr, Philip Walter: Rouge Croix Pursuivant, 1928.

kettle-hat: an obs. domestic charge which, were it revived, would be blazoned as 'a tea-cosy'. It is not a form of helmet.

kettle-hook: see **cramp.**

key: [O.E.] an instrument of metal which, inserted into a lock through the aperture provided for its reception, may be turned in order to shoot the bolt either backward or forward thus unlocking, or locking the lid, door, or gate so secured. The ~, which in addition to being the insignia of St Peter and widely used in ecclesiastical coats of arms, has an extensive secular application for its ca. allusive and symbolic possibilities, and also for the sound, simple reason of the highly decorative nature of a well-drawn ~. It consists of three parts: the bow, i.e. the ornamental, or plain, square, oval, or circular pierced end-plate by which it is secured to a chain, cord, or thong; the rod or shank; and the flag-like side projection cut into a complexity of slots, called the wards.

'A ~', to which may be added 'erect', will be palewise, bow downward, wards to the dexter; 'inverted', the bow is chiefward and the wards still facing dexter: 'reversed', the bow is downward, wards to the sinister: 'inverted and reversed' is a frequent position. 'Two ~s addorsed' gives both of them in pale, bows downward, wards facing respectively dexter and sinister: a variation of this is 'addorsed with the sinister ~ inverted'. In saltire the bows are baseward the wards outward u.o.s. A pair of ~, in saltire is one charge, 'three pairs of ~s in saltire', not 'six ~s . . .'.

When orientated fesswise, bows are to the sinister and wards upward u.o.s.; hence, when a number of ~s are blazoned their orientation is essential, i.e. 'three ~s fesswise in pale' gives each ~ horizontally and arranged one above the other from base to chief: 'three ~s palewise in pale' puts them one above the other, but each erect: 'fesswise in fess', they cross the shield end to end, but 'palewise in fess' they cross the field in procession each remaining erect. The same rule applies to ~, in bend or in bend sinister.

No rule covers the shape or the appearance of the bow which may be highly ornate: ~ addorsed may be 'conjoined in the bows' or 'with bows interlaced': the wards are cut into various ornamental shapes, but for technical sense the design, whatever it may be, ought to be symmetrical for if it is not the ~ so drawn may be expected to turn in the lock from one side only of the door. ~s are sometimes crowned or enfiled with crowns and coronets; they may co-operate to form a saltire with some other appropriate object, such as a sword, and they also come humbly in as secondary items being held in the hand of a human figure (probably St Peter); the beak of a bird (particularly the ostrich); or the paw of a quadruped. (438)

keys, ashen: see **ashen keys.**

kidney dagger: a civilian weapon originated in northern Europe in the late XIV cent. Sharp on one edge only; hence, also called a Kidney knife and, occasionally, a ballock knife. Named from the shape of the quillons, which were of wood.

kil: Swd., pile.

Kildare Pursuivant: maintained by the Earl of Kildare, c. 1485; also called 'Galdare'.

kilderkin: r. alt. for a barrel or a tun (q.v.).

Kilgour, Wm: Messenger-at-Arms to the Lyon Court, 1679.

kiln: a building, generally allusive. Also blazoned as 'brick-kiln' and very often 'fumant'.

king, a: [O.E.] identifiable by robes, crown, orb, and sceptre.

King, Gregory: Lancaster Herald, 1689. Former Rouge Dragon Pursuivant, 1677.

King, Peter: Snowdoun Herald, 1692.

King, Thomas Wm: York Herald, 1949. Former Rouge Dragon Pursuivant, 1833.

Kings of arms: see **College of Arms** and **Lyon King of Arms.**

kings of arms, crowns of: each of the kings of arms possesses a crown symbolic of his office. This is placed upon his head only during a coronation ceremony at the moment of the crowning of the sovereign. It consists of a circlet of silver-gilt engraved with the words *miserere mei Deus secondum magnam misericordiam tuam*, from 'Psalmus, L. Biblia Sacra juxta Vulgatae', rendered in English in both the A. and R. Version as, 'have mercy upon me, O God, according to thy loving kindness' (Psalm li.1) and is clearly offered as prayer for the sovereign. The facetious jests concerning the use of the quotation are not occasioned by either impiety or disloyalty, but by ignorance.

~ are heightened with sixteen leaves, eight of which rise to about twice the height of the remainder and they are arranged alternately. These leaves, sometimes described as 'oak', are also described as 'acanthus', and further as 'alternate acanthus and oak'. In drawing nine leaves only are shown, those at each side in profile. The cap is of crimson satin turned-up ermine, and on top is a tassel of gold. Crown royal, peer's coronets, and ~ represent objects: the other heraldic crowns are symbolic only.

Kings of Britain Roll: (temp. K. Hen. VI) 342 shields of both British and Saxon kings, of King Arthur, foreign monarchs, and English lords as well as the attributive arms (q.v.) of saints and others.

Kintyre Pursuivant: see **Lyon Office.**

kirkenfahne: Ger., gonfannon.

Kirkwood, George: Albany Herald, 1610.

kit: [dial.] a Sussex folk-name for a fish similar to the plaice (q.v.); employed for ca. reasons.

kite: see **piddle.**

klaverkruis: Afk., trefoil.

klawerkruis: Afk., cross bottony.

klee: [O.E.] a hoof, particularly that of the boar (q.v.); alt. spelling 'cley'.

---

283. Argent, a mermaid gules crined Or, holding in her dexter hand the mirror and, in her sinister, the comb, both also Or.
Ellis.

284. Azure, a harpy Or.
Municipal Corporation of Nuremberg.
[*Note:* This is a secondary coat of arms, the municipality having two. The 'superior' achievement is depicted at No. 107.]

285. Azure, the figure of Justice, vested argent, in the dexter-hand a sword erect proper; in the sinister, a pair of scales Or, all between two estoiles of the second.
Wergman, Surrey.

286. Gules, three sirens argent.
Basford.

287. Argent, three lympagoes in pale azure.
Radford.

288. Sable, a hand proper vested argent issuant of clouds in chief of the second rayonée Or, feeling the pulse of an arm also proper vested of the second, issuant of the sinister: in base, a pomegranate of the third, all within a bordure of five demi-fleurs-de-lys of the last.
Royal College of Surgeons.

283

284

285

286

287

288

klee-stengeln: Ger., a development of the eagle's wing-bone used in Germanic heraldry; the wings (displayed) appear to be charged along the upper edge with a barrulet (q.v.) issuant of the bird's body, and terminating at the outer end in a trefoil.

kleeblattkreuz: Ger., cross bottony.

klimmend: Afk. and D., rampant.

kluven: Swd., per pale.

knee-holm: a local name for brush, broom, or heath: also called 'knee-holly'.

knife: [O.E.] a ∼ may be blazoned without qualification; on the other hand its specific use may be indicated as 'butcher's ∼', 'plumber's ∼', and so on; however, the knives drawn vary but little if at all. The blade has the back and edge parallel except at the end where the back dips in a shallow curve and the edge rises to meet it in a point. The handle (blazoned 'haft') consists of halves: a piece of wood, bone, horn, etc., riveted on each side. A ∼ proper is argent, hafted of any colour.

knight: the second rank in sub-infeudation: tenant of a tenant-in-capite; one bound to serve the king as a mounted and appropriately armed warrior; one suitably trained, and of noble blood, raised by the king to superior military rank. In modern times a rank conferred by the accolade of the sovereign. Knighthood of this kind carries the title 'Sir' before the personal name of those selected, but the rank of Knight Bachelor is not transmissible to offspring. Knighthood is also attained in Orders of Chivalry, and in certain State Orders.

Knight, Edmund: Norroy King of Arms, 1592. Former Chester Herald, 1574; former Rouge Dragon Pursuivant, 1565.

Knight, Thomas: Chester Herald, 1617. Former Rouge Croix Pursuivant, 1592.

Knight Bachelor, badge of: f. 1926; is worn as a star and possesses neither riband nor miniature. Insignia: an oval vermilion medallion enclosed by a scroll bearing a cross-hilted sword belted and sheathed, the pommel upwards between two spurs, their rowels upwards, the whole set about with the swordbelt, all gilt.

knight's helmet: see **helmet of rank.**

knitting-frame: the representation of a piece of machinery in the achievement of the Worshipful Company of Framework Knitters. Before adopting this they competed with the basket-makers (q.v.) in plumbing the depths of prosaic objects, i.e. 'two combs and as many leads of needles . . . an iron-jack and lead-sinker, a mainspring between two smaller springs'.

knoestig: Afk., raguly.

knoop: Afk., knot.

knopkruis: Afk., cross pommetty.

knots, heraldic: named after the families who originated them as cognizances, or badges, but no longer exclusive. ∼ may be 'sailor's knots', possessing a non-heraldic technical name, or they may be shapes and interlacings that have no existence except in heraldry. It is probable that ∼ were originally monograms: the most obvious being the Stafford knot (q.v.). Loosely tied and orientated palewise it is not simply like, but actually is, the cursive script capital S of the period. There seems but little room for doubt, too, that they were evolved as the cheapest and simplest method of providing a means of identifying one's own contribution of manpower to the feudal host. All that had to be supplied was a length of cord: each man made his own knot and stitched it in the appropriate place on his own garments. Badges were essential because the men-at-arms, being strangers in blood, could not parade under the leader's arms, or any part of his arms or his crest, but marked with an individual mark they had to be, and the badge served this end. Therein may be the origin of regimental badges. (431)

knowed: [Teut.) knotted, generally in a 'figure of eight', also known in heraldry as 'the knot of Savoy' and in practical use as 'the Swedish stopper-knot'. The knot is balanced in form, and is highly decorative. Heraldic cordage, as, e.g., that pendant from an ecclesiastical hat (q.v.) is ∼; the tails of beasts may be, and the entire creature when of a suitable nature may be, e.g., eels (q.v.), serpents (q.v.). The head and tail of a serpent ∼ incline upward: ∼ reversed sets the extremities downward. Alt. spelling 'nowed' (q.v.). (75)

Knox, Robert: Dingwal Pursuivant, 1668.

koek: D., roundel.

komet: Ger., comet.

komfonerad: Swd., cross.

krenelerad: Swd., embattled.

kreuz: Ger., cross.

kromzwaard: D., scimitar.

kronen: D. and Ger., crowns and coronets.

kruckenkreus: Ger., cross potent.

kruis: Afk., and D., cross.

kruis met gescherpte voet: D., cross fitchy.

kruisies: Afk., cross-crosslet.

kruislings geplass: Afk., in cross.

krukken kruis: D., cross potent.

krulkruis: Afk., cross sarcelly.

krummschwert: Ger., scimitar.

kryckgraverk: Swd., potent.

kvadrerad: Swd., quarterly.

kwartier[e]: Afk. and D., quarters.

---

label: [M.E.] a narrow band, having on the underside either three or five short branches, each of the same width as the transverse, and about three times as long as they are wide. The branches, known as points, files, pendants, or drops, may also be dovetail in form, broadening out at the lower end. The ∼ of three points is the mark of distinction (q.v.) of the heir apparent; hence, the difference (q.v.) for the eldest son: that of five points distinguishes the heir presumptive; hence, the eldest grandson, but in the event of the early death of the eldest son, making the grandson heir apparent, the latter assumes the ∼ of three points. In England (not in Scotland), the ∼ throughout argent is reserved for members of the Royal Family; all subjects use a ∼ of not more than half the width of the shield, and it appears, as a rule, in centre-chief (q.v.). The points of a ∼ sometimes carry charges, e.g. in the Royal Family where the sovereign alone bears the arms undifferenced, the heir-apparent has a plain ∼ of three points throughout, and all other members of the family, princesses as well as princes, have personal differences in the form of charges (the plain cross, the rose, the heart, the anchor in either gules or azure) on one or more points. There are one or two examples of a ∼ appearing as a charge without reference to cadency. In such cases there are generally seven points. The infulae of a mitre (q.v.) are also called labels.

laced[1]: [M.E.] braced, or secured with a string or cord, generally threaded from side to side of an opening.

laced[2]: of a hat, or a garment adorned with lace, i.e. a network of thread forming a pattern.

lacer: L., erased.

lacy knot: might be conveniently described as a double bowen knot (q.v.): to the endless line laid out square with corners twisted into loops is added another, larger, the straight sides of which are interlaced with the corner-loops of the smaller.

lady, arms of a: see **cartouche** and **lozenge.**

Lake, John: Norroy King of Arms, 1386. Former March K. of A., and used that name of office in addition to Norroy, and also in addition to Ireland K. of A., 1395. His surname is, in some records, extended to 'Othelake'.

lamb, Paschal: passant (q.v.), the dexter fore-limb flexed over a cross-staff (q.v.) inclined over the shoulder in bend sinister (q.v.) and, flotant (q.v.) therefrom, a pennon (q.v.) of St George. The ~ wears a halo, and is alt. known as the Holy lamb, and as Agnus Dei. Emblem of St John the Baptist. (24)

lambel: archaic form of 'label' (q.v.), still current in Sp. blazon. With final 's' current in Fr. blazon.

lambella: L., label.

lambello: It., label.

lambrechini: It., mantling.

lambrequin: alt. for 'mantling' (q.v.). With final 'es' current in Sp. blazon, and with final 's' only, in Fr.

laminated: of a fish, or a reptile, or a fictitious beast when the dorsal scales are to be of a colour differing from the rest of the body.

Lamont, James Keir: Bute Pursuivant, 1899.

lamp: [M.E.] of frequent, and very appropriate occurrence in the arms of educational establishments (the ~ of learning, the source of enlightenment), when the classic Roman ~ is indicated, always 'inflamed' or 'flammant'; the wick is to the dexter, the handle to the sinister. In the arms of other establishments 'a ~' may refer to the primitive wick floating in a small, shallow vessel of oil; however, between ignorance and bad drawing the appearance is of a pudding-basin full of paraffin well alight. The Tin Plate Worker's Livery Company has a large round vessel elevated on a foot which looks very much like a tea urn. This

---

289. Azure, in base waves of the sea and thereon St Columba praying in a coracle proper: in dexter-chief a star, argent.
See of the Isles.

290. Argent, a dexter-arm couped embowed proper holding a key azure.
Porter.

291. Argent, a dexter hand appaumé couped erect sable.
Manley.

292. Gules, issuant of a bank of cloud a figure of the Virgin couped at the shoulders proper, vested in a crimson robe adorned with gold the neck encircled by a jewelled necklace: crined Or, wreathed about the temples with a chaplet of roses alternately argent and of the first and crowned with a crown celestial, also gold. The whole within a bordure of cloud also proper.
The Worshipful Company of Mercers.

293. Gules, issuant from the dexter flank a sinister cubit-arm vested azure cuffed Or, the hand proper grasping a cross fitchy of the third.
O'Donell.

294. Sable, three dexter-arms conjoined at the shoulder and flexed in triangle vested Or, cuffed argent, the hands proper, clenched.
Armstrong.

289

290

291

292

293

294

illusion is strengthened if we regard the burner as the tap screwed round and inverted. A globical, or globular ∼, ship's ∼ or lantern at first glance appears like a globe terrestrial (q.v.), the equator, and a number of longitudes being strongly marked. It is, in fact, two hollow hemispheres hinged together at the 'equator', the segments between the 'meridians' being closed with thin sheets of horn. It is of greater technical than heraldic interest, being the ∼ used at sea before gimbals were invented: a heavy weight in the bottom kept the ∼ upright in spite of rolling and pitching in severe weather. The Davy, or safety ∼ (q.v.) makes numerous appearances. (192)

lampago: r. alt. spelling of 'lympago' (q.v.).

lampassé: [Fr.] in British blazon a r. alt. for 'langued' (q.v.) but having that meaning in current Fr.

lamprey: a sea creature resembling an eel (q.v.) in shape but having a dorsal fin which blends with the tail and continues along the ventral surface. A ∼ proper is of a yellowish brown colour with dull, dark green spots.

Lancaster, the Great Coucher Book of the Duchy of: (temp. K. Hen. IV) is an illustrative roll of arms (q.v.) containing representations of the arms of the honours of the county.

Lancastrian Collar: see **collar of SS's.**

lance: a long shaft with a characteristic steel head used as the cavalryman's weapon when attacking at speed; frequently blazoned as a 'spear' or as a 'tilting-spear'. The head consists of a shank or socket into which the shaft is fitted, with a slender, triangular blade. A little more than halfway along the shaft the vamplet is fitted, a hollow, cone-shape hand-guard, the shaft terminating in a conical or a hemispherical counter-weight in order to balance the weapon. Lance (or spear) heads often appear alone as charges: the normal orientation being with the point

chiefward. A 'broken spear' consists of the rear portion of the shaft, complete with vamplet, the jagged fracture towards the dexter: a 'half spear' consists of the head and a short section of shaft, the jagged fracture to the sinister. (235, 464, 465, 467, 468)

lance-rest: see **à bouché** and **clarion.**

Lanciman, Ralph: see **Langham, Ralph.**

landscape heraldry: a decadent form that dispenses with the classic figures, and introduces scenery of a prosaic type. In the late XVII cent. the officers of arms were guilty of devising such achievements: in the XVIII and XIX cents. ∼ on chiefs of augmentation (q.v.) came to disfigure hitherto austere, beautiful devices, but in these days it is only home-made heraldry that commits this offence of ugliness.

landschape: see previous entry.

landship: see **landscape heraldry.**

Lane, Henry Murray: Chester Herald, 1864. Former Bluemantle Pursuivant, 1849.

Lane, James: Richmond Herald, 1738.

Langham, Ralph: York Herald, 1567. Former Portcullis Pursuivant, 1561. Also called 'Lanciman'.

langued: [Fr.] of a beast's tongue when differing in colour from the beast itself. A lion (q.v.) will be ∼ gules u.o.s. except when either the field or the lion himself is gules, when azure will be substituted.

Lant, Thomas: Windsor Herald, 1597. Former Portcullis Pursuivant, 1589.

lanzenwimpel: Ger., pennon.

lapwing: [O.E.] a plover or pe(e)wit, *Vanellus vulgaris,* symbolic of strategy because it leads an intruder away from its nest.

largesse: [M.E.] lit. generosity; bestowal of alms; the making of free and unsolicited gifts; extended to include cash or kind given to a herald in recognition of services rendered, hence, the income an officer of arms derives from the application of his calling.

lark: [O.E.] the skylark, *Alauda arvensis,* is

generally intended; often employed in a ca. setting for the name 'Clark[e]'.

Larken, Arthur Staunton: Richmond Herald, 1882. Former Portcullis Pursuivant, 1878.

lateinisches kreus: Ger., Latin cross.

Lateran Cross: (Vatican) f. 1903 as a medal in three classes—gold, silver, and bronze— to be awarded on the recommendation of the Chapter of the Lateran Cathedral of St John. Insignia—*Badge:* a medallion depicting the head of Christ surmounting a cross, the arms of which terminate in medallions depicting SS Peter, Paul, John, and John Baptist; between the arms an ornamental band; the whole is ensigned with a plaque inscribed *Sacrosaneta Lateranensis Ecclesia—Omnium Urbis et Orbis Ecclesiarum Mater et Caput*; some versions of the badge lack the band and plaque. *Riband:* red with a narrow blue stripe near each edge.

laterculi: L., billets.

lath: [M.E.] the flexible element of an arbalest (q.v.); a small, thin board or flat stick, used in building to form a base for plaster, and to support roofing-tiles. A bunch of ∼s appears in the arms of the Worshipful Company of Bricklayers and Tilers. A bundle of ∼s, sometimes blazoned 'faggots', will be found in the arms of the Woodmongers where firewood, not building material, is probably indicated.

latijnsch kruis: D., Latin cross.

Latin cross: a cross having the upper limb, and that at each side, of equal length and the lower limb considerably longer; alt. 'Passion cross' and 'cross Calvary'.

Latina croce: It., Latin cross.

Latina cruz: Sp., Latin cross.

Latine croix: Fr., Latin cross.

lattise: r. alt. for 'trellis' (q.v.).

latwerk: Afk., fretty.

laurel: [M.E.] a name for the bay-tree;

symbolic of triumph or fame; used in heraldry largely in the arms of literary men, either in the form of a sprig (q.v.) or of a wreath (q.v.), *Laurus nobilis*. (386, III)

Laurie, Robert: Clarenceux King of Arms, 1859. Former Norroy K. of A., 1849; former Windsor Herald, 1839; former Rouge Croix Pursuivant, 1823.

laver: [Gk] a generic term applied to all edible marine plants, but particularly to edible sea-weeds, *Ulva latissima, U. lactuca*, and others; employed in heraldry for ca. reasons, as in the device of the Corporation of the City of Liverpool, and incorporated into that of Martin's Bank (see **grasshopper**).

laver-cutter: a plough-share.

laver-pot: a hot-water jug, depicted as a Grecian **v**ase with a hinged-on cover, and sometimes a tubular spout in the side in place of a lip in the neck.

lavercock: [dial.] a lark (q.v.); alt. spelling 'laveracke'.

Law, James: Snowdoun Herald, 1607.

Laweyn Pursuivant: see **Loveyn Pursuivant**.

Lawrence, St: see **gridiron**.

Lawrie, James: Ormonde Pursuivant, 1782.

Lawson, W. J.: Herald-painter to the Lyon Court, 1832.

Lazarus, cross of St: see **sinople**.

Lazarus, Military and Hospitaller Order of St: f. as Crusading Hospitaller Order in 1098 and reorganized in 1308 and 1578 under the protection of the Crown of France. An international order, with priories, bailiwicks and commanderies in many countries, it maintains its ancient chivalric, oecumenical, and charitable traditions and activities. The Order's ranks and insignia have varied from country to country but in all cases the insignia is based on the historic green cross paty notched, often surmounting a gold cross paty notched (or a star), and the badge is worn from a plain green riband. The motto of the Order is *Atavis et Armis*. The Order also confers a medal, instituted by command of Louis XIV, in gold, silver, or bronze.

Le Neve, Peter: Norroy King of Arms, 1704. Former Richmond Herald, 1703; former Rouge Croix Pursuivant, 1690.

Le Neve, Sir Wm: Clarenceux King of Arms, 1635. Former Norroy K. of A., 1634; former York Herald, 1625; former Mowbray Herald, 1624.

Le Neve's Book, Peter: (c. 1480–1500) paper book, 11 in. by 1 ft. 3 in., a general roll containing 2070 coats of arms generally depicted on shields, but there are a few on banners. Some of the shields have the crests above. Published in facsimile by Joseph Foster, with the title 'A Tudor Book of Arms . . .' being the second of his 'Two Tudor Books of Arms' (see **Holme's Book**), in the Howard de Walden Library, 1904.

Le Neve's Book, Sir Wm: (c. 1500) a book of 156 pages containing 936 shields with names over the majority of them. It is in part a general, and in part a local, roll (q.v.).

Le Neve's Equestrian Book: (XV cent.), paper book of 124 leaves 10½ in. by 1 ft. 3 in., containing names and blazons together with painted figures of eighty-eight mounted men. There are also 2072 painted shields, sixteen to the page.

Le Neve's Roll, Sir Wm: (temp. K. Ed. I) painted, 167 shields with names over.

Le Neve's Second Roll, Sir Wm: (temp. K. Ed. II), true roll 4⅕ in. by 10 ft. 3 in., painted, 118 shields with names and blazons over.

Le Sparre Pursuivant: maintained by Lord Tiptoft, and by two dukes of Exeter, all of whom held, at various times, the lordship of Le Sparre in Gascony. The first ~ visited England in the service of Florimond Lord Le Sparre in 1390.

lead-sinker: see **knitting-frame.**

leads of needles: see **knitting-frame.**

League of Mercy, Order of the: f. 1899 as 'The League of Mercy Badge' to reward services to hospitals, or for the relief of

---

295. Or, fretty sable, the interstices charged with human eyes proper.
  Formanoirs.

296. Argent, a man's leg couped at the thigh, azure.
  Haddon.

297. Or, three broken shank-bones fesswise in pale gules.
  Da Costa.

298. Azure, a human-heart gules pierced by a sword in bend proper.
  Stoneley Priory.

299. Vert, two shin-bones in saltire, that in bend surmounting that in bend sinister.
  Newton.

300. Sable, on a rock in sinister base a skeleton of human bones sitting, resting the dexter elbow on the knee, the head in the hand; the sinister hand on the hip, all Or; in dexter-chief a tower argent: on a chief of the last a cross and in the dexter canton a sword erect, gules.
  Municipal Corporation of the City of Londonderry.

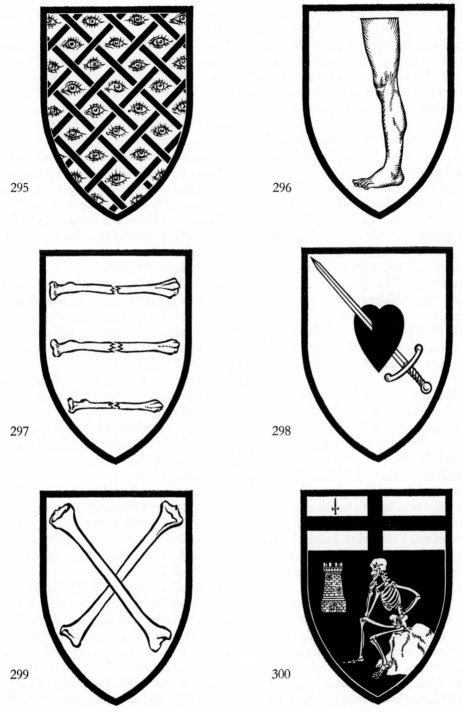

295

296

297

298

299

300

poverty, sickness, and distress. *Obverse:* a gold-rimmed Geneva cross in red enamel, ensigned with the Prince of Wales's feathers enfiled by a coronet; a central medallion surmounted by a laurel wreath depicts Charity with a child. *Reverse:* the recipient's name. *Riband:* white, black, white in equal stripes.

Leake, George Martin: Chester Herald, 1791. Succeeded his elder brother, John (see following entry).

Leake, John Martin: Chester Herald, 1752.

Leake, Stephen Martin: Garter King of Arms, 1754. Former Clarenceux K. of A., 1730; former Norroy K. of A., 1730; former Lancaster Herald, 1727.

leamed: [O.E.] suffused with light; r. obs. alt. for 'irradiated' (q.v.).

Leander, St: see **Isidore, St.**

learning, lamp of: see **lamp.**

leashed: [M.E.] complete with the thong, strap or lead by which a falcon, or a leure (q.v.), was secured. Also of a greyhound on a lead.

leather bottle: a piece of hide sewn in the form of a cylinder, flattened on one side, having closed ends, and a bottle-like neck stitched centrally. Used as a travelling-flask. Often mis-drawn.

leathered: see **book.**

leaved: pertaining to any plant when the leaves differ in colour from the stems; or indicative of the appearance of a leaf, or perhaps of two leaves when fruit is slipped (q.v.); or indicating that a plant charged is to be provided with more than a normal number of leaves.

leaves: [Teut.] of frequent occurrence for either ca. or symbolic association; the nature is always stated—'oak-leaves', 'strawberry leaves', 'maple leaves'—and the tip is in chief u.o.s.; a leaf may be of any heraldic colour, and the veins, u.o.s., sable; if some other colour is required the leaf is

described as 'nerved' of the colour. (139, 389)

Lee, Gordon Ambrose de Lisle: Clarenceux King of Arms, 1926. Former Norroy K. of A., 1922; former York Herald, 1905; former Bluemantle Pursuivant, 1889.

Lee, Richard: see **Leigh, Richard.**

Lee, Thomas: Chester Herald, 1660.

leek: a plant having a cylindrical bulbous edible root, mildly onion-like in flavour, *Allium porrum.* In Wales the ~ is a national emblem, but not a royal badge; hence, it is er. equated to the rose, the thistle, and the shamrock. The ~ is a comparatively frequent charge in the armorial bearings of Welshmen.

leeu: Afk. and D., lion.

leg: the human leg is of infrequent occurrence, is generally enclad in armour, and often flexed at the knee. Three legs, flexed at the knee, clad in armour, and conjoined at the fess point, are famous as the device of the Isle of Man. (296)

leg-bone: also referred to as a shank- or a thigh-bone; the femur is intended and is depicted naturalistically.

leg-irons: insignia of St Leonard: one of the charges in the arms of the Municipal Council of Hove, Sussex.

legato: It., jessed.

legged: see **membered.**

Legh, Roger: Clarenceux King of Arms, 1435. Former Gloucester Herald, 1431; former Rouge Croix Pursuivant; former Wallingford Pursuivant. The name is also spelt 'Lygh'.

Legion of Honour: f. 1802 by Napoleon I, since when the regulations and insignia have been revised from time to time. It is France's premier order, and when conferred for services in war carries with it the automatic award of the Croix de Guerre (q.v.). In five classes, the second of which (Grand Officers) wear their star on the right

PLATE XI *On the mantle:* Quarterly I and IV:
Argent, on a pale sable a conger eel's
head erect, couped Or and charged
with a mullet azure (for difference),
for *Gascoigne*. II: Gules, three picks
argent, for *Picot*. III: Quarterly Or
and gules a bend of the second, for
Beauchamp of Bedford.

On the kirtle: Ermine, a lion rampant sable charged on the shoulder
with a mullet Or (for difference), for
Winter.

Lady Gascoigne [née Winter] (first
wife of Sir Wm, Comptroller of the
Household to Cardinal Wolsey)
Monumental brass in Cardington
Church, Bedfordshire.

breast. Insignia—*Badge:* a white enamel five-armed ten-point pommetty star, with gold and green oak and laurel leaves between the arms; a central medallion depicts a laureated female head symbolizing the Republic, all in gold, and is surrounded by a gold-rimmed blue band inscribed *Republique Française* in gold; the badge is ensigned with a green and gold laurel wreath; the reverse of the badge depicts crossed tricolor flags and the wording *Honneur et Patrie* in gold. *Star:* five arms and ten tipped points, with a central medallion as for the badge but surrounded by the inscription *Republique Française—Honneur et Patrie*, all in silver. *Riband:* scarlet.

Legion of Merit: (U.S.A.) f. 1942 in four ranks. American Servicemen may receive only the fourth rank. Insignia—Chief Commander—a breast star only, of five arms and ten points, each point gold-ball tipped; the arms are gold-rimmed white enamel, with red edges; between the arms are crossed gold arrows; a central medallion, surrounded by an ornate gold band, bears thirteen gold-rimmed white enamel stars on a blue background; the whole surmounts a green and gold wreath, tied at the bottom with a gold bow. Commander—a smaller version of the foregoing worn at the neck, with an open laurel wreath between the uppermost points through which is attached the neck-riband. Officer—a smaller version of the Commander's badge with the wreath replaced by a gold loop for the neck-riband. Legionnaire—as for Officer, but worn as a medal. *Riband:* purple-red with white edges, bearing a gold bar and replica of the star for Chief Commander; a silver bar and star for Commander; a silver replica only for Officers.

Leicester King of Arms: served John O'Gaunt (Earl of Leicester) 1380, and at his death became one of the king's officers of arms. The name fell into desuetude c. 1415, and was revived as name of office of a herald (not a king of arms) in 1478.

Leigh, Richard: Clarenceux King of Arms, 1594. Former Richmond Herald, 1585; former Portcullis Pursuivant, 1571. The name is also spelt 'Lee'.

leiste: Ger., barrulet.

Leitch, Patrick: Ireland Herald Extraordinary, 1498.

Lenin, Order of: (Russia) f. 1930 is one class. Insignia—*Badge:* a gold and platinum medallion with Lenin's effigy, encircled by a gold rye wreath broken at the top by a banner bearing the name *Lenin* and surmounted at the base by a red hammer and sickle and, at the dexter side, by a red and gold five-point star. *Riband:* red, edged gold, with a narrow gold stripe near each edge.

Lennard, Sampson: Bluemantle Pursuivant, 1616. Former Rose Rouge, 1615.

león: Sp., lion.

Leon d'Or Pursuivant: in the service of Lord Dudley (1446).

Leonard, St: see **leg-irons.**

leone: It., lion.

leopard: see **passant.**

Leopard Herald: a name of office employed during the reigns of kings Hen. V and VI, derived from the lions passant gardant in the Royal Arms, then called 'leopards'.

leopardado, león: Sp., a lion passant.

Leopold, Order of (Belgium) f. 1832 in five classes. Insignia—*Badge:* a Maltese cross, gold-rimmed, the eight points tipped with a golden ball; a black central medallion, surrounded by the motto *Union Fait La Force* in gold on red, depicts a crowned gold lion rampant; the whole surmounts a gold and green wreath of oak and laurel leaves, and is ensigned with a crown; when awarded for military merit crossed swords appear below the crown; crossed anchors denote naval merit. *Star:* the badge's central medallion on a silver star of eight points. *Riband:* purple.

Leopold II, Order of: (Belgium) f. 1900 in five classes as a Congolese award, but absorbed by Belgium in 1908. Insignia— *Badge:* a gold cross paty notched, the eight points tipped with a golden ball; a black central medallion, surrounded by the motto *Union Fait La Force* in gold on blue, depicts a crowned lion rampant; the whole surmounts a gold wreath and is ensigned with a crown. The fifth-class badge is in silver, and attached to the Order are three medals, bearing the badge design, in gold, silver, and bronze. *Star:* the badge surmounting a star of ten points, the rays alternately gold and silver. *Riband:* blue, central black stripe.

Leslie, Patrick: Lindsay Herald Extra-ordinary, 1493.

Leslie, Robert: Albany Herald, 1623.

lettuce: [M.E.] a plant having edible leaves, *Lactuca sativa*, which is sometimes employed in heraldry.

leure: [M.E.] a device consisting of a pair of bird's wings joined with a short rod and attached to a cord, employed in falconry for training a young hawk. The normal position is with the wing-tips downward. Also blazoned as 'a hawk's ~' and as 'two wings conjoined in ~ and inverted'. A length of cord nearly always accompanies a ~ although not as a rule blazoned; when it is, the ~ is 'lined' or 'leashed'. The spelling is sometimes modernized, 'lure'. (113)

lever: see **liver-bird.**

leveret: r. alt. for a coney (q.v.).

levrier: [Fr.] see **dog.**

lewis: a device consisting of two bow-shaped steel plates, set back to back and pivoted together; each plate terminating above in a ring through both of which a short length of endless chain is passed. The purpose is to engage in a slot cut in a block of stone so that it may be suspended from a crane hook, placed in position in a building, and the ~ disengaged without the need of drawing chain from under. Generally depicted wrongly, e.g. as a single ring set permanently in the block.

leyzard: an obs. alt. name for the catamount (q.v.) and also an alt. term for the lynx (q.v.).

libarde: archaic spelling of 'leopard' (see **passant**).

Liberation, Order of (France) f. 1940 by

---

301.   Per bend azure and vert, a fish-weel in bend, Or.
      Wheler.

302.   Argent, a scythe, the blade in chief the snead in bend-sinister sable: in the fess point, a fleur-de-lys of the second.
      Sneyd, Staffordshire.

303.   Argent, three stirrups with their leathers gules.
      Gifford.

304.   Azure, three vans Or.
      Robert de Septvans.

305.   Argent, a pair of shears sable.
      Van Riebeck.

306.   Sable, a pile argent and, in base a horseshoe inverted enfiled with an annulet of the second.
      Dunstable Priory.

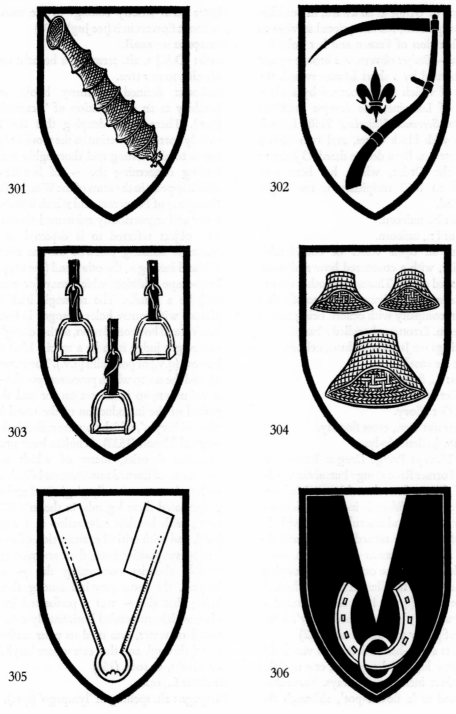

General de Gaulle as an award, in one class of Companions, for exceptional services to the liberation of France and her colonies. Insignia—*Badge:* obverse is a bronze square surmounted by a short bronze sword, the blade of which is surmounted by a black cross of Lorraine; the reverse inscribed *Patriam Servando Victoriam Tulit. Riband:* green with black edges, and two central black stripes. By a decree dated 23 January 1946 the Order, which has been presented to 1053 recipients, is no longer awarded.

licorna: It., unicorn.

licorne: Fr., unicorn.

lighter: an open vessel of considerable capacity, with a countered bow and stern, employed on the Thames and other estuarine waters for receiving the cargo of a ship and, in company with others, being towed upstream. Erroneously called a barge.

lightning: see **Jupiter's thunderbolt.**

lights: see **castle.**

liliatus: L., flory.

lilie: Ger., fleur-de-lys.

lilien: Ger., flory.

lilienkreuz: Ger., cross floretty.

lilja: Swd., fleur-de-lys.

Lilly, Henry: Rouge Dragon Pursuivant, 1638. Former Rose Rouge Pursuivant, 1634.

lily of the garden: the white, or Madonna lily, *Lilium candidum*, is indicated, depicted on a long stalk and as a rule closed, with the tips of the petals turned outward and the ends of the stamens visible: on some occasions ∼ has the outer petals drooping, thus adding to the illusion that it is the basis of the f.d.l. (q.v.). It is also blazoned as 'cultivated lily' and as 'garden lily'. Symbolic of purity and innocence. (182)

lily-pot: a two-handled Grecian vase holding three lilys of the garden, one upright, the others inclining sideways. Sometimes blazoned as 'a flower-pot', although this latter term strictly belongs to the vessel without flowers in it (see **jug**). (384)

limaçon: see **snail.**

limb: [O.E.] r. alt. term for a branch; applicable to any tree.

limbeck: defined in many books on heraldry as an abbreviation of 'alembick' (q.v.). There is no denying that this is strictly correct in relation to the word only, but is totally wrong and thoroughly misleading concerning the ∼ of heraldry, which appears in the arms of the Worshipful Company of Pewterers, and which is manifestly and mysteriously misnamed therein. The object referred to is depicted as a rectangle standing palewise on one short side and having at the other end (the top) a bow-shape addition which may (or may not) be a handle. The rectangle itself is pierced with square holes arranged in both vertical and horizontal rows, so that on sight one might judge it to be a special kind of harrow (q.v.) or portcullis (q.v.). The nature of, and the use to which pewterers put the ∼ is unknown, so is the reason for and the period of the introduction of the word in place of 'stryks', which they are called in the original blazon (1533). Scholars have propounded theories, many of which are specimens of learned nonsense, and Grub St authors have uncritically plagiarized and so perpetuated these legends. In the mid XX cent., with heraldic scholarship at a high level, and with critical examination of misleading supposition keen, there are modern, tenable theories concerning the ∼ or 'stryke', the most practical among them being that the ∼ was a perforated iron plate which, suspended horizontally over a vessel of water, was used to pour molten metal through and thus cast square 'stryks', or streaks, or rods. (156)

limbus: L., orle.

limpago: alt. spelling of 'lympago' (q.v.).

linden leaf: the heart-shape leaf of the lime tree, *Tilia europaea*, of very frequent occurrence in central European heraldry. (429)

Lindsay, Thomas[1]: Snowdoun Herald, 1571.

Lindsay, Thomas[2]: Lord Lyon Depute, 1591.

Lindsay, Wm Alexander: Clarenceux King of Arms, 1922. Former Norroy K. of A., 1919; former Windsor Herald, 1894; former Portcullis Pursuivant, 1883.

Lindsay Herald Extraordinary: an officer of arms formerly maintained by the Earl of Crawford.

Lindsay of Annatland, Sir Jerome: Lord Lyon King of Arms, 1620.

Lindsay of the Mount, Sir David[1]: Lord Lyon King of Arms, 1538. Lyon Depute, 1528, Snowdoun Herald, 1531.

Lindsay of the Mount, Sir David[2]: Lyon Depute, 1568. Former Rothesay Herald.

Lindsay of the Mount, Sir David[3]: Lord Lyon King of Arms, 1591. Former Islay Herald.

Lindsay of Rathillet, Sir David: Lord Lyon King of Arms, 1568. Rothesay Herald, 1557. Dingwal Pursuivant, 1545.

Lindsay of Trakwan, Gilbert: Islay Herald, 1534.

lined[1]: of any object to which a line, cord, or leash (q.v.) is to be attached.

lined[2]: having reference to the inner surface of a peer's cloak (q.v.), a Parliament robe (q.v.), other garment, or article of textile. Alt. such charges are blazoned as 'doubled' of fur, metal, or tincture.

ling[1]: [M.E.] a large sea-fish, *Molva vulgaris*, used as well as the cod (q.v.) in the production of stockfish (q.v.); hence, of economic importance.

ling[2]: a name applied to the freshwater turbot (q.v.).

linguado: Sp., langued.

lingue: L., langued.

linker schuinbalr: D., bend sinister.

linkerbohoek: Afk., sinister-chief.

linkeronderhoek: Afk., sinister-base.

linkerskuinsbalk: Afk., bend sinister.

links: D. and Ger., sinister.

links bo mekaar: Afk., in bend sinister.

links geschuind: D., per bend sinister.

links skuins gedeel: Afk., per bend sinister.

linksarn: Ger., sinister arm.

Linlithgow Pursuivant Extraordinary: a name of office attached to the Lyon Court.

lion: [Gk] the heraldic representation of *Panthera leo* must be a caricature, not a portrait; the attributed virtues, fierceness, bravery, regality, etc., should be expressed. When the blazon states 'a lion' without qualification, the rampant (q.v.) attitude is intended: all the other heraldic postures will be specified. A lion is armed (q.v.) and langued (q.v.) gules except when the beast is himself gules, or the field is gules, when azure is substituted, but, of course, he may be armed and langued of the other colours if so blazoned. (44, 52, 276, III, X, XII)

Lion, Royal Order of the: (Belgium) f. 1891 in five classes as a Congolese award, but absorbed by Belgium in 1908. Insignia —*Badge:* a gold-rimmed white enamel cross with blue edges, the initials in gold of Leopold II between the arms; a blue central medallion, surrounded by the motto *Travail et Progres: Arbeid en Vooruitgang* in gold, depicts a crowned lion rampant; the whole is ensigned with a crown. *Star:* the badge's medallion and motto surmounting a silver star of eight points with gold blades between the rays; a crown surmounts the top ray. *Riband:* violet with narrow borders of blue and yellow.

lion accroupi: see **accroupi.**

lion conjoined to ship: see **dimidiation.**

lion poisson: r. obs. alt. for 'sea-lion' (q.v.).

lion's face: see **face, a lion's.**

Lion of St Mark: a winged-lion (q.v.)

statant, resting the dexter fore-paw on an open book and having about the head a halo. (276)

lionced, cross: a cross humetty each limb terminating in a lion's face, but apparently existing in theory only.

lioncels: see **combatant.**

lionel: r. obs. alt. for 'lioncel'. See **combattant.**

Lisle Pursuivant: maintained by Viscount Lisle, c. 1533.

liston: lit. an edge, or extremity; in heraldry, formerly applied to the escroll (q.v.) under the arms.

Littlejohn, Andrew[1]**:** Ross Herald, 1596.

Littlejohn, Andrew[2]**:** Ross Herald, 1646. Unicorn Pursuivant, 1636.

Littlejohn, David: Albany Herald, 1837. Bute Pursuivant, 1833.

litvit: see **white.**

liver-bird: [dial.] a local name for the cormorant, or sea-raven, *Phalacrocorax carbo*, black in colour; hence, sable in arms. Ca. in the achievement of the Corporation of the City of Liverpool; also used by

Martin's Bank whose registered office is in Liverpool. Alt. spelling 'lever'. (82)

liveries: the predominant metal and tincture appearing in an achievement. (III, XVI)

Livingstone, Edward: Ormonde Pursuivant, 1834.

Livingstone, Robert Spence: Albany Herald, 1885. Bute Pursuivant, 1884.

Livingstone, Stuart Moodie: Unicorn Pursuivant, 1860.

lizard: [M.E.] a small, scaly reptile having large eyes, slender body, and long tapering tail; four legs terminating in bird-like claws. Of the order *Lacertilia*. Sometimes blazoned as 'a scaly ~', generally proper, occasionally vert, but a ~ proper is vert anyway. (76)

loach: [M.E.] a small freshwater fish, *Cobitis barbatulus*; employed in heraldry chiefly for ca. reasons.

lobster: [O.E.] a crustaceous sea-creature of the genus *Homarus*; it possesses ten legs and a long, laminated tail. Represented in heraldry by a claw which is of a highly conventionalized form, appearing like a wooden spoon erect, with a zigzag split

---

307. Azure, a fess wavy of water argent between, in chief, the sun in his splendour Or, drawing up a cloud of the second distilling drops of rain proper and, in base, a distillatory double armed of the third with two worms and bolt receivers, also of the second.
Worshipful Company of Distillers.

308. Argent, three hews sable.
Wm Chare

309. Azure, three mortars and pestles Or.
Broke, Warwickshire.

310. Azure, a tun Or, and from the bung-hole an ash-tree issuant proper.
Ashton, Cornwall.

311. Argent, three passion-nails conjoined pilewise in point embrued.
Gusthart.

312. Or, on a mount vert a windmill sable.
Wm Sampson.

307

308

309

310

311

312

descending about two-thirds of the length of the bowl. (66)

local rolls: see **rolls of arms.**

Lochaber axe: named from a locality in Inverness-shire: employed largely, but not exclusively, in Scottish heraldry. It consists of a long staff having a head shaped like a crescent, the horns of which face outward from the shank, and a spike in line with the shaft. The crescent-shaped blade was not employed in cutting at the enemy, for which purpose it was not fully adapted, but as a hook to engage in the accoutrement of a horseman who could be thus dismounted by a foot soldier. (454)

Lock, Thomas: Clarenceux King of Arms, 1784. Former Norroy K. of A. 1822; former Lancaster Herald, 1793; former Bluemantle Pursuivant 1781.

lodged: see **stag.**

log of a tree: the trunk when felled, generally having a live twig with leaves, and blazoned as 'sprouting': normally orientated fesswise and of more common occurrence in crests (q.v.) than as charges (q.v.).

loggerheads: see **face, a leopard's.**

Lomax, Michael Roger Trappes: Somerset Herald 1951. Former Rouge Dragon Pursuivant, 1946.

Longchamp Pursuivant: in the service of the Lord of Courselles, and several times engaged as messenger between England and Normandy where the major tasks of his office were performed. (1433)

London Roll: (c. 1470) painted on the dorse of the Third Calais Roll (q.v.). ($7\frac{1}{2}$ by $8\frac{1}{2}$ in.), containing 104 shields with names over, being a general roll (q.v.).

long-bow: see **bow[1].**

long-cap: a conical cap, the apex bearing a tassel and, as a rule, falling forward: often barry. Alt. terms 'infula' and 'pilia pastoralis'; of Roman origin and connected with

the fillet worn by both priest and sacrificial beast; hence, 'infulae vitae' (q.v.). The ~ has survived among wearing apparel and is known as 'brewer's cap', and as 'jelley-bag,' but is never so blazoned. (250)

long-cross: sometimes applied to the Latin cross (q.v.).

long-vair: an early form of vair (q.v.) in which the 'bells', which are curved instead of angular, are of about twice the length from base to apex as is the modern (angular) vair-bell. Also called 'old vair' and 'vair ancient'.

longé: Fr., jessed.

lopped: see **branch.**

Lord Marshal's Roll, the: (temp. K. Ed. I) a true roll, 6 in. by 9 ft $5\frac{1}{8}$ in., painted, 588 shields with names over. '~, Old', is of later date; contains forty-seven shields with names and blazons under.

Lord Marshal's Roll, Old, Part I: (temp. K. Hen. V) vellum true roll (q.v.). 6 in. by 3 ft, painted with forty-seven shields with names under. English sovereigns (including K. Ed. Confessor), dukes, earls, Irish earls, foreign dukes, and some attributed arms (q.v.), i.e. St George.

Lord Marshal's Roll, Old, Part II: (temp. K. Ed. I) vellum true roll (q.v.). 6 ft by 1 ft $3\frac{1}{4}$ in., painted with eighteen shields, each larger than those in Part I (q.v.). Names and blazons (added later) under.

lord's coronet: see **baron's coronet.**

loré: Fr., finned.

Lorimer, James: Lyon Clerk and Keeper of the Records, 1848.

Lorimer of Kellyfield, James: Rothesay Herald, 1822.

Lorraine, cross of: a cross having a double traverse, the upper being shorter than the lower, and each an equal distance from the extremity of the paler element. The ends of the limbs of ~ are sometimes of a decorative shape.

losanga: It., lozenge.

losangato: It., lozengy.

losange: Fr. and Sp., lozenge.

losangé: Fr., lozengy.

losangeodo: Sp., lozengy.

Loth, John Thomas: Bute Pursuivant, 1888.

lotus: the Asian water-lily, *Nymphaea lotus*, which has given rise to a conventionalized element of design. The ~ flower is of frequent occurrence in Indian heraldry.

loup: [Fr.] a wolf; employed in British heraldry for ca. reasons.

louterae: see **lutra.**

Loutfoot, Adam: Kintyre Pursuivant, 1494.

loutre: see **lutra.**

Louvre Pursuivant: maintained by the Duke of Bedford, Regent of France; hence, seated in the Palace of the Louvre. Employed chiefly in France, but on several occasions acted as messenger to England (c. 1430); also spelt 'Lovre' and 'Lover'.

Louw Wepener Decoration: South African award; f. 1952 as an award for exceptional deeds of courage: outside the range of purely military decorations; named after General Louw Wepener, who lost his life at Thaba Bosige in 1865. *Badge:* medal of silver, depicting Mount Thaba Bosige with two horsemen at its foot, and immediately beneath them the words *Thaba Bosige* 1865; the inscription *Louw Wepener* appears on the top edge and *Dekorasie* (Decoration) on the lower. *Riband:* six orange and five white stripes alternately.

Lover Pursuivant: see **Louvre Pursuivant.**

Loveyn Pursuivant: maintained by Henry Bourchier who was closely allied to the family of Louvaine. ~ was employed in 1455 by K. Hen. VI. Also spelt 'Laweyn'.

Lovre Pursuivant: see **Louvre Pursuivant.**

lowe: [M.E.] always 'a ~ of flame', and employed when the fire is primary. Fire that is secondary to some object may be blazoned as 'flames of fire' (q.v.), or the object may be described as 'flammant', 'fired', 'inflamed', or 'fummant'. (417)

Loyante Pursuivant: on record as having carried documents between England and France in 1444, but by whom he was maintained is unknown.

lozenge: [M.E.] a rhomboid having its major axis palewise; the shape on which the arms of a lady are emblazoned; a common charge or, according to point of view, a sub-ordinary (q.v.). (148, 405, 408)

lozengy: a variation of the field (or of an ordinary or a charge), consisting of lozenges (q.v.) set close, in barwise rows of alternate metal (or fur) and tincture; the metal should start with the first whole lozenge in dexter chief.

lucy: see **pike**[1].

Lucy's Roll: (temp. K. Hen. VI) vellum true roll (q.v.) originally containing 282 painted shields. Three membranes only survive on which appear thirty-two rows each of five shields with names over.

Luna: see **segregative blazon**; but current in both It. and Sp. with reference to the moon.

luna cornuta: L., crescent.

lune: Fr., moon.

lure: see **leure.**

lusorius latrunculus: L., zule.

lutra: r. alt. for 'otter' (q.v.); employed for ca. reasons.

Lygh Roger: see **Legh, Roger.**

lympago: see **man-lion.**

lymphad: [Gael.] lit. a long-boat, built for both rowing and sailing, used in the Isles, and highly conventionalized in heraldic art. The hull conforms to a semicircle; it has an embattled forecastle and a similar sterncastle. One central mast braced to the castles carries a yard-arm and square sail which is always furled u.o.s. Blazoned 'with oars over the side' or 'oars in action' or '~ in the water', the number to appear is four u.o.s. A ~ 'with sail spread' is also drawn with oars over the side, and the sail thus displayed is very likely to carry charges. A round-top (q.v.) is most likely to appear on the mast just above the yard-arm, and there is a tendency for artists to so arm a ~ without reference to the blazon. The ~ is clinker (or clencher) built, but quite often appears, in arms, caravel-built: no reference is, however, made to the planking; it is fortuitous, being at the artist's whim. A ~ may have in the place of, or as well as, a forecastle a figurehead, often a serpent, and may be alt. blazoned as a 'galley' or a 'galleon'. (331)

lynx: [Gk] a cat-like creature having tufted ears and a short tail carried coward (q.v.). A ~ proper is a muddy yellow, with spots of a deeper shade. He is symbolic of keensight. Identified with *Lynx caracal*.

Lyon Clerk: see **Lyon Office.**

Lyon Court: see **Court of the Lord Lyon.**

Lyon King of Arms, the Lord: chief herald of Scotland, but having wider powers and greater authority than any other king of arms in the world. He derives his title from the lion rampant in Scotland's Royal Arms and, in matters armorial, has vested in him powers equivalent to those of both Garter K. of A. and the Earl Marshal in England. Before the Act of Union ~ was *ex officio* a member of Scots Parliament and a Minister of the Crown with a seat on the Privy Council for Scotland. He is a Judge of the Realm, presiding over his own Court of Justice; he has power to make new laws of arms if those already established do not adequately provide for the particular cause being heard; he can, through his Procurator Fiscal, bring an offender to court, try and sentence him without a jury. It is among the duties of ~ to prevent the use and display of spurious armorial devices and, when necessary, destroy utterly the object on which they may be emblazoned. To be possessed of the authority is one thing, but to put it into practise quite another, particularly when the 'object' is an item of public interest with a high emotional potential, as, e.g., a war memorial, but ~ does not fail to enforce the statutes.

In addition to his being a great officer of State, ~ is a member of the Sovereign's

---

313. Sable, three awls erect, points chiefward argent hilted Or.
   Aule.

314. Argent, a fess between three pairs of pincers gules.
   Russell.

315. Gules, three claw-hammers Or, hafted argent.
   Purser.

316. Gules, three broad axes argent.
   de Renti.

317. Argent, two glazier's nippers in saltire sable between four pears Or.
   Kellaway.
   [*Note:* 'Kelway' pears being understood.]

318. Per chevron argent and sable, three anvils counterchanged.
   Smith, Abingdon.

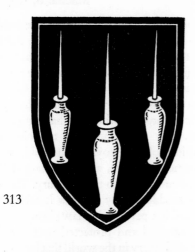

313

314

315

316

317

318

Household and is addressed by the Sovereign but by none other as 'Our Lyon'. In this aspect of his Office ~ embodies an ancient Celtic duty, i.e. that of High Sennachie, a kind of genealogist, keeper of the Sovereign's pedigree, who, before a Scottish coronation recited twenty-one generations of the claimant's ancestors. The genealogical aspect of ~ Office is still maintained, pedigree as well as armorial bearings being put on record in the Lyon Office (q.v.).

Lyon Office: the heraldic authority for Scotland, consisting originally of thirteen persons: the Lord Lyon King of Arms, six heralds, and six pursuivants; the names of office were: *Heralds*—Albany, Rothesay, Marchmont, Islay, Snowdoun, Kent; *Pursuivants*—Unicorn, Carrick, Kintyre, Bute, Dingwal, Ormond. In the mid-XIX cent. the English Parliament, in a fit of economy, unjustly and quite unnecessarily cut the ~ to seven only, i.e. the Lord Lyon assisted by three heralds and three pursuivants. The first three names of office, given above, were retained in current use, but the others are not proscribed, they are merely in abeyance, and could be taken into use at any time. Rothesay normally has the added func-

tion of Lyon Clerk: this gives him responsibility for the keeping of both 'The Public Register of all Arms and Bearings in Scotland' (known briefly as 'The Lyon Register') and also 'The Public Register of all Genealogies and Birth Brieves'. Both of these are public records to which all have right of access. The ~, in addition to being an extension of the royal household, is a department of State, and fees charged for services are paid into the Treasury. The ~ being established by statutes heraldry in Scotland is a part of civil law; hence, arms are controlled and protected by the only court of chivalry in the world that has never ceased to function, i.e. the Court of the Lord Lyon (q.v.).

Lyon Pursuivant: maintained by Thomas Burgh, Captain of Avranches, 1429. The name is derived from the Percys in right of his wife.

Lyon Register: see **Lyon Office.**

lyre: [Gk] a musical instrument consisting of a framework with balanced, S-shape sides and the strings stretched from top to bottom between them. In its symbolism it inclines not to music but to lyric poetry; hence, it is of r. occurrence.

maan: D., moon.

McCulloch, Adam: Lyon clerk and Keeper of the Records, 1554. Marchmont Herald, 1561. Bute Pursuivant 1547. Ultimately, Orkney Herald Extraordinary, 1571.

McCulloch, Alexander: Ormonde Pursuivant, 1569.

Macdonald, Alexander: Lyon Clerk Depute, 1829. Lyon Clerk and Keeper of the Records, 1845.

Macdonald, Wm Rae: Albany Herald, 1909. Carrick Pursuivant, 1898.

mace: see **civic mace** and **war mace.**

Macer: an official who bears the mace before the Lord Lyon King of Arms, and who is accorded the status of an officer of arms.

Macgeorge, Ebenezer: Bute Pursuivant, 1822.

Macgregor, John: Procurator Fiscal to the Lyon Court, 1918.

MacGregor, Malcolm Robert: Procurator Fiscal to the Lyon Court, 1933.

Machado, Roger: Clarenceux King of Arms, 1494. Former Norroy K. of A., 1486; former Richmond Herald, 1484; former Leicester Herald, 1483.

McInnes, Robert: Herald-painter to the Lyon Court, 1823.

MacKenzie, Kenneth: Snowdoun Herald, 1767.

mackerel: [M.E.] a small sea-fish, scaleless and striped, *Scomber scombrus*; employed in heraldry chiefly for ca. reasons.

Mackesone, Eleazer: Bute Pursuivant, 1616.

McKiesoun, Wm: Bute Pursuivant, 1598.

Macleod, Sir John Mackintoch Norman: Rothesay Herald, 1929. Unicorn Pursuivant, 1925.

macula: [L.] mascle.

madder: a climbing plant, *Rubia tinctorum*, imported by dye makers, and represented as in the bag (q.v.), being the crest of the Dyer's Livery Company.

magnetic needle: see **compass**².

maiden in her modesty: see following entry.

maiden's head: generally couped just below the neck, afrontée, u.o.s.; when couped below the breast blazoned as 'a ~ and bust'; as a rule vested, but when nude the fore-arm is flexed across the breast, an attitude that was formerly picturesquely blazoned as 'a maiden in her modesty'.

Maine Herald: functioned in the Province of Maine, France, and was maintained by the Duke of Bedford, 1428.

maintenance, cap of: [fm L. via Fr.] variously described as 'abacot', 'cap of dignity', 'cap of estate', and 'chapeau'; anciently the symbol of authority, and still so recognized as the lining of the crown (q.v.) and of coronets (q.v.): u.o.s., gules turned up ermine (q.v.) the rolled edge terminating in two points behind or, according to some authorities, two points in front. The ~ is sometimes employed in place of a wreath to carry a crest.

Malcolm, John: Ross Herald, 1630.

Malcolm, Wm: Bute Pursuivant, 1647.

Malcolme, Wm: Unicorn Pursuivant, 1660.

Malteserkors: Swd., Maltese cross.

Maltravers Herald: was maintained by Lord Maltravers, 1540.

Maltravers Herald Extraordinary: Mr. J. J. Howard, F.S.A., was the first to receive, under the Earl Marshal, this name of office.

Man, John: Albany Herald, 1766.

man-lion: a lion with a human face, male, bearded to blend with the lion's mane. In the XVIII cent. bad drawing gave all heraldic lions—including the dexter royal supporter—a human face, but they were not, and were not intended to be, in any example, a ~. Alt. title 'lympago'. (287)

man-tygre: an heraldic tygre having the horned head of an old-man; hence, identical with the lympago (q.v.); therefore it is contended that the ~ should be hornless. So slight a difference barely distinguishes the one from the other, it is fortunate that the ~ is r. Also called manticora.

man's head: when blazoned without specification of race or nationality a European is assumed; generally couped either at the neck or below the shoulders and facing dexter o.u.s. (195)

manacle: see **fetterlock**.

mancante: It., tronnoné.

manch: obs. alt. spelling of 'maunch' (q.v.).

manchée: see **maunch**.

mancheron: see **maunch**.

Manchester, Corporation of, v. Manchester Palace of Varieties: see **Chivalry, Court of.**

manchet: [M.E.] a bread-roll; three ~ are always depicted on a baker's peel (q.v.) and sometimes er. blazoned as 'roundels', or as 'plates' (q.v.).

Mandeville Roll: (c. 1460) paper book, containing 133 painted shields of noblemen, five rows of four each to the page, with names over.

maned: of the voluminous neck-fur of a beast, but the term is a weak substitute for 'crined' (q.v.).

mangonel: a military engine consisting of a heavy timber frame in which a sapling, or other springy medium was flexed, loaded with a stone, and then released, also named the 'ballista' or 'swepe' (often mis-spelt 'sweep').

manica: L., maunch.

manilla: a horseshoe-shape object with spatulate ends, being the archaic currency of the Gold Coast (Ghana).

maniple: an item of Eucharistic vestment being a strip of fabric about 4 ft in length, draped over and pendant from the priest's wrist: generally so depicted. More common in Fr. than in British heraldry and there spelt 'manipel' or 'manipule'.

manipolo: It., maniple.

manipule: Fr., maniple.

manipulo: Sp., maniple.

manteau: Fr., mantling.

mantelado: Sp., mantling.

mantelé: Fr., mantled.

manteliatum: L., per chevron.

mantellato: It., mantled.

mantello: It., mantling.

manticora: see **man-tygre**.

mantling: [M.E.] a curling cascade of fronds of fabric falling from below the wreath of the colours and draped at each side of the shield. In post-Tudor times ~ became coloured of the liveries, i.e. the predominant tincture and metal used in the arms, the outside being of the tincture, and doubled, or lined, of the metal (or fur). In old heraldry mantling was invariably gules doubled argent (or ermine), the colours of St George. Alt. terms 'lambrequin' and 'cappelain'.

manto: Sp., mantling.

Manuel Amador Guerrero, Order of: (Panama) f. 1953 in four classes, namely Collar, Grand Cross, Grand Officer, and Commander. Insignia—*Badge:* a gold-edged white enamel cross with narrow gold and enamel leaves between the arms, surmounted by a white central medallion depicting Dr Guerrero and bearing the name of the Order, all in gold. *Collar:* a double chain with decorated devices and leaves, all in gold. *Star:* the badge surmounting a gold

---

319. Argent, three pairs of bellows sable.
Skipton.

320. Sable, three square combs argent.
Tunstall, Cuthbert (Bishop of Durham, 1530–59).

321. Argent, a triangular trivet, sable.
Berkeley.

322. Per pale argent and azure, a ferris counterchanged.
Bogener.

323. Or, a fan displayed with a mount of various devices and colours, the sticks gules: on a chief per pale of the last and azure, dexter, a shave-iron over a bundle of fan-sticks tied together of the field and, sinister, a frame-saw in pale also Or.
Worshipful Company of Fanmakers.

324. Sable, three fleams argent.
Rendarcy.

319

320

321

322

323

324

multi-rayed star of twelve points. *Riband:* yellow with narrow blue and white central stripes.

Manwaring, George: Richmond Herald, 1635.

maple: [O.E.] a tree associated with Canada, *Acer campestre.* The ∼ leaf, which is an official badge, is of frequent occurrence in Canadian heraldry.

Mar, John Earl of: brother of K. James IV of Scotland who created for him an office of arms, namely Garrioch Pursuivant Extraordinary in 1503.

marcassin: [Fr.] a young wild boar.

March King of Arms: was maintained by Edmund Mortimer, third Earl of Mortimer on whose death (1381) he was appointed to the Crown, and ultimately had jurisdiction in Wales and Cornwall.

March Pursuivant: a name of office attached to the Lyon Court.

Marchmont Herald: see **Lyon Office.**

Marenceux Pursuivant: was maintained by the Earl of Worcester, 1462, and named from his Marenceux Lordship in Aquitaine.

Margaret, St: appears in the crest of the Municipal Corporation of Lowestoft, Suffolk. As a 'name St' her flower, the marguerite, is depicted in association with the arms of ladies.

Margrave: [Ger.] Count of the Marches; Charlemagne appointed counts (q.v.) to control vast areas of the Empire's frontiers and to organize their defence against attack. For this reason these counts were granted the military prerogatives of dukes, and by the XII cent. the title was one of great significance and was borne by princes whose lands were far removed from the marches.

marguerite: see **daisy.**

marinado león: Sp., a sea-lion.

marine lion: Fr., a sea-lion.

marined: a generic term, very seldom employed, to describe a composite fictitious beast when the sinister portion is a fish-tail, e.g. 'a lion ∼', which is neither better nor easier than a 'morse' (q.v.).

mariner's compass: see **compass**[2].

marital achievement: a combination of arms denoting marriage. In a marriage where there are no other armorial considerations the union is expressed by an impaled (q.v.) shield, dexter (q.v.), the arms of the husband, termed 'the baron' and, sinister, those of the family of the wife, termed 'femme'. Other armorial considerations, e.g. when a baron is knight of an order of chivalry (q.v.) and displays his arms within the collar of the order, or when the baron is a commoner and the femme a peeress in her own right, the union will be expressed by means of arms displayed accolée (q.v.). Before the system of impalement developed, marital achievements were marshalled (q.v.) by dimidiation (q.v.).

Mariton Herald: see **Mortain Herald.**

Mark, Lion of St: see **Lion of St Mark.**

Marleon-de-Aye Pursuivant: maintained by the Duke of Suffolk (c. 1522).

marlion: r. alt. for a 'martlet' (q.v.); possibly a corruption of 'merlin' (q.v.). Also spelt 'merlion'.

marquee: see **tent.**

Marquess: see **marquis.**

Marquis: [Fr.] lit. marcher; one who walks: the second rank in the British peerage. In France counts who had secured semi-independence of the king by virtue of their extended holdings described themselves as 'marchiones', after the margraves (q.v.), or counts of the marches, who were the only counts authorized to hold more than one county. Hence the description came to be applied to superior counts, and thus evolved a new hereditary title between count and duke. In England the lords of the Scottish and Welsh marches (march indicating a common boundary, or frontier, between

a

b

c

d

PLATE XII (a) Barry Or and azure, four fleurs-de-lys in quadrangle counterchanged.
Allhusen OF STOKE COURT

    (b) Sable, two lions passant in pale, paly of six argent and gules.
Strangwayes

    (c) Vair, a label of three points gules.
Sir Miles de Beauchamp

    (d) Vairy Or and gules.

Sir John Ferrers

two countries or estates) were occasionally termed 'marchiones', but the first creation of a marquis dates from 1 December 1385, when Robert de Vere, Earl of Oxford, was made Marquis of Dublin by Richard II and given precedence between earls and dukes.

marquis's coronet: a silver-gilt circlet heightened with alternate pearls and strawberry leaves, in drawing three of the latter and two of the former are represented: used to ensign (q.v.) a marquis's shield.

Marroffe, Martin: York Herald, 1553. Former Rouge Dragon Pursuivant, 1539; former Calais Pursuivant, 1536.

Mars: see **segregative blazon.**

Marshall, George Wm: York Herald, 1904. Former Rouge Croix Pursuivant, 1887.

marshalling: [M.E.] the arrangements in proper order of two or more coats of arms upon one shield, a multiplication that may be rendered necessary for a number of reasons, e.g. by appointment to an office that carries an armorial status; by the fusion of two armigerous bodies corporate into one organization; or by marriage, all of which bring about impalement (q.v.) of either a temporary or a permanent character; and by the inheritance of a coat of arms that is already subject to ∼ by an escutcheon of pretence (q.v.) which leads to quartering. The inheritance in such a case is not of one only, but of two coats of arms, e.g. the paternal and the maternal arms, but offspring cannot use the former with its inescutcheon because such a ∼ is the marital achievement (q.v.) of the parents; hence, the two devices must be displayed quarterly (q.v.), I and IV for the sword side, II and III for the distaff side.

In the event of this man's marriage with an heiress, he wears the escutcheon of pretence on fess point, debruising all four quarters (not on the pronominal quarter,

only), and offsprings of this marriage display I and IV their paternal arms; II, those of their grandmother, and III those of their mother. A further marriage with an heiress will ultimately put the new arms in quarter IV, and a repetition will bring in a further quarter, making five. It is customary to keep quarters even in number; hence, the new achievement in the succeeding generation will be I, the paternal arms; II, the maternal arms; III, those of the great-great-grandmother; IV, the great-grandmother, and V the grandmother; VI, a repetition of the pronominal quarter, hence, the blazon will begin 'quarterly of six: I and VI . . .'.

When an impalement (q.v.) becomes a quarter, in the event of one of the arms having had a bordure, the fourth side (omitted in impalement) is restored. Should an armiger having numerous quarters marry an heiress who brings in a similar multiplicity, all the quarters of the husband's arms will preceed all the quarters of his wife's, and if her final quarter is a repetition of her pronominal coat, and a repeat quarter is required in the ∼, it will be the husband's first quarter that does this double duty.

A very large number of quarters obviously cannot be displayed if the charges are to be visible, and many old-established armigerous families use their pronominal quarter only, keeping the others to which they may be entitled in the family archives. However, it sometimes happens that among one's quarters is to be found the arms of a very distinguished historic character with whom one desires to display affinity. This cannot be done by quartering the desired arms with one's own, but involves a display of the chain of quarters that bring about the family connection.

Ostentatious build-up of multiple quarters, though formerly treated with respect, is now looked upon as a display of armorial bad taste, and the tendency is for a reduction of numbers displayed by the best families; there are, however, sometimes special considerations (such as, e.g., a 'name and arms clause' in a will), which cause a very considerable number to remain in constant use. In central Europe, where armorial ostentation is prevalent, quarters are assumed to represent any female ancestor who was daughter of an armigerous house without reference to heirship.

Marshal's Roll, the Lord: see **Lord Marshal's Roll, the.**

martel: a war-hammer; a weapon (not a tool) consisting of a hammer head with a broad flat face and a sharp-pointed pane, or pick, secured on a long haft (q.v.). Also blazoned 'fer-de-martel', and sometimes er. applied to a craftsman's hammer.

Martello tower: the crest of the Municipal Council of Bexhill-on-Sea, Sussex.

marten: [M.E.] a generic term for animals in the *Mustela* genus and employed in heraldry for ca. reasons.

martenett: an archaic form of 'martlet' (q.v.).

Martial, St: appears in the municipal arms of Limoges.

Martin, Alexander: Islay Herald, 1725. Ormonde Pursuivant, 1710.

Martin, Francis: Clarenceux King of Arms, 1846. Former Norroy K. of A., 1839; former Windsor Herald, 1819; former Blue mantle Pursuivant, 1797.

Martin, Henry Robert Charles: Richmond Herald, 1928. Former Rouge Croix Pursuivant, 1922.

Martin, St: appears in civic arms both in Britain and on the Continent.

Martin of the West, Order of St: an international order with its headquarters in Austria. Insignia—*Badge:* a black cross potent with gold Imperial eagles between the arms, ensigned by a crown or a trophy of arms, or both according to rank and category of membership. *Star:* the unensigned badge on a silver star of eight points. *Riband:* maroon.

Martin, wheel of St: see **wheel** and **caravel.**

martlet: [Fr.] lit. the swift, *Cypselus apus;* the heraldic swallow, depicted with thighs and no claws, perpetuating the folk belief that the swallow cannot perch being thus

---

325. Gules, a cross and a saltire of chain affixed to an annulet in the fess point, and to a double orle of the same, all Or.
Navarre.

326. Gules, a chain of seven links in pale argent.
Kendall.

327. Argent, an ale-warmer within a bordure engrailed sable.
Municipal Corporation of Dunstable.

328. Argent, three annulets of chain sable.
Sir Richard de Hoo.

329. Sable, on a bend Or between two terrets in bend argent, three pheons gules.
Johnson of Twissell.

330. Argent, three door-bolts gules.
Bolton.

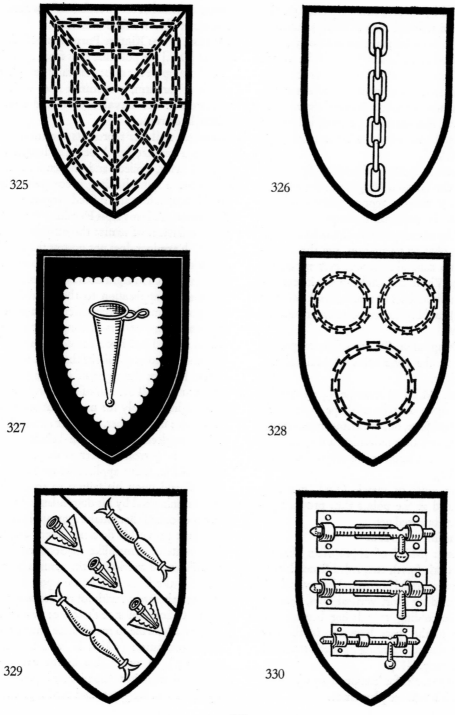

325   326

327   328

329   330

deprived by nature; strangely enough, the ~ is depicted resting on its stumps and close (q.v.). A ~ volant is almost unknown; ~ is employed as the brisure (q.v.) of the fourth son. There is a body of opinion that the ~ represents the house-martin, *Chelidon urbica*, and, when blazoned 'volant' (q.v.), the swallow, *Hirundo rustica*, is intended, and it ought to be blazoned as a 'hirondelle'. (104, 109, XIV)

martrix: alt. spelling of 'marten' (q.v.).

Mary, the Blessed Virgin: at the time of the Reformation representations of the B.V.M. in armorial bearings were concealed by alterations to both the blazon and the graphic representation. On the Continent, no concealment was ever necessary, and the Virgin and Child appear in numerous public arms. The text letters A.M. (Ave Maria), and lily flowers, often represent the B.V.M.

Mary Magdalen, St: one of the supporters (q.v.) in the civic arms of Maidenhead, Berkshire.

mascle: [M.E.] a lozenge (q.v.) voided (q.v.) often merely a shape having no special purpose, but sometimes representing a mesh, and thus indicating a net, particularly when a number are conjoined (q.v.). (422, IV)

mascly: semé of mascle (q.v.), generally conjoined at the points thus producing a conventionalized net.

mask, a fox's: see **fox.**

masoned: [M.E.] of appropriate charges, e.g. a castle (q.v.), etc., ruled from chief to base with parallel horizontal lines which are connected by short vertical lines, those in each succeeding row being beneath the centre of the space between, in the row above, thus representing bonded brickwork or masonry. (412)

masonry: r. alt. for 'masoned' (q.v.).

mason's level: see **plummet.**

mason's marks: see **merchants' marks.**

masony: obs. of a field masoned.

Masson, John: Kintyre Pursuivant, 1715.

mast: [O.E.] the pole that rises from a ship's keel to support the sails; generally complete with a yardarm, sometimes also with a square-sail. See **naval crown** and **mercantile crown.**

matches, roll of: represents the means of firing a musket (q.v.) being a length of round wick, coiled, and the end carried round in a spiral holding it compact. The end is protruding and is fired proper.

Matheson, Adam: Ross Herald, 1599.

matriculation of arms: the offspring of a Scottish armiger does not possess the birthright of taking into his own use the paternal coat of arms. His right does not exceed that of making application to the Lord Lyon King of Arms for a rematriculation of the paternal arms 'with such congruent differences as the Lord Lyon considers suitable'. In other words, he inherits the right to bear arms, but not the right of deciding what those arms shall be, and of assuming them. The right to apply for matriculation is inalienable: if the father, or other responsible adult, neglects to apply on behalf of an infant, the person concerned may, at any time of life, make application on his own behalf, and upon his failure so to do the right is inherited by his descendants. In the event of one of them making an application he must prove his descent. There are no two coats of arms alike in Scotland; the undifferenced version of the arms is borne only by the head of a house upon whose death the heir may, without reference to the Lyon Office, continue their use; nevertheless, it is advisable to matriculate arms every third generation (which is 'within living memory'), in order that in the event of failure of male issue the picture is provided by the Lyon Register, and no long, complicated, and expensive research is called for. Arms matriculated and differenced have been subject, for about a century, to a method known as the Stodart system (q.v.).

Matthew, St: appears in the municipal arms of Salerno, Italy.

Matthew Paris, arms depicted in works of: Matthew Paris became a monk of St Albans 1217, was appointed Chronicler, and was a reliable historian. His major works, *Historia Anglorum* and *Chronica Majora*, are embellished with beautifully painted shields in the margins adjacent to the notes on persons, hence his works classify as illustrative rolls (q.v.). There is also a vellum sheet 8½ by 14 in., having thirty-three shields on the face and forty-two on the dorse with names and blazons in Latin. Inverted shields in his works are indicative of the death of the armiger.

maul: see **hammer.**

Maule, Harry: Lyon Clerk and Keeper of the Records, 1709.

Maule of Melgund, Henry: Lord Lyon Depute, 1635.

maultrommel: Ger., clarion.

maunch: [M.E.] a sleeve with an elongated, hanging cuff. From XII to XIV cents. the ~, or pair of sleeves, were not built into a garment but were worn like a tubular scarf. The ~ is a romantic charge, being the article that ladies among the spectators at a tournament dropped onto the helmet of the knight of their choice as he rode round the field. A special hook was attached to the crown of a tilting helmet to support such offerings. In heraldry the sleeve itself, embowed, the elbow downward is orientated fesswise, the long, hanging-cuff, in graceful folds descends on the dexter, and, on the sinister, is balanced by a similar, but smaller, drape. In XVI cent. it was blazoned 'a half ~', and bad drawing

resulted in a beautiful and pleasing charge becoming precisely the opposite. Alt. terms, now all mercifully obs., are 'manchée', 'mancheron', 'mauchmall', 'maunch-mailtail' this last being debased French 'manch mal taille'. 'Manch' is a r. alt. but legitimate spelling. (249)

maunch-mailtail: see previous entry.

maunchmall: see **maunch.**

Maurice and Lazarus, Order of SS: (Italy) the Order of St Maurice was f. by Amadeus VIII, c. 1440, and was merged with the Italian possessions of the Order of St Lazarus (q.v.) by Pope Gregory XIII in 1572; the combined Order was reactivated in 1816 in five classes. Insignia—*Badge:* a white enamel cross pommetty, the green cross paty notched of St Lazarus appearing saltirewise, between the arms; the whole is ensigned with a gold crown, save for the fifth class. *Star:* the badge surmounting a silver star of eight points. *Riband:* green.

mautelent: see **tronnonée.**

Mawson, Charles: Chester Herald, 1690. Former Rouge Croix Pursuivant, 1686; former Blanch Lyon Pursuivant, 1680.

Mawson, Richard: Windsor Herald, 1745. Former Portcullis Pursuivant, 1717.

May, Thomas: Chester Herald, 1677. Former Rouge Dragon Pursuivant, 1675.

Mayoral cap: a representation of the fur state cap of the Lord Mayor of London is included among the exterior decorations in a full achievement of the ensigns armorial of the Corporation of the City of London.

med bård: Swd., fimbriated.

med horn: Swd., attired.

med tunga: Swd., langued.

Medaille Militaire: (France) f. 1852 for award to N.C.O.s and men of the Army and Navy, and to generals and admirals commanding armies or fleets, but not to intermediate ranks. *Badge:* a silver wreath of laurel, tied with gold ribbon at top and bottom, encircling a gold medallion depicting an enlaurelled head symbolizing the Republique Française. The badge is ensigned with a trophy of arms and an anchor. *Riband:* yellow edged with green.

Medal of Honour: (U.S.A.) f. 1861 for award to seamen and petty officers of the U.S. Navy for gallantry in action. In July 1862 the award was extended to enlisted men of the Army and Volunteer Forces; in March 1863 officers became eligible to receive the award; in 1963 the award was extended to the U.S. Air Force. All three services have different versions of the medal, and designs have been varied over the years. *Naval badge:* a bronze star of five points, each trefoil tipped and bearing laurel and oak sprays, with a central medallion, surrounded by a circle of thirty-four stars, depicting Minerva repulsing discord; the whole ensigned with an anchor. *Army badge:* a gold star of five points, each trefoil tipped and bearing a green enamel oak leaf, with a central medallion, surrounded by the inscription *United States of America*, depicting Minerva's head; the star is suspended by

two gold links from a gold bar inscribed *Valor* which is ensigned with the American eagle. *Air Force badge:* a bronze star of five points, each trefoil tipped and bearing two small gold wings with a central medallion, surrounded by a circle of thirty-four stars, depicting the head of the Statue of Liberty; the whole surmounts a green and gold laurel wreath broken at the top by a device of four bronze thunderbolts and a pair of aviator's wings, ensigned with a bronze bar inscribed *Valor*. *Riband:* various designs have been used, but now all three types are suspended from a short riband of light blue moire decorated with thirteen silver stars, behind which is attached a neck-riband of light blue.

Medjidie, Order of: (Turkey) f. 1852 in five classes. Insignia—*Badge:* a silver star of seven points, each having five rays, with a silver crescent and star between each point; a central medallion bears the Sultan's cypher on either a gold, or a silver ground. It is surmounted by a band of red enamel inscribed *For Zeal, Devotion and Loyalty* in Turkish; the whole is ensigned with a

---

331. Per fess Or and argent a lymphad sable: an escutcheon gules pendant from the sinister end of the yardarm charged with a trefoil of the second.
M'Eacharn.

332. Per pale gules and Or, two boat-oars in saltire azure.
Torrance, Scotland.

333. Argent, three playing-tops, sable.
Anvine.

334. Argent, a ship in full sail sable on waves of the sea proper.
Appleby.

335. Argent, an anchor ringed Or, surmounted by a fetterlock containing on the dexter a sword erect hilted and pommelled of the third and, on the sinister, a rose gules.
Municipal Corporation of Bewdley.

336. Chevronny argent and sable per pale counterchanged, two torches erect Or, inflamed proper.
Viscount Eccles.

331   332

333   334

335   336

crescent and star in red enamel. *Star:* a large version of the unensigned badge. *Riband:* red with a green stripe at each edge.

Meiklejohn, John: Procurator Fiscal to the Lyon Court, 1837.

Meldrum, John: Marchmont Herald, 1515.

Melusine: see **mermaid.**

Melville, Walter: Rothesay Herald, 1697. Herald-painter, 1700.

membered: referring to the colour of the claws of a non-predacious bird; the alt. term 'legged' is sometimes used.

Memorial of Merit of King Charles the Martyr: f. 1911. A body of forty-nine gentlemen, all members of the Church of England. The honour of membership is bestowed by the unanimous decision of the Chapter. Persons thus elevated use the post-nominal initials M.M.C.M. Membership is for life, and no resignation is acceptable. The government of the Memorial is by a Chapter consisting of the Chancellor, the Registrar, the Warden, and the Usher of the Purple Rod. The number forty-nine cannot be exceeded, because that was the years of the Martyr-King's age. The 19th of November and the 13th of January are kept as days of observance. The insignia is an oval medallion of gold, enamelled gules with the Martyr-King's royal cypher and ensigned with the Stuart crown-royal. Round the rim is inscribed the words *Martyred and Glorious,* which is the motto of the Memorial.

Mendell, De Corteret: Lyon Clerk Depute, 1819.

Menzies, Daniel: Snowdoun Herald, 1821. Bute Pursuivant, 1821.

mercantile crown: see **naval crown.**

merchants' marks: A general term for cyphers of identity employed from c. XII to XVI cents. by both merchants and crafts-men who, at the period, were prohibited from bearing arms. The merchants used their marks in much the same ways as a modern exporter uses his shipping mark, i.e. to establish ownership of goods in a mixed cargo: the craftsmen, masons, gold-smiths, coopers, and others added their mark to their work in lieu of a signature. It appears that a guild mark was often in-corporated in the cypher: coopers erected their geometrical, or other shape, on an annulet (q.v.) which symbolized the tun; woolmen used as a base a formalized Latin text-letter W. Many of the marks are con-structed upon a cursive Latin cross, or figure 4, which may have possessed a dual significance, being, in addition to a declaration of the merchant's religious adhesion, with its presumed high ethical standard, a conventionalized symbol of the steelyard as a guarantee of fair weights and measures. The marks were often family property, descending from father to son when the latter assumed responsibility for, or inherited, the business. As the merchant class waxed in wealth and in power and importance, the military aristocracy waned, and many a nobleman retrieved his fortunes by accepting as a son-in-law the offspring of a merchant; thus do ~ find their way into heraldry during the XIV and XV cents.; but with their increasing importance in both the national economy and social life, the merchants made their marks more like genuine heraldry than they had done hither-to, and many later ~ appear on a shield, and are formed upon ordinaries (q.v.) depicted in outline. There is a theory that ~ are based on the runes, but the simplicity of form demanded by both may have resulted in overlapping. (349–54)

mercuriusstaf: D. caduceus.

Mercury: see **segregative blazon.**

Mercury, hat of: see **petasus.**

Mercury, rod of: see **Aesculapius, rod of.**

mereltje: D., martlet.

meril: a disc used as a 'piece' in an old game similar to 'draughts'.

merillion: an implement having the appearance of a rectangular metal frame with a protruding hook at each end, the dexter inclining upward, the sinister downward, employed in the arms of the Worshipful Company of Hatband Makers.

Merit, Indian Order of: f. 1837 in three classes to reward exceptional bravery by members of the Indian Army, with a civil division in one class. The highest class was abolished in 1912 when the award of the V.C. was extended to the Indian Army. Insignia—*Badge:* a breast-worn silver star of eight points with a central medallion of blue enamel depicting in gold two crossed swords encircled by the words *For bravery*; the medallion is surrounded by a gold laurel wreath. *Ribands:* Military Division—dark blue with red edges; Civil Division—dark red with blue edges.

Merit, Order of: f. by K. Ed. VII on 23 June 1902. A gold cross globical, convexed, enamelled red with blue edges, a centre medallion bearing the words *For Merit* in gold, surrounded by white enamel pearls and a laurel wreath; the reverse bears the royal cypher centrally; the whole ensigned with a Tudor crown; silver swords with gold hilts may be added saltirewise to the cross for military recipients; the Order is worn round the neck from a 2-in. riband, half crimson, half blue.

Merit, Order of, of the Italian Republic: f. 1951 in five classes. Insignia—*Badge:* a gold-rimmed white enamel cross having gold Roman eagles between the arms from point to point; surmounted centrally by a small five-point gold star, and ensigned by three battlemented towers in gold ornamented at their base in green, red, and white. *Star:* the unensigned badge sur-

mounting a silver star of eight points. *Riband:* green with red edges.

Merit, Order of: (Chile) f. 1910 in six classes. Insignia—*Badge:* a gold-rimmed white enamel star of five points, each tipped with a gold ball, having gold laurel wreaths between the arms; a gold central medallion, surrounded by the inscription *Republica de Chile* depicts a female head symbolizing the republic; the whole ensigned by a gold condor (q.v.) with wings displayed. *Star:* a gold star of ten points surmounted by a star as for the badge, the central medallion of gold depicting Chile's coat of arms surrounded by the inscription, in gold or blue, *Orden del Merito Chile. Riband:* red, blue, white, in equal stripes.

Merit, Order of: (Germany) f. 1951 in seven classes and a medal of merit. Insignia—*Badge:* a gold-rimmed red enamel cross of eight-points with a gold central medallion depicting the German eagle in black. *Star:* a gold star of eight, six, or four points according to class, surmounted by the badge. *Riband:* red, with narrow edges of gold, black, gold: the medal is in gold, has the same riband, and bears the badge on the obverse and the legend *Fur Verdienste um die Bundesrepublik Deutschland.*

Merite, Ordre Pour Le: (Germany): f. 1665 as the Ordre de la Generosite. The name was changed in 1740 by Frederick the Great, and Frederick William III revised the Order in 1810 as Prussia's highest award for gallantry, in one class to be worn from the neck. A Grand Cross was briefly instituted in 1866 but lapsed after only three awards had been made. Insignia—*Badge:* a gold-edged blue cross paty with gold eagles between the arms; a crowned *F* appears on the top arm and *Pour le Merite* on the other arms, all in gold; some badges are ensigned with a gold oak-leaf, granted to recognize particularly outstanding gallantry, and some with a gold crown, denoting that the holder had possessed the Order for fifty years. *Riband:* black, with a broad silver stripe at each edge. The three Grand Crosses received a star of four points in gold, with a central medallion depicting the head of Frederick the Great and surrounded by the inscription *Pour le Merite* in gold on blue.

Meriton Herald: see **Mortain Herald**.

merkuriestav: D., caduceus.

merlato: It., embattled.

merlette: r. alt. for a martlet; the term is current in Fr. blazon.

Merletto: It., martlet.

merlin: see **falcon**.

Merlin, Edward: Portcullis Pursuivant, 1559.

merlion: see **marlion**.

merlon: see **embattled**.

mermaid: a composite fictitious creature, human female to the waist and fish downward, the line of juncture being consealed (decorated) with a girdle of seaweed. She is crined of her hair which she is generally engaged in dressing, holding in the dexter hand a peering-glass (q.v.) and, in the sinister, a comb. A ~ having two tails, one curling to the dexter and the other to the

sinister, is known in heraldry as a 'Melusine', although she does not conform to the Melusine of mythology. The gracefulness of the ~ is totally destroyed by the additional tail, for which reason, perhaps, the Melusine is rare. (283)

merman: variously titled 'Triton' and 'Neptune'; human to the waist and fish downward. Generally holds his dexter arm raised and, grasped in his sinister hand, a trident, tynes chiefward, in bend sinister. He is bearded and crowned of an open crown.

mertrick: alt. spelling of 'martin' (q.v.).

merula: L., martlet.

messengers-at-arms: officials who execute royal letters and other duties connected with Scottish courts of law: appointed by, and under the jurisdiction of, the Lord Lyon King of Arms (q.v.).

Messer, Wm: Procurator Fiscal to the Lyon Court, 1630.

metal: [fm Gk via L.] either gold (q.v.) or silver, respectively Or (q.v.) and argent (q.v.): the former represented in art by gold-leaf or by yellow paint; the latter, by Chinese-white or by the paper untinted.

metaller: Swd., metals.

Meyrick's Roll: (temp. K. Hen. VII)

---

337. Argent, a covered cup between four crosses paty sable.
Boteler.

338. Azure, on a chevron argent between three mortcours gold, as many roses gules barbed and seeded proper.
Worshipful Company of Wax-Chandlers.

339. Argent, three addices azure hafted Or.
Addice.

340. Azure, three water-bougets Or within a bordure ermine.
Bridges of Grodneston.

341. Argent, three hemp-breaks sable.
Hampson, Taplow.

342. Gules, three full-bottomed wigs argent.
Lord Birkett.

337

338

339

340

341

342

painted vellum true roll (q.v.) containing twenty-four shields with names over of Knights of the Garter.

Michael, Archangel: frequently confused with St Michael. The Archangel should be depicted with wings, the Saint without. Both are symbolized by the flaming sword which, strictly, is that of the Archangel, the Saint's symbol being a cross, either pommetty or bottony.

Michael and George, Most Distinguished Order of SS.: f. 1818 in three classes; originally for meritorious Ionians and Maltese, but subsequently for services abroad or in the Commonwealth. Insignia: Knights Grand Cross—a mantle of saxon blue lined with red with the star embroidered on the left, and a chapeau of blue satin lined red and embellished by black and white ostrich feathers; a collar of gold composed of crowned lions of England alternating with Maltese crosses and the cyphers *S.M.* and *S.G.*; and centrally, two winged lions each holding a book and seven arrows; a silver seven-rayed star with intermediate gold rays surmounted by a cross of St George in red enamel and centrally a medallion of St Michael holding a flaming sword and trampling on Satan, surrounded by a blue circle with the motto, in gold, *Auspicium Melioris Aevi. Badge:* gold, being a fourteen-point star with the star's central motif on one side and St George fighting the dragon on the other, worn from the collar or from the riband over the right shoulder. Knight Commanders—a silver star and a badge, both similar to those of Knights Grand Cross but smaller in size; the badge is worn from the riband round the neck. Commanders—a neck-worn badge as for Knights but smaller in size. *Riband:* blue with a central red stripe.

middenfunt: D., fess point.

mijter: D., mitre.

Military Cross: f. 1914 for officers not above substantive rank of major, for gallant and distinguished services in action. A silver cross, on each arm an Imperial crown, bearing centrally a small cross and the royal cypher. *Riband:* equal stripes of white, purple, white.

Military Medal: f. March 1916 for award to non-commissioned officers and men for bravery. The medal is silver; obverse—the words *For bravery in the Field* encircled by a wreath and ensigned with the royal cypher and cross. *Riband:* white with broad blue edges, the white bearing two narrow red stripes.

Military Roll: see **Holme's Book, Sir Thomas.**

milking pail: see **well-bucket.**

mill: see **windmill.**

mill-clack: alt. for 'mill-cog'. See **cog.**

mill-cog: see **cog.**

mill-iron: see **mill-rind.**

mill-pick: see **pick.**

mill-rind: the iron (or steel) forging that carried the mill-stone; hence, it is massive and has a primal rugged beauty. There are two conventionalized shapes; either a pair of semicircles convexity to convexity with, at the point of junction, a square protuberance pierced with a square hole to coincide with the 'eye' of the stone; or a long, narrow, rectangular plate the ends of which are cleft and turned outward: this, too, has the central square development. It is two of this latter form that, placed in cruciform juxtaposition and deprived of the central squares, make the cross moline (q.v.). Alt. terms are 'mill-iron' (which, like far too many of the drawings of the ~, is weak) and 'fer-de-moline'. (343)

mill-wheel: a pair of circular frames centrally attached to a shaft, and having suspended between them at their circumferences pivoted buckets arranged to catch the falling water and by turning in response to this impulse, impart to the mill-machinery power to turn the stone. The ~ performs the same function in the water-mill as the sails (q.v.) in a windmill. (344)

Miller, Thomas: Lancaster Herald, 1536. Former Rouge Dragon Pursuivant, 1530. Also spelt 'Milner'.

miller's thumb: see **perch**.

Milner, Thomas: see **Miller, Thomas**.

minerals: for both ca. and allusive reasons samples of unworked, or of semi-worked minerals are employed; nodules of flint ca. on the name Stone, and this substance, because of its characteristic flaking, can be recognizably drawn. Most other ~ cannot. Among semi-worked ~ are smelted metals, 'an ingot of gold', 'a cake of copper', 'a pig of lead (or of iron)', 'a block of tin', but, again, graphic art cannot make them distinguishable one from another.

miner's hew: see **pick**.

miner's lamp: see **Davy-lamp**.

miniver: a white fur used for lining garments.

minnow: [M.E.] a small, freshwater fish with a disproportionately large head, *Leuciscus phoximus*, but extended to include other small fish, particularly the stickleback (genus *Gasterosteus*); employed in heraldry chiefly for ca. reasons. Also known as the 'pink'.

mirleta: Sp., martlet.

Mirrlees, Robin Ian Evelyn Milne Stuart de la Lanne: Richmond Herald, 1961. Former Rouge Dragon Pursuivant, 1952.

mirror: see **peering-glass**.

Mitchell, James: Albany Herald, 1795. Dingwall Pursuivant, 1774.

Mitchell, Sir James Wm: Lyon Clerk and Keeper of the Records, 1890. Lyon Clerk Depute, 1886. Rothesay Herald, 1878. Carrick Pursuivant 1878.

mitra: Ger., It., and Sp., mitre.

mitre: [L.] used in place of a helmet of rank (q.v.) and a crest (q.v.) to ensign the shield of either an archbishop or a bishop, being a representation of the sacredotal headdress of those Church dignitaries, i.e. a tall cap cleft laterally, the front and back sections each taking the form of an elongated pentagon generally terminating in a pommell (q.v.) supporting a cross paty (q.v.). Descending out of the headband are two gold-edged purple ribbons, known as the *infulae vitae*. These may be developed to suggest mantling (q.v.). (242)

mitry: semé of mitres.

Mitton, Alexander Warren Dury: Rouge Dragon Pursuivant, 1919.

mittsköld: Swd., inescutcheon.

modesty, maiden in her: see **maiden's head**.

Mohammed, Order of (Morocco) f. 1956 as a one-class collar for award primarily to heads of States. Insignia—*Badge:* an ornate star of eight points in green enamel, gold edged and decorated with minute rubies; between each point appears a small gold ray, tipped with a diamond; a central medallion of green enamel, encircled by a decorative gold band, bears the arms in gold of the King of Morocco. *Collar:* a double chain with decorative devices terminating in a representation of the arms of the King of Morocco, all in gold.

Mohammed Ali, Order of (Egypt): f. 1915 in three classes, namely the Grand Collar and Cordon, the Grand Cordon, and Commander (breast star and neck badge); attached to the Order were two gallantry medals in gold and silver. Insignia—*Badge:* an ornate star of six points, gold rimmed and green edged, surmounted by a large medallion of white enamel bearing the Arabic inscription *Charity, Justice and Freedom from Strife are a Kingdom's strength*; a small central medallion of green enamel is inscribed *Mohammed Ali* in Arabic script. *Collar:* the design varies, but normally comprises en-linked versions of the badge, or decorative motifs in green and white enamel on gold. *Star:* the badge's white and green medallion superimposed on a heavily chased silver star of six points. *Riband:* light green with white stripes at the edges.

moldiwarp: [M.E.] the mole, *Talpa europaea,* a small, dark-furred, burrowing quadruped.

molet: an archaic (but alt.) spelling of 'mullet' (q.v.); quite unnecessary in modern heraldry.

moline, cross: [Fr.] a cross humetty (q.v.) having the extremities of the limbs cleft, turned outward, and each part brought to a point. ∼ is frmd of two mill-rinds (q.v.) in cruciform juxtaposition. It is employed as the brisure (q.v.) of the eighth son. (227)

molnskure: Swd., nebuly.

mon: see **Japan, heraldry in.**

Monceux Pursuivant: was functioning in 1435, but nothing further is known. Also called 'Mouncells'.

Moncrieff, David Scott: Procurator Fiscal to the Lyon Court, 1880.

mond: Ger., moon.

monstrance: r. er. alt. term for a chalice (q.v.); actually a vessel used for the display of the consecrated Host.

Montagu Herald: maintained by the Earl of Salisbury (William de Montagu), 1373.

montegre: see **man-tygre.**

months, blazon by: see **segregative blazon.**

Montignani, Wm Robert: Snowdoun Herald, 1860. Kintyre Pursuivant, 1859.

Montorgueil Herald: created by K. Hen. VII with jurisdiction in the Channel Islands.

monumental brasses: see **brasses, monumental.**

moon: a disc, argent, on which a pallid, unemotional face is depicted, surrounded by a circle of fine short lines being continued radii; represents the nocturnal luminary and is blazoned '∼ in her plenitude'; eclipsed, she is sable, retains the irradiation, and is blazoned '∼ in her detriment'. The crescent moon is rather slender, and is often within a complete circle of irradiation which is indicated by describing her as 'illuminated'. A face in profile may be depicted exterior to the concave edge. With the horns facing dexter she is (or should be) blazoned '∼ in her

---

343.   Azure a mill-rind Or.
       Brun, Kent.

344.   Azure, a watermill-wheel Or and, *in augmentation*, on a canton argent the Royal Badges of England & Scotland, *videlicit*, a rose and a thistle conjoined palewise proper.
       De Moline.

345.   Sable, a catherine-wheel argent.
       Turner.

346.   Azure, a mill-clack fesswise, Or.
       Mills.

347.   Gules, three cartwheels argent.
       Speke.

348.   Gules, three whips of three lashes each
       Swift, Scotland.

343

344

345

346

347

348

increment', and with the horns to the sinister '~ in decrement'; it must, however, be pointed out that on the numerous occasions of her being er. blazoned '~ increscent' and '~ decrescent' (and when 'decriment' is printed in place of 'detriment'), no harm is done because the intention is quite clear.

moorcock: [M.E.] the male red-grouse, *Lagopus scoticus*. The bird's tail is variously represented; either as a pair of rearward-jutting feathers or more fulsomely. This inconsistency may be the result of confusion of the numerous species. Also called 'heathcock'.

More, John: Norroy King of Arms, 1478. Former Windsor Herald, 1468; former Rouge Croix Pursuivant, c. 1460; former Antelope Pursuivant.

morian: a moorish maiden in English, but in Swd. a blackamoor.

morion: a skull or cap of steel; a form of head armour worn by a footman; close-fitting, hemispherical, and generally deeper behind, offering some protection to the back of the neck. Sometimes drawn like a distorted capital S reversed with straight back, large curl at the top and small one at the bottom: at other times drawn like an inverted basin; hence, the alt. term 'basinet' (also spelt 'basnet'). A further alt. term, 'burgonet', is also used; however, both the basinet and the burgonet were nearer to the close-helmet (q.v.) than to the ~. (247)

morion, winged: see **petasus**.

Morlee, Wm de: it is uncertain whether he was Norroy King of Arms, 1323, or a minstrel; described (16 K. Ric. II) as 'Roy de North Ministrallus Regis'.

morné: [O.F.], lit. blunt; hence, of a lion deprived of his armament and of his tongue. See also **mourne**.

Morrison, Peter: Islay Herald, 1552.

morse [Norse]: see **sea-lion**: both the word

and the idea may be connected with the walrus, *Trichechus rosmarus*.

mort[1]: er. accepted as dial. for a falcon; an assumption based on the fact that a falcon perched on a barrel was the rebus of Cardinal Morton.

mort[2]: r. alt. for a death's head (q.v.).

mort-head: r. obs. alt. for a death's head (q.v.).

Mortain Herald: served the Duke of Clarence who, from 1415 was Lieutenant of France and Normandy. Later (1449), a ~ was in the service of Edmund Beaufort, *inter alia* Count of Mortain. Also spelt 'Meriton' and 'Mariton'.

Mortar: [O.E.] a short-barrelled broad-gauge gun for firing a heavy ball at a high trajectory; a siege gun.

mortar and pestle: a strongly reinforced bowl in which materials are pounded to powder by striking repeatedly with the rounded end of a hard, heavy cylinder named the pestle. The ~ used by apothecaries during the XVIII cent. was of bronze. (309)

mortcour: the giant, mourning candlestick, large and strong enough to sustain a candle of size and weight sufficient to burn for ten, fifteen, or even twenty years. The ~ is r. in British heraldry. Those in the achievement of the Worshipful Company of Waxchandlers are represented by the heads only. They are without a central socket: in its place there rises a spike or pryck: they are hexagonal in shape, and have a kind of railing surrounding the drip-tray. Also termed 'morter'. (338)

morte: r. alt. for a lion 'morné' (q.v.).

morter: see **mortcour**.

motto: [M.E.] a word, or a phrase, generally inscribed on a ribbon, suitably draped beneath a shield (or the lozenge), that expresses a noble sentiment; supposed to represent the norm whereby members of a

France Modern
(Azure, three fleurs-de-lys Or)

PLATE XIII

France Ancient
(Azure, semé-de-lys Or)

family (or of a company) conduct their lives. Although ~ is frequently in Latin (or debased Latin) there is no rule: any language, or a dialect may be employed, and the text letters are not necessarily those of the Roman alphabet—Greek and Hebrew are to be found. ~ need not express a pious sentiment, but may be a pun on the armiger's name, or may bear reference to some notable deed performed by an ancestor. In England ~ is not normally a part of the grant of arms, and it may, therefore, be changed, or each member of a family may select his own phrase; in Scotland, however, the crest-~, or *cri-de-guerre*, a word or a phrase on an escroll over the crest, is almost universal, and this, as well as the ~ beneath the shield, is specified in the patent. In M.E. the ~ was generally described as the armiger's 'word'.

Mouncells Pursuivant: see **Monceux Pursuivant.**

mound: [M.E.] lit. the earth; hence, the regal orb; hence, a representation of this: always equatorially banded with a rising demi-meridian ensigned with a cross paty. Not to be confused with next entry. (257)

mount: [O.E.] the representation of a hillock, appearing in base (q.v.) u.o.s., and vert u.o.s. In Scotland, ~ issuant of a ducal coronet (q.v.) is the crest (q.v.) of a chief. (377, XIV)

mountain ash: see **rowan.**

mountain cat: see **catamount.**

mountain formal: the continental version of the British 'mount vert' (q.v.) of far wider application being ca. on names terminating in '-berg' of which there are very many. It is depicted as a series of small vertical rectangles with half round top lines set in close juxtaposition pyramidwise and issuant in base. The normal form is two of the sections conjoined and set fesswise with a third issuant centrally, but the number is

generally stated, e.g. ' . . . six peaks, three, two, and one . . .'. (175)

Mountjoie King of Arms: the senior heraldic officer of France; XV cent.

mourne: of a lance (q.v.) guarded by a cronel (q.v.). See also **morné.**

moussue, cross: a cross humetty having the end of each limb bulged outward in a semi-circle; alt. spelling 'musu', probably from *Musa, Musa paradisiaca*, the banana.

Mowbray Herald: originally in the service of the Duke of Norfolk; discontinued in the reign of K. Hen. VI. Revived 1623 as name of a herald extraordinary.

muhleisenkreuz: Ger., cross moline.

mulinata croce: It., cross moline.

mullet: [O.F.] the brisure (q.v.) of the third son; a figure of (normally) five triangular points representing the spur-rowel (or revel): sometimes called a 'star' solely on account of its shape, but ~ do not represent astronomical bodies: the word, being homophonous with the name of a fish, *Mullus barbatus*, has led to the statement that the heraldic ~ represents the star-fish (*Asteroidea*): it does not. ~ may be of six or more points. Mullet-fish figures in French heraldry. (43, 47, 186, IV, XI)

mundus: L., mound (orb).

münze: Ger., bezant.

muraillé: [Fr.] pertaining to a wall, and sometimes used in British heraldry as an alt. to 'masoned' (q.v.).

mural crown: a figure representing a circular, crenellated wall, having five crenellations and tapering to the lower extremity. ~ is masoned sable whether it is so blazoned or not: if it is to be masoned of another colour the blazon must state it. ~ is based upon a Roman military award granted to the first man to scale the walls of a fortified city; hence, originally of military significance; in heraldry being employed to ensign the shield of a soldier, or to act as the basis of his crest, for which purpose it is still reserved in Scottish heraldry. In England the ~ has been misapplied and has become the device that is expected to ensign the shield of a civic authority. (12, 197, X)

Murdoch, Patrick: Ormonde Pursuivant, 1641.

murices: L. caltraps.

Murray, Alexander: Dingwal Pursuivant, 1661.

Murray, Keith Wm: Portcullis Pursuivant, 1913.

Murray, Mungo: Ormonde Pursuivant, 1661.

Murray of Truim, Sir Andrew: Lord Lyon King of Arms, 1488.

murrey: see **sanguine.**

muschel: Ger., escallop.

muschetor: an ermine-spot when employed to represent the beast's tail.

mushroom: the edible fungus *Psalliota* (*Agaricus*) *compestris*; symbolic of rapid growth; more likely to be seen in continental than in British heraldry. (396)

musimon: an heraldic hybrid, thought to be the offspring of a ram and a goat, depicted with the horns of both parents: fm 'musmon' or 'moufflon', the wild sheep of Barbary, *Ammotragus tragelaphus.* Alt. title 'tityron'.

musion: see **catamount.**

musket: originally applied to the matchlock, 'a musketeer holding his matchlock together with its rest', but applied to an infantry-man's handgun of any smoothbore type; hence, the flintlock is included. The matchlock was not fired from the shoulder but from the ground, the muzzle supported on a kind of saddle fixed to one end of a rod the other end of which was pointed so as to penetrate the earth. This accessory (the matchlock-rest) has had conferred upon it the name of the major item of the combination, and, blazoned as 'a matchlock', is generally very badly drawn.

mussla: Swd., escallop.

musu cross: see **moussue, cross.**

mutilatus: L., tronnonée.

muzzled: of a beast with its mouth compulsorily closed by means of an arrangement of straps which are generally of a colour differing from that of the beast.

Mynne, John: York Herald during the reign of K. Hen. VII.

---

349. Merchant's mark, unidentified. (A Norwich Clothworker.)

350. Merchant's mark. John Beriffe, Shipowner and Master Mariner. Monumental Brass, 1521, Brightlingsea, Essex.

351. Merchant's mark. Robert Brown, Mercer, of Norwich. (Sheriff in 1535.)

352. Merchant's mark. Wm Denold, Cordwainer of Norwich, 1506.

353. Merchant's mark. John Colenge, Cooper, of London. Registerd at the Guildhall, 1428.

354. Merchant's mark. Valentine Hartnell, merchant of the Staple, 1400.

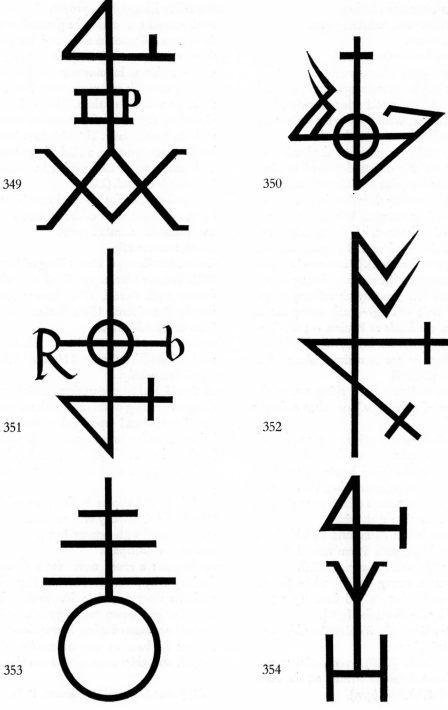

349

350

351

352

353

354

naas mekaar: Afk., in fess.

nabelstelle: Ger., nombril point.

nag: see **horse.**

nagelkopfchen: Ger., cloué.

nagelkopfgitter: Ger., trellis.

naiant: [L.] lit. swimming; hence, of a fish or a marine mammal when fesswise, head to the dexter. With head to the sinister it is blazoned 'counter-naiant'.

nails: [O.E.] represented by the heads only appear on any object described as cloué (q.v.) but a number of different kinds of ~, often blazoned by their defining names, are employed as charges. When 'a nail' unspecified is blazoned, it is drawn as having a round, flat head and the spike tapering throughout its length. 'Passion-~' are cut-~, rectangular in section, blunt-pointed, the head being merely chamfering of the broad end; closing-~ are triangular in section, the heads as Passion ~; tiler's ~ have broad, circular heads, round spikes cut to points. ~ are sometimes blazoned as 'spikes'. (95, 311)

naissant: [L.] of a beast rising out of the interior of a fess (q.v.) or other ordinary (q.v.).

name of office: the strictly correct, though rather pedantic, description of what is accepted as the 'title' bestowed upon an officer of arms on his creation. Down to the mid XVIII cent. these names were given in an act of baptism with wine.

Narboon, John: Richmond Herald, 1596. Former Bluemantle Pursuivant, 1528; former Risebank Pursuivant, 1522.

narcissus: a strong-scented white flower, *Narcissus foeticus*; in old heraldry represented by the cinquefoil (q.v.).

Nargate, Edward: Windsor Herald, 1693.

nascens: L., issuant.

Nativity Roll: (1300) seventy-nine named and blazoned shields written on the dorse of the Falkirk Roll (q.v.).

natuurlike kleur: Afk., proper.

naval crown: a circlet heightened with three sterns of wooden ships, and, between them, two masts with a square-sail rigged on the yardarms. In some versions there are three square-sails and masts with, between them, two sterns of ships. The ~ is employed in the arms of persons connected with the Royal Navy. The Merchant Navy has its own crown, i.e. a circlet heightened with three masts and sails only, named 'mercantile crown'. (232)

navel point: r. alt. for 'nombril point' (q.v.), being a lit. translation of the Fr. term.

navelpunt: D., nombril point.

navette: see **shuttle.**

Nayler, Sir George: Garter King of Arms, 1822. Former Clarenceux K. of A., 1820; former York Herald, 1794; former Bluemantle Pursuivant, 1793; former Blanc Coursier Herald, 1792.

Nazers Herald: created by K. Ed. III in celebration of the victory of Najara, 1367.

nébulé Fr., nebuly.

nebuly: [L.] a line of partition consisting of rising and falling ovals, each with the long axis fesswise and open either above or below in order to run on. An ordinary (q.v.) ~ has the 'keys' facing each other. ~ is sometimes used to represent clouds. (9, III).

needle¹: [O.E.] appear in the arms of the Worshipful Company of ~makers, where each is enfiled with a crown (q.v.).

needle²: see **compass.**

needle-gun: a crude name for a firearm discharged by percussion, invented by John Nicholas Dreyse, and so blazoned in his arms, i.e. 'gules, two needle-guns in saltire proper surmounted of an inescutcheon of Prussia: in base an antique musket also proper: on a chief azure a demi-sun issuant Or'.

Neill, John: Dingwal Pursuivant, 1830.

Neilson, Alexander: Carrick Pursuivant, 1622.

nenuphar leaf: a charge employed in teutonic heraldry being the conventionalized leaf of an aquatic plant. It is normally born with the point baseward. The representations in old heraldry are invariably sans stalk and some are notched, identifying the ~ with seeblatter (q.v.). The few remaining examples are now slipped. This expedient is an insurance against the annoyance of finding them blazoned and depicted as hearts.

Nepal, Order of the Star of: f. 1947 in three classes. Insignia—*Badge:* a twelve-point star of black and white enamel with silver and red flames between the arms; a central medallion, surrounded by a blue band enscrolled in gold, depicts a view of the Himalayas, and is surmounted by a smaller medallion, surrounded by a silver-rimmed red band, bearing two interlocked triangles in gold on white enamel; the medallions are surmounted by a gold trident. *Star:* a larger version of the badge. *Riband:* crimson in the centre, fading into white, yellow and orange at the edges.

Neptune: God of the sea, a term often employed when a merman (q.v.) is intended, but should be fully human in form, as the dexter supporter in the civic achievement of Liverpool.

Neptune's horse: r. name for the seahorse (q.v.).

nero: It., sable.

nerved: see **leaves.**

Netherlands Lion, Order of the: f. 1815 in three classes, namely Grand Cross, Commander, and Knight. Insignia—*Badge:* a gold-rimmed white cross paty pommetty, the letter W in gold appearing between the arms; a blue central medallion bears the gold inscription *Virtus Nobilitat*; the Netherlands lion appears on the reverse; the badge is ensigned with a gold crown; star, the badge, unensigned and without the W's, on a silver star of eight points. *Riband:* blue with a narrow orange stripe near each edge.

nettle: [O.E.] a profuse weed of the genus *Urtica* which grows on rough uncultivated ground and along the banks of wayside ditches. Its leaves and stems are covered with short stiff spines which, on contact exude a strong irritant, hence, 'stinging ~'; employed in heraldry in an allusive setting.

Neve, Sir Wm Le: (also Peter) see **Le Neve,** Sir Wm.

Newbald, Simon: see **Newbold, Simon.**

Newbold, Simon: Rouge Croix Pursuivant, 1547. Also spelt 'Newbald'.

Newhaven Pursuivant: name of office of the garrison pursuivant at Ambleteuse, 1544, and of a similar officer at Le Havre, 1562.

newt: [M.E.] an amphibious, long-tailed lizard-like creature, *Triton cristatus*, related to the salamander (q.v.). Also known as 'swift', 'ask', 'asker'; hence, employed frequently in a ca. setting. Generally blazoned either 'proper' or 'vert', which is the same thing.

Nichan Iftikhar, Order of: (Tunis) f. 1837 in one class as a bejewelled green medallion surrounded by the Bey's name picked out in diamonds or brilliants. The Order was revised in five classes in 1822. Insignia—*Badge:* a silver plaque surmounted by a ten-rayed star, the rays being alternately of red and green enamel, with a central green medallion, surrounded by brilliants depicting the name of the reigning Bey; the whole is ensigned with a bow in brilliants. *Star:* a large version of the unensigned badge. *Riband:* green with a double red stripe at each edge.

Nicholas: Lancaster Herald in the Service of the Black Prince, 1366.

Nicolson, Thomas: Kintyre Pursuivant, 1761.

niger: L., sable.

Niger, National Order of: f. 1959 in five classes. Insignia—*Badge:* a gold-rimmed green star of ten points pommetty, with gold sword hilts between the arms; a gold central medallion depicts the cross of Agadey in gold, surrounded by a green band inscribed *Republique du Niger*: the whole ensigned with a green and gold wreath. *Star:* the badge on a ten-point silver star. *Riband:* yellow, green, yellow, in equal stripes.

night-ape: an African innovation, occurring in public arms, with the fish-eagle (q.v.). (253)

Nile, Order of the: (Egypt) f. 1915 in five classes. Insignia—*Badge:* a nine-point faceted silver star surmounted by a five-point star of white enamel; a central medallion in gold bears an Arabic inscription in blue enamel to the glories of the Nile; prior to 1953 the badge was ensigned with a crown. *Star:* the badge surmounting a ten-point star of alternate gold and silver rays. *Riband:* light blue with a yellow stripe near each edge.

nimbe: Fr., nimbus.

nimbo: It. and Sp., nimbus.

nimbus: see **glory, a.**

ninth son, mark of difference of: see **brisure.**

Niven, Wm: Unicorn Pursuivant, 1500.

nobiliary arms: see **burgher arms.**

Nobility Roll, the Sixth: (temp. K. Ed III) vellum true roll (q.v.), damaged, painted with eighty-four shields of which number thirteen are outlines only, with names over. It measures $9\frac{1}{2}$ in. by 2 ft 5 in.

noble: [L.] in England the word 'nobleman' is normally used to describe a peer or his sons; in Scotland, and on the Continent of Europe, noble has a different connotation and can be used of all armigers.

nodoso: It., raguly.

Nogent Pursuivant: Maine Herald's (q.v.) junior, 1449.

nogmaals gevierendeel: Afk., quarterly quartered.

Noir Lyon Pursuivant: maintained by Viscount Wells, who died 1498, the name is from the lion sable in his arms.

Noir Taureau Pursuivant: maintained by the Duke of Clarence; named from the Black Bull, of that House. Also spelt 'Noyre Tauren'.

nombril point: [Fr.] an imaginary dot

---

355. Gules, three treble-violins transposed argent, stringed sable.
Sweeting.

356. Argent, three church-bells azure, the cannons and clappers gules.
Belleton.

357. Gules, three clarions Or.
Granville of Glamorgan.
(Sometimes blazoned as organ-rests, canting on glam-organ.)

358. Azure, two organ-pipes in saltire between four crosses paty argent.
Williams, Thame.

359. Sable, three hawk's bells Or.
Bellchamber.

360. Gules, three cloyshackes Or, stringed argent.
Ireland.

355

356

357

358

359

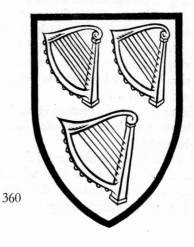

360

resting on the palar line halfway between fess point and centre-base.

nooked: lit. pointed; hence, the head of an arrow, beak of a bird, etc.

Norfolk Herald: created (and paid) by K. Hen. VII, but not accepted as a royal officer of arms, being specifically the Duke of Norfolk's servant. Subsequently the office became one of the extraordinary appointments and so it has remained. Hugh Stanford London, F.S.A., was created ~ in April 1953 (see Preface).

Norfolk and Suffolk Roll: (c. 1400) a painted true roll (q.v.) containing 150 shields of county families.

Normandy King of Arms: a French office, but a ~ was present, with Garter, functioning at the coronation of K. Hen. VII.

Norroy and Ulster King of Arms: see **College of Arms.**

North Star, Order of: (Sweden): f. 1748 in three classes: Grand Cross, Commander, Knight, and known also as the Order of the Polar Star or the Black Riband. Insignia—*Badge:* a white cross paty pommetty, with gold crown between the arms; a central blue medallion bears a white five-point star which is surmounted by the inscription in gold *Nescit Occasum*, the whole ensigned with a gold crown. *Collar:* a double chain linked by white stars and the encrowned initials F [reversed] F. *Star;* a Maltese cross, with decorated edges, surmounted in the centre by a small five-point star; stars of the first class have rays between the arms; all in silver. *Riband:* black.

Northampton Herald: served Humphrey de Bohun who was, *inter alia*, Earl of Northampton.

Northumberland Herald: served the earls of Northumberland until 1527 when he was taken into the service of the Crown and became an extraordinary officer of arms.

nose-spectacles: in the arms of the Worshipful Company of Spectacle Makers (i.e. opticians) ordinary 'reading glasses' are thus described, and they are depicted without 'sides'; it would seem that 'pince-nez' are indicated, but no clip appears on the bridge.

notched: [O.F.] provided with a broad V-shaped depression; 'a cross paty (q.v.) ~' is an alternative term for a 'cross of eight points' (q.v.). The end of the shaft of an arrow (q.v.) is actually so cut, but the detail seldom appears in drawing.

Nottingham Herald: in 1399 serving the Duke of Norfolk in his capacity of Earl of Nottingham described as a royal officer of arms when functioning at the coronation of K. Hen. V's consort, Q. Katherine (1421). K. Hen. VIII bestowed the name on a pursuivant in the service of his natural son, Henry Fitzroy, *inter alia*, Earl of Nottingham. Employed for a herald extraordinary in 1778.

noué: Fr., nowy.

nowed: [Teut.] alt. spelling of 'knowed'; since the word refers to a knot, and has no reference to the negative—not—the 'k'-spelling is to be preferred notwithstanding the possible influence of the Fr. word 'nouer', to knot.

nowy: a r. line of partition, fesswise, and rising in the centre in a semicircle of a diameter of one-third the width of the shield: of any cross having an outward quadrant at the junction of the limbs.

nowy-quadrate: often employed in blazoning a cross of any kind when quadrate (q.v.).

Noyre Fawcone: a mistake, which got into print, for 'Noir Taureau' (q.v.).

Noyre Tauren: see **Noir Taureau Pursuivant.**

nuage: r. alt. for 'nebuly' (q.v.).

nubilatum: L., nebuly.

nublado: Sp., nebuly.

Nucells Pursuivant: in the service of Anthony Woodville, Earl Rivers, Lord Scales, and Nucells, 1446.

nudado: Sp., nowy.

oak: see **trees.**

Oak Crown, Order of the: (Luxembourg) f. 1841 in five classes. Insignia—*Badge:* a white cross paty, gold-rimmed, with a green central medallion bearing in gold the encrowned initial *W. Star;* Grand Cross— a silver star of eight rays surmounted centrally by the badge's medallion which is surrounded by the inscription *Je Maintiendrai* in gold on red, within a green and gold oak wreath tied with a bow; Grand Officer—a Maltese cross of faceted silver, similarly surmounted. *Riband:* yellow with three green stripes—one central, one near each edge.

oar: [O.E.] in addition to appearing as a secondary item when a lymphad (q.v.) or other vessel is blazoned as having '~ in action', the ~ appears in its own right as a charge, generally for allusive purposes. ~ erect is palewise, blade chiefward, in bend or in bend sinister, or two in saltire, the blades remain chiefward. When the ~s are in action the blades are not only baseward, but are generally invisible beneath the surface of the water. (332, VI)

obereck: Ger., canton.

obsidional crown: appears to be another term for 'graminy chaplet' (q.v.). The ~ was the reward of the siege-breaker.

obverso ore: L., gardant.

occasional rolls: see **rolls of arms.**

occulted: [L.] alt. for 'absconded' (q.v.).

Octofoil: see **trefoil.**

offene hand: Ger., a hand appaumé.

Office, arms of: a grant-general of armorial bearings to the holder for the time being of

nut: [O.E.] any fruit, or seed, that is contained in a woody shell; blazoned by name, e.g. 'walnut', and employed in heraldry for ca. reasons.

certain official appointments; e.g. kings of arms (q.v.), regius professors of Cambridge University, and bishops. ~ impale (q.v.) personal arms; hence, a marital achievement (q.v.), on a separate shield, will be displayed accolée (q.v.).

officers of arms: the pursuivants, heralds, and kings of arms created by royal warrant, who constitute the College of Arms (q.v.). They are '~ in ordinary'.

Ogilvie, George: Albany Herald, 1677.

ogress: (unknown—not related to ogre, a fierce giant—possibly XIII–XIV cent. soldier's slang) a roundel sable, representing a cannon ball, but not to be shaded so as to appear spherical—it is a roundel, not a cannon ball proper; alt. terms 'pellet' and 'gunstone'.

Olaf, St: appears in the municipal arms of Norrkoping, Sweden.

Olav, Order of St: (Norway) f. 1847 in five classes. Insignia—*Badge:* a gold-rimmed enamel Maltese cross pommetty; between the arms is an elongated and crowned Or; on a central medallion, surrounded by a blue band with white borders, is a gold lion rampant bearing St Olav's axe; the whole is ensigned with a gold crown supporting a lion; crossed swords below the crown indicate an award for valour. *Star:* the unensigned badge on a silver star of eight points. *Riband:* red, with narrow white, blue, white stripe near the edges.

old man: used as a symbolic figure; is distinguished by a bald head and flowing grey locks at each side mingling with his beard.

Oldys, Wm: Norroy King of Arms, 1755. Former Norfolk Herald Extraordinary, 1755.

Oliphant, Alexander: Albany Herald, 1565.

Oliphant, Laurence: Lord Lyon Depute, 1631.

Oliphant, Thomas: Albany Herald, 1604.

olive: an evergreen tree, *Olea europaea*; symbolic of peace, a sprig (q.v.) of which is often carried in the beak of a dove (q.v.).

ombilico: It., nombril point.

ombiligo: Sp., nombril point.

ombre, in: see **entrailed.**

omgekeerd: Afk., reversed.

ondato: It., wavy.

ondé: Fr., wavy.

ondeado: Sp., wavy.

ondoyant: [O.F.] of a serpent erect in pale when wavy.

ondy: r. alt. spelling of 'undy' (q.v.).

ongle: r. alt. form of 'unguled' (q.v.).

oor alles heen: Afr., surmounting.

opal: see **segregative blazon.**

open book: see **book.**

open crown: see **ducal coronet.**

opinicus: a composite fictitious beast having the four limbs of a lion, a short tail, an eagle's head with ears as the griffin (q.v.), a long neck, either feathered or scaly; and wings, either feathered or membraneous. The ~, which was not evolved before the XVI cent., is, in short, a debased griffin. (191)

opressed by: r. alt. for 'surmounted by' (q.v.).

Or: [fm L. via. Fr.] gold; one of the heraldic metals, represented in art by either gold-leaf or yellow paint. Cross-hatching (q.v.) dots.

ora obventantia: L., caboshed.

orange¹: a roundel (q.v.) tenné (q.v.) employed only in continental heraldry.

orange²: a pulpy fruit enclosed in a protective skin of a red-yellow colour, *Citrus Aurantium*: always slipped and leaved (q.v.) to distinguish it from the continental roundel of the same name. (See also previous entry.)

Orange, Order of the House of: (Netherlands) f. 1905 in six classes. Insignia—*Badge:* a gold-rimmed red cross with a gold orange wreath between the arms; a gold central medallion depicts a stringed bugle-horn in blue enamel, and is surrounded by the inscription *Je Maintiendrai* in gold on white. *Star:* the medallion and inscription surmounting a gold star of eight points. *Riband:* orange.

oranje: Afk., tenné.

---

361. Paly Or and gules, on a canton argent a rat salient sable.
Trat, Cornwall.

362. Argent, on a pale gules a cross Or.
Looker.

363. Paly of six argent and azure per fess counterchanged.
Posingworth.

364. Gules, a pale ermine charged with a bend azure.
Greer.

365. Paly wavy of six gules and argent.
Gernon.

366. Argent, five lozenges conjoined in pale; in dexter-chief an escutcheon of the second.
Lorraine of Kirk-Harle.

361

362

363

364

365

366

orbiculi segmentum: L., flaunch.

Order of Merit: see **Merit, Order of.**

Order of Merit (Chile): see **Merit, Order of** (Chile).

Order of Merit (Indian): see **Merit, Order of** (Indian).

Order of Merit (National, France): see **Merit, Order of** (National, France).

orders of chivalry: see under the various keywords, e.g. **Garter,** etc.

ordinaries: [M.E.] geometric shapes, being the earliest form of heraldic device; see **bar, bend, chevron, chief, pale,** etc. ~ have diminutives (q.v.), but sub-~ (q.v.) are not related.

ordinary of arms: a roll, register, or directory cataloguing armigers (q.v.) and their bearings, arranged according to ordinaries or major charges, e.g. all achievements having a bend (q.v.) will be grouped: all with a fess (q.v.), a chevron (q.v.), etc., all crosses, all saltires, all lions, swords, etc., etc., together without reference to a, b, c order.

ordinary, officers of arms in: any officer of arms created by royal warrant and in the service of the Crown. A 'regular' officer of arms, not one in private service, nor of 'extraordinary' status.

orinatus: L., ranged.

organ rest: see **clarion.**

orieller: see **cushion.**

orielles: [Fr.] lit. a little ear; hence, the ears or hinges of an escallop.

organ pipes: the frontal, ornamental pipes of the grand organ are depicted. A single ~, which is less common than a range, may be either pale, or bendwise; a range of ~, the number of which will be stated, are palewise, graded in size, the shortest on the dexter. Two ~ in saltire (q.v.) is comparatively frequent. (358)

orientation: charges on a bend (q.v.), bend sinister (q.v.) or a chevron (q.v.), or, in the absence of an ordinary (q.v.) are, e.g., 'bendwise' or 'in bend', follow the direction of the ordinary; '. . . on a bend, three billets', the long sides of the charges will be parallel with the sides of the bend, or, if 'bendwise', will be tilted in the same way. '. . . on a chevron, three billets', one at each side will be tilted, the third, occupying the apex of the chevron will remain palar in relation to the field. When a bend is of a fur the elements of the fur slope with the ordinary, but a chevron of fur has the elements palar of the field.

orifiamma: It., orriflamme.

oriflama: Sp., orriflamme.

Orkney Herald Extraordinary: a name of office formerly employed in Scotland.

orla: Sp., orle.

orlado: Sp., fimbriated.

orle: [O.F.] the inner half of a bordure (q.v.) split through its width; said to be a sub-ordinary (q.v.) and also described as a diminutive (q.v.) of the bordure; but actually a large inescutcheon (q.v.) generously voided (q.v.). An ~ blazoned as of a line of partition, e.g. wavy (q.v.), undulates on both the inner and the outer edge, but these two edges may vary as, e.g., an ~ wavy on its outer, and engrailed (q.v.) on its inner edge. An ~ is too narrow to carry charges, but a number of objects, normally eight, may be blazoned as 'an orle of . . .', however, the same arrangement is often given as 'eight (objects) in orle'. The term 'false escutcheon', which is sometimes used as an alternative, refers to its origin. (441, IV)

Ormonde Pursuivant: see **Lyon Office.**

orn: Swd., eagle.

Oro: Fr. and Sp., Or.

or(ri)flamme: the sacred banner of St Denis to which was attributed magical properties: carried by the King of France when on a military enterprise. The ~ was a gonfanon (q.v.) of red (or orange) silk, which, in time of peace, reposed at St Denis's Priory.

osier: [M.E.] one of the titles of the willow-tree, *Salix viminalis*.

Osmania, Order of: (Turkey) f. 1862 in five classes. Insignia—*Badge:* a green enamel star of seven points, gold-rimmed and pommetty; between the rays are leaves in brilliants; a red central medallion, in a gold-edged green band, bears a Turkish inscription of Abdul Aziz Khan over a Turkish crescent and star. *Star:* the badge's central medallion surmounting a silver star of eight points. *Riband:* green with red stripes near the edges.

osprey: see **eagle**.

ostrich: a gigantic, long-legged, long-necked flightless bird, *Struthio camelus*, found in both Africa and Asia. Distinguished in heraldry by holding in the beak some article of iron—horseshoe, sword, key, and the like. (125)

ostrich-feather: see **feather**.

Otherlake, John: see **Lake, John**.

otter: [O.E.] a piscivorous mammal, having webbed feet and a long, flat paddlelike tail, *Lutra vulgaris*. r. ca. in the arms of Luterell.

ouched [M.E.] r. obs. alt. for 'garnished' (q.v.), but particularly garnished of jewelled buckles (q.v.).

ounce: [M.E.] a name applied to various members of the cat family, but specifically to *Felis uncia*, the mountain panther, or snow-leopard; also applied to the cheetah. (61)

oundy: [O.F.] r. alt. spelling of 'undy' (q.v.).

outsticker: see **basket makers' tools**.

over alles: D., overall.

Owen, George: intruded upon the office of Norroy King of Arms under Cromwell: was nominated Clarenceux King of Arms and, at the Restoration, was allowed to resume as York Herald which he had been created in 1634. Former Rouge Croix Pursuivant, 1626.

owl: [O.E.] a bird of the sub-order Striges, both nocturnal and raptorial: of characteristic appearance, having a large broad head and big staring eyes. Known variously as barn ~, church ~, hissing ~, and screech ~. The tawny ~ is also called beech ~, brown ~, ferry ~, grey ~, hooting ~, and wood ~. There is, in addition, the horned or long-eared ~. The bird, symbolic of wisdom, is usually depicted perched and close, but irrespective of his orientation he is always gardant.

Ox: [O.F.] the castrated male of the Bovidae; often having a ca. value.

P: abvn. for 'purpure' (q.v.) for which 'pur.' is also used.

paal: Afr. and D., pale.

paalsgewyse: Afk., in pale.

pack-saddle: a dish-shape tray, built up of staves, mounted on a padded frame fitting the back of a pack-horse or a mule, on which a considerable load could be carried. The heraldic ~ is drawn like half a barrel mounted on short legs.

Paddy, Nicholas: Lancaster Herald, 1588. Former Rouge Dragon Pursuivant, 1574.

padlock: see **quadrangular lock**.

pail: see **well-bucket**.

pairle: see **shakefork** and **tierced**.

pairle, disposed in: see **triangle**.

Pakistan, Order of: f. 1957 in four classes. Insignia—*Badges:* first class—a gold star of ten-point rays; a green band surrounds the white central medallion depicting

Pakistan's coat of arms; ensigned with a gold crescent and star; second class—a smaller version of the first-class badge, ensigned with a gold crescent; third class—as for second class but ensigned with a star; fourth class—a gold medallion depicting Pakistan's coat of arms. *Ribands:* first class—white with green edges; second class—equal widths of green, white, green white, green; third class—green with three white stripes; fourth class—green with four white stripes.

pal: Fr., pale.

palar line: see **pale²**

pale¹: [M.E.] an ordinary one-third of the width of the shield, vertical and central. (362, 364)

pale²: a vertical central line, either real or imaginary, by which a shield is parted; the palar line.

pale, in: of an object erect in the centre of the shield: of a number of objects occupying the position of a pale. (366, IV, VIII, XII)

palificato: It., urdy.

palis exoratus: L., paly.

palisadenformig: Ger., urdy.

palisadevormig: D., urdy.

palisado, crown: a circlet having attached to the outer surface fourteen vertical, square-section rods cut off at the top to form a blunt point, and representing a palisade. Seven only of the palings appear in drawing, those at the sides being in profile, and all being cloué. Based on a Roman military award to the first soldier to break through the outer defences of a fortified position. Employed in heraldry both to ensign the shield and replace the crest-wreath.

palizado: Sp., urdy.

pall: [O.E. fm L.] a conventionalized representation of the archbishop's pallium, being in the form of a capital Roman text letter Y, issuant (q.v.) of the dexter- and the sinister-chief corners but couped in base. ~ may be bordered, fringed, and tasselled; it may also carry charges. It is given the status of a sub-ordinary, and it appears only in ecclesiastical heraldry. (404)

pall, per: see **tierced.**

pallet: first diminutive of the pale (q.v.), being half the width of the parent. (370)

pallisadé: Fr., urdy.

palm-tree: [O.E.] a tropical monocotyledon; a sprig or a leaf of which is symbolic of triumph. Trees not of the order Palmae are used in celebration of Palm Sunday, particularly the willow (q.v.). The coconut-~ is to be found in heraldry, but by its own name, not in the category of ~. (374)

palmer: a 'palmer-worm', i.e. a caterpillar.

palmer's staff: [O.E.] a pilgrim's staff, tapering slightly and terminating at the top in a pommel, just below which a leather thong is often depicted flotant; ~ is the symbol of a traveller.

palo: It. and Sp., pale.

palo disgiunto: It., trononné.

palus: L., pale.

palus minutus: L., palet.

paly: of a field (q.v.), an ordinary (q.v.), or a charge carrying an equal number of pallets (q.v.) of alternate metal and tincture: six is the standard, and no number need be given, but for more (say eight) or less (not less than four), the number must be stated and the word 'pieces' may be added: ~ is one of the major variations of the field (q.v.), and may consist of alternate fur and tincture. (164, 365, 445, II, XII)

paly-bendy: a compound variation of the field created by lines drawn in pale (as though for paly) crossed by lines drawn in bend (as though for bendy (q.v.)), producing a series of lozenges that incline to the sinister. ~ may be of either metal or fur, and a tincture. The metal (or fur) commencing in the first whole lozenge in dexter-chief. ∼ sinister creates shapes that incline to the dexter, and commence with metal in sinister-chief. (441, 448)

pame: r. alt. for 'langued' (q.v.).

panache: see **feather.**

Pancras, St: functions as the crest of the municipal council of the Borough of ∼, London.

pannon: see **pennon.**

pannonceaux: [Fr.] a term used by French heralds to describe an armorial vane (q.v.). It was probably first applied only to a knight's pennon-shaped vane.

panon: see **pennon.**

pansrad: Swd., vambraced.

pansy: the cultivated variety of *Viola tricolor,* the petals of which are bigger and more highly coloured than those of the wild variety, is indicated.

pantheon: a semi-fictitious heraldic beast based on a combination of the natural panther, a large leopard, *Felis pardus,* and the natural cheetah, the Indian hunting leopard, *Felis jubatus.* To the heraldic pantheon is attributed enormous strength and ferocity; hence, it normally is portrayed incensed without mention in the blazon. The ∼ is generally purpure, but it may be sable and in either colour is invariably semé of stars. It possesses a r. alt. title, i.e. 'papion'. (XIV)

panter: D., panther.

pantera: It. and Sp., panther.

panthère: Fr., panther.

Papal cross: a plain cross having two additional traverses on the upper limb, the highest being the shortest. The eight limbs are sometimes made pommetty, and sometimes trefly. The ∼ is employed in continental arms, but not normally in British.

Papal tiara: see **triple crown.**

papegay: see **popinjay.**

papelonné: [Fr.] fesswise rows of downward curving semicircles; in each row the horns of these loops are conjoined to the centre of the arcs above. It is a variation of the field (q.v.) employed on the Continent and is sometimes blazoned as 'escaillée', i.e., having scales but, even in Fr. heraldry, a fish is never ∼ but is 'escaillée'.

paper, a roll of: see **parchment, a roll of.**

papillon: [Fr.] a butterfly, any member of the Lepidoptera having four wings, which it holds addorsed (q.v.) when resting, and antennae terminating with pommels (q.v.), generally depicted with wings spread (volant) and the legs invisible. (80)

Papillon Pursuivant: in the service of the Earl of Langueville, K.G., 1423.

papion: see **pantheon.**

papyrus: [Gk] a sedge, reed or rush that grows in running water, from which the Egyptians produced a woven and pressed sheet of writing material. The ∼ plant is used in heraldry often to represent papermaking interests.

paradise, bird of: to be found in Russian and Baltic-area heraldry, and to a small extent in other parts of Europe; not employed in British heraldry.

paradise tree: a specific apple-tree, fructed proper, e.g. that in the armorial achievement of the Worshipful Company of Fruiterers; not a general alt. for an apple-tree.

parado, leon: It., a lion statant.

parchment, a roll of: represented by a loosely rolled skin, usually belled outward rather at each end and tied in the middle by a binder which may or may not be specified in the blazon; frequently in bend, or in bend sinister; when fesswise part of the roll may be pendant, and a seal (q.v., 1) specified. A roll of paper is treated in precisely the same way, and is drawn the same, hence, the substitution of paper for ∼ is probably without significance; both carry the same symbolism of literature and law. (130)

paré: Fr., vested.

park-pales: the representation of an open fence, being a row of stakes, pointed at the top, driven into the ground, and secured with horizontal wires at both top and bottom. (32)

parlantes, armes: see **canting arms.**

Parliament robe: a long cape, generally gules and provided with a collar and front edges of ermine; blazoned as 'purflued' (q.v.) of the fur. A ~ or 'mantle' hangs empty from an invisible peg, the front facing outward, but it is the same garment that is depicted about the shoulders of an exalted personage, e.g. a king 'in his robes'. When a ~ is not 'purflued', it may be mistaken for 'a piece of cloth', which is a r. but separate and distinct charge.

Parliamentary Roll: (c. 1312) in book form, having nineteen vellum leaves, 6 in. by eight and a quarter inches containing 1110 names and French blazons.

parsley: a herb, *Petroselinum sativum*, widely used for garnishing, and also for flavouring, certain articles of food. In the XIX cent. it became the basis of a conventionalized pattern used on printed cotton fabric, and both the plant and the pattern appear in arms. The Corporation of Accrington, Lancashire, has, *inter alia*, a length of fabric of ~ pattern.

parrot: see **popinjay.**

parted and fretty: of a cross (or a saltire) composed of interlaced diminutives (two endorses (q.v.) interlaced with two barrulets, or two costs with two bastons): when three or more diminutives are employed in this manner the resultant cross is described as of, e.g., so many endorses interlaced with so many barrulets.

parti: Fr., per pale.

partido: Sp., per pale.

partition, lines of: a field 'party per . . . need not be divided by a straight line, neither need an ordinary, nor a subordinary consist of the space enclosed by two straight lines: there are fourteen standardized deviations, ten of which are employed with great frequency in British heraldry. See **angled, bevilled, dancetty, dovetailed, embattled, engrailed, indented, invected, nebuly, nowy, potent, quadrate, rayonny,** and **wavy.**

partito: It., per pale.

partridge: [M.E.] a game-bird, *Perdix cinerea*, having the alt. name of 'gregor'; hence, of use in ca. settings.

---

367. Azure, three fleurs-de-lys Or, impaling ermine.
Municipal Corporation of Brest.

368. Erminois, a cinquefoil ermine.
Flower, Sussex.

369. Azure, a garb Or.
Grosvenor (Duke of Westminster).

370. Argent, two pallets gules: on a chief of the last, as many mullets of the field.
Algie.

371. Gules, three teasels Or.
Woller.

372. Argent, a woolpack encircled by two branches of cotton-tree fructed proper, all within a bordure sable, charged with eight martlets Or.
Municipal Corporation of Rochdale.

367

368

369

370

371

372

party: [M.E.] divided, parted, indicating that the field (q.v.) is of two colours; invariably followed by 'per' and the direction of an ordinary; hence, 'party per fess', 'party per bend', 'party per pale', but because of the English tendency to ellipsis, the word 'party' is very frequently omitted, the blazon commencing at 'per'. In old heraldry, ~, without qualification, meant 'per pale'.

Pascal lamb: see **lamb, Paschal.**

pascuant: [L.] lit. at pasture; hence, of cattle when represented as feeding.

passant: [Fr.] lit. passing; hence, of a beast represented as walking, 'to the dexter' understood. (Counter-~. to the sinister.) Very little exaggeration of the attitude assumed by some beasts when walking distinguishes them in heraldry; others, however, are highly conventionalized. The lion ~ has his sinister hind-leg stretched well to the rear, the dexter brought abnormally forward: the dexter fore-limb is raised and flexed, the sinister carried either forward or backward, according to taste, and also to the space available. The tail is flourished along the back and turned over to the sinister; there is much in its attitude to suggest that ~ was a development of rampant (q.v.). The old Fr. term for a lion passant was 'léopardé-lionné', which gave rise to the term 'a leopard' for a lion ~ gardant. 'The "leopards" of England' are three lions passant-gardant in pale. When the true leopard (*Felis pardus*) makes his appearance he is distinguished by the typical spots. In old heraldry ~ was sometimes used for 'throughout' (q.v.).

Passavant Pursuivant: was maintained by Sir Thomas Stainer, 1431.

Passion cross: see **Latin cross.**

Passion nails: see **nails.**

pastomides: L., barnacles.

pastoral staff: [L.] strictly, the insigne of a bishop, but used indiscriminately for an archbishop: a crook, generally enhanced with web-decoration thus producing what at a distance cannot be distinguished from a crosier (q.v.), raised upon a staff and carried in procession.

patens: L., paty.

patent of arms: the document confirming that a petition for a grant of arms has been successful, wherein the matter between Rex and the petitioner is published, and the resultant arms exemplified. A ~ is not merely a legal instrument as, e.g., is a patent of invention, but it is, and has been from its inception, a work of art of considerable merit. The earliest ~ to survive is that of the Worshipful Company of Drapers, under the hand and seal of Sir William Bruges (Bridges) the first Garter King of Arms in 1439. It is a notable example of herald-painting and of manuscript illumination.

The form of a ~, in both its phraseology and its physical size and shape has, in the 500 years of its existence, made many changes, but basically in its intention it has never altered. The medium is vellum, the script is executed by a first-class scrivener in the best pen-letter that is admired at the period, and the illustrations are the work of the most competent herald-painters whose services can be secured.

A modern English ~ normally consists of a sheet of vellum measuring 20 by 16 in., which may be used in either the 'portrait' (long sides vertical) or the 'landscape' (long sides horizontal) position. The 'heading' comprises three achievements of arms: centrally, the Royal Arms; dexter, the arms of the Earl Marshal (His Grace the Duke of Norfolk) displayed in front of two batons of office in saltire and, sinister, the arms of the College as a body corporate. Beneath this, executed in a bold pen-letter (generally by the artist) in colour with capital letters gilded occur the opening words, 'To all and singular'. At that point the scrivener takes over and in a most beautiful, firm copperplate cursive hand continues; 'unto whom these presents do come . . .' and onward to the conclusion.

This first paragraph is the approach: 'To all and singular unto whom these presents do come, We . . .'—then follows the names, titles, and honours of Garter, and the appropriate provincial king of arms, the paragraph ending '. . . send greetings'. The second section states the name of and all details relating to the petitioner, and the reason for and the nature of his approach to the Earl Marshal whose titles, authority, and the like follow. Next comes the declaration that the petition has been accepted and the nature of the grant to be made is delineated, e.g. for himself and his legally begotten offspring forever, or, again, with extended limitations to his father (or his grandfather) and all legitimate offspring. The kings of arms 'do devise and grant the arms following, that is to say . . .' here follows, written in a rather larger, stronger, darker script, the blazon 'as in the margin hereof may be more plainly seen'. 'The margin' referred to is not the narrow strip of white between the left-hand edge of the skin and the commencement of the script block, but is a goodly area ruled off level with the words 'to all and singular', and cutting into the text. In this square is painted the graphic representation of the achievement blazoned in the text: shield, helmet, crest, mantling, the escroll under the arms, but not the motto thereon which is not subject to grant.

If there is to be a badge and a standard, these will be blazoned and depicted in the text; and the patent ends by declaring it done on behalf of the sovereign whose

style and regnal year is given followed by the date Anno Domeni.

The two signatures are added, the foot of the skin turned up, pierced and threaded with the ribands to which the pendant seals, in their skipettes, are attached. The whole document is rolled from the head, bound with crimson silk ribbon tied with a bow-knot, and placed in a long, rectangular wooden box having a hinged lid, covered with red Morocco leather, and embossed on the top with the royal cypher.

The preparation of a ~, the painting, writing, sealing, together with the cost of the materials, represents the outlay of a considerable sum of money; hence, the critics, antagonistic to the English armorial system, who decry the fees payable by a grantee, should learn to do simple subtraction. A ~ is alt. titled 'a patent of gentility' (see **right to bear arms**).

Patent of Gentility: see **right to bear arms, the.**

paternoster, cross: the representation of a string of beads in pale (q.v.) throughout (q.v.) surmounted (q.v.) by another in fess.

Paterson, Andrew: Ormonde Pursuivant, 1840.

Pat(t)erson, John: Snowdoun Herald, 1543. Carrick Pursuivant, 1538.

patibulatum: L., potent.

patonce, cross: a cross consisting of four limbs concave on each side, and at the ends convex and notched twice, thus having the appearance of a very shallow f.d.l. The word may be frmd on Fr. 'potence', related to 'potent' (q.v.), and the cross itself took several different forms in old heraldry. There are XII cent. examples of what is today unquestionably a cross flory (q.v.) being quoted as ~. The cross in the arms attributed to K. Ed. the Confessor is variously given as flory and ~. (215)

patriacale, croce: It., patriarchal cross.

patriarcal(e), croix: Fr., patriarchal cross.

patriarcal(e) cruz: Sp., patriarchal cross.

patriarchal cross: a plain cross having an additional short traverse on the upper limb, thus named from the symbol used in the Greek Orthodox Church. (210)

Patrick, cross of St: see saltire.

Patrick, Most Illustrious Order of St: f. by K. Geo. IV in 1783. Insignia: a silver eight-point star bearing centrally on a white field a red cross of St Patrick, charged with a green trefoil, on each leaf a gold crown, surrounded by a sky-blue circle with the motto *Quis Separabit*; a mantle of sky-blue satin lined with white silk, the Order's star being embroidered on the left side; a gold collar of five enamelled roses and six harps tied together with knots of gold; a badge depicting the central portion of the star, oval in shape, wreathed in trefoil, to be worn from the collar or a riband of sky-blue over the right shoulder.

patten: a device consisting of a foot-shape platform raised on transverse ridges beneath and provided above with straps and buckles to attach to the foot; the object was to enable a person to walk through the dung and mire of the streets without becoming soiled. They appear, notably, in the achievement of the Worshipful Company of Pattenmakers.

Patten, Mercury: Bluemantle Pursuivant, 1597.

paty, cross: [Fr.] a cross, each limb of which expands as progress outward from the centre is made, finishing as four truncated triangles, the bases outward; alt. spelling 'patty' and 'pattée': alt. term 'cross formy (or formée)'. This cross is familiar as the Victoria Cross.

Paul, St: represented by a sword in the dexter chief of the civic arms of the City of London; and by a demi-figure, issuant of a square tower, representing the donjon of the Tower of London, in the arms of the Port of London Authority.

Paul, sword of St: see **sword.**

paulownia: the more important, private, and exclusive of the two Japanese royal mon, the other, the conventionalized chrysanthemum, having become a State mon. The conventionalized trumpet-shaped flower of the tree, *Paulownia imperialis*, which is indigenous to Japan and flowers in early spring. The ~ is named after Anna Paulovna, daughter of Tsar Paul I.

paune: an alt. term for the peacock (q.v.) employed chiefly in Scottish blazon. Also spelt 'pawn'.

pavilion: see **tent.**

pavinated: see **peacock.**

paviour's maul: see **hammer.**

paviour's pick: see **pick.**

pavon: applied to a flag, the shape of a 45° triangle, the 90° being in the hoist at the foot. Of it, the *Oxford English Dictionary* says: 'a spurious word, originating in a mis-reading by Meyrick, *Ancient Armour* III Gloss., of O.F. *panon*, PENNON. Hence accepted by Fairholt *Costume Eng.* (1860) 97, new edn. (1885) (where a supposed figure is given), by Cussans, *Handbk of Heraldry* (1882) 275, Preble *Hist. Flag* (1880), in Ogilvie's *Imperial*, Cassell's *Encyclopaedic*, Webster's *Century*, and Funk's *Standard Dictionaries*', which we quote by courtesy of the Clarendon Press. However, in Scotland, where armigers are expected to fly flags of various kinds, there was felt to be a need for a flag of that shape, and the word was officially adopted.

pawn: see **paune.**

peacock: male bird of the genus *Pavo*. Presents an imposing spectacle when the fan, or train (mis-called 'the tail'), is raised. Generally depicted affrontée, the fan expanded, and the head turned to face dexter. ~ is crested (q.v.) of five points each terminating in a small sphere, which is not mentioned in the blazon. It is 'eyed' of the iridescent ocelli that bespangle the feathers of the train, which, when proper, may be blazoned as 'pavinated'. The foregoing is the usual heraldic representation of the ~, and is blazoned 'a ~ in his pride'; he may, however, also be depicted in profile, proceeding to the dexter, with the train lowered, when he is blazoned as passant (q.v.). (406)

peaked shield: see **tilting shield.**

pean: see **ermine.**

pear: the fruit of the tree *Pyrus communis*; there are numerous varieties, each individually named, hence the ~ is a widely applied ca. device not only for the name Perry and its variations, but e.g., for Warden, etc. The tree itself is also employed (373).

pearl¹: [M.E.] a silver-gilt ball, generally 1 inch in diameter, used, *inter alia*, to heighten the coronet of certain peers.

pearl²: see **segregative blazon.**

peascod: the skin, sac, pod, or legume in which the pea, the edible seed of the climbing plant, *Pisum sativum*, develops.

peel: [M.E.] a baker's long-handled shovel by the use of which he placed dough in the oven and drew the baked loaves out. There is frequently depicted on the blade three manchets (q.v.) drawn as circles and sometimes blazoned as roundels (q.v.).

peering-glass: a lady's oval hand-mirror, having a handle extending at one end of the major-axis; appears erect, the handle baseward u.o.s. The frame, which may be ornamental, follows the curvature of the glass. Sometimes blazoned simply as a 'mirror'. The Worshipful Company of Glass-sellers have a mirror in a rectangular frame, fluted on the inner edge, but this is a private charge.

Peer's helmet: see **helmet of rank.**

peewit: (also spelt with a single 'e') see **lapwing.**

Pegasus: [Gk] a winged horse, differing in no way from that which in Greek mythology sprang from the blood of Medusa. In heraldic art the wings are inclined to be drawn too small, which is a fault, and spoils the effect. ~ may be in any heraldic attitude, including sejant, but is seen to its best advantage when rampant, salient, or courant. The device of the Knights Templars, said to be from the belief that two men, mounted on one horse, and viewed from afar gave the impression of a ~. (275)

pelican: [L.], a large white piscivorous water-bird, believed in antiquity to wound her breast with her long, curved bill in order to draw blood for the purpose of feeding her young; hence, a symbol of piety, self-sacrifice, and christian virtue. In heraldic art she is depicted resting upon her nest; her long slender bill is depressed upon her chest which is invariably 'guttae de sang' (q.v.). Her wings, when elevated, are grandly over-drawn and generally addorsed, rivalling those of the eagle (q.v.). When represented as surrounded by her chicks, each with open beak uplifted, she is blazoned 'a ~ in her piety'; when alone, as 'a ~ vulning herself'. A ~ head, either couped (q.v.) or erased (q.v.) retains the neck and a portion of her breast which remains 'guttae de sang'. (193, XVI)

pellet: see **ogress.**

Pembroke Herald: maintained, 1424 by Humphrey, Duke of Gloucester, Earl of Pembroke.

pen¹: [L.] see **feather.**

pen²: a female swan.

pendant¹: [M.E.] hanging; suspended at one end only; hence, an object may be blazoned as ~, i.e. 'a buckle with tongue ~' or 'a spur with leathers ~'.

pendant²: the end of the garter, or other strap, that often passing through the buckle is draped round the loop so formed and permitted to hang down.

pendant³: one of the descending branches from a label (q.v.).

pendant⁴: a shape of the word 'pennant', itself a shape of the word 'pennon' (q.v.); employed in the Royal Navy (see following entry).

pendant⁵: a naval formation on pennon (q.v.). A broad ∼ fits into a square, and tapers slightly to the fly which remains straight: that of a commodore of the first class is charged with the cross of St George, to which a commodore of the second class adds a torteau in the first quarter. A narrow ∼ (or pennant), flown by a ship of war in commission is a comparatively long tapering triangle charged in the hoist with the cross of St George.

pendon: Sp., pennon.

pennae: L., mantling.

pennant: see **pennon**.

penner and ink-horn: a dual charge, attached one to another by a cord which is not necessarily mentioned in the blazon; the former is a leather case, pouch, or tube in which the scrivener carried his quills; the latter, a short, curving length cut from the point of a horn, and fitted with a metal-cover over the open end, in which he conveyed his ink. These hung at his waist from a cord which also served the purpose of a girdle, and which may, subject to available space, be elaborately drawn in heraldry. (120)

pennon: [M.E.] a narrow tapering flag, the fly of which might be split, forming two points, or finished in one point only, and emblazoned with the arms of the knight who carried it. The hoist of the ∼ corresponded to the chief of the shield; hence, a knight in transit, with his ∼ attached to his lance which he carried erect, might be unrecognizable since a fess seemed to be a pale; however, in war, or at the tournament, the lance was held horizontally, and the identity of the rider became manifest. In modern times the ∼ has been selected as the flag of Lancers, and the guidon (q.v.) as that of Dragoons. 'Pannon' is an alt. spelling; 'panon', also an alt., is the French form of the word; 'pennant' and 'pendant' are the spellings used in the Navy where a ∼ of great length, e.g. 'paying off ∼', is known as a 'whip'.

---

373. Or, on a mount a pear-tree vert fructed proper.
Pyrton.

374. Argent, on a mount vert a palm-tree, therefrom a serpent descending proper.
Going.

375. On a mount vert the stump of a tree; thereon a dove holding in the beak a slip of laurel between two pine-trees all proper.
Akerly.

376. Argent, a tree eradicated proper.
de Peyster.

377. Argent, issuant of a mount vert, an oak-tree, the trunk entwined with two serpents interwoven and respecting.
Duignan, Cambridge, N.Z.

378. Argent two Eastern crowns within a bordure engrailed gules: in base, issuant of a mount, an oak tree debruised of a sword in bend proper.
Macgregor.

373

374

375

376

377

378

pennoncel: a small, light-weight pennon (q.v.) suitable for carrying on the lance.

pennone: It., pennon.

penny-yard-penny: a r. obs. charge being a coin stamped with a cross moline: the name is derived from Penny-yard Castle, Ross, Herefordshire, on the assumption that the coins were minted there.

penoun: [M.E.] the feather of an arrow, a bird-bolt or a cross-bow-bolt.

pensel: the ultimate reduction in size of a pennon (q.v.), being merely a length of coloured ribbon tapered to a point; still in use upon the lances of Her Majesty's Household Cavalry.

Penson, Wm: Lancaster Herald, 1613. Former Chester Herald, 1603.

pentagon: see following entry.

pentagram: a five-point figure, being an interlaced lattice of straight lines connecting five points equidistant round the circumference of a circle; one of the mystical, potent sigils employed in arcane activities of alchemists, astrologers, magicians, and warlocks; the text-letters, S.A.L.U.S., may be inscribed one in each of the five triangular points. Alt. term 'pentacle', but frequently described er. as a 'pentagon'. This last is very misleading: a pentagon is a plane figure having five equal sides and five equal angles, a shape created in the central enclosure of the ∼, but it must not be regarded as a pentagon extended by a triangle erected on each face.

pentalpha: r. alt. term for a pentagram (q.v.)

pentacle: see **pentagram.**

peppercorn: [Gk] the dried berry of the West Indian climbing shrub, *Piper Nigrum*: reduced to powder and used (now) for culinary purposes and (anciently) as a medicine. ∼ (or short form 'peppers') are blazoned 'in the pod' notwithstanding that it does not grow in pods.

perch: [M.E.] a freshwater fish *Perca*

fluviatilis; also known as 'miller's thumb', due to its blunt, broad head, and may be so blazoned. The ∼ has two heraldic titles, i.e. 'chabot', and 'gull'. Always depicted haurient, with the dorsal surface affrontée.

perclose: see **garter.**

Percy Herald: maintained in the service of the House of Percy by the Earl of Northumberland, 1385.

perfluent: flowing: applied to 'water proper' when a stream is intended; r. alt. for 'transfluent'.

perspective, in: [L.] drawn in depth; with lines bounding horizontal planes converging; applied generally to massive charges such as buildings of various kinds.

petasus: a hat; in shape and style the same as an ecclesiastical hat (q.v.); applied specifically to the winged hat of Hermes. Sometime blazoned, loosely, as 'Mercury's hat' and er. as a winged morion (q.v.).

Peter, fish of St: see **dory.**

Peter, insignia of St: see **key.**

Peterborough Roll: (c. 1321–9) an illustrative (q.v.) roll being the Chronicle and Cartulary of ∼ Abbey. The work of Walter of Whittlesey. Arms of the Abbey and of some tenants painted in the margin.

petronel: lit. of a cavalryman's heavy pistol but applied in heraldry to any pistol: a flint-lock is generally depicted, which may, at the artist's discretion, be chased. 'Pistol' is an alt. term.

pettettée: originally an uncorrected printer's error, copied blindly and ignorantly in several later books and defined as an alt. spelling of 'pellettée', i.e. semé of pellets (q.v.).

Pettigrew, Sir John: Kintyre Pursuivant, 1536.

Pettigrew, Thomas[1]: Angus Herald Extraordinary, 1492.

Pettigrew, Thomas[2]: Unicorn Pursuivant, 1507.

Pettigrew of Magdalensyde, Thomas:

Lord Lyon King of Arms, 1519. Former Angus Herald Extraordinary.

pewter-pot: the drinking vessel of familiar shape, the handle of which, u.o.s., is to the sinister; they are also blazoned 'drinking-pot', 'possenet', or 'college-pot'.

pfahl: Ger., pale.

pheasant: [M.E.] a game-bird, *Phasianus colchicus*, with an alt. name, 'francolin'; hence, of value in ca. settings.

pheon: identical with a broad-arrow (q.v.) except that the backs of blades are engrailed. (140)

philip: [dial.] a folk name for the sparrow; employed for ca. reasons.

Philipot, John: Somerset Herald, 1624. Former Rouge Dragon Pursuivant, 1618.

Phillips, James Monson: Rouge Dragon Pursuivant, 1786.

Philp, George: Snowdoun Herald, 1712.

phlegme: see **fleam.**

phoenix: [Gk] a legendary sexless, immortal bird who, at the end of a period of time built in the desert a pyre of spice-wood which became ignited through the fanning of ~ wings. In this fire the bird plunged and was burned to ashes out of which there arose a rejuvenated ~. It is symbolic of immortality, of rebirth, renewal, renascence; is always depicted as a demi-eagle, with tufted head, wings elevated, issuant of flames of fire proper. It is either Or, or argent, occasionally gules. (271)

Phoenix, Order of the: (Greece) f. 1926 in five classes. Insignia—*Badge:* a gold-rimmed white cross, surmounted by a central phoenix in gold, with a five-point gold star on the upper arm of the cross; since 1936, when the monarchy was restored, the badge is ensigned with a gold crown. *Star:* of silver with eight points, surmounted centrally by a gold phoenix, encrowned since 1936. *Riband:* gold with black edges.

pick: [M.E.] a breaking tool, consisting of a curved steel bar drawn to a point at each end, or at one only, the other being specialized by a chisel-edge, a cross-piece, or other shape, having a central socket from which a haft (q.v.) emerges on the concave side. The ~ is subject to specializing blazon as '~-axe', 'coal-~', 'mill-~', 'miner's-~', paviour's-~', and, in addition, without such technical reference, the ~ is a ca. device on such surnames as Piggott. The word 'hew' is not a general alt. term; it applies only to the 'miners-~'. (266, XI)

piddle: [dial.] a kite, *Milvus ictinus*, a member of the family Falconidae, having long wings and a bifurcated tail. The kite, also known as the 'puttock', makes the majority of his entrances on the heraldic stage for ca. reasons.

pie: [M.E.] the magpie, *Pica caudata*; applied to any bird having black and white plumage.

pie, sea: the oyster-catcher, *Haematopus ostralegus*; r. but generally 'proper', i.e. brown with red head and neck and white wings.

piece of cloth: see **Parliament robe.**

pieces: sometimes added after the statement of number in variations of the field (q.v.).

pied: of a beast whose coat is of two colours, e.g. 'a bull argent, ~ sable', extended to include any two colours.

Piedmantle Pursuivant: a fictitious character created by Ben Jonson in *The Staple of News.*

Piedmont, bale of: r. alt. for a bale of silk.

pieficcato, croce: It., cross fitchy.

piegato: It., embowed.

pierced: [M.E.] of an object having a round hole in the centre: '~ round' gives to some charges a specific name; a lozenge (q.v.) ~ round is a rustre; a mullet (q.v.) ~ round is sometimes blazoned as a spur rowel or revel. (96)

piety, in her: see **pelican.**

pignonne: Fr., indented.

pike¹: [M.E.] the thrusting weapon carried by footmen who were not archers: consists of a long shaft headed with a socket, or shank, out of which rises a double blade; first, a narrow oval in line with the shaft, and, secondly, a hook-shaped blade set at right angles, giving the pike-head the appearance of a demi-f.d.l. The ~ may be blazoned as 'war-bill' or 'halberd'. The wood-bill, which is a tool—not a weapon—is drawn in precisely the same way, carrying the inference that even were the 'spear beaten into the pruning hook', that tool could be conscripted to act as a spear in time of war. There are examples of a pike-staff, without the head, but since the staff is without characteristics of any kind, it might be any rod or shaft. (452)

pike²: [M.E.] an aggressive freshwater fish, *Esox lucius*, named, in heraldry, the 'luce' (or 'lucy'), and depicted with a sharp, dog-like head and long snap with teeth. Originally it was the ca. device of the Norman family of Lucy, but now it has a wider application; however, under its alt. titles, i.e. (gad) (or 'ged') and 'Jack', it appears only for ca. reasons. (70)

pila pontis: It., L., and Sp., pile.

pile: [L.] a sub-ordinary being an isosceles triangle which, u.o.s., is issuant in centre-chief, one-third of the width of the shield and tapering to its apex at nombril point: the ~ may be broader, if it has to carry charges, but ought never to reach the corners of the shield and so give the appearance of party per chevron (q.v.) inverted; if blazoned 'throughout' it will reach the base point. The ~ may issue from any part of the shield, a number may appear together, and the point may be floriated (q.v.). The ~ is a most adaptable shape; hence, it is in frequent use and conforms to many different settings. (90, 263, 420, II, XIV)

pilgrim's staff: see **palmer's staff.**

pilia pastoralis: r. alt. for 'long cap' (q.v.).

pillar: [M.E.] in addition to appearing, of necessity, to support an arch (q.v.), the ~, also termed 'column', appears alone as a charge: the order—Doric, Ionic, or Corinthian—may be stated. The ~ generally acts as a support for some other charge, even a prosaic object representing a trade or a craft. A whole pillar is likely to be on a mount (q.v.), but the demi-column is issuant (q.v.). (V)

pillow: see **cushion.**

pincell: a small pennon (q.v.) charged with crest and badge.

pincers: a woodworking tool consisting of a pair of curved jaws with rod-shaped handles extending and pivoted together. Used primarily for withdrawing nails. (Often mispronounced and sometimes misspelt 'pinchers'.) (314)

pine: [O.E.] a generic name given to trees of genus *Pinus*, which have needle-leaves. Often fructed of its cones. The spruce is included. (375)

Pine, John: Bluemantle Pursuivant, 1743.

pine-apple¹: an heraldic name for a pine-cone.

pine-apple²: see **ananas.**

Pingo, Benjamin: York Herald, 1786. Former Rouge Dragon Pursuivant, 1780.

pink¹: a name for the gilliflower (q.v.); used to imply excellence.

pink²: see **minnow.**

pinnatus: L., embattled.

pinonada: Sp., indented.

pinson: [dial.] the chaffinch, *Fringilla coelebs*; alt. spelling 'pinyon'.

pinyon: see previous entry.

Pisan Cross: a cross cleché pommetty on a field gules. Generally depicted faceted (q.v.).

pismire: see **emmet.**

Pisore Pursuivant: see **Salisbury Herald.**

Pisow Pursuivant: see **Salisbury Herald.**

pisseled: formerly applied to a beast's penis when of a colour differing from that of the beast itself.

pistol: see **petronel.**

pitcher: see **jug.**

Pius, Order of: (Vatican) f. 1847 by Pius IX in honour of Pius IV (1559–65) who had created an Ordo Pianus. Originally in two classes, the Order was revised by Pius X into four classes: Grand Cross; Knight Commander with star; Knight Commander with neck-riband; Knight with badge worn at the breast. Insignia—*Badge:* an eight-point star of gold-rimmed blue enamel, having gold flames between the points; a white central medallion is inscribed *Pius IX* in gold, surrounded by a gold band lettered *Virtuti et Merito. Star:* larger version of the badge, silver rays being substituted for the gold flames. *Riband:* blue with two red stripes near each edge.

plaice: [M.E.] a flat-fish, *Pleuronectes platessa,* employed in heraldry chiefly for ca. reasons.

plain cross: see **cross.**

plain-point: see **rebatements of honour.**

plane: a carpenter's surfacing tool; the type depicted is the 'jack-~' or the 'try-~', being a long 'stock', of square section, the 'iron' and 'wedge' projecting upward from the 'mouth', a vertical handle at the rear end. The ~ is depicted fesswise, as though resting on its 'sole' (or face), and the visible side is often diapered. (It was not uncommon for a workman to carve a pattern in low-relief on the sides of his ~.)

Planché, James Robinson: Somerset Herald, 1866. Former Rouge Croix, 1854.

planets, blazon by: see **segregative blazon.**

planta genista: see **broom.**

plate: [M.E.] a roundel (q.v.) argent, representing a silver coin, particularly those of old Spain and Barbary: by 1606 'Real de plata'—the one-eighth of a piastre—were in circulation over an extensive cultural and economic area: ~ is not shaded.

platty: semé (q.v.) of plates (q.v.).

playing-card: see **card².**

playing-top: see **top.**

Playnford, Rowland: York Herald during the reign of K. Hen. VII. Former Bluemantle Pursuivant and Calais Pursuivant (K. Ed. IV).

plenitude: see **moon.**

plomb, à: of a bend (q.v.) or a bend sinister embattled, when the crenellations remain palar of the field instead of rising at 90° from the line of partition; r. in British but frequent in continental heraldry. (85)

ploughshare: the curved blade which, drawn through the earth, cuts the furrow, and turns the earth over; is naturally present when 'a plough' is blazoned, but also appears as a charge in its own right.

plover: see **lapwing.**

ployé: of a chevron the two limbs of which are concave, giving a knock-kneed appearance; r. in British heraldry; in Fr. blazon it is extended to cover 'embowed' (q.v.).

plum: the fruit of the tree, *Prunus domestica;* employed in heraldry for ca. reasons.

plumber's iron: see **soldering-iron.**

plume: see **feather.**

plumetty: a field (q.v.) of feathers (q.v.), a form that did not survive, and of which the few examples preserved from the feudal period contradict each other in appearance: one form is semé (q.v.) of feathers; another consists of barwise rows of feathers conjoined laterally; yet a third displays a field totally covered with overlapping feathers.

plummet: [M.E.] a lead weight, attached to a cord suspended upon a straight-edged board, used for testing verticality. The whole apparatus appears blazoned as 'a mason's level' with a spherical ~ which may be of another colour; but the ~ appears alone and is then given more attention: it is drawn as pear-shape, broad end, to which a ring is attached, upward, and a pointer extending beyond the apex. Often drawn hexagonal in section, but maintaining the tapering (pear-shape) elevation. Symbolic, like the square (q.v.), of uprightness of character, rectitude, simple honesty.

point: an heraldic preservation of an archaic term for the junction of the arms and the shank (q.v.) of an anchor; the locality, now called the 'crown', was actually a point when the smith forged each arm, and the shank, from straight rod, welded in the form of a crow's foot. The point might be pierced and have a ring introduced for tripping; hence, 'an anchor ringed' referred originally to the tripping ring, but now is applied to the cable ring.

point-champain: see **rebatements of honour.**

point-champion: see **rebatements of honour.**

point-chapourne: see **rebatements of honour.**

point-dexter: see **rebatements of honour.**

point-eared shield: see **prick-eared.**

point-in-point: see **rebatements of honour.**

pointe: Fr., base.

pointed: alt. for 'urdy' (q.v.).

points¹: rods, or pillars, set upon the rim of a coronet, or of an heraldic crown, and terminating in a shape such as a trefoil or a pearl (q.v.). (XII)

points²: see **label.**

points³: see **ermine.**

points⁴: see **wyre-drawers' tools.**

Polar Medal: f. 1904 in succession to earlier Arctic medals; can be awarded in silver and bronze, and recipients of both can wear them together. *Badge:* obverse—octagonal, bearing the effigy of the awarding sovereign with the appropriate inscription; reverse— a sledging party, and the ship 'Discovery'. *Riband:* white.

Pole star: see **Antarctic and Arctic Stars.**

pole-axe: consists of a battle-axe (q.v.) mounted on a long shaft. It is merely another name for the halberd (or halbert). (456).

polecat: [M.E.] a kind of weasel (q.v.) *Putorius foetidus*; also called 'fitchet'; employed in heraldry generally for ca. reasons.

Police Medal, Queen's: f. 1909. *Badge:* a silver medal having the sovereign's effigy and legend on the obverse, and on the reverse a watchman, before a fortified city, leaning on a sword and supporting a shield inscribed *To guard my people*. *Riband:* dark

---

379. Argent, three daisies stalked and leaved vert.
Daisie.

380. Or, three primroses within a double tressure, flory-counter-fleury gules.
Primrose.

381. Argent, two columbine slips crossed in saltire and drooping proper, flowered purpure.
Bessell.

382. Argent, three carnations gules stalked and leaved vert.
Noyce.

383. Azure, three fraises argent.
Fraser of Pitcallain.

384. Azure, a lily-pot argent.
Corporation of Dundee.

379

380

381

382

383

384

blue, with a broad white stripe centrally and at each edge; when awarded for gallantry, as a posthumous award, a thin red line bisects the white sections of the riband.

Polonia Restituta, Order of: f. 1921 in five classes. Insignia—*Badge:* a gold-rimmed Maltese cross, pommetty; a red central medallion depicts a white eagle displayed, and is surrounded by a blue band inscribed in gold *Polonia Restituta*; the reverse has the date 1944: prior to 1944 the eagle was crowned and the reverse bore the date 1918. *Star:* a multirayed star of eight points, having a white central medallion with the initials *RP* in gold, surmounted by a green band inscribed in gold *Polonia Restituta. Riband:* red with a narrow white stripe near the edges.

pomegranate: [M.E.] brought into British heraldry by Katherine of Aragon: always slipped (q.v.) and leaved (q.v.) and having a strip of skin removed to reveal the contents, i.e. seeds or grain: if the ~ itself is not proper it will be 'seeded proper', i.e. gules; its alt. title is 'apple of Granada', *Punica Granatum*. (391)

Pomfret, Richard: Rouge Croix Pursuivant, 1725.

pommé: [Fr.] a roundel (q.v.) vert, representing an apple; drawn as a disc, but shaded for thickness.

pommé, cross: a cross humetty (q.v.) having a circular terminal to each limb; also termed 'pommetty' and 'pommelé'. (216)

pommel: see **sword.**

pommelé, cross: see **pommé, cross.**

pommetty cross: see **pommé, cross.**

Ponde, John: Somerset Herald, 1511; also spelt 'Pound'.

poniard: see **sword.**

popeler: a water-bird; a duck with a spatulate bill; hence, identified with the spoonbill, *Platalea leucorodia*, and, in modern heraldry, included in the generic term 'shoveller' (*Spatula clypeata*) (q.v.).

popinjay: [M.E.] the title generally given to a parrot; alt. 'papegay'. When proper the bird is vert, beaked, and membered gules. (122)

poppy: the common wild flower of the cornfields, *Papaver rhoeas*, having red petals and a hairy stem is generally meant, but specific varieties are also used in arms. See also **grady.**

porch: see **church.**

porcupine: [L.] a creature which, like the hedgehog, defends itself by means of stiff, erectile, pointed spines. It was believed to discharge these at a pursuing enemy. Of the genus *Hystrix*, and not to be confused with the hedgehog, genus *Erinaceus*.

porfled: r. alt. spelling of 'purfled' (q.v.).

porpora: It., purpure.

porridge pot: see **cauldron.**

port between two towers: a castle (q.v.) without a central tower; also described as a 'wall [to which 'with battlements and a gate' may be added] between two towers'.

portate: lit. being carried; applied to objects, but particularly to a Latin cross, disposed in bend, as though resting over the shoulder of a porter unseen.

portcullis: a massive grid, or grille, having rings at each top corner, and a row of spikes at the foot, which, suspended by chains over a castle, or a city, gateway could be dropped as a means of defence. The ~ in heraldry must always have its rings which were part of the construction, but may be without its supporting chains if blazoned 'sans chain'; normally they depend on each side and, like all heraldic chains, are of rectangular links. (202)

Portcullis's Book: (c. 1440) paper book of seventy-five leaves, $5\frac{1}{2}$–6 by $7\frac{3}{4}$ in. Part 1 contains 576 painted shields with names over, six to the page. Part 2 has twelve shields to the page, the majority of which are painted and the others in trick (q.v.); this section, 108 shields is a local roll (Cheshire). Part 3 has four shields to the page, painted, with names over. It also illustrates twenty-eight different types of cross, and twenty lions in various attitudes. This section is a general roll (q.v.) exemplifying arms of saints as well as English and continental nobility.

Portcullis Pursuivant: see **College of Arms.**

Porteous, Robert: Snowdoun Herald, 1661.

Porteous of Craiglockhart, George: Marchmont Herald, 1674. Herald-painter, 1674.

Portington's Roll: (temp. K. Hen. VI) of which there are three copies, each differing from the other, and all, doubtless, from the original which was painted on vellum. Copy A contains 982 shields, a general roll (q.v.) in trick. B has, on each of the first sixty-two pages, sixteen tricked shields, and continues with a Yorkshire local roll (q.v.) and extracts from the Parliamentary Roll (q.v.). C is a general roll (q.v.) of 851 shields.

Portsmouth Pursuivant: an extraordinary office, created in 1604, and filled by John Guillim, the famous author of *A Display of Heraldry.*

posé: in British heraldry a r. alt. for 'statant' (q.v.), but current in Fr. blazon with that meaning.

possenet: see **pewter-pot.**

postament: Swd., compartment.

posto d'onore: It., honour point.

pot: see **cauldron.**

pot-gun: a sporting gun, that is to say, any form of musket (q.v.) that is to be employed in bringing down a bird for the pot rather than as a weapon of war.

potencée, croix: Fr., cross potent.

potent[1]: [M.E.] lit. a crutch-head; hence, a T-shaped object or terminal development.

potent[2]: a line of partition consisting of rising and falling rectangles, each with the major axis fesswise, and open, either above or below in order to run on; a rectilineal development of 'nebuly' (q.v.). An ordinary ~ has the 'keys' facing each other.

potent[3]: an heraldic fur (q.v.) organized and coloured on the basis of 'vair' (q.v.).

potent, cross: a cross humetty having a traverse forming the terminal of each limb. (218)

potenza: It., potent.

potenzada: Sp., potent.

poudre: a shape of the word 'powdered'; hence, sometimes (though seldom) employed to express 'semé' (q.v.).

pounce[1]: the claw of a bird of prey; a hawk's anterior claws; a lion's paw.

pounce[2]: a leather shield or sheath for a fighting-cock's spur.

pounce[3]: charcoal, or other powder, used for dusting through the holes of a design perforated in an appropriate medium thus transferring a copy onto each of numerous objects; hence, extended to a sheet of thin metal cut with lines, curves, and shapes to guide the pencil, and so enable those unskilled in drawing to make neat sketches of arms.

Pound, John: see **Ponde, John.**

pourpre: Fr., purpure.

Povey's Roll: (temp. K. Ed. II) eighty-two shields (or parts) cut from a vellum true roll and mounted in book form; painted, surnames only, over.

powdered: dusted over with; alt. for 'semé' (q.v.).

Powell's Roll: (c. 1350) in book form, twenty-eight vellum leaves each 5½ by 12 in., painted with 672 shields with names over.

powert: [M.E.] frog, *Rana*, normally orientated to the dexter (q.v.) and sejant (q.v.), may be sejant-affrontée (q.v.), and if blazoned as 'displayed' the back is presented to view and the limbs are stretched, as though leaping, head chiefward.

ppr: abvn for 'proper'.

prawn: [M.E.] a sea-creature like a large shrimp, *Palaemon senatus*; employed in heraldry chiefly for ca. reasons.

preen: [M.E.] lit. to make tidy; hence, a tool formerly used in the process of cloth-finishing which, being in appearance like a hay-rake or a garden-rake (q.v.) which has curved teeth, may easily be mistaken for such.

prescriptive right: a claim made by some of the numerous people who, in England, make use of armorial bearings that have not been the subject of a legitimate grant and have not been recorded at the Visitations of the Heralds. Those who apply this non-existent term to their right to bear arms are, as a rule, respectable people who believe themselves to be armigerous, and who, confronted with the fact of the absence of a record existing, claim ~, and condemn the officers of arms who were so careless as to overlook their ancestors at the time of the visitations.

Many of these deluded people are second, third, or even fourth generation descendants of a victim of an 'heraldic stationer'. These tradesmen flourished exceedingly in the XIX cent. not only devising arms for all who came to them, but generously bestowing existing arms upon total strangers of the same (or a closely similar) surname. The modern heraldic stationer supplies writing paper printed with arms at a customer's request; he does not initiate the arms. Spurious arms are still being devised and granted to the unwary by charlatans operating under grandiose titles.

Prester John: see **sacred and legendary figures.**

Pèeston, Thomas: Ulster King of Arms, 1633. Former Portcullis Pursuivant, 1625.

pretence, escutcheon of: an inescutcheon whereon is displayed the arms brought in by an heraldic heiress (q.v.). On the death of the wife's father the impalement (q.v.) is broken, the husband's arms again occupy the whole area of the shield and the wife's arms are displayed on an ~ because the husband has become 'pretender' to the wife's family fame and honour; he is the only living male who will defend the good name of his wife's family. Secondarily, the ~ may represent title or estate that comes to the armiger by some process other than direct lineal inheritance. This is more likely to apply in Scotland or on the Continent than in England.

preying upon: see **falcon.**

prick-eared shield: made its appearance towards the end of the Stewart period and became almost universal in the Georgian era. It consists of straight lines; the chiefmost line overruns the width of the shield which is joined to it by connecting lines thus forming two little triangles overhanging as a roof does the walls, and giving the style its name. The base descends in the form of a broad triangle. The entire effect is that of a distorted and disproportionate vair-bell; hence it is sometimes referred to as a 'vair-bell shield'. Another alt. term is 'point-eared shield'. Perhaps one of the reasons why this angular and ugly shape was so prevalent in the XVIII cent. was the facility with which the copper-plate engraver could construct it; in a collection of armorial book-plates of the period it is hard to find a shield having any curvature. It lingered through the XIX cent. and is not dead yet.

pricket: a candlestick having, instead of

PLATE XIV   Sable platty, a pile throughout barry of eight dancetty Or and gules: ensigned with a tilting-helmet mantled of the liveries whereon, upon a wreath of the colours, is set for CREST, the sun in his splendour Or charged with an escutcheon of the same on which a martlet sable within a bordure gules, the whole between.

SUPPORTERS: Two pantheons, also gules unguled Or, each charged with fifteen mullets, of which thirteen of six points and two of seven points, argent: gorged with a crown palisado and chained gold, the chain passing between the fore-limbs and reflexed over the back, the terminal annulet resting upon the compartment, a mount vert.

United Kingdom Atomic Energy Authority

sconces, spikes on which the candle was impaled.

pride, peacock in his: see **peacock.**

prime: see **basket makers' tools.**

primrose: see **trefoil.**

Prince Henry the Navigator, Order of: (Portugal) f. 1960 in five classes. Insignia—*Badge:* a gold-edged red cross paty ensigned with a small acorn and oak-leaves in gold. *Star:* a multirayed gold plaque of nine points, surmounted by a gold star of nine points, with a white central medallion bearing the unensigned badge and surrounded by the legend *Talant de Bien Faire* in gold on a black band; the legend is surrounded by a gold wreath. *Riband:* blue, white, black, in equal widths.

Prince of Wales's coronet: a circlet crusted with gems, embellished with alternate f.d.l. and crosses paty, and heightened with one arch. The cap is crimson, turned up ermine, but when the ~ appears in an armorial achievement, it is generally without the cap.

princes' and princesses' coronets: sons and daughters of the sovereign (other than the heir apparent) have a circlet encrusted with gems and embellished with alternate f.d.l. and crosses paty. Grandsons and granddaughters, being offsprings of princes, have a circlet with alternate f.d.l. and strawberry leaves: offspring of princesses—strawberry leaves only. Nephews of the sovereign, being offspring of brothers, have circlets embellished with alternate crosses paty and strawberry leaves. The caps are crimson, turned-up ermine, but when ~ are used in arms the cap is generally omitted.

promiscuously volant: see **bee.**

pronominal quarters: see **quarterly.**

pronunciation: see **spelling.**

propeller, aeroplane: an ~ erect and winged is the crest of the Municipal Corporation of Hendon.

proper: [M.E.] of a charge to be depicted in its natural colour instead of a metal (q.v.) or a tincture (q.v.). When ~ is applied to beasts it is er. extended to cover natural form or attitude. For natural movement, 'at random' should be employed.

proportion of ordinaries: such instruction as 'one-third of the width of the shield', etc., must be given, but ought not to be accepted as hard-and-fast rigid rules. ~ are approximate and flexible: if the ordinary has to accommodate a broad charge, it should exceed one-third; on the other hand, if it is between two bulky charges, e.g. lymphads (q.v.), it may with advantage be less than one-third. Artistic expediency takes precedence over geometry.

prosaic objects: heraldry being a symbolic art, very rich in material, it ought never to be necessary to introduce ~ as charges because what is to be expressed can emerge from an intelligent display of the time-honoured figures that have, for centuries, conveyed ideas to men at all levels of intelligence. However, pride of achievement is a compulsive force that may override all considerations of art and tradition put forward by the most diplomatic officer of arms; hence, civic heraldry unblushingly parades its sewing-machines, its battleships, its railway-engines, and various other items of machinery of interest mainly to the citizens of that town who are justly proud of having supplied the world with locomotives and the world's wife with sewing machines. A great drawback is that such ~ cannot be blazoned, for 'a midland railway locomotive proper' is not blazon. Who but the railway historian can, without research, say what is the 'proper' colour for such a prime-mover?

~ occur in the arms of livery companies and of industrial organizations, and, as is demonstrated in the very old bearings of some of the former, may come to mean nothing whatever to the craftsmen whose ancestors' familiar daily tools they once were. Such forgotten tools and appliances are fruitful of much scholarly speculation. It would serve no useful purpose for this work to deal in detail with individual ∼, which category must be understood to contain the majority of tools used by workmen of all kinds. Herein we deal only with ∼ that have, for one reason or another, become time-honoured and risen out of the category of ∼; also with ∼ the purpose of which has been forgotten and thus have given rise to interesting theories; and with such tools as have acquired symbolism and have changed from 'private' to common charges.

pryck-spur: see **spur.**

public arms: see **community, arms of.**

Public Register of all Arms and Bearings in Scotland: see **Lyon Office.**

Public Register of all Genealogies and Birth Brieves: see **Lyon Office.**

pugnantes: L., combatant.

Pujolas, Henry: Richmond Herald, 1763. Former Bluemantle Pursuivant, 1761.

Pulman, James: Clarenceux King of Arms, 1848. Former Norroy K. of A., 1846; former Richmond Herald, 1838; former Portcullis Pursuivant, 1822.

punt: Afk., and D., pile.

punta: It. and Sp., base.

punto de honor: Sp., honour point.

Purchase Pursuivant: was carrying documents for the Crown in 1439, and the year following was attached to the English embassy in France. He was also styled ∼ Herald. Alt. spelling 'Purchesse'.

Purchesse Herald: see previous entry.

Purdy, John: Lyon Clerk and Keeper of the Records, 1587. Ross Herald, 1593; Dingwal Pursuivant, 1590.

Purdy of Kinaldies, James: Lyon Clerk and Keeper of the Records, 1584. Islay Herald, 1572. Kintyre Pursuivant, 1569.

purfled: [frmd on 'purfle', M.E.] the decorated edge of a garment, hence of a robe or the like having an ermine (or other fur) edge; extended to include any object, not of fabric, e.g. a piece of plate-armour, with an edge decorated with other than fur, e.g. gold facings. Alt. spelling 'purflewed'.

purflewed: see previous entry.

purper: Afk., and D., purpure.

purperkoeke: Afk., a roundel purpure.

purpuna: Sp., purpure.

---

385. Azure, a heliotrope, stalked, and sprouting two leaves vert: in chief, the sun in his splendour Or.
Florio.

386. Argent, three bayleaves slipped, vert.
Foulis.

387. Per chevron argent and gules, three fig-leaves counterchanged.
Greves.

388. Argent, two gilliflowers in chief, and an escallop in base all within a bordure indented gules.
Livingstone.

389. Argent, three pairs of oak-leaves, each erect, slipped, vert, stalked sable.
Baldwin.

390. Argent, a sprig of laurel vert fructed gules, between two cinquefoils of the second.
Lorimer.

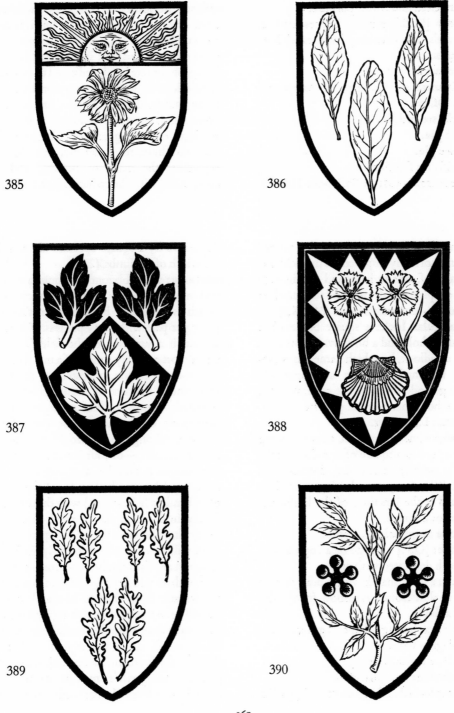

385

386

387

388

389

390

purpur: Ger., and Swd., purpure.

purpure: [M.E.] purple. Represented in engraver's cross-hatching by parallel lines in bend sinister.

purpureus: L., purpure.

Pursuivants: see **College of Arms** and **Lyon Office.**

puttock: see **piddle.**

pye: see **pie.**

pyot: see **pie.**

pyramid: see **feather.**

Pysore Pursuivant: see **Salisbury Herald.**

python, heraldic: a composite fictitious beast being a winged serpent, but it is not an amphisbaena (q.v.). The serpent in mythology is dualistic in its signification, being, on the one hand, dedicated to evil and symbolic of (as well as a metamorphasis of) Satan; hence, slain by Apollo; and, on the other hand, a symbol of divine mercy, of wisdom, of healing, and of robust health. The amphisbaena is satanic, but the ∼ represents the snake of healing, and is compatible with the caduceus (q.v.). (74)

quadrangle, in: of four objects that instead of being normally disposed on the field, i.e. one in chief, one in base, and one in each flank, are placed in dexter- and sinister-chief and dexter- and sinister-base. (240, XII)

quadrangular lock: a square box with a central keyhole and a bow over the top; in short, a padlock, by which name it is sometimes blazoned and the accompanying drawing modernized to the concave-sided convex-bottomed normal pattern.

quadrans: L., quarter.

quadrate: a line of partition, fesswise, rising in the centre in a square of one-third of the shield's width; sometimes described as 'escartellé': of any cross having, extending outward at the junctions of the limbs, the corners of a square.

quadrons angularis: L., canton.

quaintise: [O.F.] a badge or a cognizance; any cloth decorated with arms.

quarrel[1]: a short shaft having a heavy ovoid head, as shot from a crossbow (q.v.); also called a 'bolt'.

quarrel[2]: a lozenge-shape segment of a stained-glass window.

quarrel[3]: a mason's chisel.

quartefeuille: Fr., quatrefoil.

quarter-pierced: of a cross voided (q.v.) in the centre by a square aperture about half the width of the limbs. (206)

quarterly: when blazoned without a specified number, '∼ of four' is understood which is produced by a combination of party per pale with party per fess. When ∼ of four is a variation of the field (q.v.) it will almost certainly consist of a metal in the dexter-chief canton, repeated in sinister-base, and a tincture in sinister-chief, also repeated; however, this arrangement is customary only, and to use (say) four tinctures, though odd, would not be a breach of rule. ∼ of four is not necessarily a variation: it may be, and very often is, occasioned by marshalling (q.v.) the arms of an heraldic heiress (q.v.) with those of the family into which she married, and it is likely that the contents of the quarters in chief will be repeated, diagonally, in base. Quarters are distinguished one from another by numbers which progress from dexter to sinister and from chief to base and which should be represented in writing by Roman numerals: thus, a simple marshalling would be blazoned as 'Quarterly, I and IV, [blazon] for [husband's surname]. II and III [blazon] for [wife's maiden name]'. It should be observed that each quarter is blazoned separately; no attempt is made to blazon as a unit the shield in which the quarters appear.

Famous arms that need no blazon may be described as (say) 'France ancient quartering England' or 'Castile quarterly with Leon'. Notwithstanding that a quarter is a fourth part, the word embraces a wider meaning than division by four: it has, actually, no numerical signification and an object—or an armorial shield—may be ~ of any number. In old heraldry there were, in frequent use, variations of the field of six pieces and ~ of nine pieces; in each of these only two colours were used, one metal (or fur) and one tincture, starting with the metal in dexter-chief and repeating alternately.

With the passage of time ~ of six was changed in character by being blazoned as 'per fess [metal and tincture] a pale counter-changed' (q.v.). The new fashion did not appeal to all armigers with a field ~ of six; hence, the original form has survived, notably in the achievements of some of the livery companies.

~ of nine under the pressure of the passing years suffered a similar metamorphesis by becoming (say) 'argent, a cross sable quarterly pierced' (q.v.), the three quarters in pale and the three in fess being narrowed to strengthen the illusion.

Quarters accumulated by marshalling are subject in England to no limit. The greatest number held legitimately is 356, by Lloyd of Stockton. In Scotland, quarters are limited to four, but each may be a grand quarter, i.e. a quarter which is itself ~ of four sub-quarters, each of which should be represented in writing by Arabic numerals. The Scots describe such an arrangement as 'grand quarters counter quartered'; in England, in addition to the term 'grand quarters ~', we have 'quarterly quartered'.

There is an er. idea shared by all classes of society that the more quarters a man displays, the stronger the azure tincture of his blood; hence there is a tendency for people bearing genuine arms to bolster them up with spurious quarters, sometimes in good faith, they being ignorant of the rules of marshalling (q.v.) and unaware of the fact that the armiger has not the right himself to make such additions. It is correct to refer to one's own or to one's neighbour's 'quarters' or 'quartering'; it is, however, incorrect to refer to 'quarterings' notwithstanding that a great many people who ought to know better, do so. Quarter I, in any marshalling, is the pronominal quarter, being that representing the family name. (119, 406, 414, 445, 447)

quarterly pierced: of a cross voided (q.v.) of the central square, leaving the four limbs as separate pieces in cruciform juxtaposition and conjoined (q.v.) at the corners. (223)

quartier: Fr., quarter.

quarto: It., quarter.

quatrefoil: see **trefoil.**

quattrofoglie: It., quartrefoil.

quatuorfolia: L., quatrefoil.

queen, a: a female figure identifiable by robes, crown, orb, and sceptre.

Queen Margaret's Book: (c. 1445) a version (q.v.) of Thomas Jenyn's Book (q.v.), being an ordinary (q.v.) in book form having 116 paper leaves measuring $8\frac{1}{4}$ by $14\frac{1}{4}$ in. Painted with 1595 shields with names, and blazons in French, under. Made for Q. Margaret of Anjou, consort of K. Hen. VI, with a painting of her arms as a frontispiece.

Queen Margaret's version: see **rolls of arms.**

Queen's Colour: one of the two silken ensigns carried by each battalion of Brigade of Guards, and of Infantry of the Line, and by other units. For a Line Regiment the ~ is the Union Jack charged on the fess point with the crown royal and beneath it the regiment's title. The regimental colour is an ensign, the tincture of which is determined by the dress uniform facings: in the canton (q.v.) is the Union Jack; on fess point the crown royal and the regimental title; in the flanks, badges and other devices together with battle honours. The Brigade of Guards reverse this order. The colours are 3 ft in the hoist (q.v.) by 3 ft 9 in. in the fly (q.v.), the cords and tassels are of crimson and gold, the staff is 8 ft 7 in. long, the finial is a crown royal and thereon a lion statant.

querfaden: Ger., bar.

questing: of a dog statant (q.v.), the head slightly raised and turned half way between dexter and gardant; pointing.

queue fourché: see following entry.

queued: [O.F.] of the tail of a beast (generally the lion) when differing in colour from the body; also prefixed as double-~, of a beast having two tails, both rooted at the base of the spine, following each other through the same convolutions but diverging slightly throughout their length. When depicted crossing and recrossing each other they are the victims of over-elaborate draughtsmanship which destroys the purpose by making the duality invisible. A beast blazoned 'queue fourché' has one tail rooted at base of the spine: the appendage throws out a branch and is bifurcated for about three-quarters, or two-thirds of its entire length. (48, 49)

quill¹: [M.E.] a slender round rod brought to a blunt point at each end, used for winding thread; may be blazoned as 'an empty ~' or as 'a ~ of yarn'. The former appears like a stick, the latter a spool of thread.

quill²: see **penner and ink-horn.**

Quinas de Portugal: a sufficient description of the old and famous arms of Portugal: i.e. argent, on each of five escutcheons in cross azure, as many plates in saltire.

quince: fruit of the tree *Pyrus Cydonia*; employed in heraldry for ca. reasons.

quinquefolia: L., cinquefoil.

quinquefolio: Sp., cinquefoil.

quintain: [L.] a pole set up to support a target, employed in training pikemen, and used by horsemen for tilting exercise. Employed in continental heraldry. Also spelt with final 'e'.

quintana: It. and Sp., quintain.

quintefemille: Fr., cinquefoil.

quintfoil: r. alt. for 'cinquefoil' (q.v.).

quintoise: mis-spelling of 'quaintise' (q.v.).

quise, erased à la: of a bird's leg when to be depicted complete with the thigh. See also **claw.** Alt. spelling 'cuisse'.

quiver: [M.E.] a cylindrical bag closed at the lower, and attached to a shoulder-strap at the upper, end in which the archer carried his arrows: generally 'filled with arrows' when appearing as charge.

rache: [O. Norse]; see **dog.**

Racine Pursuivant: see **Rasyn Pursuivant.**

Radcliffe, Wm: Rouge Croix Pursuivant, 1803.

radial crown: see **antique crown.**

radiated crown: see **antique crown.**

radish: see **turnip.**

ragged staff: usually drawn in the round, a

staff, palewise, having lopped branches, inclining chiefward on each side; sometimes conventionalized as a pallet (q.v.) raguly (q.v.) couped at each end.

raguly: [M.E.] a line of partition consisting of three-sided rhomboidal projections at intervals of about twice their own width: 'per fess ~' the rhomboids are canted per bend, i.e. they slope to the dexter; 'per pale ~' also in bend, i.e. they slope chiefward. An ordinary has the rhomboids on the one side facing the gaps on the other. A cross has the rhomboids inclined outward from the centre. (225)

railway heraldry: with which rolling stock was emblazoned, and which appeared on the stationery of the companies, was generally spurious inasmuch as it was an unofficial marshalling of the arms of the counties and the cities served by the line. Railway engines as charges appear as emblems of a town's industrial bias in civic arms.

rainbow: sometimes rather awkwardly blazoned as 'a semicircle of various colours issuant from clouds'. It is drawn as an arch, about the width of a fess (q.v.), the ends plunging into little masses of cloud proper and coloured barry argent, vert, gules, and Or, from the convex (chiefmost) edge downward. The simple blazon, 'a ~' has taken the place of all other and more ponderous descriptions.

rake, agricultural: may be specifically named after its purpose as 'hay-~', 'tillage-~', and the like, but no difference in form is depicted; orientation (in bend, etc.) refers to the handle.

ram: [O.E.] a male sheep, distinguished by its spiral horns; its usual attitudes are statant (q.v.), passant (q.v.), and rampant. Demi-~ and ~ head, couped (q.v.), erased (q.v.), or caboshed (q.v.) are of frequent occurrence.

ramado: Sp., attired.

Ramage, Alexander Liston: Lyon Clerk Depute, 1796.

ramé: r. alt. in English blazon for 'attired' but current in Fr.

rami di cervo: It., attires.

ramoso: It., attired.

rampant: [M.E.] of any heraldic beast when depicted facing dexter, standing on the sinister hind-paw [*Note:* substitute 'hooves' for 'paws' if the beast ~ is ungulate. (44)], the dexter hind-paw raised, the trunk inclined upward at about 45°, the fore-paws elevated with the dexter above the sinister, the tail flourished upward and curved over to the sinister: all beasts in this attitude, or as near an approach as their anatomy will permit (e.g. a short tail cannot reach the sinister chief), may be blazoned ~, but some have individual descriptions. When a beast in the ~ attitude faces sinister it stands on the dexter hind-paw and raises the sinister; the sinister fore-limb is held higher than dexter. This reversed attitude may be described as 'counter-rampant', 'rampant to the sinister', or 'contourné'.

rampant to the sinister: see **rampant.**

rampante: Sp. and It., rampant.

Ramsay, John: Unicorn Pursuivant, 1599.

Ramsay, Peter: Unicorn Pursuivant, 1567.

ramure: Fr., attires.

Randle Holme's Book: see **Holme's Book, Randle.**

random, at: of a beast when depicted running, or walking, in a natural manner, not with the exaggerated postures of heraldry. (39)

rangant: of a bull with the head depressed as though in the act of charging.

Rankeillour, Wm: Kintyre Pursuivant, 1595.

Rankine, Robert: Lyon Clerk Depute, 1773.

Raphael, the archangel: employed as a ca. device for a family of that name.

rapier: see **sword.**

rased: obs. alt. for 'erased' (q.v.).

rastirillo: Sp. portcullis.

rasy: obs. alt. for 'erased' (q.v.).

Rasyn Pursuivant: in the service of John, Duke of Bedford, in 1435. Named from the eradicated (q.v.) stock badge. Also spelt 'Racine'.

rat: [O.E.] the familiar destructive rodent, *Rattus decumanus*, known also as the Norway ∼; r. in British heraldry, and by no means common on the Continent. (361)

ratch: see **dog.**

Ratcliffe, Richard: Somerset Herald, 1544. Former Bluemantle Pursuivant 1536; former Calais Pursuivant 1532; former Barnes Pursuivant, 1532.

raute: Ger., lozenge.

rautenschild: Ger., a lozenge when carrying the arms of a lady.

raven: [O.E.] the biggest European corvine bird, *Corvus corax*, popularly confused with the rook (see **rook²**), often used for ca. reasons, and (like the rook) may be given a local dialect name. (111)

Raven, John: Richmond Herald 1603. Former Rouge Dragon Pursuivant, 1888.

ravissant: of a beast passant (q.v.) and carrying in its mouth its prey.

Rawlinson Roll: (XV cent.) paper 8 by 11¼ in., a general roll (q.v.) of seventy-nine shields painted, the first twenty-nine only being named.

ray: [M.E.] lit. a beam, or pencil of light or heat; in heraldry a ray of sun is intended. In appearance a ∼ is a pile (q.v.) wavy, always issuant from its base; may erupt at any point on the periphery of the shield and taper in any direction. The ∼ may appear singly or in groups, and when issuant of a charge, e.g. along the edges of a cross, the charge is described as 'irradiated', or as 'rayonnant'. A crown 'irradiated' is sometimes applied to the 'antique crown' (q.v.). (204)

rayonée: [L.] edged with, or surrounded by, rays: a line of partition rising and falling in a shallow S-shape, the wavy peaks thus formed falling at an angle of 45° to the line along which they advance across the shield.

rayonnant: of any shape embellished by having rays (q.v.) issuant (q.v.) from behind.

reaping hook: see **sickle.**

rearing: see **horse.**

rebated: [M.E.] folded, or cut back.

rebatements of honour: certain shapes, nine in number, which when tenné may have been employed to deface the arms of one found guilty of an offence against the accepted standards of chivalry. The shapes themselves, though no longer in general use, were quite free of oblique meaning when of any but the stain and colours (q.v.), and although no examples of arms rebated can be found in the records, utterly to deny their existence in practical use is too strong.

The shapes involved are: (1) the delf (alt.

---

391. Gules, a pomegranate Or slipped, leaved and seeded proper.
      Granger.

392. Sable, a turnip leaved proper: a chief Or gutty de poix.
      Dammant.

393. Argent, issuant of a mount vert three hop-poles sustaining their fruit proper.
      Sir John Houblon.

394. Argent, a bunch of grapes pendant, stalked and leaved vert.
      Viney.

395. Azure, three cabbages Or.
      De Coole, Holland.

396. Gules, six mushrooms, three, two, and one, argent.
      Launay du Valay.

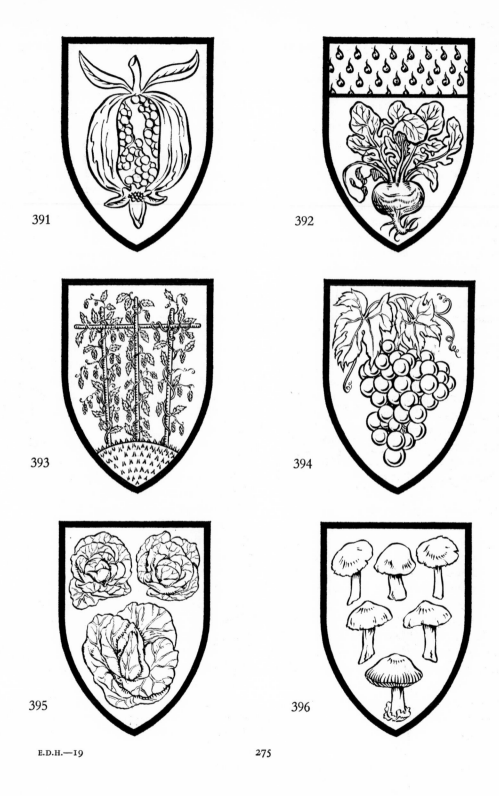

391   392

393   394

395   396

spellings 'delph' and 'delve') conforming to the dimensions of a square, but having slightly concave sides, larger than a canton but smaller than a quarter, which when tenné represented a shovelful of soil, and was, in ∼, placed on fess point: the offence was to revoke a challenge upon its being accepted. (2) An inescutcheon reversed for a deserter. (3) A plain point, being a horizontal section of the field, in base point, a little less than a third of the shield's width in its depth, tinctured tenné (the point, both plain and wavy, is of frequent occurrence in modern arms), defaced the shield of one who misled a superior. (4) Point in point, formed by two concave lines descending to the flanks at about nombril-point level, also called 'point-entee'—again of no oblique reference unless tenné—a brand for cowardice. (5) Point champaine (alt. spellings 'chapourne' and 'champion') is in effect a plain point with a downward curved line, earned by ill-treatment of a prisoner or refusal to give quarter when called upon. (6) Point dexter, a diagonal across the dexter-chief corner, for the braggart. (7) The gore, created by a drooping curve from either dexter or sinister-chief corner to fess point. The gore could thus be either dexter or sinister, but only the latter was used in rebatement—for cowardice. The gusset might be described as a gore having straight lines. (8) Is gusset dexter, the blemish for drunkenness, and 9 is gusset sinister, the mark of licentiousness, but both of these vices, 'habitual'.

Those who assent that ∼ are mere 'book' heraldry, having their origin in the imagination of some writer, and depending for their survival on the romantic-minded reader, ought to extend their knowledge of heraldry beyond England. The following is from North of the Border:

'. . . the prospective patentee was a party against whom decree of divorce had been pronounced. . . .

'*Queritur:* whether the Petitioner was a "virtuous and well-deserving person."

'*Held:* that within the meaning of the Act, . . . he was but behoved to have his arms abated [by] a *gusset sanguine.* . . .

'The present proceedings relate to a grant of arms to a divorced person. . . .'

rebus: [L.] a graphic pun; the presentation of (in heraldry) a name by pictorial suggestion. A ca. coat of arms may be, but is not necessarily, a ∼; on the other hand, an armiger whose device is not ca. may possess and use a ∼. Colonel H. A. Lewis, whose armorial bearings are herein employed as illustration to 'chalice' (q.v.), whose christian name Hexel, puns phonetically on the two text letters X and L, has, for his rebus, 'two capital Roman text letters, X and L fesswise within the circle of the bracing chain of a lewis'. A ∼, as an additional device to a coat of arms, may appear in the patent, but it need not, and is thus comparable with a monogram.

recercelé, cross [O.F.] a cross humetty with the extremity of each limb cleft, the horns thus formed pointed and turned in an inward and downward curve, as a ram's horn.

rechterarm: D., dexter arm.

rechts: D. and Ger., dexter.

rechtsoem: G r., dexter arm.

recortado: Sp., couped.

recursant: see **eagle.**

Red Banner, Order of: (U.S.S.R.) f. 1924 in one class. Insignia—*Badge:* a gold laurel wreath surrounding a centre of white enamel bearing a trophy of arms surmounted by a red star with, surtout, an enwreathed gold hammer and sickle on white enamel; a red banner at the top of the medallion is inscribed in Russian *Workers of all Nations Unite,* and a red scroll at the bottom is inscribed *CCCP. Riband:* red, white, red in equal widths, with very narrow white edges.

Red Book Roll: (c. 1580) paper book containing 548 named shields executed in trick (q.v.).

Red Eagle, Order of the: (Prussia) f. 1705 as the Order of Sincerity, and made into a four-class house order in 1712. Insignia— *Badge:* a gold-rimmed white enamel Maltese cross with a central gold medallion depicting the red eagle of Brandenberg, surrounded by a gold-rimmed blue band with the motto *Sincere et Constanter.* The Grand Cross has red eagles displayed between the limbs. *Star:* gold or silver, according to rank, surmounted by the appropriate badge. *Riband:* white with a broad red stripe near the edges.

Red Ensign: gules, with the Union in the canton; the flag to be flown at the mast-head of British ships other than those wearing either the White Ensign (q.v.) or the Blue Ensign (q.v.).

reed: see **slay.**

reefed: see **sail.**

reflexed: [L.] looped, or draped, generally of a chain or a cord attached to a beast's collar and carried over its back. (XIV)

regalienfeld: a German custom places ∼, a plain field gules, among the quarters of members of ruling families. It is indicative of sovereign rights, and has come into British heraldry in the achievements of several royal consorts. As there is not a British equivalent the word cannot be translated, it is 'Englished', however, by the phrase 'gules for regalia', which is absurd. Perhaps 'gules for regality' was originally intended. An alt. term, used on the Continent, is 'blut fahne'.

regardant: [Fr.] of a beast with its head turned completely round so that when proceeding to the dexter it looks to the sinister and vice versa. (45)

Regimental Colour: see **Queen's Colour.**

regter bohoek: Afk., dexter-chief.

regter onderhoek: Afk., dexter-base.

reindeer: [M.E.] distinguished in heraldic art by double-attires; *Rangifer tarandus.* (36)

relevé: Fr., facetted.

rematriculation: see **matriculation of arms.**

reremouse: see **bat.**

respectant: an alt. for 'respecting' (q.v.).

respecting the altar: heraldic beasts when featuring in coats of arms displayed in churches are either painted or carved so as to face the altar; hence, beasts that appear to be contourné (q.v.) may not be so according to the blazon, e.g. if pew-ends were carved with a lion rampant, that on the sermon side would be normal, i.e. facing dexter, but that on the lesson side would be turned about so as to be ∼.

respecting each other: of two beasts— usually in chief (q.v.)—the dexter being drawn contourné so as to face his companion on the sinister. The habit is not common in British heraldry, but is greatly favoured in central Europe where crest-creatures, too, often piled up in a pyramid, are subject to such discipline, facing inward from each side of the palar line.

rest[1]: alt. for 'clarion' (q.v.); also extended to 'organ rest'.

rest[2]: the support for the muzzle of a matchlock. See also **musket.**

retrospiciens: L., regardant.

revel-spur: see **spur.**

reverted: r. alt. for 'reflexed' (q.v.); also written 'verted'.

reynard: see **fox.**

rhinoceros: a bulky, thick-skinned quadruped with a short horn on the nose: native of Asia and Africa, and to be found in the arms of persons connected with these areas. It is sometimes employed as a supporter (q.v.). Its earliest appearance in heraldry seems to be that in the achievement of the Worshipful Company of Apothecaries.

Rhodes, Order of: see **Saint John of Jerusalem, Order of the Hospital of.**

rhombus: L., lozenge.

riband: see **ribbon.**

ribbed: r. alt. for 'banded' (q.v.); employed mainly in relation to the battering-ram (q.v.).

ribbon[1]: [M.E.] the third diminutive of the bend (q.v.) being a cost (or cottice) couped (q.v.) at each end to half its length: alt. spelling 'riband'; sometimes called 'baton dexter'.

ribbon[2]: the representation of a streamer, draped at each end and generally notched (q.v.) at each terminal, which extends under the shield (or the lozenge) and upon which the motto (q.v.) is inscribed; alt. term 'escroll'.

Richardson, Wm: Lyon Clerk Depute, 1751.

Richmond Herald: see **College of Arms.**

riddare: Swd., knight.

riding-boot: see **Dutch boot.**

rifesso, croce: It., cross patonce.

right to bear arms, the: with the innovation of the close-helmet the use of armorial devices became a necessity to the feudal tenants, and it was confined to that class, namely the Military Aristocracy. The application of armorial distinctiveness to seals spread the use of arms to such non-military nobility as archbishops and bishops, and impersonal arms were devised for their sees and for ecclesiastical establishments. With the passage of time the area of armorial coverage spread; men of noble birth who were neither soldiers nor priests became eligible; bodies corporate of a secular character, e.g. the governing confraternity of the chartered cities, were admitted; but the nobiliary status of armigers was stressed, the use of arms by lesser subjects of the

Crown being prohibited and infringement carrying more or less heavy punishment. The possession of wealth was not a qualification; the merchant class, notwithstanding its riches and its recognized power, was proscribed. However, even feudal military overlords found that they could not function without money, and the marriage of daughters was a good way of getting it. The merchant son-in-law, socially elevated, eluded the ban and became an armiger. Thus, ~ spread in ever-widening circles but the social eminence of the armiger was continually stressed.

Right down to the end of the XIX cent. it was gentry, and only gentry, who might display arms: a patent of arms was alternatively called a 'patent of gentility' and to protect the nobiliary aspect the officers of arms evolved a corpus of rules governing who might and who might not receive a grant. Among the prohibited were those who had not attended a university, those engaged in retail trade, and numerous other irritants of this kind, any one or all of which could be waived, overlooked, or conveniently forgotten to suit the particular case being handled.

The war of 1914–18 changed European society; now ~ has no bounds, and far from asserting the enobling effect of receiving a grant of arms, the Heraldic Authority in England, but not in Scotland, denies it.

The foregoing is a (perhaps over-simplified) statement of fact: it is neither comment nor criticism. Today ~ is possessed by every loyal adult subject of the Brittanic sovereign, irrespective of sex, class, creed, colour, calling, or educational standard. There is, however, one prohibition left that is condoned by all honest citizens, namely a petition for a grant of arms will fail if the petitioner, be he never so rich, is known to have acquired his wealth by dishonest, unsavoury, or other questionable means, or is strongly suspected of having done so, or of transacting business in a manner sub-standard of accepted commercial morality. Money ill-gotten cannot buy honour, for such, in spite of all relaxation, a grant of arms, by its very nature, remains.

ring¹: see **gem-ring.**

ring²: Afk. and Swd., annulet.

ringed¹: of a bull (q.v.) having a leading ring through the nasal septum.

ringed²: of an anchor (q.v.) having a ring through the point or crown. (N.B.: It does not refer to the eye in which the shank terminates and to which the chain, or the line, is attached.)

Risebank Pursuivant: a garrison officer of arms; named from Risban barbican of Calais.

rising: of a bird perched with wings raised as though about to take flight. A frequent alt. form of the term is 'rizant'.

Rising Sun, Order of the: (Japan) f. 1875 as an Order of Merit in eight classes. Insignia—*Badge:* a star of thirty-two white enamel rays, with a central gold-rimmed garnet, ensigned by three paulownia flowers and leaves in green; the seventh grade has green flowers and leaves and no badge pendant, the eighth grade has only silver flowers and leaves. *Star:* the badge surmounting a multirayed star of eight points. *Riband:* ivory with red edges.

Ritchie, John: Kintyre Pursuivant, 1632.

Ritchie, Walter: Kintyre Pursuivant, 1616.

Rivers Herald: maintained in the service of the Earl Rivers, 1466.

rizant: see **rising.**

roach: [M.E.] a small freshwater fish, *Leuciscus rutilus*; employed in heraldry chiefly for ca. reasons.

Robert, Thomas, Earl of Kinnoull: Lord Lyon King of Arms, 1804.

Robertson, Alexander Lambie: Lyon Clerk Depute, 1812.

Robertson, Charles: Herald-painter to the Lyon Court, 1747.

Robertson, John: Procurator Fiscal to the Lyon Court, 1851.

Robertson, Wm: Islay Herald, 1776.

robes: see **Parliament robe.**

roc: r. alt. for 'cronel' (q.v.); also spelt 'roquet'.

Roche, St: genuiant (q.v.) with St Romuald; appears in the civic arms of Suwalki, Poland.

rock: the representation of a jagged mass of basalt, often issuant (q.v.) in base (q.v.) occupying the position of a mount vert (q.v.) and acting as a platform to carry another charge which is sometimes of a ponderous character, e.g. Edinburgh Castle. (136)

rolls of arms: documents, being heraldic records compiled prior to the XVI cent. They have been classified in five groups: *Illustrative Rolls*, i.e. documents, not specifically heraldic, in which armorial records appear incidentally. *Occasional Rolls*, i.e. documents being, as it were, registers of those present on some special occasion. *Local Rolls*, i.e. documents in which arms are recorded in order of locality, such as by counties. *Ordinaries*, i.e. documents in which arms are recorded, arranged in groups by their ordinaries, or their major charges. *General Rolls*, being records of miscellaneous arms, brought together without orderly arrangement, and to perform no special purpose. As might be reasonably expected, overlapping occurs so that one document may be classifiable equally in two groups, e.g. an occasional roll might at the same time be a local roll.

All four specifically heraldic groups contain ~ that are true rolls and ~ in book-form. The former are, as the name implies, comparatively long, continuous strips produced by sewing parchment membranes head to foot, and rolling (sometimes on a wooden former) from end to end: the latter may have originally been books into which the information was written, or may consist of true rolls cut into convenient lengths and then bound.

The appearance of ~ varies from unsurpassed works of art, the shields painted and the names and blazons entered in skilfully written script, to mere 'first-draught' rough notes, hastily written in cursive hand. The information contained in the ~ is as varied as is their execution: among them is to be found the highly accurate and totally reliable historical document, and, on the other hand, documents recklessly and inexpertly compiled in which appear indiscriminate records of spurious, fictitious, and attributive arms.

Ordinaries and occasional rolls, which were likely to have been the work of heralds, are among the best; on the other extreme, the general rolls often seem to be mere students' exercise books. Every known ~ has been named and tentatively dated: neither the one nor the other is a simple task

to be undertaken lightly, for the names chosen are intended to give guidance to future scholars. Names are taken from contents, from occasions, from names of first (or of early) owners or editors. Dates can sometimes be checked by reference to the public records, but when this cannot be done dates attributed are always subject to revision. At all periods there were persons having sufficient interest in heraldry to arrange for copies of ~ to be made for inclusion in their own libraries, and it often happens that such copies have been preserved while the original has been lost or destroyed.

Copies of ~ are known as 'versions' of the particular roll, and are separately named, e.g. 'Cooke's', 'Harvey's', 'St George's', and 'Grimaldi's' versions of Glover's Roll (q.v.). Further alterations may take place when a version of a ~ is prepared for publication: a new name may be given, or sections may be omitted. These second dilutions are known as 'editions'.

The British Museum has, in its various manuscript collections, a number of ~ both originals and versions, some of which are

---

397.   Argent, on a saltire gules between four door-staples sable, an escallop Or.
Stoughton.

398.   Argent, two bendlets, the one enhanced the other abaissé azure, debruised of a saltire gules.
Dorien.

399.   Or, on a saltire couped gules five bezants: on a chief of the second a bee volant proper between two roses argent, barbed and seeded proper.
Bruce-Gardner.

400.   Per saltire argent and gules a saltire between four crosses-crosslet all counterchanged.
Twysden, of Roydon Hall.

401.   Azure, a saltire between in chief and in base a mullet and, in the flanks, an increscent and a decrescent all argent.
Earl Haig.

402.   Azure a cross humetty argent surmounted of a saltire couped gules between three mullets of the second.
Murray.

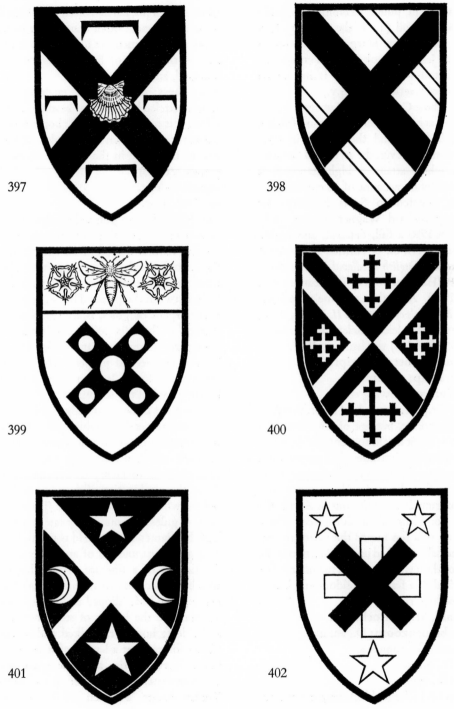

397

398

399

400

401

402

on permanent public exhibition, notably the Dering Roll (q.v.), the Military Roll (q.v.), and Queen Margaret's Version of Thomas Jenyn's Book (q.v.). Perhaps the most famous work among ~ is that named the Roll of Caerlaverock (q.v.).

The whole Continent of Europe is not so rich in ~ as is this country, and most foreign rolls fall far behind the British in their execution; however, the Armorial de Gelre (q.v.), which attains a high standard, is noteworthy on account of its containing a section devoted to Scots heraldry. Sir Anthony Richard Wagner, Garter, published in 1950 a full, detailed, and highly scholarly work on ~ entitled *Aspilogia: A Catalogue of English Medieval Rolls of Arms*, O.U.P. (Harleian Society Publication, No. 100, 1948). A further volume, *Aspilogia: Being Materials of Heraldry. II, Rolls of Arms, Henry III* (Harleian Society Publications, Nos. 113 and 114) was issued in 1967.

Roman alphabet: see **script.**

Roman lamp: see **lamp.**

Rompée: see following entry.

rompu [Fr.] cut; severed; of an ordinary, or of a diminutive, but not of a beast or of a plant: ~ is not an alt. for 'couped' (q.v.); it implies interruption rather than amputation. A chevron ~ has the central section cut and raised so that the underside of the central portion runs as a continuous line with the upper boundary of the side pieces. Three palets ~ of a fess means the palets are cut and the halves pushed up and down to make way for the fess: they are not surmounted or debruised of a fess. It is seldom employed. Alt. spelling 'rompée'.

Romuald, St: see **Roche, St.**

Ronde binnenzoom: D., annulet.

rondjies: Afk., roundles.

rood: D., gules.

rooi: Afk., gules.

rook: [O.E.] a large, black gregarious bird,

Corvus frugilegus, harsh-voiced but of handsome appearance: often confused with the raven (q.v.). Sometimes blazoned as 'crow' and, in the north of England, as 'creyke', 'docken', and 'corbie'.

rook, chess: a chess-piece, tapering to a waist encircled by a ridge or beading, above which it is bifurcated and the horns turned outward; also known as the 'zule'. Equivalent to the castle in the modern Staunton pattern set. (98)

roquet: see **roc.**

ros: Swd., rose.

rose: [O.E.] the English wild-flower u.o.s., depicted with but little conventionalization: the five natural-shaped petals extend from the central circular pod, the points of the segments of the calix extend beyond and from between the petals. The ~, normally either argent or gules, is always blazoned 'barbed' of the calix points, and 'seeded' of the centre: 'barbed vert and seeded Or', or 'barbed and seeded proper', which is the more usual form. It is employed as the brisure (q.v.) of the seventh son.

A ~ gules is the royal badge for England and roses, respectively white and red, were the badges employed by the warring houses of York and Lancaster. The marriage of Eliz. of York to Henry of Lancaster produced the combination of the white and the red ~ which is known as the Tudor ~; i.e. a ~ gules surmounted by one argent of half the diameter if the field is metal, but a ~ argent, surmounted of another gules if the field is of a tincture. 'A ~ slipped', which is a decadent form, has a short stem bearing one leaf; 'slipped and leaved' does not increase the length of stem, but does add a leaf; however, 'stalked and leaved' allows for as great a length of stalk and as many leaves as the available space will accommodate. A ~ crowned, as well as the Yorkist badge 'a ~ en soleil', i.e. sur-

PLATE XV   On a roundel, 9½ inches diameter, within a border of conventionalized
foliage: Dexter, gules, a chevron between three swans argent,
impaling azure, three horse's heads Or.

John Lyte married Edith *Horsey*, 1521

Armorial window formerly in the manor house of Lytes Cory,
Somersetshire.

rounded with rays of the sun, both still in use, are pleasing forms, but the Tudor period produced some ugly and decadent combinations that have not survived.

The cultivated ~, which may be so blazoned (or as 'garden ~' or else '~ of the garden'), is invariably stalked and leaved, and is, by comparison, a very poor thing; it ought never to be, but often is, described as 'proper', or by artist's colours, 'red', 'yellow', and 'white', which reduces a coat of arms to a florist's catalogue, for they are also 'stalked and leaved green'. (416, V)

Rose, Order of the White: (Finland) f. 1919 in five classes. Insignia—*Badge:* between the limbs of a gold-rimmed white cross-paty notched, griffins, segreant, each holding a sword erect; on a blue-rimmed, white central medallion a gold rose. *Star:* silver, having five arms of seven rays each separated by smaller rays in either gold or silver, according to class; and a central medallion, as the badge, but with a broader blue rim inscribed with the motto *Isanmaan Hyvaksi* in letters of gold. *Riband:* dark blue.

Rose Blanche Pursuivant: in 1482 served the English ambassador to France. He brought the news of the death of K. Louis XI.

Rose Herald: seems to have been a sort of temporary name of office employed during the XVI cent., and frequently confused with both Rose Blanche (q.v.) and Rose Rouge (q.v.).

Rose of Lippe, the Venerable Order of the: f. 1869 and granted in the following grades: Grand Cross, Knight Commander, Knight of Honour, Knight, Commander, Officer, and Member. Insignia—*Badge:* a gold-rimmed enamelled Maltese cross, the points gold-ball tipped, the red rose of Lippe in the centre on a white ground surrounded by the motto *Fur Treue und Verdienst* in gold on a blue circlet, which

rests on gold rays; ensigned with a gold crown. *Star:* Grand Crosses—a hexagonal star of silver with badge's central device and motto. Knights of Honour—a larger version of the unensigned badge. Knights—a Maltese cross with the red rose surmounting it centrally. *Riband:* red with gold edges.

Rose Rouge Pursuivant: was a name of office adopted for the creation of extraordinary officers of arms during the XVII cent.; derived from the Lancastrian Red Rose.

Ross, Alexander: Ross Herald, 1558.

Ross, Andrew: Marchmont Herald, 1885. Bute Pursuivant, 1885. Ross Herald 1901.

Ross Herald: a name of office formerly employed in Scotland.

rosso: It., gules.

rostratus: L., beaked.

rot: Ger., gules.

Rothesay Herald: see **Lyon Office.**

rött: Swd., gules.

rotula calcaris: L., mullet.

rouelle spur: see **spur.**

Rouen Roll: (c. 1410) a number of copies of this roll exist and differ so greatly that no opinion can be formed of the appearance of the original: the contents vary between forty-nine shields and 177. The supposition that it was a roll of arms of those engaged in the siege of Rouen is without support.

Rouge Croix Pursuivant: see **College of Arms.**

Rouge Dragon Pursuivant: see **College of Arms.**

round-tops: a mast-head fortification; in heraldic art appearing like a mural crown (q.v.), which was an advantageous position for archers and, later, musketeers.

round-tower: see **tower.**

Rous Roll: (1477–91) also known as 'Warwick Roll'. The work, of which there are two versions, is a history of the earls of Warwick, one in English and the other

Latin, both of them executed by John Rous, Chantry Priest of Guy's Cliffe, Warwickshire. They express Yorkist adherence, but the Latin copy has been toned down, by Rous himself, and given a Lancastrian aspect. This (the Latin version) is on vellum 11 in. by 24 ft 6 in., the contents arranged to read along the strip instead of, as is usual, down it. It contains portraits of kings and other friends and benefactors of Warwick; each is accompanied by a biographical note and either shields or banners of arms with numerous quarters. On the dorse is a self-portrait of Rous and forty-three banners of arms. The English version is similar: the major difference is in the identity of the kings and their consorts portrayed. There are ninety-four banners on the dorse. The spelling 'Rowse' is sometimes adopted.

rowan: a small tree having, in season, clusters of bright red berries; the mountain ash, *Pyrus aucuparia*; employed in heraldry for ca. reasons.

rowel-spur: see **spur.**

Rows Roll: see **Rous Roll.**

Roy d'Armes d'Angleterre: see **College of Arms.**

royal crown: a circlet set with gem-stones, embellished with alternate f.d.l. and crosses paty, heightened with two arches which are depressed in the middle where they are ensigned with a mound supporting a cross paty. The ~ is employed by the Stationery Office as an imprint, is to be found largely in regal heraldry, and also as a charge in the arms of commoners. (229)

Royal Arms, the British: unique in being both arms of dominion and family arms. The sovereign wears the arms undifferenced and all the other members of the Royal Family wear a label (q.v.) of three points throughout (q.v.) argent. This includes princesses. The heir-apparent has the label

plain: every other member of the family has a charge on one or more points to establish individuality. The sovereign's shield is displayed within the Garter, between the familiar supporters; dexter—the lion; sinister—the unicorn. Upon the royal helmets are three crests, England, Scotland, and Northern Ireland being thus represented. The Government for the time being employs ~ as a sort of brand, or mark of authenticity. This is not an infringement because the ~ are national arms, and the Government is but the right hand of the sovereign. Others who enjoy the privilege of displaying the ~ are the purveyors of commodities to the royal household, known in the XIX cent. as 'The Queen's Tradesmen', but now permitted to style themselves 'Royal Warrant Holders', to form an association, and to exercise vigilance that the ~ are not displayed by any manufacturers or vendors who have not been appointed. The holding of the royal warrant has become a guarantee of excellence, reliability, and integrity.

There is a striking difference between the ~ marshalled for display in England and marshalled for display in Scotland. In the former the first and fourth quarters are charged with the lions of England; in the latter, the first and fourth represents Scotland and, further, the supporters change sides: the unicorn stands on the dexter, the lion on the sinister, and each supports a banner of the national patron saint. (St George for England; St Andrew for Scotland.) (403)

royal licence: see **surname.**

Royal Red Cross: f. 27 April 1883 for ladies who render valuable services to nursing. Insignia: first class (Members)—a gold cross paty, convexed and enamelled red, with Faith, Hope, Charity, and 1883, on separate arms of the cross; centrally, a roundel with a head symbolizing nursing; the reverse bears the royal cypher and crown. Second class (Associate)—the cross of frosted silver, with a superimposed cross paty of red enamel bearing centrally the symbolic head; the reverse is as the obverse of the first class, the royal cypher replacing the head. *Riband:* red, blue, red, the red sections half the width of the blue.

Royal Standard: the name by which the sovereign's household banner is known to the public.

Royal Victorian Chain: f. 1902 as a 'pre-eminent mark of the sovereign's esteem and affection. . . .' The Chain is of two gold strands, linked by devices of lotuses, tre-foils, thistles, and roses; centrally is the cypher *VR* in red, ensigned with the Imperial crown, and surrounded by a gold laurel wreath from which hangs the badge of the Royal Victorian Order. The Chain does not confer membership of the Order.

Royal Victorian Order: f. 1896 in five classes. Insignia: Knights and Dame Grand Cross—a mantle of dark-blue silk lined with white silk and edged with red satin, with the star on the left side; a gold collar of octagonal designs, each bearing on blue enamel a gold rose jewelled with a carbuncle, alternating with gold frames containing white enamel letters that together read *Victoria. Brit. Reg. Def. Fid. Ind. Imp*; a silver star of eight points surmounted by the badge of a gold-rimmed enamel Maltese cross with a crimson central medallion bearing the gold monogram of Q. Vict.; the medallion is encircled by a blue riband inscribed *Victoria* and is ensigned with the Imperial crown; the badge is worn from the collar, or from the riband over the right shoulder. Knight Commanders—the badge, as for Grand Crosses but smaller in size, worn round the neck from the riband; a star of silver, being a cross paty with rays

between the arms, surmounted by the badge in frosted silver. The insignia for Dame Commanders is as for Knights, but the badge is worn from a bow on the left shoulder. Commanders have a badge similar to a Knight's, worn round the neck by men and from a bow by ladies. Members of the fourth class have the Commander's badge in smaller size, and Members of the fifth class have the same badge in frosted silver, both worn as medals from the riband; there are silver-gilt, silver, and bronze medals attached to the Order, being circular in shape and having the effigy of the conferring sovereign on the obverse and the royal cypher on a shield, surrounded by a wreath of laurel and below a scroll inscribed *Royal Victoria Medal*, on the reverse. *Riband* (for all classes and medals): dark blue with narrow red, white, red stripes at each edge; when a medal is awarded to a foreigner an additional narrow white stripe is added centrally.

royne: a tool used for cutting inside the staves of a barrel the grooves into which the heads fit. Also termed a drawing-board and a grose. Only in the arms of the Worshipful Company of Coopers.

ruber: L., gules.

ruby: see **segregative blazon**.

rudder: [O.E.] always drawn in association with the stern-post, but not necessarily provided with a tiller; r. and obs.

rue, crown of: a bendlet enarched vent foliated on the upper edge, being the sole change on a field barry of Or and sable, the arms of Saxony, popularized by the marshalling (q.v.) of the achievement of Albert, Prince Consort, but introduced into British heraldry by Q. Adelaide (of Saxe-Meiningen), consort of K. Wm IV. Alt. terms 'bend enarched trefly' and (r) 'crancelin'.

Rue, Order of the Crown of: (Saxony) f. 1807 in one class at Napoleon's instigation.

Insignia—*Badge:* a gold-rimmed white-edged green cross paty notched, with gold rue leaves between the arms; a white central medallion bears the encrowned initials *F.A.* (Frederick Augustus, the first K. of Saxony) in gold. *Star:* a multirayed circular silver plaque, with a gold central medallion bearing the motto *Providentiae Memor* surrounded by green rue leaves. *Riband:* dark green, worn from the right shoulder to left hip.

ruit: Afk. and D., lozenge.

ruitschild: D., lozenge carrying the arms of a lady.

ruitskild: Afk., lozenge carrying the arms of a lady.

runde schieve: Ger., roundel.

rundel: Swd., roundel.

Russell, Archibald George Blomefield: Clarenceux King of Arms, 1954. Former Lancaster Herald, 1922; former Rouge Croix Pursuivant, 1915.

rustning: Swd., armour.

rustre: see **pierced.**

rutad: Swd., lozengy.

Ryley, Francis: said to have held the office of Chester Herald under Cromwell, but there is no documentation.

Ryley, Wm: intruded upon the office of Clarenceux King of Arms, 1659, and Norroy K. of A., 1646, under Cromwell. At the Restoration resumed his office of Lancaster Herald which he had assumed in 1641. Former Bluemantle Pursuivant, 1633; former Rose Rouge Pursuivant, 1630.

---

403. Quarterly I and IV: Gules, three lions passant gardant in pale Or, for England. II: A lion rampant within a double tressure flory-counter-fleury gules, for *Scotland.* III: Azure, a harp Or stringed argent, for Northern Ireland.
Her Majesty Queen Elizabeth II.

404. On an oval cartouche azure, a crosier erect Or debruised of a pallium argent fimbriated of the second charged with four crosses paty and fringed in base sable.
Catholic Diocese of Cardiff.

405. On a lozenge argent, three trefoils slipped, in bend, vert, between two shuttles, bendwise proper.
Harvey, Miss Ida.

406. Quarterly I: Azure a lion rampant argent. II: A chevalier armed cap-a-pie, brandishing a sword in the dexter hand, at full career, argent. III: Or, a peacock in his pride proper. IV: vert, three lizards fesswise in pale Or.
Lanigan-O'Keeffe.

407. On an oval cartouche azure, three torteaux irradiated Or and in chief a hamade voided argent, flory-counter-fleury sable, therein an estoile of seven rays of the field, charged with a fleur-de-lys, also sable.
Catholic Diocese of Brentwood.

408. On a lozenge per chevron azure and argent, in chief a rose of the second barbed and seeded proper between two fleurs-de-lys also argent and, in base, three bay-leaves slipped, erect, vert.
Foulds, Miss Elise Josephine.

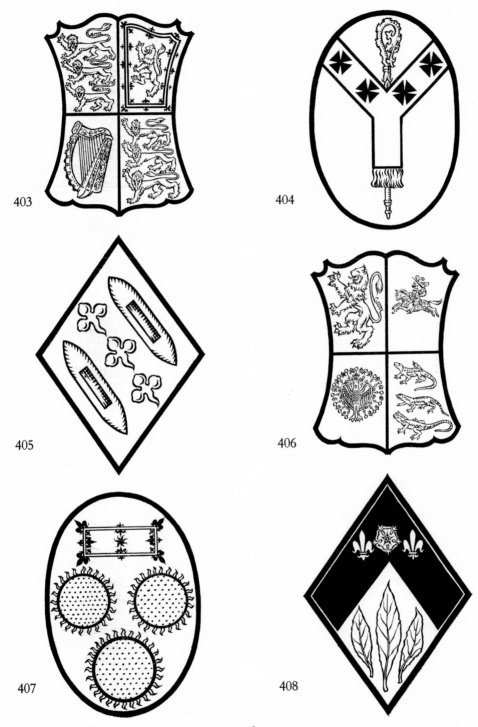

403

404

405

406

407

408

S.: abvn for 'sable' (q.v.) for which 'sa.' is also used.

sa.: see previous entry.

saamgevlegte kepers: Afk., chevrons interlaced.

sable: [Slavonic] black; represented in engraver's cross-hatching by a network of square-mesh created by palewise parallel lines in conjunction with fesswise.

sabre: a cavalry-man's curved sword, sharp on the convex edge and brought to an obtuse point. The ~ is hilted and pommelled as the sword (q.v.) and its normal orientation is fesswise, point to the dexter, cutting edge chiefward; when inverted it is generally also reversed. The ~ may be blazoned as a badelaire (or a badelar), a cutlass, a curtelace, a curtalax, a falchion, or a hanger, but a scimitar is not the same thing: it is curved, has the cutting edge on the convexity, is pommelled and hilted, but terminates in a broad, flat end, and the back (the concavity), is often engrailed. Another special curved sword is the seax: this, too, has a flat broad end, but in the back (the concavity) there is always one deep, large engrailment. The seax was a typically Anglo-Saxon weapon; hence, employed in arms of both Essex and the former County of Middlesex. (52, 100, 439, 440, 442)

sacred and legendary figures: representations of Divine beings are uncommon: the See of Chichester has '.... our Lord ... upon a throne ...', which was formerly blazoned as 'Prester John'; Inverness-shire, a crucifix; the Virgin and child occurs in some civic and other public achievements of arms. The five wounds appear as charges, and arms have been attributed to the Saviour. Angels (q.v.), saints (q.v.) ,and symbolic figures (q.v.) are in a different category. These last are of frequent occurrence in British heraldry.

Sacred Treasure, Order of the: (Japan) f. 1888 in eight classes. Insignia—*Badge:* a cross of twenty white enamel rays arranged in groups of five, representing sword blades; a central blue medallion, surrounded by a gold band, bears an eight-point silver star, representing a mirror, and is surrounded by sixteen linked rubies, representing a collar; the decoration thus symbolizes the three treasures left to his heirs by the first Emperor of Japan, i.e. a mirror, a sword, and a collar of honour. *Star:* as for the badge, but in larger size and with forty rays. *Riband:* light blue with a yellow stripe near each edge.

saddled: see **horse.**

safety lamp: see **Davy lamp.**

saffre: Fr., osprey.

saffron: the heraldic name for the autumn crocus, *Crocus sativus,* the dried stigmas of which produce edible ~, the flavouring essence.

sage: [M.E.] an aromatic herb, *Salvia officinalis,* used in the preparation of food; employed in heraldry for ca. reasons.

Sagittarius: a centaur (q.v.) bending a bow and discharging an arrow.

sagskura: Swd., indented.

sail: [O.E.] a square sail, generally complete with a yardarm; may be reefed. (189, VI)

St Antoine le Petit, church of: a church in Paris bestowed upon the French faculty of heralds, 1407.

St George, Sir Henry[1]: Garter King of Arms, 1644. Former Norroy K. of A., 1635; former Richmond Herald, 1616; former Bluemantle Pursuivant, 1611; former Rose Herald, 1610.

St George, Sir Henry[2]: Garter King of Arms, 1703. Former Clarenceux K. of A., 1679; former Norroy K. of A., 1677; former Richmond Herald, 1660.

St George, Sir Richard: Clarenceux King of Arms, 1623. Former Norroy K. of A.,

1607; former Windsor Herald, 1602; former Berwick Pursuivant, 1602.

St George, Sir Thomas: Garter King of Arms, 1686. Former Norroy K. of A., 1680; former Somerset Herald, 1660.

St George's Roll: (c. 1285), vellum true roll, 9¾ in. by 8 ft 9½ in., painted, 677 shields names over.

St George's Version: see **rolls of arms.**

St Hilda's snakes: see **shell.**

Saint John of Jerusalem, Order of the Hospital of: the Order dates from the XI cent., when the Blessed Gerard assisted the crusaders who laid siege to Jerusalem, wherein he ran a hospice for Christian pilgrims. When the city fell Gerard used his influence to attract support for his venture which grew rapidly in size. He organized its staff into a community of lay brothers for whom he adopted the Augustinian rule, and who became known as the Hospitallers of St John, after St John the Almoner, the patron saint of their church. Later the Order was to adopt St John the Baptist as its patron saint. Pope Paschal II took the Order under his protection in 1113, from which time the possessions and wealth of the Order proliferated. Raymond de Puy, a knight from Provence, succeeded Gerard in 1120, and during his Mastership the Order maintained its hospitallery work but also played a major part in the Second Crusade.

Later Popes added further privileges to the Order, which continued to grow in power, size, and prosperity, so that during the last forty years of the Latin Kingdom of Jerusalem, the Knights of St John and the Templars together provided, almost unaided, for the defence of the Holy Land. The Order suffered severe setbacks at the hands of Saladin late in the XII cent., particularly in 1187 at the battles of Tiberias and Hittin, which saw the virtual destruction of the flower of Christian chivalry. Jerusalem

was lost shortly afterwards. There was to be a remarkable recovery from these setbacks, and the Hospitallers were prominent in the campaign which won back Acre and most of the coastline. Thereafter the Order devoted itself, for a decade or so, to rebuilding its possessions, privileges, and powers, but the ensuing years of the XIII cent. were to prove disastrous. They fought and lost in many places, from Jerusalem to Egypt, and in 1291 Acre was overrun by the Muslims. Only seven knights of St John, including the Master, survived this disaster, and they sought sanctuary in Cyprus.

Guillaume de Villaret became Master in 1296 and, by securing vast gifts from the Pope and other sovereigns, he was able to reorganize and rebuild the Order, turning it into a maritime power. With their new naval force the knights and their mercenaries conquered Rhodes, and by 1308 were finally established on the island as a sovereign power. The Order's fleet played an important part in the defence of Christendom, preventing, for about two centuries, the development of the Ottomans as a first-rate Mediterranean naval power. The island was subjected to frequent attack by the Egyptians and Turks, but it withstood all pressures until 1523 when, after a year of siege, the knights were compelled to submit to Suleiman the Magnificent.

Leaving the island, where despite their great achievements they had never numbered more than 300, the knights moved to Crete and then to Messina, Baia, Viterbo, and Nizza. In 1530 the emperor Charles V gave them the fortress of Tripoli and the island of Malta. In Malta the Order flourished for more than 200 years, and survived many attacks, notably the Great Siege of 1565. Its wealth became vast, its national branches, or langues, grew in size, and Malta was greatly enriched with auberges, churches, a cathedral, chapels, forts, a palace, and a great library. In 1792 the Order lost, as a result of the Revolution, its vast possessions in France, and six years later Napoleon took the island without meeting any resistance.

The Sovereign and Military Order of Malta was homeless, but again its knights survived expulsion and moving from Messina to Catania and Ferrara they eventually established their headquarters in Rome in 1834. They have been there ever since, still recognized as sovereign by over thirty countries with whom ambassadors are exchanged, and the Order is now one of the greatest and richest of the world's charitable organizations, supporting numerous hospitals, homes, child centres, schools, and missions, as well as maintaining its position as a continuing chivalric order of the highest standing.

In addition to the Sovereign Order there are other branches of the Order of St John of Jerusalem. At the Reformation the Master and knights of the Brandenburg Bailiwick of the Order converted to protestantism, although for some time they continued to acknowledge and contribute dues to the grand preceptor of the German langue. Eventually they became a semi-independent order, known as the Venerable Order of St John in Prussia, or the Johanniterorden, enjoying the protection of the Crown of Prussia. The Johanniter Order exists actively today, as do other descendant orders, notably the Venerable Order of St John in the Netherlands, and the Grand Priory in the British Realm of the Most Venerable Order of the Hospital of St John of Jerusalem.

This latter has its roots in the original Order's English Tongue, which until its sequestration by Henry VIII owned at least 1900 properties in England. The Tongue

existed nominally henceforth, until it was actively revived in 1831 at the instigation of a commission of French knights of Malta; subsequently the Order of Malta withdrew recognition of this step, and the Tongue continued autonomously.

It flourished and grew rapidly, and in a comparatively short space of time had recovered its pre-Reformation Priory headquarters at St John's Gate in Clerkenwell, where it now has a rich collection of historic items connected with the Order, and has established itself as a major force in voluntary and charitable work. The Order founded the St John Ambulance Association in 1877, the St John Ambulance Brigade in 1887, and established its ophthalmic hospital in Jerusalem in 1881. A Royal Charter of Incorporation was granted in 1888, and the sovereign has since then been Head of the Grand Priory in the British realm of the Venerable Order of the Hospital of St John of Jerusalem.

Insignia: all the foregoing orders use the Maltese cross with a black riband as their basic insignia; the badges are differenced in various ways, e.g. the Sovereign Order has f.d.l., the Johanniter Order has the Imperial eagle, and the Most Venerable Order has lions and unicorns alternately, between the arms of the cross; the badges are for some grades ensigned with crowns, trophies, or wreaths; the star is a large white Maltese cross, sometimes bearing devices to show a particular grade of knighthood; e.g. the Most Venerable Order permits the plain cross for Knights of Justice, whereas Knights of Grace have lions and unicorns between the arms of the cross. The Sovereign Order also confers a Cross of Merit (which does not grant membership of the Order), in five classes: Grand Cross, Grand Officer, Commander, Officer, and Cross. Insignia—*Badge:* a gold-edged white cross moline, with a red central medallion bearing a Maltese cross and surrounded by the legend, in gold on white, *Mil. Ordo Equitum Melit. Bene Merenti*, the whole ensigned with a gold crown; swords can be placed in saltire behind the cross to denote the military division. *Star:* of eight points, multirayed and facetted, surmounted by the ensigned badge. *Riband:* white with broad red stripes near the edges, or red with white stripes.

St Michael King of Arms: a complimentary distinction bestowed upon a member of the Order of St Michael and St George (q.v.).

Saints[1] : not commonly employed in British heraldry as ca. devices for families of that particular surname as is customary on the Continent, but they are to be found in public arms, generally referring to the patron saint of municipality or of a livery company.

Saints[2] : see under various names—**Andrew, George**, etc.

Saints, Arms of: see **attribution, arms of.**

saker: a falcon (q.v.).

salade: see **sallet.**

salamander: [Gk] in heraldry the reference is always to the fictitious lizard that lived in fire, and it is so blazoned, i.e. 'a ~ in the fire' or '~ in flames of fire proper'. Generally argent or Or, and occasionally vert. A symbol of endurance, hence, sometimes allusive (q.v.). It is not a representation of the amphibious lizard family Salamandridae (see **newt**). (274)

salient: [L] lit. leaping upon, attacking; hence, of a beast standing firmly on both hind-paws (or hooves) the fore-limbs raised (the dexter very slightly higher for visibility), and the body inclined upward at about 45°. Any beast depicted in this naturalistic attitude may be described as ~, but some have special terms. (50)

salions: L., salient.

Salisbury Herald: in the service of the Earl of Salisbury (c. 1375). He was formerly Pisore Pursuivant (also spelt 'Pisow' and 'Pysore') as well as Griffin Pursuivant (q.v.) to the same master, William de Montague.

Salisbury Roll: (c. 1460) originally a vellum true roll, but cut and bound in book form having fifty pages $10\frac{1}{2}$ in. by 1 ft $1\frac{1}{4}$ in., painted with figures of earls of Salisbury generally accompanied by their wives. The masculine costume is armour covered by an emblazoned tabard: some wear their helmets complete with the crest, others have it beside them, nearly all hold a lance from which floatant is a banner of their arms. The ladies, like those portrayed in brasses (q.v.), wear an armorial mantle of the marital achievement (q.v.). Inscriptions reveal names and give brief genealogical notes. The ~ is part VI of Writhe's Garter Book (q.v.).

salix: [M.E.] a term used to describe the willow-tree, *Salix viminalis.*

sallet: [L.] a light-weight, close-fitting, open helmet, having a hemispherical crown and no crest; extended to an outward-curving neck-guard behind. Also termed 'salade' and 'morion'. (247)

salmon: [L.] a large sea-fish that ascends rivers in the breeding season, *Salmo salar.* His objective progress up-stream secures him a place in ca. heraldry, being so used in arms of families named Way. In folk-lore he is connected with the story of a finger-ring the loss of which endangered a lady's life, hence, he is often depicted holding in the mouth a gem-ring (q.v.). ~, particularly when holding a gem-ring, may be embowed (q.v.).

salmon-fly: neither the one nor the other, but a type of dressed fish-hook; among the prosaic objects of municipal heraldry.

saltant: r. obs. term supposed to be descriptive of small animals, as the coney (q.v.),the rat, etc., when crouched to spring.

saltire: [L. via O.E.] the fusion of a bend (q.v.) and a bend sinister giving an X-shaped cross: 'azure a saltire argent' is the cross of St Andrew and the national cross of Scotland: 'argent a saltire gules' is termed 'the cross of St Patrick' and is the national cross of Ireland; however, St P. was not a martyr and had no cross—it is actually that of the Fitzgeralds. These two, counterchanged (q.v.) quarterly and surmounted (q.v.) by the cross of St George (q.v.) constitute the Union Jack (q.v.) of Gt Britain. (400, 436)

saltire, in: of two objects (say) swords (q.v.) one in bend (q.v.) and one in bend sinister, thus occupying the position of and assuming the form of a cross ∼. (The object in bend surmounts (q.v.) that in bend sinister u.o.s.). Of a number of objects, five or nine, placed upon the shield in the position of a ∼.

saltirewise: orientated diagonally as a saltire (q.v.). What appears to be a saltire couped

and the ends of the limbs decorated is, in fact, a cross of that particular kind, say flory, etc., ∼.

salts: vessels for containing table-salt; of a somewhat ponderous and ornate nature, being depicted rather like covered cups (q.v.). The salt is sometimes represented as pouring out of apertures in the sides of the container. Often blazoned as 'sprinkling salts'. (163)

salus: see **pentagram.**

Samson, Alfred George Law: Herald-painter to the Lyon Court, 1927.

Sand-glass: see **hour-glass.**

San Marino, Equestrian Order of: f. 1859 in five class. Insignia—*Badge:* white-enamelled cross, each arm terminated by a gold ball and separated by a gold tower; a central medallion depicts San Marino, and the badge is ensigned by a crown. *Star:* the cross surmounting a laurel wreath with a medallion inscribed *Relinquo vos liberos ab utroque homine,* the whole surmounting an eight-point silver star. *Riband:* seven alternate stripes of blue and white.

---

409. Gules, three church-spires argent, each terminating in a ball and cross-paty Or. *Dakeham.*

410. Gules, a bridge of one arch heightened with three towers and, in chief, a fleur-de-lys Or between two roses argent: in base, barry-wavy of four of the last and azure and thereon three ships, each of one mast the sail furled sable. *Corporation of the City of Cambridge.*

411. Gules, upon the battlements of a tower issuant in base, a lion passant gardant Or, armed and langued azure. *Government of Singapore.*

412. Argent, masoned sable: on a chief azure a demi-lion issuant Or. *Beaw, Wm* (Bishop of Llandaff, 1679–1706).

413. Gules, three arches, two in chief and, in base, one double, argent; the imposts Or. *Arches.*

414. Quarterly I and IV: Gules, a castle triple-towered Or, for *Castile*: II and III, Argent, a lion rampant gules, for *Leon*. *Castile and Leon.*

409

410

411

412

413

414

Sandford, Francis: Lancaster Herald, 1675. Former Rouge Dragon Pursuivant, 1661.

sammanställd: Swd., impaled.

sanglier: see **boar**.

sanguine: [M.E.] murrey, or mulberry colour; one of the two stainand (q.v.) colours.

sans chain: see **portcullis**.

sans nombre: of charges by which a field is rendered semé (q.v.).

sapphire: see **segregative blazon**.

Saracen: [Gk] assumed to be of Caucasian race but black haired (and bearded): he is wreathed about the temples and habited. Demi-~ and ~ heads, when they appear, are coupéd (q.v.); ~ may act as supporters (q.v.), but also appear among crests (q.v.) and charges.

saracinesca: It., portcullis.

sarcelled: [Fr.] of a cross moline (q.v.) voided (q.v.) throughout (q.v.); of any figure made to conform to a circle.

sardonyx: obs. alt. for 'sanguine' (q.v.).

Saturn: see **segregative blazon**.

satyr: [Gk] a man to the waist and a goat downward. The ~ should carry a pair of short, curved horns, but these are sometimes omitted: a ~ head without them might be that of a savage (q.v.).

satyral: [Gk] an heraldic form of satyr, being a lion with the bald head of an old man (q.v.) to which a pair of short, curved horns are added.

säule: Ger., column.

saum: Ger., bordure.

sautoir: Fr., saltire.

Sava, Order of St: (Serbia and Jugoslavia) f. 1883 in five classes. Insignia—*Badge:* a gold-rimmed, blue-edged Maltese cross pommetty; between each arm is a crowned double-headed **eagle in gold**, surmounted by a white cross; a white central medallion depicts St Sava, and is surrounded by a blue band bearing a Cyrillic inscription; the

badge is ensigned with a gold crown. *Star:* the unensigned badge surmounting a silver star of eight points. *Riband:* white, a blue stripe near each edge.

savage: [L.] assumed to be of Caucasian race, brown haired (and bearded): he is naked, wreathed about the loins and temples, and generally supports a club, the position of which will be stated: his normal function is that of acting as a supporter (q.v.)

Savoy, knot of: see **knowed**.

saw: [O.E.] the general name for cutting tools consisting, in the main, of a strip of steel filed into triangular teeth along one edge and provided with a handle. There is a very wide variety of styles, and a ~ is generally blazoned by its defining name as, e.g., a hand ~, a frame ~, a tenon ~, a cross-cut ~. Although the ~ is often merely a prosaic object (q.v.) appearing in the arms of an industrial organization, it has also a wider application: it might be symbolic of a nation's productivity, as, e.g., the provision of timber; it might be allusive or it might be ca. (It is not unknown for it to be a creature of error, the ~ in the arms having been originally a sword.)

Sawers, James: Carrick Pursuivant, 1650.

Sawers, John[1]: Herald-painter to the Lyon Court, 1599.

Sawers, John[2]: Snowdoun Herald, 1643. Carrick Pursuivant, 1637. Herald-painter, 1638.

Saxon: always blond; generally habited in a long-robe; most likely to do duty among supporters (q.v.); seldom bearded.

Saxon crown: a plain gold circlet heightened with four points terminating in trefoils. These are attached to the outer surface of the circlet, and are cloué. Three points only appear in drawing: one in the centre, and one at each side, the latter being in profile. (11)

sbarra: It., bend sinister.

scabbard, sword in: see **sword**.

scaglione: It., chevron.

scaled: of a dolphin (q.v.), fish or composite creature that is in part piscine, when the dorsal scales are to be of a colour differing from that of the creature itself.

scales: see **hand-balance.**

Scales Pursuivant: maintained by the Earl Rivers who was also Lord Scales in right of his wife. ~ was taken prisoner in 1475 and his papers read by K. Louis XI, who was no respecter of the rules of chivalry.

scaling-ladder: a short length of ladder having, on the back of each string, a stout hook. ~ generally appear in bend, without support, but may be 'against a wall' or 'against a tower'. (466)

scallop: a truncated form of 'escallop' (q.v.).

scaly lizard: see **lizard.**

scanalato: It., invected.

scarpe: [O.F.] first diminutive (q.v.) of the bend sinister (q.v.) being half the width of the parent. The term is obs.

scent, a hound on: of a dog trippant with head lowered and nose to the ground.

schabracke: Ger., comparisoned.

schackrutad: Swd., chequy.

schelp: D., escallop.

schildfuss: Ger., base.

schildhalter: Ger., supporters.

schildhaupt: Ger., chief.

schildhoofd: D., chief.

schildhouders: D., supporters.

schildpaal: D., quintain.

schildrand: Ger., bordure.

schlange: Ger., serpent.

schlüsselkreuz: Ger., cross of Toulouse.

scholar's cap: the square, tasselled cap as worn at the universities; a college-cap, academic cap, or trencher cap.

schooner: see **ship.**

Schoriswood, George: see **Hailes Pursuivant, Extraordinary.**

schotsche degen: D., claymore.

schragbalken: Ger., bend.

schragfaden: Ger., baston.

schräggeteilt: Ger., per bend.

schräggeviert: Ger., per saltire.

schräggitter: Ger., fretty.

schrägleiste: Ger., bendlet.

schräglinksbalken: Ger., bend sinister.

schraglinksfaden: Ger., baston sinister.

schräglinksgeteilt: Ger., per bend sinister.

schreitender: Ger., passant.

schuinbalk: D., bend.

schuinkruis gevierendeeld: D., per saltire.

schuinstreep: D., riband.

schwarz: Ger., sable.

schwebend: Ger., couped.

schwenkel: a long triangular tail extending from the fly (q.v.) at, and in line with, the head of a banner; employed in continental heraldry.

scimitar: see **sabre.**

scimitarra: It., scimitar.

scintillant: of a firebrand (q.v.), or other burning object, when it is to be depicted emitting sparks; hence r.

scissors: uncommon in British heraldry but having currency on the Continent.

sconce: earthworks, entrenchments, fortifications; employed only for ca. reasons.

scorciato: It., couped.

scorpion: an arachnid related to the spider, of the genus *Scorpio*. Having eight legs and a pair of powerful claws it has the appearance of a lobster (q.v.). Its sting (situated in the tail) is not fatal but is most painful. It is usually orientated with the claws chiefward.

Scotch-spur: see **spur.**

Scott-Gatty: see **Gatty, Sir Alfred.**

scourge: [M.E.] depicted as a short, stocky rod having attached to the top end three tails, or lashes, each of which is sometimes tied with three knots; representing the whip (by which name it may be blazoned) whereby certain saints and martyrs suffered, and which was self-inflicted by the flagellants. (348)

scribed: see **tilting-shield.**

Scrimgeour of Glaster, John: Snowdown Herald, 1511. Ormonde Pursuivant, 1501.

scrip, a palmer's: see **palmer's staff.**

script: letters of more than one alphabet have, from an early period, been introduced into arms for their symbolic value: Latin, Greek, and Hebrew are time-honoured, and Arabic is not far behind. Later, the inclusion of script in arms began to trespass upon the function of symbolism, it requiring but little knowledge and no imagination to make a plain statement of merit, e.g. '. . . . and on a fess . . . inscribed in Roman capital text letters gold, the word WATERLOO'. This was a form of decadence that marred the heraldic compositions of the XIX cent. and, in the XX cent. by the wider distribution of armorial bearings to bodies corporate being limited companies, came near to reducing heraldry to brands, imprints, or trade marks. The shadow of impending disaster fell darkly over the armorial landscape; hence, the authorities in England decided to resist and restrict the inclusion of text letters in arms; in Scotland it was prohibited. (128, 129, 131)

scrog: [M.E.] sometimes used in Scottish blazon for the branch of a tree.

Scrope v. Carminow: Between 1375 and 1380 Lord Scrope, returning from an overseas campaign, met on the vessel a Cornishman named Carminow bearing arms 'azure a bend Or' which he, Scrope, claimed as his arms. A committee of knights was set up to arbitrate the matter which they most conscientiously did. Antiquity of usage being the major claim to arms, they took the word of honour of each claimant. Scrope claimed 'time out of mind' which then meant back as far as the Norman Invasion. Carminow claimed that he inherited his arms from ancestors who receive them by gift from none other than King Arthur. The knights,

in a quandary, may have considered that Cornwall was a foreign country, and that under different allegiance the same arms might be legitimately borne, for they declared both claimants fully entitled to 'azure a bend Or'. Both families continued the use until Carminow became extinct in the XIX cent. This arbitration may have had some effect on Scrope's reaction towards Grosvenor (see following entry).

Scrope v. Grosvenor: legal proceedings instituted in August 1385 by Sir Richard, first Baron Scrope of Bolton, against Sir Robert Grosvenor of Cheshire, to prohibit the use by the latter of armorial bearings, namely 'azure a bend Or', claimed by the former as his exclusive property. The Court of Chivalry (q.v.), then the Military Court of the Constable and Earl Marshal, was the appropriate body to hear and determine this cause, and Thomas, Duke of Gloucester, Constable of England and President of the Court, gave orders for depositions to be taken. This gathering of evidence continued over four years through special commissions set up severally at York, Chester, Leicester, Nottingham, Tiverton, Plymouth, and Westminster. The evidence on each side was about equal in quantity and in importance, and, indeed, both contending parties bore the device in right of ancestors, and neither could in justice be declared an infringement of the other; however, the spirit of the times was to bring all armorial bearings under control, and considerations other than antiquity of usage seem to have influenced the judgement.

Lord Scrope and his armorial achievement were well known abroad; he had been Lord Treasurer of England, he was still Chancellor, and Steward of the King's Household; any change in his arms was going to be troublesome, and even embarrassing; but Grosvenor was quite unknown even a few miles beyond his own estate, and a change would thus involve much less trouble and no international complications.

Thomas, Duke of Gloucester's judgement was, therefore, admirably diplomatic: 'azure a bend Or' to Scrope, and the same, within a 'plain bordure argent', to Grosvenor. The judgement admits that both men have an equal right to the arms, and simply differences (q.v.) the one from the other.

Grosvenor was not satisfied and appealed against the Constable's decision. There was but one court of appeal, namely the king in person, before whom on 27 May 1390 the matter was reopened. The final judgement in the matter was that a plain bordure argent was not a sufficient difference for a stranger in blood; hence, Grosvenor was prohibited from further use of 'azure a bend Or'. In its place he substituted 'azure a garb Or', which today will be seen distinguishing the arms of the Duke of Westminster, head of the House of Grosvenor.

scruttle: see **vannet**.

scudo: It., shield.

scudo femminile: It., lozenge when carrying the arms of a lady.

scutulum: L., inescutcheon.

scutum: L., escutcheon.

scythe: [O.E.] a long, narrow, curved blade pivoted at the end of a shaft having two cross-handles; operated by a long, swinging stroke that mows standing crops and all that grows among them; a tool that cuts down indiscriminately; hence, symbolic in the hands of Father Time and of Death. The shaft, named the snead, is employed as a ca. device, and is commonly mis-spelt 'sned', which is a different word meaning to lop branches or prune trees. (302)

sea pie: see **bustard**.

sea-bull: r. composite fictitious beast.

sea-dog: a composite fictitious beast, basically the talbot (q.v.) but provided with webbed feet, a pronounced dorsal fin from neck to tail which latter, carried erect is paddle-shaped like that of the beaver. There is a belief that a ~ represents the otter.

sea-dragon: a composite fictitious beast having the fore-quarters and membraneous wings of a dragon (q.v.) conjoined to the hind-part of a fish.

sea-griffin: a composite fictitious creature; eagle (with ears) to the waist and the hind-part fish; employed only in continental heraldry. See also **griffin**.

sea-horse: a composite fictitious beast having the head, shoulders, and breast of a horse, the fore-limbs terminating in webbed feet, and from the waist downward the form of a fish. The ~ may be either crined (q.v.) of his mane, or provided with a dorsal fin commencing between the ears when he is blazoned as 'finned'. Generally semi-erect, facing dexter, resting on its curled tail and blazoned sejant.

sea-lion: a composite fictitious beast having the upper part (except for webbed, water-bird-like feet in place of fore-paws) the form of a lion and from the waist downward the shape of a fish, and terminating in dolphin-like flukes. Facing dexter with tail curled, his normal attitude, he is blazoned sejant (q.v.); either extended or embowed (q.v.) in fess (q.v.) he is naiant (q.v.); and when represented as emerging from water, assurgeant. Always 'crined' (q.v.)—never 'finned'. Alt. title 'morse'. (277)

sea-pellok: alt. term for a dolphin, but only in Scottish blazon.

sea-stag: a composite fictitious beast, stag to the waist and fish downward, having webbed feet in place of hooves; based on the sea-lion (q.v.).

sea-urchin: a globe-fish having erectile spines; hence, also called sea-hedgehog.

seal¹: [L.] an impression of a die upon a disc of heated wax either to authenticate or secure a document. A ∼, being representative of a person, was normally emblazoned with arms; hence, they are a valuable source of information on old heraldry. (435)

seal²: [O.E.] the marine mammal, *Phoca vitulina*, represented in British heraldry by its head, either couped (q.v.) or erased (q.v.), and its paw. The latter, drawn like a hand having four fingers, is clearly not a representation of the ∼ flipper, nor is it strictly a paw. It is believed to have originated in the misnaming of a mole's 'hand', there being a remote connection in the uses and appearance of seal's-skin and mole's-skin. The whole beast is employed in continental arms.

seal³: the clasp of a book (q.v.).

seal's head: see **seal²**.

seal's paw: see **seal²**.

seasons, blazon by: see **segregative blazon.**

seax: see **sabre.**

second son, mark of difference of: see **brisure.**

Secret Pursuivant: maintained by Sir John Fastalf, 1425; also spelt 'Segret'.

sedens: L., sejant.

seeadler: Ger., osprey.

seeblatter: a conventionalized water-plant leaf, heart-shape, pointed baseward, and having a cruciform incision at the point where the stalk would normally be attached. 'Argent, three seeblatter gules, for Brena' was the fourteenth quarter in the premarital achievement of Prince Albert of Saxe-Coburg and Gotha, consort of Q. Vic.

seeded: specifically having reference to the central disc of an heraldic rose (q.v.) but applicable to any flower or any plant when the area of the seed-pod is to differ in colour from the petals. (180, 391, 408, V)

Seel, Henry Harrington Molyneux: Richmond Herald, 1873. Former Bluemantle Pursuivant, 1864.

seelöwe: Ger., sea-lion.

Segar, Sir Wm: Garter King of Arms, 1607. Former Norroy K. of A., 1602; former Somerset Herald, 1589; former Portcullis Pursuivant, 1585.

Segar Roll, the Second: (c. 1460) a general

---

415. Gules, a fret argent.
      Fleming of Rydal.

416. Argent, a shakefork sable, and in chief a rose gules barbed and seeded proper.
      Cunninghame of Brownhill.

417. Pean, a pile lozengy argent and azure issuant in base ensigned with a mullet of six points Or between two lowes of flame gules: on a chief vert, seven piles of the fourth.
      Field.

418. Azure, nine billets argent, four, three, and two within a bordure gules.
      Bess.

419. Per fess argent and ermine, three piles, one issuant in chief and two in base, sable.
      Hulse.

420. Or, three piles sable each charged with a fountain: in base, four barrulets wavy alternately gules and vert.
      Caldwell.

415

416

417

418

419

420

roll (q.v.) in book form painted with 150 named shields.

Segar's Roll: (c. 1282), vellum true roll 6½ in. by 9 ft 4¾ in., painted, 212 shields with names over.

segreant: see **griffin**.

segregative blazon: a form of blazon whereby royalty, nobility, and commoners were segregated, introduced in the mid XV cent. by Sicily Herald; remained in use until early in the XVII cent. Blazon by colours, i.e. metal and tinctures, as now normally employed, was reserved to describe the arms of knights and gentlemen: the arms of nobility were blazoned by the names of gem-stones, and those of royalty by the names of planets, the equivalents being as hereunder:

Planets	Gems	Colours
Sol (the sun)	topaz	Or
Luna (the moon)	pearl	argent
Mars	ruby	gules
Jupiter	sapphire	azure
Saturn	diamond	sable
Venus	emerald	vert
Mercury	opal	purpure

Such segregation was both useful and reasonable, and the foregoing three groups were, on occasions, employed by officers of arms. There grew up, however, numerous travesties, quite pointless and cryptic, that were not extensively used. Among these were blazon by virtues, signs of the Zodiac, months, days of the week, ages, flowers, seasons, elements, complexions, and Arabic numerals.

Segret Pursuivant: see **Secret, Pursuivant**.

sehne: Ger., stringed.

seize-quartiers: [Fr.] lit. sixteen quarters; applied to a form of genealogical record in which the subject, his two parents, four grandparents, eight great-grandparents and sixteen great-great-grandparents are shown. At first acquaintance this seems to be quite easy, but it is not. The average person would experience severe difficulty in providing the names only, without dates and the other usual items of information, for even eight great-grandparents.

A ~ chart may vary from a rough note on scrap paper to a highly finished work of art on vellum. When skilfully laid out, the script in more than one colour consisting of an expertly executed pen-letter, and coats of arms painted beside each name, a ~ chart is, indeed, a work of art. A complete chart with adequate information on each person up to the great-great-grandparents is not commonly achieved, and for each of the sixteen names to be accompanied by a coat of arms is rare indeed. When it is it has no effect whatever on the achievement of the subject; he does not receive, as a sort of prize, a marshalling quarterly of sixteen. In British heraldry addition of quarters is influenced by heiresses (q.v.); on the Continent, particularly in central Europe, overcrowded shields are much admired. The Lyon Office (q.v.) keeps a register of ~, called 'birth-brieves', and produces very finely executed documents.

sejant: [O.F.] of a beast squatting on its haunches, its back inclined forward, its forelegs upright. ~-erect, the back is vertical, the fore-limbs held up as when rampant (q.v.). ~-erect-affrontée, implies that the beast faces out of the shield. (56)

sekelmaan: Afk., crescent.

sembrado: Sp., semé.

semé: [Fr.] seeded; hence, of a field covered from chief to base with repetitions of a charge displayed in barwise rows, those in each succeeding row being disposed under the spaces between those in the preceeding row. The number of such charges is never stated in blazon, but the rule is there shall appear too many to count at a glance, but not so many that they will become too small for instant recognition, nor so close together that they become visually inseparable. The charges may all be whole, or those coming to the edge of the shield may be cut, e.g. in contact with the line in chief (issuant, as it were), there may appear the lower half only of the charges: the charges on the ends of rows will be cut palewise, and in base point will appear the upper-half only. It seems that ~ of charges cut by the edge of the shield is older than ~ of whole charges; hence, the latter may be a debased form, or it may be only a style of drawing.

There are a number of alt. methods of expressing ~, and attempts have been made in the past to show that true ~ is the style with charges cut and that one or another of the alt. terms should be used to describe the whole charge style. Alt. terms are 'powdered with', 'aspersed', 'gerated', and 'sans nombre'. Although there is no prohibition against any particular figure making a field ~, custom and usage have curtailed the selection, and many of the accepted forms either shorten the title of the charge; e.g. 'semé-de-lys', not '~ of fleurs-de-lys', or have a one-word title of their own. In early heraldry fields were often aspersed to create a difference (q.v.). (67, 79, III, VIII, XIII)

seminato: It., semé.

senestre: Fr., sinister.

senestrochère: Fr., sinister arm.

sengreen: an evergreen rock-plant in a compact circle of thick, moist leaves which, when overcrowded, throws up a stout stem crowned with a pink flower, the seeds from which become wind borne; the *Sempervivum tectorum*, also called 'houseleek', and used as a symbol of immortality in the arms of Dr Caius (grant 1560 by Laurence Dalton, Norroy). Perpetuated

in the impaled (q.v.) achievement of Gonville and Caius College, Cambridge.

Sennachie, the High: see **Lyon King of Arms.**

senois: an obs. and ill-defined colour in the borderland between gold and red.

sephium: a name for the chrysanthemum, a form of cultivated ox-eye daisy. In British heraldry it is drawn without conventionalization, but as the national mon (q.v.) of Japan, it is highly formal.

sepulchral brasses: see **brasses, monumental.**

seraph: see **cherub.**

Seraphim, Order of the: (Sweden) possibly f. c. 1260 by K. Magnus I; reactivated by K. Frederick I in 1748 in one class. Insignia—*Collar:* linked gold seraphim heads alternating with blue enamel patriarchal crosses. *Badge:* a gold-rimmed Maltese cross pommetty, with gold seraphim heads between the arms; a blue central medallion bears the letters *I.H.S.* between three crowns, a Latin cross rising from the cross-bar of the *H. Star:* the unensigned badge in silver throughout, save for the medallion. *Riband:* light blue.

serise: see **seruse.**

serpent: [L.] a generic term for any snake; 'knowed' (q.v.), 'glissant', (q.v.) 'ondoyant' (q.v.), and 'involved' (q.v.) are its usual attitudes. (75)

Serreshall Pursuivant: maintained in the service of Sir Richard Monfort, Deputy Lieutenant of Calais (c. 1500).

seruse: r. obs. alt. for a roundel gules; also spelt 'cerise' and 'serise'.

Seton, Sir Alexander Hay: Carrick Pursuivant, 1935.

seventh son, mark of difference of: see **brisure.**

sexfoil: see **trefoil.**

shackbolt: see **fetterlock.**

shacklebolt: see **fetterlock.**

shading: objects appearing on the armorial field have substance and will cast a shadow: the heraldic light falls from dexter-chief, bendwise, and shadows are cast to the sinister and baseward. Great discretion is required in applying ∼; too much is disastrous: ordinaries and charges are given the appearance of floating in space above the shield and casting shadows down onto it. No ∼ is far better than too much. There are, however, some situations in which ∼ helps greatly, e.g. a cross voided of the field, and a cross charged with another humetty of the field cannot be distinguished one from another without ∼. There are a few figures that must not be ∼, e.g. a fountain (q.v.) and a bezant (q.v.).

shaft: [M.E.] lit. a missile; hence, the barrel of a thunderbolt (q.v.) which may be described as 'shafted'.

shag: [dial.] one of the various dialectal names applied to the cormorant, and employed for ca. reasons. The most important is 'liver-bird' (q.v.).

shakefork: an object the shape of a capital Roman text-letter Y, couped per pale and per fess at each extremity making a point of 90° (as cross urdy (q.v.)), er. described as a pall (q.v.) couped, is in fact, the representation of a primitive agricultural implement; a thresher's fork for removing the straw from the grain. In continental heraldry precisely the same drawing represents a vine-prop and is so blazoned. ∼ debruises (q.v.) the shield of all branches of the House of Cunningham, and it appears to be exclusive to that family. Sometimes ∼ is described as a sub-ordinary, and is given the title of a 'pairle'. (416)

shamrock: [Gael.] the royal badge for Northern Ireland; a form of clover having a trifoliate leaf. Adopted, according to legend, as the national emblem of Ireland because it was used by St Patrick to illus-

trate the Trinitarian idea; *Trifolium minus.* Seldom blazoned as ∼, it makes, however, many appearances in arms, not only in Ireland, under the name 'trefoil' (q.v.).

shank: see **beam.**

shank-bone: see **leg-bone.**

shark: a gigantic fish, *Selachii*; also blazoned 'dog-fish'; generally in the act of 'swallowing a man' or 'a Negro'.

shave, currier's: a long knife with a handle at each end, used for dressing leather. It figures in the achievement of the Worshipful Company of Curriers.

shawm: alt. term for a cymbal (q.v.); also employed in ca. heraldry and more likely to be found in continental than in British arms.

sheaf: [Teut.] a unit consisting of three objects; 'a sheaf of arrows', one erect debruising (q.v.) two in saltire (q.v.); a 'sheaf of holly', three holly-leaves bound together by their stems. Holly-leaves also appear singly and in pairs. (223) (For 'sheaf of grain' see **garb.**)

shears: weaver's shears, not sheep shears, are intended; sometimes blazoned 'weaver's ∼'. Two oblong blades facing inward attached to the ends of rods which extend out of a semicircular spring. The only difference observable is that modern sheep shears have triangular blades. (305)

sheldrake: see **shoveller.**

shell: in addition to the shells of the escallop (q.v.) and of the whelk (q.v.), each blazoned by name, 'a ∼' refers to a conventionalized representation of the fossil-ammonite, a mineralized prehistoric cephalopod, abundant in the chalk in the vicinity of Whitby. They are also blazoned as 'snakestones' and as 'St Hilda's snakes'; occasionally as 'coiled snakes'.

Shepherd, Arthur: Rouge Dragon Pursuivant, 1721. Former Blanche Lion Pursuivant, 1720.

Sheborne Missal Shields: (c. 1400) a roll of arms illustrating a missal written by John Whas and illuminated by John Siferwast for the Abbey of Sherborne, Dorset. Shields with names on scrolls include English sovereigns, earls, and lords; among unnamed shields are those of Sherborne Abbey itself, and of Milton Abbey.

shepherd's pipes: see **clarion.**

Sherriff, Thomas: Rouge Dragon Pursuivant, 1758.

shin-bone: the tibia; depicted naturalistically. (299)

ship: [O.E.] generally defined in the blazon; 'a ~ in full sail proper' refers to a clipper, and though heraldry is not the place for marine architecture, some measure of accuracy is desirable. There should be a bowsprit and not less than three tri-sails set thereon; there should be three masts each having not less than four square-sails braced to the yardarms and pulling. If ensigns and pennons are flotant, then the ensign, a rectangular flag, will be at the main mast head, the pennons one each on fore and mizzen masts.

Since the ~ will be making headway to the dexter u.o.s., the ensign and pennons will be flotant to the dexter because the wind (in spite of sailor's yarns) does not blow in two directions at once. The term '~' has become generic and may be used when some other rig is intended, e.g. a barque which is square-rigged forward and on the main mast, but fore and aft on the mizzen; or a brigantine, two-masted, square-rigged on the fore, and schooner-rigged aft. The schooner itself, and other fore-and-aft rigs, appear. It is often some specific vessel that is intended, the achievement being allusive—and this the blazon will make clear. Ensigns and pennons are often charged, and sails may be, though it is uncommon when a ~ represents a merchantman. Battleships are sometimes blazoned by name, and are drawn with high freeboard to accommodate three decks. Either a merchantman or a man-o'-war may be depicted with square gun-ports closed. (334, VI). (See also **shrouded.**)

ship's lamp, see **lamp.**

Shirley's Roll: (XV cent.) paper book of seventy leaves $5\frac{1}{2}$ by $6\frac{1}{2}$ in., containing shields and crests of a general nature, some painted and others in trick (q.v.). There are nineteen drawings each occupying a page of shields, helmets, crests, and mantling of monarchs, with names and blazons written in red ink.

shoe: the heraldic ~, also blazoned 'brogue', is drawn as an ankle-boot opening at the side, the toe brought to a long, upward-inclining point.

shovel: see **spade.**

shoveller: [O.E.] in modern heraldry applied indiscriminately to any duck, but originally only to the spoonbill, *Platalea leucorodia*; alt. spelling 'shovelard', from which ~ is derived. The duck is also blazoned specifically as 'a mallard' or 'a sheldrake', generally for ca. reasons.

Shrewsbury Herald: a name of office applied, with the ascent of K. Hen. IV, to the officer of arms in the service of Dunbar, Scots Earl of March (1403). In 1442 John Talbot, Earl of Shrewsbury, maintained an officer of arms who may have been known as ~ as well as Talbot Herald.

shrouded: a term often added, for no reason other than habit, to the blazon of a clipper ship (q.v.). 'A ship of three masts in full-sail ~.' Lit. shrouds are the upper and lower standing rigging, always in pairs, collared to the mast-heads, the ends dead-eyed and lanyarded to the chain-plates. Their purpose is to provide lateral support for the masts; hence, it follows that if a ship were not ~ it would not be rigged and could not be 'in full sail'. It must, however, be allowed that the ratlines, the short lengths of rope that are clove-hitched from one leg of the shrouds to the other, forming a rope-ladder abaft the mast, may be intended when the word ~ is used, but if so, the draughtsmen ignore the instruction, and, in any case, such minute detail is conspicuously bad heraldry.

It is safe to assert that young officers of arms adding ~ to the blazon of a ship are sometimes not remotely aware of the word's meaning, and use the term simply because they take it for granted that it is the correct form of blazon. It is most remarkable, however, that the term was employed constantly in the XIX cent. when London's river was full of sail.

shuttle: [O.E.] a cylindrical box, or case, with tapering ends, which contains the weft thread and is thrown back and forth between the warp threads in weaving. In heraldic drawing the spool of thread is often visible through an opening in the side. Also blazoned as 'weaver's ~' and as 'navette'. (405)

Sicily Herald: Jean de Courtais (*ob.* 1435),

who originated the term 'false heraldry' (q.v.).

sickle: [O.E.] a thin, curved blade, the tang bent up at right angles so that when the blade is parallel with the ground the short handle is upright: strictly, the ~ has a serrated cutting-edge; when smooth the correct description is 'a reaping hook', but no such discrimination is known to heraldry where ~ is blazoned and generally a reaping hook drawn. The tool is for harvesting a crop of minor dimensions and is symbolic of peasant farming or husbandry.

side: the dexter (q.v.) third of a shield when tierced (q.v.) per pale (q.v.), assuming the status of a sub-ordinary; r. in British heraldry.

sierpe: Sp., serpent.

signatures: see **hatching**.

silbern: Ger., argent.

silberne scheibe: Ger., plate.

silver: Swd., argent.

silwer: Afk., argent.

Sinclair, James: Albany Herald, 1859. Unicorn Pursuivant, 1845.

siniestra: Sp., sinister.

siniestrocero: Sp., sinister arm.

---

421.   Argent, five escutcheons in cross azure each charged with as many plates in saltire. *Portugal.*
[*Note:* Known shortly as 'the quinas'. Cf. canton of England', 'France ancient', 'Bordure of Castile', etc.]

422.   Gules, seven mascles Or, three, three, and one. *Ferrers of Groby.*

423.   Azure, six annulets, Or, three, two, and one. *Musgrave, of Eden Hall.*

424.   Argent, an inescutcheon within a double tressure flory-counter-fleury gules. *David* (Earl of Huntingdon).

425.   Gyronny sable and argent an annulet counterchanged. *Doolan*, Ireland.

426.   Azure, ten annulets interlaced four, three, two, and one, Or. *Gibbon.*

421

422

423

424

425

426

sinister: [L. via M.E.] pertaining to the left-hand, hence the right-hand side of a shield when depicted (The armed man carrying the shield is behind it.)

sinister-base: the area of the shield to the observer's right, in the lower portion of the shield. (300, II)

sinister-chief: an area of about a third of the shield's width and roughly square, situated at the top of the shield, to the observer's right. (435, IV)

sinistra: It., sinister.

sinoper: [M.E.] red; hence, a r. alt. for 'gules' (q.v.).

sinople: [O.F.] green; hence an alt. for 'vert' (q.v.). A cross ~ is either a plain cross or a cross paty vert on a field argent: the cross of St Lazarus.

siren: [Gk.] a woman to the pelvis, but having a pair of gull's wings erupting at the shoulder-blades and carried with the tips downward; and below the pelvis the legs of a sea-bird with webbed feet. (286)

sittande: Swd., sejant.

sittende: Afk., sejant.

Sitwell Campbell Swinton, George: Lord Lyon King of Arms, 1927. Former Albany Herald.

sitzender: Ger., sejant.

sixth son, mark of difference of: see **brisure.**

Sizer, Theodoro: first Yale Pursuivant.

sjöblad: Swd., water-lily leaf.

skart: [dial.] a name given to the cormorant in the Hebrides; hence, ca. in Scottish heraldry.

skates: employed in continental heraldry in ca. settings.

skeleton: symbolic of famine and of suffering for which reason it is to be seen in the civic arms of the City of Londonderry. (300)

skene: see **sword.**

Skene, James: Lord Lyon Depute, 1655 and 1677.

Skene, John: Kintyre Pursuivant, 1706.

skiff: see **boat.**

skild: Afk., shield.

skild hoof: Afk., chief.

skild houers: Afk., supporters.

skild nawel: Afk., nombril point.

skild punt: Afk., centre-base.

skild voet: Afk., base.

skild-hoek: Afk., canton.

skillet: [M.E.] a comparatively shallow circular vessel of copper, raised upon feet and provided with a long handle, used for cooking meat; a stew-pan; a frying pan. (162)

skipetts: [frmd on 'skep', M.E., a basket] lit. a small basket; applied to the bag, basket, box, or other container that protects a pendant seal (q.v.). Those that are attached to a patent of arms (q.v.) are said to be of silver-gilt, and are embossed on the lids with representations in relief of a king of arms's crown.

skipping: an ambiguous term: an unconvincing definition copied from book to book is 'the crocodile, salamander, camelion, newt, asker, spider, ant, and all other egg-breeding reptiles, are said to be erected, mounting, leaping, or skipping'. Allowing for heraldic extravaganza and for the contortionistic ability with which its beasts are endowed, it is difficult to imagine either the crocodile or the newt behaving in so frolicsome a manner and, what is of greater significance, a search through the ordinaries and the armorials does not reveal any ~ reptiles.

The rather generous list of 'egg-breeding reptiles' does not go so far as to include dogs, yet both the talbot and the greyhound are to be found ~, and it requires no grotesque imagination to think of a dog in playful mood dancing up and down waiting to leap and seize the strap. The attitude implied by the term ~ seems to be crouching a little on the hind-limbs, the body inclined upward, the fore-paws clear of the ground, but neither rampant nor salient. (46)

sköld: Swd., shield.

sköldhållare: Swd., supporters.

skuins bo mekaar: Afk., in bend.

skuins gedeel: Afk., per bend.

skuinsbalk: Afk., bend.

skuinsgekruis: Afk., in saltire.

skuinsgevierendeel: Afk., per saltire.

skuinskruis: Afk., a saltire.

skuinstreep: Afk., cost.

skull: see **death's head.**

skura: Swd., a line of partition; plural 'skuror'.

Slacke, Richard: Windsor Herald, 1486. Former Rouge Croix Pursuivant, former Comfort Pursuivant (K. Ed. IV).

Slains Pursuivant: an officer of arms maintained by the Lord High Constable of Scotland.

slaughter-axe: see **axe.**

slay: a technical charge employed by weavers, and appearing only in the arms of the Exeter Weavers' Livery Company. It is variously spelt 'slea' and is sometimes called a reed.

slea: see previous entry.

sledge-hammer: see **hammer.**

sling: sometimes extended to 'sling-staff' and depicted as a rod with a strap attached to one end: by its use stones could be hurled to a greater distance than would have been possible without its aid.

slip: [Teut.] a twig, generally bearing three leaves.

slipped[1]**:** [Teut.] of a branch or a twig torn from the parent plant; indicated by an extended oval termination.

slipped[2]**:** of an item of fruit, or a flower, having the stem attached; often '~ and leaved'.

slippers: in British heraldry ~ are the bearings on which the spindle (or wharrow-

spindle) of a spinning-wheel runs, but in continental arms the reference is to easy footwear.

smal drawsbalkic: Afk., barrulet.

smal infattning: Swd., tressure.

smal keper: Afk., chevronel.

smal skuinbalk: Afk., bendlet.

Small, Thomas: Lyon Clerk Depute, 1804. Marchmont Herald, 1801.

smalle linkerskoinsbalk: Afk., scarpe.

Smallpiece's Roll: (temp. K. Ed. I) painted, 168 shields with names over.

smelt: [O.E.] a small, strong-flavoured fish, *Osmerus eparlanus*; also called 'sparling' (q.v.) by which name it may be blazoned; employed in heraldry chiefly for ca. reasons.

Smert, John: Garter King of Arms, 1450. Former Guyenne Herald, c. 1445.

smew: a merganser duck, *Mergus albellus*, which, being piscivorous, is a strong diver. It is distinguished by a long serrated beak with a formidable hook terminating the upper mandible.

Smith, Wm[1]**:** Rouge Dragon Pursuivant, 1597.

Smith, Wm[2]**:** Ormonde Pursuivant, 1701.

Smith, Wm[3]**:** Lyon Clerk Depute, 1823.

Smith of Gibleston, Robert: Lyon Clerk and Keeper of the Records, 1663.

smolt: [dial.] a young salmon (q.v.) when it makes its first journey to the sea; employed in heraldry for ca. reasons.

snail: [O.E.] a terrestrial gastropod carrying upon its back a spiral shell, *Helix hortensis*, the common ~ of the garden. Blazoned as 'house-~', but is uncommon and obs. in British heraldry. In France a ~ (not necessarily a common garden ~) makes its entry under the title of 'limaçon'.

snake: see **serpent.**

snake-stones: see **shell.**

snead: see **scythe.**

sned: see **scythe.**

snipe: [M.E.] a bird of the marshes, *Gal-*

linago media; employed in heraldry for ca. reasons and characterized by its long, straight beak.

Snowden Herald: the spelling form normally employed in England with reference to the Scottish Officer of Arms named, in Scotland, as in the following entry.

Snowdoun Herald: a name of office formerly employed in Scotland where it is so written and pronounced.

sobre el todo: Sp., over all.

Sol¹: see **segregative blazon.**

Sol²: Swd., the sun in his splendour.

soldering-iron: r., probably only in the achievement of the Worshipful Company of Plumbers: depicted as an oval knob on the end of a short rod that terminates in a hook. This is thought by the uninitiated to be an error, for it is not the modern tool called a ~ and could not be used as such. The plumber of old was not concerned only with water-supply and disposal: he did more than mend winter's burst pipes: he put the roof on the cathedral, and the heraldic ~, also called 'plumber's iron', is the ideal tool for drawing along the seams between the sheets of metal.

sole¹: [M.E.] a flat-fish, *Solea vulgaris*, also known as the 'whiff' and 'conter'; employed in heraldry for ca. reasons.

sole²: It., the sun in his splendour.

soleil: Fr., the sun in his splendour.

soleil, a rose in: see **rose.**

Somerset Herald: see **College of Arms.**

sonne: Ger., the sun in his splendour.

soom: Afk., bordure.

soom belaai met blare, blomme of vrugte: Afk., verdoye.

soom met voëls: Afk., enaluron.

soomsgewys geplaas: Afk., orle.

soportes: Sp., supporters.

sopra il tutto: It., over all.

sopravest: a long cassock-like garment worn, normally under a mantle, by members of certain orders, e.g. the Most Venerable Order of the Hospital of St John of Jerusalem.

sotuer: Sp., saltire.

South Africa, heraldry in the Republic of: In January 1962 the Government of the newly fledged Republic of South Africa heard the second reading of the Heraldry Bill to which, there being no opposition, the Government in the normal course of business set its seal. By the Republic Constitution Act, the President for the time being becomes the titular head of heraldry, and under him is a Council of Heraldry and Bureau of Heraldry. The head of the Bureau is the State Herald who is also a member of the Council. There are seven assistants—not yet given the titles of Pursuivants.

The State Herald has the support of both civil and criminal law in preventing the use of unofficial arms and in suppressing the duplication of those made the subject of a grant from the Bureau. Portuguese, French, Dutch, English, and other European states have all, from time to time, given population to the Cape. Some were, of course, armigerous; others, with prosperity, made themselves so; hence, the rectification of arms in the Republic is going to be a long and arduous task.

South Africa, Star of: f. 1962 in one class to be worn as a medal. *Badge:* eight silver stars surmounting each other at different angles. *Riband:* orange with three central narrow strips of green.

Southern Cross, Order of the: (Brazil) f. 1822 by the Emperor Don Pedro I and re-established under the Republic in 1932 in five classes. Insignia—*Badge:* a gold-rimmed white enamel star of ten points pommetty, with a red-berried green wreath between the arms; a blue central medallion depicts, in white, the five stars of the

Southern Constellation, and is surrounded by the motto, in gold and dark blue, *Benemerentium Praemium*; the badge is ensigned with a laurel wreath. *Star:* the badge in larger size, the wreath being replaced by gold rays. *Riband:* light blue.

soutiens: see **supporters.**

spade: the primitive digging implement, the blade of which is heart-shape. A square or a rectangular blade makes of it a shovel. Palewise u.o.s., the handle terminates in either a short bar attached at its centre.. making a T-shape; or it is bifurcated and the cross-piece supported at both ends. A half-~ consists of a ~ split palewise from hand-grip to blade point; the dexter half appears u.o.s. A ~-iron is an ornamental frame following the contours of the blade. (99)

spade-iron: see previous entry.

spancelled: of a horse having a log of wood suspended behind at fetlock level to act as a hobble.

Spark, Hugh: Dingwal Pursuivant, 1747.

sparsus: L., semé.

sparling: [M.E.] strictly an alt. name for the smelt (q.v.) but extended to include other small fish, particularly the sprat (*Clupea sprattus*); employed in heraldry chiefly for ca. reasons.

sparre: Swd., chevron.

sparren: Ger., chevron.

sparrenleiste: Ger., chevronel.

spater: a spatula or palette-knife, so blazoned in the arms of the Worshipful Company of Barbers; also spelt 'spattor'.

spattor: see previous entry.

spear: see **lance.**

spear-head: see **lance.**

speed, at: see **stag.**

spelling: the ~ of the language of heraldry has not become standardized, with the result that each writer upon the subject follows his own fancy which sometimes has

the effect of confusing the newcomer to the subject who is confronted with the task of discovering whether a cross formée fitchée is exactly the same as a cross formy fitchy. He does not recognize in a molet, a mullet; and he hesitates to write 'fess' in case the final 'e' ought to appear. British heraldry should be expressed in as English a manner as possible notwithstanding that some of the words—actually but few—are derived from, or actually are, unaltered Old French. The terminal 'y' is less jarring to the English mind than is 'ée'; however, total consistency is impossible due to the homophonous nature of some of the words—cross bottonnée is preferable to cross bottony—and those words that are clearly French in origin ought to be pronounced phonetically, as spelt. The modern French accent is as far removed from that of Anglo–Norman as normal English is.

Spence, James: Ormonde Pursuivant, 1668.

Spence of Brunstane, Hierome: Rothesay Herald, 1667.

Spence of Brunstane, John: Carrick Pursuivant, 1633.

Spence of Worministon, John: Rothesay Herald, 1633.

Spens, David: Dingwal Pursuivant, 1545.

Spenser, Richard: Heraud Mariscall del Suth, i.e. Clarenceux King of Arms, 1383.

sperver: see **tent.**

spetsruta: Swd., fusil.

spetsrutad: Swd., fusily.

spherical object: i.e. cannon-balls, should be shaded to appear spherical and should cast an oval shadow, quite distinct from any of the roundels (q.v.), including the ogress.

Sphinx: a composite fictitious creature having the head and breast of a woman merging into the body of a winged lion The head is generally covered with a capelain; the tail flexed over the back; the wings sometimes addorsed.

spider: [O.E.] an insectivorous eight-legged creature that spins a web of gossamer to catch its prey. The ~ seldom appears in person in British heraldry, but the web, which is drawn covering the entire field, suggests his presence. Sometimes blazoned 'cob-web'. (83)

spikes: see **nails.**

spinato: It., engrailed.

spindle: [O.E.] a tapering dowel; a cigar-shaped wooden instrument, part of a spinning wheel, made to revolve by means of a grooved pulley, called the wharrow, which is connected by an endless band to the treadle-operated fly-wheel; hence, sometimes blazoned as 'wharrow-spindle'. Supposed to be the model on which the fusil (q.v.) is based.

spink: [M.E.] the chaffinch; hence, chaffinches are employed to ca. on the name ~.

spinning cog: see **cog, mill.**

spinning top: see **top.**

spirling: see **sparling.**

spitsgeruite: Afk., fusily.

spitskruis: Afk., cross pointed.

spitsruit: Afk. and D., fusil.

spitsruiten: D., fusily.

spitze: Ger., chape.

spjut: Swd., spear.

spokeshave: a woodworking tool, one example only of which occurs in the arms of Kelway, but the family's arms, 'argent, two spokeshaves in saltire sable between four pears pendent Or within a bordure engrailed of the second', are also blazoned as shankbones and glazier's nippers (q.v.).

spornschnalle: Ger., buckle.

sporre: Swd., spur.

sporrklinga: Swd., mullet.

spotted-cat: see **catamount.**

sprat: see **sparling.**

sprekende wapens: Afk., canting arms.

Spret, Robert: see **Fayery, Robert.**

sprig: [M.E.] a twig bearing leaves of which there ought to be five, but either more or less may appear. (390)

springbok: an antelope indigenous to South Africa, *Antilope euchore*, distinguished in

---

427. Argent, three acorns slipped and leaved vert between two flaunches gules each charged with a thistle slipped and leaved Or.
Aikenhead.

428. Or, a gonfannon gules fringed vert.
Count of Boulogne.

429. Or, three linden leaves in triangle, slipped the stems conjoined at fess point, within a bordure vert.
Lindgren.

430. Sable, an escarbuncle Or within an orle of bezants.
Arthur.

431. Gyronny Or and gules, on a bend sable a Lacy knot between two martlets of the first.
Lacy.

432. Argent, upon a rock proper a castle triple-towered sable, masoned of the field, windows, ports, turrets, caps, and vanes gules.
Corporation of the City of Edinburgh.
(IV quarter in the arms of H.R.H. Prince Philip, Duke of Edinburgh.)

427

428

429

430

431

432

heraldic art by its broad, flat tyneless antlers.

springing: see **stag**.

springs: see **knitting-frame**.

sprinkling salt: see **salts**.

sprouting: see **log of a tree**.

spruce tree: see **pine**.

spur: [O.E.] the Anglo–Norman 'pryck ~' consisted of a U-shaped heel-iron provided with strap and buckle at the open end, and having, extending backward and upward, a sharp-pointed spike. This, sometimes mis-named Scotch-~, was a dangerous imple-ment with which to stimulate one's charger since the animal might fall dead under one due to loss of blood. The earliest representa-tion of a rowel-~ is on the Great Seal of K. Ric. I. In heraldry the ~ is drawn without conventionalization or distortion; the rowel (alt. spellings 'revel' and 'rouelle') is chief-ward and the leathers, i.e. strap and buckle for fixing to the riding boot, are flotant. The symbolism of the winged-~ is self-evident. The ~ and its leathers are not altered, and the wings rise from each side of the heel-iron. The mullet (q.v.) is de-rived from the ~ rowel. (178)

spurious arms: see **prescriptive right**.

square: a tool for draughting right-angles; the heraldic ~ is the carpenter's tool con-sisting of a stout stock with, erected at one end, a slender blade having parallel sides. Because the word has acquired the second-ary meaning of 'honest' or 'exemplary', the ~ is employed in arms in a symbolic setting, but there being no standard orien-tation the blazon must always state the position of the 'corner' or 'angle', or 'point' as, e.g. 'corner chiefward to the dexter' or '. . . . baseward to the sinister'.

square comb: see **comb**.

square hammer: see **hammer**.

square tower: a slightly conventionalized representation of a Norman donjon, or keep, always in perspective to enable the

extensions in height at each corner to be visible. Blazoned as a '~ towered', it is completely arraswise with two of the small towers in fess and two in pale which may be detailed in the blazon.

squatting: sometimes used to blazon a coney's (q.v.) attitude when sejant.

Squibb, Arthur: Clarenceux King of Arms under Cromwell.

squirrel: [M.E.] a tree-climbing furry rodent having a large bushy tail, *Sciurus vulgaris*. His characteristic habit, that of storing nuts to ensure a supply of food during the winter, makes him symbolic of both thrift and cautiousness. He is always sejant, and often depicted with his fore-paws raised to his face when he is blazoned (q.v.) as 'sejant, cracking a nut'. (28)

staak: Afk. and D., pallet.

staande: D., statant.

stab: Ger., pallet.

Stacey, Joseph: Ross Herald, 1663. Herald-painter, 1663.

staende: Swd., statant.

staff: [Teut.] a descriptive term that may be applied to any mast, pole, rod, shaft, stick, or wand notwithstanding that the par-ticular staff may be otherwise blazoned normally. It may also be applied to the handles of both weapons and tools to which 'stave' (q.v.) and 'staved' are generally applied.

staff, archbishop's: see **crosier**.

staff, palmer's: see **palmer's staff**.

staff, pike: see **pike¹**.

staff, pilgrim's: see **palmer's staff**.

staff, pastoral: see **pastoral staff**.

staff, rectorial: the rod, or baton of office of a university rector; pointed at the foot, terminating above with a potent (q.v.) or crutch-head.

staff of Hermes: see **Aesculapius, rod of**.

staff of Mercury: see **Aesculapius, rod of**.

Stafford knot: a half-hitch, or overhand

knot, generally orientated fesswise, the bight and two ends upward.

stag: [M.E.] a generic term covering all species of the genus *Cervus*: specifically the male red deer, depicted with pointed tynes (q.v.). ~ is 'attired' of his antlers and 'unguled' of his hooves when these are of a different colour from the beast himself. He may be blazoned as posed in any of the heraldic attitudes, but he has a special set of terms which should, in preference, be applied; when couchant, he is 'lodged', and instead of extending his fore-limbs he rests with them folded, the hooves concealed beneath his chest; when passant (q.v.) he is described as trippant; courant (q.v.) he is 'at speed'; 'springing', although not intended to represent him attacking, may be blazoned as salient (q.v.). When standing facing dexter he is statant (q.v.) but standing and facing out of the shield, i.e. gardant (q.v.) he is 'at gaze'. With head lowered and muzzle touching the ground (feeding) he is blazoned as 'pascuant'. He is frequently collared, or gorged, and chained, as well as crowned. (32, 35, 37, 40)

stainard: [L. via O.F.] stained, blemished; disgrace; stigma; applied only to the colours tenné (q.v.) and sanguine (q.v.) which in archaic blazon were euphemized as alternatively 'dragon's head' and 'dragon's tail'.

stalked: of a flower, or of foliage that is to be depicted as having a long stem. See also **strawed.**

stam: Swd., base.

Stamford, Roger: Chester Herald, Rouge Croix, and Guisnes Pursuivant during the reign of K. Ed. IV.

standar: Swd., banner.

standard: [M.E.] a large flag, generally about six times as long from hoist (q.v.) to fly (q.v.) as in the dip, tapering, and bifurcated in the fly, fringed of the colours. In feudal warfare the ~ was equivalent to the modern headquarters flag; beneath it was pitched the tent, or pavilion, of the leader; behind it his retainers had marched; round it they would gather after the mêle to reform, and under it they would, at worst, make their last heroic stand and die in its defence. The 'field' of a ~ was divided into three sections by means of two bends which remained white irrespective of the colour of the ground, and on which appeared the motto, or else the war-cry of the leader. The section in the hoist was argent, a cross gules for St George, being the patron saint of England and of Englishmen; the second and third sections (i.e. centre and fly) bore the badges, generally a beast badge, and a plant badge or, in place of the latter, a simple object, or a knot (q.v.); the second badge was also to be seen on breast and back of the men-at-arms. In the later Middle Ages the arms of the leader were substituted for the St George in the fly, and the crest appeared centrally in place of the beast badge. During the Tudor period the Standing Army came into being and the ~ ceased to be employed in war, but the ceremonial ~ continued in use by those who were entitled to fly them.

The right to fly a ~ is determined by the possession of an armorial badge and, although badges were granted only to bodies corporate for a number of years, the custom of granting them to private persons has, since the Second World War, been revived, and the form to be taken by the resultant ~ is depicted on the patent. The modern tendency is for the fly to be rounded instead of bifurcated, which is not a new idea, such shapes being sometimes employed in the Middle Ages.

The statement that ~ were not carried as war flags, which will be found in a number of books, is an error: the size of a ~ varied according to rank, and the rules governing dimensions are detailed in some of the surviving medieval manuscripts where there is sometimes a note stating 'not to be borne in war', which means only that a ~ of that particular size was for ceremonial use only, there being greater freedom in time of war.

standarte: Ger., banner.

standing: see **horse.**

standing bowl: see **bowl.**

standish: the heraldic name for a charger or platter; ca. in the arms of the family of Standish: lit. a tray to hold pens and ink.

Stanton, Richard: Chester Herald, towards the end of the reign of K. Hen. VI, or beginning K. Ed. IV. He was both Bluemantle and Wallingford Pursuivant to K. Hen. VI. March King of Arms, 1480.

staple: [O.E.] a bar of iron, the ends bent downward at 90° and pointed, used in rough carpentry to join two wooden beams, or for holding together other component parts of a temporary wooden structure. They may be interlaced in triangle (q.v.) or with other objects. Also blazoned as 'door staple', and sometimes described as affixed, in which case the two teeth are to be of half the normal length and finished with a flat end instead of a point, indicating that the ~ is half-driven into the timber. (397)

star: see **estoile** and **mullet.**

star-shot: a cannon-ball having spikes rising from its surface; sometimes described as a 'star-stone'.

Starkey's Roll: (c. 1460) there are three copies each of which may or may not have been taken from a vellum true roll (q.v.) containing 1127 coats of arms. Copy A, also known as 'Gybbon's Ordinary', has 1124 shields in trick (q.v.); B has 771, also tricked; and C also has 1124. It is a general roll (q.v.) covering much the same ground as most others.

starved: see **branch.**

statant: [L.] of a beast standing, facing dexter being understood u.o.s. The lion ~ flourishes his tail as when either passant (q.v.) or rampant (q.v.); 'a lion ~ with tail extended' holds it straight out towards the sinister. (58)

State, Sword of: see **sword.**

stave: [M.E.] lit. a staff, rod, or shaft; in heraldry applied to the handles of certain tools and weapons; similar in usage to 'haft' (q.v.). Also one of the curved boards that go to the making of a tun (q.v.). There is one example of the musical ~, blazoned as 'five musical lines'.

Stebbing, Samuel: Somerset Herald, 1600. Former Rose Rouge Pursuivant 1598.

steeple: see **church.**

stehender: Ger., statant.

steigender: Ger., rampant.

Steill, James: Islay Herald, 1701.

stella: It., estoile.

stellion: [M.E.] an Asiatic lizard, of the genus *Stellio*; depicted with star-shape spots.

stellula: L., estoile.

stem: see **beam.**

stendardo: It., standard.

Stephen: Windsor Herald, c. 1366.

Stephen, Order of St: (Tuscany) f. 1562 with statutes based on the Benedictine rule and on those of the Order of St John, for the purpose of defending the Catholic Church and destroying pirates who threatened ruin to Tuscan trade. Insignia—*Badge:* a gold-edged red cross paty notched with f.d.l. between the arms, ensigned overall with a gold crown. *Star:* a multirayed gold plaque surmounted by the unensigned badge. *Riband:* red.

Stephen, St: appears in the municipal arms of Györ, Hungary.

ster: D., estoile.

Sterling Roll: 102 named and blazoned coats of arms, 1304.

Stevenson, Alexander James: Carrick Pursuivant, 1939.

PLATE XVI Or, a fess chequy argent and azure, between, in chief, a pelican in her piety gules and, in base, a cinquefoil ermine pierced round of the field: ensigned with a helmet befitting his degree mantled of his liveries whereon is set for CREST, upon a wreath of the colours a demi-pelican with wings addorsed Or collared chequy as in the arms. On an escroll accompanying the crest, inscribed in Celtic text-letters sable, the words *Sanguine Cuo*.

Stewart of Inchmahome

Stevenson, John Horne: Marchmont Herald, 1924. Unicorn Pursuivant, 1902.

Stevenson, Thomas: Rouge Croix Pursuivant, 1538. Former Berwick Pursuivant, 1536.

Stewart, George: Kintyre Pursuivant, 1641.

Stewart, Gilbert: Lord Lyon Depute, 1660.

Stewart, Sir Wm: Lord Lyon King of Arms, 1567. Former Ross Herald, 1565.

Stewart, Wm: Kintyre Pursuivant, 1633.

Stibbs, Edward: Chester Herald, 1720.

stickleback: see **minnow**.

sticks, bundle of: as used in various trades appear among the prosaic objects employed in the achievements of livery companies and civic authorities.

stipatus: L. cantoned.

stirrup: [O.E.] a U-shaped iron suspended, curve upward, by a strap attached on each side of a riding saddle. The horns of the U are bridged by a flat rod, or plate, on which the rider's feet rest. A ~ is always pendant from its leathers (which may be decorated with a buckle about halfway up), but the leather itself is attached to nothing. Blazoned as a '~-iron' the leather is to be omitted whereupon the rectangular slot through which it engages needs to be drawn. In a XV cent. manuscript ~-irons appear and are slightly different in form. The arch is not U-shape but is flat at the top, and this section is engrailed on the underside thus indicating that ~s were sometimes suspended on cords (instead of leathers), which were prevented from slipping by engaging in the engrailment. (303)

stjörna: Swd., estoile.

stoat: the ermine when in its brown summer coat (*Mustela erminea*); hence, regarded in heraldry as a different creature.

stock¹: [Teut.] the stump of a tree; the part left standing on its roots when a tree has been felled: ca. on 'Woodstock'; hence, a badge of K. Hen. IV (of Woodstock). ~ may be either issuant or eradicated.

stock²: see **timber**.

stock-card: see **card¹**.

stock-fish: salted, dried cod (q.v.) depicted open, the shape of the familiar smoked haddock.

Stodart, Robert Riddle: Lyon Clerk Depute, 1864. The distinguished deviser of the Stodart system of differencing. See following entry.

Stodart system, the: a method of differencing evolved by Robert Riddle Stodart, appointed Lyon Clerk Depute in 1864. It has been in constant use in Scotland for about a century and has proved practicable and inexhaustible. The heir-apparent is exempt: he differences with a label of three points (q.v.) and will ultimately wear the arms undifferenced, but all cadets (q.v.) on rematriculation (q.v.) are granted the paternal arms 'with such congruent difference as the Lord Lyon thinks fit', and the ~ is universally applied. All the brothers receive a plain bordure, each being distinguished by its colour. The sons of the heir-apparent, being scions of the first house, do not use bordures, but the ordinary varies its lines of demarcation. The younger sons of the second son vary their bordures in the same way. Descendants in the first house continue to difference by additional charges, those in the junior branches retain the characteristic bordure and part it of two colours. The next generation quarter it. It will be seen from the foregoing outline that the combination and ramifications possible are arithmetically enormous, and if in a number of generations, each rich in male issue, every facet of the system had been used, a total counterchange or the addition of a charge from the mother's arms would start it off again.

The most adverse criticism levelled against the ∼ is that due to its application there is scarcely a Scottish achievement not confined within a bordure. Even if this were wholly true, the advantages outweigh it, for even identical twins bear different arms, yet those arms declare them sons of the same father and members of the same clan.

stolpe: Swd., pale.

stoned: see **gem-ring.**

stork: [O.E.] a long-legged, long-necked, long-billed water-bird, characterized by his having a humped back; *Ciconia alba*. It has black wing-tip and tail feathers, red legs, and is depicted holding a snake in the bill. (179)

stortar gaffelkors: Swd., tierced per graft.

Strachan, James: Unicorn Pursuivant, 1760.

Strachan, Joseph: Snowdoun Herald, 1750.

stralenwerpende ster: D., comet.

strap and buckle: see **badge.**

strappato: It., erased.

strawberry flower: see **trefoil.**

strawberry leaf: has a special status among leaves (q.v.) being used, in a conventionalized form, to heighten coronets.

strawed: of the stems of a garb (q.v.) when differing in colour from the head. The word 'stalked' is also applied.

streepbinnesoom: Afk., tressure.

streepkeeper: Afk., couple close.

striatus: L., engrailed.

string-bow: see **bow**[1].

stringed: either pertaining to the stretched wires (or gut-lines) that emit the notes of a musical instrument, or of the cord by which an object, e.g. a buglehorn, is suspended. Of the draw-cord attached to an archer's bow (q.v.).

stryks: see **limbeck.**

Stuart Royal Arms: on the accession in 1603 to the throne of England by James VI of Scotland, a re-marshalling of the Royal Arms took place: the first and fourth became grand-quarters quarterly; 1 and 4, France Modern; 2 and 3, England: II, Scotland: IV, Ireland. The Act of Union (1706), necessitated a further change, i.e. I and IV,

---

433.   Argent, a sword erect azure, hilted and pomelled Or.
Deuchar, Edinburgh.

434.   Argent, two swords in their scabbards in saltire sable, hilted and pomelled and chaped Or.
Gellibrand.

435.   Quarterly argent and gules, in sinister-chief a deed unrolled having two pendant seals proper: in dexter-base a Roman lamp of the first. Overall a sword, point chiefward, in bend of the second.
The Worshipful Company of Solicitors.

436.   Argent, a sword erect azure hilted and pomelled Or ensigned with a mullet gules and debruised by a saltire couped sable.
Garran.

437.   Gules, three swords conjoined in pairle, issuant of a pommel at fess point.
Brisac.

438.   Gules, two keys addorsed and conjoined in the bows, the upper Or the lower argent in bend sinister interlaced with a sword of the third pommelled and hilted of the second.
See of Winchester.

433

434

435

436

437

438

England impaling Scotland; II, France; III, Ireland.

stufenformig: Ger., indented.

stukke: Afk., charges.

sturgeon: [M.E.] the royal fish. Uncommon, and depicted with a swordfish-like bill and spiny hide.

Styward's Roll: (temp. K. Ed. III) also called 'Sir Symonds d'Ewes Roll' and 'Second Calais Roll'. Vellum true roll, 4½ in. by 7 ft 4½ in., painted, 135 shields with names over.

styckad: Swd., per bend.

sub-ordinaries: shapes of all kinds that appear in various settings, alone or in numbers, in numerous coats of arms; they range from a simple rectangle (see **billet**) to comparatively ornate compositions taking in their stride the roundles (q.v.), gouttae (q.v.), mullets (q.v.), fusils (q.v.), lozenges (q.v.), and even crescents and f.d.l.: there is no hard and fast line between ∼ and common charges (q.v.); hence, into which category an object falls is largely a matter of opinion.

sub-quarters: see **quarterly**.

succession, arms of: arms attached to estate, or to title, that may (or must) be displayed by the holder for the time being of such estate or title, instead of, or together with, his arms of descent. Arms of office (q.v.) are in this category.

Suffolk Herald: maintained, XIV to XV cents., by both earls and dukes of Suffolk. In early XVIII cent. was revived as name of office of an officer extraordinary.

sugar: [M.E.] a conical casting of hard ∼, blazoned as a ∼-loaf: culms of the giant grass, *Saccharum officinarum*, blazoned as ∼-cane; employed for ca. and also for allusive reasons.

summo, in: L., in chief.

summum: L., chief.

sun in his splendour, the: a disc, repre-
senting the solar body, completely surrounded by a series of alternate straight and wavy rays (q.v.) representing the corona. The disc itself may be drawn as a gentle, smiling kindly face; or it may carry a charge which will be described as (say) a gauntlet 'in the sun'. The ∼ is not, as stated in numerous textbooks 'always Or'. It is frequently Or, and equally frequently gules: there are occasions, too, when it is sable, and blazoned as 'the sun eclipsed', the corona realistically remaining Or (or gules) which is often covered in the blazon, 'the sun eclipsed, the beams Or (or gules)'. 'Half eclipsed', the disc is per pale, the second colour being sable. A demi-sun issuant may emerge from any position: chief, base, or either flank: it may also be confined to one of the top corners of the shield where, although still blazoned 'demi', it actually reveals only a quarter. As the sun's face is optional when the full disc appears, so it is with a half or a quarter when only that part of the features appropriate to the half or the quarter will be seen; e.g. 'issuant in chief' reveals the mouth and nostrils; 'issuant in base' the brow, eyes, and bridge of the nose.

In continental heraldry the presence or absence of features is not optional: when plain it is described in Fr. blazon as 'ombre de soleil'. When issuant, a demi-sun may be associated with a bank of cloud which is either argent or proper. It is usual for the beams to break through, not in a solid mass, but at intervals.

This effect is, too, secured without the sun itself: a small mass of cloud, either proper in appearance or conventionalized to a small, more or less oval shape filled with a nebuly (q.v.) pattern rather like folded cotton wool, and beneath it a section of the corona, is known as 'a sunburst'.

Sun of Peru, Order of The: f. 1821 in five classes. Insignia—*Badge:* eighteen gold rays in the form of a sun-burst; a central medallion depicts, in gold, the arms of Peru and is surrounded by a blue band inscribed in gold *El Sol Del Peru* and, on an insert of white enamel, the date 1821; the medallion is surrounded by, and the whole is also ensigned with, a green and gold laurel wreath. *Star:* a larger version of the unensigned badge. *Riband:* purple.

sunburst : see **sun in his splendour, the**

supporters: animals, real or imaginary; human figures either representative or symbolic; or inanimate objects placed one on each side of the shield and depicted as holding it up to view: the use of ~ is confined to peers of the realm, to knights grand cross in an order of chivalry, and to certain bodies corporate, e.g. municipal councils or companies, trusts, and the like whose business may be considered a 'service'—not merely that of manufacturing and vending for profit.

~ are normally borne in pairs, either two representations of the same creature or two quite unrelated to each other: in the former case there is a regrettable and growing tendency for officers of arms to make use in the blazon of the colloquial and rather sloven expression 'on either side a (say) lion'. This means that only one lion is provided and that he may parade on either side; e.g. on the dexter on Sunday and on the sinister all the week. What is intended is two lions, and the blazon ought to state 'on each side, a lion'.

In England single ~ are not used, but there are some Scottish examples. On the continent only beasts are ~ : human beings doing that duty are called 'tenants'; and vegetation and inanimate objects are 'soutiens'. Down to the end of the XIX cent. for two creatures to stand on nothing and hold up the shield did not seem out of place; in modern times there is always a 'compart-

ment' (q.v.), generally a mount (q.v.), but there are no restrictions.

In the XIX cent. the royal ~ were provided with a compartment of scrollwork which came to be known as 'the gas-bracket'. In continental, and particularly in German representations of arms, there is a tendency to place figures about a shield as though they were official ~ ; the object is not to deceive the observer but to 'decorate' the arms; as the figures chosen are generally amorini, their value is a matter of taste. There was a minor epidemic of this disease in England during the XVIII cent.

supporti: It., supporters.

supports: Fr., supporters.

surcoat: [O.F.] a long, shirtlike garment worn over a suit of armour. On it, back and front, the armorial bearings of the wearer were emblazoned thus giving rise to the term 'coat of arms'. The tabard (q.v.) has its origin in a development of the ~. From the XI to the XV cents., ladies' garments were also embellished with armorials.

surgens: L., risant.

surgerant: see **falcon.**

surmounted: [M.E.] of a charge, or an ordinary that is in part concealed by another figure passing over; of two swords in saltire (q.v.), u.o.s., that in bend sinister (q.v.) is ~ by that in bend (q.v.), the latter surmounting the former. Alt. terms are 'debruised' and 'debruising', but '~ by' is frequently er. and misleadingly used in place of 'ensigned' (q.v.). (402, IV)

surname: a name additional to the personal, given, or Christian name; a name shared by all members of a family, and which is normally transmitted from male parent to offspring of either sex but which is not established by law. A ~, having no legal status, cannot be changed by a legal instrument, and its change at will cannot be prevented by the law. A ~ depends for its stability on custom and usage; an assumed name, having been accepted and employed in relation to the assumer by his peers, is his although his previous ~ may have been that by which his ancestors had been known.

Documents having relationship to change of name are of two sorts: the deed poll, which is not an instrument of change of name but merely a statement that such a change has taken place, and in the event of the person making the change being an armiger no armorial considerations are involved. The other relevant document is the royal licence which must be 'exemplified in our Royal College of Arms, otherwise this, our royal licence, to be void and of none effect'. Notwithstanding the high dignity and the importance of such a document it, too, is not an instrument of change, for when all is completed change of mind may prevent change of name. Since the royal licence can take effect only if implemented by an officer of arms, it follows that armorial bearings are invariably involved, and the changes exemplified by the royal licence are made in response to a 'name and arms' clause in a will. Often a heraldic heiress (q.v.) had a shrewd father who was not willing to trust the perpetuation of his arms and his name to the method of marshalling (q.v.) and the good will of his son-in-law, but who took the precaution of making a will whereby his fortune would go to a charity if his name and arms were not maintained in constant daily use by his son-in-law. The normal procedure under royal licence is for the ~ of both husband and wife to be linked by a hyphen, the husband's preceding the wife's, and the pronominal quarters (q.v.) of each of their achievements to be remarshalled quarterly and granted anew as one coat of arms; hence, such a combination is indivisible and becomes a grand-quarter (q.v.) in any subse-

quent marshalling into which it may become incorporated. The hyphenated ~, having that of the wife second, causes her family ~ to become the name by which her husband, and all her offspring, will in future be known. Mr Thomas Franklyn-Tanner, F.S.A., will be called 'Tanner': in an ABC list he will come under the letter T, thus 'Tanner, Thomas Franklyn-'. This rule does not pertain in U.S.A. where, there being no royal licence, there are no genuine hyphenated ~. It is a regrettable but incontestable fact that some people believe that a 'double-barrelled ~' is, like many quarters to the coat of arms, very high-class and admirable; hence, they hyphenate their mother's and their father's ~ in that order and by so doing reveal to the initiated their fraud. There is, however, a group of 'self-hyphenatees' who are fully justified, namely the Clarks and the Smiths. It is likely that in a community of twenty-five people there will be three of each, and their voluntary assumption of their mother's ~ is an act *pro bono publico*: Jackson-Clark, Thompson-Clark, and Clitheroe-Clark, make life easier for all concerned.

Surrey Herald: name of office employed in mid XIX cent. for an extraordinary officer of arms, the Duke of Norfolk being also Earl of Surrey.

Surrogate, Earl Marshal's: see **Chivalry, Court of.**

surtout: [Fr.] overall; hence, indicative of an inescutcheon: when the shield of pretence itself carried such an addition, the latter's blazon is preceeded by the term 'surtout-de-tout'.

Suvorov, Order of: (Russia) f. 1942 in three classes; worn as a star only. Insignia: first class—a platinum star of five points, a red star surmounting the uppermost; a gold central medallion depicts the effigy and name of Alexander Suvorov above sprays of laurel and oak. *Riband:* green, with a central orange stripe. Second class—the star in gold and the medallion in silver. *Riband:* green, with orange stripes at the edges. Third class—the star and medallion in silver. *Riband:* green, with orange stripes at the edges and centrally.

svard: Swd., sword.

svart: Swd., sable.

swan: [O.E.] a large, short-legged, web-footed water-bird of the genus *Cygnus*. It has a long, elegantly curved neck and is most graceful when swimming; hence, in heraldry, symbolic thereof. In classical antiquity sacred to Apollo, and to Venus; hence, symbolic of excellence. The ~ is frequently gorged (q.v.) of a coronet; in the capacity of a royal badge, gorged and chained. The ~ is frequently close (q.v.) but may also be rizant (q.v.) or with wings addorsed. (117)

swart: Afk., sable.

swastika [Indian] a plain cross having each limb bent at 90° in a clockwise direction. It is an ancient sun and fire symbol, and it was much esteemed as a 'luck' charm throughout the world until brought into disrepute in central Europe. The spelling 'svastika' is believed to indicate counter-clockwise bending, but in heraldry it is merely an alt. and does not carry significance. Alt. terms are 'fylfot' and 'gammadion', which term leads to a difference of opinion. Cross gammadion, it is said, is not a ~ at all, but is a cross potent (q.v.) rebated and consequently it should be drawn with the turned-over sections of only half the length of those of the ~ which fits into a square.

sweep: mis-spelling of 'swepe'. See **man-gonel.**

swift: see **newt.**

Swinton, George Sitwell Campbell: Albany Herald, 1923. March Pursuivant, 1901.

swivels: appear notably in the arms of the Worshipful Company of Ironmongers; a pair of links joined by a rod upon which they are free to turn; hence, the means of joining or securing chains subject to a rotating load, e.g. ships riding at anchor. Badly drawn ~, mistaken for fetter-locks (q.v.), have been blazoned as manacles.

sword: [O.E.] a long, slender, pointed steel blade secured to a handle, or grip, called the hilt, which is ovoid and generally corded to prevent the weapon slipping. Between the blade and the hilt is a short transverse bar, generally drawn as turned upward at one end and downward at the other, but its pattern is not standardized, as the actual quillons were not in the feudal period. The ~, which is normally proper, i.e. argent, refers to the blade only; it is 'hilted' of the grip and the quillons. The hilt terminates in a ball, hence, the ~ is blazoned 'hilted and pommelled'. The point of a ~ is always chiefward u.o.s., and it is erect in most of its appearances; however, the ~ may be inverted (point in base) and fesswise, when, u.o.s., the point is to the dexter. Two ~ in saltire, a very common combination, maintain the point upwards custom, the dexter surmounting the sinister.

Although the ~ is likely to be found in the arms of a family having military association, it is, on account of its high symbolism, found in many non-military settings, i.e. symbolic of the Church militant, in ecclesiastical coats of arms, specifically named as the 'sword of Justice', 'sword of State', and the like. 'A sword in its scabbard' is also symbolic. A broken ~ consists of the hilt and pommel and half the blade only which finishes with a jagged line. A ~ wavy has short-pitched undulations.

When blazoned as 'a rapier' no difference is made in drawing, but 'a claymore' is drawn with a 'basket' hand-guard; hence without quillons. The dagger, the Scot's skene, the dirk (or durk), and the poniard are each, in appearance, but diminutive swords, and they make their several appearances in heraldry with no visual distinguishing feature; hence, the idea that the ~ of St Paul in the dexter-chief canton of the arms of the City of London is the dagger of Sir William Walworth will never die. The distinction between these ~ that is unmistakable, no matter how bad the drawing may be, is that the foregoing are all straight-bladed weapons (irrespective of a ~ wavy), and cannot be confused with the curved swords, of which the sabre (q.v.) is typical. (267, 433, 434)

Sword, Order of the: (Sweden) f. 1522 in five classes. Insignia—*Badge:* a gold-rimmed Maltese cross, set saltirewise, with gold crowns between the arms; a blue central medallion bears a sword between three crowns in gold; the top points of the badge are joined by crossed swords, and the first- and second-class badges also have swords joining the other points and linked by a gold ribbon; the badge is ensigned with a crown; the fifth class has the gold portions replaced by silver. *Star:* a silver cross paty, with small points between the arms surmounted by gold crowns; a central medallion as for the badge. *Riband:* yellow with a blue stripe near the edges.

syke: [M.E.] lit. a runnel or small stream: applied to the fountain (q.v.) when employed in the arms of families with the surname Sykes, but not in any other setting. (141)

symbolic figures: all the figures conventionalized in art and accepted as representative of virtues, emotions, attributes, etc. are used in heraldry, not so much as charges, but as crests (q.v.) and supporters (q.v.): figures such as Justice, Time, and the like are known to all levels of culture throughout the world; such representative forms are often in the arms of public bodies and of commercial undertakings. Personages such as kings (q.v.), queens (q.v.) and bishops (q.v.) are presented in a conventionalized form. (285)

Symm, Robert: Procurator Fiscal to the Lyon Court, 1668.

syren: see **siren.**

---

439. Gules, three seaxes inverted and reversed: in chief a Saxon crown gold.
Former *County Council of Middlesex.*

440. Azure, a falchion in pale argent, hilted gules.
Tatnell (2).

441. Paly bendy azure and gules, an orle of martlets, Or.
Hendley, Cranbrook.

442. Azure, three scimitars in pale argent, hilted and pommelled Or, points to the sinister.
Hodgson.

443. Azure, a sword wavy erect hilted and pommelled Or between two mullets in fess pierced argent.
Dick.

444. Barry bendy of eight Or and gules.
Bermingham.

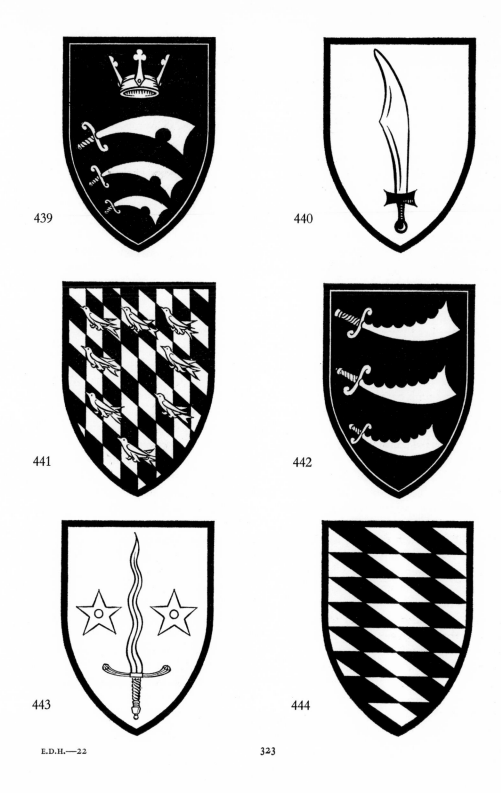

439

440

441

442

443

444

tabard: see **College of Arms.**

tabby: see **catamount.**

tabor: [Persian] the archaic name of the drum; later, specializing for a small drum to accompany the fife (q.v.) retained in heraldry for ca. value, and drawn as a modern side-drum. (150)

tadpole: [M.E.] the larva of both the frog and the toad, blazoned as haurient (q.v.), naiant (q.v.), and urinant (q.v.), but of r. occurrence.

taenia: L., bend.

taeniola: L., cotice.

tagliato: It., per bend sinister.

Tailefer, John: Marchmont Herald, 1661. Herald-painter, 1661. Also spelt 'Tailzefer'.

taille: Fr., per bend sinister.

Tailzefer, John: see **Tailefer, John.**

Tait, George: Lord Lyon Depute, 1819.

tajado: Sp., per bend sinister.

talbot: see **dog.**

Talbot Banners: (c. 1442) paper book 7½ by 10 in., painted with banners, in each I and IV, Talbot; II and III, the arms of either a family or a lordship connected with John Talbot, first Earl of Salisbury. The quarters brought in have names over.

Talbot Herald: see **Shrewsbury Herald.**

talent: r. alt. for 'bezant' (q.v.).

taper-candlestick: see **pricket.**

targe: Scottish circular shield.

tassel: [M.E.] a bunch of short lengths of thin cord issuant of a pommel, which is itself a terminal decoration of a length of thick cord. ∼s are attached to the cords of an ecclesiastical hat (q.v.), the corners of a cushion (q.v.), and in such-like secondary positions; they sometimes appear alone as a primary charge (q.v.).

tasselled: [M.E.] of any object provided with tassels, notably the cords of an ecclesiastical hat (q.v.), but also other cords and cushions.

tau-cross: The Greek text letter τ which,

to distinguish it from the Roman capital T, is always represented with all surfaces concave. It is also blazoned as 'the cross of St Anthony'. (220)

Tax on armorial bearings: in the mid XIX cent. a tax on all armorial devices, whether the subject of a grant or used without authority, was imposed so that the wearing of a signet-ring was likely to cost £1. 1s. 0d. per annum. By accepting tax on spurious arms the Treasury became party to fraud, but the Act was not repealed until the mid XX cent.

Taylor, David: Ross Herald, 1825. Unicorn Pursuivant, 1806.

teal: [M.E.] a freshwater bird of the duck family, *Querquedula crecca*; employed in heraldry largely for ca. reasons.

teasel: [M.E.] a plant, *Dipsacus fullonum*, having an egg-shape burr with stiff, sharp spines; used in dressing cloth, and figuring notably in the arms of the Worshipful Company of Clothworkers. (371)

teengekruk: Afk., counter-potent.

teenhermelyn: Afk., pean.

tegenvair: D., counter-vair.

telescope, forty feet reflecting: granted, 'with its apparatus proper', to Sir John Herschel, Bt, in 1838: an outstanding example of a 'prosaic object'.

tenantes: Sp., supporters.

tenants: see **supporters.**

tench: a freshwater fish, *Tinca vulgaris*, inhabiting deep waters, as the rivers Elbe, Rhine, and Weser. Confused in British heraldry with the barbel, and represented stout of girth and armed with a pair of barbs attached one each side of the mouth. In continental heraldry it is named the bar and is a ca. device. (67)

Tendale, Wm: see **Tyndale, Wm.**

tenente: It., supporters.

tenné: [Fr.] tawny, orange-brown, or chestnut-brown; the paramount stainand colour; not to be confused with 'brunatre' (q.v.) or with any shade of brown resulting from 'proper' (q.v.).

tent: [L.] a portable dwelling or shelter consisting of canvas or similar fabric; formerly of either felt or leather. The heraldic $\sim$ is the classic form as seen depicted in medieval manuscripts. A central pole, terminating at the top (usually) in a truck (a disc-shaped finial) supports a sharply conical roof finished with a vandyked drop from behind which the comparatively long curtain falls, in folds, to the ground. The fly is generally open revealing the lining, which may differ in colour from the exterior, and the base of the pole where sometimes there sits a beast. The $\sim$ stands firm without guy-lines and may carry a pennon flotant from the upper portion of the pole. It is variously styled '$\sim$ royal', 'pavilion', and 'sperver'. This last word is of considerable interest: in both O.E. and early Teut. it means a hawk, specifically a sparrow-hawk. The word was applied to a bed-canopy by association of ideas—the wide spread wings hovering overhead, and from there, in natural sequence, to a tent. Modern pattern $\sim$ also appear in arms and are blazoned by name, e.g., 'a marquee-$\sim$'. (241)

tenter-hook: a clothworker's peg; in appearance like a wire-nail with but half a head.

term-man: a figure of a man (or a woman) to the waist where it blends into a pillar, generally of square section, tapering downward, and standing on a plinth. In the XVIII cent. a $\sim$ and a term-woman often acted as pseudo-supporters (q.v.) and were a popular theme in bookplates. Not genuine heraldry.

terrace: a plain point vert; employed mainly in continental arms.

terret: [M.E.] a D-ring attached to an article

of leather, as a dog's collar, or a hawk's jesses (q.v.) for the purpose of engaging a hook on the end of a lead: similar rings on a horse's harness through which the reins pass: also, in heraldry, a shaped dowel, spindle, or toggle attached to the end of a lead for passing through a ring and, by its setting at right-angles to its strap (or chain), acting as a stopper. (329)

Territorial Decoration: f. 1908. *Badge:* within an oval silver wreath of oak-leaves tied at the top, bottom, and sides with gold riband, is the gold-crowned royal cypher of the conferring sovereign. *Riband:* green with a broad yellow centre stripe. The Honourable Artillery Company has the distinction of a riband based on K. Ed. VII's racing colours: half red, half royal-blue with yellow edges.

Terry, James: Athlone Herald, 1690.

tertaitum: L., tierced.

tesselatum: L., chequy.

Teutonic Order, the: the Order of the Teutonic Knights of the Hospital of St Mary of Jerusalem was f. in 1199, having grown from a fraternity of German charitable workers who, under Meister Sigebrand operated a field hospital during the siege of Acre. By the XIII cent. the Order ruled vast possessions, particularly on the Baltic coast, and the Grand Master was a sovereign *de jure et de facto*. Later the Order suffered severe blows through military defeats, the apostasy of certain high officers, and at the hands of Napoleon. In 1929 the Order became a religious community, with the continuing power to confer its knighthood and other honours, notably the Marian Cross. Insignia—*Badge:* a silver-edged black cross paty in narrow elongated form ensigned with a knight's helmet coroneted and plumed. *Star:* a larger version of the unensigned badge. *Riband:* black; the Marian Cross is similar in design, but has a central medallion depicting a red Latin cross on a white ground, and is suspended from a black and silver riband.

Teutonic Order in the Netherlands, the Bailiwick of Utrecht of the: The Teutonic knights in the Low Countries separated themselves and their portion of the Order's possessions from the Grand Master's control at the time of the Reformation, and eventually became a Protestant Bailiwick, which now flourishes under the protection of the Crown of the Netherlands.

text-letters: see **script.**

thatchaver: [dial.] a folk-name used in Worcestershire for a sparrow, and used in ca. settings for the name of Thatcher.

Themis: see **Vulcan.**

theow: a composite fictitious beast being a mastiff with cloven hoofs; the tail is described as 'that of a cow and a collie combined'. Alt. spellings 'thoye' and 'thos'.

thigh-bone: see **leg-bone.**

third son, mark of difference of: see **brisure.**

thistle: [O.E.] a wild plant; the royal badge for Scotland which, like the English rose (q.v.), is adaptable to heraldic design without (or with but slight) conventionalization. The leaves are long, narrow, and engrailed (q.v.), the head globular and green, and the flower, which consists of a mass of thread-like upstanding petals, is purple. A ～ proper is vert, flowered gules, but it may be of any heraldic colour. The ～ is armed in all its parts with prickly spines, and according to legend became Scotland's national emblem because, at the battle of Largs (1262), when King Harco, having made a landing, was advancing inland under cover of darkness, one of his barefooted followers trod on a thistle and gave a howl of pain that raised the alarm. The date of its first appearance as a royal badge is 1474, when it supplied the dorse of a silver coin of James III. A ～,

u.o.s., is accompanied by a pair of leaves, one rising on each side (41)

Thistle, Most Noble and Ancient Order of the: of legendary foundation; revived in 1687 by James II. Insignia: a star of four points, St Andrew's cross superimposed, bearing centrally an enamelled thistle on a gold background surrounded by a green circle bearing the motto *Nemo me impune lacessit*; a gold collar of alternate enamelled thistles and sprigs of rue; a gold badge of St Andrew in green gown and purple surcoat bearing his cross enamelled white surrounded by rays of gold, to be worn from the collar, or from a riband of dark green over the left shoulder; a mantle of green velvet taffeta bound, having on its left side St Andrew bearing his cross surrounded by a circlet of gold with the motto.

Thomas, James: Chester Herald, 1590. Former Bluemantle Pursuivant, 1587; and ultimately March King of Arms, 1592.

Thomas, St: appears in the municipal arms of Dobris, Bohemia (the town's status was established in the Saint's day), and in the arms of Zamose, Poland.

Thomas Beckit, St: see **Beckit, St Thomas.**

Thomas Jenyn's Book: see **Jenyn's Book, Thomas,** and **Rolls of arms.**

Thompson, Samuel: Windsor Herald, 1606. Former Portcullis Pursuivant, 1602.

Thompson, Thomas: Lancaster Herald, 1637. Former Rouge Dragon Pursuivant, 1624.

Thomson, Alexander: Bute Pursuivant, 1724.

Thomson, John: Bute Pursuivant, 1636.

Thomson, Peter: Islay Herald, 1531.

Thomson, Robert: Dingwal Pursuivant, 1795.

Thomson, Wm: Lyon Clerk Depute, 1812.

Thomson of Fairliehope, Wm: Lord Lyon Depute, 1666.

Thomson of Keillour, Henry: Lord Lyon King of Arms, 1496. Former Islay Herald.

Thor: God of Thunder; is one of the supporters of the municipal arms of the City of Sheffield, England.

Thorburn, Archibald: Carrick Pursuivant, 1864.

Thornbery, Thomas: Windsor Herald, 1745. Former Portcullis Pursuivant, 1745.

thos: see **theow.**

thoye: see **theow.**

threaded: of a spindle (q.v.), wound with thread.

throughout: see **voided.**

thunder-cross: see **Jupiter's cross.**

thunderbolt: see **Jupiter's thunderbolt.**

Thury Pursuivant: in the service of Sir John Salveyn, Bailiff and Justicar of Rouen during the second quarter of the XV cent. The name is derived from the Thury Lordship in Normandy of which, it seems, Sir John was seized. Also spelt 'Tury'.

Thynne, Francis: Lancaster Herald, 1602. Former Blanch Lyon Pursuivant, 1602.

Tibbetts, Hugh Gray: Kintyre Pursuivant, 1866.

tibiatus: L., membered.

tierced: [L.] of a shield parted by three: this may be achieved by 'per chevron, and in chief per pale', alt. 'per graft'; per graft inverted (the palar line baseward instead of chiefward) gives a field '~ in pairle' or ~, or party, per pall. There are a few examples of '~ per pale' and '~ per fess' in British heraldry (particularly during the Tudor period), but it is now considered to be a continental form, the British version being per pale (or per fess), a pale (or a fess). (450)

tiercefeuille: Fr., trefoil.

tiger proper: see **Bengal tiger.**

tiler's nails: see **nails.**

tillbakaseend: Swd., regardant.

tilting shield: Tudor: a shield of specific shape, developed in the Tudor period and which has survived because it is particularly adapted to carry an achievement quarterly of four, when the pronominal quarter (q.v.) is repeated in the fourth, and is charged with (say) three beasts passant, as in the British Royal Arms (q.v.). A heater-shape (q.v.) shield, or even a square-top round-bottom shield distorts the basemost beast in IV: a ~, however, provides ample space. It has concave flanks, and in chief it rises to an apex. The upward slope is never plain: it may be engrailed (q.v.), invected (q.v.), or 'scribed', i.e. the slopes may be formed of shallow S's or, as the term suggests, of two printer's long-brackets placed end to end. Further variations of shape in the peak are not prohibited, however; the apex in chief is reversed and repeated in base. It is sometimes termed 'a peaked shield', and some good specimens appear on English silver coinage. (403, 406)

tilting-helmet: see **helmet of rank.**

tilting-spear: see **lance.**

timber: an heraldic term for the stock of an anchor; tapering towards the extremities and bound lashed or whipped with wire seizings; also blazoned 'stock'.

timbre: [O.F.] lit. a crest (q.v.); hence, the exterior decoration of a shield of arms above the motto-scroll (q.v.) and the compartment (q.v.).

tincture: [M.E. fm L.] colour (exclusive of metal (q.v.)), to the employment of which heraldic art is restricted: there are five only in general use: gules (q.v.), sable (q.v.), vert (q.v.), azure (q.v.), purpure (q.v.).

tinktur: Swd., tincture.

Title Badges, Indian: f. 1911 at K. Geo. V's Coronation Durbar at Delhi. The badge was awarded in three classes and was worn round the neck. Titles: first class, Diwan Bahadur (Moslem), or Sardar Bahadur (Hindu)—*riband:* light blue, edged dark blue; the badge in silver-gilt. Second class—

Kahn Bahadur (Moslem) or Rai or Rao Bahadur (Hindu)—*riband:* red, edged dark red, the badge in silver-gilt. Third class, Khan Sahib (Moslem) or Rai or Rao Sahib (Hindu)—*riband:* dark blue, edge light blue; the badge in silver; *badge:* a five-point star, with a central medallion bearing the crowned effigy of the emperor surrounded by a band inscribed with the name of the appropriate title; the badge is ensigned with the Imperial crown.

tityron: see **musimon.**

tod [M.E.] alt. for a fox (q.v.).

Tod, Thomas: Snowdoun Herald, 1579.

toegewend: Afk., affrontée.

Toell Volland Pursuivant: see **Estoile Volant Pursuivant.**

Toison d'Or[1]: a king of arms created c. 1420 by the Duke of Burgundy.

toison d'Or[2]: see **fleece.**

toison d'Or[3]: see **Fleece, Order of Golden**

Tolosa, croce di: It., cross of Toulouse.

tomahawk: an all-purpose axe (q.v.) de-

veloped by the North American Indians: the haft (q.v.) between 2 and 3 ft in length, the head originally of stone, bone, or horn (later, iron), used as both a weapon and a tool. A specialized form, having a hollow haft, and the butt of the head converted into a bowl, known as a 'pipe ~', is used in the ceremonial smoking of 'the pipe of peace', and is the type generally intended in heraldry.

Toms, Peter: Portcullis Pursuivant, 1745.

Tonge, Thomas: Clarenceux King of Arms, 1534. Former Norroy K. of A., 1522; former York Herald, 1513.

tongs: [O.E.] a tool or implement consisting of two limbs which, brought into opposition, grip, and enable to be lifted, an object that cannot, or ought not, to be grasped in the hand. The insignia of St Dunstan who, being a smith, tweaked the devil's nose with his ~. As a tool, used by both the blacksmith and the founder; hence, symbolic of both callings.

tools and machines: see **prosaic objects.**

top: the masculine toy, the pear-shape, long-

---

445.   Quarterly per grand quarters: I and IV, quarterly: 1 and 4, per pale indented argent and gules: 2 and 3 azure, a lion rampant Or: II, on a chevron sable between three mascles as many mullets argent; III, paly argent and azure, a bend, also sable.
Lord Mounteagle of Brandon.

446.   Chequy Or and azure, a fess gules.
Lord Clifford of Chudleigh.

447.   Quarterly Or and gules a cross flory between I and IV, a fleur-de-lys and, II and III, a fret all counterchanged.
Municipal Corporation of Worthing.

448.   Paly-bendy argent and gules, two flaunches Or: on a chief of the last an annulet between two cinquefoils of the second.
Hagge.

449.   Quarterly, per fess indented, argent and gules: in dexter-chief a bugle-horn sable.
Foster.

450.   Tierced in pairle azure gules and sable, three trefoils Or.
Foyle.

445

446

447

448

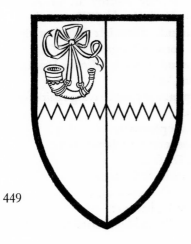

449

450

pegged top, not the short whipping top, being depicted: also blazoned as 'playing ~' and 'spinning ~'. (333)

top-boot: see **Dutch boot.**

Topaz: see **segregative blazon.**

Toppin, Aubrey John: Norroy and Ulster King of Arms, 1957. Former York Herald, 1932, former Bluemantle Pursuivant, 1923.

torch: see **firebrand.**

tornerkrage: Swd., label.

torqued: lit. twisted into an elongated spiral; hence, an alt. term—though r.—for ondoyant (q.v.), and also for 'cabley' or 'wreathed' (q.v.).

torre: Sp., tower.

Torrington Pursuivant: (c. 1430) maintained by Earl of Huntingdon, Duke of Exeter, and named from the town in Devon on the Earl's estate.

torse: [L.] r. alt. for a wreath of the colours (q.v.).

torta: It., roundels of any tincture.

torteau: [L.] a roundel (q.v.) gules, representing a round loaf of bread, or a tart: ~ should be discreetly shaded. (Plural— torteaux.)

tortella: L., torteau.

tortile: L., wreath.

tortoise: [L.] a reptile protected by a carapace, covered with horny skin called its 'shell'. Symbolic of slow but sure progress. Generally blazoned as turgiant (q.v.) but may also be passant (q.v.) and erect (q.v.). (73)

tortrixy: r. obs. for semé (q.v.) of torteaux (q.v.).

toti superinductum: L., overall.

Touch, John Edward: Lyon Clerk Depute, 1807.

Toulon, John: Ross Herald, 1746.

Toulouse cross: a cross cleché (q.v.) voided (q.v.) and pommetty (q.v.).

tournament-barrier: a fence along which the contestants in a joust rode. Being of a temporary nature, it was generally flimsily constructed of nailed planks, and it was sometimes covered with fabric. A very r. charge; sometimes employed on the continent. (110)

tower: invariably a round-~ having lights (q.v.) and a port (q.v.) which may be in front or at the side and out of which something may be emerging. 'A ~ triple towered' has, on the roof, within the battlements, three small round ~. (152)

tower, church: see **church.**

Tower and the Sword, Military Order of the: (Portugal) f. 1459 and re-activated in 1832 in five classes. Insignia—*Badge:* a gold-rimmed white star of five points, pommetty; surmounting a green and gold laurel wreath; a white central medallion depicts a curved sword horizontally between green and gold leaves, and is surrounded by blue and gold bands, the blue one being inscribed *Valor Lealdade e Merito* in gold: the badge is ensigned, between its uppermost arms, with a gold tower. *Star:* the badge surmounting a gold star of five points. *Riband:* blue.

Townley, Charles: Lancaster Herald, 1781. Former Bluemantle Pursuivant, 1774.

Townley, Sir Charles: Garter King of Arms, 1773. Former Clarenceux K. of A., 1755; former Norroy K. of A., 1751; former York Herald, 1735.

Townsend, Francis[1]: Windsor Herald, 1784. Former Rouge Croix, 1778.

Townsend, Francis[2]: Rouge Dragon Pursuivant, 1820.

tragopan: a pheasant having a pair of erectile horns.

train: see **peacock.**

train-aspect: see **trian-aspect.**

tralie: D., fret.

traliewark: Afk., trellis.

tranché: Fr., per bend.

trangla: It., barrulet.

trangle: Fr. and Sp., barrulet.

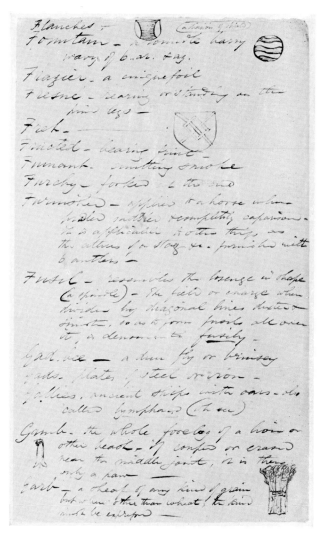

Photograph by Colin Relph

Plate XVII A page from a manuscript glossary of heraldry, anonymous and undated, but probably executed c. mid XVIII century. There are fifteen leaves measuring 8¾ by 5⅜ inches, fourteen of which are closely written on both sides, the fifteenth on the top half recto only. (In Julian Franklyn's collection.)

transfixed: pierced with a pointed implement, generally of a beast ~ with an arrow; alt. form 'transpierced'.

transfluent: of water pouring through the arches of a bridge (q.v.).

transmutatus: L., counterchanged.

transpierced: see **transfixed.**

transverse sectum: L., per fess.

trapper, horse: [M.E.] a covering, often of rich velvet, emblazoned with the rider's arms, for a war-horse, the purpose of which was to inhibit sword-cuts at the animal's legs. A horse trapper-clad is sometimes described as 'barded' (q.v.).

trapvormig: D., indented.

traverse: [M.E.] a cross-piece; particularly the horizontal element of a cross.

treblading: Swd., trefoil.

treble violent: see **violin.**

treble violin: see **violin.**

trebol: Sp., trefoil.

trebolada, cruz: Sp., cross trefly.

tree of paradise: see **paradise tree.**

tree trunk: see **log of a tree.**

trees: [O.E.] all kinds of ~ are made use of, not only those indigenous to or transplanted to our own soil, but tropical and other growths. They are generally employed for ca. reasons or as symbolic of some distant part of the world in which a man has spent a lifetime in the service of that country. Plants that to the botanist would rank as shrubs, or as bushes, are, to the heraldist, ~; and there are two fictitious plants so styled: one is known as the 'china-cocker ~', of which no specimen is known in current heraldry, the other as the 'grain ~'. When the blazon (q.v.) gives 'a tree' without specifying, the oak is to be understood. ~ are visually identifiable by their being drawn with disproportionately large leaves and, when fructed (q.v.), even more gigantic fruits. ~ may be either issuant (q.v.) or eradicated (q.v.); may appear singly or associated in groups blazoned as a hurst (q.v.) of ~. (260)

trefly, cross: see **bottony, cross.**

trefoglie: It., trefoil.

trefoil: [M.E.] a device consisting of three more or less circular leaves, each tapering to a neck and conjoined in the centre to a short stem, tapering to a point. The vector of two incessant forces pressing heavily on heraldic art, namely ignorance and plagiarism, results in crosses paty fitchy (q.v.) being drawn as ~, and ~ as crosses paty fitchy. A modified ~ terminating the limbs of a cross humetty (q.v.) makes cross trefly or bottony (q.v.).

The addition of a fourth petal makes the quatrefoil, which, unlike the ~, is never slipped: a further petal produces the cinquefoil, which may represent the narcissus, the primrose, or the strawberry flower. These last, under their alt. title 'fraises', are common in Scottish heraldry, ca. on the name Fraser. A sixth petal makes the sexfoil, also named angemmes. There is no figure having seven petals, but there is one of eight petals, the octofoil, generally called 'double quatrefoil', and employed as the brisure (q.v.) of the ninth son. (368, 380, 383)

Tregoz Roll: (XV cent.) painted vellum true roll (q.v.) of twenty-four shields; none is named, but most are those of families allied with Tregoz and Grandison.

Treheron, Thomas: Somerset Herald, 1532. Former Nottingham Pursuivant, 1530 maintained by Duke of Richmond and Somerset.

treillissé: Fr., trellis.

trellis: a debased form of fretty (q.v.) in which all the costs surmount all the bastons: when of a metal, inclined to be given a dot of tincture at the cross-overs to represent a nail-head, and blazoned 'cloué' (q.v.).

trellisado: Sp., trellis.

tressure: [M.E.] a narrow band, being the inner quarter of a bordure (q.v.) split through its width into four, which surrounds the shield. A ~ is sometimes stated to be the diminutive of an orle (q.v.). One ~ seldom appears: a second, running parallel with the first, the gap between them of the same width as each, completes a single unit known as a double-~ which is generally decorated with charges that cross the two parts. Fleurs-de-lys serving this purpose produce a double-~ flory-counter-flory: the f.d.l. in the dexter-chief corner has its head outward; that in centre-chief, its head inward and onward round the shield, eight of them alternately inward and outward.

A single ~, on the few occasions of its use, is decorated on the outer edge only, which gives rise to the supposition that a double ~ ought to be flory-counter-flory of sixteen: eight for each ~. If it is admissible the one eight is absconded (q.v.) by the other. Where space permits, as in a flag, sixteen, or any other even number may be used to advantage.

Figures other than f.d.l. may provide the decoration for a double ~, e.g. crescents, f.d.l., being in the Scottish Royal Arms, are the most well known. All figures so used appear on the outside and on the inside of the two parallel bands, but not in the gap between them.

The ~ is employed more frequently in Scottish than in English heraldry: its appearance in the achievement of a commoner is assumed to indicate a royal descent no matter how remote the relationship may be. (403—second quarter, 424)

Treswell, Robert: Somerset Herald, 1597. Former Bluemantle Pursuivant, 1589.

triam-aspect: see following entry.

trian-aspect: an obs. term, formerly applied chiefly to the eagle when displayed (q.v.)

with the head poised three-quarter face, i.e. halfway between facing dexter and affronté. Frequently mis-spelt in either of two ways, 'train' or 'triam'.

triangle, disposed in: of three objects extending from fess point towards the corners of the shield; also described as 'disposed in' or shortly as 'in pairle' (q.v.). (294, 437)

triangle, interlaced in: see **herring.**

triangular fret: three arcs, convexity inward, interlaced and conjoined at the points.

triangular tower: similar to a square tower (q.v.) but having three sides only, and always set arraswise (q.v.).

tribolo: It., caltrap.

tribuli: L., caltraps.

trick: [M.E.] a rough sketch of a coat of arms; strictly, in pen and ink, but extended to cover other writing media, and understood to include abbreviated indications of metals and tinctures to be employed.

tricorporate: see **bicorporate.**

tricuspida: Sp., bottony.

trident: a fish-spear having three barbed tynes; Poseidon's (Neptune's) sceptre.

trifogliata, croce: It., cross bottonée.

trifolium: L., trefoil.

trinciato: It., per bend.

triple arch: see **arch.**

triple crown: a crown of three tiers, each being a ducal coronet (q.v.) evolved during the Reformation in order to eliminate the Papal tiara without fundamentally altering the appearance of the arms. The achievement of the Worshipful Company of Drapers exemplifies such a charge. (234)

triple-towered: see **castle** and **tower.**

trippant: equivalent of passant (q.v.) and applicable to a dog (q.v.) or a stag (q.v.). It is also used for courant (q.v.). (33)

Tristram knot: any symmetrical interlacing of endless cordage, very often of bad design and nearly always overcrowded. The ~ is r. in British heraldry, but it has its admirers on the Continent. Alt. term 'true lover's knot'.

Triton: alt. name for a merman (q.v.).

triumphal crown: a wreath of laurel.

trivet: [M.E.] an iron frame provided with three short legs on the underside; used for supporting a cooking pot on a fire. A ~ may be either triangular, a leg at each corner, or round, and the blazon should, but does not always, specify. Symbolic of firmness, immovability. (321)

trochleated: [Gk] lit. pertaining to the wheel, or to rotation; hence, of a serpent coiled in an advancing spiral like a screw-thread; not 'ondoyant (q.v.) fesswise'.

trogodise: a stag having the attires inverted, i.e. disposed forward and downward.

trompeta: Sp., bugle-horn.

tronchado: Sp., per bend.

troncone: cut in pieces; hence a r. alt. for 'trononné' (q.v.).

trononné: dissected, disjointed, dismembered; of a beast (usually a lion) cut at every joint and the parts reassembled showing a narrow line of the field through: of any figure thus cut and reassembled: a cross sarcelled (q.v.) may be so blazoned. An alt. term, 'dechausse', is obs. In the arms of the family of Maitland the lion ~ is of ca. significance, from 'mautelent', i.e. mutilated. (47)

trotting: see **horse**.

trout: [O.E.] a freshwater fish, *Salmo fario*, the head and sides spotted black and red; considered to be a sporting fish (as well as a table delicacy); it occurs frequently in English arms.

trowel: a tool employed in working cement, plaster, and the like; generally triangular steel, provided with a raised handle. Found chiefly in Livery company arms. A 'garden ~' is a small scoop. May be ca.

true lover's knot: see **Tristram knot**.

true roll: see **rolls of arms**.

truffle: [Fr.] an edible fungus; sometimes employed for ca. reasons.

trumpet: see **hautboy**.

trumpet-banner: see **banderole**.

truncated: [L.] alt. for 'couped' (q.v.); applied to a branch (q.v.) of a tree.

truncheon: a baton of office, particularly that of the Earl Marshal.

trundle: a ball of gold thread, drawn with crossing series of parallel lines, and finishing oval, the long axis palewise. 'Or' need never be added, for if it is not, it is not a ~.

trunk: see **elephant**.

Trupour, John: Carrick Pursuivant, 1364.

trussing: see **falcon**.

Tryphonius, St: appears in the municipal arms of Kotor, Yugoslavia.

tub: see **tun**.

tub-fish: see **gurnard**.

Tubman, Nicholas: Lancaster Herald, 1553. Former Rouge Croix Pursuivant, 1550; former Hampnes Pursuivant, 1545.

tuck: alt. for a rapier; a light dress-sword.

Tucker, Stephen Isaacson: Somerset Herald, 1880. Former Rouge Croix, 1872.

Tudor Book of Arms, A: see **Holme's Book, Randle**.

Tudor Rose: the Lancastrian red and the Yorkist white ~ combined, the one debruising the other; on a field of tincture, a Yorkist ~ carries a Lancastrian, and vice versa on a field of metal.

tufted: of any beast having bunches of hair extending from the limbs, particularly at the joints. Beasts are sometimes ~ without it being specified in the blazon: the lion is a most unfortunate victim of this kind of artist's licence, sometimes being ~ at all points, and in between them, until the contour is lost and the drawing needs careful study to find out what it is intended to represent.

tulip: a plant having bell-shaped flowers and long, narrow, pointed leaves. *Tulipa gesneriana*, unknown in old and uncommon in modern heraldry, having been transplanted on to European soil (from Turkey) late in the XVI cent.

tun: a barrel as used to hold beer or wine. Depicted resting on the bilge, the bungstave facing outward. It may stand upright, but rarely does so; and it may be blazoned as 'a barrel', 'a tub', 'a hogshead', or 'a cask' but rarely is because, under any of those alt. descriptions it would represent a utility article, but as a ~ it is an object of ca. value in most of its appearances. The hoops may be of a colour differing from that of the staves. (310)

turbot: [M.E.] a large flat fish, *Psetta maxima*; employed in heraldry chiefly for ca. reasons.

turgiant: [L.] of a tortoise when passant; blazoned as displayed ~ in either fess or pale; presenting his back view with head to the named direction.

turm: Ger., tower.

turned-up: of a cap's lining revealed at the lower edge.

Turner, John: Ormonde Pursuivant, 1708.

turnierkragen: Ger., label.

turnierpfahl: Ger., Quintain.

turnip: [O.E.] a plant having a large,

spheroidal edible root, and tender leaves, *Brassica rapa*, which latter are also edible; formerly employed in British, but now only in continental heraldry. The foregoing reference to the usage of the ~ may also be applied to the carrot, the radish, and to watercress. (392)

turnstile: an upright post provided at the top with a crank-handle and crossed by a number of transverse bars extending to an equal distance on each side.

Turpin, Richard: Windsor Herald, 1565. Former Bluemantle Pursuivant, 1559; former Hampnes Pursuivant, 1549.

Tury Pursuivant: see **Thury Pursuivant.**

tusk: see **elephant.**

tweelingsbalke: Afk., bars-gemel.

two wings conjoined: see **leure.**

tygre, heraldic: a composite fictitious beast having the tail, body, and limbs of a lion, the maned neck of a horse, and the head of a wolf, but the upper jaw develops into a frontal horn: this may be either corkscrew-shaped or curved downward, like the upper mandible of an eagle. Self-appointed reformers of heraldry (and particularly of blazon), who do not see why the archaic spelling should be retained, themselves dispense with it. This may be disastrous for the ~, when proper, is by no

---

451. Sable, three chapes Or.
      Adderton.

452. Argent, two halberts in saltire azure.
      Eccles.

453. Gules, five Danish axes palewise in saltire.
      Machado.

454. Argent, a Lochaber axe between three boar's heads couped gules.
      Rankine.

455. Gules, three battle-axes argent between as many of each fleurs-de-lys and mullets Or.
      Tregold.

456. Gules, two pole-axes in saltire Or, between four martlets argent.
      Pickman.

451

452

453

454

455

456

means the Bengal tiger (q.v.). There is a legend that the tygre is a conceited creature that may be easily taken, or the cubs taken from the mother, by the simple expedient of placing a mirror on the ground; hence, 'a tygre looking at a mirror' is an occasional way in which the ~ appears. (281)

Tyndale, Wm¹: Lancaster Herald, Rouge Dragon Pursuivant, and Guisner Pursuivant during the reign of K. Hen. VII. Also spelt 'Tendale'.

Tyndale, Wm²: Lancaster King of Arms, 1450. Former Chester K. of A., 1447; former Chester Herald, 1443; former Collar Pursuivant, 1436. Also spelt 'Tendale'.

tynes: [O.E.] sharp points in a row, as the prongs of a fork; hence, the branches of a stag's attires (q.v.).

tyrwhytt: [dial.] a name for the lapwing (q.v.).

Tytler of Woodhouselee: Lord Lyon Depute, 1827.

Udwart, Martin: Ormonde Pursuivant, 1566.

uitgeschulpt: D., engrailed.

uitkomend: Afk., issuant.

Ulster King of Arms: see following entry.

Ulster Office: the heraldic authority for all Ireland before the secession. The department's business was transacted from the Record Tower, Dublin Castle. There were two official appointments; Ulster King of Arms and Keeper of State Papers (the last to hold office was Sir Neville Wilkinson), and Athlone Pursuivant. Some early writers on the subject record a Colombus Pursuivant and a Drake Pursuivant: if such there indeed were, they must have held an office similar to that of an extraordinary officer of arms. What is more important is that some contemporaneous writers record Dublin Herald and Cork Pursuivant among the Irish officers of arms: they were not. These titles were held by members of the Order of St Patrick (q.v.), and whatever duties they may have had were not connected with the control of the armorial bearings of other members of the Order.

During the revolution the chambers were seized by the rebels who did not touch the records (they may have been too ignorant to know there were such things), but were content to steal the office stationery, and they spoiled the carpet in Ulster King of Arms's room by cooking sausages and spilling the fat.

When southern Ireland became an autonomous State, England claimed the Records of the ~, but the Irish Government (justifiably) repudiated the claim on the grounds that the documents were Irish Records. They proceeded to set up their own authority which transacts its business from the same chambers, is designated 'The Irish Genealogical Office', and is under the jurisdiction of 'The Chief Herald of Ireland'. When the smart had receded from the wounds, photostatic copies were made of all the documents in the office, and these were most generously presented to England.

The title 'Ulster King of Arms' went into abeyance, but the province of Ulster was added to the territory of Norroy King of Arms (q.v.) whose title was accordingly enhanced.

Ulster Roll: (temp. K. Hen. V) in book form, painted on paper, $7\frac{5}{8}$ by $11\frac{1}{2}$ in., containing 672 shields with names over. A general roll (q.v.) depicting arms of attribution with those of English kings, queens, dukes, earls, and armigerous commoners.

umbra, in: see **entrailed.**

umbra leonis: see **entrailed.**

uncinata croce: It., swastika.

undulatory: [L.] r. alt. for 'wavy' (q.v.); more frequent, but still r., in its shortened form, i.e. 'undy'.

undulatus: L., wavy.

undy: obs. alt. for 'wavy' (q.v.), being an abbreviation of the common word 'undulatory' (q.v.). Alt. spellings 'onde' and 'unde', but ~ is often confused with 'urdy' (q.v.).

unguled: [L.] of the hooves when of a colour differing from that of the beast itself. (27, 30, 272, 280, XIV)

unicorn: [L.] a mythological beast having one horn erupting in the centre of the brow. Frequently, but er., both described and depicted as a horse thus armed. The ~ is basically a goat, having cloven hooves and being bearded; further, when in the rampant attitude the ~ may be blazoned as clymant (q.v.). In mythology the ~ was the water-conner, having in the horn the magical power of purification. In the Middle Ages a piece of ~ horn was believed to be an antidote to all forms of poison; because of this the ~ often appears in arms as a symbol of purity, e.g. as the supporters of the arms of the Society of Apothecaries. The ~ tail is that of the heraldic lion, and the beast is familiar as the sinister supporter of the Royal Arms, where it is rampant, but it also appears as a charge in both the statant and the courant attitude. The head alone, either couped or erased, is also employed. The ~ is blazoned as armed, unguled, and bearded. (272)

Unicorn Pursuivant: see **Lyon Office.**

unicornio: Sp., **unicorn.**

uniform: [L.] military and naval ~ of many periods are preserved in the figures of supporters, and the ~ of various occupations likewise have an honoured place—often in the achievements (q.v.) of peers.

Union Jack: a name first used in an official document concerning flags in the reign of Queen Anne, and adopted as the popular description of the Union Flag of Great Britain and Northern Ireland. Upon the union of the thrones of Scotland and England, K. James VI and I had ships of the Royal Scottish Navy flying at the mast-head a banner of St Andrew (q.v.) and ships of the Royal English Navy flying a banner of St George (q.v.). To regularize the position the first union flag, being the combined crosses of the two patron saints was evolved, and this, known as the Jacobean Union, remained 'the British flag' until 1801. In that year the Act of Union with Ireland necessitated the addition of the banner of St Patrick, and the blazon of the present Union Jack was promulgated, viz.: 'azure, the crosses saltire of St Andrew and St Patrick, quarterly per saltire, counterchanged argent and gules, the latter fimbriated of the second, surmounted by the cross of St George of the third, fimbriated as the saltire'. Ships of the Royal Navy display 'at the bowsprit end', i.e. well forward at the vessel's stem, flying from the jackstaff, a ~ when in harbour.

uppatbojd: Swd., enarched.

upprätt: Swd., rampant.

upright: see **horse.**

urcheon: [O.E.] archaic spelling, current in heraldry, of 'urchin', a hedgehog. Genus *Erinaceus*. (41)

urdy: a line of partition consisting of open vair-bells (q.v.) alternately inverted and conjoined; r. in British heraldry because of its homophony with 'undy' (q.v.). Cross urdy is a cross humetty with the extremity of each limb brought to a 90° point by cutting each side at an angle of 45°. Crown vallary (q.v.) is sometimes blazoned 'crown

~'. Alt. spellings, urde(e) and onde(e). Sometimes used er. for indented. (207)

urinant: [L.] lit. to dive; hence, of a fish or a marine mammal when palewise with head in base.

urn: see **jug.**

utatseende: Swd., affrontée.

utrinque-pinnatus: L., counter-embattled.

utroque latere accinctus: L., cottised.

V.: abvn for 'vert' (q.v.), for which 'ver.' is also used.

vocaido: Sp., voided.

vågskura: Swd., wavy.

Vaillant King of Arms: (c. 1350) a not very well authenticated office, no province being on record as under ~ jurisdiction. Also spelt 'Volant', unless this last was a separate name of office of another equally ill-defined king of arms.

vair: [Fr.] representing squirrel fur, a pattern of angular church-bell shapes crossing the field: along the line of the chief there should be five upright bells; hence, in dexter-chief (q.v.) the first shape is half an inverted bell. The next row is arranged base to base with the first, the two together forming a 'track' of which four should reach from chief to base, the number of bells in the track becoming reduced by the curvature of the shield. The colour scheme is argent and azure, the metal commencing in the first upright bell in the chiefmost row: in the second row the upright bells remain argent, but appear below the azure, thus metal and tincture bells are base to base, and apex to apex. When tincture and tincture, and metal and metal bells are base to base, the fur is counter-vair, and any other tincture or metal gives vairy and counter-vairy, followed by 'of' and a statement of the colours. Alt. 'verry'. (XII)

vair ancient: a term used for 'old vair' or 'long vair' (q.v.).

vair-bell shield: see **prick-eared.**

vairy: see **vair.**

vajo: It., vair.

vallary, crown: a circlet heightened by ten vair bells, five only of which appear in drawing, those at the sides being in profile. Probably an heraldic development of crown palisado (q.v.). (230)

valpoort: D., portcullis.

vambraced: of an arm (q.v.) clad in plate-armour, the hand gauntleted normally, but when proper almost certainly clenched. (243, 246, III)

vamplet: see **lance.**

van: see **vannet.**

van die een in die ander: Afk., counter-changed.

Van Riebeeck Decoration: (South Africa) f. 1952 to be awarded for distinguished service in battle. *Badge:* a silver-gilt five-point star with a central medallion depicting Jan Van Riebeeck in full length, and holding a walking-stick, against a background of circles representing his three ships; the medallion is surrounded by a band inscribed *Uitnemende Diens—Distinguished Services. Riband:* blue.

Vanbrugh, Sir John: (the dramatist) Clarenceux King of Arms, 1704. Former Carlisle Herald, 1703. He was, too, nominated Garter K. of A. These offices were improperly bestowed since ~ knew nothing of heraldry.

vane: [M.E.] a thin plate of metal fretted with an armorial device, having an arrow-head, or other pointer, extending outward on the dexter, which, mounted upon a shaft round which it could revolve was set upon a pinnacle, or roof-crown, to indicate the direction of the wind. Such wind-indicators were not erected at will but by permission and under the supervision of the heralds; hence, the shape of the ~ on castle or on grange was indicative of the rank of the occupier. A knight's ~ was triangular, as his pennon (q.v.); that of higher ranks, square or rectangular as their banners (q.v.). There is no information on the form of the ~ of a gentleman or esquire.

vannet: [frmd on L., 'fan'] a winnowing basket; a fan of basketwork broad, and convex, at the base, tapering upward and at the top turned over (forward) to form a hand-hold. Great skill is demanded in drawing the ~ or it has the appearance of an escallop (q.v.) without the hinges. Alt. terms are 'fan', 'fruttle', 'van', and 'scruttle'. (304)

vanster: Swd., sinister.

vapenbeskrivning: Swd., blazon.

vapenförande person: Swd., armiger.

vara: Sp., pallet.

variations of the field: when the field (q.v.) is composed of equal numbers of the diminutives (q.v.) or the ordinaries (q.v.), or of combinations of these: a field thus varied is neither of metal (q.v.) nor of tincture (q.v.) but partakes of both; hence, it may carry charges (q.v.) of either metal or tincture; however, the colours forming the ~ should be avoided.

variegatus: L., vair.

Vasa, Order of: (Sweden) f. 1772; nominally in three classes, but two are sub-divided to correspond with the usual five classes of state orders. Insignia—*Badge:* a gold-rimmed Maltese cross pommetty, with gold crowns between the arms; an oval blue central medallion depicts in gold a wheat-sheaf with handles, from the arms of the Vasa family, and is surrounded by a red band inscribed in gold *Gustav Den III Instiktare*

MDCCLXXII. Star: a Maltese cross, decorated between the arms, surmounted centrally by a wheatsheaf with handles, all in silver. *Riband:* green.

vase: see **jug.**

vectis: L., bar.

veld: Afk., field.

Venables, Robert: see **Fayery, Robert.**

venera: Sp., escallop.

Venetian glass cup: only in the arms of the Worshipful Company of Glass-sellers.

Venus: see **segregative blazon.**

ver.: see **V.** and **vert.**

verbroken: D., trononné.

verde: It., vert.

verdon knot: a term sometimes applied to the Harrington fret (q.v.).

verdoy: [O.F.] obs. for a bordure (q.v.) charged with any form of vegetation.

vergette: Fr., pallet.

verghetta: It., pallet.

verhaven: D., facetted.

verhoog(d): Afk. and D., enhanced.

verkort: Afk. and D., couped.

verkorte breedarminge kruis: Afk., cross paty.

verkorte gaffel: Afk., shakefork.

verkorte kruis: Afk., cross humetty.

verkorte skuinstaak: Afk., ribbon.

verlaagd: D., in base.

verolled: lit. ferruled; hence, of metal bands surrounding objects, particularly the bugle-horn (q.v.); alt. spelling 'virolled'. Substitutional for 'banded' (q.v.).

veros: Sp., vair (q.v.).

verres: [L.] a boar (q.v.) used for ca. reasons.

Verrey Pursuivant: known only as one who accompanied a herald carrying letters to the Duke of Brittany in 1468.

verry: see **vair.**

verry, cross: four vair-bells (q.v.) set in cruciform juxtaposition, apex to apex, but not conjoined (q.v.).

verschlingend: Ger., vorant.

verschoven paal: D., fracted.

versions of rolls: see **rolls of arms.**

verslindend: D., vorant.

versmalde balk: D., bar.

versmalde dwarsbalk: D., barrulet.

versmalde keper: D., chevronel.

vert: [L.] emerald green; represented in engraver's cross-hatching by parallel lines per bend (q.v.).

verted: see **reverted.**

vervelled: see **jessed.**

vested: [M.E.] an alt. for 'habited' (q.v.).

vestido: Sp., vested.

vestito: It., vested.

vexillum: [L.] a streamer or ribbon attached to a crosier just below the head, and wound about the staff.

Victoria and Albert, Royal Order of: f. by Q. Vic. in 1862 in four classes, for ladies. Insignia of first two classes being an onyx cameo of Q. Vict. and the Prince Consort bordered by diamonds and ensigned with the Imperial crown; for third class, the border is of pearls; the fourth class is a V & A monogram set with pearls, ensigned with the Imperial crown; the riband of white moiré is worn as a bow on the left shoulder.

Victoria Cross: f. by Q. Vic. on 29 January 1856, is the highest British award for valour, and takes precedence over all other British orders and decorations. It is a breast-worn bronze cross paty, struck from the metal of Russian guns captured during the Crimean War: the obverse bears a lion passant gardant standing on the royal crown, over an escroll inscribed *For Valour*; the reverse has a circle with the date of the action for which the award was granted. The riband is crimson-red (pre First World War naval awards were issued with a blue riband) and when worn without the decoration bears centrally a miniature of the Cross.

vidé: Fr., voided.

vierblad: D., quatrefoil.

vierblatt: Ger., quatrefoil.

viertel: Ger., quarter.

vigilance: see **crane.**

vijf blad: D., cinquefoil.

vildman: Swd., savage.

---

457. Or, three caltraps gules.
Bellwood.

458. Azure, three field-pieces on their carriages in pale Or; on a chief argent as many cannon balls sable.
Royal Ordnance Corps.

459. Gules, a sheaf of three arrows Or, barbed and flighted argent.
Goodrich.

460. Argent, three battering-rams fesswise in pale proper headed and garnished azure within a bordure of the last.
Bertie, of Nether Hall.

461. Argent, two guns in saltire proper between, in chief, the monogram 'GP' and, in base, the text-letter V, both regally crowned: on the dexter a barrel of gunpowder and, on the sinister, three gunstones, one and two in pyramid, all sable.
Worshipful Company of Gunmakers.

462. Azure, an archer's bow in fess, string chiefward, the arrow in pale, argent.
Muller.

457

458

459

460

461

462

vilenado: Sp., membered.

viléné: Fr., membered.

Villebon Pursuivant: known to have served under Maine Herald (q.v.) in 1449.

Vincent, Augustine: Windsor Herald, 1624. Former Rouge Croix Pursuivant, 1621; former Rose Rouge Pursuivant, 1616.

violet: the sweet-smelling wild violet, *Viola odorata*, is intended; drawn without conventionalization.

violin: the familiar musical instrument drawn naturalistically, palewise, the body chiefward. When reversed it is described as 'transposed'. The M.E. word 'fiddle' is used in blazon as frequently as is ∼. 'A treble violin' refers to the violoncello, and is sometimes written 'treble violent'. May be 'stringed' of a different colour. (355)

viper: see **serpent**.

Virgin and child: see **sacred and legendary figures.**

viridis color: L., vert.

virolled: see **verolled.**

virtues, blazon by: see **segregative blazon.**

Virtuti Militari, Order of: (Poland) f. 1792 and reactivated in 1919 in five classes; until 1944 the eagle was crowned. Insignia —*Badge:* a gold-edged black cross paty pommetty, on the arms of the cross is the Order's name in gold; a gold central medallion surrounded by a green wreath, depicts a white eagle displayed; the badge is ensigned with a gold plaque, surrounded by a wreath, bearing the letters *RP*. 4th and 5th classes, badges gilt and silver respectively. *Star:* the badge, without the gold balls and with the addition of the Order's motto *Honor I Ojczyzna* around the eagle, surmounting a silver star of eight points. *Riband:* blue with broad black stripes near the edge.

Viscount: [L.] viscounts rank fourth in the five ranks of the peerage. Originally the title was French, applied to the deputy of a count (q.v.) or a duke (q.v.), and was introduced into England after the Norman conquest when it was used in connection with the sheriffs and high sheriffs. It was first used as an English peerage style in 1440 when Lord Beaumont, Count of Boulogne, was elevated to precedence over all barons in the style of Viscount Beaumont.

viscount's coronet: a circlet heightened with pearls (q.v.) to the number of either fourteen or sixteen. In drawing seven only.

visitations of the heralds: the duty of investigating the right by which persons used and displayed armorial bearings within the province was inherent in the office of a king of arms from its inception, but no such investigation on a large scale was undertaken before Thos Benolt, Clarenceux, appealed to K. Hen. VIII for a warrant confirming him in his powers; a step made necessary by internal friction in the College of Arms. The resultant warrant, dated 6 April 1530, confirmed the right and duty of a king of arms to visit his province and to summon to appear before him all persons using arms, or styling themselves esquires or gentlemen and bring with them sufficient proof of their authority to do so. It further declared that the K. of A. was empowered to enter castles, houses, churches, and other buildings to survey armorial devices displayed therein and to deface, pull-down, or otherwise destroy all representations of arms used without authority. Spurious arms might be eliminated from plate, jewels, glass, paper, and parchment. There was nothing new in all this: it was merely in confirmation of existing powers, but the provision in the warrant of aids to the implementation of these powers was an innovation.

Visiting officers of arms, by virtue of this royal warrant, were empowered to enlist the aid of the sheriff who, by it, is called upon to provide lists of persons bearing arms or styled gentlemen. The sheriffs in turn were empowered to localize the gathering of information by calling upon the bailiffs to make a return reporting on their own bailiwicks. Because of this division of responsibility it is reasonably certain that none having the smallest pretensions failed to receive a summons. To have ignored it would have been ill advised as the result would have been an order to appear before the Earl Marshal, at its best troublesome and costly: at its worst, an entry to the Marshalsea Prison.

The fact of the list of persons being compiled by local people for the guidance of the visiting herald is either overlooked by, or is unknown to, people claiming arms by 'prescriptive right' (q.v.). They maintain that at the visitation their family was neglected because the herald was (say) a Yorkshireman who knew but little of (say) Kent. Persons examined either had their arms confirmed as they were, or, in the event of some slight irregularity, such as, e.g., the interpolation of quarters, their arms were 'rectified at the time'. Persons using arms without authority, or styled esquire, had no need to ignore the herald's summons. No terrible fate would befall them; they were simply asked to sign a 'disclaimer' which was to be displayed in the market place of the nearest town. This was not a matter to occasion distress. The local gentry and the local rustics were fully informed in the matter anyway. If the pretender was one who knew how to behave, and had been accepted as a neighbour by the gentry, they were not likely to travel to town to read the disclaimer, and the rustics, who could not read anyway, would continue to doff the cap.

Whether the arms were confirmed or rectified, or a disclaimer was signed, careful and copious notes were taken by the heralds who, on their return to London, had the whole of these notes copied in fair hand, and satisfactorily illustrated in colour in big, strongly bound permanent books, which have been kept up to date and which constitute the library of Visitation Books and Records of the College of Arms. After transcription the rough notes were returned to the heralds concerned and ultimately many of them found their way into one or another of the great manuscript collections known as the Harleian and the Cottonian collections of the British Museum. Many of these notes on visitations have been printed and published, some by private enterprise, but most by courtesy of learned societies whose interest is in this particular branch of archaeology. All students are grateful for such publications, but it must be borne in mind that they are not reproductions of the Official Records of the College of Arms, and may have had spurious matter interpolated by (say) a child, or by a servant; hence, if the information is required for some serious purpose, e.g. to establish a claim to title or property, confirmation will need to be obtained from the College of Arms.

The royal warrant of 1530 was renewed in 1555 and again in 1558. The major ∼ were organized to take place once in a generation, i.e. thirty years, and between these tours of armorial oversight, minor journeys were made to fill in the gaps, as it were. The last of the ∼ was made in 1686. The strong feeling in favour of the Stuart dynasty is attested by the lists of non-jurors, and ∼ at that time might have had an irritant effect. No visitations have been made in Scotland notwithstanding that the officers of arms are empowered to make them by Act of Parliament, 1592.

visor: [M.E.] the movable face-guard of the helmet: raised, open; lowered, closed.

vitta: L., bend sinister.

vittae infulae: [L.] the two purple ribbons, edged with gold, that descend from out of the headband of a mitre (q.v.).

viverra: L., wyvern.

vlamwijse: D., wavy.

vlug: Afk., two wings conjoined.

voetangel: D., caltrap.

voided: [M.E.] lit. emptied; hence, of a figure having the central portion cut away: a cross ~ had about one-third of its width removed leaving a framework that is continuous, i.e. the extremities of the limbs are intact; but '~ throughout' describes a cross the extremities of which are severed leaving four disconnected pieces. A cross humetty ~ throughout has the appearance of four Roman sans serif capital text letters L. (207)

voider: [M.E.] lit. a fender, screen, or other means of defence. The second diminutive of the flanch (q.v.) being, at its greatest width, one-third of the parent; half of a flasque (q.v.)s ~ are always borne in pairs, one each side of the shield. (N.B.—see note at **flasque.**)

vol, demi: [Fr.] a single wing, the tip chiefward unless blazoned as 'inverted'.

vol banneret: a wing elevated and cut

square at the tip; generally plural, being used on the Continent for flanking a crest.

volans: L., volant.

volant: [Fr.] on the wing; in flight; applied both to birds and insects.

Volant King of Arms: see **Vailant King of Arms.**

voluted: [L.] formed into a spiral, either loose and flat, as the ornament of an Ionic capital (which is lit. ~) or in an advancing, screw-like spiral; hence, applied to a serpent (q.v.) in either of its customary attitudes.

vorans: L., vorant.

vorant: feeding, devouring; of predacious beasts swallowing their prey.

voutée: r. alt. for 'enarched' (q.v.).

vruchten: D., fructed.

vrykwartier: Afk., quarter.

Vulcan: Greek god of fire; employed in arms generally as a supporter (q.v.): accompanied by Thor (q.v.) for Sheffield, Yorkshire; by Themis, goddess of civic authority for Workington, Cumberland; and, for Slough, Buckinghamshire, by Mercury.

vulning herself: see **pelican.**

vulst: Swd., torse.

vuoto: It., voided.

vuurstaal: D., ferris.

vyfpuntige ster: Afk., mullet.

---

wahlspruch: Ger., motto.

Waiting, Officer of Arms in: see **College of Arms.**

Wake and Ormond knot: a double Carrick-bend.

Wales Herald: a name of office employed during the last decade of the XIV cent. and revived as an 'extraordinary,' 1963.

Walford's Roll: (c. 1275) a vellum true roll containing 180 names and blazons.

Walker, John: Procurator Fiscal to the Lyon Court, 1876.

Walker, Sir Edward: Garter King of Arms, 1645. Former Norroy K. of A., 1644; former Chester Herald, 1638; former Rouge Dragon Pursuivant, 1637; former Blanch Lyon Pursuivant, 1635.

Walker, Wm: Lyon Clerk Depute, 1769.

Wall, Thomas[1]: Norroy King of Arms, 1516. Former Lancaster Herald, 1510; former Guisnes Pursuivant, 1506.

Wall, Thomas[2]: Garter King of Arms, 1534. Former Windsor Herald, 1525; former Rouge Croix Pursuivant, 1521.

wall between two towers: see **port between two towers.**

Wallace, James: Carrick Pursuivant, 1531.

Wallace, Robert: Procurator Fiscal to the Lyon Court, 1685.

Wallace of Craigie, Adam: Unicorn Pursuivant, 1467.

wallflower: see **gillyflower** and **heartsease.**

Wallingford Pursuivant: may have been in the service of Kings Hen. V and VI, but cannot be authenticated before 1489. Wallingford Castle, from which the name derives, was the property of the Prince of Wales, as Duke of Cornwall, till the 31st regnal year of K. Hen. VIII.

walnut: the tree, *Juglans regia*; its fruit and its leaves are all employed for ca. reasons, particularly for the name Waller. (106)

Walter, John: see **Water, John.**

wand: [M.E.] a willow branch, *Salix viminalis.*

wapen: Afk., achievement.

wap(p)enmantel: D. and Ger., mantling.

wapenschild: D. achievement.

wapensprenk: Afk., motto.

war mace: a weapon consisting of a spiked, globular head cast in one piece with the haft the end of which is generally provided with a hole to which a short length of square-linked chain is attached. (188)

war-bell: r. obs. alt. for a church bell (q.v.).

war-bill: see **pike**[1].

Warburton, John: Somerset Herald, 1720.

Ward, Knox: Clarenceux King of Arms, 1726.

warden: the name of a hard, cooking pear; employed in heraldry for ca. reasons.

Wark Pursuivant: maintained (1454) by Lord Grey of Powis who held Wark Castle, Northumberland; also spelt 'Werk'.

Warwick Herald: maintained during the first half of the XV cent. by the earls of **Warwick.**

Warwick Roll: see **Rous Roll.**

wassail bowl: see **bowl.**

wassenaar: D., crescent.

wastel-cake: [M.E.] white bread, having no standardized form, and generally secondary to a bread-basket (q.v.). Torteaux sometimes represent ~.

water: see **assurgeant.**

Water, John[1]**:** Chester Herald, 1455. Former Warwick Herald. Also spelt 'Walter'.

Water, John[2]**:** York Herald, 1484. Former Rouge Croix Pursuivant and Rose Blanche Pursuivant during the reign of K. Ed. IV. Also spelt 'Walter'.

water-bouget: [M.E.] lit. a water bag. Drinking water was carried, when on a military expedition, in bags made from the skin of a goat or a sheep. One of these was attached to each side of a pack-saddle, and the girth of the sumpter mule forced them outward. Since the bags were soft and could not be tilted to obtain the contents, a thong was sewn into the bottom inside and left hanging out at the neck. To draw water the thong was pulled thus raising the bottom of the bag, and causing an overflow at the neck. The heraldic ~ is a highly conventionalized representation of the pack-saddle, the two bags (inclining outward) and the flotant thongs. The attempts that have been made from time to time to simplify, to rationalize, and to modernize the ~ have all understandably failed. (340)

watercress: see **turnip.**

waterpot: see **jug.**

Watkins, Thomas Morgan Joseph: Chester Herald, 1913. Former Portcullis Pursuivant, 1894.

Watson, George: Lyon Clerk and Keeper of the Records, 1630.

Watson, John: Bluemantle Pursuivant, 1646.

wattled: sometimes used in place of 'jowlopped' (q.v.).

wave: obs. alt. for a fess wavy.

wavy: [O.E.] a line of partition undulating from flank to flank, or from chief to base; when an ordinary (q.v.) or a charge (q.v.) is ~, the two edges run parallel. An obs.alt. is 'undy'. (265, 443, II, X)

Waysford Pursuivant: see **Wexford Pursuivant.**

weare: see **weir.**

weasel: [O.E.] a member of the family *Mustelidae*; similar in appearance to the stoat (q.v.) with which it is often identified.

weaver's shuttle: see **shuttle.**

web: see **spider.**

wecken: Ger., fusil.

wedge: a triangular shape, exactly the same as a pile (q.v.), but never issuant nor conjoined.

weel: [M.E.] a cylindrical net, closed at one end and held open at the other—and along its full length—by wicker rings which placed in the overflow of a fish-nursery, prevented the stock from swimming downstream; may also be blazoned as 'filled with fish' when a number are represented as naiant (q.v.) within it. Alt. terms 'fish-basket', 'weir-basket', and 'eel-pot'. (301)

weir: [M.E.] a fence of pales woven with osier that was constructed across a stream forming a dam for the purpose either of creating a mill-race, or creating a fish conservatory. Alt. spelling 'weare'; alt. term, 'haie'. Of ca. value in heraldry and depicted without conventionalization.

weir-basket: see **weel.**

Weldon, Sir Wm Henry: Clarenceux King of Arms, 1911. Former Norroy K. of A., 1894; former Windsor Herald, 1880; former Rouge Dragon Pursuivant, 1870.

well: generally proper, a rustic drinking-water shaft, depicted with coping of brickwork and the crank, drum, and rope mechanism for raising and lowering the bucket (q.v.).

well-bucket: a circular vessel tapering towards the bottom, constructed by the cooper; hence, being of staves held in hoops. Two staves protrude upward, are

---

463. Or, three bird-bolts gules, nooked of the first and, in chief, a label of three points throughout gules.
Berum.

464. Ermine a spear-head in pale azure, embrued.
Jackson.

465. Quarterly gules and azure: in the second and third two bars wavy argent, the whole debruised by as many tilting-spears in saltire between, in chief, a fleur-de-lys; in fess, two annulets and, in base an anchor erect, all Or.
Lind.

466. Argent, three scaling-ladders bendwise in bend sinister gules.
Killingworth.

467. Vert, four tilting-spears fesswise in bend, surmounted by as many fesswise in bend sinister, Or.
Breakspear.

468. Azure, a trident erect in pale Or, surmounted at the fess point by a crescent argent between two Indian curved swords proper pommelled and hilted gold.
Thakore (Sahib of Palitana).

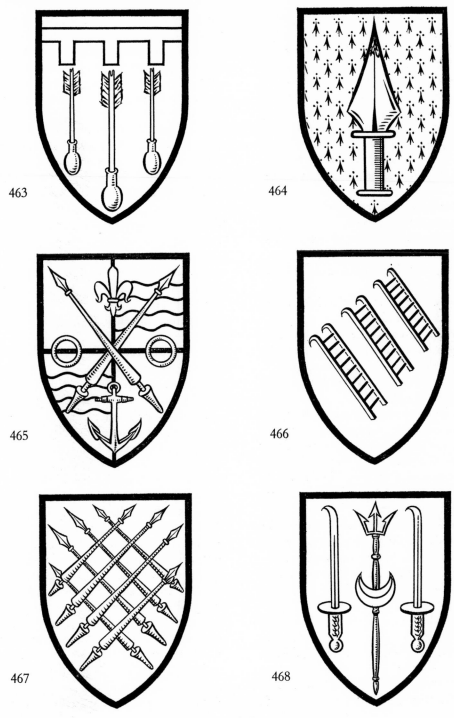

463   464

465   466

467   468

347

drilled and threaded with a rope-handle, three protrude downward forming feet. Sometimes blazoned simply as 'a bucket', and also as 'a pail'. There is a suggestion that in base it is a ~, but in chief a milking pail, and that it ought to be blazoned accordingly; however, milking pails are to be found in base and ~ in chief. Precisely the same drawing is made for a 'dosser', which is assumed to be merely an alternative term; however, a dosser is actually not a bucket, but a pannier.

wellenbalken: Ger., fess wavy.

wellengeteilt: Ger., wavy.

Wellington boot: see **Dutch boot.**

welted: r. obs. alt. for 'fimbriated'.

Wemyss, David: Marchmont Herald, 1482.

Wenceslas, St: appears in the civic arms of Stora-Boleslav, Bohemia.

werewolf: a composite fictitious beast having a human head on a wolf's body; based on the belief in shape-changing.

Werk Pursuivant: see **Wark Pursuivant.**

werpspies: D., javelin.

Westminster Tournament Roll: not a roll of arms (q.v.): a painted panorama of the procession proceeding to the 'solem jousts held at Westminster 13 day of February in the first year of King Henry VIII in honour of his Queen, Katherine'. College of Arms manuscript.

Wexford Pursuivant: maintained by John Talbot, Earl of Shrewsbury and Waterford, who was styled Earl of Wexford. ~ brought dispatches home from overseas in 1430. Also spelt 'Waysford'.

wharrow-spindle: see **spindle.**

wheel: when a ~ is blazoned without specializing, a wagon ~ is intended having a massive nave, eight stout spokes, the rim segmented into felloes and held in an iron rim or tyre. Special ~ each have their own character: an artillery ~ is without a nave, the spokes being fitted into a flat iron socket; a naval gun-~ is cast in one piece, a rimmed disc without spokes; a barrow ~ is like a wagon-~, but has four spokes only; a fly ~ is of cast-iron having S-shaped spokes, a cog- or gear-~ has a toothed edge. When a demi-~ is blazoned the dexter half appears u.o.s. The ~ is symbolic and may be both ca. and allusive. It is also the emblem of St Martin de Tours, who is patron saint of Vintners; hence, the ~ is part of the crest of that livery company. See also **caravel.** (347, 469)

whelk: [O.E.] a sea-snail, *Buccinum undatum*, represented in heraldry by its turbinate shell, and employed in ca. settings to cover the syllable 'shel' or 'shall', in a surname. Normally orientated erect, with the opening chiefward. (151)

Whinyates, Charles: Richmond Herald, 1722.

whip¹: see **pennon.**

whip²: see **scourge.**

whirlpool: see **gurge.**

whistle, boatswain's: intended to represent the bo'sun's 'call', but never drawn convincingly: the object depicted might be a dog-whistle, which is not quite suitable for piping the admiral over the side.

White, Valentine: Islay Herald, 1757.

White Elephant, Order of: (Thailand) f., 1861 in eight classes. Insignia—*Badge:* Grand Crosses—a gold-rimmed green enamel cross urdy with long silver flames between the arms; a gold central medallion depicts three white elephants and is surrounded by a band of brilliants which is ensigned with a star of thirty-two points, alternately pink and red; the whole is ensigned by the Thai crown and a symbolic sunburst. Other classes—three overlapping multipointed stars making a circular badge; a **central** medallion depicts one white elephant; ensigned with the Thai crown and a sunburst. *Star:* Grand Crosses—a star of eight points, alternately silver and gold, surmounted by the badge and crown. Other classes—of sixteen rays, with lotus leaves between each; a central medallion depicts a white elephant and the Thai crown between two symbolic temple devices. *Riband:* red with narrow green and gold striped edges.

White Ensign: the flag of the Royal Navy (and the Royal Yacht Squadron): 'argent, the cross of St George, and in the canton, the Union'. Trinity House vessels, when escorting a royal yacht, are permitted to fly the ∼.

White Lion, Order of the: (Czechoslovakia) f. 1922 in five classes. Insignia—*Badge:* a five-armed red enamel cross of fifteen points pommetty, with leaves between the arms, surmounted by a silver lion rampant; ensigned with a gold wreath, and crossed swords for the military division. *Star:* of silver, eight-point, having a red central medallion bearing the lion and surrounded by the inscription, in silver, *Pravda Vitezi. Riband:* red with two broad white stripes near the edges.

white nun: name of a specific breed of duck.

whiting: a small fish of the genus *Merlangus*; employed in heraldry for ca. reasons.

Whiting, Thomas: Chester Herald, 1471. Former Nucelles Pursuivant, 1462.

Whiting, Wm: Chester Herald during the reign of K. Hen. VI. Former Huntingdon Herald, c. 1441.

Whitwick, Thomas: see **Wightwick, Thomas.**

Whyte, John: Lyon Clerk Depute, 1863.

wicker-basket: roughly hemispherical, provided with a ring at the bottom to form a foot and prevent rolling when standing, and an arched handle twisted, or plaited, attached to the top rim. The ∼, also named 'hand-basket', differs but little, if at all, from a practical modern shopping basket.

wiedergeviert: Ger., quarterly per grand quarters.

wiggin tree: [dial.] a name for rowan, *Pyrus aucuparia*; depicted, for ca. reasons, in the civic arms of Wigan, Lancashire.

Wight, George: Unicorn Pursuivant, 1635.

Wightwick, Thomas: York Herald, 1717. Former Portcullis Pursuivant, 1713. Also spelt 'Whitwick'.

wild cat: see **catamount.**

Willement's Roll: (c. 1395) vellum true roll (q.v.) containing 601 painted shields with names over: the first twenty-five, being the arms of the founder knights of the Order of the Garter (q.v.), are displayed within the Garter. These are followed by the arms of dukes, earls, lords, and knights.

William, Military Order of: (Netherlands) f. 1815 in four classes. Insignia—*Badge:* a gold-rimmed enamel Maltese cross pommetty, with gold-edged green leaves between the arms; the words *Voor Moed Beleid Trouw* appear on the arms; a gold crown surmounts the badge centrally, and another ensigns the whole. *Star:* the unensigned badge on a silver star of eight points. *Riband:* gold with a blue stripe near each edge.

Williamson, James: Procurator Fiscal to the Lyon Court, 1809.

Williamson, Wm Kilgour: Herald-painter to the Lyon Court, 1853.

Williamson of Mylnehill, Thomas: Ross Herald, 1616.

willow-tree: generally blazoned as either 'salix' (q.v.) or 'ozier' (q.v.). See also **palm.**

Wilson, Adam: Procurator Fiscal to the Lyon Court, 1823.

Wilson, Henry: Islay Herald, 1864. Carrick Pursuivant, 1855.

Wilson, John Jeffers: Kintyre Pursuivant, 1860.

Wilson, Patrick: Carrick Pursuivant, 1679.

wimble: see **auger.**

windmill: the entire structure, complete with sails and backstay, sometimes appears as a charge: the type thus employed is the post-mill, a square, wooden building, the planking running laterally, poised upon a massive post round which it turns to face the wind. (312)

windmill sails: the combination of four constitute a unit, and it is generally orientated saltirewise (q.v.). There are two types, and the blazon does not specify which is to be represented. The old form was a timber frame having bars through its length and across its width to which a canvas sail was rigged and which had to be reefed (as the sails of a ship) to 'spill the wind', when blowing hard. The modern form was a similar frame carrying from end to end closely set slats, each of which was spring-loaded, and controlled by a screw-rod, actuated with a crank-handle, from the outer end. Both types were 'weathered', i.e. slightly twisted, and they are consequently drawn as though tapering slightly. ~ are more common as crests than as charges on the field.

Windram, Robert: Albany Herald, 1613.

Windsor Herald: see **College of Arms.**

wing: see **vol.**

winged bull: a bull provided with wings; based on Pegasus (q.v.). The symbol of St Luke.

winged horse: see **Pegasus.**

winged lion: a lion generally either statant or sejant, provided with a pair of wings (which should be of ample proportions) either elevated or addorsed. ~ is sometimes er. described as the lion of St Mark (q.v.). (276)

winged stag: a stag provided with wings; based on Pegasus (q.v.).

Wingfield, John: York Herald, 1674. Former Portcullis Pursuivant, 1660.

wings conjoined in leure, two: see **leure.**

winkelmasskreuz: Ger., swastika.

winnowing basket: see **vannet.**

Winram, James: Lyon Clerk and Keeper of the Records, 1657.

Winram, Robert: Lyon Clerk and Keeper of the Records, 1625.

wire, bundle of: only in the achievement of the Society of Mineral and Battery Workers.

(N.B.—The term 'battery workers' is, in modern times, misleading, suggesting a chemico–electric generator. The 'battery' referred to is to batter, crush minerals for smelting.)

wire-drawers' tools: see **wyre-drawers' tools.**

wisall: heraldic spelling, with the variation 'wisom', of Old Dutch 'wizle', the green tops of any edible roots such as carrots, turnips, and the like.

wisom: see previous entry.

withered: see **branch.**

Withers, Richard: Portcullis Pursuivant, 1550.

wodehouse: [Teut.] a wild-man of the woods, sub-human, but superior to the beasts. Always depicted as covered from head to foot with shaggy, brown hair and, if 'wreathed' (q.v.), he has 'an apron' of foliage about the loins. He generally carries a large, crude club. Alt. spellings 'wode-wose' and (more correctly) 'woodwose'; alt. term 'woodman'.

wolf: [O.E.] a member of the dog family, *Canis lupus*, drawn with sharply tapering snout and protruding tongue: the coat is rough; the ears large and shaggy on the lower edge; the bushy tail is ragged and carried gay. Demi-~ and ~ head either couped or erased are of more frequent occurrence than is the complete beast who, punning on his French name, 'loup', is often ca. for the name 'Lewis'. ~ may be passant, statant, courant, salient, rampant, and combatant. (15)

wolf-hook: see **cramp**.

Wollaston, Sir Gerald Woods: Garter King of Arms, 1930. Former Norroy K. of A., 1928; former Richmond Herald, 1919; former Bluemantle Pursuivant, 1905; former Fitzalan Pursuivant Extraordinary, 1902. ~ retired in 1944 and reverted to the office of Norroy and Ulster K. of A., 1944.

wolverene: a giant weasel (q.v.) or marten (q.v.), *Gulo luscus*, known also as the glutton, which is a very prevalent charge, both in its natural form and conventionalized, in Hungarian heraldry.

Wood, George: Messenger-at-Arms to the Lyon Court, 1749.

Wood, John: Procurator Fiscal to the Lyon Court, 1802.

wood-bill: see **pike¹**.

wood-louse: a crustaceous isopod, *Oniscus asellus*, always found in association with decaying timber, whose defence mechanism is to roll itself up into a tight ball. Allusive, uncommon, and depicted extended, fesswise, proceeding to the dexter. It is also termed a cheese-slip, but for reasons unknown.

woodbine: a name applied to the honeysuckle, *Lonicera periclymenum*; a climbing plant having yellow trumpet-shaped flowers.

Woodhead, Laird of: Lord Lyon King of Arms, 1471.

woodman: see **wodehouse**.

woodman's axe: see **axe**.

Woods, Albert Wm: Rouge Dragon Pursuivant, 1886.

Woods, Sir Albert Wm: Garter King of Arms, 1869. Formerly both Brunswick and Lancaster Herald, November 1841; also Norfolk Herald Extraordinary, October 1841; former Portcullis Pursuivant, 1838; former Fitzalan Pursuivant Extraordinary, 1837.

Woods, Sir Wm: Garter King of Arms, 1838. Former Clarenceux K. of A., 1831; former Bluemantle Pursuivant, 1819, and, at the same time, Norfolk Herald Extraordinary.

woodwose: see **wodehouse**.

woolcard: see **card¹**.

woolpack: identical in appearance to a bag (q.v.) but never corded. It is symbolic of all aspects of the woollen industry from sheepfarming to cloth manufacture. In the Middle Ages it was, in effect, a guild mark. It is a frequent indicator of a man's calling in monumental brasses (q.v.), where it is generally a foot-rest. (372)

Worcester Herald: in the service of John Tiptoft, Earl of Worcester, mid XV cent.

word: see **motto**.

Workman, James: Herald-painter to the Lyon Court, 1592. Marchmont Herald, 1597.

worms: see **distillatory**.

wound: according to an early writer, a ~ was one 'of the seven arms round', i.e. a roundel purpure, but it is open to doubt whether the term was ever employed in practical heraldry.

wounds: see **sacred and legendary figures**.

wreath¹: a circlet of foliage, oak, u.o.s., depicted upright with stems crossed and tied with ribbon, the ends flotant: the semicircle of leaves on one side may differ from the other, e.g. 'a wreath of laurel on the dexter and olive on the sinister'. A ~ may be of any heraldic colour. The ~, the chaplet (q.v.), and the garland (q.v.) each have characteristics that put them in classes apart from each other; however, the three terms are frequently confused one with another, and they are beginning to be accepted as interchangeable. (236, 239)

wreath²: a charge consisting of a large annulet (q.v.) gyronny (q.v.): a conventionalized representation of the crest-wreath (q.v.) seen from above; hence, in full circle.

The term ~ is also applied to a 'joscelyn' (q.v.).

wreath of the colours: a representation of two (or three) lengths of fabric twisted together like the strands of a rope with which the helmet of rank (q.v.) is encircled, and out of, or upon, which the crest is set. The ~ is of six pieces, alternate metal and tincture, these being the major colours of the shields, generally those of the field and of the ordinary. When the ~ is of three colours (all from the arms), two (different) metals will take precedence over two tinctures. ~ accompanies the crest when it is displayed apart from the achievement, and it ought always to be drawn with the ends falling below the centre to indicate curvature: a rigid, straight ~, as favoured by the copperplate engravers of the XVIII cent., is both wrong and ugly, and is facetiously but justly called 'the barber's pole'. Alt. terms 'torse' and 'bandeau'.

wreathed: see **cabley.**

Wright, John: Bute Pursuivant, 1704.

Wriothesley, Charles: Windsor Herald, 1534. Former Rouge Croix Pursuivant, 1524.

Wriothesley, Sir Thomas: see **Wrythe, Sir Thomas.**

Wriothesley, Wm: York Herald, 1509. Former Rouge Croix Pursuivant, 1505. Also known as Wm Wrythe.

Writhe's Book of Knights: (temp. K. Hen. VII) paper book of 208 leaves, 8 by 10½ in. Contains painted shields and crests of knights, commencing with those dubbed in 1460.

Writhe's Garter Book: (c. 1488) a painted book on leaves of both vellum and paper of varying dimensions, all mounted and standardized at 1 ft 8¾ in. by 2 ft 2¾ in. The contents are the bearings of Knights of the Garter beginning with the founders and arranged stall by stall; shields, crests, badges, and banners appear with biographical notes.

wrong: Afk. and D., wreath.

Wrythe, John: Garter King of Arms, 1478; he resigned in January 1485 and returned in August of that year. Former Norroy K. of A. (q.v.), 1477; former Falcon Herald (q.v.), 1473; former Rouge Croix Pursuivant (q.v.); former Antelope Pursuivant (q.v.).

Wrythe, Sir Thomas: Garter King of Arms, 1505, when he changed his name to Wriothesley. Former Wallingford Pursuivant (q.v.), 1489.

Wrythe, Wm: see **Wriothesley, Wm.**

wulst: Ger., wreath of the colours.

---

469. Gules, a chevron between three cart-wheels Or: on a chief argent, an axe fesswise, proper, the head to the dexter.
Worshipful Company of Wheelwrights.

470. Argent, a plume of six feathers three two and one sable.
Jervis.

471. Or, three billets gules within a bordure sable bezanty.
Basset.

472. Argent, three estoiles azure.
Innes.

473. Vert, in chief the Holy Bible expanded; in base, a sand-glass running argent.
Joass.

474. Argent, three buckets sable.
Follage.

469

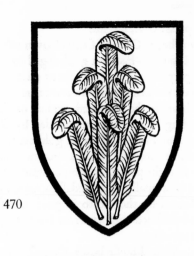

470

471

472

473

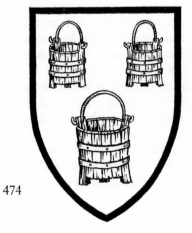

474

wurfspiess: Ger., javelin.

Würtemberg, Order of the Crown of: f. 1818. Insignia—*Badge:* a gold-edged white cross paty with gold lions passant guardant between the arms; a white central medallion, bearing the crowned cypher of the conferring monarch, is surrounded by the motto *Furchtlos Und Trew* in gold on red; the whole ensigned with a crown. *Star:* silver of eight points, bearing centrally the badge on a small white medallion which is surrounded by the motto in gold on red. *Riband:* dark red with a narrow black stripe near each edge.

Wylie, Wm Macfarlane: Carrick Pursuivant, 1884.

wyre-drawers' tools: only in the achievement of the Worshipful Company of Gold and Silver Wire-drawers, who run neck and neck, for an array of prosaic objects, with the Basket Makers (q.v.). The ~ are 'coppers', 'points', 'drawing-iron', 'rings' and an 'engrossing block'. Such inartistic arms have at least a justification in their antiquity, and the governing bodies of the companies are to be commended in not abandoning them in favour of a new and more 'heraldic' grant.

Wyrley, Wm: Rouge Croix Pursuivant, 1604. Former Rose Rouge Pursuivant, 1603.

wyvern: [O.E.] a composite fictitious beast having a pug dog-like head with a short, backward curved horn on the snout, a bird-like neck, and breast covered with scales instead of feathers and the body tapering away in a long, scaly, snakelike tail, curling towards the end, and terminating in a barb. It has two legs only which are those of an eagle, a pair of membraneous wings, and the tongue, which protrudes, is also barbed. The usual attitude is sejant, the claws and curled tail on the ground: erect, the claws are held in the rampant (q.v.) attitude, and the beast is supported by its tail only. The ~ is symbolic of malice. (279)

yale: a composite fictitious beast, in appearance an heraldic tygre (q.v.) having the curved horns of a bull (q.v.) or the spiral horns of a ram (q.v.) or both types together. The horns, whether two or four, are supposed to be attached to the head by a ball-and-socket joint, and to be, therefore, lacking in utility. In defence the ~ flees, voiding excrement into which his pursuer carelessly steps, being unaware of its corrosive nature, and is thereby burned to death. Alt. spelling 'yall'.

Yale Pursuivant: an office created in 1963 by Yale University and filled by Theodoro Sizer, professor emeritus of the history of art.

Yall: see **yale**.

Yeater, Thomas: Herald-painter to the Lyon Court, 1847.

Yellowlees, John: Dingwal Pursuivant, 1603.

yelmo: Sp., helmet.

yoke: [O.E.] a stout log of wood, cut and curved to fit upon the massive shoulders of an ox, having the ends whittled down and provided with hooks to engage the traces, and so harness the animal to the plough: any version of this as, e.g. a shaped log or board, placed on the shoulders of a human being to help in carrying two buckets. A ~ is the armorial badge of Clan Hay, one having been used in an emergency as a weapon wherewith to defeat the king's enemies.

Yonge, John: Norroy King of Arms, 1510.

Former Somerset Herald, 1494; former Falcon Pursuivant, 1486. Also spelt 'Young'.

York Herald: see **College of Arms.**

Yorkist collar: a neck ornament consisting of alternate suns and roses linked together by short runs of chain at top and bottom.

Young, John[1]: Carrick Pursuivant, 1678.

Young, John[2]: Albany Herald, 1827. Carrick Pursuivant, 1818.

Young, John[3]: see **Yonge, John.**

Young, Sir Charles George: Garter King of Arms, 1842. Former York Herald, 1820; former Rouge Dragon Pursuivant, 1813.

Ypotryll: a r. fictitious beast having an ox-like body and head but, instead of horns, two humps upon its back, rather like those of a camel, covered with rough hair. The tail, thick at the root, is of about the same length as the body, smooth, hairless, and tapering to a point.

zebra: a black and white striped wild horse of South Africa, *Hippotigris zebra*; to be found in the achievements of persons connected with that country.

zerspalten: Ger., tronnoné.

zilver: D., argent.

zilveren besant: D., plate.

zine: D., column.

zinnenförmig: Ger., embattled.

zinsprenk: D., motto.

zittende: D., sejant.

Zodiac, blazon by signs of the: see **segregative blazon.**

Zodiac, signs of: the cyphers employed to signify the twelve ~ are occasionally used as charges: they are, aquarius, ♒, the water-carrier; aries, ♈, the ram; capricorn, ♑, the goat; cancer, ♋, the crab; gemini, ♊ the twins; leo, ♌ the lion; libra, ♎ the scales; pisces, ♓, the fish; sagittarius, ♐, the archer; scorpio, ♏, the scorpion; taurus, ♉, the bull; virgo, ♍ the virgin. It will be observed that sagittarius appears also in the form of a centaur drawing a bow, in which form he is not necessarily a ~, although he may be.

zon: D., the sun in his splendour.

zoom: D., bordure.

zule: [Teut.] a chess rook (q.v.); ca. on the name Zulenstein; gules, three zules argent and a label of three points of the last, is worn in pretence (q.v.) by the Earl of Rochford.

zwart: D., sable.

Disposition of Illustrations

Disposition of Colour Plates

Analysis of Blazon

NOTE: entries appearing in square brackets, as [**canting**], [**diapering**], do not occur in blazon, but they are included in order to help with visual reference.

abaissé, 398.
[**absconded**]: 55.
[**accolée**]: X.
[**achievement**]: I, III, V, VII, X, XIV, XVI.
acorn[ed]: 171, 239, 427.
addice: 339.
addorsed: 67, 115, 279, 438; XVI.
Aesculapius, rod of: 78.
ale-warmer: 327.
alembic: 199, 228.
aloe: 228
ananas: 146.
anchor: 232, 335, 465.
annulet: 96, 201, 306, 325, 328, 423, 425, 426, 448, 465; XIV.
antelope, heraldic: 280.
antique crown: 231, 235, 378.
anvil: 318.
ape: 190, 352.
à plomb: 85.
appaumé: 291; IV.
arch: 413.
archiepiscopal cross: V.
argent: I, II, IV, V, VI, IX, X, XI, XII, XV, XVI.
arm: 201, 243, 246, 288, 290, 293, 294; III.
armed: 23, 27, 30, 34, 118, 124, 272, 406, 411.
[**armorial stained glass**]: XV.
arrow: 94, 105, 459; IV.
ass: 256.
astronomical symbols: 138.
attired: 37, 38, 165, 259.
augmentation: 55, 168, 243, 344.
awl: 313.

axe: 268, 316, 453, 454, 456, 469.
azure: II, IV, V, VI, VIII, IX, X, XI, XII, XIII, XV, XVI.

[**badge:**] 1, 2, 3, 4, 5, 6, 344.
banded: 130, 257.
banner: 20, 243.
bar: 253, 465; II.
barbed: [arrow and rose], 94, 180, 338, 399, 408, 416, 459; IV, V.
barbel: 67.
barnacles: 144.
Baronet, badge of: IV.
barrel: see **tun.**
barrulet: 12, 77, 420; IV.
barry: 8, 9, 10, 11; X, XII, XIV.
barry-bendy: 444.
barry-wavy: 8, 11, 30, 55, 64, 94, 108, 270, 410.
bars-gemel: see **gemel.**
base, centre: 47.
base, in: 43, 105, 108, 133, 134, 136, 144, 158, 161, 162, 164, 166, 171, 172, 236, 241, 253, 261, 267, 288, 289, 306, 307, 378, 388, 401, 408, 410, 411, 413, 417, 419, 420, 461, 465; IV, VXI.
bat: 143.
battering-ram, 460.
battle-axe: 108, 455.
battlement: 411.
bay: see **laurel.**
beak[ed]: 92, 107, 116, 117, 119, 120, 125, 175, 176, 228, 282, 375; V.
bear: 13, 16.
bearded: 195.

garland: 238.
garnished: 120, 127, 132, 134, 163, 241.
garter: 217.
gate: 32, 269.
gauntlet: 75; III.
gaze, at: 37.
gemel: 7, 129, 153, 187.
gillyflower: 388.
glazier's nippers: 317.
globe: see terrestrial.
glove: 252.
goat: 21.
gobony: see compony.
gonfannon: 428.
gorged: 1, 6, 197; XIV.
goshawk: see falcon.
grady, 164.
grape(vine): 181, 394.
grasshopper: 82.
grenade: 203.
greyhound: see hound.
griffin: 188; V.
gules: I, II, III, IV, V, VI, VII, VIII, IX, X, XI, XII, XIV, XV.
gun (musket): 461.
gun-stone: see cannon-ball.
gurge: 222.
gutty: 94, 193, 267, 392.
gyronny: 185, 425, 431.

habited: 201.
haft(ed): 108, 315, 339.
halbert: 452.
hamade: 407.
hammer: 315.
hand: 201, 246, 283, 285, 288, 293, 294, 300, 406; IV.
harp: 59, 360, 403.
harpy: 284.
hart: 1, 33.
hat, ecclesiastical: V.
haurient: 70, 71, 72.
hazel-leaves: 139.
head(ed): 7, 12, 13, 31, 34, 38, 71, 93, 116, 145, 165, 166, 172, 178, 195, 268, 276, 300, 454, 469; VI, XV.
heart: 221, 298.
heightened: 410.
heliotrope: 385.
helmet: 254; III, XIV, XVI.
hemp-break: 341.
heron: 126.

hew: see pick-axe.
hilted: 100, 313, 335, 433, 434, 436, 438, 440, 442, 443, 468.
hive, bee: 79.
holly: 233.
hop-pole: 393.
horned: 164, 280.
horse: 18, 19, 22, 93, 257; XV.
horseshoe: 101, 125, 306.
hound: 39, 42, 43 46.
hulk: see ship.
humetty, cross: 218, 402.
hunting-horn: see bugle-horn.
hurst: 177.

impaled(ing): 43, 367; XV.
Imperial crown: see crown royal.
Imperial eagle: see eagle.
impost: 413.
increscent: 401.
indented: 164, 183, 201, 388, 445, 449.
inescutcheon: 71, 424; IV.
infant: 198.
inflamed: 336.
ink-horn: 120.
interlaced: 59, 222, 426, 438.
interstices: 295.
interwoven: 377.
intradented: VI.
invected: 134.
inverted: 63, 174, 267, 306, 439.
irradiated: 204, 234, 288, 407.
issuant: 43, 108, 118, 133, 136, 197, 214, 243, 271, 288, 292, 293, 377, 378, 393, 411, 412, 417, 419, 437; II, III.

jelloped: 124, 282.
jessant-de-lys: 60, 63; III.
jessed: 115, 118.
jewelled: 108.
John the Baptist, St: 204.
joscelyn: 158.
Julian, cross of St: 211.
Jupiter's thunderbolt: 137.
[jupon]: VIII.
Justice (figure of): 285.

key: 290, 438.
[kirtle (lady's) emblazoned]: XI.
knot: 431.
knowed: 48, 75, 105, 239.

label: 463; XII.
lamb: 20, 241.
lamp: 192, 435.
langued: 411.
laurel: 238, 375, 386, 390, 408; III.
laver: 82.
leathered: 127, 132, 178, 303.
leaved: 59, 112, 132, 164, 181, 379, 382, 385, 391, 392, 394, 427.
leg(ged): 92, 296.
legantine cross: V.
leopard: 60, 63, 136; II, III, V.
leure: 113.
light: 108, 432.
lily (of the garden): 59, 182.
lily-pot: 384.
limbeck: 156.
linden leaf: 429.
lion: 8, 44, 45, 47, 48, 49, 50, 51, 52, 53, 54, 55, 56, 58, 59, 78, 108, 128, 176, 182, 194, 197, 217, 243, 273, 403, 406, 411, 412, 414, 445; IV, V, VII, VIII, X, XI, XII.
liver-bird: 82.
liveries: III, XIV, XVI.
lizard: 76, 406.
lobster-claws: 66.
lodged: 1, 32, 228.
loggerheads: 62.
lozenge: 148, 366.
lozenge, on a: 405, 408.
lozengewise: 224, 244.
lozengy: 417.
lucy: 70, 71.
lympagoe: 287.
lymphad: see ship.

mace: 188.
mallard: 196.
[mantle (lady's) emblazoned]: XI.
mantled: III, XIV, XVI.
martlet: 109, 255, 372, 431, 441, 456; XIV.
mascle: 422, 445; IV.
masoned: 108, 152, 197, 199, 412, 432.
mast: 189, 410.
maunch: 249.
membered: 107, 119, 175, 176, 282.
merchant's mark: 349, 350, 351, 352, 353, 354.
mermaid: 283.
mill-clack: 346.
mill-rind: 343.
mirror: 283.

mitre: 167, 242.
moline, cross: 206, 227; I.
monkey: see ape.
morion: 247.
morse: 277.
mortar: 309.
mortcour: 338.
mound: 257.
mount: 20, 32, 35, 177, 179, 181, 202, 260, 323, 373, 374, 375, 377, 378, 393; XIV.
mountain: 175.
mullet: 43, 47, 76, 96, 168, 181, 184, 186, 260, 261, 370, 401, 402, 417, 436, 443, 445, 455; IV, XI, XIV.
mural crown: 12, 197, 232, 233; X.
mushroom: 396.
muzzled: 13, 16.

nag: see horses.
naiant: 68, 69, 117, 277.
nail: 95, 311.
nebuly: 9; III.
needle (magnetic): 102.
nimbus: 276.
nooked: 463.
nowed: see knowed.

oak-leaves: 171, 389.
oak-tree: see tree.
oar: 332; VI.
[occulted]: 55.
ogress: 152, 205.
olive: 119, 175, 228.
open-crown: see coronet.
opinicus: 191.
Or: I, II, III, IV, V, VI, VII, VIII, IX, X, XI, XII, XIII, XIV, XV, XVI.
oreiller: see cushion.
organ-pipe: 358.
orle: 232, 325, 430, 441; IV.
ostrich: 125.
ostrich-feather: see feather.
ounce: 61.
owl: 172.
ox: 30.

padlock: 167.
pairle: 437, 450.
pale: 78, 362, 364.
pale, in: 54, 61, 69, 76, 111, 246, 252, 268, 287,

297, 323, 326, 366, 403, 406, 440, 442, 458, 460, 464, 468; IV, VIII, XII.
pale, on a: 78, XI.
pale, per: 14, 60, 129, 151, 182, 201, 214, 219, 227, 237, 323, 332, 336, 445; II.
palewise: 344, 453.
pallet: 370.
palmer's staff: see **staff.**
paly: 361, 363, 365, 445; II, XII.
paly-bendy: 441, 448.
pantheon: XIV.
papillon: 80.
parchment: see **roll of paper.**
park-pales: 32.
Paschal lamb: see **lamb.**
pascuant: 35.
passant: 8, 17, 24, 26, 27, 29, 30, 51, 53, 54, 55, 128, 176, 182, 187, 217, 243, 258, 403, 411; V, VII, VIII, X, XII.
patonce, cross: 215.
patriarchal cross: 116, 210.
paty, cross: 162, 165, 187, 241, 337, 358, 409.
paw: 45, 52, 108, 276.
peacock in his pride: 406.
peak: 175.
[peaked shield]: 403, 406.
pean: 417.
pear: 317, 373.
Pegasus: 275.
pelican in her piety: 193; XVI.
pendant: 252, 331, 394, 435.
penner: 120.
pennon: 189.
pestle: 309.
pheon, 31, 140, 238, 329.
phoenix, 271.
pick(axe): 266, 308; XI.
pierced (round): 96, 258, 298, 443; XVI.
pile: 90, 263, 306, 417, 419, 420; II, XIV.
pilewise: 311.
pilia pastoralis: 250.
pillar: V.
pincers: 314.
plate: 421.
platty: XIV.
plinth: see **compartment.**
plume: 470.
point(s): 30, 55, 108, 442, 463; XII.
point, in: 90, 263, 311; II.
Pole star: 102.
pomegranate: 288, 391.
pom(m)el(led): 100, 335, 433, 434, 436, 437, 438, 442, 443, 468.

pommetty, cross: 216.
popinjay: 122.
poppy: 164.
port: 108, 432.
portcullis: 202.
potent, cross: 218.
preying: 196, 198.
primrose: 380.
pyramid: 461.
python: 74.

quadrangle, in: 240; XII.
quarter-pierced: 206.
quarterly: 47, 119, 250, 403, 406, 414, 435, 445, 447, 449, 465; I, II, IV, VII, XI.
quarterly pierced: 223.
quarters, grand: 445.
queue(ued): 48, 49.

raguly: 225.
ram: 23; VI.
rampant: 44, 47, 48, 49, 52, 78, 403, 406, 414, 445; IV, XI.
random, at: 39.
rat: 361.
raven: 111.
ray: 407.
rayonée: see **irradiated.**
reflexed: XIV.
regardant: 45, 74, 253.
reindeer: 36.
respecting: 239, 377.
reversed: 439.
ringed: 335.
rizant: 121, 177.
rock: 136, 300, 432.
roll of paper (parchment or vellum): 130, 435.
rook (chess): 98.
rose: 72, 112, 144, 180, 236, 292, 335, 338, 344, 399, 408, 410, 416; V.
roundel: XV.

sable: I, II, V, XI, XII, XIV, XVI.
sabre: 52.
sail: 189, 410; VI.
salamander: 274.
salient: 25, 50, 259, 275, 361.
salt, covered (sprinkling): 163.
saltire: 325, 397, 398, 399, 400, 401, 402, 436.
saltire, in: 25, 130, 183, 299, 317, 332, 358, 381, 421, 434, 452, 453, 461, 465; IV, V.

tressure, double: 52, 380, 403, 424.
triangle (in): 59, 294, 429.
trident: 468.
trippant: 33, 36, 42, 105, 230.
trivet: 321.
trononné: 47.
trotting: 19.
tufted: V.
tulip: 132, 392.
tun: 189, 310, 461.
turgiant: 73.
turned up: 195, 198, 248, 251.
turret: 432.
tusked: 280.
tygre, heraldic: 281.

unguled: 27, 30, 272, 280; XIV.
unicorn: 272.
upright: 22.
urcheon: 41.

vair: 86, 185; XII.
vairy: XII.
vallary, crown: 230.
vambraced: 243, 246; III.
van: 304.
vane: 432.
vert: II, III, XIV.
vested: 285, 288, 292, 293, 294.
violin: 355.

Virgin (figure of the): 292.
voided: 207, 210, 227, 407.
volant: 105, 130, 399.

walnut leaves: 106.
water: 117, 307.
water-bouget: 202, 340.
wattled: 178.
waves of the sea: 105, 186, 289, 334.
wavy: 8, 11, 30, 47, 55, 108, 129, 136, 253, 263, 270, 307, 365, 410, 420, 465; II, X.
weel, fish: 301.
wheel: 171, 189, 344, 345, 347, 469.
whelk-shell: 151.
whip: 348.
wig: 342.
windmill: 312.
wine-flask: 5.
wing(ed): 137, 190, 196, 198, 203, 276, 278, 279; V, XVI.
wolf: 12, 15, 172.
woolpack: 372.
worm: 307.
wreath: 220, 236, 239, 240.
wreath of the colours: 187, 188, 189, 190, 191, 192, 193, 196, 199, 200, 201, 202, 203, 204; III, XIV, XVI.
wreathed: 259, 292.
wrist, the: IV.

zule: see **rook, chess.**